NITRO

THE INCREDIBLE RISE
AND INEVITABLE COLLAPSE
OF TED TURNER'S WCW

GUY EVANS

CW00823409

ISBN-10: 0692139176
ISBN-13: 978-0-692-13917-2

For Aysha and Nicky

CONTENTS

THE OFFER 1

AN ETERNAL QUESTION 8

THE ROAD TO WAR 18

BETTER THAN, LESS THAN, DIFFERENT THAN 22

THE TASKMASTER 33

SURPRISE, SURPRISE 40

THE DOC 49

TRASHED 58

AN AGE-OLD PROBLEM 64

HEEL 78

DIAMOND IN THE ROUGH 87

OUTSIDERS 94

YOU WANT A WAR? 99

LIGHTNING IN DAYTONA 117

HEAT 127

FLYING HIGH 142

CALL ME TED 149

ALL SOULED OUT 159

POWER STRUGGLES 170

THE DISEASE OF MORE 178

FIVE SLAMS ON THE BANKED TRACK 184

GOLDBERG 190

A NEW STANDARD 196

MATCH OF THE CENTURY 205

MR. PRESIDENT 211

TAKING ON WATER 223

CALLING OUT NAMES 244

COUNTED OUT 253

A MADE MAN 265
THE TURNING POINT 271
DAMAGE CONTROL 277
FINGERPOKE 287
I QUIT 302
FLUORESCENT VOMIT 315
CATCH UP TIME 326
BOUT IT, BOUT IT 341
THE HOLY SHIT FILE 349
GO HOME 359
A BRAVE NEW WORLD 368
VICIOUS VINCENT 381
THE POWERS THAT BE 392
COLLISION COURSE 402
PAYING ATTENTION 418
MUTINY 426
THE NEXT BIG IDEA 432
THE NIGHT THE WORLD CHANGED 448
ARQUETTE 454
THE BIG SURPRISE 463
OH, WHAT A NIGHT 475
LET ME BUY IT 492
LENITA, LENITA 503
FUSIENT 511
IT AIN'T OVER 'TIL IT'S OVER 515
TWO FRIDAYS APART 521
CONSPIRACY 541
ONE MONDAY IN FLORIDA 549
EPILOGUE 557
POSTSCRIPT 560
ACKNOWLEDGEMENTS 567
SOURCES AND REFERENCES 571

Chapter 1:
The Offer

May, 1995 —

1 CNN Center, North Tower, 14th Floor
Atlanta, GA

Y OU COULD ALMOST be excused for missing it.

After all, it stood rather inconspicuous amidst a sea of decorative souvenirs. Indeed, some eyes were first drawn to the accolades on display - the prime-time Emmy, the CableACE award, TIME Magazine's Man of the Year cover - while others stared more intently at Jane Fonda's image, showcased alluringly in a framed photograph. Perhaps most captivating, however, was the sight of 'Leo', a full-bodied stuffed lion who curiously resembled - and increasingly so, with each passing glance - the one whose roar set the stage for those classic MGM movies. A persistent rumor posited that it could be *the actual lion*, who by now had clearly seen better days. '*Leo looks sick*', thought some recent visitors.

But there it was, silently demanding your attention in the middle of the room. At the front of the desk in this top-floor office, a solid brown plaque displayed an insightful refrain:

Either lead, follow or get out of the way.

The artifact was as revealing as it was succinct. The plaque, the office, and the building (for all intents and purposes) belonged to Robert Edward Turner III - better known to the public as the eccentric media mogul, Ted Turner. On a particularly humid Atlanta day, Ted surveyed the downtown district and contemplated the standing of his pioneering cable television enterprise, *Turner Broadcasting System (TBS, Inc)*. Ted's broadcasting empire, which included ownership of New Line Cinema, CNN, and the Atlanta Braves, seemed to be under

1

no immediate threat. For now, there was the simple matter of an executive committee meeting, a monthly gathering that functioned as a pep rally of sorts for both the charismatic Chairman and his high-level suits.

As a faction of key executives entered the room, Ted cast his 56-year old pale blue eyes at a veritable 'who's who' of TBS, Inc. Among those in attendance were Terry Foster McGuirk, Turner's Director and Executive Vice President; Randolph 'Randy' L. Booth, a former Chief Financial Officer now working as an adviser; and the Director and Vice President of Turner Entertainment Group, Scott Sassa, widely considered to be the heir apparent to Turner's throne.

As the agenda moved to AOB - any other business - Booth announced with palpable glee that an unsolicited offer had been received for one of Turner's subsidiary companies. It was an offer to purchase the organization whose televised presence - for many of the TBS corporate brass, at least - had been nothing but a constant source of embarrassment. In an ironic allusion to its place in the organizational hierarchy, this particular entity was listed last on the company's inventory of 150 controlled assets (the list was compiled of course, as is standard for the SEC, in alphabetical order).

Booth reported that an offer had been made to purchase *World Championship Wrestling (WCW), Inc.* - the Turner-controlled pro wrestling outfit and notoriously inept money-loser. Since its official inception some seven years earlier, WCW had never so much as made a single dollar in profit, and to many, its continued survival was as perplexing as its creation.

———

Apparently, Ted possessed a soft spot for his wrestlers - or *rasslers* as he would call them - because WCW had simply never gone away. Its origins could be traced back to 1972, when a regional organization known as *Georgia Championship Wrestling (GCW)* produced a self-titled television program on the Turner-owned WTCG station. The wrestling show, in addition to Atlanta Braves coverage and 'Andy

2

Griffith Show' reruns, propelled WTCG to become the *original* cable network, reinventing the entire television industry.

In 1979, following the network's re-branding to WTBS (and eventually, simply TBS), GCW's show - now billed as *World Championship Wrestling* - became the first wrestling program to be broadcast across America. By 1982, the series achieved the unprecedented distinction of attracting a million viewers on cable, solidifying its status as a legitimate cultural institution in the South. But in April 1984, following some tumultuous internal strife, GCW (and its hallowed 6:05pm Saturday timeslot) was sold to Vince McMahon, Jr., newly minted owner of the Connecticut-based *World Wrestling Federation* (WWF). Three months later, on July 14, 1984, McMahon stunned the loyal GCW audience with an unannounced appearance on TBS television - an occurrence that came to be known as *Black Saturday*. While previously, fans had been used to bouts produced intimately in an Atlanta sound studio, the new show featured taped matches from Madison Square Garden. It was still wrestling, but it wasn't *rasslin'*, and consequently, the reaction to the change was catastrophic.

In response to mounting complaints and sinking ratings, an angry Ted Turner looked for restorative action. He decided to effectively compete against McMahon on his own network, providing rival promoters with air time around the Saturday night show. Hampered by Turner's decree, the WWF ceased to enjoy exclusivity on TBS, and so with his financial incentive dwindling, McMahon begrudgingly sold the time slot rights (and *World Championship Wrestling* name) to promoter Jim Crockett, Jr. in March 1985 (attaching the promise, according to wrestling lore, that Crockett would live to "choke" on his investment).

After the purchase, Crockett's company - *Jim Crockett Promotions* (JCP) - became the second-biggest wrestling organization in the country. But after several years of unsuccessful competition with the WWF, talks began to engineer a sale of JCP to Turner Broadcasting. For Ted Turner, whose growing empire demanded the need for popular (and cheap) entertainment programming, the opportunity to

3

acquire a wrestling company seemed like a fairly logical strategic move. After all, his guiding principle, formed in the early days of running his father's billboard business, was to constantly seek to acquire assets. His famous refusal to sell the library of old films that eventually became Turner Classic Movies showed that the approach appeared to work.

Besides, his aides thought, Ted simply got a kick out of the populist pageantry, over-the-top characters, and soap opera-type storylines that accompanied the pre-determined bouts of wrestling. And so, on November 2, 1988, a reported $9 million sale of JCP to Turner was made official. Using the *World Championship Wrestling* moniker as the name of the new company, WCW was officially born, and soon it began to separate from its historic territorial roots.

But after a mostly well-received first year in operation, a series of horrendous managerial decisions and bizarre on-screen stories entrenched WCW as a distant number two, trailing pitifully behind McMahon's WWF. Undoubtedly, TBS' wrestling outfit - to a sizable number of its own executives, no less - was already an absolute joke, often failing to ensure sufficient crowds despite *giving away* tickets en masse.

And then there were the demographics. Oh, the demographics! While an oft-repeated gag theorized that WCW exhibited the *opposite* of 'PBS syndrome' (far more people, as indicated by the Nielsen television ratings, watched the programming than were willing to admit), those that apparently *did* watch represented a portion of the audience that simply repelled advertisers. While the viewership for WCW's various syndicated programming and its flagship show on TBS - *WCW Saturday Night* - significantly contributed to the network's overall numbers, an inherent stigma associated with pro wrestling suggested that it appealed mostly to a low-income, low-education, low-on-sophistication crowd.

The content of WCW programming did little to help its perception. In one indelible moment, Robocop (no typo) came to the aid of wrestler Sting, only to walk backstage and never be seen again. In another plot,

4

a dastardly one-eyed dwarf named *Cheatum* engineered a terrorist bombing, presumably in an effort to *kill* two good-guy wrestlers. And in perhaps the most infamous happening of them all, a debuting character named The Shockmaster crashed embarrassingly through a prop wall on live television, losing his helmet (and dignity) in the process.

For the account executives within 'Turner Ad Sales' - the branch of Ted's empire tasked with selling commercial time on his networks - it became increasingly difficult to rationalize keeping WCW afloat. It would be unwise, many agreed, to aggressively pitch wrestling to traditional advertisers, at the risk of losing their overall business. The idea of presenting Proctor & Gamble, for example, or General Motors, with the concept of taking out spots on WCW's shows was uniformly laughed at. The outcome seemed as predictable as a Hulk Hogan match. Besides, *didn't everyone know it was all fake?*

And so, in what became practically a yearly tradition, the TBS elite proposed removing WCW from the airwaves. It stayed that way, of course, until early 1992, when one such plea ended almost as soon as it began. The conversation ceased, several attendees would recall, with Ted reminding his subordinates whose name was on the front door.

Those close to Turner had rarely seen him as enraged as on that day. He had previously promised his *rasslers*, in a rare visit to a television taping, that WCW would have a home as long as he retained power. But as the name on the front door remained, so did the resentment of WCW's existence.

———

"We have received an offer for W-C-"

The cumulative history of TBS wrestling set the stage for Booth's announcement. He could barely finish delivering the news before Scott Sassa leapt to his feet, high-fiving Terry McGuirk in a display of pure elation. Sassa enjoyed a particularly close rapport with Ted, but he seemed to be acting on behalf of everyone now. *This is it,* the group agreed with their eyes. *We can finally be done with wrestling.* A communal sense of relief filled the room, tempered just slightly by a cautious optimism. When push came to shove, their billionaire boss would still have the final say.

Ted's eyes narrowed. His instincts, well honed after a lifetime of making decisions based on *feel,* urged him to embrace his spontaneous nature. Before it became cliché, he was a true maverick, totally unaffected by the opinions of others, and characteristically unafraid to make decisions. While his brain wave to popularize 24-hour news with CNN was now hailed, for example, as a decided stroke of genius, he recalled the complete lack of support when he first broached the idea. "Uh, Mr. Turner," he remembered hearing. "People can barely watch 20 minutes of news. You want to run news *all day?*"

Dubbed by the national press as 'Captain Outrageous' (or alternatively, 'The Mouth of the South'), Ted never could quite hold his tongue, once casually suggesting to Atlanta Braves pitcher Andy Messersmith that he change his last name to "Channel" (Messersmith wore no. 17, the same number as WTCG). And true to his nature, The Mouth wasn't going to stay quiet at this moment.

It was time to start taking WCW seriously, he decided. *USA Network* were achieving impressive prime-time numbers for the WWF's flagship show, *Monday Night Raw,* even despite the wrestling industry experiencing a depressing downturn in popularity. We *own* a wrestling company, the Chairman said on occasion. *We* should be getting these numbers on prime-time - wrestling should be *our* thing.

Ted leaned forward as the Sassa-McGuirk high-five reverberated around him.

*"**You've** now got wrestling,"* he told Sassa matter-of-factly.

But Sassa provided oversight to both the TBS network - traditionally, home to WCW programming - *and* TNT (Turner Network Television), the latter of which had been positioned as an upscale

6

basic cable option (or *'gold standard'*). To this end, TNT defined itself internally with a clear mission statement, by virtue of its iconic classic film library, big budget original cable movies, and elite professional sports coverage:

TNT is for upscale adult couples and families looking for quality-driven television. TNT is that premiere basic cable network offering a variety of blue-chip sports and entertainment programs.

"You've now got wrestling," Turner clarified to Sassa. *"On **TNT**. In prime time."*

The suits paused in disbelief. Such a proposal, it was widely believed, completely contradicted TNT's efforts to position itself, especially in an increasingly crowded cable marketplace. The cross pollination of Turner's NBA coverage, whereby TNT telecasts augmented airings on TBS, already made the task of showing differentiation difficult. Therefore, aside from Ted, the consensus was rather clear - WCW on TNT would only muddy the waters further.

But that hardly mattered to Ted. His career accomplishments had developed an unshakable belief in his own convictions, no matter how spontaneous. He was a cable television pioneer after all, founder of CNN, *and* husband to Jane Fonda! Indeed, his was a very *American* story; the tale of the self-made entrepreneur with a genuine courage to take chances. And so, the decision would be final.

TNT would air World Championship Wrestling in prime-time, and they would have to make it work. In perhaps the most unlikely of tag team combinations, upscale and downscale would have to co-exist.

Chapter 2:
An Eternal Question

May, 1995 —

1 CNN Center, South Tower, 13th Floor
Atlanta, GA

ACROSS THE STREET, a younger visionary grappled with an eternal question: how would *WCW* ever make any money?

The visionary's name was Eric Bischoff, WCW's 40-year old Executive Vice President. Born and raised in Detroit, Michigan, Bischoff had hustled his way from a childhood gig sweeping a corner store driveway - earning 75 cents a shift for his efforts - to become the enterprising leader of Ted Turner's beleaguered professional wrestling franchise. To the TBS executives, he presented a charming public image; that of the handsome, articulate and ambitious trailblazer who spoke their language with a reassuring ease. But upon closer analysis, looking past the jet-black dyed hair and charismatic smile, Bischoff appeared to have more in common with his roster of wrestlers than the corporate suits that presided over him.

Fiercely independent, tough-minded and driven, Bischoff had taken a long and winding path to WCW. His decidedly lower-class upbringing, situated just two miles from the infamous 8 mile district in Detroit, provided the backdrop for a daily ritual of adversity and hardship. Each morning as a child, Bischoff could recall, his six-block walk to school attracted older bullies who reveled in taking advantage of his smaller stature. If he somehow managed to escape unscathed, he was usually beat up for his lunch money at midday, licking his wounds just long enough to suffer another assault on the way home.

Bischoff's father, born as a premature infant in the Depression Era, suffered from paralysis, the eventual result of life-long spinal

8

problems and later, a bungled brain surgery aimed to correct his condition. Stirringly, the elder Bischoff refused to quit working, even when he could no longer so much as brush his teeth without the assistance of wife Carol. He became a remarkably successful purchasing agent, and after receiving a job opportunity in 1968, moved his family to Penn Hills, an eastern suburb of Pittsburgh, PA.

Meanwhile, son Eric, now in the eighth grade, quickly found his new surroundings unable to prevent the threat of physical combat. While his new trek to school required transportation by bus, the old Detroit memories resurfaced one day as a member of the football team tested his mettle. Each time the bus came to a stop, Bischoff's tormentor - sitting menacingly in the seat behind him - jabbed and prodded the new kid to the delight of his sycophantic classmates. Over and again, an audible '*thump!*' gave way to a chorus of laughter, while Bischoff, cruelly preyed on once more, simmered impassively as the only student sitting alone.

As the bus chugged toward its final stop, and with the prospect of another year of harassment ahead, the kid from Detroit finally reached his breaking point. To the shock of everyone - not least the bully himself - Bischoff turned and socked the resident jock directly in the mouth, following up with a kick to the groin for good measure. The driver, leaving his post temporarily, descended on the scene to drag the scrappy underdog away, leaving Bischoff to hear the bully promise vengeance the very next day. But surprisingly, their subsequent showdown didn't go quite as expected - Bischoff simply pummeled his adversary in front of an assembled crowd, and from that day forward, saw himself no longer as a target.

In later years, Bischoff realized that his stand against the school menace enabled a powerful personal epiphany: *don't ever let anyone bully you like that again*, he told himself.

––––

Academically, Bischoff barely pulled through high school ("I was lucky enough to catch the tail end of the hippy era," he once quipped

9

- in reference to the faculty), and lasted only a year in college before embarking on a series of odd jobs and entrepreneurial schemes. His resume soon became filled with an admirable assortment of eclectic occupations; there was a period bouncing boozy patrons in Chicago, a stint running a tanning salon in Minneapolis, and a time operating a landscape construction company. From his teenage years onwards, he had flipped pancakes, taught karate, sold Christmas trees, and hustled, scratched and clawed in an effort to achieve financial stability; first for himself, and later, for his wife and two small children.

Physically, Bischoff matured into a classic 'late bloomer', allowing for an unlikely (albeit brief) career as a martial artist. He competed in several televised bouts broadcast by ESPN, and while on the circuit, met Sonny Onoo, an Iowa businessman and eventual life-long friend. After a particularly enthusiastic late-night drinking session, the duo hatched an ingenious proposal to develop a children's game, based on one Onoo played while growing up in Japan. They labeled the game *Ninja-Star Wars* - fitting for a diversion involving vested players launching 'ninja stars' at each other - and rubber-stamped an optimistic production order of some 10000 units.

But despite Bischoff's best efforts – including Saturdays spent outside supermarkets, launching *ninja stars* at his wife – retailers were largely disinterested. Now 32, Bischoff found himself living with thousands of impossible-to-sell boxes, stacking inventory in every room of his house. Any savings accrued from his last vocation (managing a food processing company) had vanished, but improbably, a remarkable solution was about to reveal itself.

While watching television one weekday afternoon, Bischoff stumbled across a pro wrestling show produced by the American Wrestling Association (AWA). He had enjoyed watching wrestling as a child, and maintained a level of interest as an adult, believing the genre to be 'the purest form of entertainment.' Ever the resourceful salesman, Bischoff sat through a commercial break and became convinced of an opportunity to market his game to the AWA's audience, a demographic predominately made up of children.

And so, with typical moxie and determination, Bischoff arranged a meeting with the AWA's owner, the legendary wrestler and promoter Verne Gagne. Subsequently, his eventual pitch was so impressive - so polished - that he left the room with a job offer to run the company's syndication sales department. Soon enough, in another improbable break, Bischoff began appearing on-camera as a straight-laced backstage interviewer. At first, however, his reliable self-assuredness failed - albeit temporarily - to impress a locker room of wrestlers who teased him for his 'Ken Doll'-like physical appearance. Bischoff tried to sound convincing on the microphone, but in response, as he would later recall, 'the boys' could barely contain their laughter.

In time, the 'Ken Doll' proved himself as a valuable, curious and dedicated employee. However, Gagne's organization was ailing. At one stage, Bischoff worked for six months without a pay check, and with the AWA standing on the verge of collapse, he answered a call to audition with the WWF. He tried out as an announcer with Vince McMahon, who clearly enjoyed - in a variation of the 'sell me this pen' interview question - instructing Bischoff to 'interview' a broom instead. "Hey Eric, why don't you try to 'sell' me that broom over there?" grinned McMahon. "This doesn't mean I'm going home..." replied a nervous Bischoff, "does it Vince?"

Admittedly unseasoned, Bischoff would indeed return home - empty-handed – and braced himself for an uncertain future. Financially, his life was spiraling, with missed mortgage payments accompanying the litany of bills that would result in his car being repossessed. Children Garett and Montana, five and six years old respectively, sufficed only on rice and beans, and in a particularly solemn moment, the heat to the Bischoff home was unceremoniously cut off. "I needed a miracle, or I needed to get out of pro wrestling...maybe both," Bischoff would later reflect.

Finally, Bischoff left the AWA and on a whim, sent an audition tape to WCW. It was 1991, and the company was struggling for an identity under the unpopular leadership of Jim Herd, an ex-Pizza Hut impresario with a reputation for adopting off-the-wall ideas. Luckily for Bischoff, Herd liked what he saw ("you look like a movie star" he told the desperate hopeful), before offering a generous $70,000 salary to play backup announcer. The miracle had arrived, but Herd's reign of power proved utterly disastrous. His successor, Kip Frey, failed in similar fashion, only further cementing WCW's status as the 'red-headed stepchild' of TBS.

Two years later, in 1993, WCW was suffering through its latest embarrassment. Executive Vice President Bill Watts, an old-school promoter known for allegedly wearing a gun to work and urinating out of his office window, was ousted after making racially charged comments to a journalist. In response, WCW President Bill Shaw announced his intention to empower a new leader for the company - a person with a fresh vision for televised wrestling, but not a *wrestling person* - and thus began a search to hire the company's first-ever Executive Producer. "[WCW] is going to be run like a television company, [and] not a wrestling company," he reportedly told employees gathered at CNN Center. "In general terms," observed Bischoff in a contemporaneous interview, "there's been a realization that we need to compete on a broader level - as a television product."

After contemplating an exit from wrestling during the Watts era, Bischoff applied for the new role and shockingly, to the surprise of the entire industry, was chosen by Shaw as the successful candidate. During the selection process, Shaw had consulted Mike Shields, the former head of production for the now-defunct AWA. "I told Bill that Eric...will do whatever it takes to keep his job," recalls Shields. "[I told him that Eric] will build relationships. He will manage egos. He is smart enough to hire people to do things [he can't]. He will think outside the box, because he knows what WCW is doing is not working, and will [eventually] lead to the company shutting down."

Incredibly, Bischoff was now responsible for WCW's entire on-screen product. As a perceived outsider to the business, his rise to power energized an array of detractors who would consistently make claims of resume embellishment. But to those who knew him well, Bischoff's ascent was not altogether unexpected. "Eric always was a great salesman - a *great* salesman," emphasizes Sonny Onoo.

Bischoff was also extremely competitive - a self-described Type A personality with a preference, he often told friends, for a good fight over good sex. "I met Eric Bischoff in a pull apart fight - me and him," laughs Diamond Dallas Page, one of WCW's biggest ever stars.

"Next morning I wake-up, and I can't get it out of my head. I'm [thinking], 'I'm gonna go knock on his fuckin' door and see how bad he is at eight in the morning'. And as I'm walking out my door, I heard it knock. It was him.

"He said, 'I heard I was a real asshole last night'. I said, 'yeah, you were - I was just on my way to see you'. He said, 'I saved you the walk. So there's one of two things we can do here.

"'One - accept my apology and shake my hand. Or two-'

"And [at this point]," Page continues, "he pulled his front three [fake] teeth out of his mouth. He said, 'or punch me in the face. You do whatever you feel is right'.

"That's who Eric Bischoff is.

"I said, 'I'd much rather shake your hand, because that's the best comeback I've ever heard!'"

———

Despite Bischoff's inexperience, his energy and enthusiasm as Executive Producer instantly impressed even the most jaded of WCW employees. In outlining a clear vision and fresh philosophical approach, he spoke of making the company a truly viable national promotion for the first time. A co-branding effort with Disney MGM studios, while logistically problematic, did much to chip away at the dull company image. Cost-cutting measures, such as reducing the number of untelevised events, coupled with a dramatic curtailing of travel expenses, pleased the higher-ups concerned with WCW's hemorrhaging of funds. But Bischoff's most important move was yet to come. On June 6, 1994, he finalized a deal to sign Terry Bollea,

13

better known to fans as the immortal Hulk Hogan - the driving force behind the WWF's national expansion and subsequent 'boom period' for pro wrestling in the mid-to-late 1980s.

Suddenly, WCW's marketing arm could flaunt the acquisition of the *Hulkster*, an enormously popular superstar whose *Wrestlemania III* battle with Andre the Giant drew in excess of 78,000 spectators to Detroit's Pontiac Silverdome. Hogan's distinctive persona, characterized by his familiar red-and-yellow apparel and purported '24-inch pythons', resulted in Hulkamania becoming a legitimate cultural touchstone in '80s America.

But for all of the ballyhoo that accompanied WCW's announcement of his signing, which Disney-MGM hosted as part of a ticker-tape parade, Hogan's influence and ability to interest casual viewers had waned. While his initial *Bash at the Beach* showdown with bleach-blonde legend Ric Flair helped spike one of the largest buy rates in company history, a 1.02, it soon became evident that Hogan's all-too-familiar act failed to resonate with WCW's television audience. For fans whose interest traced back to the *Georgia* Championship Wrestling days, Hogan's shtick came across as tired, formulaic, and far too identified with the style of his former employer, the WWF.

Nevertheless, the impact of Hogan's signing was seen in WCW's ability to use his highly recognizable persona as a means to achieve new media and advertising opportunities. His appearance at the annual NATPE (National Association of Television Program Executives) convention, now as a representative of WCW, was not lost on the suits in attendance. Licensing and merchandising, revenue streams that were woefully undeveloped prior to his arrival, expanded dramatically. By early 1995, a profitable WCW, previously inconceivable in the days of Robocop run-ins, appeared within reach.

Harry Anderson didn't think it could be done. As the Executive VP of Finance and Operations for Turner Entertainment, Anderson observed Bischoff's moves with interest. He felt strongly, however, that WCW, a money-losing proposition since day one, would never so much as break-even - much less make a dollar in profit. During a meeting involving Bill Shaw, the executive responsible for promoting Bischoff, Anderson sat in amazement as he witnessed Bischoff boldly proclaim that in 1995, WCW would do exactly that.

"Listen, Eric," Anderson interrupted. *"I hear what you're saying, but...there's no way. It just isn't possible."* Bischoff, relishing the thought of being able to prove himself further, looked Anderson squarely in the eye. "Harry," he said through a smile, "I can tell you that it *will* happen."

In the most cordial tone possible, Bischoff proposed a friendly wager. "I'm going to bet you a dollar that it happens," he continued, "and if it does, you agree to pay me that dollar at the company Christmas party. You're going to have to get down on one knee, and hand that dollar to me." Anderson, one of the most senior members of the Turner executive committee, could only chuckle to himself. *"You got it,"* he responded. *"I'll betcha'."*

Bischoff exited the meeting with a renewed sense of purpose. The Hulk Hogan signing, combined with the subsequent debut of another ex-WWF mainstay, Randy 'Macho Man' Savage, put WCW in a position to improve its international distribution. An opportunity soon arose with a network that had transformed itself, over the preceding two years, from a regional broadcaster to a powerful global entity. According to Bischoff, an offer from *Star TV* - Asia's pioneer satellite television service - was believed so lucrative as to potentially push WCW into the black.

But there was still one fairly imposing hurdle to overcome. In 1993, Australian business magnate Rupert Murdoch took over *Star* as part of his purported ambition to establish the world's first global television empire. Aside from an estimated $3.3 billion fortune, he also owned a long-standing dislike for Ted Turner, who would later characterize Murdoch as a "very dangerous person...dangerous to democracy, dangerous to [America]," in an interview with Larry King.

"At one point, Ted publicly said he wanted to challenge Rupert

Murdoch to a boxing match," recalls Bill Burke, President of the TBS network from 1995 to 1999. "Someone said to him, 'Ted, you don't want to box - wrestle him! We'll put [the event] on'. Ted goes, 'nah, I don't wanna wrestle...I [really] wanna hit him!'"

Mindful of the tension between Turner and Murdoch, Bischoff knew that he needed approval to make the *Star* deal happen. Unaware of Ted's prior mandate, in an executive committee meeting, that WCW would expand to TNT on prime-time, Bischoff enlisted a tight-lipped Scott Sassa to arrange a conference with the tycoon and Dr. Harvey Schiller - the Head of Turner Sports - on Monday June 5th, 1995.

The summit would mark almost three years to the day when Bischoff, still recovering from the AWA experience and a significant tax issue with the IRS, filed for Chapter 7 bankruptcy in the district of Minnesota. In an almost surreal reversal of fortunes, the former Blue Ribbon Foods salesman now faced the prospect of addressing one of the 50 richest men in the country.

Bischoff prepared diligently for the pitch, repeatedly rehearsing his presentation with thoughtful consideration of any and all possible objections. Moments into the talk, however, he was swiftly interrupted by Ted. "*Uh, Eric...*" began Turner, "*what do we need to do to become competitive with Vince [McMahon] and the WWF?*" The question lingered ominously in the air, as Bischoff saw his professional life flash before his eyes. "Well...Ted...I think we need to have prime-time," he eventually babbled, trying hard to conceal his own uncertainty. To Bischoff's astonishment, Turner then announced what had already been privately determined, but with one caveat: "*Scott [Sassa], give Eric prime-time - every **Monday** on TNT.*"

The implications of the statement were clear - WCW, by order of its owner, was set to compete *directly* against the WWF and its established program on USA network, *Monday Night Raw*.

Once the parties dispersed, Bischoff found himself alone in the hallway, suddenly a man with enough rope to hang himself with. For as far as both he and WCW had progressed, one prevailing thought

16

flashed across his mind.

"'What the fuck do I do now?'"

Chapter 3:
The Road To War

Bischoff's DEPARTMENT HEADS did a double take upon hearing the news. It would take a monumental effort, they thought, to compete for ratings supremacy with the WWF, who despite suffering a marked drop-off in business, awaited them as the familiar incumbent.

In fact, the previous decade had been an astounding one for Vince McMahon's company. The advent of pay-per-view and increased penetration of cable television provided an ideal platform for iconic stars such as Hulk Hogan, Randy 'Macho Man' Savage, 'Rowdy' Roddy Piper, and Andre the Giant to become household names. By virtue of a timely association with MTV - and specifically, the pop singer Cyndi Lauper - the Stamford, Connecticut-based promotion transformed itself into a pop culture phenomenon. In 1985, McMahon successfully gambled everything on the promise of the first *Wrestlemania*, "changing the landscape," according to Bischoff. "Wrestling was no longer the regional territory model it had been up to the point," reflects Bischoff. "The 80s saw an amazing amount of growth - an explosion in popularity - with the *Wrestlemania* format and [McMahon's] efforts on cable."

McMahon was relentless in his desire to dominate the American wrestling scene, breaking the unwritten rules of the industry as quickly as he did attendance records. He poached talent from regional organizations, displaced existing wrestling programming by buying up local airtime, and committed to a grueling schedule that often featured multiple live events occurring simultaneously around the country. It was an aggressive approach, seen as predatory in the eyes of rival promoters, and one that would have disappointed Vince McMahon *Sr.*, the widely respected boss who ran the company until 1982. "Had my father known what I was going to do," Vince Jr. revealed to *Sports Illustrated*, "he never would have sold his stock to

18

me." As a result of the younger McMahon's audacious tactics, his company was a juggernaut by the end of the decade, grossing an estimated $150 million in 1989.

"For years, the very mention of pro wrestling would cause the eyes to roll, and the voice to chuckle," said Bob Costas in an NBC feature on the WWF-sparked '80s wrestling boom, inferring that the widespread perception of the spectacle was at last evolving. But televised wrestling had enjoyed a long history in the United States. Network executives in the late 1940s first realized its potential as an inexpensive form of popular programming, with the pioneering Dumont Television Network drawing huge viewership for their weekly airing of matches from Chicago's Marigold Gardens. "The rise to prominence of pro wrestling came alongside the whole idea of spectator entertainment," says Sam Ford, Professor of an MIT course on professional wrestling. "The idea of the arena as this huge, spectator sport *locale* is something that accompanied the rise of mass media."

In the 1950s, similar to how the advent of television popularized the 'slugger' style of fighting in boxing, professional wrestlers of the time also adapted their presentation. The televised wrestler, now more than ever, played the role of a *performer*, with the narcissistic villain Gorgeous George becoming the first break out star of the genre. His flamboyant antics made him a hated bad-guy, or *heel* in wrestling parlance, as he masterfully exploited the social conservatism of the period. *Gorgeous George Gets Hair Curled*, protested one Washington Post headline, seemingly inviting fury from its male readership.

George antagonized fans so much that he is credited for generating more sales of television sets than any other factor of the time, thus making pro wrestling the first real TV 'hit'. He was admired by fellow showmen Muhammad Ali, who studied his act as a young Cassius Clay, and James Brown, who incorporated his theatrics on stage. Bob Dylan would even write in his autobiography that "[George gave me] all the recognition and encouragement I would need for years to come."

At its peak in the '50s, more than 200 stations carried wrestling. However, by the end of the decade, its popularity declined. Networks that had eagerly moved to cash in on the fad's novelty caused the programming to be overexposed, and new, alternative programming caught the interest of casual viewers. The wrestling promoters of the '60s, forced to accept that the 'golden age' was no more, moved to produce their shows for the purpose of syndication, with small, local stations able to provide them with cheap late-night time slots. Regional mega stars such as Verne Gagne, in the Midwest, and Bruno Sammartino, throughout the North East, were created as a result of breakaway organizations from the National Wrestling Alliance (NWA), a powerful body of independent promotions. Gagne and Sammartino represented the most significant of these entities, the American Wrestling Association (AWA), and the World Wide Wrestling Federation (WWWF), respectively; the latter of which would eventually become the World Wrestling Federation (WWF).

But even with the WWF's expansion nationally - and internationally - throughout the 1980s, and Ted Turner's eventual entrance into the *rasslin'* business, pro wrestling found itself on a downswing by the early 1990s. A series of sex and drug scandals cooled the WWF's momentum, while the impotence of WCW did little to inspire an industry revival.

It was a state of affairs not lost on WCW management. In one late 1992 memo, Executive Vice President Bill Watts unloaded in frustration, emphasizing the need to finally realize Ted's vision:

As professional athletes and independent contractors, it signifies you have attained the highest level in your sport.

...While WCW does want each of you it has contracted, you are not indispensable except possibly in your own mind and in the minds of a few you may happen to influence.

...Our industry is in a crisis - you have been a part in getting it there - you cannot just blame it all on management as some are wont to do.

...[So] may 1993 bring us all together on a mission to make WCW set the standard and to save our industry. Read the signs and dedicate yourself to helping us make WCW a profitable entity for TBS.

...The bottom line here at WCW is "our way or the highway" and you had better make your bookings and once there give it your all to make the event (not just yourself) successful for the fans, your peers, and WCW. If you do that, 1993 will be remembered as the year WCW began resurrecting wrestling from the ashes of ridicule and chaos on the verge of collapse. TBS has invested millions in WCW, '93 is the year we begin justifying Ted's vision.

By 1994, mainstream publications were lamenting the industry's decline, with one challenging its readers, 'quick, name the World Wrestling Federation's champion.' In mid-year, McMahon narrowly avoided jail time on steroid distribution charges. "I think mainly because of some of the challenges that the WWF experienced, the popularity of the product began to diminish somewhat," reflects Bischoff. "It just got stale, as a result of some of the distractions."

The WWF looked increasingly to its overseas markets, and WCW, losing as much as $10 million in one year, remained a remote number two, achieving approximately a quarter of the revenue of its competitor. "WCW might as well have been number twenty two," jokes Bischoff. "It could have been considered, at that time, a national brand because of its distribution with [TBS], but it wasn't nearly as popular as the WWF was, even though the WWF had been suffering diminished success."

Understandably, there existed "some apprehension" about competing with the WWF, recalls Alan Sharp, WCW's former Head of Public Relations. "It was like, 'what have we done? We're gonna go head-to-head against *Raw*?'

"We thought, 'this could get ugly'.

"It was daunting."

21

Chapter 4:
Better Than, Less Than,
Different Than

As WORD of WCW's expansion filtered down to TNT's Executive Vice President, Bradley J. Siegel, it seemed as though Bischoff would face some serious resistance. "Brad [initially] said, 'I don't want it'," recalls Bill Burke, who was early in his tenure heading up TBS.

"Ad Sales and TNT's leadership were opposed to it," agrees Scot Safon, TNT's VP of Advertising. "It felt too downscale, didn't draw any of the audience we were doing well with - older men and women watching movies, or young urban/suburban men watching the NBA - [and so] 'Ad Sales' didn't know how we would sell it."

"We were also trying to differentiate [TNT and TBS]," continues Burke. "TBS was sort of more fun…baseball, wrestling…'movies for guys who like movies' was one of the things that we did. [Conversely], TNT was the best movie studio on television. They were making these kind of high-brow cool films, [for example]."

"There was a lot of competition between sister networks," remembers Tom Karsch, VP of Sports Marketing for TNT. "It wasn't a malicious competition, but it was a friendly and healthy one. At TNT, we really looked at ourselves as kind of the 'Tiffany network' of basic cable. We were spending more money on original movies, [and our] whole pitch to the Hollywood community and the stars was that they could bring their special projects to us.

"Not to mention, because we were carrying such good sports packages, it was one of the most expensive television networks for cable affiliates. [Therefore], it was really up to us to create real value for what they were paying.

"So we kind of looked at ourselves in a very snobby way. We were the gold standard of basic cable, and we looked down a little bit on the TBS guys because they were still doing their Elvis Presley marathons, and their James Bond marathons...Gilligan's Island...Andy Griffith [Show], that kind of stuff.

"At the time, wrestling kind of murkied the waters for us. We kind of thumbed our nose at it. It wasn't a sport, and at the network, we just thought it flew in the face of our brand positioning."

"[While] Ted started by strongly suggesting that TNT or TBS consider putting WCW on live in prime-time, he finally just mandated it," says Safon. "USA Network was drawing enormous numbers to prime-time with [*Monday Night Raw*] - multiples of what anyone was drawing with movies or old series. This was before major sports franchises were being presented on cable, and so the WWF numbers were unprecedented - [representing] the closest cable could come to those sports numbers.

"Ted was a fiercely competitive guy and had a strong belief that sports [type] programming, especially live sports, was very valuable on television. He also liked larger-than-life characters and grand gestures, and so he appreciated the more over-the-top aspects of what WCW was doing. I think he saw a lot of potential there, especially as the WWF started to draw enormous ratings, in prime-time, on USA."

Interestingly, the call for the new show to air on TNT occurred, according to Burke, only as a result of TBS' Monday night baseball coverage. "[WCW on Mondays] would have been on TBS, but we couldn't do it because of baseball," he recalls.

With the option of TBS carrying the program an impossibility, TNT head Siegel conceded that any resistance was futile. Besides, it wasn't as if the boss ever showed a tendency to deviate once a course of action had been determined. "Ted was a great decision maker," says Burke, "because whether you liked his decisions or not, he [unreservedly] made decisions, and then the company moved on."

The Chairman's decision-making process was often rather comedic (and admirable) in its simplicity. In 1992, he ordered the creation of the first 24-hour single-genre channel with animation as its main theme. While his marketing gurus deliberated the various options for its name, Ted made things easy for them. The network of cartoons became, well, *Cartoon Network*.

A year later, as his staff began to prepare for the launch of yet another cable network - this time, a platform designed to capitalize on Turner's impressive film library of some 3,500 titles - brainstorming began on what to call the new channel. The innovative American Movie Classics (AMC), with Brad Siegel, incidentally, as its head of programming, had already established its dominance in the small but profitable niche of old movies on television. With Siegel now working for Turner, and the example of AMC's success to learn from, focus groups were planned in a number of markets across the country. Turner's research department prepared a shortlist of eight potential names for the channel, but once word of the activity got back to Ted, he quickly sent out the following memo:

TO: Scott Sassa, Bradley J. Siegel
FROM: R.E. Turner
Subject: New channel

Turner Classic Movies is the name of the new channel.

Needless to say, the focus groups were immediately canceled.

———

For WCW's foray on TNT to be successful, its prime-time offerings had to become *event programming*, thought Siegel. The new show, he argued, needed to be live every week, and had to emanate from major arenas around the country. In essence, as he would later explain to *Broadcasting and Cable*, TNT had to create pro wrestling's version of the NFL's *Monday Night Football*.

Ironically, the network already carried the NFL's Sunday night games, originally marketed using the tag line *Sunday Nitro*. Seeing a clear opportunity to leverage an already established theme, TNT's VP of Public Relations, Jim Weiss, suggested that WCW adopt a similar show title: *WCW Monday Nitro Live!*

Meanwhile, Eric Bischoff began to digest the gravity of the task ahead of him. He knew that his future in professional wrestling depended wholly on the success (or lack thereof) of *Monday Nitro*. "There was a ton of pressure on me," Bischoff admits. "I'd be lying to suggest that I wasn't concerned about my job."

Bischoff wasn't the only one with concern, as in the industry publications read by the most hardcore of fans, the pundits were forecasting a gloomy road ahead. "Time is running out on the chances for a break-even year," wrote Bruce Mitchell of the *Pro Wrestling Torch*. "Eric Bischoff has to produce. After seven long years, [Turner] is serious about WCW finally breaking even." Dave Meltzer, editor of the revered *Wrestling Observer Newsletter*, was even more direct about the potential consequences of WCW's Monday move. "Turner has a lot of money," Meltzer told the *Philadelphia Inquirer*. "But this may be difficult, even suicidal, for WCW."

At a pair of WCW Executive Committee meetings (June 14th and June 29th, 1995, to be exact), Bischoff began to outline his strategy. Then, in early July - less than two months away from showtime - he detached himself for a short spell alone, hoping that further inspiration would arise from solitude. Sitting down with a legal pad, Bischoff arrived at a lucid realization: while WCW would perhaps never be perceived as *better* than the WWF, it certainly could be perceived as *different*.

It was an approach reminiscent of Al Ries and Jack Trout's *immutable laws of marketing*. For decades, big business realized that marketplace success was not so much about presenting a product as *better* than the competition, as much as it was about being first in a category - in other words, being seen as being the best at something *unique to itself*. The technology company Dell demonstrated this by creating the new paradigm of selling computers by phone, being flexible enough to differentiate themselves in an already crowded PC market. Ironically, Vince McMahon would later promote the WWF as being *sports entertainment* (as opposed to pro wrestling), in a controversial effort to be first in a category (and, not so coincidentally, to avoid the athletic commission taxes associated with 'real' sports).

Similarly, Bischoff was unlikely to find success positioning *Nitro*, at least at the beginning, solely as the *best* professional wrestling on prime-time television. Despite WCW's base of support in the South, the WWF brand **was** professional wrestling to the mainstream. Simply put, since McMahon's circuit was already perceived as the most prestigious national wrestling promotion, Bischoff needed to find a new category, or *space*, for *Nitro* to occupy.

If our competitor wants to appeal to children, he reasoned, *we can be wrestling for eighteen-to-thirty-nine-year-old males. If our competitor wants to present cartoonish, animated characters, we can present them with a keen sense of realism. If our competitor wants to continue its taped format for Monday Night Raw, we can take advantage of our status as live programming.*

The final point was of particular importance to Bischoff. An earlier discussion with Siegel led to the implementation of a research project to devise *Nitro*'s creative formula (Ted Turner, presumably, was kept in the dark). The outcomes of the study were clear - WCW's target audience wanted a feeling of spontaneity to permeate the new program. They wanted 'can't miss TV', a drastically different television format (as compared to the WWF strategy of giving away 'squash matches', i.e. bouts where established superstars predictably beat up on hapless underdogs), and an avoidance of the tried-and-true tactic of reserving the major, often more unpredictable match-ups for pay-per-view.

"I was fascinated by that research," remembers Bischoff. "It helped us really understand more about the psychology of *why* people really watch wrestling. As opposed to [basic questions such as] 'what do you like?' or 'what characters do you like?', it got into the emotional elements that they liked most about [the genre], especially compared

26

to other forms of television. I got very excited about it, because I was able to focus on the key elements that drove the audience."

As Bischoff considered the stylistic elements that would give *Nitro* a competitive edge, Pat McNeely, a highly respected Turner graphic design artist and director, was tasked with creating the show's opening sequence. "We met with the TNT higher-ups," McNeely recalls, "and it was a little strange. They were like, 'what else have you worked on?' and 'we [really] need to be involved'.

"TNT didn't want [the open] to look like Atlanta. They wanted it to look like 'anytown USA' - bigger. So we came up with an idea where there was this cityscape...and kind of a desolate opening. All of a sudden, you see this fire comin' down the street, and as the fire comes, explosions go off, and on the buildings you see sort of 'mapped' wrestling footage. We pitched it as a storyboard and drew everything we could think of! It was like a 15-second open, and at the end, there would be a line of fire going through every frame, hitting this huge, 50-foot tall logo. It was like, '*Nitro* is here!'

"We went down to Disney in Orlando, where they had a kind of 'forced perspective' city street back lot. At the end of this [constructed] three-block street at a right angle, they had built this huge plaque of New York City. It looked like walking down the street in Manhattan...just a huge skyline...but it was only about 20-feet tall. We thought, 'this is perfect!'"

When McNeely and his director Karl Horstmann returned to the Disney site in early August, however, the entire cityscape had been destroyed, a casualty of Hurricane Erin. "Buildings were torn off, chunks of metal were showing," laughs McNeely, who also designed the *Nitro* logo. "We worked until late that night, trying to figure out how to solve this problem, re-drawing storyboards [and so on]. We said, 'this is gonna cost extra money, because instead of using that backdrop, we have to now put one in'. We have to *add a cityscape*, which at the time, was a little bit of a bigger deal that it would be now.

"We called Eric Bischoff at about 10 o'clock at night. We said, 'there's a problem. The hurricane has knocked down part of our set here, and it's gonna cost 50 thousand dollars extra to fix it'.

Bischoff had only one question, recalls McNeely.

"He just asked, 'is it still gonna look cool?'"

———

Bischoff approved the additional cost, his attention more likely focused on an escalating psychological battle with Vince McMahon, a man with a drive so relentless, it was believed without parallel.

Vince doesn't sleep, new WWF recruits were often warned.

He never stops working.

He can't stop working.

Oh, and don't sneeze.

He hates when people can't control themselves.

Cleverly, McMahon, ever the spin doctor, revealingly failed to mention Bischoff by name in an appearance on Chet Coppock's *NewSport Talk* show. By skillfully directing his comments towards Ted Turner, who despite numerous public statements of approval, had no direct involvement in WCW's day-to-day affairs, he was able to frame the WWF as the underdog. "That was the perception McMahon wanted to create, and the media ate that up," observes Alan Sharp. "They didn't wanna hear that Vince McMahon was competing with Eric Bischoff, [rather], he was 'competing against Billionaire Ted'. I would literally have conversations with reporters and say, 'you know that Ted Turner has nothing to do with our wrestling product, right'?"

"We love the sports entertainment business," McMahon stated in the *NewSport* interview. "It's a family owned business. It's something you almost have to grow up in to really understand. It's not just another business venture, as it is with Ted Turner." As for Hulk Hogan, his former cash cow, McMahon provided his blunt assessment, labeling Hogan's WCW run as a "disaster."

A week later, Bischoff made his own appearance on the show, enjoying a billing as "Ted Turner's right hand man, in charge of one of Ted's favorite companies." WCW, according to Bischoff, had already proven itself worthy of doing battle in the ratings contest. "We're [already] neck and neck with them," he boasted, in reference to the historically strong ratings on TBS. "I'm sure [that] I'm going to develop a product that is very unique and different from what we're doing right now. It's going to be *different* from anything our competition's doing, and it's something I think will be exciting for the viewers.

"It's an alternative - a choice. I'm excited about giving viewers and fans that choice."

To fully ensure his rhetoric agreed with reality, Bischoff decided to appoint himself as *Nitro*'s play-by-play announcer. Given his commitment to divergence, it was hardly a surprising move; rather, it was downright necessary, he thought. Besides, to be frank, Bischoff viewed himself as the best option available, despite some fans' expectation that Tony Schiavone - a commentator closely identified with the company lineage - would be offered the role instead.

Schiavone was many things - intelligent, hard-working, and often stunningly believable - but *Nitro* was in need of a fresh voice. After all, for all the talk of its decline, the WWF had *owned* Monday night wrestling since the debut of *Raw* in 1993. For WCW, therefore, the need to shake things up - and, more importantly, convince fans to change their viewing habits - innately necessitated an original, perhaps even audacious kind of presentation. And so, with the cocksure Bischoff as its visionary, leader and mouthpiece, a novel production style enveloping the program, and a roster of stars led by Hulk Hogan, *Nitro* figured to be - at the very least - immediately intriguing.

29

However, to what extent *Nitro* could be *competitive* was certainly in question. Ultimately, its success would be measured by its *Nielsen rating*, specifically as compared to *Monday Night Raw*. According to *Nielsen*'s formula (which incidentally, provoked skepticism as far back as the '60s), one ratings 'point' reflected one *percent* of the potential TV market (approximately 954,000 households, as of September 1995). In other words, a show recording a 1.5 rating, for example, theoretically attracted 1,431,000 households. A separate but oft-cited statistic, the audience *share*, revealed the percentage allocation of the *viewing audience* (i.e. households actively viewing television) who tuned in to a particular show. Indispensable as a gauge of popularity, both metrics provided the basis for advertising rates throughout the industry.

Contrary to popular belief, the Nielsen company did not arrive at its figures through ubiquitous measurement. Rather, it utilized a sample size of some 5,000 households, chosen randomly from U.S. census statistics, to collect its data. Specially installed meter boxes reported the preferences of so-called 'Nielsen families', using telephone lines to send viewing data digitally. According to the company, channel changes were tracked to the nearest minute, although the particulars - as well as the rating and share itself - became available only during the next business day.

Another misnomer concerned the relationship between audience size and advertising rates. One common interpretation propounded that programs with higher ratings produced higher *revenues* - a logical fallacy insofar as it flagrantly disregarded crucial influencing factors (notably, content and demographics). In 1994, to cite one illustrative example, *Seinfeld* commanded $390,000 for a 30-second spot - $40,000 more than *Home Improvement* - despite attracting fewer overall viewers. Its ability to draw more young viewers (often defined as the 'highly desirable' 18-49 demographic) instead made all the difference. In sum, as industry experts realized, advertisers bought 'demos' before they did households.

Despite its purported commitment to accuracy, the inherent flaws in *Nielsen*'s system seemed rather obvious. Its method of extrapolation (derisively referred to as 'voodoo' in some circles) almost invited manipulation. To prove this point, a Los Angeles TV station once aired a series on 'Nielsen families', who subsequently tuned in with undivided attention. Needless to say, the station numbers skyrocketed overnight.

"*Nielsen* was the only game in town at the time," sighs one former WCW employee. "People had their doubts about its efficacy and the methodology, but it was the only benchmark that existed. The tools were clunky and the servers prone to crashing, but what choice did we have? Everyone was resigned that it was a bad system…it was the only system."

As it was the only system, there was little choice but to conquer it. To this end, a host of auxiliary considerations would require careful monitoring from production staff. "At the time," begins Richard Steinberg, TBS' Director of Corporate Intelligence from 1989 to 1995, "the television ratings business was done in 15 minute intervals. If you had a viewer for eight or more minutes of that time period, you got credited for the whole 15 minutes - whether people were switching or not. [Therefore], the key was to retain the audience.

"You had some limitations on the cable network side. There are 'interconnects', where the local commercials come in after :25 past the hour, then :35 after, and :55 after. Those are hard breaks - you can't get away from those things - because that's when the cable networks sell their local advertising. So you have to be cognizant of how to program around those breaks that naturally come in to your program.

"[But] we were literally going head-to-head with Vince on the same night, so we wanted to start slightly earlier. [By doing so], we could capture the audience ahead of time, and then keep them throughout the program. You had to keep people, so the smart move was to [strategically] put on a strong enough match, to stop people from switching the dial."

As Vince McMahon eagerly pointed out, WCW benefited from its

31

parent company owning the TNT network. It offered the opportunity, as Steinberg noted, to start early, or - if necessary - even run late. For those within WCW that had seen darker days, it was refreshing to finally be the aggressor. "TNT was a different environment than being on TBS," says Rob Garner, WCW's former VP of TV Programming and Sales. "We thought, 'we've got a station with incredible coverage in TNT' and 'we've got a brand that's different from the WWF'. With *Raw* being on Monday nights forever, we felt that there was an audience there."

Chapter 5:
The Taskmaster

WHILE BISCHOFF CONTINUED to develop the overall vision for *Nitro*, the week-to-week content of the program would largely be handled by Kevin Sullivan - WCW's head matchmaker, or *booker* in wrestling vernacular. As a notorious heel wrestler in the Florida territory a decade earlier, Sullivan employed a ruthless devil worshiping persona with such believability that fans quickly overlooked his billed height of only 5 feet, 8 inches. Known as the 'Prince of Darkness', Sullivan emerged in Florida amidst the backdrop of a moral panic surrounding supposed satanic cult-based abuse, a mostly mass-media fueled hysteria that followed a growing occult fascination throughout the '70s. His nefarious character carried an iron spike to the ring, mercilessly beat female valets, and existed in sharp contrast to other contemporary villains, whose character motivations - in large part - tended to revolve around cheating to capture championships from sympathetic crowd favorites.

Sullivan's most frequent foil was the beloved Dusty Rhodes, an overweight 'son of a plumber' whose intensely charismatic interviews bonded him strongly with the region's working-class people. Their long-running feud throughout 1982 set-up a sell-out clash in St. Petersburg, FL. on Christmas Day, with a stipulation that the loser would leave the state for 60 days. Festivities be damned, Sullivan sent Rhodes packing in a stunning twist ending, pinning the popular protagonist after help from 'Santa Claus' (a costume in fact occupied by Jake 'The Snake' Roberts).

While in Florida, Sullivan learned under the tutelage of promoter Eddie Graham, whose philosophy emphasized the importance of maintaining *kayfabe*, the pretense that the staged rivalries and performances of professional wrestling were entirely authentic. As such, Sullivan, as was commonplace among wrestlers for generations, vigorously maintained the aura of his on-screen character at all times. While pro wrestling, as evidenced by newspaper accounts as early as the 1930s, generally operated under the suspicion (and later widespread public understanding) that its events were pre-conceived, promoters across the country believed strongly in the sanctity of preserving its illusory existence as a legitimate sport.

The belief was, it could be argued, entirely well founded - after all, wrestling had its roots in genuine competition, and the 20th century offered numerous examples (harness racing, perhaps most famously) of popular spectacles whose decline correlated with a rise in public mistrust regarding its authenticity. Moreover, the kayfabe practice was part of a wider rallying cry to *protect the business*, an ethos achieved by never acknowledging that conflicts were manipulated, wrestling in a believable style, and preventing curious outsiders from being 'smartened up'.

But Graham's brilliance transcended his adherence to the credo that wrestling should be presented as real. He had an uncanny feel for the Floridian audience, Sullivan thought, seemingly knowing instinctively when to progress or conclude a popular storyline. His ability to instruct wrestlers how to build to the finish of matches - thus baiting the audience towards a logical, and eventually, satisfying finale - was thought to be singular. In most cases, his 'finishes' would raise even more interest in the next chapter of a story, and in later years, Sullivan would adopt a similar mentality when constructing his most important shows. *If you can't book the match, the finish, and the return*, he would tell his assistants, *then don't book the match at all.*

On Super Bowl Sunday, 1985, Graham stunningly committed suicide, the apparent consequence of mounting personal and business-related issues. His death rocked Sullivan, who was ultimately given the chance to book the territory later in the year. Similar to his mentor, Sullivan ensured that each televised twist and turn occurred amidst the facade of legitimate athletic competition. For that reason, his shows almost always began with a technical wrestling match, saving the heavy blood-and-guts violence for the main event. After all, he grew fond of saying, *it still says wrestling on the marquee.*

In February 1987, Championship Wrestling from Florida (CWF) - the corporate name for the Florida territory - closed after being bought by Jim Crockett Promotions. Ironically, Sullivan's on-screen adversary Dusty Rhodes would play a role in JCP's own demise (and subsequent purchase by TBS the following year). In his own spell as a booker, Rhodes heavily relied on a match finish originally devised by Eddie Graham; a trick ending intended to gain sympathy for an unlucky babyface. Fans soon caught on to the routine - their hero would persevere to triumph in a title match, only to have the decision (and thus, the title win) reversed due to a technicality, often involving a conveniently unconscious referee. In time, a variation of *The Dusty Finish*, as it would later become known, treated fans to an ambiguous ending whereby the actual victor of a match was left unclear. Sullivan, whose role as a performer continued after the CWF sale, understood clearly why the pattern of confusing finishes was occurring. Backstage politics were rife, and too often, the solution to resolving tensions among top-tier talent was to effectively have neither party win or lose. But in the end, of course, there *was* a clear loser - the fans themselves.

———

In the territory era, wrestling bookers stayed in power as long as their creative output resulted in good business. By deciding the match-ups, constructing finishes, and building *programs* - a series of matches between two opponents - bookers aimed to build fan interest by alternatively building and 'paying-off' conflicts over the course of several months (and in rare cases, even longer).

Televised programming, which mainly served as a platform to advertise the frequent *untelevised* shows throughout the region, was notable for the use of judicious (and impactful) *angles* (wrestling plots designed to introduce or advance stories), and impassioned interviews or *promos* used by wrestlers to promote their upcoming fights (in the case of Dusty Rhodes, such interviews could take on an almost spiritual form). With minimal instructions from the booker - typically, only the interview subject (e.g. "you're wrestling Ric Flair on Sunday, and he cheated to beat you last time") and the available time (e.g. "you've got three minutes") - the inherently spontaneous trash-talking often became the most realistic and entertaining portion of a wrestling program.

Rather than writing a script, bookers opted to produce a *format* for their TV shows, sometimes as short as one page in length. Nevertheless, booking was arguably the most difficult job in wrestling. Great bookers had to not only manipulate the fans, but in many cases, the actual performers; due to the pre-determined (and live) nature of pro wrestling, a wrestler could theoretically refuse to play the role of loser, potentially ruining months of careful build-up. Successful bookers had to be able to identify talent - more importantly, *money-drawing talent* - and convince supporting acts that their position, which could include being a perpetual 'loser', was of great value.

Kevin Sullivan, many people thought, possessed these qualities in spades. In the early years of his career, while working as a fresh-faced midcarder in New York, he stumbled across a notebook after arriving early to an arena show. Inside the book, he found plans detailing the upcoming matches and feuds for the company he wrestled for, the WWWF. Almost as quickly as he perused its contents, however, he was interrupted by its owner - a bemused Vince McMahon, Sr.

To Sullivan's surprise, McMahon Sr. calmly explained his overall philosophy towards booking the territory, apparently appreciative of his young wrestler's curiosity. Sullivan listened intently, only speaking briefly to ask another question. *Why do you have these two guys wrestling each other three times, and these guys only twice? How do you know whose gonna face Bruno (Sammartino) next month at the Garden? How do you get these guys to work together?*

McMahon, Sr., evidently, could provide a clear rationale to support all of his major matchmaking decisions, and Sullivan, influenced immensely by the conversation, began a career-long trajectory towards his appointment as WCW's head booker in September 1994. By that time, Sullivan, a native Bostonian with a knack for starting a sentence with 'brother…' and ending it with 'y'know what I mean?', was more than familiar with the cautious backstage maneuvering needed to promote locker room harmony. On a tour of Germany at the start of his tenure, he projected a sense of welcomed self-assuredness in a conversation with his biggest star, Hulk Hogan. "Hulk came to me," Sullivan remembers, "and asked, 'can you take us there?' I said, 'yeah, I can take you to the promised land, just [leave] it to me'."

Proud of his Irish roots, Sullivan claimed to be from the same family tree as John L. Sullivan, the 'Boston Strong Boy' and first heavyweight champion of gloved boxing in 1882. Perhaps because of his family ties, the modern-day Sullivan professed a keen interest in boxing, often referring to the sport as the 'first cousin' of pro wrestling. He drew inspiration from the great fighters, especially Muhammad Ali, and even while booking WCW, he could still be affected by a great bout. As one wrestler remembers, an emotional Sullivan applauded with tears in his eyes - no doubt while hatching his next great creative idea - at the conclusion of a particularly stunning Evander Holyfield performance.

Through a thick Boston accent and a distinctive cadence of speech which frequently made reference to historical events, Sullivan could effectively communicate the minutiae of an angle to an intrinsically cagey performer. He believed that plot points could be subtle in their emergence, nuanced in their execution, and perhaps even subliminal in their presentation. In general, however, his philosophy remained, in the tradition of Eddie Graham, to present wrestling as a real sport. When all else failed - assuming his approach failed to make sense to others - he would articulate an idea by using an analogy from baseball, another favorite pastime.

As Sullivan saw it, his ability to improve WCW's creative fortunes could potentially be hampered by two forces - which paradoxically, could have also been seen as WCW's two biggest assets - Hulk Hogan, and TBS itself. Sullivan had particular disregard for Turner's financial people, or 'North Tower bean counters' as he referred to them, after an accountant allegedly advised him to prominently feature (or 'push') wrestlers only towards the top of the pay scale. *A talent* *making $200,000 can't pin one making $500,000*, he remembers being told. *That way, we can at least try to rationalize our investments in talent.*

The concept of determining wrestlers' position on the card by salary, if indeed encouraged, would appear to fly in the face of conventional wrestling booking. In order to maximize profitability, it would stand to reason that bookers would pay close attention to fan reactions (and more importantly, purchase habits) when deciding upon an appropriate role for a particular wrestler. Furthermore, there were often clear indicators as to who patrons wished to see in high-profile matches, as attendance numbers, pay-per-view buy rates, television ratings and merchandise sales could - to a reasonable extent - be correlated with which stars occupied the main event slots.

As for Hogan, his contract with WCW contained a crucial clause, one that would seemingly ensure his status as the company's top star in perpetuity. His agreement contained language which gave him complete *creative control* over his character. Therefore, if a younger star, for example, began to connect strongly with fans and showed potential to draw serious money, the outcome of an eventual match with Hogan could not be decided wholly by Sullivan (or even, for that matter, Eric Bischoff). While Sullivan eventually found Hogan to be generally receptive of his ideas, he also conceded that Hulk would naturally be reluctant to risk his spot as the 'top guy', as crucially, his contract called for sizable pay-per-view and attendance-based bonuses. With millions of dollars in incentives at stake, *any* main eventer was likely to trust themselves first to draw money, Sullivan thought. Unfortunately for WCW, the provision in Hogan's deal was a necessity to secure his services, as without relinquishing this power - it was widely believed - the signing never would have occurred in the first place.

And so, in an effort to gain Hogan's trust, Sullivan contends, WCW's on-air product in 1995 featured a cartoonish stable of heel wrestlers, commonly banded together to thwart the aging Hulkster at every turn. The group, billed as the 'Dungeon of Doom', curiously resembled the goofy collection of bad guys Hogan dispatched during his 80's WWF run. Reluctantly, he says, Sullivan agreed to spearhead the evil alliance, and via an on-screen persona called *The Taskmaster*, he told viewers his goal was to rid the world - permanently - of *Hulkamania*.

Behind the curtain, ironically, Sullivan *did* realize that his star's good-guy act had worn thin. With the *Dungeon* storyline bombing throughout the summer of '95, Hulk's colorful routine, undoubtedly a relic from the previous decade, only served further to galvanize a noticeable contempt among WCW loyalists. Increasingly, before the cameras began to roll, and as the ring announcer informed fans of Hogan's presence, the negative reaction was painfully perceptible; meanwhile, in the locker room backstage, while the resonant sound of a thousand 'boos' echoed around them, a group of younger wrestlers raised their eyebrows in resigned frustration.

Chapter 6:
Surprise, Surprise

WITH ONLY WEEKS REMAINING until the *Nitro* debut, Bischoff continued to ponder TNT's research findings. Time and again, he kept returning to a theme of the focus group discussions - *surprises*. Quite simply, observed Bischoff, wrestling fans loved to be surprised. If he could regularly keep viewers guessing, manufacturing astonishment with narrative twists and turns, *Nitro* could surely establish itself as 'must-see' programming. In this regard, the first episode offered a chance to set the tone, but it was - as grand plans often are - easier said than done.

But then, Bischoff received a phone call from Steve Borden, better known as the flamboyant babyface Sting. A holdover from the Crockett days, Sting survived all the management shake-ups and company embarrassments to become WCW's most popular 'home-grown' star, earning $750,000 annually (a figure known colloquially as *Sting money*) in the process.

In between matches, Sting often spent time on the phone with Larry Pfohl, aka Lex Luger, a former WCW talent and one of the WWF's headline stars. During one such talk on an August afternoon, Pfohl let it slip that he was currently working without a written agreement. *I haven't been under contract for six months*, he told Borden. *Vince [McMahon] and I are working on a handshake deal*. In total disbelief, Borden gathered himself, and suggested that a return to WCW might be a good career move. *So contractually, you're a free agent right now*, Borden clarified. *If you don't mind, I'll speak with Eric Bischoff*.

But despite seeing the potential in signing a key WWF performer - and certainly setting up a shocking surprise - Bischoff was decidedly indifferent. In his prior dealings with 'Lex', a dedicated bodybuilder who once portrayed a character known as *The Narcissist* (it wasn't a stretch, according to those who knew him well), Bischoff found the star to be insufferably arrogant. In their first meeting regarding a potential move - a clandestine discussion housed in Borden's garage - Bischoff recalls offering a paltry $150,000 a year contract, some $350,000 *less* than Lex had been making with the WWF. Moreover, the offer was a conditional one, based only on his willingness to leave McMahon's company without trace. *Are you saying I can't give Vince [McMahon] any kind of notice?* Lex purportedly asked.

That is correct, replied Bischoff.

If Luger couldn't keep quiet, word of a possible 'jump' would surely reach the WWF. Although *Nitro* would emanate as a live program, secretive plans leaked frequently in wrestling, spawning a humorous expression in the process: *telephone, telegram, tell-a-wrestler...*

Such disclosures were often reported by the *wrestling media*, a collection of newsletters, magazines and radio shows that Bischoff mostly loathed. "I had absolutely no respect for them," he says, "nor did I value their opinions at all. There was no reason to, quite frankly."

On Monday, August 14th, 1995, WCW organized a press event for 'legitimate' media members - the formal launch of *Monday Nitro*. At a press conference held at the Harley Davidson Cafe in New York - for all intents and purposes, the WWF's backyard - Brad Siegel valiantly professed that WCW was an ideal fit for his network. "We actually went to WCW and said, 'we want a show that will be the best wrestling event on television, and we wanna put it on Monday nights'," the network president claimed.

Strategically, TNT selected a start date for *Nitro* to air unopposed; in other words, *without competition*, as in a fortuitous occurrence, *Raw* was set to be pre-empted by the U.S. Open, leaving the entire wrestling audience up for grabs (for one week, at least).

"We'd like to make an announcement today that I'm very, very pleased to make," continued Siegel. "Starting Labor Day night - Monday September 4th - TNT will once again live up to its name in a very explosive way. WCW wrestling comes to our network, live every week, in prime time and from a different city."

"*WCW Monday Nitro Live!* will be seen Monday nights live at 9pm Eastern, and will originate - as we said - from a different city, every single week. The one hour telecast will be replayed at midnight Eastern, nine o'clock Pacific, [and] WCW's debut on TNT will be live from the Mall of America in Minneapolis, Minnesota. [It] will be called the 'Brawl at the Mall'."

The choice of venue for the first show was, in the eyes of many wrestling purists, an unusual one. But located near the Minneapolis-Saint Paul metropolitan area, the 4.2 million sq. ft. Mall would provide a glittering backdrop for the spectacle - and with over 30,000 daily visitors to the plaza, a curious and suitably large crowd for the show could be expected. Interestingly, the Mall became a viable idea only after initial discussions regarding a New York City debut were swiftly thwarted, the consequence of the WWF's exclusivity agreement with Madison Square Garden. "There are a lot of interesting things in the business of booking arenas," smirked Bischoff, standing confidently at the press podium. "We will come from New York [in the future]," he promised.

"WCW wrestling will become the centerpiece of a brand new franchise on TNT called *Monday Nitro*," continued Siegel. "Each week at eight o'clock - leading in to the telecast - we will present the action adventure television series *Thunder and Paradise* which stars Hulk Hogan. After both airings of WCW on TNT, we will present a very heavy duty action movie to make *Monday Nitro* a very action-driven night [of television].

"TNT is becoming known for a network that has the best of its kind. We've got the best sports franchises with the NFL and the NBA. We're quickly becoming the best maker of original movies on TV....we have the best cartoons...the best movie library available. [And so] we thought it was about time to put the best wrestling on TNT."

42

"It's a heck of an opportunity," beamed Bischoff in support several minutes later. "Those of you who...have watched our growth over the last 12 months know that there's a lot of momentum here. I wanna thank Brad. I wanna thank everybody at TNT.

"There's a lot of great people [working at TNT]. They're creative. They're driven. They're aggressive...and that's the kind of combination we felt we needed to take WCW to the next level. And that's exactly what we intend to do."

As the press conference wore on, a stoic Siegel witnessed a buoyant Bischoff boldly predict a competitive ratings battle from the start. "Since the addition of Hulk Hogan and Randy Savage, [WCW] has really closed the gap [with the WWF]," argued Bischoff. "We're coming on strong and we have a lot of momentum. We believe that we've got the biggest stars in our industry...and that's what entertainment is all about. [People are] entertained by stars, and we've got 'em in WCW. Now [fans are] going to have a choice. They can watch whatever else is going on...or they can flip on over and watch *Monday Nitro* on TNT.

"This show is gonna be in your face...up to the edge...over the edge...[there's gonna be a] surprise every single Monday. It's gonna be live and when I tell you it's 'in your face', I mean it's gonna be *in your face*...this is an incredibly different product.

"I think the fact that we have the biggest stars in the industry already differentiates us from the WWF and *Monday Night Raw*. A lot of the people they have over there are kind of...WCW has-beens. We're gonna be live every week - they're not. We're gonna take the show all over the country.

"All I can say is tune in. September 4th, you'll see the difference. I can stand up here and talk all afternoon long about creatively, all of the different things that we're gonna do...but we're gonna give the show an edge. This show is gonna be more like rock-and-roll than meat and potatoes. [It's a] faster pace, more of an MTV-type of show.

"[So] how long do I think it's gonna take [to become number one]? Hey, I'm not gonna [instantly] overtake a company that's done a pretty good job of branding themselves in this position for the last couple of years. This is a long-term project for us. We're not doing this to just see if it's gonna work for six months. This is a long-term project, and we've got a big commitment from the Turner organization, Brad Siegel, and some very aggressive creative people over at TNT.

"The only thing I like better than competition is winning, and we look forward to [winning]."

But it would not be Bischoff, however, who would deliver the most biting comment in the WWF's direction. Mindful of the potential impact of a Lex Luger defection, Sting - representing the stars of WCW along with Hulk Hogan and Randy Savage - presciently foreshadowed what was about to come.

"All I gotta say to sum it up," Sting bellowed at the media, "[is] somebody is in for a *Raw deal*."

———

Returning to the New York market in his red-and-yellow garb, Hulk Hogan generated significant attention at the press conference. Showcasing the affable charm that long endeared him to decision makers - both in and out of the industry - since the early 1980s, Hogan took to the podium with ease. "Now I've got Mr. Siegel right where I want him," he joked, demonstrating a headlock before teasing an eventual match with Savage, almost in the very next breath. After a deft Harley Davidson plug, Hogan prepared to conclude his comments with a modification of a catch phrase he made famous in an earlier time. "What are you gonna do," he asked rhetorically, "when Hulk Hogan and *Monday Nitro* run wild on you?"

Curiously, the line was delivered, but devoid of reaction. Hogan's eyes darted as he repeated himself, fighting back against an apparent glitch in the matrix. "What are you gonna do when Hulk Hogan and

44

Monday Nitro run wild on you?" he demanded again, achieving some mild applause in response. For the first time in a long time - maybe forever - the usually willing media greeted the Hulkster routine with a collective yawn.

Nevertheless, and despite WCW entering a new era, there appeared no sign of phasing out the Hulk Hogan character. Observers noted the intriguing coincidence of a Hogan-themed restaurant, *Pastamania*, situated conveniently inside the Mall of America doors. It stood as a telling reminder that despite the aging champion's failure to connect with the hardcores, his sheer recognizability still created opportunities that no other wrestler could enjoy. To the casual mainstream audience, he remained the most famous performer of his genre, the *Michael Jordan of wrestling*, it could easily be argued. For that reason, Bischoff decreed that the inaugural *Nitro* feature a rare Hogan title defense, effectively giving away a pay-per-view match on television.

Meanwhile, in the time since his summit with Bischoff, Lex Luger received a formal contract offer from Vince McMahon. In an unusual lapse of attention, McMahon was oblivious to the possibility of covert Atlanta talks, but regardless, his offer failed to address several (preexisting) points of contention. On Friday, September 1st, Lex called Sting to inquire about Bischoff's earlier proposal. Two days later, on Sunday, September 3rd, 24 hours before the Minneapolis *Nitro* and incredibly, the same day as Luger was advertised to appear on a WWF card in New Brunswick, Canada, Bischoff reiterated the terms of the deal: *$150,000 per year, no notice, and everything must be kept under wraps. I'm in*, Lex confirmed, confident that eventually, his performance would warrant a commensurate raise.

During the following morning, Luger boarded a plane headed for Minneapolis. At the airport, he was bundled into a van and driven to a hotel separate from the other wrestlers, minimizing the risk of being seen by fans camping out in the lobby for autographs and pictures. To ensure that no one - not even 'the boys' themselves - could potentially leak out word of his defection, he was instructed to wait in his room until just before show time. Upon arrival at the Mall, he was escorted to an isolated area away from detection, a towel covering his head for good measure. Bischoff then delivered the pertinent instructions - at the outset of a match involving Ric Flair and Sting, Luger would first appear, and then, at the very end of the show, *"you'll come out again and get nose-to-nose with Hulk,"* Bischoff told him.

At 8:00pm EST, the *Nitro* era was officially under way. Pat McNeely's brilliantly designed opening sequence, featuring a hearty dose of explosions and pyro effects, preceded sweeping aerial shots of downtown Minneapolis. *"From the land of ten thousand lakes..."* narrated an exuberant Eric Bischoff, *"...Minneapolis, Minnesota...the Mall of America..."* he continued, as an establishing shot of the Mall exterior filled the screen. *"The only building big enough to hold the debut edition of WCW Monday Nitro!"*

The shot faded to an impressive overhead of the ring, surrounded by an enthusiastic crowd, sparkling lights, and the striking image of captivated patrons on board a huge ascending escalator. *"We are coming to you live,"* emphasized Bischoff, *"here on TNT!"*

On the undercard, the show kicked off with a fast-paced clash between the colorful Jushin 'Thunder' Liger, and the unpredictable Brian Pillman. "I knew we were gonna do well with that," says Sullivan, "because Liger was the darling of the [wrestling media] at the time. I also knew that I wanted [Ric] Flair to wrestle Sting."

Since fighting each other to a 45-minute draw in a legendary bout at *Clash of the Champions* in 1988, Flair and Sting had been inexorably linked in the minds of wrestling fans. They possessed a unique chemistry, with Flair's methodical style contrasting perfectly with the upbeat, enthusiastic and highly athletic Sting. More importantly, in a time of great need, they could be relied on faithfully to attract an audience, a fact not lost on Sullivan. "Since the *Clash of the Champions*, you could just put them down [to wrestle] and they were gonna draw a number," he shrugs. "It didn't take any genius to figure that out."

The presentation looked major league, and the action lived up the hype. The Pillman-Liger opener, conducted at a frantic pace with exciting high flying moves, could hardly be mistaken for the plodding style of a typical *Raw* match. Next, in a complete shock to viewers at home - not to mention Vince McMahon himself - Lex Luger emerged in the entrance aisle as Flair and Sting prepared to do battle. *"What the hell is he doing here!?"* exclaimed Bischoff coyly in his announcing role. *"Get the camera off of him! Get the security and get him outta here!"*

"I think I'm the only person who can say that I attended every single *Nitro*," says David Penzer, the long-time company ring announcer. "When Lex Luger walked down that aisle, it sent a message to everyone that 'hey, we're for real'."

In the main event, a predictable paint-by-numbers Hogan match ended with the Hulk-Luger confrontation, and in a clever move, director Craig Leathers cut to break shortly after the two stars collided. As the commercials rolled on TNT, however, the in-ring face off almost got real; a relaxed Luger broke character as the cameras turned away, smiling at WCW's biggest star in a moment of satisfied tranquility. *Wipe that grin off your face, or I'll knock it off,* threatened the Hulkster through gritted teeth. *You're stealing money from me and my family right now.*

Once the show resumed, the venerable 'Mean' Gene Okerlund, a peerless on-screen interviewer beloved in wrestling circles, entered the fray to uncover some answers. *"I am sick and tired of playing around with 'kids',"* Luger announced over Okerlund's microphone, alluding to the younger, less established roster of his most recent employer. *"I'm here to get it on with the big boys, and that means you,"* he directed at Hogan. A title match was announced for the *following week* - an intrepid move considering the bout's perceived importance.

After the show, a concerned Lex attempted to apologize for breaking character, but the old-school Hogan unceremoniously brushed him aside, bristling at the notion that someone would endanger kayfabe. Nonetheless, Luger's dramatic entrance had given Bischoff the element of *unpredictability* that the pre-*Nitro* research study suggested he needed. To several confidants, Bischoff quietly predicted that a 2.5 rating - precisely 2,385,000 viewers, according to Nielsen's ratings formula, could be within reach once the head-to-head competition began proper the following week.

But no one quite knew what number to expect for the first (unopposed) show. In the hotel bar afterwards, Kevin Sullivan tempered expectations, telling *Pro Wrestling Torch* reporter Wade Keller that it would take months for the TBS viewership to find *Nitro* on TNT. Across the bar, Eric Bischoff watched its replay on a television screen, digesting the finished product as a viewer for the first time. "He was glued to the screen like a parent watching their child perform in a high school play," Keller wrote years later. "[But he was] surely critiquing it in his mind, too."

Chapter 7:
The Doc

ON TUESDAY AFTERNOON, the number came in: *Nitro* scored a *2.9*, roughly 2.75 million viewers, in its debut edition. Suddenly caught blindsided by Luger's departure - not to mention the strong first week rating - the WWF were reeling heading into week two, the first official head-to-head battle. Tantalizingly, however, McMahon could do little to combat the advertised Hogan vs. Luger match on September 11th. *Raw* was already taped in advance, meaning he could only watch as *Nitro*, building serious momentum already, triumphed with a 2.5-2.2 win.

It was a remarkable achievement for WCW, TNT, and perhaps above all, Eric Bischoff, whose self-belief and vision was already paying big dividends. "When Eric told me about going head-to-head originally," reveals Diamond Dallas Page, "I told him, 'dude, I don't think that's a good idea'. I'm thinking, 'what, are we gonna get a '1', and they're gonna get like a '1.8?' Who's gonna give a fuck? If anything, it's gonna bring down wrestling.

"But I didn't understand the 'clicker effect'. I didn't understand what kind of impact Lex Luger coming in from day one would have. Nobody knew about that but Lex, Sting, and Bischoff - I didn't even know that, back then. All Bischoff said was 'watch tonight, there's gonna be a surprise'.

"But when it actually went on, head-to-head, it really showed - and this is something we would learn over time - if there's 10 fans, three weren't gonna watch anything but WCW. Three or four were WWF fans, and they weren't gonna watch anything but WWF. Then there were three or four fans who bounced back and forth. [The competition] pulled some of those [undecided] fans to watch WCW, and vice versa."

According to the Nielsen numbers, 4.7% of the television audience (on average) watched wrestling on September 11th, 1995, the first head-to-head ratings battle. Interestingly, however, many believed (including Bischoff himself) that the percentage was misleading. "There was a ton of duplication in that number," Bischoff said years later, referencing the phenomenon of viewers switching back-and-forth.

In this case, "duplication" meant that some audience members, through their decision to rapidly change programs, could effectively be accounted for *twice* in the rating. "I think that's impossible, let's put it that way," clarifies Mike Ciraldo, former Sales Manager for WCW. "I think that the Nielsen model is sophisticated enough…so that it would never happen. There is no way that if I switch from the Yankee game to CNN, then back-and-forth several times, that these programs are gonna get twice the number."

Although a resurgent WWF triumphed with its *Raw* offering on September 18th - registering a 2.5 to *Nitro*'s 2.4, the difference of some one hundred thousand viewers - Bischoff became even more determined to live up to his original mandate. "I was there on Eric Bischoff's couch...because we lived on the other side of the hill from each other," continues Page, "and he told me, 'I'm gonna knock Vince out. I'm gonna beat him. *We are gonna beat the WWF*'. I used to think to myself, 'what the fuck is he smoking?' Nobody can compete with McMahon. Pepsi can't compete with Coke, y'know?"

If Bischoff was indeed aiming for a knockout, it appeared to be of the first round variety. His inflammatory on-air comments, which included giving away results from the taped *Raw* show in opposition, set the tone for the gamesmanship to come. "*By the way*," he brashly advised viewers as Sting entered the ring for a match, "*in case you're tempted to grab the remote control, check out the competition, don't bother.*

"*[Their show] is two or three weeks old. Shawn Michaels beat [Sid Vicious] with a superkick that you couldn't earn a green belt with in*

50

a local YMCA. Stay right here - it's live, it's where the action is!"

With all the subtlety of a body slam, the Monday Night Wars were underway. Suddenly, after pilfering the industry for talent in the 1980's, McMahon professed that "Ted Turner" was driving him out of business, as lest anyone forget it for a second, his WWF was a privately-owned, "family business" - seemingly ill-equipped to compete on financial terms with TBS.

And so, with comparatively limited resources, the WWF's best recourse was simply to produce more compelling programming. However, going live was an impossibility - at least for the moment - and every business metric was trending downward. "More bad news for Titan Sports," reported Mike Tenay, referring to the WWF's corporate name, on the *WCW Hotline*. "Attendances continue to plummet at arena shows, coming off one of the worst tours in recent memory - a Florida swing that saw several shows canceled, and several crowds of under 1000 fans."

It was ironic, thought Bischoff, that McMahon now painted himself as a victim, a 'little guy' bullied by the merciless Turner. After all, even ignoring the fact that for years, McMahon engaged in many behaviors he now decried, the WWF still possessed some advantages. First, as a company, it retained incredible brand recognition. During the '80s, the term 'WWF' had become widely synonymous with wrestling itself, and that association would be difficult to alter. Secondly, its maturity as a business - from an infrastructure standpoint especially - dwarfed that of WCW.

But undoubtedly, the WWF's trump card was Vince McMahon himself. Perhaps, when it was all said and done, the threat he perceived as existential could become beneficial. Maniacally motivated, McMahon slept with a notepad next to his bed, desperate to document the ideas produced by his subconscious, prepared quite literally to work around-the-clock. But meanwhile, as McMahon obsessed over his sole area of professional focus, Ted Turner was focused on other priorities.

51

Turner was busy contemplating an unexpected merger with Time Warner Inc., once the world's largest media and entertainment company. Now under the direction of Gerald "Jerry" M. Levin, its uncomfortably reserved 56 year old CEO, Time Warner was in a state of disarray, with company debts said to be in excess of $15 billion. In mid-August 1995, after Walt Disney Corp. offered $19 billion to buy Capital Cities/ABC, Levin redoubled his prior efforts to sell Time Warner's 21.9% stake in TBS, Inc., an attempt that began some several months earlier. It was a rather obvious move to shore up the balance sheet, but one day, without any prior indication, Levin hatched an ingenuous plan to do one better. Rather than shopping Time Warner's stake in TBS, Levin decided, he would make overtures towards purchasing the 78.1% stake that Time *didn't own*. It was a hastily conceived idea, one developed without the consultation of executives, nor the input of investment bankers. On the surface, it appeared a move straight out of the Ted Turner playbook.

But the differences between Levin and Turner could hardly have been more pronounced. Whereas the insecure Jerry fretted over his public image, Ted could hardly have thought less about his coverage in the media. While Turner possessed charisma in spades, Levin was rather bland, stoic, and stunted in his ability to connect with a crowd. More importantly, despite of (or perhaps because of) his most recent brain wave, Levin's aptitude as a decision-maker remained in doubt, a charge that was unlikely to be levied towards Ted.

Turner thought little of Levin, but over the course of a five-week courtship, he considered the impact of the rapidly changing media landscape on TBS, Inc. Throughout his adult life, one achievement had remained elusive for Ted - his ultimate dream of owning one of the big three television networks. In an era of significant media consolidation, including the Disney acquisition of Cap-Cities/ABC, and the $5.4 billion sale of CBS to Westinghouse a day later, Turner grew concerned that TBS was simply too small to compete. Levin, desperate to save his career, sweetened the deal by offering Ted the distinction of becoming Time Warner's Vice Chairman and largest (10%) individual shareholder. Considering Levin's anemic performance as CEO, Ted pictured himself as ultimately being in charge of the new company anyway; and so, on September 22nd, 1995, TBS, Inc. announced it would merge into Time Warner, Inc. in a $7.5 billion deal.

————

With Time Warner as its parent company, the nature of Turner Broadcasting was destined to change. Traditionally, its operations split into two distinct categories, with one partition housing its respected news division, consisting of CNN and various ancillary entities, and the other unit organizing its seemingly endless entertainment properties - including its networks (TBS and TNT), assorted film libraries, and Turner Sports - collectively categorized as *Turner Entertainment Group.*

World Championship Wrestling, the most-maligned entity of TBS, Inc., functioned curiously as a branch of Turner Sports. Under this structure, Bischoff's position could not be viewed as analogous to Vince McMahon, as despite any indications otherwise, he did not enjoy complete autonomy over company affairs. Furthermore, Bischoff reported regularly to a superior - the President of Turner Sports (and, by proxy, WCW) - Dr. Harvey Schiller.

Inside the corporate offices, Schiller, an athletic, 6-foot-4 renaissance man of sorts, responded almost always to 'The Doc' (sometimes 'Dr. Schiller', a former subordinate reveals, but *never* simply 'Harvey'). His resume read like the bullet points of a screenplay; indeed, it was hard *not* to respect a man who served in Vietnam as a war pilot, earned a PhD in chemistry, taught at the Air Force Academy, ran the SEC conference, oversaw the United States Olympic Committee, *and* completed marathons in his spare time. As one author breathlessly described his exploits, "think Indiana Jones....James Bond...still, you have not reached Dr. Harvey Schiller. Simply, he is the most interesting man alive." Perhaps Dos Equis were also paying attention.

A personal appointee of Ted himself, The Doc arrived at TBS in 1994 to oversee more than 900 hours of sports programming - including WCW - despite possessing no direct television experience. In the early days, perhaps expectant of a militaristic style of leadership, his staff advised he drop the implementation of a sign-in sheet for the Turner TV people, many of whom kept unorthodox travel schedules (not to mention unusual work hours). But before long, while a periodic table displayed in his office remained, Schiller started to loosen up, adapting to his new surroundings and growing to appreciate Turner's entrepreneurial culture. Interviews with job candidates featured chemistry questions and a challenge to stand next to a line marked on an adjacent wall. "Oh, I'm sorry," the towering Doc would joke. "You're not tall enough."

At his first social event with TBS, a Christmas party involving other prominent executives, Schiller found himself cornered by a new coworker. *"Did you hear what happened on the wrestling show last night?"* the executive asked. "No, what happened?" answered Schiller. *"One of your wrestlers fell out of the ring and broke his back."*

Puzzled, the Doc placed a concerned phone call to Eric Bischoff. "Eric," Schiller began. "I'm now - on paper - the President [of WCW - as well as Turner Sports]. When things like this happen, you should inform me."

"Oh...," Schiller recalls Bischoff responding. "You believed it?"

"Eric..." Schiller replied after a pause. "'I'm coming to your office tomorrow morning, and you're gonna tell me everything you know about professional wrestling'."

Early the next day, Schiller made good on his promise. "What's the most important thing for me to know?" he asked Bischoff.

"It's very simple," Bischoff replied. "If you can't 'talk', you can't wrestle."

Schiller considered the concept, and decided to trust Bischoff implicitly. "He knew more than I did about wrestling," Schiller acknowledges.

While The Doc admittedly had lots to learn, his presence as theoretical boss constituted a genuine coup for WCW, even representing a "huge step for the [wrestling] industry towards regaining legitimacy," according to one trade publication. Within TBS, however, a respectable wrestling group remained an unfathomable possibility.

"From day one of my employment, all I heard was how executives at the *SuperStation* wanted to get rid of wrestling from their network," offers Richard Steinberg. "They viewed it as a joke...I literally heard this from the President of Turner Networks to the lowest programming employee."

"In some ways, I think WCW was viewed as a joke organization," agrees David Albritton, a former Media Manager at TBS. "The CNN and CNN International folks had a much more formal business culture. WCW was definitely an outlier, was [traditionally] less organized, and seemed to have weaker leadership than CNN, TBS, TNT, and so on."

"One story that always makes me laugh," begins Brian Welch, former Executive Producer of TBS Promotions, "happened around 1988. I worked at CNN at the time, which was located in the basement of the 'Techwood' building. Studio A was just above, and that's where they'd set up a ring for the NWA/WCW television tapings each week. During the CNN newscasts downstairs, you could see the studio lights shaking every time someone was body slammed!"

"You'd hear people tell stories," remembers Greg Daniel, a Turner producer, "about coming in to work after the tapings. There would be blood, towels and all that kind of stuff just laying around. You'd have to clean up first, just to get to work!"

The clash in cultures could have easily provided enough material for a successful sitcom. "When you got off the elevator at CNN Center," says Scott Sergent, WCW's Interactive Communications Manager, "there was this long hallway, and WCW was at the end of the hallway. There was this huge dent in the wall, like someone had taken a sledgehammer and just knocked the crap out of it. I was asking people like, 'what happened here?' They said, 'well, Ole [Anderson] and one of his old buddies were recreating one of their old wrestling matches, and it got a little out of hand!'"

"The offices for TBS and the master control room were right next to the studio," remembers Brian Welch. "Right across the hall from the studio, one of the office bathrooms had been expanded to include a shower for the wrestlers. A female associate of mine was working one weekend, and came around the corner just as Ric Flair was coming out of the bathroom, with only a towel around his waist.

"He dropped his towel and stood in front of her, feigning embarrassment, an 'oops, sorry about that', [kinda thing]. She rolled her eyes, turned and walked away - but not before [offering] a sarcastic, 'thanks Ric'.

"It was a different time - way before sexual harassment lawsuits!"

The jokes were not all in one direction, however, especially when TBS hired Jim Herd - a former Pizza Hut manager - to run WCW in 1989. "When WCW was based at CNN Center," laughs former feature producer Neal Pruitt, "our production facilities were downstairs. We had a code that we always had to 'punch in', just to get in the front door. When you left the building, you had to wait for this little 'click', so that the door sensor could figure there was motion going towards it.

"Well, for whatever reason, Mr. Herd - Mr. 'Hot Head' - always left the lobby as fast as he could. But every time he would do that, the door sensor wouldn't trigger quick enough. [Consequently], he'd end up acting like he was trying to go through a locked door.

"[WCW producer] Keith Mitchell said to him, 'Mr. Herd, here's what you have to do. You have to take your hand, put it over your head, and wave it back and forth. That's the only way this thing really works'.

"So every now and then, you'd see Mr. Herd come down - storming towards the door - and then waving his hand back and forth above his head! It was hilarious to watch. Everyone tried to gather in the lobby, if we got word he was going out the door!"

Like many of the WCW production staff, Pruitt took exception to attempts to belittle his livelihood. "I once matched my paycheck up against a CNN producer," he says, "and he was saying, 'Neal, you work with goofy wrestling - why do you do that? It's just so stupid'.

"I said, 'you think it's stupid, huh?'

"He said, 'yeah, I do'.

"I said, 'you know what the difference is between wrestling and CNN?'

"He goes, 'no, what?'

"I said, 'at least we admit we make it up!'"

Chapter 8:
Trashed

SIX SHOWS INTO THE Monday night experiment, WCW was neck-and-neck with the WWF. *Nitro* emerged victorious on two occasions, was defeated twice, and tied twice with *Raw*, meaning by any realistic measure, its 2.6 average rating constituted a resounding early success. Moreover, the program was genuinely revolutionizing televised wrestling, with marquee names including Hulk Hogan, Sting, Lex Luger and Randy Savage appearing often, sometimes in match-ups traditionally reserved for pay-per-view. On the undercard, dazzling technicians such as Eddy Guerrero, Dean Malenko, and Chris Benoit wrestled in a legitimate style that provided a solid foundation to offset the goofy Dungeon of Doom antics elsewhere in the show. Consistently, *Nitro* was exciting, colorful, fast-paced, unpredictable, and above all else, *live*.

"It was genuinely fun, unpredictable, and lively," adds Scot Safon, TNT's VP of Marketing. "It was like an action spectacle that would surprise all the time. It had fewer rules and regulations than pro sports, so the action was non-stop, and it had a narrative that included characters, plot twists and dialogue. So it was a drama too. Sometimes a comedy. I totally understood why it worked as live event television."

As part of a difficult balancing act, WCW needed to maintain its focus on beating *Raw*, while simultaneously presenting attractive events on pay-per-view. At *Halloween Havoc*, the traditional October special, Hogan was booked to defend his World Title against newcomer *The Giant* - supposedly the 'son' of WWF legend Andre The Giant. In reality, Giant, real name Paul Wight, was a Hulk Hogan project from day one. Standing at a legitimate seven-feet tall, Wight was answering phones for a karaoke company when he got the chance to play in a celebrity basketball game. Fortuitously, he subsequently met Hogan, and a WCW contract followed in short order.

His showdown against Hogan would be Wight's in-ring debut - on pay-per-view no less - but to his utter surprise, he would be booked to win the championship at his very first attempt. Before the match, however, the two warriors engaged in a 'monster truck battle' on the roof of the building, resulting in Giant (in storyline) falling off the side of Detroit's Joe Louis Arena.

For many fans, it was a farcical visual, setting the stage for more outlandish happenings in the main event. Despite his fall, The Giant miraculously returned to face Hogan in the ring, but after a plodding 13-minute encounter, a newcomer labeled as *The Yeti* lumbered into the fray. What followed can be best described as resembling a fever dream - The Yeti attacked Hogan from behind with some aggressive hugging, while Giant throttled the champion with his bare hands. In a convoluted and cartoonish finish, the title changed hands on a disqualification.

Such top-of-the-card antics seemed to contradict, rather jarringly, Bischoff's stated goal to present a more realistic product. He looked to Japan, where wrestling was covered authentically, as an example of how to heighten viewers' *suspension of disbelief.* "You hear people in wrestling often use that phrase," observes Professor Sam Ford, a research affiliate at MIT. "It's the idea that while they're watching, fans put aside the fact they know it's not real."

Along those lines, Bischoff also sought to benefit from an existing company alliance with New Japan Pro Wrestling (NJPW). Fortunately - as of 1995 - the relationship was on good terms, but previous to Bischoff, WCW angered NJPW officials with its blatant disregard of their agreement. "New Japan paid WCW upwards of $400,000 a year to do a talent exchange program," remembers Sonny Onoo, "so that WCW talent could go on some New Japan tours. But it turns out the prior management of WCW took the money and never sent the talent."

Eager to mend fences, Bischoff recruited Onoo for a do-or-die meeting. "He called me from Atlanta," Onoo says, "driving his new Black Corvette back home. I'm not sure if he had a couple drinks -

I'm not saying he was - but he left me a message first about this car and how fast it was!

"I called back and we're talkin', just shootin' [with each other]. He said, 'oh, by the way, I need to take care of some business in Japan - do you wanna go?' I said, 'sure, I'll go to Japan'. At one point, we thought about doing a martial arts show on television together, so we had that in the back of our heads [too]. So Eric said, 'ok, I'll get it set up and we'll leave in two weeks'. I said, 'great!'

"So now we're supposed to leave in like three days - and I'm not hearing anything from Eric. I finally called him up and said, 'hey, are we still going to Japan in three days?' His answer was, 'oh - *you* were the guy I was talking to!'"

Upon arriving in the country, Onoo says, the pair realized the extent of the previously caused hostilities. "We were in front of five of the scariest looking Japanese persons…[Seiji] Sakaguchi who was a ['65 World Judo Champion]…you got Masa Saito, who was in the '64 Olympics, Greco-Roman…a real famous Japanese wrestler. You had [Riki] Choshu. These guys are sitting across from us and they *tower* over us.

"There was a guy named Masao Hattori. He was their referee, but he lives in New York so he's fluent in English. I'm not there to translate - as far as I know, I'm there to talk about this karate show we wanna put together.

"But Eric starts to speak, and I'm listening to him…and then Hattori looks at me and says, 'ok, Sonny - you translate'. I left Japan when I was like 11 years old, and I was educated in the United States…so I'm fluent - but not *that* fluent…[at least] to discuss business.

"So I'm translating what Eric is saying, simultaneously in Japanese, and I'm hearing about the previous issues for the first time. Now I know why these people wanted to kill us! None of them were smiling.

"As the meeting went on, Eric acknowledged that he wanted a new

60

start. Masa Saito said, 'ok, that's all good and dandy, but are you gonna make up for the money we gave you?' He said, 'and [another] problem was scheduling - you guys were always doing a conflicting show'. He said, 'we need better communication'. Without skipping a beat, Eric says, 'oh, that'll be Sonny. You can just call Sonny direct - he'll make sure you guys don't have any issues'.

"I'm looking at Eric like, 'I don't work for you!' He said, 'you do now!'"

Consequently, Onoo became the contact person for the WCW-NJPW partnership, securing an eventual $1 million in annual revenue. "I think the initial year was just making up for the money we accepted," he remembers. "Obviously, it became a great relationship, and New Japan was an amazing part of the growth for WCW. When *Nitro* happened, we needed more talent, and through the talent exchange program, we got to use their biggest talent in Japan.

"Eric proposed putting some of the most popular cruiserweights working in Japan - Eddie Guerrero, Chris Benoit, Dean Malenko, Ultimo Dragon and Chris Jericho - under WCW contract. Once we did that, New Japan freed themselves from paying these guys. Under the talent exchange program, New Japan then had access to these guys, along with the rest of the WCW talent, for one 'lump sum' payment. From a management standpoint, it was a pretty brilliant way to maximize the [relationship]."

As a side benefit, Bischoff got to experience NJPW up close, at a time when creatively, the company was promoting an interpromotional feud with its rival, UWFI. Back home, conversely, WCW had yet to find its 'sweet spot', Bischoff believed, in reference to offsetting its more theatrical elements against a sports-like presentation.

For his own part, Sullivan - still involved with the Dungeon of Doom storyline - detected some hesitance on the part of Hogan, whose on-screen hijinks had previously resulted in great success. In the coming weeks, however, things would only get weirder, as the Hulkster, experimenting in a radical all-black look, appeared on *Nitro* to

61

proclaim he was embracing his 'dark side'.

Soon enough, the concept was abandoned, and Hogan returned to his colorful babyface get-up. Nonetheless, it had come time, Bischoff and Sullivan agreed, for a long-overdue heel turn. The notion met further support in Jerry Jarrett, a legendary promoter, booker and businessman now working as a WCW consultant. In recent years, Jarrett had served in a similar capacity for the WWF, famously being tapped to take over if Vince McMahon - fighting steroid distribution charges - went to prison.

"Eric called me," remembers Jarrett, "and advised that he heard that I left the WWF. He inquired if I would be interested in working for WCW...and asked if I would serve as a consultant...[stating] that I could stay at home and we could work together on the phone. I advised that I would have to think about it.

"I called Vince [McMahon] and reported the Bischoff offer. Vince [said to] take their generous offer, because [with] the course they were on, even Ted Turner would go broke. I took the job, yet Vince continued to send me a check during the entire time I was getting a check from WCW...It was the easiest $125,000 I ever made.

"During my tenure, I only went to Atlanta one time. Eric and I would talk weekly, [however]. One call pertained to Eric wanting Hulk to turn heel. Eric asked if I would call Hulk and talk him into the role change."

In the meantime, WCW was holding up well on Monday nights, recording back-to-back wins to end November. As the year drew to a close, profitability appeared within reach for Bischoff, while antithetically, the outlook was bleak for Vince McMahon. For the first time ever, as the WWF prepared to report an annual loss, its costs were being slashed in all directions. "The truth was," remembers Bischoff, "that things were so bad for them financially, they literally couldn't afford to have the water coolers serviced any longer. They were cutting back on everything they could, and they literally took the water coolers out of the building. That's how bad things were."

Shortly before Christmas, McMahon was forced to release Debra Miceli - his current Women's Champion - from her WWF contract. With the title belt still in her possession, Miceli contacted Bischoff looking for work, and on December 18th, in a clip that would be played and discussed for years to come, she debuted on *Nitro* in shocking fashion. *"I am Madusa,"* she said at the announce table, referencing a previous ring name. *"Always have been Madusa, always will be Madusa. This is the WWF Women's Championship belt…"*

With that, Madusa looked directly at the camera, and unceremoniously dumped the belt into a garbage can. In some ways, it was a callback to 1991, when Ric Flair - signed by McMahon after a dispute with WCW management - showed up wearing the World Heavyweight title on WWF programming. But in concert with the Luger signing, giving away *Raw* results, and baiting McMahon at every turn, Bischoff now significantly upped the ante. Live on *Nitro*, he had literally *trashed* a WWF title, catching McMahon with his pants down yet again (ironically, Miceli negotiated her deal with Bischoff, without McMahon's foreknowledge, during a casual trip to the bathroom).

Christmas had come early for Eric Bischoff, but his biggest triumph was yet to come. At the Turner holiday party, as promised, Harry Anderson presented Bischoff with a single dollar, reflecting WCW's status as a profitable entity. Surprising *Nitro* viewers was fun, and fooling McMahon a thrill, but to prove a Turner executive wrong…Bischoff was on cloud nine.

As 1995 ended, Bischoff's next goal became clear - establishing WCW, undisputedly, as the world's greatest wrestling company.

Chapter 9:
An Age-Old Problem

UNDER THE LEADERSHIP of Eric Bischoff, WCW achieved the impossible in 1995 - profitability. However, in an important contrast to McMahon's WWF, its financial picture could not be measured by a simple accounting of revenues and expenses. Rather, as a 'downstream operating entity', its bottom-line picture resulted from meeting a complex set of monthly allocations determined at the corporate accounting level, a kind of forecasting based on prior performance.

Inherently, it appeared that the system, although in concert with Generally Accepted Accounting Principles (GAAP), *could* offer a means to obscure any true accounting of marketplace performance. Suppositionally, if a certain item of revenue, for example, was credited to one TBS subsidiary - as opposed to another - this shifting of income could not be detected by the financial experts downstream. "We weren't there," clarifies Greg Prince, WCW's controller, "to watch how the 'sausage' was made."

According to Dick Cheatham CPA, a certified forensic accountant and former group controller at TBS, accounting issues pervaded across the company. "When I got there, there were *a lot* of accounting problems - serious accounting problems," he reports.

"A lot of that had to do with the fact that Ted didn't care much for accountants. The way he saw accountants was that they were necessary - [in that] they built financial statements you could use to borrow money with - but they weren't risk-takers. Now that's true…as a group, accountants are not risk-takers. We're just record keepers, [or] scribes. But at TBS, there weren't very many *real* accountants, although there were a lot of bookkeepers.

"I came in with a consultant - Jack Zimmermann and Associates - and our take was, 'if your books aren't any good, you can't rely on the information that's in there to make decisions ...because the books are no good!'

"So our first nine months to a year was just cleaning stuff up. For example, we had something like $15 million in accounts receivable at Turner International. We asked, 'when was the last time we got a *payment* on any of these receivables?'

"[The response was] 'Well, I don't know, we haven't heard from any of these people in about three years'.

"Ok, wait a minute. We haven't heard from any of these people in three years that owe us $15 million. What we're looking at then is an *impaired asset*. We can't carry this on our books at face value, because we don't know where these guys are that owe us this money...and because we haven't received a payment in three years, we may have to charge the damn thing off! That was the kind of mess we walked in to, [because] from the perspective of some people who worked at Turner, collecting was not as important as selling. [It's like], 'if I can sell it, then I've earned my bonus, my commission...I'm a hero...and somebody else can collect the mess'.

"Sales was everything. Their deal was, 'a dollar of sales revenue is worth more than a dollar of expense cutting'. To me, the impact on the bottom line is the same, but their deal was, 'no - I need a dollar more in revenue, even if it takes me two more dollars in expenses to create it'. It was all *revenue-driven* - the *whole company* was revenue-driven."

Interestingly - although the public may not have realized it - there existed a logical reason for such an attitude. "Underneath everything, Turner Broadcasting never really made a whole lot of money," Cheatham reveals. "It was all revenue, and it's hard to report to shareholders when you're not really making net income. You know, when you're not really making money!

65

"But let's say you're the President of Turner Home Entertainment, and your bonus is based on revenue. Well, you're gonna 'jawbone' the hell out of your controller to make it happen. It doesn't matter what actually happened - the [statement] has got to reflect that, because there's your bonus. In those days, that's another reason why we had bad accounting, because the line executives were beating the crap out of their accountants.

"The [financial] characteristics of the whole company bled through every one of its entities. Probably one out of every five transactions had been improperly recorded. You couldn't rely on the information, and you [certainly] couldn't rely on it for decision making. So there was this other issue, too...[we asked ourselves], 'are we sure that we're accurately reporting the condition of the company to our shareholders and regulators?'

As a result, Cheatham says, TBS' corporate overlords worked to popularize a performance measure called *EBITDA* - Earnings Before Interest, Taxes, Depreciation and Amortization. "[They said], 'Ok, what can we do that will tell people that we're really doing a good job?' With EBITDA, what you end up with is a modified form of cash accounting."

In other words, executive management promoted a measure of profit derived from stripping certain expenses away from the total cost of business - interest, tax paid, depreciation (the loss in value of operational assets), and amortization (the outlay for various intangible assets, spread over a number of years) - and then subtracting that figure from total revenue:

EBITDA = Revenue - Expenses (excluding interest, tax, depreciation and amortization)

In terms of being able to show how much cash a company produced - based solely around its current assets and operations - EBITDA's proponents trumpeted its merits. "You want to be able to report *something*," concedes Cheatham, "and we were *cash flowing*. That's the thing about Turner - it 'cash flowed' pretty good."

Conversely, EBITDA's critics - Warren Buffett famously among them - pointed out its ability to obscure reality. "People who use EBITDA," Buffett reportedly observed at a shareholder meeting, "are either trying to con you, or they're conning themselves. Interest and taxes are real costs."

Moreover, the willful ignorance of capital expenditures - money spent in acquiring or maintaining fixed assets such as land, buildings and equipment – often raised the alarm of more seasoned accountants. "A lot of us 'traditional people'," chuckles Cheatham, "were saying, 'what the hell is this EBITDA stuff?' At some point down the road, there's a *reckoning*. If you have more expenses than you have income - whether it's cash or not - you're gonna hit a wall."

Cheatham could remember only a handful of staff raising their concerns - "us three old guys", he jokes - noting that TBS tended to employ younger, more inexperienced accountants, some of whom were not even certified (a measure taken, ironically, to save money). "We were saying 'this is bullshit', guys," says Cheatham, "unless we [actually] make *net income*'."

"[But] we would have done probably anything in those days, to find a way to show we were 'good'," he laughs. "You pull interest out because that's a function of how you're financed," he says sardonically. "You're not responsible for taxes - god knows, you didn't make the decision for how much taxes you have to pay - the government did that, so we can't count that as an expense. You know, amortization and depreciation…you can't count that stuff, because the money has already been spent - so it doesn't affect current operations. Again, that was the reasoning and logic behind this modified number that we would kind of celebrate. But that was Turner Broadcasting as a whole. We were selling a new concept, a new idea…that this was a better measure."

In regards to WCW's financial performance in 1995, its year-end income statement clearly showed a profit of $283,466:

Total Revenue: 43,937,499
Total Expense: 43,654,033

However, when factoring in interest, tax, depreciation and amortization, a net *loss* was actually recorded:

Net Income: -9,803,128

In any event, Bischoff understood that internally, WCW had finally been recognized for *exceeding* its foregoing projections. In 1996, therefore, he looked to receive both an increase in terms of resources - *and* expectations - an apparent double-edged sword if not for Ted's ultimate position as financial arbiter. For as many company veterans would recall, a personal guarantee offered by the Chairman during the lean years provided all the assurances necessary, regardless of whether WCW made money or not.

"We always had the young 'MBA's' who would charge after WCW," Cheatham says, "making the case for why wrestling needed to go away. They took this to Ted on [numerous occasions]. They said, 'we gotta get rid of wrestling. It's not sophisticated enough for us…it's not for us…it's lowbrow'. If you were in corporate and were completely indifferent to wrestling, you better learn to hate it, because the guys at the top hated it.

"Well, Ted would say things like, 'where else can I get original programming for $300,000-a-week?

"He'd say, 'and on top of that, I like it - so it stays!'"

"Ted threw a meeting one day for all the wrestlers," recounts Marcus 'Buff' Bagwell. "It was at CNN Center. The Atlanta Braves had just made the World Series, so this must have been like '91. We all show up and we're thinking, 'we're getting fired'. That's what we - 'the boys' - thought.

"[Anyway], we get into this meeting, and it's kind of a 'Q & A' with Ted Turner. He starts talking for a minute, and somebody raises their hand and says, 'are we getting fired?' Ted said, 'no, there's no way I'm giving up on y'all!'

"[He said], 'look what just happened to the Braves. For years, people tried to get me to give up on [them]...but I didn't, and look what happened'. He said, 'heck no, I'm in it for the gusto!'"

The promise bolstered a common perception that for Ted, his continued involvement in wrestling revealed a true affinity for the genre. "Ted *was* a wrestling fan," states legendary promoter Jerry Jarrett. "His long term love of wrestling is why he first put it in his programming lineup. Many times in interviews, Ted would give wrestling credit for the initial success of the *SuperStation*. [But] this in no way reflected that he was not a fan himself."

"Look, if it had done a lousy rating, he would have dropped any affinity really quickly," offers Bill Burke, former President of TBS. "He understood the ratings [wrestling garnered], but he also thought it was *fun* and it was inexpensive. It was harmless."

According to Burke, the historical success of wrestling on the TBS network also allowed its founder to indulge in a favorite pastime: proving people wrong. "He thrived on people turning their noses up at stuff," reveals Burke. "Take 'Andy Griffith', for example. [Critics would say], 'you country bumpkins...', and then the ratings would be really good.

"There's some great early stories of him in his sales days. When American Express, for example, wouldn't buy advertising on TBS because they were 'too downscale'...and 'too this, too that'...Ted pulls out an American Express card, slides it across the table and says, 'I use your product, but you don't use mine. I have a real problem with that'.

"They were saying our audience was downscale, and he's like, '*I*

69

watch TBS, and I'm worth half a billion dollars, pal!' He rejected people's snobbery of 'it's gotta be this fancy programming'. He was like 'look, I'm doing a '3' rating at 6:05, so screw you'."

"Ted would show up late at night, and sit in the control room to watch my edit sessions of our wrestling show," adds Jarrett. "This would be strange behavior if his only appreciation of professional wrestling was the ratings it garnered.

"Ted [also] arranged for Johnny Walker - 'Mr. Wrestling II' - to meet with President Jimmy Carter. President Carter's mother was a big wrestling fan and loved Mr. Wrestling II...so this meeting indicated that President Carter and Ted Turner discussed professional wrestling on a personal level.

"[Another] supporting story...[involves] Edward Welch (aka Buddy Fuller) and Ray Gunkle who were partners in the Atlanta territory. Ray died and [wife] Ann refused to sell her interest, instead [taking] an active role in the promotion. This lead to trouble. Buddy decided to sell his interest to Lester Welch, his uncle, in the hopes he could better get along with Ann.

"[But] Ann and Lester escalated their fight to an all-out war...to the point that Ann came into the office at night and changed the locks on the doors. Now what was poor Ted to do regarding his television wrestling show? He did what any wrestling fan would do. He gave *both* partners television time.

"[Later on], I was selling out the old city auditorium when Ann folded her promotion. This is when Ted started coming to the studio, and he told me personally that he was intrigued by my storylines. I still consider this perhaps the greatest compliment of my career."

One former TBS executive, speaking under the condition of anonymity, claims that notions of Ted's fandom have been greatly exaggerated. "Wrestling didn't matter to him at all," the executive argues. "He didn't care about it. He only cared about the ratings it delivered."

"Look," summarizes Burke, "I don't think he could walk into his office and rattle off a bunch of names...or tell you who the champ was...he wasn't *that* kind of fan. It's funny...Ted fancied himself as a programmer, but he wasn't. He liked ratings and he liked making a little noise, getting a little press, being a little controversial. I think he thought [wrestling] was fun."

In what Burke describes as the 'age-old' problem with WCW, consistent difficulties in converting the ratings to ad dollars caused much of the disdain within TBS. "First of all, advertisers couldn't get their head around the fact that wealthy people were watching WCW," Burke laments. "In fact, this one sales guy wanted to do a sales tape where we would film the cars at a WCW event...with the Range Rovers, the Mercedes, [and so on]. His point was, 'this looks like an NFL parking lot', and the NFL gets the highest CPM's (cost per thousand impressions) on television.

"It drove [Turner Ad Sales] nuts. They could not get advertisers over the hump that this was not a 'downscale' [property]. So it didn't drive ad sales rates, and the other thing to remember is that we got paid by cable companies - we got a subscription fee. Those fees were driven primarily by sports, but then also by more prestige [programming] like *Seinfeld*. WCW didn't get you anything, because they had the downscale perception.

"The funny thing is though, the advertisers themselves would be like, 'nobody cares if Diamond Dallas Page just beat...'. It was like, 'you wouldn't have been watching last week, would you?' I mean, if you gave everyone truth serum...[I mean], I watched it. It was *fun!*

"It was huge on college campuses - *huge*. I used to give a talk once a year at Emory University in Atlanta as head of TBS. I'd say, 'raise your hand if you watched wrestling in the last seven days'. There was a sea of hands raised. And that is a *very* attractive audience - you just couldn't convince advertisers [of that]."

"The reality within the ad sales environment," Eric Bischoff reveals,

71

"was always challenging. Part of that was because if you look at wrestling at its core...what is it? It's good versus evil. It's violence. It's physicality. It's characters and storylines.

"But one of the biggest challenges with wrestling then - and even now - is that it doesn't fit into a bucket that people understand. With scripted television [for example], everybody understands [that] - they know what a drama is. They know what an action series is. They can give themselves permission to be involved from an advertising point-of-view, in a program or genre that is easy for them to understand.

"Wrestling is scripted...but it isn't scripted. It's a sport - at least, it's presented as a sport - but it's not a sport. It's a little bit of everything, even though, as a producer, I know it can be highly scripted and well-disciplined, in terms of the [story] arcs you develop over a six-month period or a nine-month period. The character development can be just as disciplined as a lot of things that people watch on television in a scripted environment.

"But to the untrained eye, or to someone who's not in the business, it's like...[just] big guys in their underwear beating each other up with chairs. [Because] it doesn't fit into a category, it's hard for people to commit millions of dollars into ad campaigns over a long period of time, or invest that money into a product that they really don't understand. Very few people, including the ad sales community, really understand why wrestling works.

"You have to remember [too] that Turner ad sales was based in New York, and they were completely autonomous. [WCW] had no relationship with them whatsoever. Their job was to sell the commercial inventory on our show, and there was very little dialogue, communication, or strategy - *anything* - between ad sales and myself."

According to Greg Scordato, a sales account executive at Turner during Bischoff's tenure, a persistent stigma among advertisers contributed to the unattractiveness of WCW's product. "For many, selling WCW was a burden. Although [they] had a crop of shows that helped our ratings overall, there was a stigma for many advertisers to buy commercial time in wrestling. There was a feeling, among many of the salespeople, that it did not fit the image of the rest of the network, especially TNT which we were trying to position as upscale at the time. A large majority of our major advertisers were [also] targeting a female audience...[so] selling wrestling was extremely difficult with our existing advertiser base.

"If you had clients who were fans, there was a whole different experience. I think the sales office in Chicago, Detroit, and Los Angeles had an easier time with WCW, but that's just speculation. In New York, we were proud to talk about being number one in the ratings with the help of WCW, yet embarrassed by the program from a content standpoint - and even an audience standpoint - [it felt] downscale, country, [and so on]."

In comparing the difference between ad rates for wrestling and other programming, the discrepancy was "significant," says Bill Burke, who estimates that an alternative show with similar ratings could command a rate three times that of WCW. Consequently, income derived from ad sales - one of the four primary revenue drivers for a contemporary pro wrestling organization (alongside pay-per-views, live attendance, and licensing and merchandising) - consistently failed to reflect the size of the audience.

In regards to pay-per-view buy rates, WCW had seen a marked increase since the Hogan signing in mid-1994. With the right match-up and promotion, the major events - traditionally, *Halloween Havoc*, *Bash at the Beach*, *SuperBrawl* and *Starrcade* - tended to produce an absolute windfall for the company (*Bash at the Beach '95*, for example, with Hulk Hogan defending the WCW belt in a cage match, grossed an estimated $4.8 million in revenue). But interestingly, according to Bischoff, the resultant income (split 50/50 with the pay-per-view provider) would typically *not* be credited to WCW, but rather to a division of TBS, Inc. known as Turner Home Entertainment.

"I really can't speak to how [the revenue] might have flowed through Turner Entertainment," responds Greg Prince. "Eric may have been recalling other things that did flow through [that unit], as there were a lot of significant revenue items flowing into our income statement that were straight allocations from 'up above'. That would be true for revenues *and* certain expense items. [So] what [Turner's financial staff] were doing and eventually sending down to us...who's to say [if that was true]?

"Jay Hassman was our pay-per-view director, and we would work with the pay-per-view industry to develop as tight an estimate of pay-per-view revenue as possible. Then you would have the [revenue] 'tail' wind out over time, as all of the pay-per-view buys got reported, and then ultimately 'booked'. [So in terms] of what went into the income statement for pay-per-view revenue, that really wasn't an allocation through Turner Home Entertainment, it was really more us trying to make the best initial estimate - based on those initial pay-per-view buys that were reported - and then trying to estimate how that 'tail' would work as the [other] buys crystallized over the next three or four months."

Gradually, and incrementally over his tenure, Bischoff expanded the number of WCW pay-per-view events to 10 (and ultimately, 12) per year. If nothing else, the sheer frequency of the 'super shows' presented a multitude of potential issues, regardless of their short-term viability. Creatively, Sullivan would have to balance presenting major matches on 'free' television with a need to retain others for pay-per-view. Secondly, in accordance with the law of supply and demand, it seemed inevitable that charging $29.95 for a show every four weeks could potentially lessen the perceived value of each, causing fans to eventually lose interest in the latest 'biggest match ever'.

But the most worrying possible outcome foretold Bischoff, even with a dramatic proliferation in revenues, effectively becoming a victim of his own success. Due to the accounting methodology employed at TBS - the projections, allocations, clandestine calculations, and the like - a successful pay-per-view in July, for example, could be used as a baseline for a forecast of the following year. As an oft-repeated axiom articulated however, the wrestling business was known for being *cyclical* in nature, vulnerable especially to a top star losing his popularity or succumbing to injury.

Bischoff also saw himself hamstrung by WCW's woefully underdeveloped licensing and merchandising infrastructure, one that paled in comparison to McMahon's WWF. Shrewdly, and during a time of rapid expansion no less, McMahon had carefully controlled his labor costs by structuring contracts with a 'minimum downside guarantee', crucially incentivizing an unlimited 'upside' in the process. In addition to being rewarded when business was good, much of the additional remuneration earned by WWF wrestlers resulted from ancillary sources - action figures, video games, t-shirts, and the like - whereas in WCW, Bischoff inherited a very different arrangement.

Similar to the structure employed by Turner's Atlanta Braves and other professional franchises, the large majority of WCW wrestlers worked under guaranteed contracts, employed essentially as salaried individuals despite their official classification as independent contractors. Although in time, bonus compensation from auxiliary activities would come to supplement certain deals, such earnings were dwarfed by the 'fixed' salary paid irrespective of company performance (wrestler Booker T., for example, on payroll for over $150,000, received only $2,668 from licensing and merchandising in 1996, according to company records).

According to one company insider, the rationale informing such a structure was two-fold. Firstly, and most practically, viewing WCW contracts as analogous to those used in 'real' sports enabled a consistency of operations within Turner Sports. Secondly, and more plainly, it was perhaps the inevitable consequence of a persistent ignorance about professional wrestling and its participants. For that reason, the guaranteed deal approach concerned many in the industry, who believed it to be in opposition with the very nature of the performers themselves. "There are some basic principles that cause instant failure when broken," argues Jerry Jarrett. "Wrestlers are fueled by hope and optimism. A salary without incentives takes the heart and soul from the talent. The rhetorical question might be, 'if I'm making a million dollars each year, why risk injury at the most, and pain and suffering at the least?'"

"Historically," says Greg Prince, WCW's controller, "the guys that made the money were the guys out there, working their asses off and taking the 'bumps'. [In WCW], the big name stars were on pretty good guaranteed contracts. You can just imagine how this would play out. When you go from what [the wrestlers] were accustomed to in the industry, now the mindset is 'well, I'm getting paid 'x' amount per year, it's probably in my long-term best interests to try to stick around as long as possible'. It was like this backward incentive to make guaranteed money, but work as little as possible."

"Picture me for a second," says Buff Bagwell, "you're Marcus Alexander Bagwell, making $150,000 a year, and it's '91, '92. [WCW] have got to *beg* people to come in - off the streets - so they've got 500 people in the stands to tape a wrestling show. On the card is Sting, Lex Luger, Dusty Rhodes...top names! Kevin Sullivan, Brian Pillman, Ricky Steamboat, Dustin Rhodes, Barry Windham, Marcus Bagwell, Ric Flair! I mean, we had a card, y'know? But we had to beg people to come in to watch *free* wrestling.

"There was a guy named Chip Burnham that handled a lot of our marketing. I would sit on the curb with him to get people to come in for free - give them free pictures, free autographs and stuff. Well Chip's job also was to have people who had their teeth...so we had to hire models for coming in and out of commercial break. So when you come out of commercial, you have two people clapping at the wrestling show that have their teeth. They would get paid 75 dollars a piece. You gotta realize, we're in the middle of Atlanta. There's drug addicts and all kinds of stuff [around]...we're just trying to fill the seats so we can tape a show.

"The point of this story is - be me - you're making $150,000! *How!? How in the heck are we doin' this!?* That's why I would ask Sting stuff like, 'how are we playing golf [on our days off]?' Sting would explain it to me that we were 'TV', and it was different [than traditional wrestling companies]. The way he explained it, it made sense but still we're playing golf...making $150,000 to $200,000 dollars a year...back then and even now, that is a *ton* of money!"

Although implementation of the guaranteed contract structure would often be attributed to him specifically, Bischoff would remind his detractors that the practice existed before he ever arose to power. Memorably, and during his very first day with WCW in fact, he quickly learned why so many opportunists flocked to get a roster spot in the first place.

This is the greatest place ever, veteran grappler Larry Zybysko told Bischoff, almost in a state of jubilant disbelief.

Just keep your head down, stay out of trouble, and you'll have a job for life.

Chapter 10:
Heel

Aˢ 1996 BEGAN, WCW experienced a surge in attendance to its non-televised events. In February, an average of 3,830 fans attended a 'house show' in their local market, the highest figure in the history of the company under Turner. The increase could be correlated with an intense Ric Flair-Randy Savage feud, a story which also encompassed the heel turn of Savage's former (real life) wife Elizabeth. But upon closer analysis, attendance numbers had generally been trending upwards since 1994, when an unsung marketing wizard named Zane Bresloff began promoting WCW shows.

Affectionately known as 'Insane Zane', Bresloff personified the 'in-your-face' attitude that was starting to characterize '90s pro wrestling (and, for that matter, mainstream pop culture). Although he was, at heart, a hugely enthusiastic fan, he never showed himself to be a *mark* around the wrestlers, realizing that portraying himself as anything less than an equal would be fatally ineffectual. While WCW had traditionally done little to promote its shows locally, opting to announce the date, time and location of an event before essentially *hoping* that word would travel, Bresloff revolutionized the entire process. In a tactic borrowed from the world of concert promotions (where, not so coincidentally, Bresloff got his start), the mere commencement of tickets going on sale soon became an event in itself. Top stars were flown around the country to sign autographs, meet fans, and appear on local radio stations in an effort to drive interest. And where others may have had difficulty convincing 350-pound behemoths to get excited about guesting on *Joe's Morning Drive* in say, Biloxi, Mississippi, Zane rarely ran into problems. "There were times when he would be up in some of the wrestlers' faces," recalls son Sean, speaking of his late father. "He could be very intimidating when he wanted to be. The wrestlers knew that you couldn't mess with him, and realized that if he said he was going to

78

do something, he did it."

But humorously, Zane's reputation contrasted sharply with both his physical appearance and the more nuanced details of his personality. As a diminutive, red-headed Jewish man with a curious dislike for large crowds, he could hardly have been considered a likely candidate to become the most revered events promoter in wrestling. But in 1985, after several years working as an executive for *Select-A-Seat* - the precursor to *Ticketmaster* - Bresloff single-handedly enabled Vince McMahon to gain a foothold in the Denver, CO market. Before long, Bresloff was booking and promoting arenas for the WWF nationwide, highlighted by his instrumental role in hyping the seminal *Wrestlemania III*.

Eventually, however, Bresloff became yet another of McMahon's key assets to head for Atlanta. In November 1993, when 'Mean' Gene Okerlund, a pivotal on-screen figure with the WWF during its boom period, debuted in WCW as a backstage interviewer, he recommended Zane as an essential acquisition. "A lot of those [former WWF] guys said, 'we're not going [to WCW] - unless you bring in Zane'," claims Sean Bresloff. Subsequently, in late 1993, WCW offered Zane a significant retainer - plus substantial percentage points - in a so-called 'Godfather' offer for his services. "I saw the contract," reveals one of Bresloff's close friends. "No one would have turned it down."

In the eight months (May-December '93) preceding Bresloff's hiring, WCW managed to attract only 615 fans, on average, to pay for its house shows. Post-Bresloff, the average rocketed up to 2,040 within a month, representing an immediate 230% increase. At first, he initiated a simple strategy, focusing mostly on the markets where historically, WCW had actually drawn fans, and cutting back on the areas in which the opposite was true. By the time of *Nitro*'s debut on TNT, Bresloff's influence expanded greatly, leading to a perpetually productive phone relationship with Eric Bischoff.

"It was daily [communication] - 365 days a year," reports Sean of his father's discussions with Bischoff. "They had a very solid working relationship and talked constantly. From what I recall, a lot of it was

Eric calling my Dad to pick his brains, and their conversations would literally be [like] 30 seconds [or so], [like] 'what do you think about this idea?' They would hang up, brainstorm some new idea and talk again in five minutes. With Eric being in Atlanta, and us being in Denver, there's a two-hour time difference - but it didn't matter. There were times when my Dad would be on the phone at midnight...five-in-the-morning...and he would fly out to Atlanta four or five times a year to talk about stuff with Eric [in person]. I wish I was a fly-on-the-wall for some of those conversations. I'm sure they were very entertaining, but also very positive and groundbreaking at the time."

Throughout his career, Zane's concepts had so often been hailed as "awesome" that he decided to adopt the term in forming his own company, *Awesome Promotions*. On a typical day, friends say, he worked until about 2:00pm in his work office, before returning home to field a relentless stream of calls from Bischoff and stars like Randy Savage and Diamond Dallas Page. With the phone pressed to his ear, Bresloff often stared at the continuous flicker of the home television set, while a selection of vintage hockey and wrestling VHS tapes played on heavy rotation. Only a close game involving his beloved Montreal Canadiens would result in a call ever going unanswered ("the first piece of clothing I ever wore," laughs Sean, in a testament to his father's passion for the NHL franchise, "was a Canadiens shirt, at two days old!").

For all of Bresloff's status and affluence, he cared little about materialistic pursuits, usually sporting a trademark t-shirt-and-shorts combination at home or in public. His quirks, like refusing to wear socks and leaving shows as soon as they started, all became part of the charm. But ultimately, and perhaps in a manner reminiscent of Don Draper's smooth self-assuredness in *Mad Men*, Bresloff's most successful sales act was to sell *himself*. While physically he more resembled a character from an earlier age (unfortunately, the principal in *Ferris Bueller's Day Off*, as evidenced by the relatively frequent requests for his autograph), Zane's sheer competency garnered universal respect amongst his peers.

One of Bresloff's most inspired interventions appeared, at least on the surface, to be blatantly counterintuitive. He advised Bischoff to closely examine the ticket prices for WCW's live events, arguing that if fans could obtain great seats for $10, or $12, for example, the prestige associated with attending dropped accordingly - making it more difficult for the shows to become *cool*. Bresloff's time promoting rock concerts taught him that lesson; insofar as cheap tickets actually cheapened the perception of the entire experience. *We should triple ticket prices*, he told Bischoff, understanding that young women were unlikely to feel insulted - regardless of what they thought of wrestling - if they knew their dates spent $35 for a ticket. With the new philosophy in effect, the live event revenue stream could become lucrative, Bresloff thought.

———

Meanwhile, in a departure from custom, Bresloff's former employer was engaging in a public effort to ridicule WCW and its owner. In a biting lampoon of Ted Turner's persona and business practices, the WWF produced a series of skits entitled *Billionaire Ted's rasslin' Warroom*, each presenting exaggerated caricatures of Hogan, Savage and Okerlund (labeled as 'The Huckster', 'The Nacho Man' and 'Scheme Gene' respectively).

But the most targeted of attacks focused on Turner himself. "*I built this company…by doing one thing well,*" drawled 'Billionaire Ted' in the first televised sketch. "*That's buying old assets, and repackaging them. Buying old movies…buying old cartoons…well heck, I even bought old rasslers!*"

Despite deliberately escalating tensions with WCW, the sendup drew little reaction from Ted, recalls Bill Burke of TBS. "Everything was about Rupert Murdoch back then," Burke says. "I'm sure it was on his radar, but Ted would have seen himself here," he motions, extending his arm upwards, "and McMahon down here."

Undeterred, McMahon continued his offensive by purchasing a quarter-page ad in the *New York Times,* asking its readers to consider Turner's "personal vendetta against the World Wrestling Federation."

But while it appeared dubious that Ted, irrespective of the time-slot flap a decade earlier, harbored any substantial ill feelings towards McMahon, his underlings wondered if it was Bischoff with the real score to settle.

After all, some observers noted, it was McMahon who had effectively forced Verne Gagne out of business. Then there was the matter of Bischoff's failed announcer audition, a humbling experience if there ever was one. But the perception amounted to nothing more than "bullshit," according to Bischoff. "The idea that I had some kind of vendetta because Vince didn't hire me…that is so much bullshit," he says. "The thought never crossed my mind. It had nothing to do with things, really. The only thing going through my mind was that I was given this opportunity to turn this company around…it worked, and now I want my company to be number one. I didn't want to be number two.

"It had nothing at all to do with a personal vendetta, or me getting back at Vince for not hiring me. That's just so childish, but it makes for a good [story]."

———

As the two sides continued to trade ratings wins into mid-February, the ongoing wrestling war was generating an exponential amount of mainstream attention. "In this corner," announced a *Wall Street Journal* headline, "Ted 'Hulk' Turner; in the other, Vince 'Titan' McMahon. A no-holds-barred fight is shaking up the world of championship wrestling, but the rumble isn't in the ring."

The media buzz intensified following the WWF's issuance of a formal complaint to the Federal Trade Commission on February 8. In an accompanying press release, McMahon alleged that TBS had executed "a systematic plan, implemented by a series of steps, to destroy the WWF…[and] achieve a monopoly over the professional wrestling business."

"The theatrics have turned serious," wrote journalist Mark Robichaux.

"Among Titan's most pointed charges: Turner has told some TV stations who want to buy [ads] from its popular CNN service that they must also buy World Championship Wrestling programs. [The] timing could be painful...[as] FTC investigators are busy combing over Time Warner's merger agreement with [Turner Broadcasting]. Antitrust lawyers at the FTC are known to be taking the wrestling petition seriously, concerned that the combined company could use its vast store of programming content to bully rivals and manipulate cable operators."

"I'm not trying to be a stumbling block to the merger," McMahon responded in comments to the *Pro Wrestling Torch*. "I'm not trying to anger the stockholders. We're trying to fight because we're tired of being beat on...in our complaint filed with the FTC, we included a lot of issues, but not all of them. We left some out, because the list was so overwhelming."

After previously eliminating so much of his competition, McMahon now portrayed himself as a helpless victim, persecuted ruthlessly at the hands of an oppressive outside entity. It was an irony not lost on Eric Bischoff, who in a *WCW Magazine* article lauding his 'marketing genius', took aim at the suddenly out-of-touch promoter. "I was there when Verne [Gagne] refused to accept...[that] there was someone out there who was smarter, thinking bigger and with more resources," Bischoff noted. "Verne reacted much the same way to Vince McMahon that Vince...is now reacting to World Championship Wrestling. There's a real parallel there - Vince McMahon is clearly becoming the Verne Gagne of the 1990's.

"It's unfortunate that a man could miscalculate an industry so badly, [and] make so many mistakes and so many bad moves in such a short period of time. Clearly, the only thing that he's got that anyone is talking about is the 'Billionaire Ted' skits. That speaks volumes about his television product, the quality of his talent and the general lack of confidence he has in his ability to create good, solid programming.

"I think Vince McMahon now has to see that WCW is number one. I think the pressure…is forcing him into a real reactionary mode. He obviously [isn't] thinking clearly. It's unfortunate - McMahon has reached the desperation stage."

Concurrent to the back-and-forth rhetoric, hardcore fans were buzzing about a brilliant angle involving Kevin Sullivan, who ahead of *SuperBrawl* on February 11, booked himself to wrestle the eccentric 'Four Horsemen' member Brian Pillman. In a clever amalgamation of two classic 'gimmick matches', the bout promised a leather strap binding each man around the wrist, teasing a violent encounter that in a unique twist, could only be ended with a formal proclamation of 'respect'.

But less than a minute into the match, Pillman spinned away from Sullivan to grab the microphone. "*I Respect You-*," he declared to a stunned St. Petersburg crowd, before apparently defying *kayfabe* with two additional words: "*Booker Man.*"

Immediately, Sullivan looked shell-shocked as Pillman exited the ring. In reality, they had concocted the stunt together, at once maintaining both creative consistency (in his 'Loose Cannon' persona, Pillman's unpredictability had already been established, and his muffled enunciation of "Booker Man" could have easily gone unnoticed), while simultaneously causing the most fervent of fans to question what they were seeing.

Many of the latter category of fans, despite constituting only a minuscule portion of the overall audience, frequently enjoyed discussing storylines, exchanging rumors, and providing snarky analysis on primitive web-based interfaces such as *Usenet* - a precursor to the online discussion 'boards' that would later host such discourse. On *rec.sport.pro.wrestling*, a popular community or 'newsgroup' for wrestling fans, speculation abounded that the *Booker Man* incident was not meant for public consumption.

"Maybe I'm a mark," began one user, referencing an industry term for an over-enthusiastic or naive fan, "[but] Sullivan…looked genuinely bewildered. "I taped the show, and my lip reading had Kevin say, 'what's wrong with him?'" offered another post. "I think it goes without saying that we'll never see Brian Pillman in a WCW ring anytime in the next century," laughed another take. "I guess you gotta respect the guy for having the guts to go out like that...but you gotta question [his] brains!"

Remarkably, word traveled to Sullivan that a contingent of WWF wrestlers believed Pillman's actions to be a *shoot* - a deliberate attempt to veer off-script - an impression that gained legitimacy when Pillman convinced Bischoff to offer him a contractual release (coupled with WCW's decision to remove the outburst from its *SuperBrawl* VHS release). Pillman eventually ended up in the WWF - much to the chagrin of Eric Bischoff - but *Booker Man* remained as part of WCW folklore. In isolation at least, the incident embodied - as author David Shoemaker later memorialized - a "beautiful singular moment in which pro wrestling's innocence was recaptured."

Conversely, and painfully devoid of any comparable sophistication, the top of the card remained dominated by Hogan and his medley of familiar foes. By the spring, concerns circulated that several Hogan 'dream' matches looked already passé, an inevitability - some wondered - of WCW's attitude towards the ratings contest.

In the first three months of *Nitro*, after all, Hogan had squared off against an array of popular nemeses - Lex Luger, Sting and Ric Flair among them - meaning that unless some new blood entered the upper card, Sullivan risked booking without a fresh 'money match' to build towards. Given the company salary structure - not to mention the gulf in name recognition between the established stars and midcarders - it looked to be an untenable situation.

Alternatively, it remained possible that an *existing* main-eventer could get a new coat of paint, essentially allowing for a repackaging of matches under novel circumstances. Therefore, after a convoluted cage match involving Hogan and nine other wrestlers headlined *Uncensored* on March 24th, Bischoff traveled to Tampa to resume a difficult discussion with his highest paid star.

In concert with repeated pleas from Sullivan ("I told [Hogan], 'you *have* to do this'," the booker remembers) and a personal phone call from Jerry Jarrett ("I called Hulk [to suggest] a turn might revitalize his career"), Bischoff entered Terry Bollea's palatial home to deliver an uncomfortable message. If there was to be any remaining mileage, he argued, in a Hogan-WCW relationship, it was time to execute an unequivocal heel turn.

Bollea listened attentively to the pitch, at first pausing to comment but eventually looking up to say, according to Bischoff:

Until you've walked a mile in my red and yellow boots, you'll never really understand.

With that, Bischoff retreated to Atlanta, wary of the path ahead.

Chapter 11:
Diamond in the Rough

1987 -

Norma Jean's Nightclub
Fort Myers, FL

HE TRIED. Oh, how he tried. Anything to stop *that* feeling - the incessant sorrow, the searing pain of regret. It wore on him, gnawed at him, *showed* on him. It was just another night in a string of, well, just-another-nights, each second a reminder of a second-rate existence.

Oh sure, for a Jersey kid, it wasn't *that* bad of a gig - the booze, the broads, the bullshit. As far as the patrons knew, he just about had it made - pretty Floridian chicks in every direction, a '62 pink Cadillac outside, and his name above the door out front. On occasion, he even traded shots with a brigade of pro wrestlers who loved to frequent his club, *the* hottest club in all of Fort Myers, *Norma Jean's*. From afar, he could even be mistaken for one of them - a star.

Except, he wasn't. He stared solemnly at the corner television set, his gaudy jewelry glistening, a drink half-attended to. He smirked at the screen. Four years after its 1983 release, 'Girls Just Want to Have Fun' was still getting some burn, and the music video was playing loudly. As part of the video, Cyndi Lauper frolicked around a make-believe house, lip-syncing the words and putting her Dad into an arm lock.

But 'Dad' was no stranger to the maneuver. He was, famously, the bombastic 'Captain' Lou Albano, one of the most outlandish and successful managers in WWF history. As history would show it, Albano's cameo in the video - one that ultimately precipitated Lauper's own involvement in the ring - acted as the perfect catalyst to a revolutionary WWF marketing campaign: *Rock and Wrestling*.

87

Inside the club, *Norma Jean's* was having a slow night - hardly a Norma or Jean in sight. Its part-owner - the Jersey kid - looked up to gaze at Albano, stopping to consider the bottom of the glass instead.

That could have been me.

In the least subdued of surroundings, his predicament was almost poetic. Perhaps he was the soul that Henry David Thoreau lamented for; something about those men who lead lives of quiet desperation. It had been a while since he had seen Albano - at least, ever since the *last* time he quit watching that damn wrestling show. Or was it the time before? He couldn't keep track any longer.

With nothing left to do but wonder, he looked up again, his self-talk getting louder:

That should have been me.

In the background, Lauper continued to wail - *That's all we really waaaaant* - but within a few minutes, his subconscious chatter subsided. A new video was playing, and it was time for the Jersey kid to count the night's takings, huddled amongst his buddies in a back room. Before long, with the drinks still flowing and the crowd now growing, the room would became his stage. *Wrestling, man,* he lamented. *I tried it when I was 22...*

His voice trailed off. Well, to the first set of ears it did, anyway. The next witness heard something about a failed 'gimmick', the next something about a plan to be a manager. One after another, they dropped off like flies - bar flies - passing out before story time was done. It was a familiar tale, after all, the 30-something booze hound musing on what could have been. But didn't they know that dreams - like *diamonds* - last forever?

The orator could only hold court for so long, eventually drifting off to sleep too. But with the vision of Albano and Lauper arresting his psyche, he had first managed to write down a vision of his own. He awoke to scribbles on a notepad, face pressed against the page, a new attitude arriving with the new day.

*That's **gonna** be me.*

———

Something changed that night for the dreamer, one Page Joseph Falkinburg. Within a week, a series of zany radio commercials he produced for *Norma's* led to the first of many helpful coincidences - an interview with the *Party News Network*. With his notepad still open on the desk, Falkinburg metamorphosized on camera, using the local cable show to trial a new persona. *The voice...*, he began, referencing his comical verbal cadence in the radio spots, *comes from Diamond Dallas Page, daddy. I was born to be a professional wrestling manager!*

Remarkably, less than a day after the interview aired, 'Dallas' - nicknamed after his childhood love for the NFL's Cowboys - received an impromptu invite to guest on a Fort Myers radio show. Even more serendipitous was that he would appear alongside an *actual* pro wrestling manager - none other than 'Captain' Lou Albano himself.

"I was going in there to get Norma's as a sponsor," remembers the host of the radio show, James 'Smitty' Smith. "I heard a little about Page, but as soon as I laid my eyes on him - and spoke to him - I realized that this is a guy with tremendous potential.

"I may have heard that he was interested in pursuing wrestling, and I had just started to integrate wrestling into my sports talk show. But when I met with him, I was *convinced* that he could get into professional wrestling and be successful.

"I also figured that this would be a wonderful way to seal the deal and get [the club] as a sponsor, [by offering] the opportunity to be on my show. I basically just said, 'look, I'm gonna have Sgt. Slaughter and Captain Lou on, and you can come on, be a manager - whatever'.

"He said, 'well, wait a minute. I'm not a *real* professional wrestling manager. How do I do this?'

"I said, 'you just fake it. Fake it! You can create a script…we'll go over it…we'll just go on the air and do it'.

"It was not long after, maybe several weeks at the most, when he came on the show. He did a wonderful job of interacting with the legendary Albano and Sgt. Slaughter, and when I called them afterwards, they said [Page] had tremendous potential, too."

Subsequently, Smith advised Page to put together a formal audition tape for Rob Russen, a friend and Vice-President of the American Wrestling Association. "I said, 'my advice to you is to create a video'," Smith remembers. "I said, 'you have all the resources. You've got beautiful women at your disposal…you've got a midget at your disposal…you've got all kinds of other…*people*…to [help] put something together'.

"Page took the ball and ran with it. He did every one of those things I said. He put together a wonderful little low-budget video, and knocked it out of the park. The rest, as they say, is history."

When the AWA's premier manager, Paul Heyman, departed the company for Jim Crockett Promotions, the budding hopeful received an affirmative response. "Page was way over the top," remembers Russen, who encouraged the hopeful to bring his ragtag crew for a Las Vegas tryout. "[He was] very much in the mold of Jesse Ventura who left a big personality void at the AWA when he left for WWF. Page was exciting…high energy…and Verne and Greg Gagne loved his gimmick with the 'Diamond Dolls'."

Making it to the AWA would mean national television exposure, an unheard of accomplishment for a rookie with no prior connections in the business. But characteristically, Page rose to the challenge, acing the tryout and later debuting on television in 1988. As leader of the *Diamond Exchange*, and with a stable of female valets at his side, he promptly rose the company ladder to manage Badd Company, the

AWA World Tag Team Champions.

After a year of regular run-ins on ESPN - home of the AWA's weekly show - Page's talent caught the attention of legendary wrestler-come-booker Dusty Rhodes. Over the phone, Dallas wowed the icon, throwing together every *rasslin'* cliché and catch phrase he could think of. Breathlessly, the awestruck newcomer demonstrated his ability in one memorable call:

Good Gawd! Dusty Rhodes! The American Dream! The Tower of Power! The Man of the Hour, Too Sweet To Be Sour...Getting Funky Like A Monkey in Florida Championship Wrestling with D-D-P - Diamond Dallas Page! Good GAWD!

In his trademark southern drawl, Rhodes responded to the promo quizzically:

Was that a recordin', kid?

Although heavily influenced by Rhodes, Page was the real deal, and the phone call would spark a lasting friendship. In 1991, after Rhodes gained booking power in WCW, Dallas was signed to manage The Fabulous Freebirds, a tag team with an enormous pedigree and recognition. Unfortunately, however, and gradually over time, a perception developed that at 6-foot-5, Page was destined to overshadow the very performers his role aimed to enhance. To stay in the business, it became clear that there would be only one option: becoming a wrestler himself at the age of 35, an age when most performers had one eye on the finish line.

News of his sudden desire to wrestle provoked laughter across the locker room. For some, like Michael 'P.S.' Hayes of the Freebirds, the thought was so preposterous as to justify *literally* rolling on the floor in hysterics. But once Page made his televised wrestling debut - partnering with Mike Graham for a tag-team encounter at *Starrcade* 1991 - the initial response was promising. *For your first match*, Dallas heard from announcer Tony Schiavone, *that was great.*

But don't get me wrong. If you're still that good in six months, you suck.

Despite showing measured improvement throughout 1992 - the product of countless hours invested at WCW's 'Power Plant' training facility - an injured Page was out of work at year's end. He would soon hatch a plan to regain his job, however, forming an unlikely bond with the venerable villain Jake 'The Snake' Roberts, a man reeling himself from a recent divorce. Their association first began during the previous decade, with Roberts patronizing *Norma's* on occasion in Fort Myers, but now it blossomed as the heavy-hearted Snake moved in to Page's spare room.

Their living arrangement (ultimately terminated when an actual snake, used by Roberts as part of his gimmick, went missing inside the home) allowed for daily discussion of wrestling psychology, showmanship and the tricks of the trade used to elicit passionate reactions from fans ('getting over', as per wrestling lingo). Subsequently, at the hands of Eric Bischoff, Page made his way back to the roster, and set out to demonstrate his development to a curious Dusty Rhodes.

You know, D, Rhodes stated matter-of-factly following a training match at the Power Plant, *I know you always saw yourself as a top performer in our business...but I never saw it.*

Until yesterday.

Keep doin' what you're doin'.

"I had no idea, in the beginning, that Page was going to put on the tights himself," admits Russen. "But looking back, it did not surprise me, because I knew he could achieve anything he set his mind on doing."

Encouraged by Rhodes' feedback, Page redoubled his efforts, soon adding a signature move to his repertoire: *The Diamond Cutter*. In an unlikely coincidence, he also purchased a house next door to Bischoff, enabling habitual socializing (and brainstorming) sessions whenever possible. As ever, Dallas' enthusiasm was unparalleled, with Saturday morning phone calls to friends containing an endless supply of creative ideas (so endless, joked Bischoff, that he could remove himself from the receiver, only to return minutes later to hear a partially developed concept in progress).

But unlike many of his contemporaries, Page generated an equal number of schemes designed to further the careers of *other* wrestlers. In this way, his attitude typified a philosophy that would reveal itself constantly in the years to come. It was one forged at 22 years of age - about the time of Dallas' first venture into wrestling - when he was first made aware of the author and motivational speaker Hilary 'Zig' Ziglar. One of Ziglar's more popular adages, repeated ad infinitum as part of an inspiring message of hope and humor, recognized the ambition of his listeners while highlighting the need to help others:

You can have everything in life you want, if you will just help enough other people get what they want.

Decades later, Page would credit the mantra with changing his entire mind set. "We continue to be amazed - and inspired - by the number of people who let us know they have adopted that mantra," remarks Laurie Magers, Ziglar's dedicated executive assistant. "We believe it has contributed much to the success [people] enjoy in life.

"Mr. Ziglar was already using that maxim when I came to work for him over 40 years ago, but none of us know when he first began using it. Basically, it's simply the 'Golden Rule' - voiced as he understood it - [demonstrating that] doing for others ultimately brings the rewards we seek and desire."

As Memorial Day approached in the spring of 1996, Page would act on the mantra with dramatic effect.

For Bischoff, it would be a call worth staying on the line for.

Chapter 12: Outsiders

The rootless children of warriors grow up with confused and incomplete notions of what it is to belong - but they know all too well what it means to be an outsider.
-Mary Edwards Wertsch, *Military Brats*

WITHOUT A SENSE OF BELONGING, he packed up his belongings. It was time to move on once again, start over once again, fit in once again. For the fifteenth time - maybe more, on second thought - Scott Oliver Hall prepared to be the *new kid* once again.

By now, he couldn't remember all of the bases he lived on. But such was the life of an army brat, a label he would eventually embrace as an adult. It meant never getting too sentimental, too comfortable, or too content. After all, there would always be *another* base to live on, *another* culture to be exposed to. Perhaps, in the end, the only thing he would be attached to was the feeling of unattachment.

It wasn't all heartache and disruption though - far from it, in fact. One of his fondest memories was October 20th, 1966 - Scott's eighth birthday - and the day Dad took him to see his first wrestling match. Mr. Hall was posted at Fort Rucker, Alabama, and in a peculiar irony, he joined an audience of mostly crew cuts in awaiting the main event - a Hair vs. Hair match.

Despite what his friends said, little Scott was sure - no, *adamant* - that wrestling was as authentic as his father's uniform. *Would you let someone shave your hair?* he asked the foolish nonbelievers, running eagerly to scoop up strands strewn all over the ring mat. Over time, his naiveté departed, but curiously, even in middle age, the souvenir never did. Perhaps it was something to hold on to.

As it turned out, it wasn't the only early memory to persist. Words can be especially difficult to forget, especially when Dad, the latest in a line of alcoholics, tells you:

You're gonna slip.
You're gonna fall, son.

Try to fall forward.

As little Scott became teenage Scott, the vagabond lifestyle manifested itself in a deep desire to avoid the inevitable: *a real job.* Life on the road, while once a symbol for constant upheaval, didn't look so bad anymore. His travels brought him to Florida, where at 17, his days could be spent lifting weights and laying in the sun. Pretty *sweet,* as he would become known to say.

At 22, Scott achieved a decent compromise for a kid eager to avoid a nine-to-five. For three nights a week, he tended bar at *The Doll House,* a popular (and especially seedy) strip joint in Orlando. But still, there was something missing. He had his days free, but at night...well, he always *had* liked the idea of being an entertainer. Maybe it was time to revisit something from the army days. Maybe it was time to revisit wrestling.

Then came January 15th, 1983. A dispute over a girl led to an altercation with a patron outside the club. Words were exchanged, and then blows. When the patron reached for his .45 caliber, Scott grabbed it instead. Only one man walked away.

Despite a charge of 2nd degree murder, the homicide case was eventually dismissed. It was time for a change, so Scott moved to Tampa, the home of Championship Wrestling from Florida. He joined every gym in town, hoping to rub elbows with a wrestler, and before long, he did just that - running in to Kevin Sullivan, no less. A year later, he was in the business.

For the first seven years of his new career, Scott moved around territories like his family once had around outposts. Stints in Florida, the AWA, the NWA, Puerto Rico and Germany led to an opportunity with WCW in 1991. Now renamed as *The Diamond Studd* - the star pupil of one Diamond Dallas Page - Scott showed potential but never could quite catch a break. It was time to move on once again.

In 1992, Scott joined the WWF as the ultra-charismatic Razor Ramon, a stylish Cuban-American heel billed from Miami. Heavily influenced by *Scarface*, and in particular, its lead character, Tony Montana, Ramon's catch phrases and bravado ultimately made him a fan favorite. He became a perennial Intercontinental champion - not quite *the* man, but very close to it.

By 1996, Scott was recognized as one of the most gifted performers in the industry. When he was on, he was *on*, dazzling crowds with an effortless wrestling style, impeccable ring psychology, and devastatingly quick-witted interviews. When he unleashed a trademark right hand across the jaw of an opponent, even the most apathetic had to wonder: *would you let someone hit you like that?*

There was, as there always was, just one small problem. Scott was married with two young children, and the punishing WWF schedule didn't allow for much time at home. To compound matters, his pay had started to level off. *If we move the decimal point a little this way*, he remembered asking Vince McMahon, *would it be so bad for the McMahon family? 'Cos I know it would be great for the Hall family.*

Enter an old friend - Diamond Dallas Page. One Saturday afternoon, Page informed Eric Bischoff that Scott wanted out, and as a go-between, relayed the subsequent offer: $750,000 per year - guaranteed - with a maximum of 180 dates.

———

A father's death is the most important event, the most heartbreaking and poignant loss in a man's life.
-Sigmund Freud, *The Interpretation of Dreams*

IT STARTED JUST LIKE any other Thursday, with one unusual difference.

For the first time he could remember, Kevin Nash traveled to school with his father Robert. It was April 4th, 1968, and eight-year old

96

Kevin enjoyed the chance to spend some extra time with Dad, an employee of the stereotypically *Detroit* Ford Motor Company. Usually, their fondest moments together arose in the evening, upon Mr. Nash's return from work, sparking a night of toy soldier battles and, if the impulse dictated, a trip to the ice cream shop.

Shortly before lunch on this otherwise normal school day, however, Kevin was visited in class by his principal, who immediately asked him to step outside the room. As Kevin gazed down the long hallway of his school, he saw brother Mark, himself only ten, being pulled out of *his* class. *You gotta be strong*, he could make out Mark being told.

The brothers headed outside to the parking lot, where they were greeted by a family friend and their father's boss at Ford. It was there that they learned the news. It was there they learned their father had died.

That night, Kevin returned home and in the back bedroom, away from grieving family members, he turned on a black-and-white television set. His father, just 36, had suffered a massive heart attack, but as he watched the screen, he discovered he wasn't the only child suffering from loss. In Memphis, Tennessee, at approximately 7:05pm, Martin Luther King Jr. was also pronounced dead.

Throughout his adolescence, Kevin grew rapidly, quickly reaching six-feet-eight at the age of 14. His height - and strength - made him a natural on the basketball court, enabling participation on the Varsity team as a freshman. As a Senior, he received over 200 scholarship offers, but in an effort to stay relatively close to home, he chose the University of Tennessee in 1977.

For three years at Tennessee, the now six-foot-ten Kevin fulfilled the unlikely role of underdog, averaging a paltry 5.1 points and 4.2 rebounds per game. Whereas other Centers faced double-teams, he mostly faced only boos, precipitating an attempt to transfer to Bowling Green State University. Perhaps the Tennessee fans couldn't appreciate his wit, intelligence, or talent for quoting obscure movie passages. Or maybe, the small matter of shoving the Head Coach had something to do with it.

After college, Kevin spent a season playing in Germany, before a devastating ACL injury ended his career prematurely. After a spell in the army, and a stint at Ford on the assembly line, he eventually settled as the floor manager of a strip club. One Friday night, he went to Joe Louis Arena in downtown Detroit to catch a WWF show, and there, he witnessed Hulk Hogan. Inspired, Kevin decided he wanted to try wrestling.

As in basketball, Kevin's size made him well-suited for his new endeavor. In 1990, he debuted in WCW as the orange-mohawked 'Steel', before cycling through a series of uninspired gimmicks: The Master Blaster, Oz and Vinnic Vegas. After convincing WCW that he wanted out of the business, Kevin secured his release and signed a WWF contract in 1993.

His initial WWF deal, consistent with McMahon's typical offer to an unproven commodity, represented a stiff decline from the $120,000 he was making in WCW. Nonetheless, McMahon told Kevin that he would *make him a star*, and on November 26, 1994, the former Tennessee troublemaker (under the gimmick name 'Diesel') secured his first WWF Championship.

One night after a show in early 1996, an unhappy Scott told Kevin that he was going to WCW. *I got favored nations*, he said, referring to a clause indicating that if another wrestler received better terms, he would be entitled to the same terms. *If you wanna go too, push the envelope in your negotiations. It only bumps my pay up.*

Together, Scott and Kevin were about to make history.

Not as conformists.

But as *Outsiders*.

Chapter 13:
You Want A War?

KEVIN NASH STILL SMILES AT IT, the memory of first meeting
Vince McMahon. He can still picture the prideful walk, the confident
demeanor, even the cut-off sweat shirt. McMahon was so composed,
Nash thought, so *in control*, that as he outlined his plans for the future,
he couldn't help but believe every single word. *I'm looking at
Steinbrenner*, Nash realized, the vision of a sprawling Greenwich
estate surrounding him.

It was the start of a famously close bond between owner and
performer, one that would see Nash view himself - in time - as more
than just an employee. "Vince was the first person to ever believe in
me," he declares. "Vince was the first person to ever 'push' me. If
Vince McMahon didn't create Diesel, and make him what he was,
Kevin Nash wouldn't have even been in the situation to make a move
[to WCW]. I owed all that to the WWF and to Vince McMahon. He
was my friend, my mentor...he was like a *father* to me.

"I loved that company. It was a wrestling company doing wrestling,
not an entertainment company doing wrestling, or a television
company doing wrestling. It was probably, to this day, the hardest
decision I've ever made in my life."

Despite his loyalty to McMahon, other, more salient considerations
were pulling at Nash's conscience. "I felt very much like a Benedict
Arnold, like I was a traitor to the WWF," he says. "At the same time,
my wife was six months pregnant when I made the decision. So from
that point of view, instead of working 310 days a year, I could be
working 180 days a year [based on WCW's offer].

"Dallas talked to Scott, because they just weren't paying us very much
at the WWF. Scott was very unhappy. Scott asked Vince if he could

go to Japan, or do other things [to earn additional income]. Vince said 'no', and then Scott came to me in the showers. He said he was probably gonna go to WCW. I was just like, 'wow'."

"I wasn't talking to both of them at the same time," clarifies DDP. "I was talking to them one at a time. I didn't know which one would actually really come."

"Scott told me the offer they gave him," continues Nash, "and I was just like 'wooooah'. He said, 'I have *favored nations*, if you wanna go and wanna push the envelope, it just bumps my pay up'. I had no intention whatsoever to go to WCW."

A defection to WCW meant returning to the company that had - under a previous regime - badly underutilized his potential. "It was always a situation where you were at WCW like, 'man, they're just not using me right'," reveals Nash. "Guys would always say 'you should go to Titan [Sports - the former corporate name of the WWF]', because to go to the WWF was like the big time.

"But when I got the call from [WWF star] Shawn Michaels saying he wanted me to be his [storyline] bodyguard, I had to kind of 'hoodwink' my way through the system [to leave WCW in 1993]. But it didn't take much - I basically asked for my release and they gave it to me."

In fact, Nash's prior departure from WCW had not occurred without controversy. He had, admittedly, misrepresented his reasons for wanting out of his deal, telling staffers that he was looking to quit wrestling completely. Consequently, to Eric Bischoff, Nash could hardly be considered as trustworthy. "'Bisch' thought that from how Kevin left there, he was a lying piece of shit," states DDP. "I was like, 'no, he's not', and he was like, 'yes he is!'"

"I said, 'the guy went from making 120 thousand dollars a year [in WCW]' - and that ain't a lot of money when you have to pay for everything - 'to making 60 [in the WWF]'. I said to 'Bisch', 'they fucked him over, and fucked him over, and fucked him over [in

WCW]. Would you give him his release if you knew he was going up there? Fuck no! But you weren't gonna use him here either though'. He did what he had to do for his family."

Ultimately, the impetus for Nash's decision came, he says, as a result of a backstage disagreement with Bret 'The Hitman' Hart, the Canadian main-eventer and company mainstay. At *In Your House 6*, the final pay-per-view before the WWF's annual showcase, *Wrestlemania*, Nash and Bret faced off in a cage match to further the company's top two storylines. "I was going to *Wrestlemania* [to face] the Undertaker," Nash says. "We're the co-main event with Bret and Shawn [Michaels]. I had cost 'Taker the match at the Royal Rumble, so [the plan] was to do a 'tit for tat'."

After interfering in the Undertaker's match a month earlier - and thus causing him to lose - Nash proposed a repeat of the angle, involving an effective defeat of Hart before receiving his comeuppance. "I would powerbomb Bret, basically have him beat," he says, "and then 'Taker comes through the bottom of the ring. Then he pulls me underneath long enough for Bret to recover, crawl through the ring and win."

Although Hart, according to Nash, emerged victorious in the planned scenario, he expressed hesitance at being the beneficiary of a 'fluke' victory. "Bret says, 'no, I'm not doing that. What does that do for me?'" Nash recalls. "We had a meeting that day, and it was one of the few times I've seen 'Taker go off. He said, 'man, it's not always about you, Bret'. At the beginning of the day, they said Bret was gonna take the finish, but as the day went on, Vince came to me and said 'no, Bret isn't gonna take the finish - it isn't needed'.

"As soon as I heard that, I said 'ok'. I did my match...busted my ass. But I already called Eric that day from a pay telephone. I said, 'I'm coming'.

"Eric watched the match, and saw me bust my ass against Bret. He said, 'are you *sure* you're coming?' I'm like, 'yeah!'

"So that night I'm in the showers with Scott and I said, 'I'm coming'. He said, 'what? Ask for more money'. I said, 'I already have!'"

On February 28th, 1996 - ten days after his match with Bret Hart - Nash penned his resignation letter to McMahon:

Re: Written Notice to Terminate Titan Sports, Inc. Booking Contract by and between Titan Sports, Inc. d/b/a/ The World Wrestling Federation ("Titan") and Kevin Nash (a/k/a/ "Diesel"), dated June 6, 1993 (the "Agreement")

Dear Vince:

As you know, under paragraph 6 of the Agreement, I am required to provide Titan with written notice at least ninety (90) days prior to the end of the term or any successive one year term of the Agreement of my decision to terminate the Agreement effective as of the end of any such term. As we have recently spoke about, I am providing you with such written notice to terminate the Agreement, effective as of June 6, 1996.

As I have mentioned to you many times in the past, you have been instrumental in furthering my wrestling career, and I thank you for all your time and efforts in promoting me. I deeply value the friendship that we have established and I hope that you can understand how difficult this decision has been for me. Although this letter terminates our business relationship, I look forward to continuing our friendship on a personal level.

Very truly yours,
Kevin Nash.

Nash would enter WCW mostly unimpressed with the prior creative direction. "We were," he says, speaking of the WWF, "by far, *the show*. The first *Nitro* was from the Mall of America, and I [thought] it was kind of cheesy. But they brought Luger out who was on our show like maybe a week earlier. We were like 'woah'. [But] *Nitro* was like 'Dungeon of Doom'...Giant was in a monster truck battle with Hogan, and got knocked off the top of Kobo Hall which was like fifteen stories [high]. He came back and fought in the main event, then the Yeti came down in ace bandages and bear hugged him. I mean, it was *bad*.

"We were going from doing Jackson Pollock [paintings] to doing lithographs. We were just like, 'ok, let's take the money. We've already played the starving artist thing so y'know, let's just go for the money'."

Despite the fortuitous fact that Nash and Hall's WWF contracts expired just six days apart, there would be no opportunity to replicate a *total* surprise, as with Lex Luger's *Nitro* debut. On this occasion, each performer had to provide written notice, meaning that word of their departure soon leaked to the wrestling media. Nonetheless, not *every* fan would be aware of their status, and for the handful that were, there would be huge anticipation for their arrival anyway. Therefore, Bischoff flew to Arizona to meet with Nash (ending the night, as Bischoff would recall, in a local strip joint), while outlining his vision in broad strokes. "He pitched that to me in my home in Arizona," Nash confirms. "He had the whole concept. Eric had the whole thing mapped out."

"I don't know if 'Bisch' would admit this or not," remembers Page, "but at one point, he wanted to call Kevin 'Axle' [as a play on *Diesel*]. I don't remember the name they had for Hall. I was like, 'everybody knows who the fuck they are. You don't need to call them anything right now, and if you are [going to], call them Nash and Hall, 'cos those are two cool fuckin' names!'"

For Bischoff, capitalizing on the new signings was of paramount importance, especially in light of the WWF rallying to five consecutive ratings wins on Monday nights. Furthermore, he was still processing a recent directive from Ted dictating a previously unthinkable scenario, as in an aggressive effort to increase audience share, *Nitro* was set to expand to *two* hours (8-10pm) from Memorial Day onwards. "The advantage is [having] a head-start on *Raw*," noted Alex Marvez of the *Dayton Daily News*, "but WCW officials might struggle to present an entertaining show for two hours each week."

But such concerns quickly evaporated after an unforgettable *Nitro* aired on May 27th, the first of the two-hour format. To gauge the mindset of Hall, a man whose reputation - vis-à-vis his role in causing backstage turmoil - certainly preceded him, Bischoff (now driving a black Porsche 911) personally escorted him to the arena. *Scott*, warned

Bischoff as they zoomed down the road, *if you're gonna come here and cause the trouble that I've heard you cause…I don't need it, and I don't want it.*

Only hours later - at exactly 8:34pm EST - TNT viewers rejoined *Nitro* after commercial break. A match between journeymen Steve Doll and Mike Enos was in progress, but as the combatants grappled for superiority mid-ring, a shadowy figure appeared in the top left corner of the screen. Slowly, without first being shown on camera, the figure began descending through a dumbfounded Macon Coliseum crowd.

It was Scott Hall, last seen on WWF television as Razor Ramon, making the most unique of entrances possible. As opposed to simply walking down the entranceway, his emergence through the crowd suggested that something *unplanned*, perhaps even unwanted, was in progress. Casually, Hall hopped over the guardrail separating the fans from the performers, and strutted confidently into the ring.

Whereas traditionally, promoters looked to exploit the signing of a new wrestler by promoting his arrival ahead of time ("coming next week!"), Bischoff recaptured the impact of the Luger surprise with a refrain of such hype. There was also another reason for the decision, as in a brilliant inversion of the 'Billionaire Ted' skits, he would have Hall present himself as an outside entity, an "invader," says Kevin Sullivan, apparently sent by Vince McMahon and the WWF.

"I think we all kicked it around," reports Sullivan, "and agreed that if he wasn't 'signed' by WCW, then you couldn't have him come out any other way. You couldn't promote him, and we needed the shock of the announcers to sell it."

On color commentary, Larry Zybysko convincingly feigned ignorance *("what the hell…what's with this?")*, even though ironically, he had actually suggested Hall enter through the crowd. Amid a stunned silence, Hall grabbed a microphone as the wrestlers dispersed, a visual never before employed on a professional wrestling telecast. *"You people know who I am,"* he taunted, *"but you don't know why I'm here."*

Backstage, Diamond Dallas Page, warming up for a match with Craig Pittman, froze in a state of disbelief. "I didn't know ahead of time," he remembers. "'Bisch' wanted me to be surprised, and to get my [real] reaction. I was stretching out when I heard his voice. It was like, 'get the fuck out! *This* is the place?'"

Hall continued his diatribe, making specific reference - in accordance with Bischoff's instructions (conveyed on a single piece of paper, typed on his assistant Janie Engle's computer, just moments before airtime) - to the WWF's 'Billionaire Ted' skits: *Where is Billionaire Ted? Where is the Nacho Man? That punk can't even get in the building. Me - I go wherever I want - whenever I want. And where, oh where, is Scheme Gene? 'Cos I got a scoop for you.*

"When that Ken doll lookalike, when that weatherman wannabe comes out here later tonight, I got a challenge for him, for Billionaire Ted, for the Nacho Man and for anyone else in uh...dubya-cee-dubya.

"Hey...you want to go to war?

"You want a war?

"You're going to get one."

"I have no idea what to say," responded Tony Schiavone on commentary. *"Stay with us,"* he implored as TNT returned to commercial break.

TNT 117 Page #3 (Rvd. 5/27/96 5pm)
Macon, GA/Airs: Monday, May 27, 1996   Air Time & Program Length: 8:00pm-9:59:50pm eastern

RING: (2:30)   1-M   2-M
                   STEVE DOLL   vs.   MIKE ENOS w/Col. Parker
Match Note: Match Continues & Ends In This Segment...Tony Pitch To Gene
                             (2:30) includes A :45 Interruption....
                             Ring Interruption @ 8:37:04...
             Note: Break to Interruption (8:33:45- 8:34:10)
             Break to bell (8:33:45 - 8:34:10)
             8:34:00 - Large man spotted in audience makes his way to the ring - he requests a microphone
             8:34:26 - Col. in ring w/ Enos - Doll leaves - large man in ring - he makes references to "Billionaire Ted/Nacho Man, etc." It is apparent
he   is [was] a wrestler from WWF. He declares war w/ WCW/WWF - ref gets him to leave. Announcers are speechless - match is
completely   interrupted - go to break.
             Result of match: No winner!
             Break @ 8:36:40   8:36:04

Above: Scott Hall's debut, as outlined in the show format ("he declares war w/ WCW/WWF...")

Later in the episode, Hall returned to confront Bischoff at the announce table. *"Hey, lookie here, Ken Doll,"* he goaded. *"You got such a big mouth and **we** are sick of it."*

"What do you mean?" responded Bischoff. *"Who's we?"*

"You know who," Hall replied. *"This is where the 'big boys play'? What a joke! I tell you what...you go get Billionaire Ted [and] tell him [to] get three of his very best.*

"We are taking over. You wanna war? Let's do it right. In the ring, where it matters. Not on no microphones. Not in those newspapers or 'dirtsheets'. Let's do it in the ring where it matters.

"We are coming down here and like it or not, we are taking over."

Seven days later in Asheville, North Carolina, Hall returned on *Nitro* in dramatic fashion. *"Yo, Ken Doll,"* he badgered to Bischoff. *"I had such a good time last week that I came back for more."* Hall promised to return again in the next episode, but this time, indicated he would not be alone. *"I got a little...no...I got a big surprise for you next week,"* he warned ominously as the show went off the air.

By now, the intimation of a cross-promotional 'invasion' - coupled with the presentation of Hall's character - drew the attention of Jerry McDevitt, the WWF's lead attorney. In a June 7th letter addressed to Nicholas Lambros, TBS' VP of Development and Administration, McDevitt advised that WCW drop the angle immediately:

Dear Mr. Lambros:

I am writing to you in regard to the most recent deliberate attempt of the WCW to infringe upon Titan's intellectual property rights and create confusion among consumers. Specifically, I am writing to you regarding the ongoing storyline being promoted by the WCW the past two weeks on the *Nitro* show as well as the WCW 900 lines that Razor Ramon, a trademark belonging to Titan Sports, is now appearing on Turner's networks as part of some interpromotional warfare between

WCW talent and WWF talent. In Mr. Hall's appearance, his reference to "Billionaire Ted" and "Nacho Man", and his character portrayal, all were intended to, and did, further the inference that the WWF character Razor Ramon was appearing on WCW shows because, in his words, "you wanted war."

To add to this confusion, WCW evidently intends to bring Kevin Nash, who performed at Titan under the trademarks Diesel and Big Daddy Cool, onto its show this coming Monday to further the false suggestion that "Team WWF" is now engaging in matches with WCW wrestlers on Turner's networks. The entire purpose of the storyline is clearly crafted to confuse the public, and has confused the public. As you and your organization well know, Scott Hall and Kevin Nash are no longer under a contract to the WWF and their appearances on your show have nothing to do with the WWF or any contest between WWF wrestlers and WCW wrestlers, and falsely suggests endorsement and sponsorship by the WWF in violation of the Lanham Act and other laws...

...Under the law, since the intent was and is clearly to confuse the public, it would be the burden of the WCW to prove consumers are not in fact confused. Given the actual confusion that exists, WCW will not be able to do so. I would further note that WCW's actions in this regard make it amenable to suit under state unfair competition laws and for punitive damages.

Accordingly, this letter is to demand the immediate cessation of the particular infringement of Titan's rights and the false suggestion of WWF sponsorship or endorsement. Moreover, this is to demand corrective action by the WCW to eliminate all confusion in the marketplace as a result of their activities.

Should the WCW fail to take immediate action to cease this angle, we will file an action against the WCW and TNT in which we will seek injunctive, monetary and exemplary relief. This letter is written with a full reservation of all other legal rights Titan may have.

Yours very truly,
Jerry S. McDevitt.

Unmoved, WCW moved ahead with its plan to introduce Hall's big surprise - Kevin Nash. In his June 10th *Nitro* debut, Nash furthered the perception of a WWF takeover, referencing a possible 'winner take all' match in the process. *"You've been sitting out here for six months running your mouth,"* barked Nash at Bischoff. *"This is where the big boys play, huh? Look at the adjective, play [sic]. We ain't here to play! Now, [Hall] said last week that he was going to bring somebody out here. I'm here, [but] you still don't have your three people and do you know why? Because nobody wants to face us!"*

"*No trouble tonight, man*," mumbled Bischoff softly. "*Speak your piece and...*"

"*Yeah, no trouble*," responded Nash, "*'cos you know I'll kick your teeth down your throat. Where are these three guys? You couldn't get a paleontologist to get these fossils cleared? You ain't got enough guys off a dialysis machine to get a team? Where's Hogan? Where's the Macho Man?*"

"*Look*," pleaded Bischoff, "*I don't have [that] authority, right here, right now. [But] you wanna face three guys? Tomorrow morning at 9:00am, I'm going to be in Atlanta. I'll be in the offices of WCW, [and] I'll try and get you your fight. You know what? Live this Sunday in Baltimore, [at the] Great American Bash, you guys want to show up? You want a fight? You show up and I'll see if I can get you your fight.*"

In a cleverly subtle (yet scripted) use of body language, the telecast terminated with Bischoff signaling for the cameras to cut:

10:00:21 - Nash pushes EB back and leaves
10:00:30 - Music up - EB motions to "cut" - go to crane shot and close.

(:10)Copyright   10:00:47

Above: From the show script - "EB motions to 'cut'"

"When Kevin showed up," remembers DDP, "people thought it was real! It blew my mind how many people were like, 'you guys are doing business with New York now'. The WCW and WWF are merging - that's what they thought!"

————

On Wednesday, June 12th, McDevitt wrote to David Payne, Turner's Senior Counsel, advising that the WWF's prior threat to sue would materialize:

Dear Mr. Payne:

108

Per your prior advice, enclosed please find a copy of a letter sent to Mr. Lambros last week regarding the recent actions of the WCW as they relate to confusing the consuming public by infringing on Titan's intellectual property. As usual, Mr. Lambros was unable to respond.

I am in the midst of drafting a lawsuit regarding these activities which I anticipate filing late this week or early next week. Among other forms or relief, we will be asking for preliminary injunctive relief. Accordingly, please advise who you would like to receive notice upon the filing of this lawsuit so that TBS and WCW may appear and defend its interests.

Yours very truly,
Jerry S. McDevitt.

As alluded to in McDevitt's initial correspondence, the WWF claimed that in their presentation of Hall and Nash, WCW were portraying them in a manner not dissimilar from their WWF characters. To counter this claim, the evidence suggested that WCW was considering - in accordance with their own internal e-mails - to bill the duo as 'The Bad Guy' and 'AXCEL/AXEL'.

At 10:14am on June 12th, for example, WCW VP Gary Juster CC'ed Bischoff on the following e-mail, addressed primarily to Ellen Morrisey Hughes, a Turner legal assistant (incidentally, WCW's own Hotline referred to Hall as 'The Bad Guy' on four separate occasions that night):

Subject: Registrations

Per our conversation, please conduct the computer search for "Bad Guy" and "The Bad Guy" ASAP. If this preliminary search is OK then please proceed with the full search (fastest search available) and then registration.

Re: AXCEL please go forth with the fastest full search possible and then on to registration.

We are in a time-critical situation and appreciate your help.

Thanks!
GJ

At 8:02am the next morning - Thursday, June 13th - Lambros sent out a similar e-mail from his desk:

Subject: Wrestler Names

Please request a computer tm search of "AXCEL" for a wrestler name. Also, please request a FULL T&T search (including copyright), 7 day turn-around, for "THE BAD GUY".

THX
Nl

In the interim, WCW had taken to referring to Hall (in its format for *Nitro*) as 'Razor Ramone':

9:57:06 - BH leaves - enter Razor Ramone EB asks him about the "big surprise" he promised last week.
9:58:53 - EB says he doesn't want any trouble - but Nash says "yeah,don't cause any trouble cuz' I'll kick your teeth down your throat." and then asks about WCW's 3 guys to wrestle.
9:59:35 - RR keeps patting EB on the head

Above: For one episode, WCW used the name 'Razor Ramone' to describe Hall in its production notes

Soon, TBS filed an official title and trademark search for 'THE BAD GUY':

...on behalf of World Championship Wrestling, Inc. ("WCW"). The proposed mark will be used as the name of a wrestler...and for related merchandise classes...

But a later e-mail from Lambros indicated that WCW were having second thoughts:

Please do not register or make any application to register The Bad Guy or Axle without discussing with me first.

Thanks,
Nick

Finally, TBS' legal division advised against 'The Bad Guy' moniker, according to an internal memo:

The full search came in from outside counsel for The Bad Guy. Outside counsel recommends that we don't use the mark because of a pending application [by] Wrestling Bad Guys for magazines relating to wrestling owned by London Publishing Co. and a registration for Bad Guys for clothing, namely, jackets, jumpsuits, sweatshirts, sweaters and pants owned by Bad Boys Wear B.V.

110

And thus, in an added touch of realism, the interlopers would eventually wrestle under their real names after all: Kevin Nash and Scott Hall.

———

On Sunday, June 16th, in the middle of its *Great American Bash* pay-per-view from Baltimore, MD, WCW acknowledged - on the advice of legal counsel - that the 'invaders' were no longer signed to their primary competition. The admission did little to slow the momentum of the angle, however, as in a thrilling spectacle, Nash responded to Bischoff's formal announcement of the 3-on-3 match by power bombing him off the stage.

24 hours later on *Nitro*, it was announced that WCW would determine - as part of a 'random drawing' - 3 wrestlers to fight at *Bash at the Beach*, the July 7th pay-per-view from Daytona Beach, Florida. At the conclusion of the show, 'Mean' Gene Okerlund revealed the final team as Sting, Lex Luger and Randy Savage, provoking questions over who would join Hall and Nash on the opposite side (via the WWF Hotline, Vince McMahon attempted to convince fans that it would be Jeff Jarrett, a wrestler currently without attachment).

On Monday, June 24th - mere hours before the latest head-to-head competition - wrestling's real-life war moved officially into the courts, spurred by a WWF complaint accusing WCW of "defamation, slander, trademark infringement, and unfair competition." As part of the complaint, the WWF requested an immediate temporary restraining order against "further use of Scott Hall and Kevin Nash, in ways that could deceive or confuse the wrestling public into thinking the WWF was affiliated with their ongoing WCW storyline":

The creative genius in the development and portrayal of distinctive characters and personas is effectively the principal method by which the WWF competes with the enormous financial and network power of TBS. Unlike the WWF, WCW has no reputation for creativity in developing and then promoting wrestlers as distinctive characters and personas.

WCW thereafter began systematically copying virtually everything done by the

WWF, raiding its talent, pawning off the WWF's reputation, and infringing Titan's rights.

From inception, TBS and WCW utilized the Nitro show as a vehicle to disparage, defame, and libel the WWF and its talent rather than promote its own product on its own merits. A constant and on-going theme of Nitro was that WWF wrestlers were leaving the WWF to join WCW because that was 'where the big boys play.' At the same time, TBS and WCW agents, employees, and operatives constantly used their media power and unlimited checkbook to suggest that WWF talent should join WCW with promises of lucrative contracts. As part of its systematic corporate plan to harm the WWF as opposed to promoting its own product on its own merits, WCW employees and agents constantly circulated phony and false rumors of Titan's supposed impending bankruptcy so as to maximize its chances of luring talent away from the WWF.

In a humorously expansive request for restorative action, the suit continued:

WCW [should] be required to state at the beginning, middle, and end of every Nitro program and for upcoming pay-per-views for the immediate future that:

(a) Hall and Nash are both under contract to WCW and that all their actions since May 27, 1996 have been at the direction of WCW;
(b) Any suggestion by Defendants that Hall and Nash were with or affiliated with the WWF since May 27, 1996 were false and misleading;
(c) The WWF was not and has not been in any way affiliated with the portrayal of Hall and Nash since May 27, 1996;
(d) That there will be no interpromotional matches between WCW and the WWF and that any suggestions to that effect by WCW and TBS personnel were false; and
(e) That consumers who wish to view WWF wrestlers should watch the WWF's programs including Monday Night Raw which airs on the USA Network Monday nights at 9:00 p.m. EST."

"The suggestion that the WWF is somehow affiliated [with the storyline] never goes away," argued WWF attorney Jerry McDevitt in front of Chief U.S. District Judge Peter C. Dorsey. "It's like Batman or Superman. We created these characters and wrestling fans have come to associate them with the WWF. Why would anyone like Ted Turner pay them $750,000 a year, put them in the trade dress of Diesel and Razor Ramon, and not give them a name? [If they don't stop], the way it affects the WWF is incalculable."

Later that evening, Hall and Nash continued to interrupt *Nitro*, showing up with baseball bats and causing the ring to fill up with police officers. "I remember [that night] in Charlotte," reminisces Nash. "We had to make it *real*...so Sullivan, Scott and myself came up with using aluminum baseball bats. I don't care how many guys there are, you've still gotta come through the ropes, and two guys swinging baseball bats...you're gonna do some serious damage! That was the only way it possibly made sense...that these two thugs from the other organization could hold off the entire company.

"I remember Eric saying, 'eh...I don't know', but Sullivan was shaking his head 'yes' and saying, 'do not bring the baseball bats', [at the same time]. *He was shaking his head 'yes' while saying 'no!'*"

With less than two weeks until the pay-per-view, WCW was providing few hints as to who the *third man* might be. However, as Bischoff boarded a midweek flight to Los Angeles, he believed a commitment from another ex-WWF star was near.

Bischoff was in LA to visit Terry Bollea, who despite not appearing on television since the *Uncensored* debacle, occupied himself with filming *Santa with Muscles*, a production that eventually found itself on a variety of 'worst movie ever' lists ("working [with] an irredeemably bland screenplay," wrote one critic, "John Murlowski directs with all the enthusiasm of someone going through the motions to pay off a debt").

In between takes, Bollea had been keeping up with the happenings on *Nitro*, as evidenced by the stack of VHS tapes littered around his trailer. At the end of a *long* day of 'action' (for all involved, evidently, given the eventual film reviews), Bischoff arrived on set to find the Hulkster enjoying a beer, with a handful of Cuban cigars - Montecristo No. 4's - sitting out for good measure.

So, brother, Bollea pondered, *who's the third guy?*

I don't know yet, confessed Bischoff. *I haven't made up my mind.*

Well, I know who the third guy should be, Bollea teased.

You're looking at him.

"I remember me and 'Bisch' having some beers at the Longhorn Saloon (in Atlanta)," says DDP. "I remember him saying, 'Terry [Bollea] is thinking about being a part of this whole outsider thing'. There was no name for the group yet. I said, 'yeah, that would be good. But *I'm* the fucking guy that should be number three!

"I said, 'I'm the only guy with any real affiliation to these two guys!'

"He's like, 'no, we can't do that'.

"I go, 'why not?'

"He goes, 'you don't mean anything'.

"At the time, he was right. I was getting hotter and hotter and hotter, but he was absolutely right.

"It had to be Hulk to really mean something."

As Page quickly accepted, the consequences of a Hulk Hogan heel turn could *really* mean something. With over a decade of character back story to leverage, it could potentially send shock waves throughout the entire wrestling world - and beyond - if the execution was handled correctly. The debut of Lex Luger had been a surprise, for sure - and the Madusa stunt certainly shocking - but the prospect of a *bad* Hulk Hogan was almost inconceivable.

"I got in the business because of Hulk Hogan," reveals Kevin Nash. "He's the reason I started watching pro wrestling again. I remember my first night in Albany with the WWF, I walked by the first locker room, and there was Hulk and a couple other guys there. It was just like, 'wow, *that's Hulk Hogan*'."

114

As Terry Bollea knew well, a heel turn carried with it - to say the least - significant risk. Since the 1980's, he had built his career on the 'train, say your prayers, and take your vitamins' credo that made him a hero to children worldwide. His remarkable popularity, reinforced every time he triumphed against the odds, had enabled an ongoing transition into television and film. Alternatively, maybe those children - now teenagers, or perhaps even young adults, by this point - would identify more with a character possessing some edge. Maybe the time to be an All-American babyface had passed; besides, Bollea's contract was up in October, anyway, and with no real interest from his former employer, joining Hall and Nash could be an act of self-preservation.

While the hardcores recalled his earlier run as a villain - some 16 years earlier before his star began to rise - mainstream America had known only a virtuous Hogan, whose matches tended to follow a familiar pattern. Time after time, he would struggle mightily against a brutish wrongdoer, before experiencing a sudden second wind, instantaneously becoming impervious to pain. With the *Hulkamaniacs* on his side, Hogan would then execute his trademark finishing sequence - three punches, an Irish whip, a big boot, and the atomic *leg drop* - ensuring almost certain victory while validating his shtick once more.

With such a squeaky-clean track record, there was probably no going back if a heel turn failed. A star of Hogan's magnitude could not be repackaged, or newly represented as another character, assuming the move didn't catch on. Provided that the angle succeeded, however, history dictated that it could be huge for business. In January 1980, when Larry Zybysko turned on mentor Bruno Sammartino in the WWF, the event generated such contempt in fans that Zybysko suffered a stabbing and repeated damage to his car (36,295 fans paid to see the eventual blow-off match at Shea Stadium). Hogan himself benefited from similar plot twists, as betrayals from Andre The Giant and Randy 'Macho Man' Savage contributed spectacularly to the success of *Wrestlemania III* and *V* respectively.

With this in mind, Bollea confirmed to Bischoff, just days before the Sunday pay-per-view, that he was 'in'. In response, a skeptical Sullivan, mindful of his star's tendency to second-guess himself - often a consequence of listening to others, including his wife - suggested that Bollea spend Saturday at his Daytona home. *It's a mile from the building*, Sullivan implored.

Bollea showed up on Saturday, but he wasn't alone.

He was with his agent, Peter Young, and he had a message for Sullivan:

We need to talk.

Chapter 14:
Lightning in Daytona

As DAY BECAME NIGHT at the Sullivan home, Bollea deliberated his participation in the pay-per-view. "Everybody was telling him that it was the wrong thing to do," Sullivan says. "He was getting booed out of the arena, but they were all saying, 'this is gonna kill him'."

With no end to the discussion in sight, the wily booker casually suggested that Bollea and Young make use of his two guest rooms until the morning. "I isolated [them]," Sullivan admits. "I was just afraid that at the last minute, he was going to use his creative control [clause] and pull out."

If Sullivan could deliver Bollea to the arena by showtime, the finish of the match called for Hogan to star in the most dramatic of surprise endings. In a sequence devised by Kevin Nash, an unannounced Hulkster would shockingly interfere in the match, but only after the heels gained an unfair advantage through cheating. It would be a brilliant misdirection, Nash thought, as fans would instinctively believe Hogan's appearance to be in support of the babyface team. "I knew there were gonna be 55 different ideas," Nash says, thinking back to the eve of the event, "[so] I actually put a lot of thought into it. I called Scott [Hall] two or three days before that, and said 'what do you think about this?'

"We had to make it a 2-on-2 match with [Lex] Luger getting injured [during the match] and going out. We would cheat to get Macho [Man] in trouble and all of a sudden Hulk comes down, which of course would mean 'ok, here comes Hulk to make the save'. [Hall] said, 'I love   it'."

There was, however, the looming possibility that Bollea could reject his turn at the eleventh hour. Thinking ahead, Bischoff developed a contingency plan in which Sting would play the role, ultimately revealing himself - despite not having prior experience with the WWF - as the 'third man' instead.

"I remember Eric came in to the locker room," recalls Marcus 'Buff' Bagwell, "and said [to Sting], 'I wanna talk to you about something'. I could hear them going over the idea, and then when they got done, Sting told me what they were talking about. He said that [Eric said], 'there are only two guys that could turn heel where it would really matter'. That would be Hogan and Sting."

"He was offering Sting the job first, [as I recall], and Sting didn't wanna do it. He didn't really say it wouldn't work, but he just said, 'it doesn't intrigue me. I don't wanna do it'."

According to Andre Freitas, a special effects artist who worked in costume design and character development for WCW, the proposed Sting swerve was to involve the use of a doppelganger - or 'phony' Sting - presumably in an effort to fool fans that the real character had switched sides. "That was their original plan," says Freitas. "Eric showed me a picture of Jeff Farmer (a lower-card wrestler) and said 'can you make him Sting?' I told him that they have similar bodies...then we looked at Sting's hair and Jeff's hair...and talked about all that stuff. I did a head cast for [Farmer] and some prosthetic and test make-ups. But when they secured Hogan, we didn't do [the angle]."

———

Amazingly, even as *Bash at the Beach* began, Bischoff continued to consider Plan B. "I remember walking by this perforated wall in the Ocean Center," divulges Nash, "and Eric said to me, 'Hulk is with Sullivan, and he's not sure he's gonna do it yet'. It was up in the air."

Meanwhile, viewers of the pay-per-view - and, for that matter, WCW's own production staff - speculated as to the identity of the third man. "They were trying to 'work' everyone," asserts Jason

Douglas, a WCW producer backstage at his first pay-per-view event. "'Rocket' (staff member Rick Sancher) came up to me - they were kinda testing me because I was new on the road - and said 'hey, I think it's gonna be [WWF wrestler] Bret Hart'. I guess it was to see if I would leak something, and so I was just like 'oh, cool, Bret Hart'."

In reality, aside from Bischoff, Bollea, Young, Hall, Nash and Sullivan, the turn would be concealed from *everyone* - even the announcers, according to orders from Bischoff - as to ensure their most realistic reactions.

With less than an hour before the main event began, production staffer Woody Kearce discovered a revealing clue in the parking lot. A Hulk Hogan motorcycle had appeared mysteriously in one of the spaces, sparking another round of backstage conjecture. Finally, with what Sullivan recalls as "thirty minutes" and Bischoff remembers as "forty-five to sixty minutes" left on the air, Bollea belatedly arrived at the Ocean Center.

The mood suddenly changed. Upon realizing that his star had been convinced, Bischoff began to relax. "Once he got to the building, I recall a sense of calm," he reveals. "All of the anxiety, all of the tension, all of the worry, all of the effort to make sure things stayed quiet...all of that just kind of dissipated. It was like fog lifting when the sun comes out - it all just went away. I was thinking, 'it is what it is, there's nothing more I can do...so let's just roll with it'."

To cement the turn, Bollea knew, he would have to deliver a monumental post-match promo to explain his actions. While typically, he enjoyed using Bischoff as a sounding board to rehearse interviews, the need for complete privacy - on this occasion - was unquestionably paramount. And so, away from prying eyes - and ears - the two met up in the most unglamorous of clandestine locations - a utility closet. In the midst of the run-through, Bischoff stopped to emphasize an important point:

When you grab that microphone, I want you to say... 'this is the beginning of the new...world...order'.

119

The phrase - 'new world order' - lingered auspiciously in the air. Bischoff surprised himself with the utterance, realizing slowly that the term encapsulated everything that the invasion storyline could represent. In 1990, then-president George H.W. Bush famously utilized the same expression in a speech to Congress, although its origin could actually be traced back to the 28th President, Woodrow Wilson. But if Bischoff was unsure as to the source of his spontaneous inspiration, perhaps the answer could be found closer to home - on the preceding *Nitro*, just six days earlier, announcer Larry Zybysko serendipitously made the following proclamation: *"This Sunday, I promise you, there will be a new world order of wrestling..."*

Fans at the Ocean Center waited anxiously to see if Zybysko's prophecy would materialize; for after all the hoopla, it was suddenly time for the main event. Before the opening bell, the audience was already on its feet for ring announcer Michael Buffer's pre-match introductions. As Hall and Nash sauntered to the ring for *The Hostile Takeover match*, Buffer set the scene with theatrical aplomb:

"Ladies and gentleman, at this time, let me introduce the men whose plan and goal is to takeover the WCW with force and hostility. We were told there would be three of these interlopers, and I must apologize as I have been informed - as you can see - there are only two. Ladies and gentleman, introducing...the Outsiiiiiders!"

In a moment that played off perfectly on television, Sting's entrance music began - and quickly ended - as 'Mean Gene' Okerlund traipsed cautiously into the ring. After exchanging quizzical looks with Buffer and referee Randy Anderson, Okerlund confronted the Outsiders to get some answers, an inspired plot device designed to build the tension even further. *"Gentleman,"* began Okerlund, *"if I could have your attention...I don't have police protection with me at this time, but I wanna confront you in front of this full house here at the Ocean Center, and millions of others watching across the country and around the world. I don't see three men here tonight. Where is your partner?"*

Responding in a manner consistent with their WWF characters, Hall and Nash assured Okerlund that the third man was present - and ready. "*Let me tell you something,*" announced a confident Nash, "*we got enough to handle it right now, right here.*" Once more, Sting's entrance music blared from the arena speakers, this time preceding the man himself, accompanied by Luger and Savage. "*Here we go!*" screamed color commentator Bobby Heenan as the wrestlers passed an unusually large contingent of security personnel on the entrance way. "*The war is on!*"

Less than two minutes into the bout, Luger collapsed to the outside, a move in accordance with Nash's plan to even the sides before the climactic reveal. "*Now it's two against two!*" yelled Heenan. After a brief delay, the concerned crowd looked on as Luger left the arena on a stretcher, leaving Sting and Savage alone to fight valiantly for WCW. As the match progressed, the contemptible Outsiders used every trick to stall their opponent's momentum, until a revitalized Savage began a furious rally at the fifteen-and-a-half minute mark. The invaders were suddenly down, but not out - as with the referee distracted, Nash landed a low-blow to bring the Macho Man to his knees. All four men lay on the canvas, exhausted, as referee Anderson started a ten count.

As Anderson yelled '*ONE*', several rows of spectators rose to their feet. Within seconds, the reaction diffused from section to section, the noise level increasing with each passing beat. On the live broadcast, viewers at home caught glimpse of a familiar figure making his way down the ramp. "*Hulkamania!*" screamed Dusty Rhodes on commentary while Hogan walked methodically towards the ring. Noticeably, the Hulkster seemed oddly disaffected - even *out-of-character* - but after exchanging the briefest of glances with the crowd, he continued stride with the din reaching fever pitch.

"*Whose side is he on?*" bellowed Heenan, a question that seemed inexplicable given the history of Hogan's on-screen persona. "*Whose side is he on?*" repeated Heenan, who as longtime fans could recall, had opposed Hogan for years as a manager in the WWF. For that reason, the comment flew over the heads of most (but not all) viewers;

meanwhile, the live crowd was cheering as if their team had won the World Series.

Nash and Hall retreated to the floor as Hogan tore off his shirt, an apparent signal that the archetypal good guy was here to save the day again. "*Whose bad now boys?*" taunted play-by-play man Tony Schiavone on commentary, confident that WCW's honor was no longer in jeopardy.

Savage lay prone on the mat as Hogan surveyed the scene. Above the cheapest of cheap seats, peeking through a curtain with palpable anticipation, was Eric Bischoff. "I knew that something big was about to happen," he recalls. "It was either gonna be a big failure, or a big success."

Seemingly out of nowhere, with his unsuspecting devotees enveloped in celebration, Hulk backed up to the corner. With the coldness of a serial killer, the once-honorable hero shockingly shoved referee Anderson, and executed his patented finishing move - the leg drop - to the helpless Macho Man below.

The audience became completely, utterly unglued. "I was standing back with the announcers," remembers Michelle Baines, newly hired as a production assistant. "One of the producers turned to me and said, 'you need to go to the back'.

"'I said, 'what do you mean?'

"She said, 'it's gonna get ugly real quick'."

"She was right - the crowd turned ugly *quick*."

In retrospect, it was clear that even as Hogan's body approached the canvas - contact with Savage just milliseconds away - the gravity of the assault started to hit home. "*What has he done?*" questioned a crestfallen Rhodes, "*is he the third man? What the hell is going on here?*" Heenan was even more direct - "*Hulk Hogan has betrayed WCW! He is the third man in this picture!*"

122

A breathless Schiavone could barely muster more than three words: *Oh My God*, he repeated. *Oh My God*, he continued, as Hogan high-fived a grinning Hall and Nash. The courageous Sting, stumbling to his feet to stop the injustice, was quickly dispatched, and in the coup de grace, Hogan tossed Anderson to the floor. Sardonically, he covered Savage for the pin, the contest now clearly a farce. "*I hope you love it*," a disappointed Rhodes wailed on commentary. "*You just sold your soul to the devil.*"

The third man was a mystery no more, and Hall, Nash, and Hogan raised their hands in victory to a genuinely astonished audience. The immediate outrage, which first gave way to shock, was now inspiring unmitigated rage. Simultaneously, the evil trio continued to taunt, pose, and antagonize while the announcers lamented WCW's future. As Sting and Savage hobbled back to the locker room, a visibly distraught Okerlund returned to conduct an explanatory interview, based around the one Hogan and Bischoff had mapped out earlier. "*Mean Gene*," commanded Hogan, "*the first thing you need to do is to tell these people to shut up if you wanna hear what I gotta say.*"

For the next four minutes, Hogan rationalized his turn with remarkable clarity. "*The first thing you gotta realize, brother, is this right here is the future of wrestling. You can call this the new...world...order of wrestling. These two men right here came from a great big organization up north, and everybody was wondering who the third man was. Well, who knows more about that organization than me, brother? I made that organization a monster. I made people rich up there. I made the people that ran that organization rich up there. And when it all came to pass, the name Hulk Hogan, the man Hulk Hogan, got bigger than the whole organization!*"

Bischoff watched from his secretive seat in amazement - he had not seen, nor had anyone, this intensity of emotion on display at a wrestling show before. It was almost as if the assembled masses had lost themselves in the performance, perhaps even forgetting, if only for a moment, that they were witnesses to a pre-determined event. Hogan's actions had ostensibly interrupted their critical faculties; in other words, they had *suspended their disbelief* by reacting to the incident *as if* it were real. Moreover, the shock was manifesting in the most volatile ways imaginable, as in an incident edited out of future showings of the pay-per-view, a rather large man, likely intoxicated, ran into the ring before being knocked down by Hall and Nash. Concurrently, a stream of debris rained down from the stands, with one object hitting Okerlund, and the rest filling the ring in a stunningly unique visual.

Hogan continued as the trash piled up around him, even referencing Ted Turner in his diatribe:

"Billionaire Ted promised me movies brother. Billionaire Ted promised me millions of dollars. And Billionaire Ted promised me world caliber matches. And as far as Billionaire Ted, Eric Bischoff, and the entire WCW goes, I'm bored brother! That's why I want these two guys here, these so called Outsiders. These are the men I want as my friends. They are the new blood of professional wrestling, and not only are we going to take over the whole wrestling business...with Hulk Hogan, the new blood and the monsters with me, we will destroy everything in our path, Mean Gene."

"Look at all the crap in this ring," responded Okerlund. *"This is what's in the future for you if you want to hang around the likes of this man Hall, and this man Nash."* Hogan raised his finger as if to stop the interviewer midstream, the perfect line instantly coming to mind. *"As far as I'm concerned, all this crap in the ring represents these fans out here,"* he boomed defiantly.

"For two years, I held my head high," ranted Hogan, alluding to his rather uninspired WCW tenure. *"I did everything for the charities. I did everything for the kids. And the reception I got when I came out here, you fans can stick it brother! Because if it wasn't for Hulk Hogan, you people wouldn't be here. If it wasn't for Hulk Hogan, Eric Bischoff would still be selling meat from a truck in Minneapolis. And if it wasn't for Hulk Hogan, all of these 'Johnny come latelys' that you see out here wrestling wouldn't be here. I was selling the world out, brother, while they were bumming gas to put in their car to get to high*

124

school!"

In closing, Hogan foreshadowed the future state of affairs in WCW with a prophetic preview of coming storylines: *"With Hulk Hogan and the new world organization of wrestling, brother...me and the new blood by my side...whatcha gonna do when the new world organization runs wild on you? Whatcha gonna do? What are you gonna do??"*

Despite mistakenly bungling the 'new world order' phrase at the conclusion of his speech, Hogan still provided the perfect punctuation to a sensational heel turn. His promo, inarguably the most dynamic of his career, came across as strikingly authentic ("it felt real, because it *was* real'," offered a proud Eric Bischoff upon reflection years later). On commentary, Schiavone - who most inspiredly suggested that Hogan had planned to double-cross WCW all along, since his debut in 1994 no less - added to the realism with some mournful final comments: *"We have seen the end of Hulkamania,"* he grieved. *"Hulk Hogan, you can go to hell! We're outta here.*

"Straight to hell."

––––

To the layman, there appeared an obvious explanation for the feverous crowd response that accompanied Hogan's turn. Clearly, the element of surprise - one of the key elements of *Nitro*'s success - had been exploited to a masterful degree ("nobody on earth thought that the third man was going to be Hulk Hogan," highlights Nash).

To Kevin Sullivan, however, there were several layers of story at play. "People thought that it was an invasion from the WWF," he begins, implying that the success of the angle could be correlated to its realism. "They really bought into it, and when Hogan turned heel...they were *sure* of it.

"So while Hogan gets the credit for the reaction, it was [Nash and Hall] who set the whole thing up. Those guys built the foundation of heat, and when Hogan came down, it just blew up."

"We were red hot coming off WWF television," agrees Nash, "and then you had the biggest turn in the world on top of that. The biggest babyface of all-time finally turned heel!"

To the ever-meticulous Sullivan, always a keen observer of the nuances present in a wrestling angle, an often overlooked element was also noteworthy. "He did it to *Randy* [Savage]," the booker emphasizes, speaking of Hogan's betrayal. "People knew there was real-life heat there. That helped out too, but everyone played an intricate part.

"Lightning...you can't catch it in a bottle but one time."

126

Chapter 15:
Heat

AFTER MONTHS of careful deliberation, Bischoff's 'third man' storyline had played out in spectacular fashion. The reaction had been swift, intense, and limited not only to Daytona. "TBS was flooded with phone calls...letters...e-mails...chastising the company for letting Hogan be a bad guy," remembers DDP. "I mean, wow - you talk about changing the game!"

"I can remember when Hulk Hogan showed up in black one day," recalls Turner executive Joe Uva. "All of a sudden, Hulk went bad! That was a big thing. I think it really intensified the interest in WCW."

But somewhat lost amidst the commotion of Hogan's treachery was the memory of a match earlier in the night - the show opener, specifically, between cruiserweights Rey Mysterio, Jr. and Psychosis. Only 21 and 25 years old respectively, the spectacular *luchadores* put on a breathtaking clinic in aerial acrobatics, with daring dives and high-risk moves that were still novel to an American audience. Their performance rivaled the previous month's pay-per-view clash between Mysterio and master technician Dean Malenko, a match that moved the entire locker room to stand and applaud both competitors afterwards - the first time anyone associated with WCW could remember such an occurrence.

A Malenko-Mysterio rematch kicked off the July 8th *Nitro*, less than 24 hours since the leg drop heard around the world. Before each man made his entrance, announcer Tony Schiavone professed his sorrow at the events of the preceding evening:

"Ladies and gentleman, we are one day removed from one of the most shocking...one of the most startling...one of the most disappointing, disheartening events in the history of our sport."

As part of an episode-long theme, various WCW wrestlers - regardless of their face/heel orientation - derided the Hulkster's actions in heartfelt interviews. *"I'm lost for words,"* bemoaned Hulk's former manager, Jimmy Hart. *"What I saw...made me wanna puke,"* offered Arn Anderson. *"Last night, you wiped out and trashed every little kid, and every person...that patterned their lives after you!"* fumed an irate Sting. But perhaps the most biting comment came from the 'Macho Man' Randy Savage, who in an off-the-cuff remark, sarcastically referred to his former friend as *'Hollywood'* Hogan.

Within weeks, Bollea incorporated the put-down into his new heel persona. To accompany his all black attire - a remarkable contrast from the iconic red-and-yellow getup he sported as the consummate babyface - Bollea's character would now be billed as *Hollywood Hogan* after all. The change, however subtle, alluded cleverly to the aging star's involvement in a series of B-movies and straight-to-video releases. While Hulk was, in accordance with *kayfabe*, a wrestler first and foremost, his *Hollywood* character would eventually morph into an insufferable egomaniac, often projecting his status as being bigger than the sport itself ("I believe [Hogan] is back on the set, doing a movie tonight," smiled Nash in an interview to end the post-Bash *Nitro*).

―――

As the New World Order storyline progressed, the integration of various spontaneous, unplanned and even fortuitous occurrences advanced the plot as much as the most premeditated of creative decisions. Undoubtedly, its genesis involved a striking degree of good fortune - the expiration of Scott Hall's WWF contract, just six days prior to the end of Kevin Nash's own deal - and throughout the summer of '96, *Nitro* epitomized the sense of unpredictability that Bischoff so desired. "A lot of this shit would write itself," says Diamond Dallas Page, alluding to the way in which story arcs tended to emerge organically. "Some things were mapped out six months in advance, but sometimes it didn't always work out that way."

128

"You can sit in a room with four, five, or six people and convince yourself you're on the right track," reveals Bischoff, "but you never know until you see how the audience responds. So my approach then - as it is now - is to have a plan, have an arc, plan your stuff out three months in advance, or six months in advance...have a great idea where you're going, work backwards from there, but stay flexible enough to adjust to whatever variables come your way. That variable could be an injury. It could be a contract conflict. It could be [someone saying] 'I just got a better idea'.

"But more often than not, that variable comes in the form of an audience reaction. So you've got to have a great idea of where you're going. You've got to have a sense, a tone, an idea of generally what you're looking for, and a good solid arc to aim at. But you can't be so rigid in your approach that you don't know what to do if it doesn't work. You can't just start over every week. You've got to be flexible.

"That was one of the fun things about producing wrestling live every week, because not only did you have the opportunity to utilize the ratings, the research, the 'demos', the quarter hour numbers, the minute-by-minute numbers...you had a live audience, so you could sit in the arena, feel the energy and know intuitively whether you were on the right track [or not]. So, my instinct was - and probably still is - to know your audience, listen to them, but also have a pretty good idea of where you're going and what you want to achieve."

Remarkably, and with some notable exceptions granted, each week of WCW programming was rather seamless in its transition into the next. "In some ways it was hard, because of just the sheer volume of [WCW programming on the Turner networks]," continues Bischoff, in reference to achieving continuity. "But we were doing it *every week*. We were done on Monday night and by Tuesday morning, we were already laying out, or fine-tuning, the details for the following week's show."

Unplanned occurrences aside, the matchmaking and week-to-week storytelling continued to be handled by Kevin Sullivan, with Bischoff maintaining the overall creative vision. On a typical week in '96,

Sullivan says, the upcoming edition of *Nitro* was generally 'formatted' (or outlined) by Thursday afternoon ("that was *never* the case," retorts one WCW producer. "I ran laps around arenas getting the latest format out every week, sometimes while the pyro(technics) started.") In an exceptional case - Lex Luger becoming available to debut on the inaugural *Nitro* at the last minute, for example - Sullivan could reach WCW's travel department on a private line to amend his plan. In any event, the booker contends, his directions were usually - in those days - carried out without too much resistance from talent. With Bollea revitalized in his new role, and WCW pulling away from its competition in the ratings, backstage morale was approaching an all-time high.

It was summer, it was scorching, and *Nitro* was emanating weekly from the Disney-MGM Studios in Orlando. With Atlanta preparing to host the Olympics - the so-called 'Glitch Games' due to a host of logistical calamities - many of the Turner Sports production staff found themselves away on assignment, and therefore, unable to assist in running WCW's marquee show. Consequently, to manage the lack of personnel and facilities available, a makeshift outdoor arena was constructed at the iconic theme park, an inspired innovation in terms of its presentation. For the staffers remaining on site, downtime was filled with poolside relaxation and tipsy go-cart rides. "My favorite summer ever," is how production assistant Michelle Baines describes the time. "I worked 15 to 20 hours a day, but it was always a great time. It was a family thing...it was just so much fun."

The MGM setting also provided the use of an iconic production facility, an amenity utilized in recent years by towering Hollywood figures like Robin Williams and James Earl Jones. One afternoon before a show, feature producer Neal Pruitt entered the space to experiment with some voice-over work. To Pruitt, a highly respected figure with a colossal command of the production elements required for television, the New World Order storyline was capturing the imagination of fans in a distinctly visceral manner ("people were just in *awe*," Pruitt emphasizes upon recollection of Hogan's initial turn).

But glaringly, a crucial component of the invasion narrative seemed, at least at first, to be conspicuously absent. For while the villainy perpetrated by the Outsiders and Hogan was, unequivocally, revolutionary in its execution, it appeared logical that the trio required a similarly pioneering approach towards their visual presentation.

"I started giving my input right away," continues Pruitt, "and had a vision in mind when I first got the project. I had a lot of ideas that they used, like when Hogan talked about how Atlanta used to be Ted Turner's place and now they're taking over. I gave Kevin Nash a paintbrush and canvas to paint on, and he painted the world being taken over by the group. I actually brought in the spray paint idea, [too], kinda going off how gangs would tag their territory."

After Scott Hall foreshadowed, in another extemporaneous boast on *Nitro*, that the invaders were willing to pay for air time on WCW programming ("this portion of *WCW Monday Nitro* [is] brought to you by the Outsiders and [Hollywood] Hogan"), discussion began around the potential visual, aural and textural content of a standalone New World Order segment. Lending from a famous commercial for *Paul Mitchell* hair products, it was determined that the first such vignette would be shown in black-and-white - a paradoxically *new* mode of display within the context of a wrestling show. And so, on the July 27th edition of *WCW Saturday Night*, a four-minute video aired featuring the fearful threesome; instantly, however, viewers registered that this was hardly any run-of-the-mill promo. Hogan, Nash, and Hall laughed, threatened, and sneered at their babyface challengers - all familiar tropes of heel interviews - but rather than ramble endlessly, their scathing quotes came quickly - and often. They were talking in *sound bites*, creating an almost psychedelic experience when coupled with the rapid fire edits and effects deployed by Pruitt and Senior Editor Kemper Rogers.

"The way it was cut was almost a necessity," reveals Pruitt, reflecting on the production, "because there were so many egos in the room that needed to get their point across. [Furthermore], if you're a new organization [like the New World Order], you don't have a whole lot of money to spend. Sometimes you don't necessarily get the best people - it was like a college kid on a 'switcher' going crazy!"

131

The techniques would prove particularly beneficial in curtailing the long, winding tirades of Bollea, who in the eyes of Hall and Nash, was having difficulty in adjusting to the quicker, punchier delivery required of a contemporary bad-guy. "The style of [the video] ended up being fair towards all of the group," continues Pruitt. "Somebody could dominate the conversation for 20 minutes, but then when we got into the edit room, we were able to make it make sense - using only the highlights of each person."

"Y'know the way Hulk talks," adds DDP, "'brother this', 'brother that'. He had canned stuff, stuff that had been working for 20 years. So why change it?

"But Terry Bollea was one of the coolest motherfuckers you've *ever* known. Like, Hulk Hogan was a caricature of himself. But Terry Bollea, man...that motherfucker is as cool as it gets! All he had to do was bring more Terry Bollea through the black-and-white."

In the background, for the first time, the opening riffs of the New World Order theme song could be heard. The composition, labeled as 'FCD 115, Track 14' in the Turner Production Music Library (and officially titled 'Rockhouse' by Frank Shelley), was in fact an amalgamation of five Jimi Hendrix records: 'Highway Chile', 'Purple Haze', 'Hey Joe', 'Stone Free' and 'The Stars That Play With Laughing Sam's Dice'. Despite being a piece of stock music that was, ostensibly, picked rather casually, the tune, like everything else in the mini-movie, worked perfectly in contributing to the overall ambiance.

At approximately the 25-second mark of the first segment, a previously unseen logo engulfed the screen as Hogan continued to rant and rave. The letters 'nWo' - stylized in scratchy lettering inside an equally rugged-looking rectangle - graced a WCW telecast for the very first time.

The logo, according to various accounts, was the self-effacing work of Rob Wright, a Senior Editor formerly with the WWF, with an assist from an unknown graphic designer from Disney MGM studios. The resulting design, beautifully simplistic in its conception, added significantly to the group's perceived appeal.

While the storyline was beginning to take off, a lingering question still remained: how could WCW have permitted airtime to these renegades on their own transmission?

Hall's utterance several weeks earlier ("this portion of *WCW Monday Nitro* [is] brought to you by...") offered a plausible explanation. In their quest to takeover WCW, the nWo would naturally advertise their superiority by paying TBS for the right to air their own infomercials. It would enable the group to speak uninterrupted about their plans for destruction, a kind of propagandistic ploy in the war against Ted Turner's beloved *rasslers*.

To the viewing audience at home, thought director Craig Leathers, the storytelling device used to introduce the videos was paramount. Leathers sensed that if the voice of a WCW announcer preceded the grainy black-and-white footage, there would be a jarring disconnect - therefore, an ambiguous spokesperson would be much better served in the role.

It was for that reason that Neal Pruitt found himself in front of the microphone at MGM. "Craig said 'I'd like something different, something more modern than your typical pro wrestling announcer'," reveals Pruitt. "He said, 'what would *you* like it to sound like?' I said, 'well, there's this dude (Keith Eubanks) on (alternative rock station) 99X in Atlanta, and every now and then, they throw his voice on the air'. Craig said, 'well what does it sound like?' I said, 'it sounds like...(raspily) ninety...nine...x'. It's real breathy and...I wouldn't say emotionless but...it was just *that* voice - I don't know how to describe it! So he said 'why don't you do [the nWo voiceover]?'"

Leaning into the mic, the naturally-raspy Pruitt whispered the words that would forever signal the nWo's on-screen arrival, simultaneously securing his spot in wrestling folklore: *The following announcement has been paid for by the New World Order.*

———

With *Nitro*'s run at Disney coming to an end, Sullivan contemplated an angle that would exemplify his underlying philosophy - and illustrate his overwhelming success - as WCW's head booker. Above all else, Sullivan's unwavering conviction in generating *heat* - vitriolic crowd responses towards his top villains - served as his guiding principle; as in order to draw money, he often quipped, *my babyfaces need to slay fire-breathing dragons - not salamanders*. The matchmaker likened the process to guiding a hot-air balloon skyward, indicating that for WCW's rise to continue, it remained imperative to develop formidable heels to oppose the crowd favorites.

"There was a movie that really influenced my thinking," imparts Sullivan. "It was the original *Straw Dogs* with Dustin Hoffman. There was a couple in the movie that moved from America to England, and lived in the country. These people picked on them...and picked on them...and picked on them. Halfway through the movie, I almost left - I said, 'this is ridiculous'. But then [Hoffman's character] made a comeback, and it was like, 'woah!' I said 'well, that's the way it should be for babyfaces and heels'.

"If you look at boxing, when Ali first came around, everybody paid to see him get beat. They weren't paying to see him win. It was because he was arrogant, a black man in America...at the time, we were [experiencing] a lot of social unrest...so my philosophy was 'you can't have good guys be good guys, unless they go through the *Twelve Labors of Hercules*'."

Whereas Sullivan's angle with Brian Pillman blurred the lines between reality and fiction, the July 29th *Nitro* made the distinction almost unrecognizable. During a match involving Sting, Luger, Savage and the Four Horsemen, heel manager Jimmy Hart rushed to the ring in a state of absolute panic. "*We need help - the Outsiders are in the back!*" screamed Hart, jumping up and down on the ring apron. "*Please! We need help!*"

Suddenly, the camera angle shifted to reveal the menacing figures of

134

Hall and Nash, baseball bats in hand, standing over a fallen Arn Anderson in the backstage area. "Everything was implied - it was [reminiscent] of Hitchcock," remembers Nash. After the duo quickly dispatched of midcarder Scotty Riggs, the diminutive body of Rey Mysterio, Jr. launched a patented aerial assault from the top of a nearby production truck. Unfortunately for the cruiserweight, Nash caught his lifeless frame in mid-air, before hurling the masked star - almost like a lawn dart - remorselessly into the truck itself (but not into its windows, as per Sullivan's original plan). Having made their assault, the Outsiders slinked away in their limousine, prompting a fired up Savage - in a risky and completely improvised move - to dive upon the vehicle as it sped away.

As Sting and his team descended on the scene, it became clear that the attack had affected more than a select few. Indiscriminately, it seemed, Hall and Nash had taken out as many WCW wrestlers as they could find - irrespective of each character's virtue. In other words, both faces *and* heels lay wounded on the concrete, prompting several concerned viewers to place calls to local law enforcement ("people watching in the Orlando area called in like, 'hey, you've got some guys causing some shit on the Disney property!'" laughs Nash).

Amidst a cacophony of sirens and a panorama of ambulances, the sympathetic Rey Jr. sold the beatdown magnificently. "*There were four!*" he implored, shortly before medics removed his ever-present mask (which in itself, was a profound indication that something *real* could be happening). While a solemn announce team struggled to make sense of the carnage, several previously advertised matches were thrown out, causing - as planned - a 20 minute delay in the action.

Years later, a wistful Sullivan would refer to the angle as "the greatest thing I ever did in my [wrestling] life." In essence, he had done the unthinkable - deliberately broken *kayfabe* - in an effort to uniquely establish the severity of the nWo threat. The message was clear: even arch-enemies become allies when it was time to fight an invading force.

But for a history buff like Sullivan, the scattering of bodies reminded him not of a wrestling plot, but of Custer's Last Stand, a battle of the Great Sioux War of 1876.

———

The construction of an angle like the 'lawn dart' incident (although, in truth, no-one could remember a scene *quite* like that before) had long mystified wrestling fans, who remained isolated from the inner mechanics of story development. On this night, ironically, the production truck that aided the Nash-Mysterio stunt was the site of a small conference on the afternoon of the show. Away from prying eyes, Sullivan first pitched the concept to Craig Leathers, Keith Mitchell, Pruitt, Nash, and Tony Schiavone, before initiating an exchange of ideas to propel the vision further. These ideas, as would often be the case, were recorded on a single sheet of paper, effectively enabling a 'mind map' to be developed on the page. Soon, an order of events could be assembled - not a storyboard, per se - but a sequential list of how the most viable suggestions could be connected.

At this stage, it would become imperative for the Head Booker - in this case, Sullivan - to take charge in order to prevent confusion. Group members would be asked to verify (and clarify) the intricacies of their contributions, which once settled, precipitated a basic walk-through in the proposed areas of filming. Production staff, like Pruitt, would conceptualize the visual end product by viewing each area through the lens of an imagined camera, visualizing the framing of each shot with an assist from wrestlers involved in the scene. Invariably, the chance to survey the environment would inspire additional input, or, as in the case of this particular gathering, refine the execution of each planned action. *Here's how I'll throw him*, Nash demonstrated as the contingent looked on.

Due to the inherent nature of live television production - each shot inexorably linked to the last - the timing of each sequence was essential. To guide the transition between shots, particular actions would be designated as *triggers*, signaling to the performers and production staff that the 'active' camera was about to change. Once these cues were determined, an on-site cameraman would record aspects of the dry run back to the production truck; meanwhile, in slow motion, the performers practiced their role to remove any remaining ambiguity.

During the actual transmission, hidden carefully from view, pre-assigned stagehands facilitated the changeover of shots by alerting participants of an imminent live camera. For that reason, it was typically necessary to plan for some *leeway time*, a buffer of sorts to prevent the potentially kayfabe-shattering broadcast of a wrestler acting out of character.

In an effort to manufacture a realistic feeling of legitimacy, and in concert with Sullivan's creative philosophy, even off-camera personnel dedicated themselves to the illusion. Senior members of the production staff conversed with concern etched on their faces, contributing to a discernible unease permeating the entire setting. But ultimately, once *Nitro* concluded with a slow motion montage of the dramatic attack, the entire production team celebrated, high-fiving in a state of collective euphoria.

———

Within a matter of two months, the nWo takeover narrative had taken suspension of disbelief to new levels. But the shockingly *real* tenor of WCW programming appeared to be part of a larger trend gripping the public, occurring amid a renewed interest in the prevalence of televised violence. Although questions over the content of television dated back almost to the advent of the medium, taking shape in the form of congressional hearings (mid '50's), commissions ('60's), advisory committees ('70's) and task forces ('80s'), the latest wave of concerns bordered on the hysterical. "We have reached the point," argued Presidential candidate Bob Dole during the previous year, "where our popular culture threatens to undermine our character as a nation."

Dole's comments, however hyperbolic, hardly existed in isolation; indeed, across the political, media and academic spectrum, various authorities on the subject roundly shook their heads in condemnation. Even Ted Turner, never to be mistaken for a conformist, had to accept that the discussion possessed some validity. "At the end of the day," he conceded in a press conference at the House of Blues, the site of a weekly TBS music show, "I'm not proud of everything we make. But in order to stop, I want everyone to stop.

"[But] how can [Dole] be for assault weapons," Turner protested, unable to resist a zinger in the Senator's direction, "and yet [be] against violence on television? I'm personally against assault weapons. I don't think the criminals should be better armed than the police. Maybe I'm crazy."

Incrementally, in anticipation of the inevitability that pro wrestling itself face congressional pressure, the WWF had positioned itself as the *socially responsible* alternative to WCW. At the behest of Michael Ortman, its Vice President for Distribution, Vince McMahon endorsed a corporate manifesto entitled *The Principles*, a document that pledged to ban, among other things, "the use of a foreign object as a weapon, blood employed for dramatic effect, and aggressive behavior towards women."

To that end, McMahon goaded Turner in a series of correspondences designed to provoke his stockholders. "On Sunday," began one such communication. "Turner Broadcasting will kick off the cable industry's *Voices Against Violence* week by presenting its most violent pay-per-view ever…this tasteless event is being marketed by describing how bones pierce through skin, eyes might be displaced, a person's head may be dragged on asphalt from a moving vehicle, and a leather strap could cut through flesh like a machete.

"The reputation of the company you built will be shaken," directed McMahon at Ted, "if this event is allowed to go on as promoted. This letter marks my fourth written attempt to privately implore your company to reduce the incidents of gratuitous violence and unethical solicitation. While I initially held out hope that things were improving, I must now conclude that a consensus decision has been made by your WCW to fill a creative voice with increased violent content. In order to further distance my product from yours, WCW's actions have left me no choice but to place your product under a more public microscope."

"Dear Ted," began another McMahon missive, "since there has been no response to my repeated request that you and your pro-rasslin' company stop the practice of self mutilation, I can only assume based upon the last two weeks of *Nitro* that the practice of self mutilation (slicing oneself with a razor blade) is not only condoned but encouraged.

"This [practice] is disgusting, violent, potentially infectious, and completely contradictory to your testimony before Congress in June of 1993 and contrary to your 1995 participation of 'Voices against Violence'. Notwithstanding numerous unprecedented predatory practices against the World Wrestling Federation, if you continue to promote self mutilation, I hope your stockholders hold you accountable for this unethically, guttural, potentially unhealthy practice."

―――

Concurrent to the apparent rise in 'visual violence', a coalition of public figures induced a resumption of an earlier moral panic: *gangsta rap*. Describing their latest efforts as 'Round 2' in an ongoing anti-rap war, a group led by former US Education Secretary William Bennett attacked five premier record companies for their involvement in the genre. "Music conglomerates [are] putting money before the overall welfare of our children and the community," argued C. Delores Tucker, a civil rights activist and politician. "These companies have the blood of our children on their hands."

Earlier in the decade, the scrutiny of hardcore rap lyrics reached its zenith following the release of 'Cop Killer', a song recorded by a metal band fronted by rapper Ice-T. "Here is a very influential corporation," observed then-Vice President Dan Quayle in reference to Time Warner Inc., owner of the record label backing the song, "supporting and making money off a record that suggests its 'OK' to kill cops. I find that outrageous."

Ultimately, citing concerns over its content, Time Warner began to distance itself from the music by selling its 50 percent stake in *Interscope Records*, home to the particularly controversial subsidiary label, *Death Row Records*. "It's a great victory for our children and for America's future," proclaimed Tucker at the time of the sale. "It shows that Time Warner has a corporate soul."

But throughout the summer of 1996, despite a purported drop in sales and relevancy ("gangsta rap is done," proclaimed Darryl McDaniels of the pioneering group Run DMC), the genre remained prevalent on the Billboard music charts. Tupac Shakur owned the airwaves with 'How Do You Want It', a song that ironically - or perhaps tellingly - pointed its second verse squarely at Tucker and Dole. "*C. Delores Tucker, you's a motherfucker,*" rhymed Shakur over a slick instrumental. "*Mister Bob Dole, you're too old to understand the way the game's told…*"

Some 2000 miles away from Shakur's adopted home of Los Angeles, Kevin Nash and Scott Hall took note. "Scott and I were listening to a lot of West Coast rap," remembers Kevin Nash of the time. "It was that whole 'Thug Life' kind of thing ...it was pop culture. That's why I wore a bandanna, but turned it backwards like Tupac did. I think the masses looked at that and were like 'wow, these guys are kind of playing [up] the 'Thug Life' thing'. When we said, '4 Life', that came from [rapper] Mac 10."

On Saturday, August 10th, the thugs continued their dominance at *Hog Wild*, a WCW pay-per-view broadcast from South Dakota's annual motorcycle rally in Sturgis. "The only time I tried to be creative, I probably screwed it up," says Harvey Schiller of the event. "A lot of the wrestlers had motorcycles, so I was the guy who said, 'why don't we do a show up at Sturgis, South Dakota when they do the big motorcycle get together?' We did it outdoors and I don't think it did as great as I thought it would do. Most of wrestling appeals to a younger generation, [rather] than people on the back of motorcycles."

Such an observation became obvious as the crowd - free attendees who revved their bikes up intermittently - cheered Hogan upon his main event entrance. Nonetheless, despite the rather flat atmosphere, Hogan dethroned The Giant to become WCW champion for the second time. In a further act of aggression after the match, Hollywood defaced the prestigious WCW title by spray-painting the letters 'nWo' over it - a highly disrespectful move given its lineage (which, in *kayfabe*, traced back almost a hundred years). "For some reason," laughs Neal Pruitt, "when using the spray paint, Hogan could never write the small 'n' in nWo!"

On August 26th, mid-way through an episode of *Nitro*, and coincidentally, on a night when USA Network preempted *Raw*, 'The Million Dollar Man' Ted Dibiase - another highly recognizable ex-WWF figure from the past decade - shocked fans by appearing ringside during a match. With a cold and impassive look, Dibiase held up four fingers to signify that he was the next member of the nWo, before showing five fingers and mouthing to the camera: '*next week*'.

In the final shot of the episode, the scene was dramatically replayed to viewers in a gripping omen of what was to come: *now there were apparently four, who was number five?*

On September 2nd, *Nitro* ended in what was becoming a familiar sight - Hogan, Hall and Nash, in an unannounced yet callously coordinated attack, viciously assaulting a string of WCW's top stars. Apparently tired of the onslaught, The Giant marched to the ring in order to even the odds; however, in a completely unforeseen swerve, the former champion aided the nWo, revealing himself to be the fifth member. Although his membership signaled a departure from the pattern - wrestlers who were identified most with WCW's real-life competition, the WWF, acting cooperatively as an invading force - the capacity crowd in Chattanooga, TN roared disbelievingly in amazement.

It was a classic ending, and with *Raw* preempted for the second straight week, *Nitro* scored a 4.3 in the ratings - a massive TV audience, and the highest since the TNT experiment began.

Chapter 16:
Flying High

Wɪᴛʜ ᴛʜᴇ ɴᴇxᴛ major pay-per-view event, *Fall Brawl*, set to feature a long-awaited nWo vs. WCW 'War Games' match - pitting Hogan, Nash, Hall and a mystery partner against Sting, Luger, Flair and Arn Anderson - the September 9th *Nitro* featured another shocking plot twist. In an apparent blow to Team WCW, Sting - the ultimate company loyalist - appeared to attack Luger after shockingly emerging from an nWo limousine. "*No! No! No!*" exclaimed Bischoff on commentary. "*Sting has turned!*"

It was an unimaginable betrayal, one with dramatic consequences for the *Fall Brawl* main event. "*I'm standing here in shock*," lamented Anderson in a backstage interview with Gene Okerlund. "*The only constant over the last ten years since [Turner] bought the company was you! People went here, people went there...the only thing you could always count on was Sting! I got a sick feeling in my stomach - I'm in shock! I guess the only thing I can say, for the first time in my life...is I'm outta words...I'm speechless!*"

In reality, the assault was a well-cloaked facade, as although Hogan's turn quelled earlier plans to incorporate an imitation 'Sting', the bogus Sting plan would now be implemented - to great effect. "Eric Bischoff told me, 'if [this plan] gets out - if we don't keep it to ourselves - I'm gonna squash it'," recalls Jeff Farmer, selected to play Sting's double. "I said, 'whatever you want'. At that time, I had no power or influence in the company, and so when he approached me with [the idea], I said 'sure'. I think it was going to be a limited time thing [originally]."

Two years earlier, Farmer, the younger brother of Paul, a famous anthropologist and Harvard grad, exited WCW under uncomfortable circumstances. Fresh off a moderately successful mini-run as *Lightning*, the tag-team partner of *Thunder*, Farmer embarked on

142

contentious contract negotiations with newly-promoted Eric Bischoff. "It was really silly," Farmer remembers. "We didn't have an attorney, and we just thought it was only professional to [have one]. We didn't know the business at the time...[and didn't know] not to use leverage when you really didn't have any. We probably stepped on some toes, in retrospect, and didn't handle the situation the best way.

"We had an attorney from Orlando that looked at the contract. Of course, it was very one-sided towards WCW. They had all the power to use your likeness, produce action figures, market you and so on. The attorney didn't think it was very good, and so there was some back-and-forth. Anyway, WCW withdrew their offer. We had been there for a long time, so that was pretty devastating for my partner and I."

In the summer of 1995, Farmer returned briefly to WCW as the paramilitary character Cobra, a short-lived role that quietly fizzled out on the syndicated show *WCW Worldwide*. "The character wasn't really pushed, and it was a difficult time in WCW for new characters to get rolling," he reflects. "I thought the character had some potential, but it wasn't really being utilized right."

For Farmer, whose prior industry success ranked as relatively meager, joining the nWo represented a huge career break. Suitably, the preparation for his debut had been meticulous - in the make-up chair, special effects artist Andre Freitas placed contact lenses, those closely resembling the irises of the real Sting, on top of Farmer's eyes. "When I hit Lex [on *Nitro*]," Farmer laughs, "the contacts shifted to one side. I couldn't see out of one eye!"

Despite the mishap, Farmer recognized clearly that the nWo story was evolving in a thrillingly uncertain direction. "It seemed to me that they were doing a lot of stuff...off-the-cuff, or impromptu," he observes. "It appeared as if they were basing the [plot points] on audience reaction, which is good. If it's working, you do it, [as opposed to] planning something that doesn't work, and then forcing it down their throat...that happens in wrestling a lot. But I don't think there was a real plan for me."

As part of an interview segment during the pay-per-view broadcast, Sting pleaded his innocence to a disbelieving Luger. However, in an apparent contradiction, 'Sting' then entered War Games to help the nWo, delivering a series of signature maneuvers in his familiar ring attire. Suddenly, however, the impostor would be exposed. Evening the score, the *real* Sting stormed down the entrance way, swiftly ending the charade and single-handedly destroying the nWo in the process. But rather than securing a WCW victory, the consummate babyface - to the shock of the assembled crowd and viewers at home - left his allies to fight the battle shorthanded. *"Is that good enough for you right there?"* he exhorted to Luger before withdrawing from the contest. *"Is that proof enough?"*

Ultimately, the nWo would be victorious again, its 4-on-3 advantage too difficult to overcome. On *Nitro* the following night, in an unannounced appearance devoid of his usual music and pyrotechnics, an irate Sting launched an impassioned tirade about the events of the previous week:

"I want a chance to explain something that happened last Monday night at Nitro. I was on an airplane flying from L.A. to Atlanta. When I got to Atlanta, I tuned in the TV to Nitro.

"I thought I was watching a rerun! It was a very convincing film. Often imitated but never duplicated, though! I saw people...I saw wrestlers...I saw commentators...and I saw best friends doubt the Stinger. That's right, [they] doubted the Stinger!

"I heard Lex Luger say, 'I know where he lives, I know where he works out, I'm gonna go get him'. So I said to myself, 'I'll just go into seclusion. I'll wait and see what happens on [WCW] Saturday night, and I tuned in Saturday night, and what did I see? More of the same...more doubt.

"I knew I had to get to Fall Brawl and get face to face with [Luger] to let him know that it wasn't me. And what I got out of that was, 'No Sting, I don't believe you Sting!' Well, all I gotta say is I have been

144

[a] mediator...I have been [a] babysitter for Lex Luger, and I've given him the benefit of the doubt about a thousand times in the last twelve months! And I've carried the WCW banner, and I have given my blood, my sweat, and my tears for WCW!"

In a brilliantly understated detail, Sting continued to rant with his back turned away from the hard camera, symbolically indicating disappointment not only with his fellow wrestlers, but also, perhaps with his fans:

"So for all of those fans out there and all those wrestlers and people that never doubted the Stinger, I'll stand by you if you stand by me! But for all of the people, all of the commentators, all of the wrestlers, and all of the best friends who did doubt me...you can stick it! From now on, I consider myself a free agent.

"But that doesn't mean that you won't see the Stinger.

"From time to time...I'm gonna pop in when you least expect it."

Bizarrely, the WWF's response to WCW reaching its creative zenith was to introduce a 'doppelganger' storyline of its own. In a head-scratching decision, one made, presumably, as a means to support their ongoing litigation efforts, the WWF announced it would reintroduce 'Razor Ramon' and 'Diesel' on the September 23rd edition of *Monday Night Raw*.

According to Kevin Nash, WCW officials were so concerned that he and Hall had secretly negotiated a return with McMahon, that the duo were soon presented with new contracts containing $400,000 raises (Bischoff, for his part, vehemently denies the claim). Nonetheless, the 'new' Ramon and Diesel - portrayed by Rick Bognar and Glen Jacobs respectively - debuted to an overwhelmingly negative reaction, reinforcing the perception that McMahon was finally out of ideas.

"This is the honest-to-God's truth," begins Marcus 'Buff' Bagwell. "I remember us - as 'the boys' - being *worried* that we were gonna put Vince [McMahon] out of business.

145

"Now, think about it - it's not that crazy. Here's Vince with a fake Kevin Nash and a fake Razor! I mean, he's reachin', brother! He's really against the ropes, and we know - as 'the boys' - we *need* two teams. We need two companies. We know that we're screwed without that.

"So we're high-fiving Eric Bischoff that our ratings are good, but really we're going, 'ok, let's just back off a little bit!'"

———

McMahon was surely on the ropes, and as if anyone thought otherwise, Bischoff was convinced of it. With *Nitro* simply dominating the ratings war since the Outsiders debut - outdrawing *Raw* by almost a million viewers each week, Bischoff had again shown his mettle in a situation where others most certainly would have folded. Ever since his dispatch of the school bullies decades earlier, he had learned that the best way to approach fear was to approach it head on. For that reason, while he was soaring professionally, he decided to tackle a persistent phobia that had bothered him since adolescence.

Although few were aware of it, Bischoff's nights were often filled with recurring nightmares, the kind involving air travel (and, more specifically, journeys involving a catastrophic ending). He would see himself as the pilot, but at some point in the trip, something would go terribly wrong, and the plane would descend terrifyingly towards the ground. To Bischoff, there appeared only one practical solution - learning to fly a plane himself.

And so, one September afternoon, Bischoff stared at his computer screen, completing a test necessary to receive his pilot's license. Midway through the task, he was informed of a visitor - James Morrison - a former WCW on-screen personality and more recently, a departed Vice President of the WWF. Better known as J.J. Dillon, his stage name, Morrison showed up to the pre-arranged meeting ten minutes past the scheduled appointment time. According to Dillon,

146

his tardiness was not lost on Bischoff, who immediately drew attention to it before commenting on Dillon's attire. *We don't dress up very often around here*, Bischoff allegedly stated.

Clearly, the meeting was off to an inauspicious start, but what happened next is a matter of contention. According to Bischoff, a desperate Dillon, eager for a job and supporting a special needs child at home, demonstrated his potential value by revealing proprietary information relevant to the WWF. Specifically, Bischoff says, Dillon opened a folder containing salary information for McMahon's top superstars, a set of data that Dillon would, theoretically, have been privy to in his previous role as VP of Talent Relations.

As per Dillon's account, the reveal of such valuable details never occurred. Instead, he recalls an arrogant Bischoff, otherwise engaged with the computer test and indifferent towards his credentials, hogging most of the interview time by asking and answering his own questions. There was one question, however, that Bischoff could apparently not answer on his own accord. He looked across his desk, remembers Dillon, and inquired of the following information:

How much longer can Vince last?

With the Turner-Time Warner merger just weeks away from approval, Bischoff advised Dillon that WCW, as per all other TBS divisions, was currently operating under a hiring freeze. Therefore, he hired Dillon as a consultant for the month of October, an appointment that eventually converted into a full-time salary of $165,000 (and post-1997, an on-screen role as WCW commissioner).

But regardless of the veracity of Dillon's claim - that which pertained to the private obsession of his new boss to finally topple McMahon - a number of public comments indicated that Bischoff believed the war to be almost over. "I really don't know how much longer Vince McMahon has," offered Bischoff in an online interview. "Digging out of that hole can be a long and painful process...and to date, he has not demonstrated to me that he has the creative ability - or resources - to get out of that hole anytime in the near future.

"He is certainly overrated when it comes to creative ability, [and] that is showing with the recent problems. As a business man, I think he [once] had a tremendous opportunity and took advantage of it.

"The world changed.

"And he didn't."

Chapter 17:
Call Me Ted

ON OCTOBER, 10th, 1996, shareholders officially approved the Turner-Time Warner merger. Immediately, Ted Turner's net worth increased by a billion dollars, and with entities such as HBO - Jerry Levin's baby - reporting to him, the Mouth of the South "was just *loving* life," emphasizes Bill Burke. At the first post-merger executive committee meeting, Turner, although no longer technically *the* boss, headed up the gathering regardless. "We're going around the table, and Ted's running the meeting," Burke remembers. "He goes, *'ok, let's hear it from the king of the number one paid cable service in the world, HBO - go ahead Jeff'* [Bewkes, its CEO].

"...'now *let's hear it from the king of the number one network in basic cable during prime-time [TNT], Brad Siegel - go ahead Brad!'*"

Finally, Ted turned his attention towards Burke, the President of the TBS network, which was suffering from an unusual ratings slump. *"'And let's hear it from the king of the network that's... number one with 18-49 year old one-eyed cocksuckers - go ahead Bill!'"*

The Turner execs doubled over in laughter. *"Well Ted, that's a very important constituency,"* Burke responded, playing along as Jerry Levin looked dumbfounded. *"'I know pal, you gotta be number one in somethin'!'"* Ted yelled uproariously, diffusing, as only he could, a potentially damaging source of conflict.

While certainly unconventional, the exchange was typical of Ted's leadership, reports Joe Uva, President of Turner Entertainment Sales and Marketing at the time. "TBS was a company," reminisces Uva, "where really the culture, attitude, and [how we worked] really came from Ted himself. He was hard charging, he really believed in the company, and he had so much passion for it. He was a guy who could see things other people couldn't, and he was [masterful] in recruiting people who could implement his vision.

"At the same time, people weren't afraid to tell him when they disagreed. Ted was a guy that liked spirited debate! Something that I really learned from him - and have tried to take with me throughout my career - is that when things were going really well, he would [actually] be the toughest on people. He wanted you to keep the 'pedal to the metal', because he realized that it wouldn't last forever.

"When times got tough - and there *were* challenging economic times - he would be the first guy to wrap his arm around you and say 'don't worry about it pal, things are gonna get better'. He would never, *ever* chastise people when times were tough. He was just the opposite, [in fact], he would simply just encourage.

"So you wanted to succeed for him, and I found that to be true throughout the company. His name was on the front door, but it was more than that. He was a bigger than life personality, and he created an incredible company."

Despite a *New York Times* report that Ted was 'ceding control' of his networks, behind the scenes, little had changed. Ted's force of personality continued to define the organizational culture, and his famous entrepreneurial spirit seemed rejuvenated by the addition of HBO. Simultaneously, however, cost-cutting measures quietly began, with management consultants looking to trim the fat wherever possible. "Cutting costs had *never* been instituted before the Time Warner merger," one Turner employee remembers.

Unfortunately, it was a common post-merger practice, and as Ted began working with Levin - technically his superior, at least on paper - a thorough examination began of all Turner-Time Warner divisions (and their associated operating costs). A more surprising revelation, however, concerned Ted's professional treatment of his own son, Teddy. As rumors of downsizing swirled around the company, Teddy, an employee of 'Turner Home Video' (effectively a redundant entity following the merger, a consolidation that yielded Warner Brothers, after all) inquired of his future at a dinner involving his father. *"What happens to us?"* he asked.

"You're toast," responded Dad, devoid of sentimentality.

Turner Home Video disappeared - as did Teddy, at least temporarily - in an illustrative example of one of Ted's core business values. Unlike other successful impresarios, he believed that preferential handling of his children could only lead to charges of nepotism, damaging his reputation as an equal opportunist. To drive home the point further, he ordered the removal of a collection of expensive artwork displayed in the corporate offices in New York, furious about the underlying message. *So while we're laying off $30,000 a year employees in Atlanta*, Ted reportedly challenged in the board room, *we have multi-million dollar oil paintings hanging from the walls in New York?*

For several months thereafter, empty dark rectangles on the walls served as a constant reminder of Ted's ordinance. But while unfamiliar outsiders may have considered his empathy to be of mysterious origin (Ted was, his critics cried, the son of a wealthy billboard salesman, hardly the recipe for a compassionate existence), the truth revealed his formative years to be much more fraught than first evident.

As a child, although he rarely discussed it publicly, Ted had been the victim of physical abuse at the hands of his father - Ed Turner. It only perpetuated his various (but extremely well-guarded) insecurities, first developed after being sent to attend a Cincinnati boarding school at just four years old (Ed was enrolled in the Navy by then, spurred by the Japanese attack on Pearl Harbor).

Alone, and without his parents or infant sister (who herself would pass away at age 12), Ted experienced a searing loneliness that carried through to his adult life. "Given everything that happened to Ted," wrote actress Jane Fonda, his wife for almost a decade, "the beatings, the psychological manipulations...his father asking him to beat him, his mother screaming outside the door, his father coming home drunk at night and telling him stories about women - there was [just] complete toxicity [there].

"As a result of his upbringing, for Ted, there's a fear of abandonment that is deeper than with anyone I've ever known. He can't sit still...because if you sit still, the demons catch up with you. He needs constant companionship."

For Ed, a sufferer of bipolar disorder, depression was his constant compatriot. He had many insecurities of his own, but believed it to be beneficial in enabling professional success. "He thought that people who were insecure worked harder," Ted told *The New Yorker*, "and I think that's probably true. I don't think I ever met a 'superachiever' who wasn't insecure to some degree."

Ed's instability manifested itself further upon Ted's enrollment at Brown University. Already disappointed that his son failed to gain entrance to Harvard, he became irate upon learning of Ted's choice to master in classics. In a letter sent to his dorm room, the elder Turner wrote:

I am appalled, even horrified, that you have adopted Classics as a Major. As a matter of fact, I almost puked on the way home today.

I am a practical man, and for the life of me I cannot possibly understand why you should wish to speak Greek. With whom will you communicate in Greek? I have read, in recent years, the deliberations of Plato and Aristotle, and was interested to learn that the old bastards had minds which worked very similarly to the way our minds work today. I was amazed that they had so much time for deliberating and thinking and [were] interested in the kind of civilization that would permit such useless deliberation...I suppose everybody has to be a snob of some sort, and I suppose you will feel that you are distinguishing yourself from the herd by becoming a Classical snob.

I can see you drifting into a bar, belting down a few, turning around to a guy on the stool next to you - a contemporary billboard baron from Podunk, Iowa - and saying, "Well, what do you think about old Leonidas?"

It isn't really important what I think. It's important what you wish to do with the rest of your life. I just wish I could feel that the influence of those odd-ball professors and the ivory towers were developing you into the kind of man we can both be proud of...I think you are rapidly becoming a jackass, and the sooner you get out of that filthy atmosphere, the better it will suit me.

Before long, after smuggling a coed in to his room (and publishing his father's letter anonymously in the student newspaper), Ted was expelled from the institution. He returned home to work with Ed in the billboard business, but found his Dad drowning in a daily ritual of alcohol, cigarettes and a copious amount of prescription pills. On March 5, 1963, following an apparently routine breakfast with his wife, Ed walked upstairs and pulled the trigger of a .38-calibre silver pistol on himself. He was 52.

After willing himself through months of grieving, Ted became determined to save - and expand upon - his father's business. He believed that at least some of Ed's troubles could be credited to a malaise that gripped him following early success. "My father strongly recommended," Ted would reveal decades later, "that I set my goals so high, [insofar as] I couldn't achieve them in my lifetime.

"He set a goal, after the depression, that he would be a millionaire and have a yacht and a plantation. [Well], he had a small plantation...he had a small yacht...*and* he was a millionaire, [but] he couldn't refocus his life. He said, 'I'm having a lot of trouble now, because I've achieved my goals'. He said, 'please set your goals so high that you can't achieve them'."

Even after launching WTCG, acquiring the Braves, embarking on The SuperStation, establishing CNN, and reaching the cover of TIME magazine, Ted still looked to his departed Dad for validation.

"I made the cover of *Success Magazine*," he later revealed, holding his arms skywards, "and held a copy up to 'Dad'.

"I said, *'Dad, is that enough?'*"

———

Ted's success inspired his entire workforce, not least of which Eric Bischoff, who was getting used to receiving his (admittedly brief) congratulatory phone calls on Tuesday afternoons. Taking more of the creative reigns than ever, Bischoff was steering the nWo storyline towards a Hollywood Hogan title defense at *Halloween Havoc*. Meanwhile, Kevin Sullivan, observers noted, appeared to be less involved in the main event scene than ever, despite retaining the official title of Head Booker.

"Kevin had nothing to do with the creation of *Nitro*," Bischoff says dismissively. "He had nothing to do with the format. He had nothing to do with the strategic or tactical decisions that really made the brand work. He wasn't involved in the research. He wasn't in any of the big meetings. He wasn't involved in anything other than fundamental matchmaking for the undercard. That was it.

"Kevin's job was basically to take the undercard and lay out the matches, in a way that was coherent and made sense from a wrestling point of view. But he was not - by any means - the architect [of *Nitro*]. In fact, he didn't even have a pencil in that regard."

Speaking generally on the subject, ring announcer David Penzer - a frequent travel partner of Sullivan - describes the booker as "directly responsible - as much as anybody," in regards to the content of *Nitro*.

"I drove with Kevin a lot," says Penzer, "and he would be writing the 'TVs' as we drove from town to town. Sometimes I even wrote them for him - he would say, 'Penzer, write this down', and sort of dictate for me. He was literally writing the shows that you would watch every week.

"I think that he would plan out what he saw, take that to Eric and say, 'you wanna do this?' As opposed to Eric saying, 'this is what I wanna do'. I'm not saying that a lot of it didn't get tweaked by Eric - because he had the last say - but Kevin created it, and then Eric approved it…or tweaked it.

"But especially with the nWo, I think Eric took that as his pet project."

Bischoff's decision to exercise more control over the booking, while simultaneously maintaining his role as lead announcer and - more importantly - retaining his job as Executive Vice President, concerned many who believed the added responsibility would invariably become overwhelming. Furthermore, with his roster swelling in size, and locker room egos growing by the day, he was still forced to deal with an unrelenting array of talent concerns and inquiries.

And contrary to counsel, he was about to add even more onto his plate. "I was sitting in my office one day," reveals TBS group controller Dick Cheatham, who recalls being "close" with Bischoff for some time. "I got a phone call from Eric. He said, 'I'm thinking about joining the program'. I said, 'ok, what do you mean?' He said, 'I'm gonna be part of the storyline. I'm not gonna be an announcer anymore - I'm gonna be part of the nWo. What do you think?'

"What I told him was, 'I think it's a bad idea, Eric. Right now, you're in a company that nobody likes, but what you've done is virtually impossible. You've turned it around and inside of Turner Broadcasting, there's only two people that have had this kind of success. One is John Schuerholz who took the Braves, and turned them around from last in the league to winning the World Series in a year. And you - *you* have taken WCW that was nothing, and you beat the industry leader.

"I said, 'right now, we don't have a lot of people inside of [TBS] that are great executives, and you have a hell of a story'. Not as part of a wrestling story, but as a turnaround executive inside of Turner Broadcasting. That was the pitch I made, because right or wrong, I thought that was the best possible way for Eric to do career planning. At the time, Scott Sassa ran our entertainment side and while Scott was a very talented young man, he was flirting with Sony at the time. I was thinking, 'this guy is gonna leave, and that's gonna open up a hole at the top of the pyramid in [Turner] Entertainment…Eric's had such success, this might be a natural [fit]'.

"There's a lot of people that don't like Eric, but I always liked him. [But] that was probably the last time Eric and I were really on a close basis, because he had made up his mind, and didn't really care about my opinion. I still thought it was the best thing for him at the time.

"You gotta remember, it was still *wrestling* - and the [Turner higher-ups] *didn't like wrestling*...[so] the more he became associated with wrestling, I thought - long-term - that was a career damaging deal."

"At that time," begins Brendon Hamlin, a former TBS producer, "the perception was, 'WCW is doing great...Eric Bischoff is a big part of that...but at the end of the day, it's wrestling'.

"Its popularity was great, and there were some great stars that came out of there. But it maybe got bigger than it ever really should have been."

"In fact, the guy that I worked for - a corporate controller - counseled me on this," continues Dick Cheatham. "He said, 'you don't wanna be working so closely with wrestling, because it's gonna damage your career'. I said, 'wait a minute - how does that damage my career if I help these guys make money?' He said, 'everybody hates it. It doesn't matter if WCW makes money or not - they hate it'."

———

On Saturday, October 26th, a day before the big *Havoc* show, Bischoff visited the hotel room of Randy Poffo - better known as Randy 'Macho Man' Savage - a character who had been consistently downtrodden since Hogan's *Bash at the Beach* betrayal. As Bischoff surveyed the scene, he reminded himself that Savage's contract was soon to expire, before noting that the often aberrant star - set to fight Hogan in the *Havoc* main event - quizzically emerged from his shower stark naked. *We need to talk, brother*, Savage growled, making no mention of his unusual appearance.

With beer bottles, clothing, and apparently, the evidence of several rounds of room service strewn across the room, Bischoff prepared himself for an interesting negotiation. But things were about to get more interesting, as within moments, a knock on the door signaled the arrival of even *more* food. Hesitant to leave a hotel employee standing outside, Bischoff opened the door, and stood red-faced while the staffer awkwardly wheeled in his cart. All the while, and in all of his glory, a willfully oblivious Savage relaxed comfortably on the bed, ostensibly indifferent to the presence of a visitor. For once, Eric Bischoff was left speechless, as far apart in etiquette as he was from Savage on financial terms (eventually, 'Macho' would return in January, earning $1.9 million over the next 12 months).

But the hotel worker was not the only one getting a shock, as on Sunday night, WCW fans witnessed the return of 'Rowdy' Roddy Piper, formerly a huge mainstream star with the WWF. Before long, Piper would make a dramatic impact on *Nitro*, and in a memorable ending to a November episode, he forced Bischoff - in storyline - to admit his role as a covert member of the nWo.

Now self-cast as an on-screen villain, Bischoff enraged fans with a smarmy, insincere countenance. *"Not only am I the highest ranking executive in the nWo,"* he beamed to a sold-out Salisbury, MD crowd on *Nitro*, *"I'm the highest ranking executive in WCW! What a wonderful country!*

"Back in Baltimore...in June," he explained, *"I got jackknifed through a stage by one of the most powerful men on the planet. And the next day, I woke up and...asked myself one very important question: Do I wanna be consumed by the power...or do I wanna be part of the force?*

"[So] a couple of days later, Mr. Hall, Mr. Nash and myself got together. We had a little summit. We did some talking...we did some thinking...we did some planning...and we decided to consolidate power. We are going to build a dynasty!"

In actuality, it appeared as if Bischoff really was building a dynasty. While in his on-screen persona, he spoke of clandestine meetings and plans for global dominance, he was simultaneously receiving recognition for showing real-life effectiveness as a change agent, relative to Turner's corporate structure. In an incredible turn of events - especially given the historic contempt for WCW among Ted's henchmen - the vaunted goal of mere profitability seemed almost comical in retrospect.

After all, a year ago, shortly before Harry Anderson made good on his profitability wager, Bischoff could recall a Jerry Levin proclamation that instead of following a road towards stifling overgrowth, the new Turner-Time Warner conglomerate would retain Ted's entrepreneurial philosophy. As someone more comfortable in jeans than a suit - more partial to cowboy boots than wing-tip shoes - the promise played like music to Bischoff's ears.

Now at the conclusion of 1996, morale stood *unquestionably* at an all-time high. Backstage before shows, wrestlers described the atmosphere as akin to a sports locker room, seeing themselves as team members working towards a common goal. Even Hogan himself was getting in to the act, excitedly agreeing to lose to Piper in their eventual *Starrcade* clash (a loss that occurred, as fans would carefully note, in a *non-title* match).

But in the limo ride back from the arena, a joyous Hogan marveled about *putting over* Piper, apparently elated to approve a rare loss. For both Hogan - the man with creative control - and WCW itself, the road ahead looked to be nothing but promising. The foundation for a brilliant long-term storyline involving Sting - suddenly presented (in a manner reminiscent of Brandon Lee's *Crow*) as a brooding, dark anti-hero with a propensity to strike at the most opportune of occasions - figured to be a major part of future programming. The high-flying daredevils of the cruiserweight division continued thrilling audiences with evermore incredible maneuvers. And most importantly, with the competition grasping at straws for a commensurate response, *Nitro* closed the year with its 27th consecutive ratings victory.

Chapter 18:
All Souled Out

DEPENDING ON WHICH internal income statement you believed, WCW reported a divisional profit of either $3.5 or $5.0 million for 1996 - representing over a ten-fold increase on 1995. Whereas weeks before the nWo invasion, initial year-end projections estimated a net *loss* of $940,000, the added investment in talent was clearly paying off spectacularly. On January 13th, 1997, *Nitro* in New Orleans attracted over $100,000 in ticket sales alone - the first such achievement in the program's history. The Nielsen numbers showed no sign of declining interest either, with an average of almost 3.4 million viewers watching the two-hour broadcast. In a particular highlight, DDP became the first WCW wrestler to embarrass the nWo, refusing to join the group in an inventive deception. From any objective standard, everything seemed to be clicking.

A day later, the nWo were a huge hit at the annual NATPE convention, this year held conveniently across town in New Orleans. Outside a booth designated for Warner Brothers and other Turner properties, cameras flashed as Hogan, Hall and Nash posed for pictures among a giddy assemblage of paparazzi. Inside the booth, a small troupe of WCW salespeople met in a modest display area with prospective customers, providing each with a press kit entitled *WCW - Where the Big Boys Play.*

Nearby, representatives of Turner Ad Sales distributed a separate document, one aimed at educating specific advertisers about WCW. It touted *Nitro* as an undoubted ratings winner, attracting 'more teens than MTV', 'more men than ESPN' and an average of 1.2 million viewers in the coveted 18-49 male demographic. Through a variety of charts, figures and statistics, it showcased the "endless marketing possibilities" available to advertisers, reporting 675,000 annual home video sales and "unbelievable growth" on the recently-launched WCW website (1.5 million monthly impressions as of November '96).

Fittingly, and with considerably less ballyhoo, a cohort of WWF officials chatted with potential buyers on Wednesday. During some downtime in the afternoon, its Senior VP of North American Sales, James Rothschild, surreptitiously came across the Turner-produced packet. A noted sports marketing expert, Rothschild decided to review its contents carefully on his plane ride home, eager to view the written sales pitch for himself.

When he finally did peruse the pages, Rothschild couldn't believe what he was reading. At the top of the fourth page, a caption read *'THE OUTSIDERS - SCOTT HALL AND KEVIN NASH. FORMERLY RAZOR RAMON AND DIESEL IN THE WWF'*. On the surface, this reference appeared to contradict a court-ordered 'Consent Order' that WCW agreed to several months prior:

CONSENT ORDER (August 20, 1996)
1.....[I]n connection with any television programming WCW produces, public statements WCW makes or authorizes and statements and commentary made on "900" number telephone lines WCW controls:

a. WCW, its officers, agents and employees shall not refer to the wrestler Scott Hall as Razor Ramon or The Bad Guy and WCW will instruct its independent contractors not to refer to Mr. Hall by those names;

b. WCW, its officers, agents and employees shall not refer to Kevin Nash as Diesel or Big Daddy Cool, and WCW will instruct its independent contractors not to refer to Mr. Nash by those names;

c. WCW, its officers, agents and employees shall not in connection with any appearance by Mr. Hall and Mr. Nash state that Mr. Hall or Mr. Nash are currently employed by, affiliated with or any appearance by them is sponsored, approved or authorized by Titan or the World Wrestling Federation, and WCW shall instruct its independent contractors not to make any such statement.

Soon after the Consent Order was filed, all WCW employees and independent contractors had been instructed to comply with its terms. At first, this guidance failed to reach other subsidiaries of TBS, Inc., but a November 8th memo from Mike Ciraldo, a sales manager for WCW, stated the situation clearly. "We CANNOT use their WWF names when talking about them," wrote Ciraldo to executive Mark Harrad. "They are simply [to be] known as Hall and Nash."

Nonetheless, just a month before NATPE, a copy of the offending booklet was presented at a Turner sales meeting in New York City. The allusions to Razor and Diesel remained in the document, but without a WCW employee present, the language passed without objection. Therefore, on January 7th, 1997 - only a week before the convention - approximately 100 Turner Ad Sales employees received the materials, unaware of the inherent issue.

The mix-up provided a poignant reminder of the disconnect present between WCW and its parent company. But as Rothschild continued reading on the plane, he noticed something even more eye-catching: a series of highly inflammatory statements that seemed to support the WWF's claim of unfair competition. *'WCW's COVERAGE GROWS, WHILE WWF'S FALTERS'*, exclaimed the title of one page, noting a "defection of many WWF station affiliates for their two weekly syndicated shows." Another page cited *'DECLINE OF WWF'* as a key factor in *Nitro*'s success, alongside *'CLOSET VIEWER PHENOMENON'* and *'GREAT STORYLINE: NWO'*.

Indeed, the nWo narrative, already all-encompassing by nature, figured to feature prominently throughout 1997. According to Bischoff, its progression was following in line with its ultimate purpose, that which viewed the group as more than simply an invading entity, but rather, a separate *brand* in and of itself. Therefore, he reasoned, an expansion in group size would be necessary, although tellingly, only the most dedicated of fans could keep track of who was actually in the group (14 wrestlers in total now comprised the nWo, following an angle turning The Giant babyface).

Nonetheless, to further Bischoff's vision, WCW advertised an nWo-themed pay-per-view for January 25th, a broadcast inauspiciously produced in Cedar Rapids, Iowa. Comprised of eight matches featuring wrestlers from each organization, *nWo Souled Out* promised to deliver on its promotional tagline - *The World Ain't Big Enough For The Both Of Us* - with the presentation of a unique spectacle designed to create interest in similar spin-off events.

In an unusual pre-recorded video, the show opened with an assortment of nWo villains making their way to the arena on top of garbage trucks. Nash, Hall and other auxiliary members preened and posed at the camera, delivering an assortment of sound bites eventually edited together by WCW's production team. But it was Bischoff who would make perhaps the most memorable of taunts, providing an especially grating quip in reference to the procession around him - *"A whole fleet of dirtbags!"* he sneered derisively.

The parade faded into a live shot backstage, as Hogan and company strutted confidently into the building, conjuring more the image of a street gang than a stable of pro wrestlers (although in an amusing production gaffe, an unidentified bald man momentarily wound up among them). Moments later, the voice of feature producer Neal Pruitt introduced an nWo video package filmed during the previous week in Chicago. The piece featured Eric Bischoff, positioned at a podium in front of several large microphones, delivering a State of the Union-type address inspired by a scene in *Citizen Kane*. *"Thank you - thank you very much,"* began Bischoff in an almost stately disposition. *"I stand before you today…humbled by the premier event that is about to take place.*

"We are in control. [So] to those of you who have risen to the challenge, and have joined the ranks of the nWo…to you I say - thank you, one and all…"

Five days earlier, Pruitt, along with Kemper Rogers and several other production staffers, kicked around ideas for the video at *Uno's* in Chicago. "We wrote every word Eric said," Pruitt remembers. "As a boss, he may not have listened to people…he might have rushed down the hallway, not really talking to anybody or saying 'hi' - because he was in deep thought - but when he was a talent, he took direction."

As a producer and editor on similar videos, Pruitt often stressed the importance of a memorable closing line. But on this occasion, the brainstorming at *Uno's* failed to generate such a remark, leaving the production team in a state of malaise. "I remember we really needed inspiration to figure out the last line," Pruitt says. "We just couldn't think of it.

"Well, there were two guys with us that were unsung heroes backstage. William was one of them, and Moses the other. After a while, the beer had started to flow a little bit, and William looked at [our script]. Out of nowhere, he said, '*what the hell were you thinkin'?*'

The serendipitous one-liner became "the perfect line to end it all," says Pruitt. And so, at the conclusion of the monologue, Bischoff looked directly into the camera for his parting shot.

"*To those of who who have offered yourself as opponents,*" he concluded. "*What the hell were you thinking?*"

"It hit so well, and it was just so...*nasty* like the nWo would be," marvels Pruitt, who would feature heavily in the event as a sarcastic ring announcer. "Eric delivered it really well."

Behind the stage, Kemper Rogers prepared nervously for another innovative video presentation. He would be required to simultaneously trigger the playback of three separate tapes - each containing pre-recorded comments from Hogan, Nash and Hall - in order to broadcast an effective 'conversation' across three large video screens. Miraculously, he timed the effect perfectly, contributing to a novel and highly successful opening to the pay-per-view.

"It started off with a bang," acknowledges Pruitt, "but unfortunately, it soon went downhill." Indeed, in the eyes of many fans, *Souled Out* would unfold as one of the more bizarre telecasts in company history, with a mostly flat crowd, ambiguous match finishes, and a puzzling 'Miss nWo' contest featuring middle-aged housewives. "The 'Miss nWo' contest was a disaster," Pruitt states matter-of-factly, noting its questionable inclusion in the show format.

Still theoretically the Head Booker, Kevin Sullivan recalls having no input in the event. He remembers advising against the nWo expansion, fearing that it could only lead to overexposure, although he conceded

163

that the original concept had been, at least technically speaking, already bastardized. After all, it had been months since the nWo boasted an exclusive membership of ex-WWF stars invading their Southern competition, and perhaps for that reason, Sullivan's warning fell on deaf ears.

"In retrospect," Sullivan says, "I think Eric thought - and he might have been right - that this was a way to get guys 'over' quickly. Well, to me, how much steak can you eat? The Rolling Stones are still playing in their '70s, but what if they had 12 other guys singing the songs with them? I don't think they'd draw!"

———

In the final analysis, some 170,000 viewers purchased *Souled Out*, a relatively poor outcome when measured against contemporary WCW pay-per-views (a drop of some 80,000 buys, in fact, compared to the average figure in the nWo era). Nonetheless, the following major event seemed destined to perform well, as Bischoff decided to promote a rematch of Hogan and Piper for *Superbrawl* in San Francisco.

In preparation for the match, Piper - in kayfabe - locked himself in a cell on Alcatraz Island, once site of an infamous federal prison and after 1972, a public landmark managed by the National Park Service. With *Nitro*, of course, occurring live each Monday, combined with an unrelenting schedule of syndicated programming, plus the monthly pay-per-view cards - all produced without the prospect of any tangible 'off-season' - various staffers started to question where the line separating spontaneity and chaos could be found.

"I don't think we often had a plan," concedes Pruitt, who was asked to make sense of a paltry set of instructions while filming at Alcatraz. "I just think [the creative team] were kind of running out of their hip pocket, so to speak, and that was kinda scary. In the case of Piper at Alcatraz, they wanted us to film him leaving the cell and running outside to a boat - all in one shot. Well, that's impossible."

164

On the day of filming, production manager David Crockett secured the all-important boat, provided to WCW at a cost of $1,000 per hour. In a memorable scene, Pruitt (along with cameraman Bill Tinsley and audio tech Mike Filosa) captured Piper ranting maniacally about his rematch, a battle he would ultimately lose. "Piper was fired up," recalls Pruitt. "He's so fired up in fact, that he gets on to the front of the ship and hangs on to the mast! He's saying, 'Hogan, I'm comin' to get you! It's just a matter of hours until we see each other face-to-face in the ring!'

"We videotaped that part, and then he looks at us and goes, 'Neal, I don't know...I didn't like it'. At that time, the captain of the ship comes up [and goes], 'what in the hell are you doin', hangin' off that mast? That mast could have easily broken off! Don't you know how old these ships are? If you would have fallen down in that water, it's about 60 degrees. You wouldn't last but a couple minutes!'

"[Now] if you're standing there - on Alcatraz - and you're looking at the water, it is *rushing away* from San Francisco towards the Golden Gate Bridge...where all the sharks are waiting for you. I can see why about nobody escaped from Alcatraz. [But] Piper goes, 'Neal, I really think we need to do that again'.

"So I had to go knock on the captain's door, and say 'captain, can you come out here for a second?' I said, 'ok Piper, here's the situation. You're saying that you wanna do another take. The captain has just told us that if you fall overboard, and you go into that water, you could *die* in a matter of minutes. There's no turning this boat around very easily to get you back. You're willing to take that risk to get a better take?' We pointed the camera at Piper and he said, 'yep, I am'.

"The captain just looked at us like, 'you guys are nuts!'"

Piper's bravery - or lunacy, depending on one's perspective - illustrated clearly how he maintained his position as what wrestlers called 'a top guy'. But while his personality laid bare a host of idiosyncrasies - as Pruitt, who noticed Piper scooping up a souvenir of prison dirt upon leaving the island, could surely attest to - this kind of dedication was a reflection of a deeper sacrifice made by most top wrestlers. For all the glitz and glamour, it remained a very tough life, and one that functioned within a world of contradictions - competition with cooperation, premeditation and consternation, physicality and choreography.

Mentally, the stress involved in maintaining a roster 'spot' could be debilitating on a performer, but it paled next to the very corporeal effect on the human body. As Diamond Dallas Page would later observe, although wrestlers seemed destined to answer the charge of their profession being *fake*, gravity itself could not be manipulated. The talk show hosts would never know it, but a long-standing tradition instructed wrestlers to shake hands following a match, demonstrating their mutual appreciation for making it through another supposedly fake contest. *Thanks for taking care of me, brother.*

But any notion of locker rooms filled with conscientious choirboys, operating innocently in the pursuit of common harmony, could only be described as naive at best. Rather, like many entertainers, a great number of wrestlers suffered with dependencies, compulsions, and addictions they believed to be inseparable from the business itself. But more perniciously, and perhaps the result of continued success under unyielding pressure, a *party culture* unique to WCW threatened to become unmanageable. "There were overdoses and so on that we dealt with," says a company source, speaking on the condition of anonymity. "I have some stories about the partying that are really beyond belief."

"WCW has had the same policy in existence for the past several years," defended Bischoff in a February '97 interview, referencing a drug testing protocol first introduced by Dr. Harvey Schiller. "We have random testing on a regular basis. Talent under fully executed contracts are tested when they come in to WCW."

In practice, however, the policing of illicit drugs appeared to be flawed in its design, as typically, testing would occur only when WCW shows occurred near Atlanta. Tate Nurkin, an arena promotions coordinator in his early 20's, was often asked to help organize and monitor the tests (alongside, of course, a professional drug screening firm). "Just about every time we had a show in Gainesville," Nurkin remembers,

166

"or Rome...or Dalton...[Vice-President] Gary Juster would hand me a piece of paper with six names on it. These six people had theoretically been pulled out of our contract database. I would have to drive up to wherever the show was and say, 'you've been selected for a random drug screening'.

"We'd have drug screeners there - people who would take the samples and collect them. But I would go stand in the restroom with the wrestlers. I remember the humorous - although belittling - comments that I received from some wrestlers. They preferred that someone wasn't watching them pee in a cup!

"The wrestlers would have three strikes basically. I don't know if the rules were different for Ric Flair [for example], [as opposed to] the newest guys that we brought in...but I do know that I pulled some big names while I was there. Randy Savage, Kevin Sullivan, Lex Luger...their names got pulled. I don't know why they would test Kevin Sullivan, though. He was running the booking committee. If they had a problem with him, why wouldn't you just talk to him and go sort it out? Don't go to me, and have him go to the bathroom in a cup [while I'm there].

"[Nonetheless], I have faith that there was some effort to...at least keep in the back of their minds that if they were doing something illicit or illegal...you would have to be very careful about it. But we had wrestlers who tested positive, and I could have made a lot of money actually accepting their bribe attempts."

With *Nitro* taking place in Atlanta on March 3rd, Schiller planned to witness the backstage environment for himself. In a surprising turn of events, he would also be called to appear on the live broadcast, but only after - in accordance with the rumor mill - attempts to entice a cameo from Ted proved unsuccessful. For his part, Schiller would portray an unimpressed TBS executive, visibly furious with the conduct of Eric Bischoff. The intervention appeared rather necessary, as in storyline, Bischoff was in the midst of a serious power trip, intermittently ordering the reversal of match outcomes, callously suspending WCW wrestlers, and even 'firing' referee Randy Anderson in front of his family (the latter stunt resulting in Turner PR

167

receiving mail from Anderson's real-life church).

"My production people all told me not to do it," says Schiller. "They thought that it would diminish the view of Turner Sports…but I felt it was entertainment. [I thought], 'let's have some fun with it'."

Shortly before the start of *Raw*, Bischoff gloated to almost 14,000 fans at the Omni Coliseum about his recent successes. "*I am the most powerful man in this industry*," he bragged. "*If it wasn't for Eric Bischoff and the nWo…you people wouldn't be here. You owe me a debt of gratitude, and you're welcome!*"

Suddenly, at the top of the entrance way, Dr. Schiller emerged to deliver some justice. Unexpectedly, the home-town Atlanta fans erupted at his interruption, setting the scene for a momentous showdown. "I have no idea why the live crowd reacted like that," says Schiller. "The announcers really didn't say much [about me either], if you listen to it carefully. It was really remarkable."

"*We need to talk*," commanded the Doc to Bischoff on camera. "*This is the President of Turner Sports - your boss*," interjected the venerable 'Mean' Gene Okerlund, chosen wisely to commandeer the confrontation.

"*Do you think [that] just because you have a contract, you have total control of World Championship Wrestling?*" Schiller challenged.

"*Well, it's my understanding - according to [my] agreement - that I'm Executive Vice-President and I run WCW,*" responded Bischoff.

"*You think just because you have a contract*," continued Schiller, "*you can fire referees any time you want? You can break the rules of professional wrestling? You can take titles away from people at will? You may have a contract, but as of right now, you're suspended!*"

"There was almost no rehearsal," reveals Schiller of the segment. "Eric Bischoff was the designer of it - [it was supposed to be] the point and counter-point [to the nWo]. Gene Okerlund and all those people are true professionals, and they knew what they were doing…and

Harvey's standing there not knowing what he was doing! If you look at it real carefully, you can see that I'm biting my lip. I'm not sure if I wanna laugh - or not laugh - as it's going through the paces.

"When I got home, my wife was angry, because people were calling our home wanting to know what would happen next. I called Eric and said 'what do I tell 'em?' He said, 'oh, just tell them you've turned it over to the Executive Committee' - whatever that meant!"

Before exiting the arena, Schiller decided to stop by the locker room. "We were all smoking cigars and drinking wine in the back," says Kevin Nash. "He came in, and he was just...*appalled.* I could just see this 'oh my god' [look on his face].

"I think it was kinda hard for him to digest the digression of what was needed for people to be their character. I mean, you go on a movie set, and if somebody's playing Jim Morrison, they're Jim Morrison...[but] guys are playing characters [in wrestling too], and we're not hitting curve balls, you know.

"So it was hard for [executives] to differentiate between sports and *sports entertainment.* But my whole thing is if I'm an executive, and I'm doing television, and I'm looking at the cable ratings...and my two hours of wrestling are 'number one' and 'number two'...I think I'd have a little bit more compassion to whatever they're doing to make this happen.

"There was never that much live 'TV' before. When we were doing *Raw* [at the time of its debut], it was an hour-long show, and we never gave away a pay-per-view [caliber] match. [By 1997], we were doing two hours on *Nitro,* and we were giving away pay-per-view matches every hour. So [that pressure] was just like, 'holy shit!'

"They knew it was a hot entity. They knew celebrities were coming...and *paying* to get tickets.

"But pro wrestling...when it gets that hot...it's like the world's biggest pirate ship."

169

Chapter 19:
Power Struggles

AT *UNCENSORED* ON March 16th, the nWo triumphed again in a 'triangle elimination' main event match, ensuring an ability - as per the match stipulations - to challenge for any title at any time. Bolstered by the addition of Randy Savage - a character recently turned heel in a rather ambiguous storyline - their dominance appeared to have no bounds. Furthermore, and in a particularly troubling development for WCW, Sting looked to be following suit, showing a supposed allegiance to the nWo on episodes of *Nitro*.

But in a stunning finale to the pay-per-view, dressed in his now customary all-black attire with white facepaint, Sting descended from the rafters to show his true colors. With a packed North Charleston Coliseum in hysterics, the company loyalist interrupted the celebrations of the nWo, pouncing on Hall, Nash and Savage and then delivering a Scorpion Death Drop to a bewildered Hogan. Finally, eight months after the Hogan turn, WCW's savior had emerged.

The show closing surprise was big news to wrestling fans, but to the mainstream audience, an advertised appearance by Chicago Bulls forward Dennis Rodman stole all of the headlines. Fully decked out in an nWo shirt, 'The Worm' proudly wore Hogan's title belt over his shoulder, attracting significant publicity in his role as merely a bystander at ringside. While it remained unclear how WCW could possibly control Rodman in future appearances - his on-court antics, including an attack on a cameraman, were setting new records for NBA fines - the bad-boy of basketball appeared to foster a genuine affection for Hogan, effectively his counterpart in wrestling.

Indeed, a week prior to *Uncensored*, TBS viewers noted Hogan and Bischoff sitting behind the Bulls bench for a road game at Madison Square Garden. Later that night, Rodman filmed a vignette that aired on *Nitro*, contributing to an impressive pay-per-view buy rate that would easily outdraw (by almost 100,000 purchases) the WWF's flagship event in March, *Wrestlemania.*

But despite the box office success, media coverage of the event reminded Bischoff that in terms of the public consciousness, his competition retained the upper hand. "It was only inevitable - Dennis Rodman has signed on with the *WWF*," the Atlanta Journal-Constitution erroneously reported. Various international outlets repeated the misprint, demonstrating a woeful ignorance of the post-*Nitro* landscape.

"Certainly, at that time, we had a *lot* of fans," reflects Bischoff. "We had caught up to the WWF, and were neck and neck in terms of the awareness of our brand - no doubt about that. But at no time during that period did we get to the point where when [the general public] thought about wrestling, they thought about us first.

"The WWF had been around for three generations. But it wasn't just the WWF, [with] Vince McMahon and *Monday Night Raw*…it was Vince McMahon's father [before him]. He owned the business and was quite successful throughout the entire Northeast, when Vince was just a teenager. And prior to that, Vince's *father's father* was a successful wrestling promoter. So the WWF brand had been deeply embedded into the densest part of the wrestling audience's population - meaning the Northeast - for generations. There was no way that WCW was going to overcome that kind of brand stability, at least in the short term. It might have happened over the course of 10 or 20 years…but even then, it would have been a challenge to get to that point."

"I don't think I ever felt like we were *bigger* than the WWF," admits Alan Sharp - WCW's PR Chief - "but I think we were in the same sentence as them. You look back at what happened with Hulk Hogan in the '80s…they had such a long, successful run. A [sports] announcer would just unconsciously say, 'that was like something from the WWF', [for example]. You started to hear some announcers say 'WCW', but it wasn't like we took over their brand. They were still very strong, and they weren't going away quietly."

Meanwhile, in a harbinger of things to come, Scott Hall disappeared from WCW programming to address some real-life personal problems. In an effort to explain his sabbatical - and simultaneously account for Hogan being unavailable due to movie commitments - Sullivan reportedly suggested that Nash criticize Hall as part of a one-week 'breakup' of the nWo. Instead, as *Nitro* came to a close on March 31st, Nash ripped Sullivan in an impromptu (on-screen) interview, referring to the booker as 'Napoleon' - a thinly-veiled jab at his 5' 8" frame.

By early May, however, Sullivan was taking a hiatus of his own, the consequence of burnout and family difficulties hastened by a controversial storyline. Still an active wrestler, Sullivan was embroiled in a year-long feud with Chris Benoit, resulting in several brutal matches on pay-per-view. To add fuel to the conflict, Benoit was portrayed as having 'stole' Sullivan's real-life wife Nancy, a plot twist that would culminate in an *actual* affair (and later, her legitimate divorce from Kevin).

Left to cope with jibes of 'booking his own divorce', Sullivan went home amid reports of losing favor backstage. "Sullivan [has] become so unpopular in so many circles," wrote Wade Keller of *The Pro Wrestling Torch*, "that several insiders have been hard pressed to name even one remaining close ally [he has]. Already there is heated speculation that Kevin Nash and Scott Hall will end up as the main bookers."

In the interim, a makeshift committee led by Terry Taylor, an assistant of Sullivan and accomplished wrestler in his own right, took over the responsibility of formatting *Nitro*. But with the Head Booker gone, company officials feared the inevitability of a power vacuum, a particularly viable possibility in consideration of the parties involved.

As Bischoff knew all too well, Nash, Hall and Sean Waltman (or *Syxx*, as in the sixth member of the nWo) comprised three-fifths of a collective known as the *Kliq*, an informal union of sorts stretching across both companies. In the WWF, the Kliq had famously forced Vince McMahon to visit an Indianapolis house show, so as to diffuse

172

backstage tensions before show time. Rival wrestlers accused the group of sabotaging careers, while others openly fumed at their antagonistic behavior (if a wrestler complained to McMahon, for example, the group would be sure to post a 'KLIQ ONLY' sign on the locker room door).

But the most shocking of all incidents occurred on May 19, 1996, just days before Scott Hall's WWF contract expired. At the conclusion of an untelevised Madison Square Garden event, the Kliq openly embraced in front of a stunned New York crowd - displaying a total non-adherence to kayfabe in an apparent 'send-off' to Hall and Nash. In wrestling lore, the stunt became known as *the Curtain Call*.

When together, Hall and Nash could be especially insufferable. Later in the *Nitro* era, the duo teased wrestler Konnan mercilessly, following his creation of a crowd-pleasing catchphrase ("*let me speak on this!*"). For a period, Konnan - real name Carlos Ashenoff, one of the more legendary figures in Mexican wrestling - could barely utter a sentence before hearing his own mantra yelled back at him: "*LET ME SPEAK ON THIS!*"

When acting alone, Hall enjoyed antagonizing his colleagues as sport, often bragging to younger wrestlers about his contract and status (reportedly, he also believed he couldn't be fired - regardless of the reason - due to the ongoing WWF lawsuit). But for all the perceived selfishness, however, Hall (and his Kliq brethren) were nothing but intensely loyal.

In January of '97, for example, the Outsiders agreed to an important angle putting over Diamond Dallas Page, a gesture of reciprocation for Page's help earlier in the decade. The move was so effective in its execution that Page - deeply embroiled in a feud with Randy Savage - later headlined two pay-per-views within a three month span.

However, in regards to their attitude towards WCW's other wrestlers, Hall and Nash remained somewhat dismissive. "They did throw it in our face a little bit," says Marcus 'Buff' Bagwell, a long-time friend of Nash, "that we were spoiled...and they were right!

173

"We knew what kind of check we were getting every two weeks, and they made it clear that…where they came from, it was a bunch of 'sharks' attacking at all times."

———

In other news, the WWF's lawsuit was encompassing evermore ground, leading to an eventual ruling that unexpectedly, helped define the very nature of journalism itself.

As part of the discovery process, the WWF (under its corporate name 'Titan Sports, Inc.') issued a subpoena to depose Mark Madden, a WCW employee of its 900-number hotline. Madden's commentaries - delivered under the guise of an exaggerated persona ('Pro Wrestling's Only Real Journalist') - had certainly been attracting attention:

"Vince McMahon could wrestle Eric Bischoff in a true-to-life bout," Madden propounded in one update, "where Bischoff could use Ted Turner's wallet as a weapon."

"The reason why WWF can't do Raw live every week? Vince McMahon ain't got no money, honey," offered another.

"The WWF's collapse is great," Madden boasted on October 13th, 1995. "I can say anything I want to on this hotline, because they can't afford to sue me. They probably can't afford to call me."

"If things keep going like they are," he said on November 3rd, "I believe that WWF will eventually go broke, and they'll be speaking with Southern accents in Stamford, Connecticut someday."

"Let's pray for Vince McMahon," Madden teased on December 22nd. "Let's buy a pencil from him, and put a nickel in his cup."

Subsequently, when asked to identify his sources at a July 15, 1996 deposition, Madden - who admitted his commentaries (also used to promote upcoming events, announce recent results, discuss industry news and so on), were often as much "entertainment as journalism" - refused to identify such information. Through counsel, Madden invoked his 'journalist's privilege' and - based on his state of residency - protection of the Pennsylvania Journalist's 'Shield Law'.

At the district court level, Madden was found to be correct in asserting the privilege, and as such, qualified as a 'journalist', based on his intention to disseminate information to third parties. On April 11, 1997, the court concluded that "Titan…is therefore prohibited from compelling disclosure of Mr. Madden's confidential sources."

Eventually, however, the ruling would be appealed (and overturned), thus establishing *The Madden Test*, a method used to determine journalistic validity. As explained in the Appeals Court opinion:

Madden's activities in this case cannot be considered 'reporting', let alone 'investigative reporting'. By his own admission, he is an entertainer, not a reporter, disseminating hype, not news. Although Madden proclaims himself to be 'Pro Wrestling's only real journalist,' hyperbolic self-proclamation will not suffice as proof that an individual is a journalist. Moreover, the record reveals that all of Madden's information was given to him directly by WCW executives…he uncovered no story on his own nor did he independently investigate any of the information given to him by WCW executives.

…to summarize, we hold that individuals claiming the protections of journalist's privilege must demonstrate the concurrence of three elements: that they: 1) are engaged in investigative reporting; 2) are gathering news; and 3) possess the intent at the inception of the news gathering process to disseminate this news to the public.

———

As WCW geared up for *Slamboree* on May 18th, its political instability was on full display. During episodes of *Nitro*, the primary participants in the upcoming pay-per-view (headlined by a match pitting Hall, Nash and Syxx against a returning Ric Flair, Roddy Piper, and former NFL linebacker Kevin Greene) traded barbs with no little to no impediment. *"When I came into this business seven years ago,"* lamented Nash, surrounded by various nWo members, *"I looked down the road that you guys paved for us, and I saw nothing but potholes.*

You guys came into this business, strip-mined it, you took what you could get out of it...and you left the young guys behind you with nothing.

"WCW was nothing but a bunch of guys pushing their sons. If you didn't have a dad in the business, you couldn't even get an opportunity. Scott Hall was here [and] I was here. Scott Hall was ready to become a superstar. Hey, I was still a little green. But Scott Hall was ready, and you know what you did. He worked here a year, he proved himself, and you cut his salary so he went elsewhere."

With no obvious ties between the Kliq and their opponents, insiders speculated that the match was in serious jeopardy. After all, Sullivan would not be around to mediate matters, and Bischoff was busy facing the first real questions surrounding his leadership, judgment and professional conduct. "It's no secret that Eric Bischoff lives up to his rogue image in hotel bars and restaurants after the wrestling shows are over," revealed columnist Bruce Mitchell. "A lot of the illogical haze that covers WCW comes because often more energy goes into chasing the night than actually planning and executing wrestling programs.

"Bischoff, who supposedly has a Turner corporate image to uphold, puts in more bar time than many of the wrestlers he supposedly supervises. His behavior at times has been 180-degrees from what the North Tower at TBS expects from its management.

"His inexplicable decision to allow wrestlers to drink in the dressing room [exposes] TBS to the possibility of million dollar personal injury lawsuits. What do you think a jobber with a lawyer is going to do when he's injured in a match with a WCW wrestler who 'had a few' in the dressing room before the match?

"His drive to be 'one of the boys' clouds his judgment - in more ways than one."

Come *Slamboree*, 'the boys' eventually took care of business, as the nWo agreed to lose against Flair's team. Symbolically, all three heels were defeated in the *middle of the ring* - an act commonly seen as the most respected manner to lose a match among wrestlers.

176

Yet still, the tensions continued to build. As an enthralled Boston crowd buzzed to the exits after the June 9th edition of *Nitro* - a show that drew a company record of $243,946 in ticket revenue - Nash and Piper engaged in a heated confrontation backstage. According to various accounts, the trouble began when Piper decided to preemptively attack (or 'jumpstart') Hall and Nash before the bell, contradicting the match structure agreed to beforehand. Subsequently, a disjointed tag-team match - also involving Ric Flair - fizzled out disappointingly, terminating several minutes before its planned finish.

Following the match, an improvised brawl involving various WCW and nWo wrestlers followed, until a breathtaking spectacle left the Fleet Center crowd in hysterics. In a remarkable stunt, Sting descended from the rafters to save DDP, just in time to evade the nWo and facilitate an escape back to the top of the building. *"I don't believe this!"* bellowed Bobby Heenan on commentary, echoing millions of viewers at home.

Nonetheless, Nash was furious about the bout, reportedly kicking in the door to Piper's dressing room. *You think you're running things around here?* Nash allegedly challenged, causing Piper - a 24-year veteran with a reputation for being uniquely tough - to stand defiantly to his feet. Nash responded with an open-hand blow to Piper's face, and then withstood a take-down attempt before the fight was broken up.

Earlier in the night, Kevin Sullivan returned to WCW television, issuing yet another challenge to Chris Benoit. Upon hearing of the commotion backstage, he made a beeline to find Nash, who by now was reliving the incident in his dressing room. *I see you in there,* Sullivan yelled at Nash, sticking his fingers under the doorway. *Come out here now!*

Thoroughly amused by the situation, Nash couldn't help but to smile. As the tirade in the hallway persisted, he locked eyes with his allies and laughed.

Chapter 20:
The Disease of More

Success is often the first step toward disaster.
-Pat Riley, *Showtime*

MOVING QUICKLY to dispel any notion of burgeoning chaos, Bischoff downplayed the Boston incident in an online interview. "There is nothing I can do to force people to get along 100 percent of the time," he protested days later. "As I said before, we have a tremendous wealth of talent...[and we have some] very intense and competitive individuals.

"Most of the time they get along very well...but from time to time, emotions get in the way and there are flare-ups. I don't want to condone the incident, [but] this isn't grade school. I can't make them write a hundred times, 'I will not lose my temper'."

In regards to the creative situation, Bischoff clarified that since Sullivan's official leave-taking on May 12, *Nitro* had technically been produced without a booker. "Kevin [Sullivan] is not back," Bischoff explained. "He came back to do an interview in Boston. That was the beginning and the end of Kevin's involvement in that show. Terry Taylor is not the booker...Kevin Sullivan is not the booker...in fact, there is no booker in WCW [right now].

"Terry Taylor, [director] Craig Leathers and [producer] Annette Yother work together with me to lay out our television and pay-per-views. I have the final say on everything that goes on television...[and] the same will be true when - and if - Kevin Sullivan returns [officially] to WCW."

But Bischoff's most noteworthy remarks concerned Vince McMahon, whose WWF organization was reeling from its own backstage drama, the apparent departure of Shawn Michaels, and a fifty-week losing streak in the Monday night ratings competition. "Vince's ego got him in trouble, and now [he] realizes he was wrong. It's too late now," bragged Bischoff. "I gave him credit for taking a regional industry and turning it into a national promotion, and for having the vision and courage…to try to take wrestling mainstream, [but] we're not talking about the late '80s [anymore]. We're talking about the late '90s, and Vince McMahon no longer has his pulse on the industry, or for that matter, his own company. He is simply out of touch."

Rumors surrounding WCW's signing of *another* ex-WWF star - its former 'Mr. Perfect' Curt Hennig - provided further evidence of the turning tide, argued Bischoff. "Their roster is depleted, and Vince McMahon can thank himself for that," he prodded. "[McMahon] has thought for years that the WWF is more important than talent. I think the opposite - talent is what makes the product interesting."

During the previous summer and fall, much of the intrigue surrounding the nWo storyline concerned which of McMahon's talent would be next to 'jump' from the WWF, furthering a perception of WCW as the 'cool', cutting-edge wrestling organization (possessing all the mainstream stars of yesteryear, combined with an array of incredible young talent lower down the card). However, it seemed plausible that this perception could eventually become counter-productive, as quite clearly, there would invariably come a time that the well-run pipeline of defecting older stars would run dry. Moreover, even *if* Hogan, Savage, Piper and the other legends maintained their drawing power for another year or two, the novelty of their WCW involvement seemed to be limited by both their age and continued exposure. Before long, the shock value of a *bad* Hulk Hogan, for example, could become as passé as the red-and-yellow version that preceded it.

Finally, and despite being in the midst of record business, there appeared a need to balance the reliance on aging icons with a careful development of (ideally) homegrown talent. Aside from the notable exception of Diamond Dallas Page, it was difficult to find evidence of upward mobility for anyone else on the roster. While arguably, Page,

Sting and The Giant could all be considered 'WCW originals', the large majority of its main eventers owed much of their popularity to a prior WWF run. Failure to *build for the future* could have disastrous consequences, observers warned, not least of which foresaw McMahon leveraging the exodus of so many veterans to present WCW as a dumping ground - a 'retirement home' of sorts for discarded talent.

Of course, the strategy had been attempted before - the 'Billionaire Ted' skits as one obvious example - but it would figure to become only more viable as time progressed (and the WWF developed its own 'fresher' roster of wrestlers). For now, though, WCW was undoubtedly employing "a good formula," argued recently-released midcarder Disco Inferno.

"Everybody talks about WCW doing great right now," Disco stated in a *Pro Wrestling Torch* interview. "But [if] you look at the roster of the top guys - Hogan, Savage, Hall, Nash - it's really hard to compete with those names.

"They've got the big draws. People have always said, 'well, all Eric ever did was just buy all the top talent'. [But] the philosophy works. You pay for quality, you get quality - WCW is doing great."

———

Anxious to further its mainstream awareness and momentum, WCW signed Dennis Rodman to appear at July's *Bash at the Beach* pay-per-view. This time, however, Rodman would be paid to actually *wrestle*, with a deal promising $750,000 (plus 50% of revenues above $3.9 million) to get into the ring himself. "Hogan's the one that got that started," recalls Mike Weber, WCW's former Director of Marketing. "[In 1995], we did *Bash at the Beach* at Huntington Beach, and I remember it like yesterday. I'm getting on the elevator and there's Hogan with Rodman. Hogan goes, 'yeah, I'm getting Dennis drunk here, hoping to get him involved with our company!'"

"Now that he's played basketball in green hair, donned a bridal gown to marry himself, blabbed to the world about sex with Madonna and appeared on his book cover wearing nothing but tiger-striped body paint," wondered the *Orlando Sentinel*, "what's left for a muscle-bound exhibitionist like Dennis Rodman to do?"

Miraculously, Rodman starred in a tag-team main event involving Hogan, Lex Luger, and the Giant, propelling the event to achieve a .89 buy rate, highest among all WCW pay-per-views (excluding *Starrcade*) since 1995. "So now Dennis Rodman is a bonafide pro wrestler," wrote *Wrestling Observer* Editor Dave Meltzer. "The scary part is, he wasn't all that bad."

Earlier in the year, the Bulls forward looked to be WWF bound, until a timely phone call from Hogan alerted Bischoff to their negotiations. Now with the 100th episode of *Nitro* approaching, Hogan conveyed another brain wave to Bischoff - *losing* his World Heavyweight title to cap a special three-hour broadcast.

The benefactor of Hogan's plan would be Luger, who was enjoying an unlikely resurgence as a wildly popular babyface. Since returning on a $150,000 a year contract, 'The Total Package' had parlayed his way to a $700,000 a year deal, despite remaining unpopular with Bischoff (not to mention half the production staff). On this night, however, even the most skeptical would be made into believers, as with close to five million viewers watching on TNT, Luger submitted Hogan in a shocker ending - one so closely guarded that referee Randy Anderson found out just minutes before the bell. Incredibly, over two million fans watched the match *replay* at 1:30am, a figure approaching first-run numbers for *Raw*.

Five days later, Hogan regained his belt at *Road Wild*, maintaining the build-up towards an eventual match with Sting. By now, with upcoming movie commitments and a planned match against Roddy Piper at *Halloween Havoc*, the showdown seemed primed to occur at *Starrcade*, WCW's December pay-per-view. Logically, a clean loss to Sting would surely follow, but in the meantime, Hogan was reveling in regaining the industry's top spot.

"There was a promoter during the late-1980s," Hogan told the *Chicago Tribune*, "[who] was on a negative vibe most of the time. He would say, 'Terry, wrestling will never be as big as it once [was]…there will never be that [kind of] media awareness…your career will never be as great as it was during the 1980s'.

"I responded, 'short-sighted, no vision, loser, see you later', Hogan continued, his comments clearly directed at Vince McMahon. "I'm proving now that wrestling is bigger and hotter than it's ever been.

"I look at wrestling, and who and what it draws to the sport, as a magnet. Wrestling didn't show up because Rodman was there - Rodman came because wrestling was there.

"All of a sudden…[we've] become respected, and it's really cool because we work real hard. A lot of people don't realize that this thing is a 24-hour-a-day profession, not just the 10-minutes you see us jumping around the ring in a pair of tights."

Indeed, although insider fans were often quick to label Hogan as selfish, egotistical, and manipulative - based mostly on a collection of anecdotes alleging his political proclivities - he could certainly never be accused of lacking commitment to the business. Any hesitancy to 'pass the torch', several friends thought, arose partly out of his concern for the industry's future (along with the obvious decrease in financial rewards and notoriety).

At autograph signings and public appearances, Hogan was famous for being fan friendly. "One of my best memories," reveals Neal Pruitt, "is when Hogan signed autographs in Chicago for what seemed like hundreds of people. He was even willing to stay overtime and miss his flight back home, just so he could sign those autographs.

"I thanked him in our limo ride back to the hotel," continues Pruitt, who once scribbled 'nWo' - with the star's approval, of course - on Hogan's forehead before he underwent a knee surgery. "He said he hadn't passed up an autograph in 15 years, and wasn't about to do it now. I said, 'that's why you're on top'."

182

Hogan was also enjoying his association with Ted Turner, noting to the *Tribune* that Ted's own commitment to wrestling was paying off. "Many people have told [Ted] that wrestling doesn't fit in [his] 'portfolio of programming'," Hogan observed, "but Turner always stuck to his guns.

"Now he's having the last laugh, because it's paying off. We've got the hottest show on cable."

———

Despite losing Hogan to movie commitments after *Road Wild*, WCW recorded its 58th straight ratings win on August 11th. Following the show, Bischoff embarked on a short family vacation in Wyoming, his first such break in several years. While on the journey, he received a congratulatory phone call from Harvey Schiller, who counted himself as impressed with the recent programming.

Great pay-per-view, Bischoff recalls Schiller extolling.

By the way, the Doc then mentioned in passing, *I just got out of a meeting with Ted.*

Because of the success of Monday Nitro on TNT…

Ted wants to launch a new show on TBS.

Bischoff stared at the car phone.

This has to be a joke, he thought.

183

Chapter 21:
Five Slams on the Banked Track

THE DOC *HAD* to be joking. With no off-season to speak of, producing two (weekly) hours of live original programming was already arduous. The mere concept of adding an additional show seemed ludicrous, thought Bischoff, notwithstanding the obvious financial incentive for TBS. *Harvey*, he responded, *I'm on vacation, and I'm not going to let you piss me off. Come up with another joke.*

I'm serious, retorted Schiller, jabbing an incredulous Bischoff with each additional detail. *Two additional hours...live...prime time...every Thursday...*

His voice trailed off.

As with the launch of *WCW Monday Nitro* on TNT, the new show, eventually titled *WCW Thursday Thunder*, owed its creation to a directive made by Ted Turner alone. "Ted just said, 'I wanna do a second night of prime time'," reveals former TBS President Bill Burke. "Ted wanted it on Thursdays - on TBS - because we didn't have [Atlanta] Braves [coverage] that night."

"I am pretty sure that Thursday was a strategic choice," adds David Albritton, former Media Manager at Turner Broadcasting. "Many advertisers wanted event programming near the weekend for promotion advertising. I used to work for a local Atlanta ad agency called *Ad Action Group* who dealt exclusively with car dealers. These advertisers spent almost all of their ad money on Thursday [to Sunday], [in order] to promote weekend traffic. Because *WCW Thunder* was exciting and very male-targeted, it appealed to these car dealers and made for a good place to spend promotion advertising dollars."

"I [also] remember *Thunder* being created on Thursday nights," adds Greg Scordato, a former Turner account executive, "particularly to take advantage of movie advertiser money."

In a departure from the internal reaction in 1995, the possibility of *more wrestling* on the Turner networks was now being met with a curious optimism. "Brad [Siegel]...who never wanted wrestling...now you'd think he *invented* it," laughs Burke. "Brad was like, 'either do it on TNT, or don't do it - we're the prime time wrestling network!' I was like, 'you gotta be kidding me!'"

"I had my reasons for wanting it, and Brad had his reasons for wanting it [on TNT]. So I make my case...Brad makes his case...and we set up a meeting with Ted. Ted, surprisingly, patiently listens to me, and he listens to Brad. He goes, 'you haven't changed my mind - we're doing it on TBS'. Brad starts talking again and Ted goes, 'look, Brad - we're gonna have two nights of prime time wrestling. Do you want me to move them *both* to TBS? Or do you wanna keep Monday on TNT'? Brad goes, 'I wanna keep Monday on TNT'. Ted goes, 'ok, done. See ya guys'. That's how it happened."

Despite his protests to Ted, Siegel privately confided in colleagues that another show would be a bridge too far for WCW, potentially causing its product to be overexposed. "It was funny though, 'cos Brad would make that argument," remembers Burke, "and we always thought it was self-serving, because he didn't want [*Thunder*] on TBS. We were definitely *pushing it*, [though]...[in terms of leading to] overexposure, and then just absolutely exhausting everybody. But at TBS, selfishly, we were like 'we want the '3' rating or whatever it was getting. It was like, 'bring it on' - our head of programming was doing cartwheels about it.

"In fairness to him, we felt like we (TBS network) were the ones who had WCW all those years, and everyone made fun of us. Now, all of a sudden, it was the thing everyone wanted. So we embraced it."

The long-tail consequences of *Thunder* concerned Bischoff, who digested the news without knowledge of its financing. He estimated that his production staff would increase in size - by fifteen to twenty people, most likely - not to mention a commensurate escalation in talent costs. Creatively, an inability to induce anticipation (to the same degree as before) would be likely, as for the foreseeable future, only three to four days would elapse between prime-time WCW programming. Consequently, it seemed plausible that *Thunder* could become, although perhaps not at first, a *nothing show* relegated to 'B' or 'C' status. Despite WCW seemingly hitting on all cylinders, its fans could potentially get *burned out* on the product - the expansion causing a dilution of once-interesting storylines.

"We were already producing two hours of live 'TV' - every Monday," laments Bischoff. "We had two hours of *WCW Saturday Night*. We had a one hour show on Sunday night on TBS - called *WCW Main Event*. We had [various] syndicated shows, distributed domestically and internationally. We were producing so much content already, and the thought of producing another two hours - live every week - was just mind-boggling.

"My fear was that we would dilute our own brand. You can only put Hulk Hogan or Sting out there so many times a week, before people don't feel like it's special anymore."

A worrying (and famous) example of overexposure existed in Roller Derby, the once-popular spectacle that had thrilled crowds earlier in the century. In a post-World War II nation looking for escapism, competitive roller skating took America by storm after its debut on New York television in November 1948. "It is neither sport nor show biz, but a new television art form with elements of both," reported *Variety*. "It is cathartic, dramatically structured, fast-paced and classic as a John Wayne movie."

By mid-1949, 'the Derby' secured a prestigious booking at Madison Square Garden, the handiwork of its creator, Leo Seltzer. With a cumulative crowd of 55 thousand fans enjoying five summer dates, Seltzer parlayed the success in New York into the formalization of a six-team quasi-legitimate league. He sold the league's television

186

rights to ABC, but admittedly, failed to read the fine print of the agreement. According to the deal, ABC retained - in exchange for its outlay of $5,000 per week - the rights to televise up to 12 weekly hours of Derby programming. But with the network suffering from serious financial issues, it began to rely heavily on the Derby to attract viewers, soon broadcasting three and a half games per week. Before long, its executives proposed a much more drastic escalation - *daily* broadcasts with the new season beginning the day after the last (the proposal never found fruition, although coincidentally, Sullivan remembers a rare TBS executive - beginning to see revenues on the rise - suggesting the same for WCW).

In regards to Roller Derby, Seltzer appealed ABC to televise games twice per week - Friday night and Sunday afternoon - the optimal time slots to capture a relaxed adult audience. ABC President Robert Kintner was unmoved, however, ironically telling Seltzer that "no sports will ever be [televised] on Sunday." Eventually, despite maneuvering his way out of the deal, Seltzer failed to finalize a sponsorship pact with General Motors, one that would ensure the broadcast of games on NBC. "Without TV," wrote Frank Deford in the definitive Roller Derby book, *Five Strides on the Banked Track*, "...there were no more presents and flowers awaiting the skaters in the locker rooms. The fan clubs dissolved. Cab drivers stopped tooting their horns at skaters. There were no more celebrities in the box seats, posing for pictures. There were, for that matter, precious few anybodies in the box seats, or in any of the seats."

Under the leadership of Seltzer's son, Jerry, Roller Derby experienced an unlikely (and extraordinary) revival in the 1960's, before finally shutting down in 1973. During its second peak (15 million weekly television viewers in 1969), the younger Seltzer had skillfully managed to limit the league's dependency on television, viewing the medium as an opportunity to drive fans primarily to the live matches. "We use TV for exposure and publicity, but not for revenue," he stated. "We make our money by the presentation of the event, and we keep our feet on the ground. Sports such as baseball and football have continued to show profits only because of TV. It is that thin a line, and TV has let them stay in the black and justify ridiculous player salaries.

Pull TV out materially, and the whole structure could collapse."

Unlike Roller Derby, WCW could not afford to regard its televised events in the same manner. In contrast to the WWF, a privately-owned wrestling organization, WCW functioned as an entity within Turner Broadcasting, and therefore, any deliberate sacrifice of TV viewership would not be tolerated. With Turner Ad Sales reportedly promising advertisers a consistent 4.0 rating ("I don't remember that. A 4.0 sounds extremely aggressive," retorts Rob Garner, WCW's former VP of TV Programming and Sales), the inherent pressure to produce *two* 'can't miss' weekly programs was building. Besides, with no WWF competition on Thursday nights, it was unclear exactly what would drive Bischoff and his team to maintain their enthusiasm.

In the meantime, the on-screen product showed little sign of slowing down, with the August 25th *Nitro* scoring a 5.0 rating, its highest ever. Backstage, Kevin Sullivan was officially back in his role as booker, and in a memorable segment, a retiring Arn Anderson offered his Four Horsemen 'spot' to Curt Hennig.

A week later, the nWo spoofed Anderson's emotional gesture with a controversial parody of his stable mates. "I was just told, 'Andre, we're gonna do a parody - like *Saturday Night Live*'," recalls special effects artist Andre Freitas, who designed the costuming used in the segment. "That's the only input I got, so I thought, 'well, I need to make Kevin [Nash] balding, put a combover hairdo on him, make his cheeks rosy and get him a neck brace'. Kevin came up with the idea for the beer cooler.

"Arn took it very seriously, and never talked to me again after that moment. He took it personally, because he felt it was a jab at his career."

In large part due to the parody, *Fall Brawl*'s main event - Horsemen vs. the nWo - involved an inordinate amount of *heat*, but in a show-closing swerve, Curt Hennig took despicable to entirely new levels. Revealing his allegiance to be with the nWo all along, Hennig violently slammed Ric Flair's head into the cage door, causing a furious Winston-Salem crowd to erupt in displeasure. *They killed the town*, Flair later lamented, in reference to the booking decision.

Apparently, the nWo's comeuppance had been postponed - for a day still yet to come.

Chapter 22:
Goldberg

"Blow it out your ass!"

The date: Fall 1995.

The place: Main Event Fitness, 5249 Buford Highway N.E., Atlanta, Georgia.

The pissed off weightlifter: Bill Goldberg, a washed-out defensive tackle recently cut from the Carolina Panthers.

Bill GOLDBERG WASN'T HAPPY. Fresh off an unusual surgery reattaching his torn abdominal muscles, the one-time University of Georgia standout gazed incredulously over his shoulder. It may have been the methadone, but he could swear that a group of other lifters were mocking his rehabilitation. The primary culprit appeared to be one of the owners of the facility - Larry Pfohl - better known to the public as WCW's Lex Luger. It was a familiar routine; Luger would pick up a five-pound dumbbell weight, lift it above his head, and then crack up his friends with an array of exaggerated grunting sounds. His comedy act failed to resonate with Goldberg, however, whose voice bellowed threateningly across the gym:

Blow it out your ass!

Once a monster on the gridiron, the 6'3", 275 lb. Goldberg now regarded himself as a failure. He still harbored hopes of an NFL comeback, but at 30, he was now seen league-wide as 'damaged goods'. Several career 'options' remained - working as a mechanic for brother Mike, for instance - but none of them seemed particularly appealing. The next stop was depression, a sad regression for a former Psychology major and famously, the son of a Jewish OB/GYN.

Figuring he could capitalize on his name value as a former athlete, Goldberg decided to create a personal training business, using the

190

trading name *Body Mechanics*. He paid $250 to obtain the requisite certificate, but soon discovered his new vocation to be just as unappealing (the actual experience of being recognized as an *ex-athlete* proved excruciating, he told friends). At night, he drifted around the Atlanta clubs, but for the first time, paid close attention to a persistent pitchman: Diamond Dallas Page.

Along with Sting and Luger (the 'blow it out your ass' episode now resolved), Page had been working on Goldberg to give wrestling a try. It seemed like a goofy idea, but perhaps it could resemble the NFL experience, Goldberg thought, especially in regards to the locker room atmosphere. And so, on June 24th, 1996 - a Charlotte-based edition of *Monday Nitro* notable for the presence of armed security guards (necessary to keep the invading Outsiders at bay) - Goldberg visited the backstage area for the first time. Upon entering the arena, he witnessed a pleasant camaraderie reminiscent of his football days, and despite numerous reservations about a wrestling career (most notably, the sheer embarrassment of participating in a 'fake sport'), he expressed an interest to a distracted Eric Bischoff. The two had met before under much different circumstances - the hazy dance floor in Atlanta's 'upscale' strip joint, *the Gold Club* - and on that occasion, Goldberg joked that he could be WCW's next big thing. As they parted in Charlotte, however, Bischoff offered the possibility of a more serious conversation. *Call the office in two or three weeks*, he said.

Three weeks later, Goldberg did as Bischoff requested, leaving a message with the WCW offices. But a week after that - despite making a follow-up call - Goldberg had yet to receive a response. Despite still clutching to the hope of returning to football, his next call would be to Jim Ross, a fellow Oklahoman and WWF's Head of Talent Relations. Ross had interviewed Goldberg during his tenure with the Atlanta Falcons, and unreservedly arranged a meeting with Vince McMahon. After a month of negotiations with the WWF, Goldberg looked poised to finalize an agreement, but with only hours remaining until decision time, Bischoff finally got in touch.

It was nine o'clock on a Thursday morning, and at noon, the WWF was expecting an answer. *I have no desire to be some 500 dollar a week, throw-your-ass around the ring, dress-me-up-in-a-clown suit dipshit*, Goldberg told Bischoff. *I've chosen to do this because I think I can contribute to the profession, and somehow, I think it can be a lot of fun.*

At (almost) the eleventh hour, Bischoff had dodged a bullet: Goldberg agreed to terms with WCW, signing a reported six-figure deal to train five days a week before his first match.

Shortly before Christmas of 1996, Bischoff requested a progress report on Goldberg from Terry Taylor. To Bischoff's amazement, however, a confused Taylor responded with precisely zero information, stating that Goldberg had yet to report to WCW's training facility, *The Power Plant. Terry*, answered Goldberg after being reached on the phone, *I've been calling WCW every week since I signed my contract in September, and you're the first person to call me back!*

At the Plant, Goldberg learned under the tutelage of its head trainer, a diminutive yet formidable ex-wrestler known as 'Sarge' DeWayne Bruce. An unrelenting instructor, Sarge designed his workouts to commence with 45 minutes of punishing 'Hindu' squats, followed by push-ups, sit-ups and other demanding endurance exercises. He typically acted unmoved by any protest, staring stoically while hopefuls practiced 'hitting the ropes' (actually steel cables surrounding the ring) until the point of fatigue.

At occasional open tryouts, unprepared wannabes, some of whom boasted of their collegiate, or indeed, professional athletic prowess, almost always went home before lunchtime. But Goldberg was different, and although he admitted avoiding the full barbarity of Sarge's regimen, his toughness and willingness to learn earned him respect among his peers (even post-class, recruits remember, Goldberg maintained the same intensity, videotaping the practice of moves to review later).

Over the course of several months at the Plant, Goldberg slowly

192

developed the building blocks of an in-ring persona. He chose a suitably understated ring attire - black briefs, black knee pads, and black gloves - resembling the mixed martial artists he became enamored with while in training. In sum, his menacingly simple look made him feel like an Oakland Raider - one ready to rip off an opponent's helmet at a moment's notice. He paid $375 for a tribal tattoo on his shoulder, which coupled with a freshly shaved bald head, ensured there would be no further hesitation about wrestling. *If I follow through with all of these changes*, Goldberg thought, *maybe I can't back out of being a wrestler after all.*

In regards to Goldberg's in-ring repertoire, football provided the inspiration again. After violently tackling an opponent in a tryout match, Jody Hamilton, the Head of the Power Plant, instructed the rookie to incorporate the tackle (or 'spear') as a set-up for a signature finishing move - a combination suplex and power slam eventually dubbed *the Jackhammer.*

The remaining decision was perhaps most important. Goldberg was asked to come up with a ring name, and during some early brainstorming, he cycled through a series of kooky monikers like *The Beast, The Annihilator, The Mossad, The Hybrid* and even *Jack Hammer.* In dark matches throughout the summer of 1997, he then wrestled under his real name (and alternatively as 'Bill Gold'), but as plans developed for a televised introduction, his character officially remained anonymous.

On September 22nd, 1997, *Nitro* returned from an early commercial break with a mysterious figure standing in the ring. It was Goldberg, but mere moments before his debut match, the announcers were scrambling for clarification on their headsets. *What do you want me to call him?* questioned a testy Tony Schiavone, speaking off-camera to Bischoff.

Just call him Bill Goldberg, shrugged Bischoff in response.

"Bill Goldberg..." responded Schiavone to the TNT audience. *"A man we know absolutely nothing about...is making his debut here. From*

the looks of him, he is very determined and looks very powerful."

Goldberg's first opponent was chosen to be Hugh Morrus, an agile heavyweight with a reliable reputation. "I was approached by Terry Taylor, who was my agent, and he said that I was gonna have to do 'the job'," reveals Morrus, real name Bill Demott. "I think Terry at one time said I took it very negatively, but make no mistake, I knew what my job was. I've said it before, and I'll say it all these years later - I had no qualms about going out there and 'doing the favors', as we say. That's how I made my living. I'd like to think I was there for Bill, and helped him get started. I think it's pretty cool that one of the things I'm remembered for is being Goldberg's first opponent.

"It's a feather in my cap. I was flattered when years later, I heard Kevin Sullivan say I was the guy for the job and he knew it. So yeah, I think it's cool to be that guy."

Two minutes into the contest, a back elbow leveled Goldberg to the mat. To the amazement of the Salt Lake City crowd, however, the newcomer sprung to his feet, performing a backflip and then a devastating power slam. "The funny part about the match to me," Demott continues, "is that they told Bill, 'don't do the backflip!'. He had such a large presence, and to see a guy that size do a backflip kinda felt out of sorts. But it was in his mind to prove how agile he was, and how athletic he was.

"When he did the backflip, I could just imagine Sullivan back there saying 'god damn it, we told him not to do that!'"

Half a minute later, Goldberg picked up Morrus for an apparent suplex, but instead executed the Jackhammer move to set up a pin. "*Combination slam*," observed Schiavone. "*One...two...three! Bill Goldberg comes to Nitro and pulls a major upset!*"

Shunning the referee's attempt to raise his hand, Goldberg turned to the camera. *That's one*, he indicated, raising his index finger for dramatic effect. After ignoring Gene Okerlund on the entranceway - a departure in protocol for a debuting wrestler - the newcomer

194

disappeared into the backstage area. In totality, despite only five minutes of air time, he already projected the rarest of commodities: *mystique*.

Chapter 23:
A New Standard

ON SUNDAY, OCTOBER 5th, Brian Pillman was found dead in a Minneapolis hotel room. It had been over 18 months since his WCW release (a move that opened the doors for a signing with the WWF, fresh off the 'Booker Man' feud with Sullivan), but the news still hit Bischoff hard. "That man happened to be a pretty good friend of mine," he mused in an online interview. "I don't take the situation lightly."

Although eventually, a toxicology report revealed Pillman to have died from 'natural causes', Bischoff decided to address the elephant in the room. "Unfortunately, there is only so much we can do to curtail or prevent the abuse of prescription drugs, or any other drugs for that matter," he said.

"WCW does have a drug testing policy in place and wrestlers are tested when they come to WCW. They are subject to random tests at any time, and there are random test procedures in place that have been fairly effective.

"I'm not going to insult anyone's intelligence [and] say there aren't abuses, but the fact is…there isn't a problem …among people working with us now. Unfortunately, drug abuse exists not just in wrestling, but all walks of life."

Before *Nitro* on October 13th, Bischoff addressed the WCW locker room, reportedly revisiting the issue of drug use. "I hope you people don't think I'm completely naive to what goes on here," the *Pro Wrestling Torch* reported him as saying. "I've heard about it. I know there's abuse, but I don't think it's too bad."

According to the *Torch* piece, Bischoff promised confidentiality for any performer requiring rehabilitation. He clarified that no wrestler was to perform while injured, lest the potential for a painkiller addiction develop. Then, according to various sources, Bischoff added his commentary on some other topics, highlighting Hogan, Piper and Savage as the only three wrestlers capable of *putting asses in seats*. It was a comment unlikely to inspire fellowship among the rest of the roster - many of whom already dreaded the launch of *Thunder* - and one that appeared utterly illogical in composition (the snipe occurred, some reports suggested, mostly as a thinly-veiled jab at Hall and Nash).

Bischoff also made reference to the WWF, deriding McMahon's recent strategic change towards raunchier programming, and allegedly predicting his competition would face severe financial issues within six months. But such prognostication - spouted partly to motivate himself, Bischoff claims - seemed illogical upon closer consideration of the facts.

Superficially, the prevailing perception of the Monday Night Wars - from its commencement until the winter of 1997 - reflected a kind of zero-sum thinking. According to this reasoning, WCW's gain occurred at the *cost* of the WWF's business, insofar as when *Nitro* gained viewership, *Raw*'s numbers decreased in proportion. Belief in this commensurate relationship appeared rational, especially given Vince McMahon's own statements - propaganda or not - that WCW were looking to *divide* the wrestling audience with its Monday night programming. Under this paradigm, however, a fixation on audience *share* was prioritized - irrespective of total audience *size* - reflecting a 'fixed pie' fallacy in action. Through competition, the evidence suggested, the 'pie' (as defined by audience size) actually *increased* since 1995. In other words, the number of available fans was *variable* - not *fixed* - meaning that theoretically, one side could gain in a manner independent to its competitor's loss.

Conversely, the opposite notion - built on an arresting premise framing *Nitro* as an *existential* threat to the WWF - failed to materialize objectively. Quite clearly, its inherent supposition proved evidently false, as despite losing in the ratings battle, the WWF had quietly kept its ship afloat. While granted, in 1995, the company *did* lose $6 million, a remarkable stabilization then occurred in 1996, precipitating a gradual recovery throughout 1997. In fact, in reference to its key revenue drivers, McMahon's operation was on the *rise*, with average ratings (2.5 in '96 to 2.6 in '97), house show attendance (4,881 to 5,826), and buy rates (220,600 to 228,600) all up year-to-year.

As McMahon himself would later acknowledge, the competition had been "good for business." While allowing WCW to fixate on its Monday night ratings, he had skillfully maintained the WWF's fortunes, a feat explained eloquently in the book *Titan Screwed*:

With WCW prospering, the misconception was that the publicly humiliated WWF was floundering, struggling to stay afloat thanks to its frequent defeats in the weekly ratings battle. It was a myth that brazen WCW President Eric Bischoff was more than happy to perpetuate. Bischoff repeated the fallacy with such frequent gusto that many in the industry began to accept it as gospel…

…The reality of the WWF's standing was much different to the Bischoff-led allusions of their impending demise. The weekly ratings battle was a war of perception, existing purely to fuel bragging rights between networks TNT and USA about which of them was number one on cable. While there was some financial motivation behind the broadcasters vying for top spot…the effect of the war was far less detrimental to Titan's bottom line than WCW's propaganda, and indeed the WWF's own propaganda, implied.

There was little doubt that WCW's business had improved across the board since the advent of *Nitro* and particularly with Bischoff's creation of the New World Order storyline in mid-1996, but the belief that the ticket buying public had deserted the WWF was simply not the case. The WWF's performance on Monday nights had surprisingly little bearing on their prosperity in other avenues, for while McMahon watched his ratings plummet into the low 2s, his house show business was growing at a phenomenal rate.

Therefore, if Bischoff continued counting McMahon out, he did so at the risk of his own credibility; moreover, such rhetoric created a new, mostly *external* benchmark of WCW's performance. Whereas earlier, he had focused first on making WCW profitable, winning on Monday nights and later on, becoming the world's "number one" wrestling company, Bischoff's ability to control attainment of the new standard - pushing McMahon into financial peril - relied less on WCW's success and more on the WWF's *own* performance. At least, that is what the data - over two years of it, at this point - seemed to imply.

Put differently, while every goal naturally involved some outside influences (especially, as previously established, the aim to become 'profitable' within the TBS structure), the degree of difficulty soared as more externally dependent variables - an adversary's financial standing, for example - were introduced and emphasized. By definition, Bischoff could now not be successful until he ran McMahon out of business.

More fundamentally, according to Bischoff's own forecast, McMahon would presumably experience money problems around a very specific time frame - April 1998. Unsurprisingly, within a matter of days, WWF attorneys seized on the comments, referring back to language contained in its initial (June 1996) complaint:

As part of its systematic corporate plan to harm the WWF as opposed to promoting its own product on its own merits, WCW employees and agents constantly circulated phony and false rumors of Titan's supposed impending bankruptcy so as to maximize its chances of luring talent away from the WWF.

In response, TBS lawyer John Houston Pope refuted the contention in a letter:

The comments by Mr. Bischoff...did not involve any intent to put Titan out of business or to obtain a monopoly. As we understand Mr. Bischoff's comments, he explained at a meeting of a group of wrestlers (who are neither the public nor other management-level employees of WCW or TBS) that he expected that Titan would go "belly up" in six months because Titan's advertisers are disgusted with its story lines and are withdrawing from its programming.

Although six months was a lifetime in wrestling, it would certainly come around soon enough. At that time, if the WWF continued along its path, perhaps even closing the ratings gap, Bischoff could be seen - in this delicate game of perceptions, after all - as being delusional, distracted, even desperate. In case he hadn't heard, *the water coolers had been back for some time*.

For the moment, however, Bischoff appeared a step or two away from conquering - definitively - the vaunted World Wrestling Federation.

199

Misleading as it may have been, the sentiment intensified with reportage of his latest acquisition - Bret 'The Hitman' Hart, currently McMahon's champion and an iconic Canadian megastar. Renowned widely for his realistic style, staunch adherence to kayfabe and international popularity, Hart initially pondered WCW's advances in October 1996 (a charge Bischoff has alternately confirmed and denied ever since). Privately, the latest negotiations had been underway for over a month, following a meeting where Hart learned that McMahon - citing financial difficulties - could no longer honor his contract (with 19 years remaining in balance). It sounded plausible, especially given the perception of McMahon's fortunes; however, once the events of early 1998 would transpire, it seemed rather curious - perhaps flagrantly dishonest - that money could have been an issue.

Maybe McMahon was having buyer's remorse. Maybe he believed his return on a 20-year deal would be dismal. Maybe he knew something Bischoff didn't. In any event, he encouraged the Hitman to take a reported 3-year, $7.5 million offer, noting that WCW "wouldn't know what to do with a Bret Hart."

On Halloween night, Hart informed Bischoff that he was ready to sign. Simultaneously, however, he was still the reigning WWF champion, and as such, he was engaged in a tense dispute (relevant to his final match) with McMahon. On his way out, 'The Hitman' would naturally be asked to drop the belt, but he refused to do so in Canada - his home country - and not against Shawn Michaels, a wrestler with whom he held a bitter real-life hatred.

Consequently, on November 9th, one of the more infamous events in pro wrestling history occurred in Montreal, Canada. Before the WCW signing was made official, Hart was booked against Michaels in the main event of *Survivor Series*, despite his continued objections to losing in Canada.

To his credit, Hart did suggest losing to Michaels in America - before the event - or vacating the title on *Raw*. But after a long period of negotiations, Hart, McMahon and Michaels agreed to a *disqualification* finish in Montreal, enabling Hart to lose elsewhere before December 1st, his start date with WCW. According to the plan, Michaels would lock Hart in his own signature move (The 'Sharpshooter'), triggering a series of events ending in a brawl, thus leading to the match being thrown out.

However, in a shocking (and legitimate) double-cross, McMahon ordered the referee to end the match prematurely, screwing Hart without his foreknowledge. Fittingly, the incident - deconstructed, debated and dissected endlessly in the years that followed - became known idiomatically as the *Montreal Screwjob*.

As captured brilliantly in the documentary *Wrestling With Shadows*, Hart charged into the dressing room afterwards, questioning Michaels about his involvement and famously, decking McMahon with a single punch.

Meanwhile, sitting at home, Eric Bischoff answered a call from Rick Rude, a former WCW star-turned manager working for McMahon on a night-to-night deal. Rude was vociferously irate - reflective of the anger pervading the WWF locker room backstage - and so in short order, Bischoff offered him a contract.

On November 17th, Rude became the first person to ever appear on *Nitro* and *Raw* concurrently, showing up clean-shaven with the nWo on TNT (an hour later, in a taped appearance, he sported a beard on USA).

"Oh, what a difference a day makes," Rude growled in the center of the ring. *"Twenty four little hours. You know, we all have our fifteen minutes of fame, and I'd like to take a couple of my fifteen minutes to talk about the rights - and the wrongs - in the world of professional wrestling.*

"What's wrong in the world of professional wrestling is Shawn Michaels claiming to be World Champion when he never beat Bret Hart. What's wrong with the world of professional wrestling is for Vince McMahon to instruct the referee to ring the bell - in order to rob Bret Hart of his title. But on the other hand what's right in the

world of professional wrestling is for Bret Hart to abandon the Titanic and swim to the refuge of the nWo."

A week earlier on *Nitro*, Bischoff foreshadowed Hart's impending arrival, even alluding to his punching out of Vince McMahon ("you're a real *knockout* kinda guy!"). In storyline, Bischoff implied that Hart was poised to join the New World Order, and as such, he joined its members in a rendition of the Canadian National Anthem. By the time Hart appeared on WCW television, however, his debut occurred to little fanfare.

In a cross-promotional (WWF to WCW) convergence of narrative, Hart was shoehorned into Bischoff's (on-screen) feud with a semi-retired commentator, Larry Zybysko. Throughout 1997, Zybysko consistently stood up to the nWo's actions, eventually talking his way into a *Starrcade* match with Bischoff. According to the stipulations, 'ownership' of *Monday Nitro* would be at stake in the match, playing on Bischoff's real-life idea for the nWo to takeover *Nitro* (allowing, he says, WCW to 'live' on *Thunder*, the soon-to-begin *TBS* program). For his part, Hart would serve as a 'guest referee', setting up a redemption of sorts after the Montreal debacle. *"Nobody knows better than me,"* he portended to the *Nitro* crowd, *"what it's like to get screwed by a referee."*

Additionally, Hart was scripted to participate in *Starrcade*'s main event - a long-awaited showdown between Hollywood Hogan and Sting. According to journalist Dave Meltzer, Bischoff outlined the nature of Hart's involvement "five weeks before the match." At that time, Meltzer says, Bischoff envisioned Hogan 'cheating' to win the bout, before Hart - acting in the capacity of a referee - would call for the match to be restarted (thus allowing Sting to eventually triumph).

Meanwhile, to preview a future where the nWo controlled *Nitro*, Bischoff planned a one-week 'takeover' of the program on December 22nd. To maximize its effectiveness, he requested a new title sequence, graphics, and various nWo-themed production elements to accompany the stunt. "We went down to his office to pitch the idea," remembers Pat McNeely, an instrumental force in creating the original

Nitro open. "I'd done up all these storyboards…how there's this organization…this militia that comes in, takes over the city…kind of like a big brother type [thing].

"We had it all designed, but he just looked at me and was like, 'no - this is not at all what we want to do'. He just didn't get it, y'know. I was like, 'wait! But then - there's this football field…they come and there's this [and that]…explosions…I was all gung-ho about it. He was like, 'no, no, no...no'.

"I looked over at Karl [Horstmann], and Karl was already packing up. He was like, 'oh, we'll come back. We'll pitch you another idea'. I was ready to go, 'cos it just wasn't right. It needed to be a little more different for whatever Eric wanted this nWo [takeover] to *feel like*."

Interestingly, McNeely - along with Greg Daniel - another producer who worked on the concept - recalls the discussion occurring months before *Starrcade*. Evidently, the eventual *nWo Monday Nitro* title sequence actually featured Bill Goldberg, who appeared in a shot destroying the *WCW Monday Nitro* logo. "We ended up doing something," McNeely continues, "where we got a hold of Bill Goldberg - *before* he was a wrestler. He was still kind of in training, and was kind of our model for this shoot.

"[Goldberg] had a sledgehammer, in this rusty, kinda…factory or something like that. It was real grungy. He basically smashed the *Nitro* logo, and underneath was an 'nWo Nitro' version of the logo."

Upon its airing, the video highlighted a 25-minute segment in which nWo members tore down WCW signage, intimidated cameramen and posed at the crowd, staging a strikingly subdued 'takeover'. The lengthy inaction seemed to flatten the live crowd, and unmistakably, it inspired a similar response among the TNT audience. *Nitro* still won the night over *Raw* (3.5 to 3.1), but the margin of victory was the closest in seventeen months. Moreover, for the first time in 1997, more viewers watched the opposing segment on *Raw*, giving the WWF a win (3.2 to 3.0) over the final head-to-head hour. "It seemed to me," adds McNeely, "that this was when the storyline got a little confusing."

As the ratings war progressed, an accepted axiom came to describe the distinction between each company. *WCW is a television company doing wrestling*, went the refrain, or some version of it, *while WWF is a wrestling company doing wrestling.*

As if it needed performative illustration, the reaction to *Nitro* losing an hour spoke volumes, says Kevin Sullivan.

"Eric told me," he remembers, "'don't *ever* let that happen again'."

Chapter 24:
Match of the Century

It WAS BILLED as the *Match of the Century*, an apparently perfect culmination of almost 18 months of storytelling. On December 28th, 1997, in front of a sold out MCI Center in Washington, D.C., Hollywood Hogan would finally - surely - receive his comeuppance against the most loyal of WCW's soldiers, the 'Franchise', Sting. "We built that story perfectly," reminisces Bischoff. "It was totally incomprehensible to the Kevin Sullivan's of the world, to the Dusty Rhodes' of the world, and other people who were involved, at various times, in the creative process. They would have never dreamed that you could build an arc like that. It worked magnificently."

Despite the urging of Sullivan, who envisioned a buildup of several months for the match, Bischoff demonstrated tremendous patience in reserving the showdown for *Starrcade*. While some 469 days had elapsed since Steve Borden last competed in the ring, he initially appeared ready to make up for lost time. "Sting showed up on time," confirms Bischoff. "Everything was fine. He was always very good about [arriving to the arena on time]. Then he sat down with Hulk and I, to kind of talk through the details of what we had been planning."

Soon, however, Bischoff says he realized something was awry. "[As] Sting walked into the room, he was a broken man," he recalls. "He looked soft, he looked pale. He was uninspired. He wasn't into it. As an entertainer, you have to take care of yourself. Mick Jagger doesn't go out there with a beer gut, looking bloated, and not being able to move. You have to be able to perform to the audience's expectation.

"Hulk and I both looked at each other, and, y'know...we didn't articulate it, but we were both thinking the same thing. We thought, 'my god, we've built this thing for almost a year, and done a phenomenal job [in the process]. Hulk is ready to do what the audience wants us to do, and Sting doesn't look like he bothered to even bring

205

his wrestling gear'."

Unquestionably, after over a year on the sidelines (or more accurately, in the rafters), Sting did appear to be less than fully fit, as evident upon his ring entrance hours later. However, to what extent this warranted a change in narrative direction was debatable, with one perspective - shared subsequently and often by many fans - viewing Sting's condition to be irrelevant. Their hero may not have been as hulking as Hogan, but arguably, he still looked capable - on the surface - of getting the job done.

Not so, says Bischoff. "At that point, we were both really taken aback," he continues. "Hulk wasn't excited about following through with what we all agreed to. We had all agreed that Sting was gonna come in and 'right the wrong's', and defeat Hulk Hogan. That was the plan going in, but when Sting got there, it looked like he just wasn't into it. We had to re-think it."

Prior to the main event, *Starrcade '97* struggled to live up to its billing, with a disjointed undercard dampening the crowd. Originally, WCW looked to pay off a number of other feuds at the pay-per-view, including Kevin Nash vs. The Giant, Ric Flair vs. Curt Hennig, and Chris Benoit vs. Raven. On the day of the show, however, Nash called out sick, later claiming that a batch of pot brownies gave him chest pain. Flair was set to gain revenge on Hennig in a cage match, but was forced out due to injury. And in a late booking decision, Benoit and Raven didn't occur either, their rivalry pushed off for another month.

In the semi-main event, Larry Zybysko defeated Bischoff to secure the rights to *Monday Nitro*, bringing the crowd back alive for the marquee match-up. Enjoying a ring introduction from Michael Buffer, Hogan entered first for the main event, suddenly full of confidence after running from Sting all year. The returning hero came out next, stoically sauntering to the ring before locking eyes with the hated Hogan.

For the next 10 minutes, Hogan dominated a mostly flat contest, setting up a faux ending bungled up at the last minute. While earlier in the night, referee Nick Patrick had been instructed to perform a 'fast count' - effectively screwing Sting to induce the intervention of Bret Hart - he was subsequently told to do the opposite. "One guy came up to me and told me to fast count it," Patrick claimed in a later interview, "and the other guy said 'don't fast count it. Keep it nice and slow'. And so the person that was in charge evidently didn't want to make a call...didn't want to pick a side, and made themselves scarce all night long. I couldn't find them to ask them, 'hey, what do you want me to do?'"

Hart's involvement had been planned since November, but sans the 'fast count' ending, according to journalist Dave Meltzer. "[Bischoff] told me the finish in early November," he later wrote on his website, "[but the] only thing different was Nick didn't do the fast count."

Ultimately, the 'fast count' would be anything but - Patrick counted in his normal cadence, it appeared, after Hogan stunned Sting with a leg drop. Incredibly, Sting then laid on the mat as Patrick counted to '3', effectively ending the match fair-and-square. Lost in the commotion and chaos, Bret Hart wondrously emerged at ringside, restarted the match ("*I'm not gonna let someone get screwed again!*") and as Hogan submitted to Sting's Scorpion Death Lock, Hart called for the bell. Ostensibly, Hogan had finally been defeated, but due to the nature of its execution, the ending almost made his character sympathetic. Who really got screwed?

"The referee's count looked normal to me," offers Kevin Sullivan. "It wasn't supposed to be like that...somebody conned somebody.

"I knew the fix was in. I may not be the brightest bulb in the pack, but I could see through that."

"Someone had to get in Patrick's ear," suggests WCW referee Johnny Boone. "As a referee, there were plenty of times where Hogan or Macho Man would pull me in a room and say, 'hey man, this what we're going to do tonight'. They would tell you just like that. But when the finish went down at *Starrcade*, a lot of people were like, 'what the hell?'"

207

"I was very disappointed," laments Bischoff, "just like the audience was. Just like Hulk Hogan was. Just like Sting was. Everybody was disappointed in the way that it ended. A large part of that disappointment was a result of the huge investment...and the success we enjoyed in the 12 months leading up to the payoff."

Curiously, as Sting celebrated among a horde of WCW wrestlers, he turned to deliver an impromptu on-camera utterance. Although mostly unintelligible, his comments audibly included the phrase "mamacita," a statement rather incongruous with the 'Crow Sting' character. "After such a long build up," remembers WCW producer Jason Douglas, "it was confusing to us why the finish wasn't clean, why Sting spoke in Spanish at the end, and why we needed the Bret Hart involvement. Of course, we were looking for a way to inject Bret into a top-tier storyline, but I think there are multiple reasons why it just didn't work.

"Hogan dropped the belt to Luger during the summer, and this minimized the result of Sting's win. Plus I guess the thought was, 'if Sting wins clean, what reason will the viewers have to tune-in during the next few weeks?'"

When asked if Hogan "ix-nayed" a finish involving Sting winning 'clean', Bischoff responds directly. "Hulk *did* ix-nay [the finish] - so did I," he states. "But we did it for a reason. It wasn't Hulk Hogan's ego, it wasn't me being deferential to Hulk because he was Hulk Hogan. It was a very valid reason.

"I want to be really careful here. Sting - Steve Borden - is a friend of mine. He's someone whom I have a tremendous amount of respect for. But...he had some personal issues that I didn't know about, quite frankly. They were serious personal issues, involving his family, his marriage...and all kinds of chilling things that none of us who knew him well were aware of.

"During the 12 months that were leading up to the payoff, Sting would show up, do his 'scary guy' in the rafters gimmick, and we would sneak him in and out of the building. He would do his thing...it would work...and he'd go home and we'd go about our business. None of us were really aware of what was going on in his life. Now I know he was dealing with some heavy, *heavy* duty stuff.

"If you go back and look at the obvious [indicators], he wasn't in the ring wrestling. He wore that long, dark trench coat. He had a full face of make-up. We couldn't tell physically what was going on - or not going on - with Sting. Until it came time to finish off the story, at *Starrcade*."

Its latest chapter notwithstanding, the story of Sting's near-mythical metamorphosis had been incredibly successful. "World Championship Wrestling continues to astound and surprise the pay-per-view industry," wrote Thomas Umstead for *MultiChannel News*. "The show earned a preliminary 1.9 percent buy-rate...the third-biggest PPV event of 1997 [across all entertainment genres].

"The show, which pitted former World Wrestling Federation wrestler Hulk Hogan against WCW staple Sting, was aided by a yearlong story-line buildup, which WCW exploited on its *Monday Night Nitro* weekly wrestling event. At a suggested retail price of $29.95, Starrcade grossed about $18 million."

Commercially, *Starrcade* exceeded all expectations. From a critical standpoint, however, its residual effects would surely metastasize in 1998. "Maybe," summarizes Bischoff, "if we would have stuck to the plan...Sting would have come around. Maybe he would've got back into the gym, got re-motivated and all that. Maybe. But when you're sitting there, having to make a decision, and you're looking at a guy who looked like...he looked like *me* for crying out loud.

"He just didn't look like Sting, and not what the audience would have expected. As a result, Hogan wasn't as excited about doing what we had talked about doing, because he didn't feel like Sting was in the game. That's the truth.

"[Again], I didn't understand what Sting was going through at the time. I may have made a different decision, had I known. But he didn't look like he prepared. He didn't look like he was interested in [the match]. He kind of had a blasé attitude.

"People can believe me or not believe me. I really don't give two shits anymore."

Chapter 25:
Mr. President

Despite the bungled *Starrcade* finish - and a subsequent rematch where Hogan *pinned* Sting - WCW entered 1998 on top of the wrestling world. With a 76-week win streak over the competition, the leading prime-time show on basic cable, a second weekly prime-time program imminent, the signing of Bret Hart, and a seemingly endless combination of marquee names to fight on pay-per-view, all signs pointed towards continued success across every major revenue stream.

According to a source familiar with its financial records, WCW generated $112 million over the course of 1997, and for Eric Bischoff, the new year brought some additional good news. After first being hired as a third-string announcer in 1991, Bischoff's seven-year odyssey - fraught with fighting substantial doubt and disbelief along the way - culminated in a well-deserved promotion. "The leadership of Eric Bischoff has built WCW into an extremely dynamic, successful company," beamed Dr. Harvey Schiller in a company press release. "We look forward to the exciting impact his direction will bring to WCW's future."

Bischoff was on a serious roll, and not only when he rode his 'chopper' to work, parking in a spot three places removed from Ted Turner. He was earning around a half-million dollars a year, receiving Rolex watches as bonus compensation, and sporting a pair of cowboy boots at his desk. Regardless of the *Starrcade* debacle, the aura of his midas touch remained, promising a future as bright as his favorite Harley's handlebars.

More importantly, on an institutional level, the long-rooted perception of WCW was evolving. On the golf course, Bischoff learned, Turner EVP Terry McGuirk couldn't stop talking about WCW. In the halls of Techwood, Steve Heyer (the incumbent corporate CEO) was adopting the 'nWo' hand sign when passing staffers at work. With *Thunder* set to debut on January 8th, everyone apparently wanted *more* wrestling - including, in a circular irony, the network that started it all - TBS SuperStation ("we were dying for [*Thunder*]," remembers network President Bill Burke). Effective from January 26th, TNT would benefit too, *expanding* the length of *Nitro* to three hours.

Gaining *internal* acceptance of WCW's existence, an uphill battle ever since the Turner acquisition, represented a remarkable accomplishment for its new President. "It was kind of a big deal, really," Bischoff says proudly. "I was able to get more personal satisfaction out of that...than any other thing you may have read or heard about. WCW was the loud, obnoxious, red-headed stepchild that nobody in the Turner organization wanted anything to do with. It was almost like, 'oh, Ted Turner owns a little porn company'. It was *almost* that kind of a feeling amongst the other executives. The higher up you got in the organization, the more disdain there was for our division.

"When things started really turning around...I would get a phone call almost every Tuesday afternoon when the ratings came out from Ted Turner himself, and Scott Sassa. Brad Siegel certainly would call me...it was usually the three of them that would call and congratulate me. So my immediate bosses were very happy.

"But to imagine somebody at Terry McGuirk's level, playing on the golf course amongst their country club friends, talking about *Nitro* - in a positive way – that was a really, really rewarding thing for me. [Turner staff] were calling the office asking for tickets because their friends and family were coming to town, and they wanted to meet some of the wrestlers backstage. That had never happened before in WCW - *ever*.

"We were able to change the way, internally, people looked at wrestling - at least the way they looked at WCW - for the most part. We didn't convert everybody, but we did a fairly good job of converting a lot of people who never thought they'd be converted."

212

The looming *external* test - addressing the reluctance of advertisers to spend money on wrestling - remained a formidable one. "As a fan, I loved what Eric did," says Joe Uva, then-President of Turner Entertainment Sales and Marketing. "As a guy in charge of all the [ad] revenue, it was hard.

"A lot of brands looked at it as neither 'fish nor fowl'. They were upset by some of the content, namely a lot of the scantily-clad women. When some of the events got a little bit outrageous…if they started to show blood, or guys got hit over the head with chairs [or if there were] ladder matches and things like that…advertisers would get a little squeamish.

"We would bring them to live events. They would watch the shows, meet some of the folks, and they were [generally] entertained. But somewhere along the line, in their advertising guidelines, there would inevitably be [a notice stating that] 'we avoid gratuitous sex and violence'. That became a challenge."

"There were definitely some fundamental objections that advertisers had," says Mike Ciraldo, a Sales Manager for WCW. "Sometimes the storylines got a little out of hand, and you had some distasteful content - although more so on the WWF side."

On the surface, it seemed plausible that wrestling's problem of perception could actually be leveraged. To the uninitiated, there appeared to be obvious crossover potential with distinctly 'adult' brands - beer companies, for example - but according to Uva, it wasn't quite as straightforward. "I had always wanted to go to Anheuser-Busch, and Miller, and Coors, and some of the other beers," he remembers, "but because the percentage of the audience under 21 was so high, we couldn't. That eliminated potentially the biggest category of advertisers."

Alternative strategies included packaging WCW programming alongside other prime-time offerings, reveals Uva. "You'd say [to advertisers], 'ok, you're gonna get prime-time across the week -

Monday to Sunday'. But even then, some would say, 'ok, but we're not taking wrestling - it's inconsistent with who our brand is'.

"You also had some negative news that came out about the wrestlers. Guys that were beating up women, getting in brawls, using steroids…[all of this] caused advertisers to shy away. But if you found an advertiser with somebody in the marketing department or advertising services department who was a closet wrestling fan, you could leverage that. [Those people] understood what it was."

———

On January 8th, 1998, the first edition of *WCW Thunder* aired on TBS, reportedly becoming the most watched (4.0) cable debut in history. But while its launch coincided with intensified concerns over talent and staff burnout, there would also be less visible implications for Turner Ad Sales. After all, two *additional* hours of wrestling programming - the consequence of Ted's ambition to capitalize on *Nitro*'s success - meant absorbing a commensurate increase in available inventory. It would mean selling even more spots and commercial time for the property, bereft of any real growth in CPM.

Enter Neill Cameron. As President of Ogilvy & Mather South - a division of the legendary New-York based ad agency - Cameron had enjoyed a long working relationship with Turner Broadcasting. With *Nitro* helping TNT finish 1997 as the top-rated cable network in prime time, Turner executives, he recalls, approached him to work with WCW on brand advertising. "Turner [was] a hot property in Atlanta, and I ran a hot advertising agency," says Cameron, the runner-up in 1995's *Advertising Man of the Year*. "We had been involved in some very high-profile sports and entertainment activities. We had done *Wild World of Golf* - a very popular 90-minute golf 'travelogue' with golf celebrities. We did the work for the '96 Olympic Games, and I was on the organizing committee for that. I was Chairman of the Peach Bowl at that time. We also handled the marketing for four NASCAR teams.

"So my agency, and myself specifically, were involved in a lot of

214

sports and entertainment-related activity, in Atlanta, and nationally. That's why, I think, [Turner executives] came to me and said, 'help us with WCW'."

In 1980, the MLB's Houston Astros - scrambling after signing Nolan Ryan to a lucrative (for the time) $1 million per year contract - approached Cameron while he was working in Ogilvy's Houston office ("They said, 'we gotta sell 35,000 season tickets to pay for this guy'," the veteran marketer chuckles). Consequently, his agency developed the first *mini-season* ticket program in sports, enabling patrons to purchase a group of tickets - 'weekenders' for example - rather than paying for every home game.

The strategy was instantly successful - so successful, in fact, that word soon reached Ted Turner. "Ted had just got the Atlanta Braves," remembers Cameron. "I saw him one day in the airport, and obviously I introduced myself. We got to talking, and he mentioned the Houston Astros campaign. I said, 'well yeah Ted, I was involved in that when I was in the Houston Office for Ogilvy'. He said, 'well, we need to do something like that!' I said, 'well you need to hire a smart advertising agency to do that for you'. He said, 'well, I'm the smartest person I know!' I saw him later at cable TV conventions, and we laughed about that."

"But Ted was very inventive, not only in programming, but in technology also. He really got it. It's no accident that Ted is a genius and a billionaire. I've sat in the room with him, where everybody in the room disagreed with where he was going - except for him. And it turned out to be successful - CNN, for one [idea]. If you were in Atlanta in the media advertising business, and you weren't studying Ted Turner, you weren't alive!"

Although admittedly, Cameron lacked an up-to-date product knowledge in regards to its televised storylines, the surge in popularity experienced by WCW had not passed him by ("in my opinion, it was a phenomenon," he asserts). While Ted's support of the genre had long confounded others, Cameron believed a confluence of factors - both short and long-term - explained why WCW survived, and ultimately, thrived.

"Number one, Turner created a lot of properties with his *SuperStation*. He desperately needed programming - *original* programming. Ted didn't buy the Atlanta Braves and the Atlanta Hawks because he was a sports fan, he bought them because he needed original programming to populate his station. WCW [functioned] as that also. He wanted to control that inventory, versus buying syndicated programming all the time. He built some pretty successful networks, [like] the Cartoon Network, [for example], by going out and buying Hanna-Barbera's inventory. Obviously his movie channel was created through buying old movie inventory. He was constantly looking for his own wholly-owned programming, and he had a proclivity towards sports, entertainment and news. All of that suggested a type of program like this.

"Secondly, the ability of the SuperStation [played a role]. This is the time when distribution in media had gone to a totally different paradigm. My entire life growing up, we had three channels...ABC, NBC, CBS...about six magazines, and about six radio channels. Well, we know where we are today. Of course, Ted was one of the architects of taking broadcast [media] to a new level.

"Thirdly, all of a sudden, extreme sports, if you will, were becoming popular. Before that, you didn't have a lot of extreme sports. You had the sports we all grew up playing in grade school and high school. [At this time], you had NASCAR on the scene where people are flocking, in hundreds of thousands, to see people crash on the race track. You had everything from Motorcross to the snow sports, [and so on].

"Pro wrestling was kind of a niche between traditional sports and extreme sports. Now, they may not have known that - at the time - but if you look at it in hindsight, that's what it was.

"Finally, you add the personalities at play here. Vince McMahon ain't gonna let Ted Turner one-up him. So he's in this for the long run. Eric Bischoff has got a pretty big ego himself...and then you've got the talent which is over the moon [in terms of personality].

"So I thought it was a phenomenon. It wasn't just any programming alternative out of the programming department, like what happens in Hollywood for networks these days. It was the confluence of many things at that time. People may disagree, but I watched it happen.

"Advertisers didn't understand all of that, but they did understand that there was a phenomenon going on. They said, 'there's something weird going on out there'. They didn't know if wrestling could be categorized as sports, entertainment, theater, reality TV...[but in fact] this was probably your first reality TV [type of programming]!"

In his first meeting with Eric Bischoff, Cameron was immediately struck by his presence. "I've been around clients that I wouldn't wanna spend more than five minutes with. I found Bischoff to be very engaging. He was smart, confident, and very clear as to what he wanted. He said, 'we have to get the advertising time up, make it more valuable, and we gotta sell some sponsorships so we can make some money'. He said, '...because we're gonna spend it'. And he did!"

With WCW (as a Turner company) capable of producing its own marketing materials, Cameron focused mostly on two specific goals: overcoming advertiser bias, and selling sponsorships through advertising agencies. "It evolved more towards that, rather than doing the traditional 'brand advertising' and building the brand - although we did some of that," he says.

In time, Cameron found certain clients, *Snickers* as one prominent example, to be amenable towards sponsoring *specific* WCW events. From that standpoint, his contributions towards creating revenue growth - coupled with later efforts to support endorsement opportunities for wrestlers - could be ranked as significant. However, gaining a more concrete commitment from businesses proved to be difficult, with the ever-present stigma around wrestling rearing its head once more.

"The traditional big buck advertisers were *very* reluctant to get involved with [wrestling], for the obvious reasons - image [and so

217

on]," he says. "If we woulda had some of the advertisers that we have today - the *Go Daddy*'s of the world and other companies that have an edge to their brand - it would have been a lot easier. In the '90s, the people who had the money were very traditional brand marketers. They were very aware of their brand status. If we went - and we did by the way - to someone like *General Foods*...and you talk to the brand managers, and marketing director there and say, 'do you wanna do something', they would say 'oh no, we gotta think about that'.

"It seemed like everybody had a reason not to do it - even though everybody was intrigued by it."

At the same time as Cameron's intervention, a collaborative effort was underway to help further boost the cause. In early 1998, a special 'spring break' episode of *Nitro* provided the impetus, recalls Michael Polydoroff, a Marketing Project Manager for TNT. "WCW wanted to refresh, and really hit the spring break audience," he says, referencing what would become a yearly company tradition. "They were hosting an actual live wrestling event in Panama City, Florida, and we were given about eight weeks notice to create some excitement for it.

"[Previously], we had the Ad Sales people come to the marketing folks and say, 'we have got to somehow turn around the perception on this property'. They said, 'we're not sure how, but we are really losing so much revenue from people that are not booking because they have stereotypes [about wrestling]'."

"So we knew we needed to create something to engage the buyer - and the marketing person at the brand we were pitching - as well as start to show people that we have a broader audience. It was a really interesting time, because there was a lot of tolerance, a lot of patience, a lot of acceptance of the relationship between marketing and sales. It was to the point where we would start to go on calls with them to pitch ideas for WCW, and soon we started to create more in the arsenal of promotional marketing."

In an effort to recruit more desirable clients, Polydoroff says, he believed it possible to leverage the presence of existing ones at the

Panama City event. "Through sampling and signage," he details, "you could show the consumer having fun. The WCW property was being engaged, and the retailer looked good [too]. I could then use this example to get the people I really wanted to go after - people that were saying 'no' to me."

Although the concept of a 'Spring Break' *Nitro* originated in 1997, Polydoroff plotted to dramatically expand its scope for 1998. At first, however, his efforts were met with resistance from a protective Eric Bischoff. "I was completely intimidated," he admits. "Eric was very hard, very distrusting, very skeptical. Usually I had to have Brad Siegel with me to kind of temper his [objections]. [His attitude was], 'this isn't gonna work, what are you doing in my business, get out of my property'. We were trying to say, 'hey, we're here to help'. It was a very tumultuous start.

"It was intense. He cared so much, like, 'what are you gonna do for my baby?' 'How are you going to treat it?' He was very skeptical, and so I literally had to put all my heart and soul to prove [myself] to him."

In light of a recent revelation, Bischoff certainly had reason to be uptight. He was in Florida completing his pilot certification when the phone rang. It was Zane Bresloff - the marketing guru with whom he spoke compulsively - and the news was a shocker. *McMahon has signed Mike Tyson*, Bresloff advised.

Tyson's association with the WWF arose at a time when he was - unquestionably - the most controversial athlete in all of sports. He emerged from a 1997 fight with Evander Holyfield as a disgraced figure, suffering the loss of his boxing license after a bizarre ear-biting incident. Boxing was out of the question, but that said nothing of pro wrestling. For McMahon, it was a brilliant acquisition, thought Bischoff. "That was a turning point," he confesses.

The 'Iron Mike' signing fit perfectly with the gradual shift in the WWF's content. Throughout the previous year, while *Nitro* brazenly reigned supreme in the ratings, *Raw* enjoyed a quiet uptick in viewership, owing in large part to its newly risqué tone. On December

15th, McMahon officially acknowledged the new direction with an on-screen address on *Monday Night Raw*:

"It has been said that anything can happen here in the World Wrestling Federation, but now more than ever, truer words have never been spoken. This is a conscious effort on our part to 'open the creative envelope', so to speak, in order to entertain you in a more contemporary manner. Even though we call ourselves 'Sports Entertainment' because of the athleticism involved, the keyword in that phrase is 'Entertainment'. The WWF extends far beyond the strict confines of sports presentation into the wide open environment of broad based entertainment. We borrow from such programs niches like soap-operas, like 'The Days of Our Lives', or music videos such as those on MTV, Daytime talk-shows like 'Jerry Springer' and others, cartoons like 'The King of The Hill' on FOX, Sitcoms like 'Seinfeld', and other widely accepted forms of television entertainment. We, in the WWF, think that you, the audience, are quite frankly tired of having your intelligence insulted. We also think that you're tired of the same old simplistic theory of 'Good Guys' versus 'Bad Guys'...

"Therefore, we've embarked on a far more innovative and contemporary creative campaign, that is far more invigorating and extemporaneous than ever before. However, due to the live nature of 'Raw' and the 'WarZone', we encourage some degree of parental discretion, as relates to the younger audience allowed to stay up late...

"As the times have changed, so have we. I'm happy to say that this new vibrant, creative direction has resulted in a huge increase in television viewership, for which we thank the USA Network...for allowing us to have the creative freedom."

As far as Bischoff was concerned, the new era of WWF programming - eventually immortalized as *The Attitude Era* - simply adapted the formula that made *Nitro* successful. "Vince McMahon adapted the formula that we perfected, and decided to do it even bigger and better," he says. "He went after our audience, and he was willing to

220

take bigger risks. He used Mike Tyson to [help] do it, and it was *fantastic*."

Although retrospective reports have alleged that Bischoff missed out on the Tyson signing, he refutes the claim unreservedly. "I recently read," he sighs, "that Bret Hart said I told him that I had a chance to get Mike Tyson. That's fucking...[look], I never had a conversation with Mike Tyson, or any of his representatives."

Post-Montreal, McMahon was brilliantly capitalizing on fans' real-life animus towards his treatment of Hart. In his new role as 'Mr. McMahon', he now featured heavily on *Raw* as a contemptible, egomaniacal boss, a character inspired, Bischoff claims, by his own heel turn as nWo leader (McMahon already took a turn as an on-screen villain, however, in an obscure 1992 cross-promotional angle).

McMahon's most common foil was 'Stone Cold' Steve Austin, a 33-year old beer-swilling brawler and ironically, a former employee of WCW. As he would tire of being reminded, Bischoff had fired an injury-prone Austin some three years earlier, delivering the news via FedEx. It was a decision he still defended resolutely. "Steve Austin would be a midcard player in WCW," he told *Off The Record* that spring. "[He's] a big fish in a relatively small pond."

On January 19th, Tyson starred in an in-ring confrontation on *Raw*, acting apparently as an ally of McMahon. In an example of perfect casting, Austin was chosen to be his adversary, and the two engaged in a classic pull-apart scuffle. "*TYSON AND AUSTIN, TYSON AND AUSTIN!*" yelled announcer Jim Ross, himself a WCW castoff.

On *Nitro*, meanwhile, Bischoff was building towards another Sting-Hogan match, this time with the inherent promise of narrative closure. In a promotional video for the event, the slow count employed by Nick Patrick was artificially sped up, an effective attempt to atone for *Starrcade*'s sins.

———

221

Somewhere around this time - although no-one could *quite* be sure when - Turner's legal counsel prepared to make David Crockett an offer. As WCW's VP of Production, Crockett had been on staff since the Turner buyout, and in fact, Jim Crockett Promotions still maintained a minority interest in WCW (reflected in TBS' annual 10-K report, which showed JCP as owning 100 shares of 'non-voting Class B common stock').

"I was called in to Turner's in-house counsel's office one afternoon," recalls Crockett. "It was, 'this is what we will buy you out for. Say yes or no. If no, the offer goes away'. No discussion."

"It was raining money for WCW, TBS and TNT because of our shows. [Therefore], management did not want me to have time or the numbers to see if the [payout] was too low."

"It was never the intent of Turner management that WCW make money," claims Dick Cheatham of TBS, "because the Crockett family still owned a participating interest in WCW. If WCW started making *real* money, the Crockett's would have a substantial interest in those earnings.

"Of course, you can still make money that you don't have to share by recognizing ad revenue at TBS - not WCW, [for example]. But the scheme begins to deteriorate when you crank up 'PPV's' to twelve a year, with buy rates rising, and no way to recognize the cash flow at another Turner entity.

"Greed is an ugly thing, especially when your success depends on screwing a business partner or associate. If you can acquire control of a property without buying the whole thing, and then assure that it never makes income you have to share with a partner, you win.

"[But] if they actually understood the wrestling business, they would have understood the high risk business model of WCW.

"For over a year they were setting up Sting vs. Hogan.

"Nothing else was in the pipeline."

222

Chapter 26:
Taking on Water

At *SUPERBRAWL*, Sting defeated Hogan in a spirited rematch, capturing the WCW World Heavyweight Title for the fourth time. In a clever inversion of an nWo trope, the Stinger spray-painted 'WCW' on the back of Hogan, apparently alluding to the end of their personal saga. And although the *Starrcade* hype could never be recaptured, 415,000 fans paid to see him do it, establishing the event as WCW's second most successful pay-per-view ever.

Furthermore, despite the WWF's purported resurgence, *Nitro* was staying on top in the Nielsen numbers. After a close scare (4.5 to 4.0) on January 19th - Mike Tyson's introduction on *Raw* - the weekly differential surprisingly settled back to normal. By February 23rd, the gap stood at 1.4, with *Nitro* registering a 4.6 rating to a 3.2 achieved by *Raw*. On March 9th, *Nitro* cruised to its 85th straight victory with a 4.9 rating, tied for its highest (head-to-head) number of all-time.

But on Tuesday, March 10th, the Internet was abuzz with rumors of some serious discord behind the scenes. Details were sketchy, but the newsboard Micasa.com was reporting that Sean 'Syxx' Waltman had been fired. The 25-year old was still rehabilitating from an October neck injury, but despite disappearing from the screen, Hall and Nash frequently made televised references to his status. Above all else, the trio were still part of *The Kliq*, and for that reason, it figured wise to not to inflame any political tensions.

In private, however, Bischoff was furious over Waltman's attempt to renegotiate his contract, to say nothing of the involvement of his agent, Barry Bloom. During a heated conversation with Bloom the previous Friday, Bischoff reportedly made the first threat of termination, warning the representative directly that he was "gonna fire Sean."

As a matter of principle, Bischoff detested going back on a previously agreed-upon deal. *I do not renegotiate*, he told friends, a stance he would hold into his later years. Consequently, in a manner reminiscent of the Steve Austin firing, Waltman was notified - via FedEx - that his services were no longer required.

Before *Nitro* later in the day, an incredulous Hall and Nash demanded answers from the boss. *I'll fix it*, said Bischoff, whose subsequent inaction only made things worse. Backstage at *Thunder* three days later, the duo stepped up their pressure. According to Waltman, his Kliq companions trapped Bischoff in a backstage closet, culminating in Nash requesting a contractual release of his own.

The request was unheeded, and Nash went to the Internet to express his frustration. In an online chat before *Uncensored* - the latest pay-per-view produced amid all the offstage commotion - he confessed to being "irate" at the recent developments. "I had a long talk with Eric," Nash wrote, "[and he] informed me that he has people to answer to. It was coincidental that the backstage controversy and the discontinuing of his contract came within 24 hours of each other…let's just say Eric has an explosive temper."

Such flashes of anger were apparently nothing new. "There was once a situation," recalls Jason Douglas, a WCW producer, "where they announced that Hulk beat Flair - *before the match had taken place*. The producer involved in that had a very difficult conversation in Eric's office. Eric stated, 'you can leave here one of two ways.

"One - out the door, or two - over the balcony'."

Regarding his reputation for possessing a 'short fuse', Bischoff argues such a notion is erroneous. "In truth," he says, "I was probably more lenient, forgiving and tolerant than I probably should have been - given the responsibility I had to the company.

"There were people that I should have fired multiple times - Scott Hall being one of them…for some of the crazy things Scott did and said.

The way he showed up to work, [for example]. But it wasn't just Scott - it was a lot of other people. There were certain executives that I kept on, because I was aware that this was their livelihood. I was aware that they had families. I looked the other way, and tolerated things I probably shouldn't.

"But I *do* call 'bullshit'. If I feel like I'm being lied to or manipulated, I don't tolerate that. I *will* call 'bullshit' and challenge people...but that is not the same thing as being abusive, or having a 'short fuse'."

———

When truly indifferent about something, Hall and Nash - self-described 'pricks' - could be downright hilarious in their approach. In early March, Hall goofed for the camera at a deposition hearing, using the WWF's lawsuit as a chance to say "hi" to Vince McMahon. When asked to what extent he complied with an exhaustive request for documents, Hall responded thusly:

Q. How did you go about the process of complying with the subpoena in terms of locating documents that were requested, what did you do?

A. Very little.

Q. Did you do anything?

A. I brought tights.

Q. That's it?

A. Yes, sir.

For his part, Nash showcased such charm as to almost halt the proceedings. "The deposition nearly had to be stopped," says one source, "because the questioner was laughing so hard at his answers. It's still the only case I've ever seen where that's happened."

When genuinely angered, however, Hall and Nash could be practically unmanageable. Since their return to WCW, they had always provided creative input, but with Waltman now fired, the duo

225

decided to refrain. There would be no more brainstorming, swapping of ideas, or help with finishes - Hall and Nash now viewed themselves strictly as contracted talent.

Step one unfolded on Monday, March 16th - the date of the Spring Break *Nitro* in Panama City. Accompanied by a case of Budweiser and matching Hawaiian shirts, the duo showed up halfway into an all-day drinking session, causing Bischoff to reportedly blow a gasket before show time. *Are you gonna go in?* Bischoff prodded at Hall, referring to the need to attend a rehabilitation facility. Unmoved, Hall quipped back with the wit that his character was famous for, noting the presence of a swimming pool surrounding the ring. *Yeah, I'll go in the pool - make sure nobody else goes in.*

Shockingly, the Outsiders made their way on to the broadcast, cutting an obviously impaired interview that bordered on breaking the fourth wall ("*hey Giant, that's your cue,*" cracked Hall over the live microphone). But in concert with the frenetic style of *Nitro*, their involvement only added to the fun of the broadcast. Later on, in a breathtaking visual, the show featured an incredible entrance as World Champion Sting arrived for the main event. "It was like a Vietnam movie!" exclaims Mike Ciraldo. "Sting was lowered from a helicopter - down a wire and into the ring. That's how he made his entrance!"

"At *Club La Vela,*" recalls lighting director Jeff Bornstein, in reference to the venue, "we had a floating ring that we had to lower over the building - with a crane - into the swimming pool!

"Sting came in on the helicopter and rappelled down a rope into the ring. I used a rope with a sandbag on the bottom of it - as a guide for his rappel. The helicopter took off, and the sandbag got caught on one of my scaffold towers, with a spotlight on that tower. It started to lift [the spotlight] off the ground, but fortunately, it broke free."

As far as the tipsy college crowd could tell, however, the stunt acted as the perfect finale to an uproariously fun day. "We basically created an entire fan experience," remembers Michael Polydoroff, "leading up to the actual wrestling show. We had games, we had wrestler

226

appearances, and we had signage opportunities for brands. We created this atmosphere just showing people having fun.

"The net result was that advertisers were happy, because they were getting that desired demographic of college kids. The wrestlers were happy, because they didn't realize that they could sit on the beach, basically catch a tan, and sign autographs. They could engage with fans who were really passionate, and weren't...your [stereotypical] 50 year old, 500-pound guy, [for example]. It was a crowd of [college] kids that looked up to them, very awestruck and thereby an easier crowd to tame and excite."

The popularity of *Nitro* in Panama City reflected the existence of a wider trend, recalls Rob Garner, WCW's former VP of TV Programming and Sales. "We discovered that the Ivy League schools would have these '*Nitro* parties' on Monday nights," he says. "They would get together at Brown, Cornell, Princeton...and they would sit there and watch these shows. Somebody thought - and it might have been Eric - 'we oughta have people send in video of their parties'. [And] then the best ones, we'd go there - to that town or that market - and do live 'cut-ins' at these schools.

"So all of a sudden, we could go to New York ad agencies and say, 'hey, if you thought wrestling was a bunch of hicks and people in pickup trucks with two teeth and overalls, think again'. It showed that wrestling transcended everything. Everybody thought that it was just for people who were ignorant and didn't have any sense. But no, people in Ivy League schools loved it too!

"When we had a presentation to give to advertisers or potential sponsors, they couldn't believe it. We said, 'it's real - we couldn't produce this stuff!'"

While it may not have been possible for WCW to preemptively produce its 'cool factor' on college campuses, its competitor produced a stunning *Wrestlemania* pay-per-view on March 30th. Before each match, Kevin Nash remembers, video retrospectives aired to inform viewers of the attached storyline, a technique that would become a company staple ("Vince [McMahon] put a movie trailer type package that took you through everything leading up to *Wrestlemania,*" he observes). In a heart-stopping main event, 'Stone Cold' Steve Austin then captured the WWF championship, while Mike Tyson, participating as a special referee, lifted his hand in victory.

At first, initial industry estimates pegged *Mania* as drawing a 1.8 buy rate (a slightly poorer performance than *Starrcade*), leading Bischoff to deride the notion of a WWF turnaround. "That's a joke," he stated defiantly. "Given all of the publicity, and the reported $6 million that Titan spent on Tyson and Don King…the fact that it's only coming in at a 1.8 buyrate - and considering that *Nitro* still beat *Raw* by 0.6 - I hardly consider that a shift in momentum.

"In fact, I think that in a short time, *Nitro* will be back to a 1.0 to 1.5 advantage. They gave it their best shot with Tyson. Their best shot was weak at best. I don't think the future looks very bright for the WWF on USA Network."

Kevin Sullivan took a different view. For all the talk of branding, marketing, demographics and promotion, the veteran booker still understood what truly moved the dial in wrestling. He watched *Wrestlemania* intently, marveling at the integration of Tyson into the marquee match with Austin. "I remember Kevin Sullivan saw me the next day," says Nash, "and he asked me, 'brother, did you feel that?'

"I said, 'what's *that?*'

"He said, 'the water just got real cold - we're close to the iceberg'.

"I felt it that night, [too]."

By the time the final buy rate number reached the press, Sullivan's suspicions had been confirmed. Unfathomably, reports indicated that *Wrestlemania* garnered a 2.2 buy rate, its 836,000 buys ranking 18% higher than *Starrcade*.

Sullivan wondered if others could feel the iceberg yet. On March 30th, the WWF grabbed headlines when a fired-up Sean Waltman returned to the company on *Raw*. In an emotional, stunningly direct promo, he stood in the ring and on camera, took aim at Bischoff and WCW:

"Kevin Nash and Scott Hall would be standing right here...if they weren't being held hostage by World Championship Wrestling. And that's a fact, Eric Bischoff!"

Bischoff decided to issue an immediate response, one that would remove any shred of ambiguity about his motives. "I hired Sean Waltman because of Hall and Nash," he wrote in a Tuesday chat on the *Prodigy* web service. "[Then] basically, I terminated Sean Waltman because of a combination of Hall and Nash, and Waltman's neck injury.

"Both Scott Hall and Kevin Nash have a track record - both in the WWF and here in WCW - of being fairly disruptive in the locker room. I made it clear to Scott Hall on the first day he came back that one of the things I was most proud and protective of...was that the locker room and the production team was a pretty positive environment.

"...I pointed that out to Scott Hall because of his track record in the WWF and [because] I didn't want him to bring that over to WCW. I brought Sean Waltman in more as a gesture to Kevin and Scott...to create a positive environment and make them as comfortable as possible.

"...[Now], because of what I consider to be negative and disruptive behavior on their part, it was clear to me that there was nothing I could do to create a positive environment for them. In light of the fact that Waltman was [injured] more than he was able to work while with WCW, it no longer made sense to carry one of their friends under contract...it served absolutely no purpose.

"Had Sean been healthy and able to perform, I probably wouldn't have cut him loose. In light of his neck injury [though], it was a decision I felt it was time to make."

229

On Tuesday, April 7th, the Nielsen numbers revealed that *Nitro*'s lead was officially on thin ice. The show drew a 4.6, but with *Raw* climbing to a 4.4, the margin was the slimmest it had been for almost two years. Meanwhile, Bischoff was in Japan on international business, but he soon returned to encounter more unpleasantness.

WCW was in Tallahassee for *Thunder*, a weekly series that had already fallen into 'b-show' status. Earlier in the week, fans were promised that Ric Flair would make a major announcement on the broadcast, which according to various insiders, figured to concern a Four Horsemen reunion. However, in an apparent miscommunication, Flair no-showed the event, traveling to Detroit to watch his 10-year old son, Reid, compete in an AAU amateur wrestling tournament.

Flair then missed the April 13th edition of *Nitro*, an episode hosted at the Target Center in Minneapolis. Six weeks earlier, he had signed autographs at a promotional appearance in the market, helping the show sell out within 48 hours. The State Governor even declared plans to establish 'Ric Flair Day' in his honor, but before the actual show - in front of an assemblage of Flair's coworkers - Bischoff delivered his own tribute.

Only two weeks removed from the Syxx fiasco, Bischoff reportedly threatened that he would sue Flair for breach of contract. As the room full of high-price talent looked on, the rhetoric grew increasingly extreme. *I'm going to starve Flair*, Bischoff allegedly promised. *I'm gonna cause him to move out to the streets.*

Over on USA Network, meanwhile, the WWF was promoting a match between Vince McMahon and Steve Austin. Although it was eventually revealed as a ruse, their 'match' created enough interest to finally turn the tide.

At last, *Nitro*'s 88-week win streak was over.
Bischoff assured his talent that he was just getting started. *I will not*

rest, he claimed defiantly, *until I put a stake through the heart of Vince McMahon.*

Ted Turner, founder of Turner Broadcasting System

Eric Bischoff, former WCW President

Bradley J. Siegel, former President
of Turner Entertainment Networks

Bill Burke, former President of
the TBS network

232

Re: LETTER OF AGREEMENT

Dear Terry:

This letter will confirm the principal terms and conditions of the parties, World Championship Wrestling, Inc. ("WCW") and Terry Bollea p/k/a "Hulk Hogan" ("Bollea") to enter into an agreement to renew and extend the October 15, 1996 Letter of Agreement between the parties.

1.   **TERM:**   Unless otherwise extended or terminated pursuant to the terms and conditions herein, the term of this Agreement shall begin on May 29, 1998 and shall continue for a period of four (4) years through May 28, 2002 (the "Term").

2.   **BONUS:**   In consideration of Bollea's performance hereunder, WCW shall pay to Bollea a bonus in the amount of Two Million Dollars ($2,000,000) to be paid within fourteen (14) days after Bollea's execution and delivery of this Letter of Agreement (the "Agreement") to WCW.

3.   **PAY PER VIEW EVENTS**

A.   Bollea will promote, appear, wrestle and perform at six (6) pay per view ("PPV") events (the "Events") per year during Years One (1) through Three (3) of this Agreement. Bollea will be the featured wrestler at each of the Events.

An excerpt from Hulk Hogan's 1998 contract, detailing a $675,000 guarantee for pay-per-view events. *Photo Credit: Michael Sandler/Phillip*

B.   In consideration for Bollea's participation in the Events, WCW shall compensate Bollea the greater of Fifteen percent (15%) of One Hundred percent (100%) of domestic PPV cable sales received by WCW for each Event or a Six Hundred Seventy-Five Thousand Dollars ($675,000) guarantee payment (the "PPV Guarantee Payment) per Event.

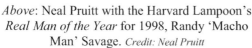

Above: Neal Pruitt with the Harvard Lampoon's *Real Man of the Year* for 1998, Randy 'Macho Man' Savage. *Credit: Neal Pruitt*

Right: Kevin Nash throws up the 'West Side' sign after defeating Goldberg at Starrcade '98. *Credit: Michael Sandler/Phillip Kidwell*

233

Left: Bill Goldberg at a promotional appearance, circa 1998. *Credit: Michael Sandler/Phillip Kidwell*

Above: The Nitro Girls entertained audiences during commercials – and on screen - from 1997 to 2000.

Note: Entrance to Break (8:52:40 - 9:00:53)
Bell to Break (8:54:47 - 9:00:53)
* During RF/AA Entrance, they come out in Kevin Greens & Steve McMichael's football jerseys.
8:55:00 - Stick of Dynamite chyron w/ digital clock appears in lower right thirds counting the seconds until the second hour of Nitro begins w/ Eric Bischoff & Bobby Heenan commentating.
8:56:00 - Lots of pyro above the ring - great pyro at Entrance
* Debut performance of Rock & Roll Express on Nitro & they have a good showing against RF/AA
8:58:14 - Ladies are shown standing in front of the VIP table during the match sipping champagne
8:59:42 - FIG 4 to RF by RRE
8:59:56 - FIG 4 to AA by other RRE
9:00:01 - AA pokes the eye of RRE that hold RF - breaks the hold
9:00:05 - Ref and RF get in a shoving match - RF leaves the ring - ref follows AA & RF - Ref smacks RF outside the ring and knocks him down.

A section of a 1996 *Nitro* format, indicating various production cues.

Neal Pruitt (far right) provides direction to Ted Turner (far left) prior to a 1994 on-screen appearance. Also pictured: Ric Flair and Bill Shaw (back to camera). *Credit: Neal Pruitt*

Surrounded by paparazzi, Kevin Nash arrives for a promotional appearance in 1998. *Credit: Michael Sandler/Phillip Kidwell*

Fans react to the commencement of *Monday Nitro* in March 1999.

Goldberg prepares to wrestle Kevin Nash at Starrcade 1998.
Credit: Michael Sandler/Phillip Kidwell

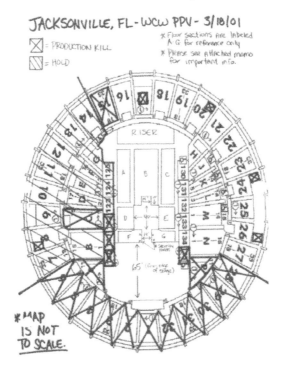

Production notes indicating camera placement for a 2001
pay-per view. *Credit: Bryan Barrera*

#40

WCW Monday Nitro

Denver, Colorado   4/10/2000

Segment #1

(1)WCW Logo Signature

(2)WCW Monday Nitro Open
Production Note:
* Rip Effect For The Open

(3)PRE-TAPE:
Establishing Shots Of Denver These Shots Include
Aerial Of Downtown
Exteriors Of The Pepsi Center
Announcer Note: These Shots Give The Announcers Time To Lay Out The Setting & Build The
Anticipation Of What's About To Go Down On Nitro

(3a)Pyro/Ballyhoo

(4)LIVE SHOT: (Ring)
WCW Talent Standing In & Around The Ring.
Talent Note:
* All Talent In Street Clothes-No Gimmicks/Talent Should Be Dressed To The Nines As Follows

3 Count	Dustin Rhodes	Disco Inferno
The Mamalukes	Screamin' Norman SmileyPG-13	
4 X 4	Stevie Ray	Big T.
Tank Abbott	Rick Steiner	Jerry Flynn
The Demon	Meng	The Artist
Paisley	Ms. Hancock	The Maestro
Symphony	La Parka	Lash LeRoux
Hammer	Chris Kanyon	Fit Finlay
Rick Fuller	Chris Candido	Horace Bolder
Crowbar	David Flair	Daffney
Juventud Guerrera	Pyschosis	Bam Bam Bigelow
The Harris Brothers	XS	Los Fabulosos
Hugh Morris	Chavo Guerrero, Jr.	Asya
Madusa	Mona	Berlyn
Kid Romeo	J Biggs	Hall

Production Note:
* No Pyro
* No Music
* Use Steady Cam For These Opening Shots Around The Ring-The Steady Cam Should Be Circling The Ring
* The Steady Cam Shots...Please Milk These Prior To Jeff Jarrett's Monologue

Announcer Note: The Announcers Should Discuss That Vince Russo Has Called This Meeting—
His Invited Guests Only!

An excerpt of the script for a 2000 *Nitro* episode.

237

```
Author:  Tony Schiavone at TBSCNNCTRWCW
Date:    3/19/96  2:07 PM
Priority: Normal
TO: Eric Bischoff
Subject: Big Boys Play
----------------------------- Message Contents -----------------------------

    Here are some more possible Big Boys Play bumps:

    --Steve Austin
    Loses to Renegade
    Loses to Ice Train in arm wrestling
    taking bumps from Flair, Arn, Steiners and Nasty Boys

    --Dustin
    loses to Arn Anderson
    taking bumps from Stevie Ray, Bobby Eaton and Lord Regal

    --Shanghai (Henry Godwin)
    Loses to Marcus Bagwell
    Loses to Sting

    --Tex (Godwin Brother)
    Loses to Savage
    Loses to Sting
    Loses to Renegade

    --Michael Hayes (Doc)
    Loses to Steiners
    Loses to Road Warriors

    --Cactus Jack
    Loses to Sting
    Loses to Taskmaster
    Loses to Orndorff

    --Badd
    Loses to Regal
    Loses to Arn
    Loses to Orndorff
    Loses to Page

    Do we want to use these, and is Cactus now with the WWF?  How about
    Badd?  Please advise.

    TONY S.
```

A Tuesday afternoon email from Tony Schiavone to Eric Bischoff, March 1996.

- V.O. NOTE: ANNOUNCE DURING MATCH THAT THE POWERS THAT BE HAVE WAIVED KEVIN NASH'S RETIREMENT, CITING IT A "RIDICULOUS ANGLE!!" THE MATCH IS NOW BOOKED FOR TONIGHT—KEVIN NASH VS. SID VICIOUS IN AN ANYTHING GOES STREET FIGHT!!!
- Creative Control Wins Match
- Creative Control Continues to Pummel Booker T.
- The Entire Arena Blacks Out and One Thundering "BONG" is heard
- When Lights Come Up, "Midnight" is standing in the middle of the Ring
1. HANDICAP TAG MATCH
    - "Midnight" Pummels Creative Control
    - Booker T. Joins the Melee
    - "Midnight" & Booker T. Clear the Ring
    - Creative Control Powders
    - Booker T. Music on Out

2. (PRE-TAPE) First Family Arguing Amongst themselves.
    - Jimmy Tnes to be Peacemaker between Jerry Flynn and Barbarian.
    - Flynn says to Barbarian: "I'll see you in the Block---and this time It won't be for fun!!!"

An excerpt from a *Monday Nitro* script, November 1999.

Diamond Dallas Page at a promotional event, circa 1998. *Credit: Michael Sandler/Phillip Kidwell*

An advertisement for WCW's '*Big Bang*' pay-per-view, planned to occur in May 2001.

Various members of WCW's production crew. From left: Kip Bissell, Neal Pruitt, Dan Bynum, Greg Leathers and Rob Wright. *Credit: Neal Pruitt*

239

THE FINKEL REPORT.....JUNE 7, 1996

DAVE MELTZER....WRESTLING OBSERVER HOT LINE

He talks about Brian Pillman, and says that "can say that the folks at WCW think they have a deal with Brian Pillman. It's been talked about, they put him on TV Monday. What the situation really is with Brian Pillman, well, time will tell. I really don't know, and if I don't know, I would say that there's probably only two or three people who do know, and maybe there's no one who knows".

He talks about Vince going on our Superstar line, saying "I have not had this story confirmed, but on his own 900 number he made some statements about Kevin Nash and Scott Hall not being part of Titan Sports, and the name Jeff Jarrett, which has fueled the rumors that Jeff Jarrett's the third man in that match. And again, those are just rumors, I don't know, but could be. The name I was given was Lex Luger" (H--Apparently there will be a six man tag team match on the July 7 pay per view in Daytona Beach, with Nash. Hall, and ?? -vs- three of WCW's talents).

An internal WWF report regarding the wrestling media, June 1996.

Left: Chad Damiani provided comic relief and insight on WCW.com.
Center: Jeff Jarrett berates David Arquette (not pictured) at the Ready to Rumble movie premiere.
Right: An overhead shot of the ring, minutes before a 2000 pay-per-view.

```
Eric Bischoff (Speaker)
We are taking a look at the/possiblity of producing another
prime time program for the TBS Network. Based on the
success of NITRO we feel that if there is an opportunity
during the week in prime time on another network that we
can generate even more interest in the WCW product.
```

Above: In a February 1997 interview, Eric Bischoff alluded to plans for a second prime-time show.

Where it all began for Eric Bischoff – sweeping the driveway at Lucy's Corner Store.

A van bearing the WCW logo followed the company to each of its events, in hopes of signing up fans to a WCW-themed credit card. *Credit: Phillip Kidwell*

Eric Bischoff (left) joins Jeremy Borash (right) for an interview on WCW.com, April 2000.

241

The revamped *Monday Nitro* logo (and its earlier iterations), developed in
spring 1999.
Credit: Stephen O'Laughlin

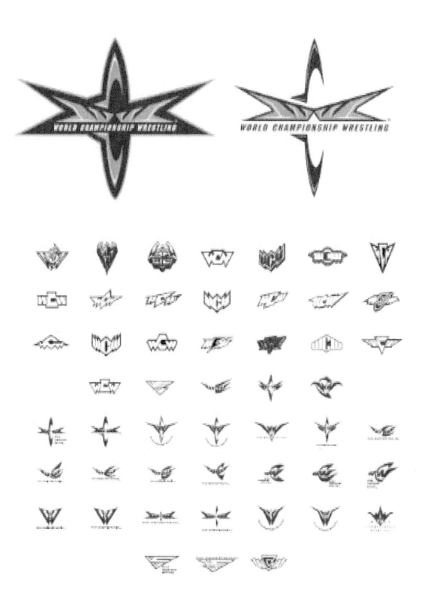

The revamped WCW logo (top left corner) and other proposed designs.
Credit: Chung Deh Tien

Chapter 27:
Calling Out Names

"THIS ISN'T what I want," stressed Eric Bischoff backstage in the locker room, his voice barely audible over the crowd's roar. "This isn't what I had in mind."

Moments before the April 20th *Nitro* - the first attempt for WCW to regain its ratings supremacy over *Raw* - Bischoff was coaching wrestler Raven on a backstage promo. Inside the arena, ring announcer David Penzer was busy getting the audience warmed up, even though the show itself was still being constructed.

"This is so out of character," lamented Raven after an aborted take. "They know he's gonna win anyway, what's the difference? Everyone knows Goldberg's winning, so I don't know…I just think the stronger [I am], the more it seems [like] he *beat* somebody."

"You're about to be killed," Bischoff stated, frustrated at Raven's inability to strike the right tone. "I don't want philosophy - I want emotion. I don't necessarily want to see you scared…that's not what I'm looking for. I don't want a 'chickenshit'. But this has gotta be…if I want people to think that he's the fuckin' shit, then you gotta react to him like he's the fuckin' shit."

The 'he' in the equation was Bill Goldberg, who since making his debut in September, had caught fire with an undefeated win streak (the brainchild, according to various sources, of announcer Mike Tenay). All of a sudden, with *Raw* the ascendant Monday night wrestling show - at least for the moment - Goldberg was penned to wrestle Raven for the United States Championship, the second most prestigious title in WCW.

"Maybe I jumped your shit and I shouldn't have," Bischoff continued with Raven, catching himself getting aggravated. "I apologize - just beat me up later.

"Please," Bischoff continued, trying to ease the mood. "Just kick my ass. It's easier...less [painful]."

"What's his record, 71-0?" Raven asked, prepping himself for another take.

"I don't know," Bischoff responded. "74, 75...78, who cares."

"74-0!" seethed Raven back in character, the cameras again rolling. "74-0! Well Goldberg, I'm not gonna be 75..."

"OK," Bischoff chimed in. "The only thing that's possibly wrong with that is we're not sure [if] it's 74, 75, or 102. So let's get the number. Where's Goldberg? Could somebody grab Goldberg for us?"

"Goldberg's on the Internet, Eric," a staffer replied.

"Fuck the Internet," Bischoff shot back. "We're doing *Nitro*."

Bischoff's views on 'the Internet' - a colloquialism meaning the subsection of fans who frequently engaged in passionate online discussions - manifested itself often in his last-minute preparations. Whereas in 1996, for example, a typical *Nitro* format would contain a half-dozen bullet points for each match - indicating important production cues - the scripts being rolled off in 1998 frequently lacked as much detail ('match begins and ends in this segment', read a common instruction).

So much as there was one, the plan could now shift numerous times before air, and even, unthinkably, as *Nitro* was in progress. Two technicians supervised the running of industrial copy machines - each traveling with the production staff to live shows - in order to maintain the distribution of oft-changed run sheets. Paranoia was becoming rampant, staffers recall, with concerns over creative ideas leaking online - or relatedly, to the wrestling media - impeding the ability to communicate.

"Most of the time, I would do the opposite of whatever position they were taking," claims Bischoff. "I would feel comfort in that, and most of the time, I was right. Not every time, but most of the time - at least from a creative perspective, especially early on.

"Mind you, all of the wrestling writers, from Dave Meltzer to Wade Keller, and everybody and anybody in between…all of them, when they heard about *Nitro*…they all said, 'there's no way it's ever gonna work'. [They said] 'Eric Bischoff doesn't have a clue what he's doing'. 'He's an announcer from Minneapolis'. It was on and on and on. 'WCW will never be successful', [and so forth], 'there's no way that it will ever work'.

"Every one of them predicted that it wouldn't last a month, or several months. I proved every one of them wrong. And once I started really listening to them, and listening to their critique of my product, it gave me a fair amount of comfort to know that I was doing the right thing."

Regardless of the rationale, many production staffers felt slighted at being kept 'out of the loop', remembers WCW VP David Crockett. "It was an insult to everybody, production wise," he says.

"It wasn't always like that. When Eric was first there, we talked all the time about what he wanted to do. [Over time, however] egos got in the way. It was more, 'look what I know, and you don't know'.

"They felt if they talked to any of the wrestling people, it's gonna get out, but to single out the rest of us…to me it was a joke.

"I had ways of finding out what was gonna go on, and I added an extra tractor trailer to carry stuff that we *might* need. Tables, chairs, garbage cans [for wrestlers to use], a stretcher, or uniforms for guys we would dress up as either security or police, [for example]."

Such unease existed about "the 'scandal sheets' getting information," laments Crockett, that WCW took to adopting an unusual travel policy. It had become common for almost the entire roster to attend *Nitro*, despite the fact that ultimately, only a quarter of that number would actually appear on television. "We were flying all these people in," he says, "and they might not even wrestle. That's how *bizarre* it got."

"I was once with the crew in Florida," remembers wrestler Bobby Blaze, "for a *Thursday Thunder*, [before] they flew me to Atlanta. I worked in Rome, Georgia - about 60 miles north of Atlanta - and then flew home [to Kentucky] on a Wednesday morning. I wasn't home more than probably two hours, and I get a call saying I need to be at *Thunder* - the next day in Salt Lake City, [Utah]. So instead of flying me from Atlanta - with the rest of the crew - out to Salt Lake City, I went from Atlanta to Huntington Tri-State...in West Virginia...and then home to Kentucky. That's a couple thousand dollars to go back to Atlanta, and then connect to Salt Lake.

"That happened to me quite a bit. They'd be days where I'd fly from Orlando back home, have a day or two there, and then go back to Atlanta for a couple of days - just sitting there. They flew me to San Bernardino, California for a taping...and I'm sitting in the back, not being used. I have to get a rental car, a hotel room and a flight back home...granted I'm being paid...but why even buy that ticket?"

"It was [essentially] like," adds Crockett, "'we've got this idea, and this is what we're gonna do...but we're not gonna tell anybody, so we're gonna just fly everybody in!'"

"I was talking with Dean Malenko one day before a show," continues Blaze, "and he said, 'so and so opened the book up, and WWF's got the next three months planned out - booked out. He said, 'you can't tell me it can't be done. This could all be planned out...three to six months in advance'.

"He said, 'with us, we're going week-to-week!'"

"We couldn't seem to book more than a couple weeks down the road," agrees Ray 'Glacier' Lloyd, a WCW wrestler from 1996-1999. "Vince

[McMahon] was several months down the road, and everything was leading to *Wrestlemania* every year…that's the formula that has worked forever.

"I remember one show at the United Center in Chicago, they sent Fit Finlay and Steve Regal out there and said, 'just go until we tell you to stop'. The board [of matches] was not even up at the time we went live. You can't do that."

Curiously, on the subject of leaked information, someone in the know *was* consistently talking, says Jason Shaya, a teenage employee of the WCW hotline. "There used to be a woman," he details, "who called herself the 'Red Shadow'. She would leave voicemails on the local Detroit wrestling hotlines, and send me emails with huge scoops and inside stuff. It was obvious [that] she was extremely close to the top…but to this day, I never found out who it was."

Nonetheless, backstage machinations, underhanded politics and secret disclosures could often be obscured in front of a live audience, most of whom cared little for any online gossip. On this night, a raucous capacity crowd in Colorado Springs erupted when Goldberg became United States champion, standing awestruck at his astounding feats of power. Undoubtedly, the match could be considered the best of Goldberg's short career, an achievement that owed itself - in no small part - to the skill of his experienced opponent. Announcer Larry Zybysko summarized the excitement with a memorable closing line: "*Goldberg is open for business!*"

In the main event, Hollywood Hogan regained the World Heavyweight title in a marquee match-up with Randy Savage. It was the second such change in 24 hours, as to conclude *Spring Stampede* the previous night, Savage defeated Sting despite legitimately tearing his ACL in the process. With the ratings streak broken, analysts theorized, Bischoff believed a babyface challenger was needed to reignite interest at the top of the card. Therefore, after only two months as the 'undisputed' champion, Sting's run was cut short.

Resetting in the direction of a Hogan title reign struck many critics as a sign of desperation. In a tangled finish, he became the beneficiary of an interfering Bret Hart, who for a rather ambiguous reason, aided him to win the match. In contrast to the Hogan turn almost two years earlier, however, Hart's apparent nWo defection occurred sans anticipation, as fans largely struggled to understand his character's motives (in a plot development that quickly fizzled out, he later suggested his interference occurred for selfish reasons - a desire to beat Hogan himself for the belt).

In any event, the episode drew a 5.11 rating, its best ever performance in a head-to-head environment. As part of winning the night over *Raw* (4.4), the final few minutes of the show - featuring Hogan's win over Savage - registered an extraordinary 6.53 rating, the second-highest number for a cable TV match in history.

But the nostalgia of two legends competing in the main event - or, for that matter, the impact of Goldberg's first title win - could not be replicated again. It would likely take a sequence of entertaining, logical and well-planned shows to convince fans that WCW was still number one. That task would be impeded, however, with the news that for several weeks, TNT would preempt *Nitro* in favor of its NBA Playoffs coverage (meaning that consequently, the WWF could air *Raw* unopposed).

The decision couldn't come at a more inopportune time, and in Norfolk, Virginia on April 27th, WCW was forced to record two 'mini-shows' - one half to air that night, and the other to broadcast on Tuesday. During an early segment, Bischoff stood in the ring for a Hogan interview when something unusual caught his attention. At ringside, production member Annette Yother was waving her hands furiously, trying to deliver him a coded message. In Yother's earpiece, backstage security was in the midst of a dialogue with the production truck, discussing a scenario that seemed as fictional as wrestling itself. Yother learned that the WWF stable 'Degeneration X' - a group of wrestlers that included Sean Waltman among them - were apparently outside the arena, mocking WCW and filming footage to air on *Raw*

249

(by the time Bischoff reached backstage, he was informed - much to his chagrin, he says, that the 'invaders' had departed).

As evidenced by its eventual airing, part of the footage included an electronic sign outside the arena, so edited to suggest *Nitro* was occurring with tickets still unsold. As an act of aggression, it was a particularly damaging inference, thought Turner's legal team, and enough to become the catalyst for TBS filing a 'mirror image' complaint against the WWF (alleging, in cleverly worded legal prose, a "Titan scheme...to combat WCW's success...[via] a campaign to compete unfairly with WCW by disparaging WCW and the wrestlers who appear on its programs.").

In terms of TBS going on the 'offensive' - vis-a-vis the lawsuit - it marked the second attempt to demonstrate that both groups used similar tactics to gain viewership. On June 30, 1997, WCW attempted to halt the WWF's upcoming 'Canadian Stampede' event - scheduled just six days later - due to its similarity in title to 'Spring Stampede'. "WCW hereby demands," wrote attorney Mark VanderBrook, representing WCW, "that WWF immediately cease and desist from using the designation...to identify or promote its July 6, 1997 pay-per-view special, and to terminate any advertising or promotions using the term."

Two days after the DX stunt, even the attorneys for both sides were taking jabs at each other:

Eric Bischoff: (on naming Scott Hall) I could have called him Porky the Pig, I could have called him anything, but I didn't.

David Dunn (representing Turner Broadcasting): This was all gone over at the prior deposition.

Jerry McDevitt (representing the WWF): And it's gonna be gone over again.

David Dunn: Well, not for very long because the object of the deposition is not to ask the same questions you've asked before. I object.

Jerry McDevitt: It will go on as long as I have questions to ask about it.

250

David Dunn: Not if you ask the same questions and don't…

Jerry McDevitt: And we'll go on as long as I cross-examine this witness on the subject matter.

David Dunn: Don't threaten me.

Jerry McDevitt: And if you want to instruct him (Bischoff), you instruct *him*, Mr. Dunn.

David Dunn: Fine.

Jerry McDevitt: …You can object, but you cannot tell me what questions I will ask.

David Dunn: Well, if you continue to ask questions you've already asked and already received answers to, we will take steps to terminate this deposition.

Jerry McDevitt: I have no doubt that you'll do what you believe to be appropriate, Mr. Dunn.

———

Bischoff had previously considered direct provocation of the WWF (specifically, purchasing ringside seats to *Raw* for his nWo members), but on this occasion - instead of planning a 'tit-for-tat' - he opted to take a different approach. After the 'DX' group showed up at WCW's headquarters on May 11th, Bischoff - in Kansas City, MO for *Nitro* - shocked fans with a televised challenge to Vince McMahon:

"For the last couple of weeks, he's been sending his little wannabes around, demanding to talk to 'moi'. The problem with that is, he always sends them where he knows I'm not going to be. That's ok, 'cos I got a solution.

"Sean Waltman - you want an apology from me? You actually show up to our offices on a Monday afternoon, when I think you probably got it figured out - even you, Sean - are smart enough to figure out I probably won't be there. And as far as the apology goes…bite me. I apologize to no-one.

"But I've got a better idea. Because Sean, I know you're just a little puppet, and you do what Vince McMahon tells you to do. So Vince

251

McMahon - this is for you.

"*I'm coming to your backyard this Sunday. That's right - Worcester, Mass. Got a little pay-per-view thing going on. And I got a hell of an idea - just a hell of an idea!*

"*You want me? I'm gonna be in your backyard. Consider this an open invitation, Vince McMahon. You show up at Slamboree, it'll be me and you, McMahon. In the ring.*

"*How 'bout it, Vinnie? But I want to warn you people right now. If you think Vince McMahon has got the guts to show up, don't buy this pay-per-view, 'cos I guarantee you, he is not man enough to step into the ring with 'moi'.*

"*But I'll be there, Vinnie Mac! I'll be waiting for ya, and I'm gonna knock you out.*"

252

Chapter 28:
Counted Out

WITHIN A DAY, McMahon responded to Bischoff on the WWF website. *IN RESPONSE TO ERIC BISCHOFF'S "CHALLENGE"*, read the May 12th headline, *A QUOTE FROM MR. MCMAHON*:

I consider Eric Bischoff's 'Challenge' a cheap and desperate tactic to increase WCW PPV Buys. I will not do anything to help WCW increase their PPV Buys. Therefore, I will not appear at Turner's next PPV as invited.

However, if Mr. Bischoff is hell bent on fighting me, then such a fight can be arranged at any time, in any parking lot in the country; void of television cameras, photographers, and public announcement.

Nonetheless, Bischoff continued to goad McMahon during WCW programming. On May 14th, he opened *Thunder* by appearing in a pre-recorded video, sparring against hapless stand-ins at the Power Plant. *"Come on Vince,"* Bischoff taunted. *"Step into the ring and do what so many other people would love to do. Get your hands around my skinny little neck..."*

If the trash-talking felt real, it's because it *was* real, argues Dick Cheatham. "His whole deal was that he really wanted to knock off WWF," he says of Bischoff. "I think a lot of that was a personal issue. He'd originally gone there to audition for a position with the folks at WWF, but they didn't care for it, [almost like] they threw the tape in the trash or something. I think that created a drive in Eric that other people didn't have. He was just *so competitive*."

"It was personal," agrees Marcus 'Buff' Bagwell. "A million percent personal - on both sides. Vince did not like Eric, and Eric did not like Vince. That's what made it real to the fans, because they knew - even though wrestling is predetermined - that there was money on the line. There were ratings on the line. Wrestling had become real again."

The perceived authenticity of Bischoff's latest challenge - packaged memorably in the *Thunder* video - also benefited from its spontaneity. More than anything, it exemplified a free-flowing production style that was becoming ever-more prevalent - the 'run-and-gun' approach as it was known internally. On this day, for example, Bischoff arrived over two hours late for the shoot, racing across the skies in a G-5 jet from Orlando. Already dressed in his kickboxing sweats, he apologized for the mishap and then proceeded - rather convincingly - to dominate an assortment of faceless trainees (with one suffering a broken jaw during filming).

Drenched in sweat, Bischoff leaned towards the camera, and as projectors beamed the nWo logo around him, he spoke slowly and directly to McMahon. "*You can do it…*" he heckled, appearing strikingly relaxed under dramatic mood lightning, "*…if you've got the guts. Do you Vince? Have you go the guts to really show up? I do…do you?*"

In his most obnoxiously charismatic delivery, Bischoff continued. "*Do you got the guts, Vince? We'll find out. We'll be waiting for ya, Vinnie Mac - with open arms.*"

Shortly thereafter, almost as quickly as he rushed in, Bischoff departed the facility on Carrol Drive. In the interim, his comments would be chopped up, repositioned and carefully organized by Kemper Rogers, WCW's immensely respected Senior Editor. In following with the nWo motif, Rogers knew that he would utilize 'jump cuts' - abrupt transitions from one phrase to another - to tell the story of Bischoff's promo. However, in a departure from other videos, Rogers was unable to 'cut' to other subjects, as Bischoff was the only speaker on camera. Therefore, to prevent the transitions from becoming distracting, he arrived at a brilliant resolution. Inspiredly, Rogers sampled, filtered and truncated the sound from his camera stabilizer, layering the audio on top of each temporal change. It amounted to a strikingly impressive audiovisual effect.

Meanwhile, while Rogers created something *ex nihilo*, Bischoff

254

remained hopeful that *Slamboree* could conjure up controversy. In his promos, he had leveraged the WWF's rhetoric against them, painting himself as a courageous challenger in the process. He also fully expected McMahon to show up, despite numerous indications suggesting otherwise - and the reservations of some talent. *He's going to take this seriously*, Hogan warned Bischoff, speaking of McMahon. *There's no way he's not going to come and try to kick your ass.*

Great, responded Bischoff. *It'll make one hell of a pay-per-view.*

Ultimately, McMahon failed to appear, skillfully side-stepping Bischoff's trap and opting instead - as if there was a choice - to attend his daughter's graduation from Boston University. Nonetheless, Bischoff continued to capitalize on his challenge, accepting the 'no-show' as a forfeit. "*Alright, get this*," he told the crowd over a house mic, before following up freudianistically, "*we're gonna have to count Vinnie Mac out. Why don't we all do it together?*"

Later that night, in the main event, Scott Hall turned on long-time partner Kevin Nash, gifting the World Tag Team belts to Sting and The Giant. It was only the latest plot twist in the nWo storyline, an epic that in recent weeks, led to the emergence of two intrafactional groups. On one side, nWo Hollywood (alternatively, 'nWo Black-and-White') furthered its original mission under Hollywood Hogan, while simultaneously, the nWo Wolfpac (or 'nWo Red-and-Black'), received favorable crowd responses under Kevin Nash.

Over the months to come, the Wolfpac - comprised originally of Nash, Randy Savage and Konnan - developed an undeniable bond with WCW fans. Upon making their way to the ring, the group bopped to a catchy, self-titled hip-hop track, often erroneously credited to rapper C-Murder. "The rapper on the Wolfpac song was a guy named Lequince Henderson," says producer Howard Helm. "I was working with him on his album at the studio [back then]."

Before his involvement in wrestling, Helm - a Canadian composer with a background in piano, French horn and Voice - toured with a variety of popular rock bands throughout the 1980s. In the early '90s, he then moved to Florida, meeting musician-turned-wrestling manager Jimmy Hart along the way (although to most fans, Hart was known best for his WWF and Memphis Wrestling exploits, he previously starred as a vocalist for 'The Gentry's', scoring a Number 4 hit in 1965). Almost immediately, Helm and Hart hit it off, and with WCW lacking a designated musical specialist, the duo dutifully began work on character-specific entrance music.

Despite much of their output resulting in hard driving rock songs, Helm and Hart chose a different approach for the Wolfpac theme. "We saw how big the rap stuff had been," notes Helm (indeed, even Lex Luger was now listening to the genre - DMX specifically, according to those in the know). "We thought, 'let's do something that's really, totally different'.

"The construction of the song was fairly simple," continues Helm. "We immediately had that hook - 'Wolfpac is back, causin' mass destruction...' - we had that hook thing together…and then it had that very simple piano. [Initially], the rap was just being sung with the piano, and then I said, 'you know, we need to make this as simple as possible'.

"We put the simplest beat [underneath], and the bass line was very simple. There's also no guitar on the song. There was a little string line, but then bit by bit, once we got the vocal [recorded], we thought, 'you know what, this thing kind of sits just the way it is'.

"Sure enough, it worked. It was an experiment at the time - trying something that was such a different direction from most of the themes - but boy, it was great. The tempo of it meant the guys could sort of come out, do that sort of slow swagger, and it seemed to just hit the show with the right tempo and the right attitude. It was always a break from all the other stuff, which tended to be very guitar driven. I think that's another reason why it stood out."

Contrary to popular belief, Helm says, 'Wolfpac' was not based on the *Militia* song 'Burn', a contemporaneous hit garnering MTV rotation. "It began with the piano," he reveals of the process. "The piano was kind of our timekeeper. Once that was there, I'm fairly certain that putting a drum beat with the piano was the next part of it. Once the drum beat was with it and it was going along, it had a motion already there. So I thought to myself, 'well you know, we don't need to get too carried away with the bass', so we tried a couple of things (hums bass). It's a synthesized bass that I played, and it seemed to do the trick. I liked the idea that it had holes in it, because it was easier to then 'pick up' the vocal. I'm almost certain the strings were added later on, to kinda give it a little bit of texture.

"There's a little 'answering' clavinet that's in there too. We had to downplay it, because it was almost like a reggae rhythm that's answering to the bassline. But it was all done on keyboards, which of course many rap records are. It was really written in a very raw form. We would have been in my workroom…going through some ideas for the words…playing the simplest thing on the piano I could think of. That's pretty much how that came together.

"It was one of those things we kind of fell into - an experiment. When we sent it in, we were waiting to see if anybody was gonna go, 'what's this?' Instead, it turned out to be very popular."

Although arguably their most popular track, 'Wolfpac' was one of 160 themes produced by the Hart and Helm partnership. One song they could not lay claim to, however, was Goldberg's 'Invasion', a piece of instrumental stock music even heard on other cable programming. "[WCW] really got caught with that situation," says Helm. "It was a 'library cut', and later on, as Goldberg got bigger and bigger and bigger…the fans really [associated] that music with him…but WCW couldn't market the song at all."

Infamously - during the mid to late '90s especially - WCW's reliance on such music was well-known. On the Internet, websites charted the number of songs either 'inspired' (or completely ripped-off) from popular mainstream tunes, including DDP's 'Self High Five' (Nirvana's 'Smells Like Teen Spirit'), Chris Jericho's 'One Crazed Anarchist' (Pearl Jam's 'Evenflow'), and The Outsiders' 'Crazed' (Seal's 'Crazy'). "What would happen," reveals Helm, "is that Library music would be created in *certain styles*. They would say, 'do something that *sounds like* Van Halen', [for example].

"Then the [wrestlers] may say, 'well, I want something that sounds like such and such'. So somebody goes and starts searching through the library and says, 'what about this?' But a lot of the guys really did want to use sounds that were done by certain artists. Only Hulk could have pushed that through, [such as] the short time he used 'Voodoo Child' by Jimi Hendrix."

According to Bischoff, WCW was able to secure worldwide rights to Hendrix's 'Voodoo Child' - and play the theme multiple times per broadcast - for the relatively paltry sum of just $100,000. However, at least until Helm and Hart took over, most other performers sufficed on production music, which in itself (as was the case with the original nWo theme) often sampled other commercial songs. Booker T's 'Rap Sheet', for example, owed its drum break to Soul II Soul's 'Back to Life (Club Mix)', its sound effects to Kwaftwerk's 'Sex Object' and 'Musique Non Stop', and its peculiar vocal effect from Hateful Head Helen's curiously-titled (and performed) 'Sweet Pussy Pauline'.

"One of the things we pointed out to [WCW]," remembers Helm, "was, 'you realize the limitations - legally - that you've got with using library music'. You have permission to use it on your broadcasts, but that's where it ends. You cannot do anything else with that music. You can't put it on a CD to sell as a separate product, which is something they really never did, and Jimmy and I could never, ever figure out why. It made no business sense, whatsoever. [WWF] were putting out music CD's with all the fans' favorite themes - I mean, people love that stuff, and it's extra money for the company. The thing is…they weren't even remotely interested in doing that.

"[At WCW], there wasn't a music department, per se…and maybe somebody knew how much of it was library music and went, 'well, we can't release it anyway'. But by the time the original stuff started getting created, that was one of the things we kept going to the company for, like, 'why don't you put these things out? You own the publishing on them!'"

Eventually, as part of a partnership with Tommy Boy Records, *WCW Mayhem: The Music* was released in 1999. "It was supposed to be theme music," says Helm, "but that was a very, very curious project. When it came originally to us, we thought that they were finally smartening up and releasing the themes from the show.

"In the end, they only ended up taking seven pieces of music from Jimmy and I. We kind of thought to ourselves, 'what are they doing? That's only gonna be 18 or 19 minutes of music...that doesn't make any sense'. I was told that Eric [Bischoff] had something going with Tommy Boy...and all these other songs that no-one had ever heard showed up on that CD. [Those songs] got attached to wrestler's names, but if you look carefully at it, every one of those artists were on Tommy Boy...it was not what the fans wanted."

As Kevin Nash points out, the issue underscored that from an infrastructural standpoint, WCW was still "far behind" its chief competitor. "I have so much respect for Eric, for that alone," he says. "Eric had no idea of the machine he was up against, in terms of the WWF."

"The WWF guys were so brilliant," marvels Matt Williams, formerly the Director of Research at Turner. "We did a content study on them, and I think we found that more than half of the commentary during shows was not even about wrestling. They were always pitching something else during the telecast - 'to learn more about this guy, pick up the latest WWF Magazine'. They were brilliant equity builders, and were always redirecting you.

"With WCW, the company had so many avenues to get *one-on-one* viewer information. The big thing was the fan mail that came in - there were boxes of it just sitting around - and I'm like, 'oh my god! These are your fans'!

"I proposed setting up a database based [on that], and by the time I was finished, we had a half a million names on there."

"We couldn't believe," adds Neal Pruitt, "that we didn't have a central location for all our art design and graphics. Insanely, we didn't have that at all, and that was a big loss of income in my mind.

"One of the things I proposed - that fell on deaf ears - was producing a 'Best of' for Ric Flair, Sting, the Steiner Brothers, whoever. I said, 'let me sit down with the wrestlers, interview them and we'll put it together'. It's been proven many times before in the record business that repackaging works…but they wouldn't listen. It was frustrating."

In comparison to the WWF, WCW's licensing and merchandising business was also regarded as lacking. "People like Hogan and others," highlights Dr. Harvey Schiller, "[actually] *owned* their character. That meant doing a deal with them on licensed products was *their* deal. We didn't own the Hulk Hogan character - he did.

"So we actually started looking [more] at creating characters," continues Schiller. "One of the funny ones, which to this day I remember," he laughs, "was…*Spam Man!* We were going to create *Spam Man* for the product 'Spam'. They thought they'd get a sponsorship for Spam, and we would have the character, but it never got anywhere."

While some innovations, in regards to merchandising specifically, were more inspired - peddling nWo shirts outside arenas via 'bootleggers' (actually company employees) to cite one prominent example - the mechanics involved in selling similar garb was cumbersome.

"They didn't operate like the WWF," states Andre Freitas, WCW's special effects expert. "Vince McMahon has a structure where he runs the whole thing, and he has divisions such as an art department, costume makers, and everything else. They help develop a character, and then they manufacture merchandise for that character.

"WCW was very fragmented. They did have an art department, but it was designed for making graphics for the show, or helping to create a 'scene' for the pay-per-views. The merchandising wasn't tied in to that.

"There were a lot of business practices that didn't make sense. There was a lady in marketing…and her brother-in-law got all the T-shirt contracts. As it became a mainstream thing and got bigger, she put out very [poor] designs, because she wasn't in the 18-35 year old demographic."

"I know an employee of WCW," adds producer Tim Tewell, on a similar note, "who had his own 'Avid' [editing machine]. He was renting his equipment to Turner - for him to use - for years. Everybody knew it, and nobody called him on it."

Amusingly, the machine almost perished in one calamitous caper, recalls Tewell. "There was someone," he says, "who came to us from another Turner division. She fucked up three or four jobs at Turner, so finally they sent her down to WCW. While she's there, she gets locked in this little square hallway that was bordered by three businesses. One of them was WCW, and the other two were companies that had contracts with WCW.

"At a certain time - when their doors locked - you could get trapped in this area. Well…this person thinks, 'I'm trapped in this hallway, so I should take my lighter and put it on the fire [sensor], and that way, I'll be saved'.

"It flooded the edit suite. It rained on all of our computers, and ruined a ton of shit. That girl kept her job, [though]. Who else would keep their job after that?"

With so much dysfunction, Andre Freitas remembers, he would be forced to explore "unbelievable channels" to develop a simple T-shirt design. "You had to bypass the marketing people," he sighs, "and sometimes give the designs to wrestlers indirectly - just so a guy could have a cool T-shirt."

One of Freitas' most successful initiatives, he says, was helping to develop the popular 'Crow Sting' persona for Steve Borden. "Since he lived in Marietta," Freitas recalls, "Steve came to see me one day. I proposed this sort of gothic character, and showed him some pictures of Marilyn Manson in extreme make-up - including the front of *Rolling Stone* with a super close-up of [Manson's] face.

"We talked about the 'Crow', and I was also thinking about the movie 'Dune'...with the Kyle MacLachlan character that had like an exo-suit. I showed Sting all of these different things on a 'Mood Board' - basically an idea board - but I know he gravitated to the Crow imagery, the gothic stuff, and the Marilyn Manson *Rolling Stone* cover.

"I did a bunch of drawings for him - even extrapolated drawings so if he eventually shifted from the black-and-white [look]...he would become these other colored versions...but still in that same style. He totally went after it.

"The reason I picked black-and-white was [two-fold]. I was into the gothic scene and dark stuff - that was sort of my lifestyle. Also, it was a complete '180' from who Sting was - so colorful as a character.

"People were saying, 'we're gonna get in trouble for ripping it off', but at one point, the guy who wrote the 'Crow' comic book [indicated] he didn't mind it. I think he saw it as another Crow manifestation, and another type of character with the Scorpion [element]."

Freitas also remembers creating the 'Sting mask', an item of merchandise sold frequently at WCW shows. "They wanted me to make a whole bunch of 'fake Stings' at once," he says, "but in reality, it was not practical to do prosthetic make-up on these millions of wrestler guys. So I took Steve's head cast, made a vacuum shell, and I invented the Sting mask - to speed up the make-up process."

Responding to the notion that Scott Hall pitched the 'Crow Sting' gimmick - a memory shared by Eric Bischoff and others - Freitas disputes its accuracy. "I don't think it's accurate," he says, "unless it's a combination of Sting showing him stuff, and saying, 'wouldn't it be cool...', or looking at drawings that I did.

262

"Scott Hall wasn't at my studio. I mean, I like Scott Hall, and maybe he saw his facepaint and said something like that. Maybe he influenced Steve in another way that I don't know about...but all the meetings I had were just Steve and I. It was me doing drawings, showing him the cover of *Rolling Stone* magazine - with Marilyn Manson in facepaint. I showed him comic book pictures, and images of the Crow that I gathered together. That had nothing to do with Scott Hall at all.

"Maybe Steve talked about it with Scott, and showed him the magazine cover at a later time. Maybe he resonated that same thinking, based on the black-and-white imagery...I don't know. I don't remember him doing that, and I don't remember Scott Hall instructing me how to do drawings that I came up with on my own."

———

Despite its immaturity as a business - as evidenced by its various operational limitations - WCW would soon be forced to find new headquarters, a consequence of TBS' purchase of the expansion Atlanta Thrashers. At the behest of Harvey Schiller, the company was at last moved out of the CNN Center - surely the culmination of many executive's fantasies - despite the recent improvement of its perception. Once employees entered the less-glamorous new location in Smyrna, GA (2865 Log Cabin Drive, to be exact), Bischoff realized that morale would likely take a dive, even assuming they ignored the still-present smell of sewage inside. "It was always," laments Kevin Sullivan, "'we'll (TBS) support them, but we don't have to have lunch with them'."

"Eric had no idea what he was up against," emphasizes Nash, before his voice trails off. "Fuckin' Log Cabin..."

At the very least, WCW looked to have a clear creative direction ahead. For the short-term, Dennis Rodman would be brought back in, leading to his disappearance from the Chicago Bulls (during the NBA Finals, no less) to appear on *Nitro*. "I asked him, 'Dennis, what should

I say to the press?'" shared Bulls Coach Phil Jackson. "He hung up on me."

For the long-term, more promisingly, there appeared to be an infinite number of possible match-ups. Hogan and Hart had yet to face off ("I think [they] are going to make a tremendous amount of money together," promised Bischoff), and a clash between the warring nWo factions seemed inevitable. Exciting younger talent, such as Chris Jericho, Chris Benoit, Eddie Guerrero and Booker T. looked close to being elevated to top spots.

Moreover, to a practically inconceivable level, Goldberg continued to build momentum. On May 29th, tickets went on sale for the July 6th edition of *Nitro*, an episode that would be broadcast in WCW's backyard - the Georgia Dome in Atlanta. Traditionally, such 'hometown' shows attracted an array of Turner executives and their families, often creating a unique pressure to put on a particularly entertaining spectacle. Within a week of their release, over 20,000 tickets were sold for the event, and before long, the number climbed to 29,000. Subsequently, however, the sales soon stagnated, opening the door for a radical suggestion.

"I remember where I was," outlines Bischoff. "I was driving to Marina Del Ray in Los Angeles, and Hulk [Hogan] called me on my cellphone.

"He said, 'hey - I got an idea'..."

Chapter 29:
A Made Man

AS HISTORY WOULD remember it, Hogan's idea involved wrestling at the Dome opposite WCW's hottest property - Bill Goldberg. According to revered journalist Dave Meltzer, the match was first proposed as a 'dark match' - occurring untelevised to the audience at home - before being added to the main card on short notice. "No, it wasn't going to be a dark match," retorts Rob Garner. "It was too good for that, and there would have been some angry people [if that were the case]."

With *Raw* looking formidable in the ratings - and enjoying a sweep of *Nitro* throughout June - WCW looked for the match to spark some momentum. On the July 2nd edition of *Thunder*, WCW commissioner J.J. Dillon announced its occurrence via an impromptu on-screen address, informing fans (and watching at home, Goldberg himself) about Hogan's forthcoming title defense:

"I would suggest that you don't miss this coming Monday night, because it is now official. Hollywood Hulk Hogan - the WCW champion - is contractually obligated to be in the Georgia Dome...this coming Monday night for Nitro...to defend the WCW Heavyweight Title belt...against what I feel is the number one contender...GOLDBERG!"

Come Monday, the atmosphere at the Dome was electric. An astonishing 41,412 fans rushed through the turnstiles - comprising the largest crowd in WCW history - although erroneously, the company claimed a number of 39,000 on its telecast. "The energy was high and there was a *lot* of anticipation," remembers Bischoff of the preparations.

While some fans could foresee the arena becoming WCW's spiritual home, it wasn't a distinct priority for the company, remembers its President. "It wasn't on the forefront of our minds," Bischoff admits. "Naturally, we wanted do really well there, but nobody ever sat around a room and said, 'ok, this is going to be *our Madison Square Garden*'. That wasn't the case - at least not from my point of view. Other people may have saw that, or had that conversation, but it wasn't a prevailing thought in my mind."

Bischoff's decision to 'give away' Hogan-Goldberg attracted a lightning rod of criticism from industry experts, who argued that WCW was neglecting millions of dollars in potential pay-per-view revenue. Interestingly, Bischoff concedes that he shared a similar outlook. "There was some trepidation," he acknowledges, "and there were some people who thought it was a mistake - business wise - to put something that big on free TV. And I was one of them. I wasn't 100% sure it was the right thing to do.

"But no-one would have ever expected a match like that on free television - just like they never expected 99% of things we did - which is [one] reason I did it."

"We started losing in the ratings just a little bit," recalls DDP, "and they figured, 'we gotta push Goldberg through the roof, so he's gonna win the U.S. title - and [later], the World title'. It's like, '*what?* He's not ready for that."

As the fans filed in, David Crockett enjoyed an aside with Bill Shaw, the Turner executive who promoted Bischoff in 1993. "I turned to Bill," remembers Crockett, "and said, 'did you ever think, three years ago, that we would be *here?*'

Backstage, the inexperienced Goldberg found Hogan in the locker room, and proceeded to ask a rather fundamental question: *what are we doing for the match?*

Don't worry, brother, responded the seasoned Hogan. *We'll call it in the ring.*

While typically self-assured, Hogan had reason to feel even more secure than usual. On May 29th - the same day as tickets to the Dome show went on sale - he signed a four-year contract extension with WCW, attaining previously unheard of terms for a wrestler:

"In consideration of Bollea's performance hereunder, WCW shall pay to Bollea a bonus in the amount of Two Million Dollars ($2,000,000) to be paid within fourteen (14) days after Bollea's execution and delivery of this Letter of Agreement...

"...in consideration of Bollea's participation in [pay-per-views], WCW shall compensate Bollea the greater of Fifteen percent (15%)...of domestic cable sales received by WCW for each Event or a Six Hundred Seventy-Five Thousand Dollars ($675,000) guarantee payment...per Event.

"...During Years One (1) through Three (3) of this Agreement, Bollea shall promote, appear, wrestle and perform...at WCW Nitro and WCW Thunder events. In consideration of Bollea's participation in any such events, WCW shall pay Bollea twenty-five percent (25%) of the (after tax) arena ticket revenues for each WCW Nitro and/or WCW Thunder in which he appears and wrestles, however, in no event will Bollea's compensation be less than Twenty-Five Thousand Dollars ($25,000) per event.

...Bollea shall receive a royalty of fifty percent (50%) of the Net Receipts (as defined herein) received by WCW on all merchandise sold directly by WCW to any consumer incorporating "Hulk Hogan," "Hollywood Hogan" or Bollea's name, likeness or character.

...During the period in which Bollea is a member of the New World Order ("NWO"), Bollea will receive a promotional fee for promoting the NWO (wearing the name while wrestling, on-air, in photo shoots, etc.) of Twenty Thousand Dollars ($20,000) per month.

...Should WCW create a 900#/call-in hotline featuring "Hulk Hogan" or "Hollywood Hogan" and should Bollea be available to provide recordings for said 900#, Bollea shall receive one hundred percent (100%) of WCW's Net Revenues (as herein defined) from Bollea's feature(s) on such Hotline.

...When required to travel for WCW as contemplated hereunder, Bollea will receive first-class air travel, first-class hotel accommodations, limousine transportation and One Hundred Seventy-Five Dollars ($175.00) per diem.

...Bollea shall have approval over the outcome of all wrestling matches in which he appears, wrestles and performs, such approval not to be unreasonably withheld.

As per the agreement, Hogan retained his creative control clause,

267

meaning that theoretically, he could end Goldberg's streak in their match. Early in the broadcast, he promised to "kill" the undefeated phenom in a hyperbolic promo, but as the challenger made his entrance - standing in the middle of sparkling pyrotechnics (following a now-customary escort from a team of security guards) - it felt palpably like Goldberg's night. *"Fans, you're not gonna have to wait much longer,"* promised Tony Schiavone on commentary. *"When we come back, the World Champ Hollywood Hogan will come out, and Goldberg and Hogan will battle for the World Title - next!"*

Moments later, a menacingly low pitched sound bite (actually taken from a clip of Bischoff enunciating 'n…W…o') introduced the cocksure champion. With the nWo music blaring in the background, Hogan looked dismissively at the ring, and then directed a rather tame threat to the ringside cameraman. *"I am gonna kick…,"* he began, his words hanging in mid-air, *"Goldberg's…butt!"*

As Schiavone would note, the Georgia Dome crowd - many of whom were familiar with Goldberg prior to wrestling, by virtue of his football prowess - erupted loudly at the bell. As the combatants locked up, there seemed to be magic in the air, and after Goldberg shoulder blocked Hogan to the canvas, the buzz reached an even higher plateau.

In a classic 'spot' to demonstrate the strength of a babyface, Goldberg then won a 'test of strength', causing Hogan to bail outside. Realizing that he couldn't outmuscle the monster, Hogan began to cheat, raking the eyes of Goldberg and whipping him with his weightlifting belt. Subsequently, in a simple yet effective use of wrestling psychology, Goldberg grabbed Hogan's belt - but only to throw it away instead. *"He doesn't want to take any shortcuts,"* observed color commentator Mike Tenay. *"He wants to earn the victory over Hogan."*

Low-blowing his way out of a Full Nelson hold, Hogan next took Goldberg down to the canvas. *"A blatant chokehold,"* protested Schiavone, *"right in front of the referee!"*

"Hogan on the outside…is a master," continued Schiavone, witnessing Hollywood use a chair to great effect. Within seconds,

268

Goldberg was sprawled on the canvas mid-ring, and Hogan seemed primed to take advantage. *"There comes a time,"* mused Schiavone as Hogan delivered his patented leg drop, *"where you gotta dig down deep...you gotta suck it up. You gotta prove without a shadow of a doubt...that you belong here. For Goldberg, the time is right now, because the Champ is leveling him with everything!"*

Suddenly, the camera cut to the entranceway, as Curt Hennig - Hogan's nWo stablemate - decided it was time to intervene; meanwhile, almost lost in the commotion, Goldberg kicked out after *three* of Hogan's leg drops. Dramatically, Hennig was soon stopped from interfering in the contest, courtesy of a timely Diamond Cutter from Karl Malone, the Utah Jazz forward who would oppose Dennis Rodman - as part of a tag-team main event match - at the upcoming *Bash at the Beach* pay-per-view.

Springing to his feet, Goldberg rebounded to deliver his spear to Hogan. *"There's part one!"* screamed Bobby Heenan on commentary. *"Now finish him off! Finish him off! This place will erupt when he picks him up..."*

"He's got him up!" rejoiced Schiavone, beholding Goldberg's Jackhammer maneuver in progress. *"Oh hell yeah!"*

Time stood still as referee Charles Robinson made the count.

"'ONE'...

'TWO'...

'THREE!'"

In the years that followed, many in attendance would contend that at this precise moment, the arena began to shake. At ringside, grown men jumped up and down in excitement, seemingly losing themselves in the spectacle. Arena security looked overwhelmed in the chaos; spectators rushed from the upper levels to the aisle way, seats buckled around the ring from the weight of standing fans, and inexplicably, a roll of toilet paper flew across the ropes - in full view of the five million people watching live on TNT.

Fireworks erupted from the ceiling, and the defeated Hogan rolled out of the fray. The crowd reaction, or *pop* in wrestling parlance, reached an extraordinary level as Goldberg hoisted both his titles. "It was pretty magical, actually," says Rob Garner. "It was electric. That place was amazing - *amazing*. It was just…gosh, it's hard to describe. It was kind of surreal…people were just going crazy. It was probably one of the best moments ever."

Much like a sporting event, the noise reflected a genuine outpouring of emotion - and eventually, even as the fans walked to the exits - they continued to serenade their new hero: *Gold-berg…Gold-berg…Gold-berg…*

By any tangible metric, the title switch appeared to have been a huge success. More people watched Goldberg's coronation than any other match in the history of cable television; moreover, the combined revenue from ticket sales and merchandise easily exceeded a million dollars, and the reported crowd of 41,412 constituted the largest ever assembled for a WCW show. In sum, it had been the single most profitable *Nitro* in the company's existence.

Recalling their conversation from several years earlier ("if you can't talk, you can't wrestle"), Harvey Schiller placed a call to Eric Bischoff.

"I said, 'Eric…', chuckles Schiller, "Goldberg just grunts - he never speaks!'"

Bischoff was quick to respond, remembers Schiller.

"Eric said, '*he* doesn't have to!'"

Chapter 30:
The Turning Point

O N THE MORNING of Tuesday, July 28th, the Atlanta Constitution was buzzing about the so-called 'Jesus deal' - CBS' $17 million investment in a miniseries depicting the life of Jesus Christ. Prior talks with TNT fizzled out, Lorenzo Minoli told the *Constitution*, after network representatives offered their own creative suggestions. "We walked away from TNT," said Minoli, executive producer for the series. "[They] wanted to fill the movie with magic and special effects, featuring a Jesus who flew through the air."

By day's end, Eric Bischoff would himself feel like calling on the son of God.

After flying back from San Antonio, TX, the site of the previous *Monday Nitro*, Bischoff drove to his office to consider the following week's program. But upon arriving at WCW's new headquarters on Log Cabin Drive, he took notice of a peculiar memo on his desk. Apparently, a group of senior TBS executives were waiting at 'Techwood' - the original Turner Broadcasting campus located closer to downtown - for reasons that were not immediately clear.

Puzzled, Bischoff returned to the road, traveling seven miles to join a summit already in progress. Cautiously taking his seat in a crowded conference room, he looked around the table with a sinking feeling. "There was probably 15 or 18 people sitting around this table, most of whom I had never heard of before, or met before," he recalls.

According to Bischoff, the assemblage then began to discuss a recently added *Nitro* segment, one that involved him (as part of the build-up for talk show host Jay Leno to become involved in WCW storylines) making several risqué references to the Clinton-Lewinsky affair. "I walked into that room," Bischoff continues, "and was told 'this is how you're going to produce your show'."

Several minutes into the discussion, a veteran TBS employee stood to introduce herself. While in the distant future, Bischoff would chuckle at her memory ('great stripper name', he would later joke), her forthcoming pronouncement would be no laughing matter at all. The Leno gags, ordered Terri Tingle, Senior Vice President of Standards and Practices ('S&P'), were no longer appropriate for WCW's programming. "This is where 'Standards and Practices' came in," laments Bischoff, who says he was previously unaware of the department's existence. "I was told, 'you are no longer going to be targeting eighteen-to-thirty-four year olds - we want to go after family friendly audiences'."

In the corner of the room, a VCR whirred into motion. *Here's an example of what you can't do anymore*, Bischoff remembers hearing, as a tape of a recent *Nitro* flickered ominously on screen. The tape had been cued to show a WCW wrestler delivering an insult - a fairly typical occurrence on a wrestling show, Bischoff thought - so as to further tensions between two rival stars.

After all, since the original nWo invasion some two years earlier, *Nitro* was in large part built on *heat*, a critical element of Kevin Sullivan's booking formula (humorously, when once asked how much heat was enough, the booker responded thusly: "the fire department will come!"). Therefore, stringent limitations regarding content, aside from the obvious and established restrictions pertaining to foul language, death threats, nudity, and the like, raised the troubling question of how exactly this success could be replicated. Without the underlying emotion accompanying a match, Bischoff ruminated, the result was something much less inspiring - two guys in their underwear fighting for ambiguous reasons. "They were basically telling me that I had to abandon the very formula that had not only worked for us, but that our competition had adapted," he says. "I was then told to have my scripts approved a month in advance."

The demand struck Bischoff as showing a demonstrable lack of understanding. "They were used to looking at feature films and traditional scripted programming," he says. "But that's not how wrestling was ever produced - it's still not. They wanted to treat it like [the TBS cartoon series] *Captain Planet*."

Excruciatingly for WCW's President, the summit rolled on, as the Turner team opted to address another perpetual problem: advertising.

"I recall we had some debate," recalls Joe Uva, described by Bischoff as the 'most vocal' participant in the room. "I think whether Eric agreed or not, I *did* know a lot about the product, and I was a fan since the time I was a young kid. I definitely knew about the audience. But that wasn't the issue.

"The issue was yes, the ratings may go down by taming it a little bit...but there's an old saying in television. You'd rather have a '2' rating that is highly desirable, and advertisers want it, [versus] a '5' rating that no advertisers would want to be associated with."

While Bischoff regards the meeting as hugely significant, Uva holds a different impression. "As far as the outcome of the meeting, I don't think there were any definitive decisions that were taken," he says. "It was more or less, 'let's just monitor this', [and] 'let's see how it goes'.

"It wasn't like, 'you have to be responsible, like everybody else in the company, to Terri Tingle', in terms of the content that goes on the air. But clearly, there were economic considerations [involved]."

"My perception [of the meeting]," opines Bill Burke, "would be...[Eric] just kept getting more and more outrageous. S&P were always waiting in the wings, but he never pushed the envelope quite that way before. WWF would do something scandalous, so he had to do something [to respond]. It was like an arms race in terms of who could do something more outrageous."

To understand the rationale for such a discussion, Burke argues, it is necessary to contextualize its occurrence in the first place. "The industry [in 1997] agreed to add content ratings to television for the first time," he says. "At that time, there was a lot of pressure on television that violence was being imitated by kids.

"Those external pressures didn't *necessarily* apply as much to wrestling, because it's 'guys hitting each with chairs'...but it *was* getting very sexualized, as I recall."

But ever since Vince McMahon's 'Attitude Era' pronouncement (and, technically speaking, even earlier than that), much of the overtly sexual content arose from WCW's competition, the WWF. Executives at the USA Network, including its Senior Vice President of Programming, Bonnie Hammer, openly defended such changes. "I think we get a bum rep," Hammer told journalist Alex Marvez. "Take a look at [any] prime-time drama series. We're not any more violent than *NYPD Blue*. [And] in terms of sexual innuendo, it's done for humor."

The environment on the Turner networks was clearly different, points out Burke. "Ted actually had trouble with stuff like that, interestingly," he says. "His personal life was...sexualized...but he didn't like a lot of that on his networks. I had young kids at the time, and I still remember watching a baseball game and a viagra ad came on. I'm like, 'come on!' If I signed up to watch a certain show [with them], then that's my fault, but I'm watching baseball and I gotta explain what a four-hour erection is."

At the time, Bischoff predicted that the WWF's new approach would "set wrestling back 20 years," suggesting that advertisers "would run" if they were paying close enough attention. In hindsight, Bischoff argues, McMahon's strategic change was a logical consequence of *Nitro*'s innovation. "We were kicking the WWF's ass," he says unequivocally. "We knew it, they knew it...the audience knew it...everybody knew it. In every way, shape, or form, we were pretty much trouncing them.

"They were watching our product closely, despite what they've said publicly in the past. I know people that are very, very high up in their production food chain, and I know that they were watching our show, literally while it was happening. For a long time, they didn't think

[*Nitro*] was going to work.

"Well, after a year and a half, almost two years, it was like, 'ok, we can't do this anymore'. I think once it got that bad for them, Vince was really looking at the downfall of his company. From what I've been told, things were horribly bad…and it was at that time that they said, 'screw it'. This is what's working…'let's do it better than them'. That's when the 'Attitude Era' came about.

"Vince McMahon turned himself heel and made himself a character - modeled after the character I had established a year and a half earlier. He couldn't wear the big buffoon kind of suits, and gaudy ties and be the straight play-by-play guy [anymore]…and [also] acknowledge that he was the President of the company. All of that was a result of what we were doing on television.

"They modeled their creative formula after ours, but they turned up the volume. They did it raunchier. They did it more aggressive. They did more spectacular things. They were willing to drink beer, and have 'Stone Cold' Steve Austin give the audience the finger. They were willing to have women expose their breasts in the ring. They were willing to go much further than we were capable of - or willing to do.

"So Vince - all of a sudden - embraced the 'Attitude Era'. [It was] nothing more than copying the formula that we had established - going after the 18-34 year old male, abandoning the child-like characters, doing more realistic storylines. All of the things that we had [proved] to be successful, Vince adapted those things…but he did them bigger, louder and more aggressively.

"[But] while Vince was making that creative decision and adapting that strategy…I've got a bunch of corporate executives who knew nothing about our product. They didn't know why people watched it. They didn't know the history of it. They didn't understand why it worked. They knew nothing at all about it.

"It couldn't have been better for Vince, and it couldn't have been worse for us."

275

Five days after the meeting, the *Constitution* ran another television story, this time addressing increases in violence, foul language and nudity across both broadcast and cable networks. In a passage that flew almost completely under the radar, Terri Tingle admitted TNT was now having 'second thoughts' about *Monday Nitro*. "We are looking into the question right now about whether it's too violent," Tingle said. "There's been a lot of publicity about wrestling, and we wouldn't be responsive if we weren't listening to what was being said."

––––––

To begin the next *Nitro* broadcast, Tony Schiavone informed fans that his announce partner, Larry Zybysko, was embroiled in a meeting with "Time Warner officials." When Zybysko returned to the announce booth later on, he explained his absence using some rather curious language, claiming that a doctored videotape had fooled the executives into believing he had behaved improperly. "People who don't belong on the set," Zybysko concluded, "should stay off the set."

Whether intentional or not, the utterance materialized amongst intense internal unrest, both within TBS, Inc. (vis-à-vis its relationship with WCW), and - evidently - within the psyche of Eric Bischoff himself. After participating in a tag-team match against Jay Leno at *Road Wild*, Bischoff returned home with a clear response in mind.

I've made up my mind, Bischoff told his wife.

I'm not going back.

Chapter 31:
Damage Control

ULTIMATELY, BISCHOFF CHANGED his mind, optimistic that he could stand his ground against the TBS suits. After all, WCW was in the midst of another wave of national attention, this time arising from Leno's involvement at *Road Wild*. Although wrestling purists claimed the match to be a farce - at one stage, Leno put Hollywood Hogan in a sustained submission hold - an estimated 365,000 fans purchased the spectacle on pay-per-view. More importantly, mainstream outlets were covering the wrestling wars like never before.

Writing for the *New York Times*, media reporter Bill Carter observed that the ratings battle existed within a wider conflict between broadcast and cable networks. "Weekly wrestling shows have become the dominant hits of cable television," Carter wrote. "The cable channels with wrestling shows - TNT, TBS and USA - are increasingly using this fact to try [and] pry more revenue from advertisers.

"Network executives, meanwhile," continued Carter, "are trying, with some forced subtlety, to reference the stereotype of the wrestling audience - lower-income, under-educated - as a reason why cable is not a place [for] premium advertisers."

In May - at the same time Eric Bischoff was engaged in his challenge towards Vince McMahon - ABC encouraged advertisers to stray away from wrestling, purchasing a persuasive full-page ad in the *Wall Street Journal*. "Thinking of shifting ad dollars from broadcast to cable?" asked the blurb, which highlighted wrestling as occupying 8 of the 15 most watched hours on cable. "By contrast," it continued, "look at the ABC shows that make up 1/3 of the top 15 broadcast network programs - *The Drew Carey Show, Home Improvement, NYPD Blue, Dharma and Greg*, and *ABC's Monday Night Football*."

"There was a lot of press around cable's ratings growth," says Joe Uva of the time, "and the fact that cable could be a cost effective substitute...to extend audience reach. ABC knew that many advertisers were squeamish over wrestling's content, and the ad was pointing out that the highest rated programs in cable prime time - other than live NFL broadcasts - were WCW and WWF telecasts. The timing of their ad and its placement in the *Wall Street Journal* coincided with the start of the annual 'Upfront' buying season, when advertisers typically buy upwards of 80% of their ad time for the following year."

In Carter's *New York Times* piece, Brad Siegel derided the ABC ad as being "borne of ignorance." He contended that he had "pounded the pavement for three years" in an effort to reach advertisers, before citing a recent deal with Pepsi as evidence of a turnaround. "Last year," Siegel revealed in a separate interview, "I visited every single advertising agency in New York. I was so frustrated by the fact that I knew we had this event every Monday night that delivered the same kind of viewers that major sporting events and ESPN and MTV were delivering, but advertisers had this sort of snob attitude about it. It was as though [advertisers] thought it wasn't good for their product. It made no sense at all."

For the moment, while unwilling to publicly support WCW's positioning as 'family-friendly' entertainment, Bischoff decided to condemn the competition instead. "Out of desperation," he told *Broadcasting and Cable*, "and in order to get bigger numbers, [the WWF] are going with gratuitous 'T' and 'A'...and women mouthing the F-word.

"I have nothing against going for hard-core, adult themes, if indeed your network will allow you to do that. I think it is irresponsible in the long term, [however], and I think Vince is shooting himself in the foot."

Ironically, Bischoff's newest acquisition was a throwback to the

WWF's more cartoonish history. In an effort to capitalize on another old *Wrestlemania* match, Jim Hellwig returned as *The Warrior* in Hartford, Connecticut, facing off with Hogan in a surprise *Nitro* segment.

Known for being as passionate as he was eccentric, Hellwig faxed nearly 50 pages of ideas to Bischoff before his comeback, and evidently, articulated many of them upon arrival. "*You were the quintessential influence of what was good, great, and heroic,*" spouted Warrior to a disbelieving Hogan. "*But [though] you may have beaten myths, legends, giants, and other great men, you never - never - beat a Warrior!*"

Warrior continued his speech for 20 minutes, taking unexpected turns here, there, and - as Eric Bischoff memorably described it - *evvverrrywhere*. Nonetheless, in the short-term, his signing looked to have been a stroke of brilliance. The stumbling soliloquy drew a 6.4 rating, more than double the competing segment on *Raw*, while setting up a nostalgic return bout with Hogan later in the year.

Additionally, more good news was to come, as following a five-month legal dispute, Ric Flair prepared to make a return of his own. Rumors abounded that Flair would play a major role at an upcoming *Nitro* in Greenville, SC - a city in which he had performed since the 1970s - and on September 14th, the conjecture came true. Skirting the line between fiction and reality, Flair exploded in front of the BI-LO Center crowd, trashing Bischoff in an intensely memorable segment:

"*Bischoff, this might be my only shot, and I gotta tell ya, I'm gonna make it my best. Is this what you call a great moment in TV? This is real! This is not bought and paid for! It's a real...life..situation!*

"*You're an overbearing asshole! That's right! You're an obnoxious...overbearing ass! Abuse of power! You! Abuse of power! Cut me off! Come on! It's called abuse of power! You suck!*

"*I hate your guts. I hate your guts. You are a liar, you're a cheat,*

279

you're a scam, you are a no...good...son of a bitch!

"Fire me! I'm already fired! Fire me! I'm already fired!"

As the show returned from commercial break, Tony Schiavone called the moment the greatest in *Nitro* history, but breathtakingly - in an ostensible effort to *guarantee* a ratings victory - Flair's promo was followed by another huge occurrence: the first-ever match between Goldberg and Sting.

In the end, Goldberg retained his title, and WCW retained its latest winning streak on Mondays, besting *Raw* for the fourth straight time in head-to-head competition. But after dropping the subsequent show on September 21st, *Nitro* returned on September 28th with an even bigger main event: Hollywood Hogan vs. Bret Hart.

Similar to Goldberg vs. Sting, Hogan vs. Hart could certainly be considered a 'dream match', and conventionally, it was a clash thought to deserve a long-term buildup. After all, fans had clamored for the latter match for the best part of a decade, and throughout 1998, WCW's own programming teased its eventuality.

But minutes into the contest, Hart went down with an apparent knee injury, causing Sting to 'substitute' for him instead. The injury was soon revealed to be a ruse, however, and despite being confusing in its internal logic, the Hitman returned to attack Sting. Signaling his renewed alliance with Hogan, Hart helped *Nitro* to best *Raw* regardless (4.6 to 4.0) - at the cost of a major novelty match-up.

Hogan's ongoing feud with Warrior - not to mention his numerous other disputes with Sting, Goldberg, Nash, and the like - continued to take center stage on *Nitro*. Meanwhile, Diamond Dallas Page secured a title shot with his win at *Fall Brawl: War Games*, the first event broadcast from WCW's new digital production truck. "David Crockett knows about this," begins Dick Cheatham, "and Neal Pruitt knows about this...but nobody else does.

"At this point, [TBS] had a freeze on capital expenditures. They were [saying], 'no more capital, because we'll be in violation of loan covenants'. They were really strict...they didn't wanna have their threshold of $100 million in capital expenditure violated, because we'd be in a world of trouble with our lenders.

"At that point, a horizon for capital expenditure was only $1,000. So if you wanted to get a new computer, [for example], you were just 'SOL' - because that was a capital expenditure. So we had to change some rules so that people could get the tools they wanted to have.

"I hate to admit this, but it's true...Neal and David were saying, 'we have gotta have this new digital truck. We gotta have it, because with the direction [production is] going, we gotta have it for just the general quality of our program'.

"My deal was, 'ok, how much?'

"They said, '2 million bucks'.

"I said, 'Don't worry - I got you covered. I'll find a way to hide it'.

"So while everybody else is not getting their couches covered, I'm doing everything I can to help these guys go first class. I remember watching the War Games pay per view, seeing the referee's coin flip and dammit...if you couldn't read the coin with that camera! That's how good it was! You couldn't lie about [the coin flip] at that point!

"So I spent 2 million dollars - of Turner's money - to improve the programming when everybody else was fighting for nickles. But my deal was...I loved wrestling - I loved it."

Also on the pay-per-view, Cheatham watched as Scott Hall - now playing a modified gimmick 'inspired' by his real-life troubles with alcohol - stumbled around the mat in a loss to Konnan. 24 hours later, he would throw up on Bischoff as part of a widely panned angle. "I think Eric," shrugs Cheatham, "was in this netherworld of performance art, by this point."

Apparently, Bischoff had even taken to 'performing' off-camera, remembers new hire Joel Edwards. "I got the whole office tour after my first couple of days," says Edwards, who was appointed as an Avid Editor and Producer. 'They said, Eric's in his office - let's introduce you to him'.

"He was in the biggest office at the Power Plant and…I guess he had been forewarned. They brought me in…and he's at his desk on the far side…wearing a Viking helmet with horns, a little mask over his eyes and a fake black wig with long hair down the back.

"So he's wearing this helmet thing, and he stands up [to greet me]. I said, 'hi, I'm Joel - I'm the new Avid editor'. He was kind of doing his best to intimidate me, and it was kinda working. He said, 'so…watch a lot of wrestling?' I said, 'no…I did as a kid, but I've been in editing and broadcasting for a while'. He said, 'you're not a mark, are you'? I said, 'no…but I can be if you want'. Maybe he just wanted to make sure I was [really] an editor, and not someone that just wanted to be around the wrestlers.

"Then, he sort of walked me to the door - being uncomfortably close, I felt - with his helmet on and everything. He did this fake punch to my chest, slapping his own chest to make the sound effect. I was sort of prepared for that, because the other producers had said to be prepared for anything. So I sold it like a pro - I fell back against the wall and clutched my chest, gasping and moaning.

"He said, 'cool - you're hired' - and walked away.

"I thought I was already hired."

Despite Bischoff and his company being sequestered from the rest of TBS - by virtue of its new Smyrna, GA headquarters - the corporate bosses still looked to maintain some oversight. One former Turner employee, speaking under anonymity, recalls being asked to create a new filing system at the WCW offices. "Bischoff came by my office and accused me of being a spy," he divulges. "He said he 'knew what I was up to'. He said I was a 'spy from corporate', and he didn't want me around. My jaw was on the floor."

"Please don't attach me to this," says another high-ranking Turner executive, "but I think Eric kinda lost it. Yeah, he was this character on TV, but people forget he was also running the company. And, from what I understand, he was coming up with the storylines...so it was just too much, I think."

With *Halloween Havoc* on the horizon, Bischoff hoped to supplement the card - which featured DDP challenging Goldberg, Kevin Nash facing Scott Hall, Bret Hart squaring off with Sting, and Hollywood Hogan meeting the Warrior - with an attention-grabbing angle like no other. "It was probably October 20th," begins TBS President Bill Burke. "It's like Tuesday...we've got *Thursday Thunder* and then *Halloween Havoc* is over the weekend or something. I come to work, and I get a message from Terri Tingle - the head of Standards and Practices - that says, 'have you talked to Eric'?

"[Terri said], 'he's got an idea that I'm not so excited about. I said, 'no', and now he wants to talk to you'.

"So I said [over the phone], 'Hey, Eric, I heard you got an idea'."

"He said, 'yeah...here's what we're gonna do. We're gonna leak it on the Internet...'"

"Remember Eric was a pilot - he had his pilot's license.

"So Eric goes, "we're gonna leak it on the Internet that I died in a plane crash with..."

"I wish I could remember the wrestler. It was a medium-level wrestler.

"He goes, "we're just gonna leak it out, and no-one's gonna know if it's real or not. Then, he and I are gonna come back as ghosts at *Halloween Havoc*, and we're gonna kick everybody's ass!'

"I was like, 'huh. Well, y'know, we generally don't deal in death...I mean, we're gonna say that Eric Bischoff *died?*'

"He said, 'yeah'.

"I said, 'well, Eric, you're also the guy who is President of WCW. So [in reality], we would have to do a press release...'

"He said, 'no press release'.

"I said, 'what if somebody calls CNN'?

"He's like, 'we'll say...we can't comment until they've notified...next of kin', or something!

"I said, 'ok, Eric...we can't tell CNN...that's like the most respected - at least then - the most respected [news outlet]...we can't do that! And I don't think we wanna deal in death. I'm really sorry - I'm with Terri on this one'.

"He's like, 'what if it's not me - it's just two wrestlers?'

"He kept pushing and pushing [for it]. I mean it was a brilliant idea...incredibly creative...but we're not dealing with death, and CNN is not gonna do that. But I'll never forget that story."

In the end, there were no ghosts at *Halloween Havoc*, but the Hogan-Warrior match - most fans agreed - was ghastly. Conversely, fan favorite Diamond Dallas Page - receiving serious consideration (courtesy of Dusty Rhodes, still a huge advocate) to end Goldberg's winning streak, electrified the crowd with a match surpassing all prior expectations. In the final moments, Goldberg (having previously knocked himself out during the contest), kicked out of Page's famed Diamond Cutter, and then hit the Jackhammer to dramatically remain champion.

But unfortunately for WCW, many fans who ordered the event didn't even see the match, as before it began, the live signal dropped out for around 20 percent of the audience. Inexplicably, *Halloween Havoc* lived up to its name - not because of an unfortunate technical glitch, but due to human error.

It later emerged that despite purchasing a three-hour time slot for the pay-per-view, WCW failed to inform cable operators that they were actually running long. "You only have a certain length of time that you're on the satellite for a pay-per-view," clarifies David Crockett. "[After that], they turn around and re-run it, or they might have another program straight after. Either way, at 11:00pm, they cut your signal. The transponder on that satellite goes to somebody else…it's like cutting a switch off."

Incredibly, Bischoff learned of the issue only after speaking with his 12-year old son, Garett, over the phone. By that point, the entire event was over. "There were people that weren't paying attention," continues Crockett. "In the production truck, we were trying to tell them. We were screaming, trying to tell them to get their act together, but it just didn't happen. They thought, 'well you can go longer…'. No - you cannot! That is one thing that is set in stone!"

According to one industry spokesperson, given appropriate notice, it would have been a "two-minute" fix to extend the time window. Instead, WCW was forced to issue millions of dollars in eventual refunds. "Cable systems wanted their money back," Crockett says, "and viewers wanted their money back. It was not a pleasant thing."

To open *Nitro* the next night, Tony Schiavone informed fans that the protracted match would replay at 9:00pm EST - for everyone - on TNT. "Unfortunately, last night," Schiavone began, "an instance occurred that was out of the control of World Championship

Wrestling. Some of the systems went down prematurely...and because of this - as you might expect - WCW officials have been in meetings all day...deciding what course of action to take. We have decided tonight - on this program, around the 9 o'clock hour - we will bring you the match between Goldberg and Diamond Dallas Page in its entirety.

"Now, our competition...would make people believe that this has been ratings ploy - that we went off the air on purpose last night, to bring you the match later on [for free]. That is not the case (ironically, years later, Schiavone believes the claim may possess some truth)."

At 8:50pm, the announcers were informed of a change. "We're going early," said associate director Mark Sanders from the TNT control truck. "Apologize to people who call in," he continued, speaking with network colleagues in Atlanta. "Y'all may be getting some irate calls from people who started their VCRs exactly at 9."

On the fly, the format for *Nitro* was changed, resulting in an upcoming match being canceled. At 8:56pm, the replay kicked in, allowing for Goldberg's entrance to counter *Raw*'s (9:00pm) start on USA. "The good news," remarked Sanders, shortly before stepping out for a cigarette, "is that it's an 18-minute tape."

On Tuesday afternoon, the numbers came in: *Nitro* recorded a 5.06 rating - reaching an unbelievable peak of 7.18 during the Goldberg vs. Page replay - seeing off *Raw* (4.48) for the first time in five weeks. A closer look at the metrics revealed that aside from the blockbuster bout, *Raw* actually would have won the night, 4.64 to 4.44; but nevertheless, with the damage control initiated, the crisis had been navigated, and the fans apparently satiated.

For now.

Chapter 32:
Fingerpoke

ON NOVEMBER 9TH, in a publicity stunt designed to remove his character from WCW television, Hollywood Hogan announced his supposed intention to 'run for President'. According to reports, Hogan believed he was flirting with overexposure, and with the Warrior experiment finished - courtesy of a bicep injury to Jim Hellwig - the leader of nWo 'Black-and-White' stepped aside for the immediate future.

Backstage at *Nitro*, Hogan still found time to participate in an impromptu sitdown with Bischoff, Goldberg and Chris Jericho, who since running through the cruiserweight division, had engaged (with the support of Terry Taylor) in an unplanned feud with Goldberg on television. In September, as a means to buttress weeks of witty promos mocking the champion, Jericho 'defeated' a Goldberg imposter - beginning a gag where he claimed himself (facetiously) as undefeated - causing an array of crowd signs to call for his destruction. *They wanna see this*, Jericho implored to the room, suggesting that Goldberg defeat him convincingly in a 'squash match'. *Let's make them pay for it!*

But unfortunately for the Canadian, the only thing to get squashed was the idea itself. The match would not take place, Bischoff decided, leaving Jericho to settle for a one-off angle where Goldberg violently speared him instead (along the way, Jericho recalls Bischoff also suggesting that Judge Judy could somehow get involved). In light of the verdict, Jericho's decision to meet secretly with Vince McMahon in October - a clear case of tampering if ever the news broke - seemed more admissible than ever. Along with The Giant (soon to be signed to a 10-year, $10 million contract), Jericho would be WWF-bound within the year.

Specifically, both performers cited frustration with WCW's 'glass ceiling' - the perception that aside from rare exceptions (DDP, Sting, Goldberg), the road to main eventing was first through Vince McMahon. "There were guys who were hungry, and wanted to do more," remembers Michelle Baines, a WCW producer. "I was working as a PA on *WCW Saturday Night*, back when Woody Kearce was the producer. The show was full of our midcard guys - except for the last match. Well, we wanted to promote these other guys…teach them how to give good interviews, [and so on].

"One day, we were in the 'war room' with everyone, and I was talking to Craig [Leathers]. We really wanted to push these ideas forward…so I said, 'these midcard guys want some time as well, and we've come up with some ideas to help them'.

"We were *shut down* - I almost got fired. I was told, 'don't worry about it - just be like a carpenter and build your little show'. I said, 'we love this show! We put our heart in to this, and we want to make it better'. I was told, 'this is not the 'A' show, and this isn't even the 'B' show, so you need to get out of the conversation'."

"If you weren't on the private plane," quips one WCW wrestler - referencing Bischoff's propensity to travel with certain wrestlers - "I don't know how much he cared about you. It was kind of like being on the independent scene, because you could really do whatever you wanted. One time, I'm sitting there with 10 minutes before we go live, and someone comes in and says, 'lace 'em up'.

"So now I'm going out there with one of the luchadores, and Kevin Sullivan tells me I'm going 'over' with my 'finish'. Two minutes later, Terry Taylor comes up to me and says, 'we're doing a 'DQ' (disqualification finish) - shove the ref and get out of there'.

"So now I'm about ready to go through the curtain, and Arn [Anderson] pulls me aside. He goes, 'you're gonna slip on a banana peel and get rolled up'. So now I don't know what the fuck I'm doing.

"In the end, I just go out there and pin the guy with my finish. Kevin had the 'pencil' at that time, so I figure to stay in line with that. Of course, I got yelled at after the match."

"I was on an airplane one day," remembers Bobby Blaze, a veteran wrestler with international experience, "and someone told me, 'Eric Bischoff don't speak to anyone who makes less than $500,000 a year'. I said, 'you know…that's about right'. I was sitting in first class with someone making *almost* that much.

"I think Eric was very, very busy. I think he did a very good job and had a lot of responsibility…but he [mostly] kept in contact with the guys who were there to draw the money, and draw the ratings.

"He spoke to me a couple of times. He said, 'hey, good match, Louie' after my tryout match, and I said, 'it's Bobby. Bobby Blaze'. A couple years went by before we actually spoke again, on a one-on-one type basis. I didn't take it any of it personally.

"When I started with WCW [in September 1997], everyone thought he was a genius, I think. The people I was around were like, 'Eric's doing a great job…this thing is really taking off'.

"[But] it got to where people were starting to understand…I can't speak for everyone…but some people were like, 'what's he doing? Where the hell did he come up with this crazy idea? Who's in his ear this week?'

"It got to where…some people thought, 'this guy's just a goof. It's kind of a fluke [thing]. He was listening to so-and-so, and now he's not listening to anyone. He thinks he's done it all himself, and he hasn't'."

"I remember trying to break the ice with Eric," shares one lower card WCW wrestler. "I was in the bathroom and he walked in. Now for whatever reason, I had recently ran into the guy who taught Eric karate in Minneapolis. So to kind of break the ice, make some waves with the boss, I go, 'hey, Eric - I heard from your karate instructor over there in Minneapolis'.

289

"He said, 'oh yeah, how's he doing?'"

"I said, 'yeah great, he's still running his gym and everything, and-'"

"Before I could finish my sentence, he just dried his hands and walked out of the room."

"I was talking to [former WCW controller and promoter] Chip Burnham one day," adds Dick Cheatham. "We used to drink a beer every now and then. Well, Chip told me that Eric had passed on Dwayne Johnson."

"It was *before* he broke loose with the WWF, doing that goofy Rocky Maivia thing. They had a chance to see his raw talent, but apparently, there was no interest. It wasn't just Eric, it was the people at the Power Plant too, which was supposedly where we developed all the talent."

———

Meanwhile, in Hogan's absence, Kevin Nash was apparently providing creative input again, as on November 24th, Mark Madden reported that along with DDP, Nash had recently joined the booking committee as an 'idea man'. "They tried to put me in that for a while," remembers Page of his involvement, "and I was like, 'fuck that - too much stress and pressure'."

In any event, Madden's revelation came just two days after *World War 3* - a pay-per-view where Nash won a battle royal to face Goldberg at *Starrcade* - and only a day after he defeated Wrath, a wrestler with a lengthy (25 matches) unbeaten streak of his own.

Therefore, the Nash push fueled speculation that he was, in fact, suddenly and unambiguously - WCW's Head Booker. But while he certainly possessed tremendous influence, the ultimate authority on creative matters remained Bischoff. To that end, with *Starrcade* ('The Granddaddy of Them All') fast approaching, Bischoff was about to sign-off on the Granddaddy of all decisions.

But concurrently, Bischoff was also engaged in an on-screen feud with Ric Flair, based deliberately around their real-life issues. Their beef ultimately produced some of Flair's most memorable promos in years, although on December 14th, the 49-year old star was asked to show some weakness on *Nitro*.

Following backstage instructions, Flair crumpled to the mat after an interview with Gene Okerlund, clutching his left arm and feigning a heart attack. Incredibly, the cameras kept rolling as the production staff - including department VP David Crockett - reacted as if it were legitimate (noticeably, Crockett appeared visibly shaken as he watched Flair on the mat, unaware of its contrivance).

Behind the stage, various staffers were becoming apoplectic, causing an altercation with a policeman perceived to be blocking an ambulance. "I could normally tell when things were contrived," agrees Neal Pruitt, "but at that point, I was sold - hook, line and sinker. I thought for sure that it was the last of Ric Flair's days there."

The reasoning, as per usual, was a familiar one. "They were so paranoid about people leaking their ideas," says one former production member, "that they had us thinking Ric was gonna die."

———

In the final stretch to *Starrcade*, WCW rolled in to St. Louis, MO for a *Nitro* episode on December 21st. Before air time, Bischoff prepared to deliver a patented pre-show speech, mindful of the nearly 30,000 fans packing the TWA Dome for the show (braving a vicious snowstorm in the process). Shockingly, as Jericho would later recount, Bischoff made further predictions of the WWF's demise, *again* guaranteeing its collapse within six months.

Two days later, it looked as though if nothing else, Bischoff was about to secure a huge coup for his company. Following Jay Leno's participation at *Road Wild* in August, NBC were apparently interested - as per a *Variety* magazine report - in airing a special WCW broadcast on February 14:

NBC is in talks with Turner Broadcasting-owned World Championship Wrestling to carry a primetime two-hour wrestling special during the February 1999 sweeps.

Although spokesmen for NBC and Turner declined to comment on the discussions, sources say NBC has penciled in the special for Feb. 14 as a replacement for the canceled NBA All-Star Game, which has fallen victim to the team owners' player lockouts. National Basketball Assn. Commissioner David Stern said Wednesday that he will recommend canceling the season unless an agreement can be reached by Jan. 7.

The NBC-Turner event has already sounded out Hollywood Hulk Hogan and Randy Savage as two of the marquee names, sources say. One source says a another reason why Turner wants to get a primetime game on NBC on Feb. 14 is to financially damage a pay-per-view event produced by Turner's cutthroat competitor, Vince McMahon's WWF (World Wrestling Federation), called the "Valentine's Day Massacre." The NBC event would be live, probably from the MGM Grand in Las Vegas.

According to a source familiar with its financial records, WCW grossed $188 million in 1998 - over *half-a-million dollars per day*. Now, with the NBC deal seemingly in place, its product could potentially be exposed to an entirely new audience, creating an array of alternative marketing and advertising opportunities. According to some reports, NBC were envisioning the broadcast of *multiple* WCW events, occurring periodically throughout 1999 (and perhaps, even beyond).

To draw viewers to the first special (tentatively titled as 'WCW Love Hurts'), Bischoff planned an inversion of a familiar wrestling trope. In the middle of the ring, Dennis Rodman would be asked to *divorce* model Carmen Electra, following his filing for annulment on November 23rd - nine days into their marriage. Subsequently, in a rematch of their now-famous Georgia Dome clash, reports suggested that Goldberg would wrestle Hogan in the finale.

For the time being, however, all of the focus was on Goldberg's title defense at *Starrcade '98*. Beforehand, the hype resembled a "heavyweight fight," recalls Kevin Nash, his opponent in the match. "Go back and watch that *Starrcade*," Nash says. "It's 50-50 that night when we go out. There's 50 percent of the people that want me to win, and 50 percent that want him to win."

10 minutes into a physical, back-and-forth contest, Goldberg looked poised to deliver his patented set-up move - the spear. Suddenly, however, Scott Hall - following earlier run-ins from Bam Bam Bigelow and Disco Inferno - interfered to stun the champion with a cattle prod (or 'stun gun'). Nash quickly capitalized, lifting the dazed Goldberg up for his Jackknife Powerbomb. Three seconds later, amid an electric crowd reaction, the streak was over.

"People wanted to see him get beat," remembers Nash of the crowd response, "[but] when he got beat, they went, 'oh shit - I'm not sure I wanted to see [that]'.

"That's only because of the 15 run-ins, cattle prods...if we went toe to toe - and I'd have beat Bill with the Powerbomb [only] - I would have been a god."

"When they gave me that finish," says Kevin Sullivan, still involved in the creative process, "I said, 'why don't we hire Barnum and Bailey and have the elephants trample on him, too?' If he had lost in a *wrestling match*...

"Anybody can lose, right? Ronda Rousey lost. Brock Lesnar lost. It's when you come back [that matters]. They coulda had three huge pay-per-views - like Ali-Frasier.

"I wasn't the booker then, and Eric and Kevin [Nash] were doing a lot of it, so it mighta been Eric's call...it mighta been Kevin's call...it mighta been somebody else's call. But when they gave me the finish, I said, 'please don't do it this way'.

"The finish should've been...Bill's got Kevin rockin' and rollin'...Kevin's slumped in the corner...Goldberg goes for the tackle...Kevin moves out of the way...he hits the 'bows...come back out, big boot to the face...Powerbomb...Kevin covers him, one, two, three."

293

"I guarantee if I had the pen - or the pencil - I'd have booked it that way," agrees Nash.

———

To begin the year, WCW's new champion addressed fans in a series of half-'shoot' (legitimate), half-'work' (in character) online commentaries. "For almost two years," wrote Nash in the first entry, dated January 1st, 1999, "we dominated the WWF and became the No. 1 promotion in North America, if not the world. Since then, they gained some momentum during the NBA playoffs while we were off, and we haven't seemed to be able to bounce back. Some people say the WWF is doing some tacky stuff; some people say they are doing some innovative stuff…but they're doing good television and this is a TV show. It's no longer a wrestling show.

"*Starrcade*, Dec. 27th, was Bill Goldberg's birthday. For him, I know losing the belt on that day was kinda upsetting…[so] Monday on Nitro from The Georgia Dome…I have to erase all doubts…I've got to stick Bill on my own, without anyone's help."

And thus, Nash helped set the scene for WCW's return to the Georgia Dome on Monday, January 4th. With *Raw* presenting a taped program, and Goldberg's highly-hyped rematch to build around, it looked as though *Nitro* could win the night for the first time since October.

Behind the curtain come Monday, half the backstage buzz concerned Scott Steiner - who decided to beat up announcer Jimmy Baron - while others watched the '99 Fiesta Bowl, a game featuring Nash's alma mater, the Tennessee Volunteers. Late in the afternoon, a *Sports Illustrated* reporter witnessed Nash, Steiner, Lex Luger, Scott Hall and Goldberg discussing creative plans for the show. As viewers would later witness, Goldberg would be first removed from the arena at the hands of Atlanta police - specifically, via a spurious 'sexual assault' claim levied by Elizabeth, an nWo manager - allowing for the surprise return of Hollywood Hogan. Nash would then campaign for a 'warm-up' match against Hogan (leveraging nine months of nWo

294

in-fighting), only to *literally* take a dive and get pinned in an elaborate ruse. This would provide the catalyst for Goldberg to save the day - only for Nash et al. to violently assault him instead. The suddenly reformed nWo would utilize handcuffs, spray paint and Hall's cattle prod (strategically covered with a thick piece of electrical tape, as to not *actually* produce a jolt) to take out the fallen Goldberg, restarting his title chase all over again.

"The whole thing was designed," begins Nash, "to put together a faction [to oppose Goldberg]. It was the old school, Hulk Hogan [philosophy] - build a team of heels that Goldberg had to fight for eight months. That's the way it was laid out."

Midway through the show, at the behest of Bischoff, Tony Schiavone implored viewers not to switch to *Raw:*

"Fans, don't even think about changing the channel, because we've learned that at our competition, Mick Foley, who used to wrestle here as Cactus Jack, is going to win their world title! Heh - talk about putting asses in the seats."

As Schiavone would constantly be reminded of (and despite WWF.com spoiling the title change themselves), an estimated 600,000 viewers immediately switched to the USA Network. For those that did stay with *Nitro*, a shocking sight then unfolded when Nash 'laid down' for Hogan, taking a single finger to the chest and collapsing to the mat. As the nWo celebrated their deception, Goldberg hit the ring to an incredible crowd response, prompting 2.1 million viewers - in a long-forgotten trivia note - to join the broadcast on TNT. But after spearing Hogan to the canvas, Goldberg was beaten mercilessly and overwhelmingly by the group, generating a level of vitriol reminiscent of Hogan's 1996 turn (to what extent this reaction consisted of *true heat* - or what wrestlers called *go-away heat* - is an opinion still debated today).

As planned, Hall leaned over to administer the cattle prod to Goldberg, only for the former Atlanta Falcon to grab its end *not* covered with tape. "He knew the tape was there to protect him," Hall later said of

295

Goldberg, "but he's such a complete psycho.

"I was sticking him, and he grabbed it and pushed it away, looked me dead in the eye and yelled, 'Come on!'

"I thought, 'whoa. Someone please tell Bill, 'this is supposed to be fake'.'"

———

The entire affair (eventually known axiomatically as *The Fingerpoke of Doom*) - combined with Goldberg's loss to Nash at *Starrcade* - have often been cited as two significant errors in WCW's booking. When asked if both were mistakes, Bischoff accepts the charge, but simultaneously downplays their importance. "Were they mistakes? Yeah - arguably - they could be considered [so]. It didn't work. But guess what? There's 52 weeks of television every year. Hundreds of hours a year. Some things work, some things don't.

"Nobody is 100% all of the time…[but] were they creative mistakes? Sure. I'll take responsibility for that. If I could've done it differently - knowing then what I know now - would I have done it differently? Of course I would! [But] were they turning points? Absolutely not.

"That's just asinine. That's - again - people who know nothing about the business, trying to sound like that they do by pointing out things like that, [retrospectively]…and making themselves sound really, really smart. It's similar to me to sitting back, the Monday morning after the Super Bowl, and talking about how I would've coached the game, and the plays I would've called differently, so we could've won the game. It's no different.

"There were several turning points. It was not one, and they certainly weren't *creative* turning points. That's just bullshit…nonsense…wrestling dirt site nonsense. The real turning point was in mid-1998 when I was told, 'you are no longer going to use the formula that got you to the dance. You are no longer going to use the formula that almost put Vince McMahon out of business.

296

You're gonna become family friendly. You're gonna abandon the creative formula that's working so well, and you're gonna adapt a new formula that's going to make us family friendly'.

"I knew my audience was gonna shit on that. I knew we were going to lose a bunch of our audience - and we did. I protested it, as loud as I could…[but] *that* was a turning point.

"Another turning point was Mike Tyson. I knew when I saw that - the game was over. That was a turning point…and when Vince McMahon adapted our formula and went after our audience. He did it better, [too] - because he was willing to take bigger risks.

"That was the [real] turning point - not the 'Fingerpoke of Doom'!"

For his part, reflecting on the events that followed *Starrcade*, Nash rejects the notion that he benefited from beating Goldberg. "Anybody that knows Kevin Nash knows I'm a pretty smart guy," he begins, "and if I'm gonna beat Bill Goldberg - after 172 or whatever wins in a row - I'm sure as fuck not gonna turn around the next Monday, and do a Fingerpoke of Doom and hand the belt to Hulk Hogan.

"What did that do for Kevin Nash? *What did Goldberg's streak do for Kevin Nash*? Now if I'm gonna book [it] myself, I'm gonna go on a 173 win streak myself, and dodge Goldberg as a heel."

Instead, the combination of injuries, inconsistent booking and eventually, multiple character turns (Hollywood Hogan to babyface, Ric Flair to heel, Diamond Dallas Page to heel, etc.) prevented Goldberg from ever achieving true vengeance against the nWo. Consequently, some observers believed his popularity to have been wasted - with announcer Bobby Heenan famously among them. *This is the beginning of the end*, Heenan lamented to colleagues after Goldberg's first loss, mindful that such a phenomenon was unlikely to be duplicated.

"I think we rushed it," reflects Mike Weber, WCW's long-time Director of Marketing. "We could have got another year or two out of his peak popularity. I mean, we had Goldberg yarmulkes as a licensed product! We sold his T-shirts like it was going out of style. We actually had WCW-themed credit cards through Capital One, and that's when I knew Goldberg was hot - because more people wanted his credit cards than Hulk Hogan."

"Hogan was trying to hold on to the twilight of his career," says Greg Prince, WCW's former controller, "but Goldberg was the phenomenon in the arenas. Every department head I would interact with - from the pay-per-view guy to merchandising to ad sales…it got to the point where it was Goldberg sort of driving things. So it was creating some friction - no doubt about it."

Indeed, even as WCW approached the new century - the new millennium - Hogan, age 45, remained a towering backstage presence. "I fought with Hogan - as a shoot backstage - trying to get things done for almost two years here," lamented Nash in a January 6th web post. "And you're not gonna beat Hogan. If it doesn't have his blessing, it ain't gonna get done.

"The only reason we got the NBC deal is because Hogan's here. For a year, I haven't been used by this company, [so] I came up with an angle that got Hogan the belt, knowing that it would put me back in the mix."

Responding to user comments three days later, Nash clarified things further. "Until Hulk Hogan completely retires from professional wrestling," he wrote, "he's *The Man*…[he] can make your life in this business very easy - if you're on his team. His money and his power can make your life a whole lot easier.

"You can either jump aboard his express, earn a ton of money and live an easy life, or try to fight him like I did for almost a year and not be used…[because] you're not gonna beat him politically. You're just not gonna be able to function in a company when he's on top, unless you're on his team. It's a business decision, and it's the right decision."

————

From an objective standpoint, although the 'Fingerpoke' episode trailed *Raw* on January 4th (5.7-5.0), viewership in subsequent weeks reflected strong interest in an nWo reformation, with *Thunder* hitting record ratings and *Nitro* maintaining its large audience (even registering a '5.0' twice more in January).

At the same time, Bischoff was apparently still convinced that time was ticking on McMahon (who incidentally, ran into Nash shortly after the 'Fingerpoke' match, joking to his former star that it was "good booking"). After USA Today published a reader's letter criticizing wrestling - specifically its more risqué tone - and subsequently, printing McMahon's rebuttal, Bischoff weighed in with a response of his own:

Mr. Fuller,

Rest assured...Mr. McMahon knows that YOU DO "GET IT"! That's his biggest fear right now. The fact that not only are viewers beginning to "get it" but advertisers will as well.

You see, Mr. McMahon found out that he didn't have the ability to compete in this industry without resorting to the type of programming that can only be compared to an "R" rated freak show. He decided that if he was going to survive he would have to change his brand and his strategy and copy that of Jerry Springer and Howard Stern. That is his right as the owner of WWF and the rights of the USA network to air it.

The hypocrisy in his position, and the reason for his fear, is that he is dependent on advertising and licensing of his product to children. Just take a look at the advertising in his programs. Look at the kind of advertising that you see in Wal-Mart and Toys R Us. Then ask yourself, or better yet, the executives of those chains, if they "get it".

The WWF uses their programming on Saturdays, Sundays and Mondays to deliver ratings commitments to their advertisers as well as promote their licensing and merchandising. If Mr. McMahon were sincere in his position he would not accept advertising that targets children.

That will never happen. He is dependent on children. He just hopes no one "gets it"... and you did!

Eric Bischoff

WCW President

On the surface, it seemed like Bischoff had been buoyed by the NBC deal, its occurrence strengthening his skepticism of McMahon's creative strategy ("our boss doesn't feel that [it's] the way to go anyway, even if it was an option," wrote Nash on his website, referencing Bischoff's take on the WWF product). But a January 11th *Electronic Media* report revealed his optimism to have been premature:

NEW YORK — NBC killed its deal with Time Warner's World Championship Wrestling unit, citing the return of the NBA. The network planned to run a WCW special on Feb. 14, the day the NBA All-Star Game was originally scheduled.

According to Bischoff's later writings, the deal was actually nixed due to the involvement of Turner Ad Sales:

I got the green light from NBC and went back to Harvey Schiller for his approval right before Christmas.

"Harvey, here's what we've got. We can do a two-hour special on NBC. It's prime time. It's a great way to reposition ourselves and do something out of the box— bigger than and different than WWF. What do you think?"

Unfortunately, Harvey was no longer in a position to make that kind of decision on his own. He had to take it to a committee of Turner execs. I got a call back right after the first of the year from ad sales. I was told, "Yeah, that's a great opportunity, but we don't want to do it."

Ad sales.

Ad sales!

They apparently felt that by putting our brand on NBC, we would put Turner salespeople at some kind of disadvantage.

"I was on the Turner executive committee," responds Joe Uva, TBS' President of Entertainment Sales and Marketing, "but I don't recall a meeting where an NBC deal for wrestling was discussed, or that Ad Sales killed it. Dick Ebersol of NBC and Vince McMahon were/are very close, [however], and Dick and Vince [once] did a deal to put WWF on Saturday nights before Saturday Night Live."

300

And so, whether owing to the NBA's return, TBS politics or McMahon's meddling, Bischoff saw NBC slip through his fingers.

It still pisses me off, he solemnly later reflected, many years removed from its consequences.

Chapter 33:
I Quit

ACCORDING TO SONNY ONOO, Bischoff's friend and international consultant, the shelved NBC deal occurred mere months after another missed opportunity. "There was a company in Japan called *Pride*," Onoo says, referring to the mixed martial arts organization founded in 1997. "It was a pretty big company. I structured a deal to bring *Pride* to the United States, and we were gonna own half of their business in [America].

"That deal was done. We had a meeting with all the department heads, and in '98, all of the *Pride* people flew into Las Vegas for [*Halloween Havoc*]. It was at the height of the nWo, and WCW was making an amazing amount of money.

"We were bursting at the seams, and everyone was doing more than one [job]…so I think it just kind of got dropped. Everybody agreed on what we were gonna do…but it never materialized."

Interestingly, Bischoff recalls an occasion in "either '98 or '99" when TBS blocked the purchase of the Ultimate Fighting Championship (UFC), an outfit later described as "bankrupt and going under," by its eventual President Dana White. While its valuation ultimately reached $4 billion, the UFC was being shopped, Bischoff believes, at around $1.5 million.

"If I could go back in time," adds Onoo, "I wish Eric would have said, 'just go and work on this *Pride* thing'. Because we were the largest content provider for pay-per-view, we would have probably…*easily* bought UFC…and *Pride* would have been *the* MMA organization in the world.

"That's what I believe, and that's what I like to think. We had the fighters with *Pride* that were very popular - top stars fought there - and then we had a 'PPV' company willing to put it on a worldwide stage. It would have been a hell of a marriage.

"You look back and say, 'what could have been'?"

———

Notwithstanding its own parent company, WCW's most significant battle remained not with the nWo, but rather - with respect to both market share and legal affairs - the WWF. On January 13th, a letter addressed to Judge Joan Margolis advised of WCW's failure to produce key evidence in the ongoing trademark lawsuit; specifically, videotapes demonstrating Scott Hall's prior presentation as a 'jobber' in the early '90s. WWF attorneys requested the tapes after Hall discussed - in a September deposition hearing - changes to his 'look' since the mid-1980s.

On the surface, the testimony invalidated an earlier claim from Bischoff that upon returning to WCW, fans would likely recognize Hall as 'Scott Hall' - and not, as was a central issue in the case - Razor Ramon.

In his correspondence to the Judge, WWF attorney Jerry McDevitt wrote:

The specific issue is WCW's refusal to produce audiovisual works in its possession of Scott Hall's persona and look on WCW programming in the early 1980s [sic]. We regard this as very critical evidence...

A central claim in this case is that WCW infringed upon Titan's copyrights in the character RAZOR RAMON by its presentation of Scott Hall on WCW programming beginning on May 27, 1996. As the Court will recall, Mr. Hall appeared on that program, and for several weeks thereafter, without being referred to by any name whatsoever. The other major claim is that Defendants deliberately violated the Lanham Act in its presentation of Hall by purposefully presenting him in a way designed to make consumers believe he was RAZOR RAMON from the

303

WWF appearing on Turner's programming on behalf of the WWF to wrestle WCW talent.

…In one of the first depositions…Mr. Bischoff was questioned at length regarding the intended and probable effects of the aforementioned scripted lines. Mr. Bischoff denied scripting the lines to make people believe it was RAZOR RAMON, and asserted, in varying and conflicting answers, that some of the fans would have recognized the unnamed performer as Scott Hall based on his prior performances as Scott Hall.

…We…believe the audiovisual tapes in WCW's possession not only are highly probative evidence of our case-in-chief, but also a powerful piece of evidence impeaching Mr. Bischoff's claim that viewers would have recognized the unnamed performer as Scott Hall.

…For the above reasons, we served WCW with a single document request tracking Mr. Hall's deposition testimony that he performed as a jobber for WCW…[requesting] 'copies of all WCW television programming…on which Scott Hall appeared in [prior to being cast as Razor Ramon]'…

….WCW has refused to produce any of those tapes, claiming that WCW's internal procedures are such a disorganized mess that it would be unduly burdensome for WCW to attempt to locate the tapes.

Responding on behalf of WCW, TBS lawyer John Pope identified the issue as rather peculiar in nature:

Regarding Titan's alleged justification for wanting the tapes, Mr. McDevitt's arguments suggest he has everything he says he needs. He has already 'caught' Mr. Bischoff in the alleged 'inconsistency', and he has the photographs showing Mr. Hall's 'look' as a 'jobber'. There is no 'unresolved issue' about Mr. Hall's appearance, because Mr. Hall expressly testified that the photographs reflect his 'look' during that period.

The fact is no one is contending that Mr. Hall's brief appearances as a jobber…established audience recognition for him. That truly is Mr. McDevitt's strawman. Mr. Hall cultivated a 'look' as 'Diamond Studd' - in the 1990s - and Titan copied that 'look' for 'Razor Ramon'. Defendants cannot be held liable for allegedly infringing a 'look' that they originated and Titan copied.

Concurrently, the Lanham Act - a federal statute of law integral to the WWF's case - made the news for a dispute involving America Online (AOL), a dominant Internet service provider with some 15 million members (not to mention a valuation three times that of Disney). The company, absolutely ubiquitous among the average net user, successfully sued an obscure marketing outfit for sending 60 million 'spam' e-mail messages over a 10 month period. Many of the messages contained the letters "aol.com" in their headers, creating a false designation and ultimately, arousing suspicion and anger within AOL's user base.

Such a practice was especially damaging to AOL, which contemporaneously, launched similar suits against a dozen or so other spammers. It stood as an inconvenient truth, but the fact remained that aside from its membership, AOL comprised of very little else. As a company, it owned practically nothing in terms of tangible assets, and with a host of rival providers emerging at a rapid rate - often advertising their services for free - its co-founder, Steve Case, worried about a possible decline. "Case always understood that this wasn't going to last forever; [and AOL needed] to merge with a traditional company," a confidant later revealed of his thought process.

And so, throughout January of 1999, AOL's VP of Corporate Development, Miles Gilburne, devoted himself to pondering the future. Regarded as a genius in a very particular way, Gilburne contemplated his office whiteboard and spent weeks scribbling diagrams, ideas and financial projections. In the end, he realized that AOL needed to commit itself to a clear identity, growing beyond its original purpose to ensure some concrete measure of security.

But such long-term planning, regardless of its efficacy, hardly stood out as unique in the corporate world. Even in the realm of popular entertainment, premeditation was considered an essential part of creation, with storyboarding used extensively across television and film (interestingly, one of the first films to benefit from this process was *Gone With the Wind*, a movie cherished by Ted Turner). But ironically, for a spectacle ostensibly based in forethought, wrestling storylines often developed as pseudo-spontaneous realizations.

Part of the problem, bookers sometimes lamented, was unpredictability, with injuries, contract issues and uncertain audience reactions causing changes in agreed-upon plans. The competitive environment of weekly ratings battles also contributed, in no small measure, to fostering a short-term focus towards programming decisions. Furthermore, in the specific case of WCW, there were added complications arising from its second weekly prime-time show. The notion of airing *Thunder* live had long been abandoned, but even as a taped show, WCW recorded two of its episodes on the same night. Consequently, in order for storylines to 'carry' from TNT and TBS, *10* hours of content would conceivably require consideration:

March 1st, 1999: Live Monday Nitro broadcast from Chapel Hill, NC

March 4th, 1999: Thursday Thunder Taping (2 episodes - to air 3/4/99 and 3/11/99) from Winston-Salem, NC

March 8th, 1999: Live Monday Nitro broadcast from Worcester, MA

"It was always my perception," begins Brendon Hamlin, a TBS promo producer from 1995-2001, "that WCW was run in a way not unlike what you saw on TV.

"There was a huge amount of confusion when we were trying to get the promos built for *Thunder*. Its premiere was a record for a cable show, but there just wasn't a lot of synergy in launching it. It was still basking in WCW's popularity, but after that, it was probably oversaturation.

"I think they were painting the airplane while it was flying in the air. They were just trying to come up with anything to 'up the ante' a little bit more, and maybe not always in a positive way.

"It was a little bit crazy, and a little bit out of control. I interacted with [WCW producer] Michael Shocket the most, and I think he brought some clarity and sanity to the whole operation. But a lot of what I did was independent of them. A lot of that stuff they were deciding on-site, in the dressing room, who was going to win the match and how it was all gonna roll out. You often questioned what was real, and what was fake there.

"Knowing what was happening in that company...I felt like three people knew...and everybody else was wondering what was gonna happen next. It felt like the company was being run like the show."

To what extent WCW's disorganization occurred as an *adaptive* response presented an intriguing conundrum. With nearly a decade of uncertainty underpinning its existence, the lack of creative planning was *technically* understandable, with fleeting pleasures and short-term gains particularly appealing under the TBS structure. To borrow from an analysis by the economist Thomas Sowell, prudence and long-range planning were unlikely to be prioritized, after all, when part of a perceptibly chaotic world.

There was also the very human problem of burnout, which Bischoff cited as influencing his decision - effective from January 21st - to designate Kevin Nash as Head Booker.

Regarded widely, among other things, as a keen connoisseur of pop culture, Nash looked to incorporate elements from an HBO show into his writing. "My conception was always to shoot wrestling like the *Larry Sanders Show*," he says. "You shoot it with two cameras. Shoot backstage [stuff] the night before - soap-opera style - just like the [Sanders] show."

Similar to how the faux talk-show recorded backstage scenes on film (interspersed with 'live' shots on videotape), Nash envisaged a clear visual distinction - within the context of a wrestling show - between 'skits' designed to advance storylines, and the actual 'in-ring' content. "I wanted," he continues, "to do things where...two guys cut a promo [backstage], and then we say 'ok, cut, thanks guys'...but then you go to a boom camera, two guys walk in and say, 'yeah, we sat at the monitor, watching you run your mouth...'. I mean, I wanted to try and cross that…bullshit reality line there, from that standpoint too."

Nash also believed he could recast Hogan, a proposal that seemed beneficial for all concerned. "I really wanted Hulk to be the commissioner," he says. "Vince [McMahon] was taking over [on *Raw*] as the 'Mr. McMahon' character, and we needed somebody to [counteract that]."

But according to Nash, he was barely given scope to implement his vision. He contends that only his first effort - an episode of *Thunder* live from Indianapolis - ranks as the single show he possessed true autonomy over.

"I got to write one show that was *my show*," he says. "That was the first *Thunder* that aired out of Indianapolis. That's where the [nWo] 'Black and White' guys were talking shit, and we had set a camera in their locker room. That was my show that I wrote from top to bottom. It was always a 'booking committee' [after that]."

Responding to why he led a committee of contributors - as opposed to functioning as a sole authority, Nash points to the initial show in question. "I think the show was successful. I pushed people that needed to be pushed. I would like somebody to pull that show up, watch it and go 'ok, well that's a lot different than what was before and what followed'.

"It was so hard to get people to see the vision. I wanted to create a different universe that wrestling was gonna be shot in, and here we are [years later], still shooting one-camera backstage shots, where the guy closest to the camera looks like the Lochness monster.

"I was [also] trying to get Hulk to play [the commissioner] part…not knowing what Hulk's contract was. Hulk's contract was based on buy rates, and this, and that. It would have cost him millions of dollars. It was just like, 'ok, we're not structured the same as [the WWF] are'."

In addition to philosophical and contractual concerns, Nash adduces an array of other factors that influenced the booking process. "They brought in 'Standards and Practices' after three weeks," he says. "On top of that, people don't realize...we came home Monday night on a private jet, landed...got up on Tuesday and had to write next Monday's show - which was three hours - and then we had to drop a two hour *Thunder* show. [However], because we shot two Thunders [at a time], we had to write up *another* three hour *Nitro* show...to piece [together] the second *Thunder* we were gonna shoot.

"So we were basically writing ten hours of TV - plus the Saturday Night show. And we're doing that in three days - you're writing 12 hours of TV in three days. It's just not possible.

"Then you've got guys with [referring to Hogan], 'it doesn't work for me, brother' in their contract. So when you get to the building and they're in four segments...and they say, 'that doesn't work for me' - because they've got creative control - now you've got to try to rewrite around that. Or they show up at five when you're on at eight."

"A lot of times," recalls Michelle Baines, a versatile member of WCW's production team, "it was, 'let's get the input of the big stars in there'. Well, no! If you're the writer of the show, write the damn show. If you wanna have a meeting after the show, to talk about the direction of characters or storylines...fine. But you don't ask those stars that day or whatever, when y'all just get on the airplane or at the arena. That's just dumb. You have to plan your stuff better - because from a production standpoint, it's a freaking nightmare."

"There were a lot of intangibles," continues Nash. "It was just very difficult, y'know...Vince [McMahon] never ever had to deal with any of those things.

"We [also] had a ton of injuries for a while, but I did the best I could for what I had. If I was in a room by myself - with maybe Sullivan and one other person - we would've been fine. But there were just so many people involved in that booking process."

Regardless of his exact power, insiders questioned Nash's creative involvement. Some predicted, in step with previous wrestler-turned-bookers, that he would invariably position himself too favorably, while others speculated he would look to submerge his political enemies (namely Bret Hart, who remained decidedly directionless on-camera).

On February 7th, Hart traveled to Atlanta for a booking meeting, so arranged as to plot the path towards a match with Hogan in the fall. But according to the Hitman, while Hogan and Bischoff initially agreed on the plan, Nash shot down the direction afterwards. Before *Nitro* the next night, Hart then learned he would lose his United States title to Roddy Piper, nixing original plans to issue an 'open' challenge for opponents at the *SuperBrawl* pay-per-view.

The title change, while surprising, occurred on a night where *Nitro* hit a record 5.7 rating, the result of *USA* preempting *Raw*. In fairness, however, the early returns on a Nash-led booking committee were disappointing. *Raw* was pulling away from *Nitro* again, winning easily on January 25th (5.5 to 5.0), and decisively on February 1st (5.9-4.7) and February 15th (5.9-3.9).

Especially damning was the discrepancy on February 15th, a night in which *Nitro* featured a controversial angle involving Ric Flair and the nWo. In storyline, Flair was lured away from the arena, attacked mercilessly by Hogan and his cronies, and then seemingly left for dead in a nondescript field. The sheer length of the beating - not to mention its gratuitous violence - struck some fans as particularly jarring, recalls feature producer Neal Pruitt.

"I was in my office, and somebody said, 'you got a letter', reveals Pruitt, who edited the segment in a manner reminiscent of a feature film. "I opened it and I kinda got a little sick to my stomach. This mother was talking about watching the whole Flair beatdown with her child. The kid was like eight years old, or something like that, and a big Ric Flair fan.

"[She talked about] how disgusting it was for us to sit there and do that to Flair...to prolong his agony, leave him in the field...and tease and torment and bully him for that long, with all those different people involved.

"Frankly, I felt the same way she did. If it had been in my control, I would have made it half as long - and it wouldn't have been quite so violent. I know we always mixed reality with fantasy in our business, but in this case, I just felt we went overboard - I really did. I knew it, and I'm kinda glad that letter was written to me to confirm my conviction, [in terms of] how I felt about the whole shoot."

———

If WCW was indeed trending downwards, the buy rate for *SuperBrawl IX* offered some hope. An estimated 485,000 viewers purchased the event - the highest pay-per-view number (Rodman notwithstanding) since *Starrcade '97* - although critically, pundits reacted mostly with ambivalence. In a hastily-thrown together tag match also involving Nash, Rey Mysterio Jr. was booked to lose his mask, preceding a heavily-hyped main event where Flair failed to defeat Hogan for the WCW title. For his part, meanwhile, Bret Hart was left off the card entirely.

As part of *Nitro* on February 22nd, Mysterio gained some measure of revenge with a shock pinfall win over Nash in singles competition. But while insiders surmised that through 'putting over' Mysterio, Nash sought to build his trust with the locker room, the loss occurred before a scheduled rematch with Goldberg, whose character was suffering overtly from a lack of purpose. Furthermore, it partly overshadowed another upset on the same night - Bret Hart losing cleanly to Booker T.

After the show, Hart learned - along with the rest of the locker room - that Bischoff planned to embark on a long-overdue vacation, a somewhat surprising development given the state of the ratings war.

For years, however, Bischoff had vowed to take his daughter to France, and with her spring break from college upcoming, he finally decided to make good on the promise.

But irrespective of his absence, the future of Bischoff's company - and, more pertinently, that of Time Warner itself - took a step towards its destiny on Tuesday, February 23rd. Covertly, a meeting was underway in Dulles, VA - headquarters of America Online - between the men who fretted about AOL's future (Steve Case and Miles Gilburne), and an investment banker named Eduardo Mestre.

To make the most of AOL's market capitalization - possibly before it was too late - Case and Gilburne outlined three strategic options: either a) merge with a media and entertainment conglomerate; b) merge with a telecommunications company; or c) merge with another established (and profitable) Internet company. The first option appealed most to Case, who believed Time Warner to be the most viable candidate (followed by Disney, whose leadership later dismissed the idea as 'ludicrous').

In considering the proposal, Mestre understood the upside for AOL, but struggled to see how a merger could benefit Time Warner. *To be honest*, he shrugged to the group, *I can't see how it can be done.*

Nonetheless, Case continued to obsess over Time Warner, a feeling that intensified after cogitations towards eBay, Citigroup and AT&T. Meanwhile, several thousand miles away, oblivious to the talks (in step with the rest of the world), Bischoff tried to keep some control over WCW. While in France, he checked in regularly with the key players by phone, but reportedly blew a gasket upon hearing of the March 8th *Nitro*, an infamous episode featuring a total lack of wrestling in the first hour. To make matters worse, Bischoff learned that *Raw* was now attaining record numbers in the Nielsen ratings (demolishing *Nitro* to the tune of two million viewers weekly), as Hogan warned ominously - and publicly - of possible 'problems' leading up to *Uncensored* on March 14th.

312

Ultimately at the pay-per-view, Hogan dropped the belt in a convoluted cage match with Flair, subsequent to an apparent (and sudden) 'double turn' in the ring (Hogan to babyface, Flair to heel). While it was long understood that Flair preferred to play a villain, Hogan's character change was much more perplexing; in particular, his abrupt adoption of mannerisms associated with his 'good-guy' run - 'Hulking up' for the crowd especially - struck some fans as puzzling.

Bischoff returned backstage for the March 15th *Nitro*, walking directly into a conflict involving an incredulous Bret Hart. According to reports, Hart stormed out after a backstage disagreement with the booking committee, before flying to Panama City on March 22nd - only to be informed his services were not required.

After much deliberation, Hart persuaded Nash to give him some interview time, and in a deliberately subtle reference, the 'Hitman' teased a future confrontation with Goldberg. In actuality, Hart had already convinced Goldberg to participate in an upcoming *Nitro* angle - set to occur at Toronto's *Air Canada Centre* - timed just before Hart was scheduled for groin surgery.

As a returning Canadian hero, Hart imagined himself calling out Goldberg in Toronto - goading him into a faceoff and absorbing a 'spear' tackle in the process - before 'pinning' the former champion in front of a raucous crowd. With the audience in quizzical disbelief, Hart would then reveal a hidden 'steel' plate under his trademark 'Hitman' jersey, setting up an inevitable feud with Goldberg out for revenge.

When an excited Hart arrived at the arena on March 29th, he claimed to witness thousands of fans chanting his name outside. But upon entering the locker room, he learned that Goldberg was suddenly having second thoughts, the apparent outcome of a discussion with Nash and Sullivan. According to Hart, he then approached Nash for clarification, but learned that the booker had actually inserted himself in the scenario, apparently in order to attack the Canadian afterwards.

313

Hart made a beeline for Eric Bischoff, declaredly expressing his astonishment at the change of plans. In response, Hart recalls, Bischoff suggested an alternative option: turning on the fans instead. *How 'bout this*, outlined Bischoff, *go out and tell the fans you don't need them anymore.*

Eric, Hart responded. *You hear that sound? That's the sound of thousands of my fans - and only my fans - standing outside on the sidewalk, in the dead of winter, chanting my name. Why would I do that?*

Bischoff then proposed *another* idea - following through, as planned, with the Goldberg angle after all, but then ending the segment with Hogan double-crossing the Hitman. *Why in God's name*, protested Hart, *would you fuck up such a great angle with something so stupid and pointless?*

You'll have to convince Terry, Hart remembers Bischoff saying. *If he says it's okay, then fine.*

Now I know who runs WCW, Hart thought to himself.

Ultimately, Hogan relented to Hart, who walked out to perform the angle sans interference. On his way through the curtain, he passed a convulsing Kevin Sullivan, who was receiving medical attention after falling to the floor in seizure. *Who could make this stuff up?* thought the Hitman, who professed little respect for Sullivan to begin with.

In a classic *Nitro* moment, the 'steel plate' angle went off without a hitch, drawing a stunning live reaction in the process. At Bischoff's request, Hart then exited the ring with one final parting shot. *Hey, WCW*, he bellowed over a house microphone. *I quit!*

Depressed over his lack of direction, Hart returned home and considered - despite a $2.5 million annual salary - whether he should actually quit for real.

Chapter 34:
Fluorescent Vomit

As THOSE AROUND HIM could surely attest, Diamond Dallas Page often cited a phone conversation with his mentor, Dusty Rhodes, occurring at a time of tremendous self-doubt.

I'm never gonna be like you, or Hogan, or Flair, Page commiserated. *I'm never gonna be the World Champion.*

If you don't think you can be World Champion, responded Rhodes, *then what the fuck are you doing this for?*

Page put down the phone and immediately recorded a goal. *Within five years*, he wrote, *I will be World Champion*. It was November 28th, 1994.

Four years, four months, and fourteen days later, his prophecy was realized. At *Spring Stampede* on April 11th, 1999, DDP captured the gold in a 'fatal four-way' match in Tacoma, WA, pinning Ric Flair en route to championship victory. In the locker room before the match, Hogan and Nash agreed it was the right call (*'it's his time'*, offered Hogan, who was set to leave for knee surgery), but afterwards, the first person to call was Dusty.

Page was driving through the Washington mountains when his phone rang. *Hey D*, began Rhodes. *How does it feeeel?*

It feels real, replied the new champ.

*That's because it **is**, baby*, Rhodes countered.

In a locker room bursting at the seams with stars, Page's triumph arose at an opportune time (although pundits would deride the move as occurring at least six months late). With WCW losing its reputation as the 'cool' wrestling promotion (even being derided as "superannuated" in one publication), it was imperative to showcase more of its 'home-grown' superstars.

Soon after, when Goldberg graced the cover of *Entertainment Weekly* (a Time Warner property, not-so-coincidentally), the publication asked its readers what many in America were surely wondering to themselves: How did *wrestling* get so big?

It was a question for which everyone seemingly had an answer for. "Since the end of the Cold War, there's no one for us to beat up on - no real hated enemy like we had with the Soviet Union," offered Alan Dundes, a professor of anthropology and folklore at the University of California at Berkley. "We've had a hard time finding outlets for our machismo."

Alternatively, in a breathless assessment of wrestling as a melodrama, MIT professor Henry Jenkins described its modern presentation as "a morality play...a spectacle of excess where one sees the externalization of emotion, the spectacle of power and powerless, treachery and revenge, and the exhilaration of the hero's victorious return from near collapse."

To others, the explanation was rather more straightforward. "Eric Bischoff is the man most responsible for the wrestling boom today," wrote Mark Madden on WCW.com. "The competition...has increased revenues and popularity for both companies. That competition is the doing of one man - Eric Bischoff."

"Look at the guys who were 'over' as fuck then," highlights DDP. "When we really started to take over, we were all in our mid-to-late 30s, or early-to-mid 40s.

"We were *men* - we weren't boys. If you look at Clint Eastwood, John

Wayne, Bruce Willis, Sylvester Stallone…in their prime, they're all in their late 30s, 40s, and 50s.

"People relate to father figures and men, and our shit was about as real as it got."

Surely at its peak, the latest wrestling boom felt like "it would never end," reminisces *Wrestleline* journalist Ben Miller. "Pro wrestling in the '90s," he says, "was like Marvel movies today. It was pervasive among teens and early-20's males.

"I recall Dave Meltzer pointing out that at some point, wrestling always seems to boom when there are advances in technology - UHF TV, then cable TV, then the Internet, [and so on]. I'm not sure if that is causality or coincidence.

"But it felt like the phenomenon would never end. The 'old timers' did seem to be grousing about how it was going to ruin the business [though]."

Indeed, while new audiences reveled in the 'can-you-top-this' mentality on Monday nights, industry veterans warned of some less visible implications. In the territory days especially, bookers historically responded to declining business by engaging in 'hot-shotting' - essentially an unbridled approach to programming - presenting out-of-the-ordinary angles with no regard for the long-term. But similar to how a soap opera, for example, couldn't 'kill off' characters every week, 'hot-shotting' ran the risk of leaving bookers without a viable means of upping the ante.

Nonetheless, from an outsider's perspective, wrestling's popularity seemed to have no bounds. Bischoff himself marveled at the memory of presenting TBS, some three years earlier, with an ambitious five-year plan - outlining specifically how WCW could transcend into other forms of entertainment. In the intervening period, his company became a legitimate pop culture sensation, and its footprints were all across the mainstream landscape.

317

In the particular arena of video games, for example, a partnership with THQ proved to be highly beneficial, with *WCW/nWo Revenge* - an N64 title released in October 1998 - selling 1.88 million copies in the US alone. While eventually, the sales figure marked a record for Nintendo (in reference to games produced by a third-party), it took only a month for *Revenge* to become the top-selling console game in North America. "The latest sales charts," beamed an IGN report on November 13th, "show just how popular WCW/nWo wrestling is."

According to Germaine Gioia, THQ's Senior Vice President of Licensing and Merchandising, the association helped put the company on the map. "WCW was the biggest thing at the time," she remembers. "It was an exciting time, and it was *hugely* successful for THQ."

Eventually, due to a dispute over royalties, the relationship between the companies would sever (and after EA Sports offered WCW $10 million, sweetened with a $5 million down payment, THQ moved on to the WWF). Regardless, *Revenge* remains a fond memory for those who enjoyed its innovation and impact.

Sanders Keel, an associate producer for the game, describes its success as an evolutionary process. "THQ were looking for other options for the N64, as well as possibly another Playstation WCW game," he says. "I was given a copy of several wrestling games being created in Japan (Virtual Pro Wrestling, Virtual Pro Wrestling 64, Touken Retsuden, Touken Road, Fire Pro Wrestling), and instantly fell in love with these games. To me, they captured more of the essence of what WCW was and how wrestling games should be made.

"For one, the game wasn't based around button mashing, punching and kicking but rather actual grappling, locking up and executing high impact moves. These games also [featured] moves from the top rope, diving out of the ring...at the time, WCW seemed to be boosting its cruiserweights and we were seeing more of those types of moves on the shows. Back then we weren't using motion capture, so an artist created each frame of animation!

318

"It was quite exciting to see such a match in vision from the Japanese developers and the style WCW was headed in. This was also the beginning of the nWo, which seemed to expand the roster greatly. Previous wrestling games usually had 6-8 characters to choose from, but our games were the first American wrestling games to really take advantage of the loaded WCW roster.

"[In 1996], *WCW vs. The World* came out for the Playstation and was getting good buzz. Sting was featured on the cover with his new darker look, which we had seen in photos long before his [Crow] character debuted. I was pretty shocked when I saw his new look...it rivaled the change to Hogan, and seemed like WCW was really going for a new look all around.

"*Nitro* was blowing up on TV, the nWo was a phenomenon, and it seemed like every week, a new wrestler showed up to push the storyline. The end of each show had the fans wanting more, and for us, this was all a goldmine for content. We were able to recreate all of the factions in the game, opening the door for more moves and scenarios in the gameplay. Entrances were also recreated with the music, and [wrestlers] walking to the ring.

"Our [first] N64 game was titled *WCW vs. nWo World Tour*. We received great reviews and awards for this game, and needless to say, the developer of these games - AKI - were set to make more games for us. We then began work on our most challenging project to date, *WCW/nWo Revenge*.

"One of the bigger challenges was to keep updating the attire for each wrestler. We would have photo shoots to get close-ups on all the details of their clothing, hairstyles, and tattoos...but all of the talent was very accommodating and patient with us.

"I was a big fan of Raven," continues Keel, who recalls pushing for his appearance on the game's cover. "He had a unique look and was a fresh face in WCW. It also [helped appeal] to some more of the

319

hardcore fans that followed all the shows."

During THQ's visits to WCW events, Gioia found herself enraptured by the atmosphere. "It was massive…pure entertainment…and very safe for children. I remember being overwhelmed by the attention those wrestlers gave to their fans, to children…I was struck by being at an event, and just feeling like you could lose your children there, and everything would just be fine. Somebody would find your child, and bring them back to you - there was just no worry in the WCW environment at Turner.

"It was just tremendous. We were at a signing event, and Randy Savage and Hulk Hogan were the kindest, most gracious, gentle-to-children people…it was *special*."

Without question, Gioia says, THQ viewed the wrestling relationship as a "pillar" of its business growth. "At the time, in the early days of the business, wrestling and video games were a beautiful mirror of each other," she says.

"There are certain times where you dovetail, most beautifully, a brand with a platform. In that sense, wrestling and video games was a perfect marriage at the perfect time.

"The WCW audience was so *broad* - it was kids, the elderly, and everybody in between."

Still, in much of the media, not everyone was convinced. "Wrestling is so big," complained Jeff Simon of *The Buffalo News*, "so seamlessly welded to American culture these days…I wanted to see what gives here. Surely I've been missing something.

"What I discovered about TV wrestling is that it's incredibly weird, and except for some dramatic wrinkles after 10pm, even more incredibly boring…for a first-time visitor, it was hilariously senseless."

Earlier in the year, Dr. Andy Gillentine, a Professor at Mississippi State University, involved himself in a series of research studies aimed at analyzing wrestling fans and their consumption habits. Initially interested in studying the wrestling phenomenon from a marketing perspective, Gillentine grew to firmly understand the root of its appeal. "In addition to the classic good vs. evil [component]," he offers, "the change in societal norms regarding acceptable behaviors reflected the uptick in the popularity of wrestling. Wrestling brought a new level of brashness to both good and bad guys, and viewers loved it. The new era of wrestling brought sex appeal, indoor fireworks, new production techniques, and great athleticism. The live television aspect created a 'can't miss this' feeling among viewers."

In one particular study, Gillentine and his colleagues collected 475 surveys from attendees to a WCW house show in College Station, Texas. The resultant findings seemed to contradict the persistent perceptions of its fanbase, as of the respondents, 62 percent either attended college or possessed a degree, over half reported an income of at least $40,000 per year, and one of out every nine made $75,000 a year. His study concluded that "[the] results indicate that the consumer of professional wrestling is middle class, family oriented, economically stable (employed), and able to make informed consumer decisions. The results of this study indicate that the wrestling fan looks a whole lot like your neighbor or the person you see in the mirror each day."

Anecdotally, the experience of Phillip Kidwell, WCW's Tour Manager from 1997-1999, supports Gillentine's findings. "Overall, I think the fans were...families taking their kids out to have a good time," he says. "I don't remember seeing one fight in the concourse. I don't remember any violence happening at the arena. No issues with security...I mean, it seemed to be, 'come on out Friday night, bring the kids, have a good time, grab some popcorn, get a shirt'...just kind of an American, middle-class thing to do."

"In my opinion," adds former TBS Marketing Manager Aline Weiller, "the typical wrestling consumer was a middle class male who was an extreme sports fan…[comparable] to perhaps a NASCAR fan.

"But certainly there were plenty of female fans and teenagers who followed WCW. As a 30-year-old woman from the Northeast, I became a 'super fan' before long, due to my involvement as Marketing Manager. The WCW atmosphere really had an enthusiasm that was contagious."

From the perspective of others, the appeal of wrestling was even broader. "A lot of people look down on wrestling fans," argues DDP, "but they may be the most diversified group of people ever. From CEO's of companies to top athletes…to doctors and lawyers. I remember one day going through the airport…this one guy said, 'I just gotta walk over and shake your hand. Every Monday night, you're my hero'. I said, 'thanks, bro! What's your name'? He said, 'Doctor so-and-so'. I thought, 'this guy saves lives for a living, and I'm his hero'."

Dick Cheatham, formerly the group controller for TBS, recalls a similar interaction in 1996. "I was at an appointment," Cheatham recalls, "and the doctor said, 'what do you do for a living'?

"I said, 'Turner Sports - Braves, Hawks…wrestling.'

"He said, 'I gotta ask you something. My son and I wanna know…are Hall and Nash really in this thing, or not?'"

"I have a neighbor - a research scientist with the CDC (Centers for Disease Control and Prevention) - and he watches wrestling," offers Matt Williams, then-Director of Audience Research and Fan Database Operations for WCW. "It's a male soap opera - just look at the product. What man wouldn't wanna be one of those wrestlers? They're buff, they usually have a hot chick on their arm, they can talk smack - they can back it up - and they can do all these incredible athletic feats."

While an oft-told joke about female fans correlated attractiveness with revenues (the better the business, the better the women, according to the wrestlers), Williams witnessed their devotion first hand. "WCW had a whole wall in their warehouse, dedicated to stuff sent in to the wrestlers. Pictures, underwear…we were like, 'we thought we've seen everything, but look at *this!*'

"I'll never forget when we were in West Virginia at a casino," recalls Brandon Woodson, former webmaster for WCW.com. "Mike Tyson was coming back to fight Francois Botha, and we were watching it at this monitor. People were just coming up left and right - just to ask the wrestlers to sign their *betting slips*!"

"I bet you my face was on toilet paper…fuckin' sheets, colognes…it was everywhere," laughs Page. "It's one of the reasons I changed my name to Dallas Page, 'cos there's no brand name in Page Falkinburg.

"One thing that pissed me off though was the 'DDP bowling ball'. When it came down to looking for your royalties, you call them up and they go, 'we don't have any bowling leagues!'"

"Let's just say the word 'paparazzi' doesn't do it [justice]," reminisces Buff Bagwell of the time period. "Pulling up with 30 really cool wrestlers at the MGM studios…it was the coolest thing in the world, man."

———

To expand WCW's reach even further, company VP Jay Hassman spearheaded a new marketing campaign in mid-April, designed to reflect an innovative, hip, *family-friendly* brand identity. Using the tag-line 'it's out there', a series of bizarre advertisements appeared in trade publications, but the more significant change was visible to a larger audience. Fans tuning in to *Nitro* were suddenly confronted with a new title sequence, a new stage, and even - rather shockingly - a new logo.

"When they showed the logo to me," remembers Pat McNeely, Design

Director for Turner Studios, "I was like, 'what is that? I can't even see the WCW letters in there'."

"The first thing I said when I saw the logo," recalls Stephen O'Laughlin, a graphic designer who subsequently created its event-specific variations, "was, 'I don't know - it's not very readable. I think we should re-work it'. They said, 'no, no - it's been approved'. It was kind of a problem thereafter."

O'Laughlin recalls a fellow employee of SME Design as having designed the new emblem. "He was a good designer," O'Laughlin says, reflecting on his time with the New York City based firm, "but he would do radical stuff like this logo. It was kind of a cool, crazy, dangerous looking thing, but I said, 'it's really not very readable'."

"I was hired at SME for only a month or so, before I was given that project," says Chung Deh Tien, the artist in question. "All the designers were locked up with other projects. I loved WCW when I was growing up, and I wanted this project.

"[Our CEO] Ed O'Hara told me the only request: the letters 'WCW' [needed to] be written in that sequence. I was a cartooning major and read comics, so Marvel and DC comic titles were an influence.

"After about 50 or so concepts, Ed wanted something wild. He [told] me to go crazy...so I came up with something heavy and dangerous in looks and appearance."

"The *old* WCW 'look', observes producer Joel Edwards, "was big and branded...lovely and masculine...but from just a style perspective, it was starting to look old - very 'early 90s'.

"I think the new logo was an attempt to get dark and edgy like the WWF...but it was like, 'we wanna be dark, but not *too* dark, because we have to maintain our ground as 'family entertainment'.

"We called it the 'spider logo'. Nobody liked it."

324

"I'll never forget being back at the Longhorn Saloon with 'E'," says DDP, speaking of Bischoff. "I said, 'dude, this new WCW branding sucks. We need to *become the nWo*.

"The nWo has to take over, and we can get a whole 'nother life out of this. WCW can be the rebels instead. I can be the rebel - Goldberg can be the rebel!' He was like, 'I know…'

"He knew it, but they had spent *millions* branding…that thing that looked like a spaceship. It was *brutal*, but they spent millions on it, so the bottom line is, they were gonna run with it."

"It did look like something from out of space," agrees Greg Prince, WCW's controller, in reference to the logo.

"It looked like a bug splat," chuckles Neal Pruitt. "I believe the story was that [Director] Craig Leathers went on a much needed vacation, and they knew he wouldn't approve of it, so they snuck it in while he was gone. Most of us production people hated it, because it really didn't fit any format of television or merchandise."

In his customary, often hilariously descriptive style, Bischoff later provided his own evaluation of the logo.

It looks like fluorescent vomit, he said with disgust.

Chapter 35:
Catch Up Time

IN THE ERA OF national wrestling organizations, promoters long observed the deferred temporal consequences of poor programming. While trends in television viewing habits reflected - almost inherently by nature - the *short-term* efficacy of an angle or show, attendance figures often displayed a delayed impact, with effects manifesting more over time.

This apparent discrepancy could be explained, it was theorized, through the fundamental nature of ticket sales themselves. With a high percentage of seats typically sold in advance, interest in a show occurring in May, for example, actually denoted fan engagement from a period weeks (or even months) earlier. During a period of 'bad' booking, this mechanism created the allusion of a 'hot' product, effectively papering over the cracks of a creaky foundation. With this in mind, observers predicted that at some point, WCW's attendance figures would start to 'catch up' with its perceptible decline.

On May 9th, compelling evidence emerged of such a trend, as *Slamboree* in St. Louis attracted less than 21,000 fans (13,789 paid) to the TWA Dome. The turnout came just five months after some 30,000 patrons - braving a significant snowstorm in the process - gleefully packed the same arena for *Nitro*.

In the interim between both shows, WCW invested in a long-running story arc concerning its on-screen 'Presidency', with Ric Flair - in kayfabe - holding the position after defeating Bischoff in December. At *Slamboree*, however, fans noticed a glaring continuity error when suddenly, Bischoff interfered to change the outcome of two matches. While according to the announcers, Bischoff derived his power from being "heavily involved in the decision making process," it appeared to contradict months of prior programming. But symbolically, the plot twist pointed to a wider set of problems, many of which would unfold in the months to come.

"It was really a chaotic time," says Jason Glast, hired in 1999 to work as a WCW publicist. "I arrived on the other side of the peak. The company was starting to become aware that they were losing the Monday night battles, but there was a lot of denial going on."

Admittedly not a wrestling fan, Glast first entered the organization looking to get a foothold within Turner Sports. "I got my Masters in Sports Administration at Ohio University, and they actually had a good pipeline to Turner Broadcasting. There were three or four Ohio grads at WCW already, including my boss, Alan Sharp.

"At Ohio, the learning procedure was, 'we're gonna do everything for the college football games. You're gonna start at six in the morning, be done at ten at night - selling tickets, raffles, and sponsorships'. It was like, 'you will work hard and do anything to get the job done'.

"To some extent, in WCW, that philosophy was necessary to survive too. You needed to do whatever it took to get the job done, but it was definitely a culture shock for me. I barely knew who any of the wrestlers actually were."

In wrestling, particularly for staff who interacted often with talent, it usually paid *not* to be an ardent follower of the spectacle, states Tim Tewell, a former WCW producer. "When you're in the entertainment business," states Tewell, "and you're around stars...you can't be 'starry-eyed' around those people. If you're gonna ask Buff Bagwell for a picture for your father-in-law, you're out."

"I probably got the job by *not* being a fan," adds fellow production team member Chris Larson. "When asked in one of my interviews who my favorite wrestler was...I answered truthfully that I hadn't really followed it since I was a kid. At first, the interviewer's facial reaction made me think I had [blown it]...but he smiled and said, 'good, I've got enough fans working for me. What I need are good producers'."

327

Indeed, the psychological game between employees and wrestlers could be as fascinating as any on-screen rivalry. Coaxing a performer into showing up on time, waking up for a radio interview, or engaging with a 'pre-tape' promo backstage, for example, meant influencing performers who were able - as Bischoff himself later lamented - to make manipulation into an *art form*. "I had to quickly change my thinking," reveals Glast. "I saw that, 'wow, these people are TV stars, making a tremendous amount of money…and many are on steroids, pills, and alcohol [as well]'.

"There were sometimes kind of unstable personalities who could be physically intimidating [too]. So I had to quickly figure out, 'how do I get what I want from somebody like that'? The challenge became getting Hulk Hogan to do local news in Des Moines, [Iowa], when he clearly would think he was above that.

"I had to figure out their soft spots, and to their credit, it would often be children. Wrestlers had the philosophy to 'comfort the afflicted, and afflict the comfortable'. They could be kind of gruff and difficult with the VP's and people that wanted stuff from them, but with the kids that saw them as superheroes…they were *tremendous*. I was able to put up with the attitude, the anger and the drama, because I saw how wonderful they could be."

In particular, Bill Goldberg was uniquely wonderful around young fans, Glast thought. Stories purporting his goodwill were innumerable, yet never deliberately constructed, revealing an admirable authenticity to an intensely believable persona. According to legend, Goldberg once (and likely many times) drove around Atlanta on a mission to visit sick and underprivileged children, taking a van filled with toys, games and stuffed animals with him. One afternoon, in another indicative story, he joined a group of awestruck teenagers for lunch at Dairy Queen, answering all of their questions with a contented smile. "I was with Goldberg in Los Angeles," remembers Glast, "and we were walking down the street. We saw a homeless man, and then I look back and Bill is giving this guy $500.

"He was big on little acts of charity that weren't about getting huge attention. It was more WCW or Turner [Broadcasting] that wanted to focus the spotlight on him, [in that regard]."

But during May and June of 1999, the spotlight - vis-à-vis Goldberg - focused mostly on his agent's attempts to secure him a better contract. Once again, following on from the Sean Waltman fiasco (and, in fact, the Ric Flair affair), it was Barry Bloom in the middle of things - despite having already achieved better terms for Goldberg the previous year (approximately $500,000-per-annum, a near four-fold increase on 1997's terms).

Bloom possessed a significant amount of control over Goldberg's career, and often booked his media appearances without involvement from WCW. He recruited Henry Holmes - a leading entertainment and sports lawyer with Terry Bollea as a client - to become involved in the negotiation process, culminating in a Beverly Hills summit at *CAA*, an agency representing WCW "in all matters related to television and film," according to Jamie Waldron, an agent with the firm from 1997-1999.

Ultimately, Bischoff and WCW had little leverage to refuse Bloom's demands. Goldberg received a 4-year, $11 million extension - notwithstanding additional bonuses for participation in WCW pay-per-views - locking him up until June 30th, 2003.

Concurrently, Bischoff's presence in Los Angeles spurred rumors of his impending departure from wrestling. According to one prominent account of the time period, "by June 1999, he was disappearing further and further into the [L.A.] music industry," ostensibly to set up an exit plan in the event of WCW's demise. Waldron doubts the veracity of such a report, but does recall Bischoff harboring some larger ambitions.

"I worked closely with Eric Bischoff and Turner in terms of placing wrestlers in programming, spin-off ideas, developing new talent, branding, [and so on]...," he says. "[But] I've never heard that Eric wanted to be in the music business, and he certainly never told me that. His idea was to start a TV Production company. That could include music, but not [as] the driving force."

In the meantime, *Nitro* was falling behind *Raw* at a rate almost incomprehensible a year earlier. It was now routine for the WWF to garner twice the audience of its competitor, with one head-to-head battle resulting in a 7.2-3.1 disparity. Surprisingly, at least at first, remembers Jason Glast, WCW's management exhibited little concern. "I think the overall philosophy was, 'well, we've still got more of the really famous guys," he says. "[It was], 'we can just keep spending tremendous amounts of money, and do all these big stunts, and all will be well."

For some, quite frankly, the party was still ongoing. A WCW employee hired contemporaneously remembers being introduced to the company culture. "I was told by [WCW PR director] Alan Sharp," he says, "to 'get to know the beers the wrestlers like, and just keep the beers coming'. I was told, 'whatever you do, don't get the beers wrong!'"

"There was this unbelievable arrogance at the time," recalls another staffer wishing to go unnamed. "Ratings were slipping - and fast - but everyone still thought they were number one. There was no fiscal responsibility, even by then. I asked if I could bring my wife on a road trip, and they said, 'sure, bring her along - y'all can stay at the Four Seasons'. I was like, 'what the fuck?'"

"When I first arrived in '99," reports Jason Glast, "I was given a company credit card and [informed], 'you can just buy anyone at the hotel bar anything they want'. It was just shocking to me, and that expense was nothing in the whole scheme of things. But you had just *carte blanche* to buy all the wrestlers, all their hangers-on, all the fans…y'know, just 'take care of everybody'. It could be anywhere up to $2,000 after a *Nitro*…that's a lot of beer in 1999.

"So I would rack up these enormous bills, and they would never really blink an eye. I would hear stories that people would turn in expenses written on a cocktail napkin…then they would just kinda create the receipt after the fact and get reimbursed. Stories like that filtered throughout the company."

"WCW were gonna do this luchador TV show, and we were hired to do the [show] open," remembers Greg Daniel, a producer who helped spearhead Turner's effects division. "There was a budget...all of that came up...and Bischoff approved it.

"But we realized that we needed more money for the open. I think Pat [McNeely] and Karl [Horstmann] asked for it, and Bischoff gave it to them. We worked on this open for a long time, had all the graphics ready...it was awesome!

"By the time we were done, we put it on Bischoff's desk and he basically just put it in the trash. He goes, 'we've decided not to do that'. It was that kind of money that we were like, 'holy crap!' They just spent tons of money...and now they're deciding not to do it."

In recent years, such stories have aggregated to inform a damning perception, one that espouses the notion that Bischoff (and other WCW executives) failed to provide the requisite financial oversight to prevent reckless spending. Responding to these claims, Bischoff (or 'ATM Eric' as some came to know him) is direct and forthright. "It's complete bullshit," he says without hesitation. "Anybody that was really there that worked in the office in '93, '94, and early '95...anybody that was honest would call 'bullshit'. It was exactly the opposite of that. There was an austerity program [then].

"This is what people don't do. They don't put things in context when they write 'The Death of WCW', [for example]. From what I've been told and heard about that book, there's no context. People don't tend to write about the state of WCW in '92, and then '93, and then early '94...*before* the acquisition of Hulk. We were a company that was generating $25 million but losing $10 million in the process, and because most of the executives in the company - including the finance committee, by the way - wanted WCW to go away...our budgets were excruciatingly tight. We were challenged - I was challenged - *daily* about expenses and losses. People were looking for excuses to pull the plug.

"Now, what happened when I was essentially given control of the company...[although] for the most part, I never had total control...that's another thing that is mischaracterized. I didn't even have control over, for example, the budget.

"Nobody that worked in the finance department - including the accountants that worked in WCW - reported to me. There was a separation of 'Church and State' - corporately speaking - that kept finance, accounting and legal completely away from anybody. If you were the President of Turner Sports, for example, you may have lawyers that work in your department, but they don't report to you. They report to legal at Turner Corporate.

"So you might have accountants working in your office, but they don't report to you. You can't make them do anything, [because] they report to the finance division.

"There was always that separation of 'Church and State', which really makes sense if you think about it. [But] when I was 'in control' of the company...making changes that were fiscally responsible and had some logic behind them...if I had an annual overall budget of $25 million in 1993, then in 1994, I might have gotten $27 million. Or $28 million. I worked to propose a budget and had to justify that increase by saying, 'ok, this is how I'm gonna use the additional 2 or 3 million dollars this year...here's what we're gonna do next year, and here's why it makes sense'.

"I would propose my budget six months in advance, or a year in advance in some cases...and once that budget was approved, I had to live within that budget.

"In '93 and 94, I was making fiscally smart, responsible decisions. I was performing against my budgets, my ideas and the growth that I proposed. [As stated], we went through a really aggressive austerity program. I remember one time, there was a large group of people in a meeting, and I made everybody get up. I said, 'go to your offices right now, and count how many pencils and how many pens you have at

332

your desk. Come back and report that to me'.

"People looked at me like I was fucking nuts. When they came back, I said, 'if you don't know what your assets are…if you don't know what your resources are…if you don't know what your limits are…there's no way we're gonna be able to build the company. You have to keep an eye on your assets, you have to keep an eye on your limitations, and you have to know when you're gonna run out of ink, [so to speak]. You have to know, and then you build from there'.

"I said, 'by the way, hold on to those pencils, because if we have to go out on street corners and sell these pencils to make our budget, then guess what? We're all gonna be standing on street corners, selling pencils at Christmas time, trying to get our revenues up to meet our forecasts. I mean, that's how tough things were.

"After the launch of *Nitro*…you gotta keep in mind…we went from shooting a little television show in a place called Center Stage - a little warn down, rat-infested theater where we gave tickets away to homeless people to come and watch wrestling…because it was air conditioned in the summertime. And they could drink their wine in brown paper bags. I mean, that was really our audience. We went from doing that…to taking the show on the road, and producing it in major arenas which required a lot more money. So of course, the budgets increased substantially from that point."

———

In the *Nitro* era, commensurate with wrestling's economic growth, the stars of both major organizations enjoyed a rapid rise in notoriety. On May 14th, Kevin Nash (often described as 'Big Sexy' on television) guested on the *Tonight Show*, continuing WCW's relationship with Jay Leno (even despite the scrapped NBC deal). As Nash relaxed opposite Leno, the interview began fairly benevolently: *where does the name 'Big Sexy' come from?*

Watching at home, Luther Biggs was dumbfounded. "I had been doing a character," the wrestler begins, "called 'Big Sexy'. I had been doing it for a while, and it was a perfect fit. I loved it - it was just *me*. On the independent circuit, I was so confident with it.

"So I went down to WCW, and literally, right before I went out [for a match], they came up to me and said, 'you can't use the name 'Big Sexy'. I was like, 'really? Where's this coming from?' They said, 'well, it's just too suggestive of a name for TV'.

"Of course, I'm getting ready to go and have a match, so I can't sit there and debate with them. They said, 'we're gonna with Luscious Luther [instead]'. I said, 'ok, whatever'.

"I'll never forget [referee] Teddy Long was standing right there. He said, 'are you kiddin' me? He's got Big Sexy written all over him'. It was on the front of my outfit and the back!

"I was very disappointed that [moniker] was stripped from me. In wrestling, everything is about that name, that gimmick…and to me, 'Luscious Luther' is *very* generic. 'Big Sexy' fit me. I'm not gonna say I'm the sexiest man in the world, but it was a nickname given to me by [wrestler] Ron Reis, and it just took off - everybody loved it.

"Now, I can't read the guy's mind, but common sense tells me 'yes', there's a [connection with Nash]. He was on the Tonight Show with Jay Leno, and they asked him how he came up with the name. The way I recall him answering that was to stumble and stammer…and say that he and his wife were watching somebody on TV who was calling himself 'sexy'…and he said, 'I just figured anyone can call themselves sexy - and I'm a big guy - so why not'?

"I was sitting there, watching that with [7' 2"] Ron Reis and his wife. Later during that interview, Jay Leno asked Nash if he was the tallest guy in WCW. He said that he was.

"So they asked where he got 'Big Sexy', and I'm thinkin', 'I know where he got it'. Then Ron – whose quite a bit taller than Nash…heard him say that.

"Again, like I said, I can't read the guy's mind - I don't know. I don't understand, though, why it was 'too suggestive' for me, but not too suggestive for him."

Another suggestion was still to come, however, as Nash used the appearance to issue a challenge towards Bret Hart (following an earlier Leno stunt where Goldberg, in a gesture that went unanswered, dared Steve Austin to a match). "He's been out of control for a while," said Nash, settling into character. "I don't know what his deal is, but he's basically said he doesn't wanna work for a Federation anymore. [So] I'll challenge Bret Hart...here, on the *Tonight Show*, and I'll put up about $250,000 of my money."

Five years earlier - in real-life - Hart put up his money to invest in the Calgary *Hitmen*, a Canadian hockey franchise inspired by his wresting persona. By 1999, the club was one of the best in Canada's Western Hockey League, and on the day before Hart planned to respond to Nash's challenge on Leno, Calgary was scheduled to face the Ottawa 67'ers in a play-off final. The solution was simple, Hart thought - *I'll go to both.*

It was Sunday, May 23rd, and while the Hitmen narrowly lost 7-6, the game went to overtime, leaving Hart precious time to fly to Los Angeles. He was about halfway in the air, however, when something ominous started to bother him. Once the cockpit flew open, Hart just knew - somehow - that he was about to receive some bad news. The pilot passed him a note with worrying instructions: *Bret Hart, please call home. Family emergency!*

When Hart reached his agent, he received news of an unimaginable nature. At a WWF pay-per-view in Kansas City, his brother Owen fell 78 feet from an elongated cable, smashing chest-first across the ropes in a stunt gone wrong. Within several minutes, despite the best efforts of paramedics, Owen was dead.

On the ground, Eric Bischoff was waiting for Hart at LAX. Upon meeting eyes with the Canadian, Bischoff knew instantly that Hart did too. He decided to immediately cancel the Leno appearance, put his star on the first flight to Calgary, and indicate, in no uncertain terms, that he should take as much time as needed.

Stunned, shattered and devastated, Hart later confessed to have been touched by Bischoff's empathy. On the other hand, he was absolutely incandescent towards Vince McMahon, who in a hugely controversial decision, opted to continue the event *after* learning of Owen's death. Days later, Calgary Sun columnist Eric Francis echoed much of the prevailing sentiment, labeling the decision as "sick, disrespectful and wrong."

"But what else," offered Francis, "would you expect from the WWF?"

Scores of similar condemnations flew in from across the media landscape. On Monday, May 24th, CNN's *Larry King Live* covered the story, featuring Bischoff as part of its discussion. "I gave [it] a lot of thought," Bischoff said, answering a question on McMahon's decision to keep the show going. "I tried to put myself in that position and ask myself what I would do. And I don't really know what I would do. I'm not surprised that they finished the evening, quite frankly. There's no easy answer to that.

"Had they not finished the evening, you would have had a whole group of people that would have been very upset that - you know - they didn't continue. Now that they made the decision to continue the show, you're going to have people who are going to criticize them for that, too.

"I was with Bret for a few hours last night and arranged for a charter to take him back to Calgary...I think he was shocked. I don't know that it really had sunk in last night when I was with him."

Once again, the wrestling business prepared to issue a premature goodbye to one of its own. Owen's funeral on May 31st drew over 1000 attendees - including representatives from both the WWF and WCW - but Bischoff wasn't one of them.

Just a month earlier, Rick Rude, still under a WCW contract and preparing for an in-ring return, died of heart failure at age 40. "Rick kept falling asleep the day before he died," says one production staffer, speaking on the condition of anonymity. "It was such a shock - to me, at least.

"But it seemed like whenever someone passed away, they'd throw up their picture at the start of the show, and then we'd move on."

At Rude's service, Bischoff was reportedly confronted by the fallen star's sister, and before long, the atmosphere turned tense, causing the President to leave early with his wife. Shaken by the experience, Bischoff decided unequivocally that he would never attend a wrestler's funeral again.

In his *Larry King Show* appearance, Bischoff revealed an insightful exchange he had with Hart. "I asked him at one point," Bischoff said, "'Bret, do you ever wonder if it's really worth it anymore?'

"Because of the emotion, and the things he was going through...he said, 'yeah, the thought has crossed my mind'."

For Bischoff, there was no time to ask himself the same question. Wrestling was a 52-week endeavor, and WCW needed help - and fast. On June 9th, he re-signed Dennis Rodman - now out of the NBA and previously, embroiled in a lawsuit with WCW over unpaid pay-per-view revenue - to a $1 million contract. But while critics slammed the move, citing it as the latest example of Turner's 'open checkbook' (in fairness, it did follow a 3-year, $2.55 million deal for big man Sid Vicious on *the same day*), Bischoff vigorously rejects such a notion.

"For anybody to suggest that there was this unlimited budget, and Eric could spend whatever he wanted to spend - on anything he wanted to spend - it's so fucking totally nonsensical. Anybody that worked in the Turner organization that was remotely honest would call 'bullshit' on that. *Nobody* got to do that - including Ted Turner himself.

"It's just so much bullshit, but it's the foundation of the narrative, because at the core of that narrative, there's an image of Eric with an unlimited checkbook to compete with Vince McMahon. At the core of that is Vince McMahon wanting people to believe that the only reason I kicked his ass for as long as I did was because money was no object for me - as it was for him. *Totally fucking false*. Totally false."

What *was* incontrovertible, however, was that by mid-1999, WCW's key business metrics were in a state of freefall. "It was almost like every single Monday," says Glast, "the ratings would just start plummeting. It kinda descended into chaos, and all of a sudden, you could feel true panic."

"There was an 'old timer'," reveals Matt Williams, formerly WCW's Director of Audience Research and Fan Database Operations, "who told me, 'these guys aren't that smart' - talking about Eric and the others. He said, 'they bottled lightning once, and now they don't know how to do it again. They're struggling'."

Ratings for *Nitro*, having reached an average of 4.95 for January, were down to a 3.45 average for May. Attendance declined over the same period, falling from 8,661 per show to 5,752, while the average live gate decreased by $50,000 per event. *Slamboree* was the lowest-drawing pay-per-view in years.

Bischoff was starting to feel the walls close in. It was becoming absolute torture, he later described it, dealing with the high-priced talent and corporate suits. "He was under more pressure," states Dick Cheatham, "than anybody I've ever seen in Corporate America. Most people have what we call a 'rabbi' - somebody up top who is your sponsor...who looks after you. Well, Eric didn't have one. Eric didn't have a rabbi.

"HR was hunting for him, corporate management didn't care for him. They were dialing in on him: 'did he say something somewhere that somebody took the wrong way?' 'Is he creating a hostile workplace?' One of 'em got a hold of me and said, 'look, uh, we see Eric is referring to himself as 'Eazy E' now'. That was back when he was part of the nWo. They said, 'this is disgusting...'. I said 'wait, wait - this is a *program*, and that's the way he wants to go'. You can knock him any way you want to, but Eric was delivering the program that was number one on cable for [88] consecutive weeks. If you end up not liking him - because he refers to himself as 'Eazy E' - then get over yourself!"

Additionally, from a creative standpoint, Bischoff seemed to have no more answers for the WWF, whose ratings were climbing astronomically. To add insult to injury, his competition managed to secure a *Raw* booking at the Georgia Dome. "In mid-99," begins Cheatham, "The WWF was holding a press conference at the Georgia Dome. I knew enough of the guys, so I thought to go over. One of the peculiar things about the business is…if you wear a suit, a tie, and your hair is short - no-one is going to stop you from going anywhere. A lot of that has to do with the mystique among wrestlers which is…the suits are how you get paid, and the suits can screw your life up. So don't mess with the suits. I'd wander around everywhere like I owned the place, and nobody was gonna challenge me - because *I looked like somebody important*!

"After the press conference broke up, I got to talking with 'Stone Cold' [Steve Austin]. I'd known Steve for a number of years. I asked him, 'Steve, what do you think of our programming lately'? He looked at me and said, 'it looks like Eric Bischoff is out of ideas'.

"I think he was exactly right. And if you look at our shows - at the end - you would have a bad taste in your mouth. The good guys would get beat up, and that was just it. Vince McMahon even said that once. Vince said, 'they just don't get it down there. There's a formula for how you do this, and they just don't get it'."

In regards to the organizational culture of both companies, their differences were perhaps never more apparent than when *Playboy* visited both offices in July. "Bill Pryor was doing an article," says Cheatham, "on why wrestling was big…why it was important. I talked to him later and he said, 'you're not gonna believe the difference between the two companies'. He said, 'everyone is really sort of tight around Eric - this is not a fun company. But if you go to see Vince McMahon…here comes Stephanie, here comes Shane…everybody's playing 'grab-ass', having a ball…this is just *fun* for them'."

Meanwhile, in Atlanta - or, more accurately, Smyrna - it hadn't been fun in a while.

If something didn't change, Bischoff's position would invariably be under threat.

Moreover, although he didn't yet know it, his safety would be too.

Chapter 36:
Bout It, Bout It

"I want to be the ghetto Bill Gates," Percy Miller told *The New York Times*. "There ain't no goal to stop at."

For the 29-year old Miller - otherwise known as New Orleans-based rap mogul *Master P* - just about any goal seemed possible. A self-made millionaire, Miller began 1999 presiding over one of the world's biggest independent music labels, *No Limit Records*. Having been raised in the now-demolished Calliope Projects, 'P' now lived in a stately mansion located on the grounds of a Baton Rouge Country Club. With an estimated worth of $361 million, his portfolio included ownership of a film company, commercial properties, and a fashion label, along with a host of ancillary businesses.

Unlike many of his contemporaries, however, Miller had ascended to rap royalty without compromising his message. Although his music, quite obviously, drew inspiration from a range of similar artists - most blatantly, Tupac Shakur - he had yet to release anything resembling a 'pop' single (his breakout hit 'Ice Cream Man', for example, addressed not the occupation implied in the song's title, but rather, the trials of selling crack cocaine).

His growing legend appeared to be, in one sense at least, more akin to Ted Turner than Ice-T. In a way not too dissimilar from Turner's focus on aggregating content, Miller's own business ethic emphasized ownership of *everything* - his master tapes, his studio, even the film negatives for his straight-to-video movies. In an era where shiny suits and flashy chains reigned supreme, he focused his efforts on a less fleeting call to action - building *generational wealth* for his historically poor family.

It all started, famously, with an unexpected inheritance of $10,000, the outcome of a malpractice suit involving Miller's grandfather.

341

After using the money to open a record store in Richmond, California, within two years, 'P' was releasing music of his own - first directly out of his trunk - and eventually, through negotiating an historic '80/20' distribution deal with Priority Records (a pact in which, crucially, Miller maintained 100 percent ownership of his master recordings).

By the end of decade, some $120 million in record sales later, the intrepid entrepreneur saw his influence expand further. In the NBA, the Charlotte Hornets, eager to generate publicity after a painfully onerous league lockout, signed the 6-foot-4 magnate to a contract in pre-season. Upon the announcement of his involvement in a free intra-squad scrimmage, over 15 thousand fans - some lining up as early as 7am - flocked to the Charlotte Coliseum to see Miller suit up in uniform. Despite scoring 9 points on 3-of-6 shooting, the rapper was quickly cut, in an expected move, four days prior to the season opener (years later, Miller would defend his viability as a pro, maintaining his departure to be "all politics").

Meanwhile, in WCW, former nWo member Konnan was entertaining audiences with a rapturous pre-match routine. "Orale!", he yelled in a call-and-response to announce his presence. "Arriba la raza! We are los vatos locos forever! But more importantly than all that, [Insert city] is 'bout it, 'bout it, and rowdy, rowdy!"

Watching from home on television one night, Randy Thornton sat up to take notice. Konnan's 'bout it, 'bout it tagline - clearly borrowed from Master P's film (and soundtrack) containing the same phrase - signaled to the *No Limit* member that a business opportunity could be imminent. *Hey P*, said Thornton, a childhood friend of the rap star. *I think I can get us in WCW.*

"[Miller] was like, 'you crazy'," remembers Thornton, a former NFL linebacker with a little-known tenure in *New Japan Pro Wrestling*. "I called [retired wrestler] Brad Rheingans, as Brad was my trainer and had connections with WCW. He gave me some numbers to call, so I called WCW and told them who I was. [Shortly thereafter], I flew to Atlanta with my attorney, and it so happened that I met with Randy

342

Savage and Dusty Rhodes [upon arrival].

"I told them that I wrestled for *New Japan*, and I had trained with Brad. Back then, Master P was super hot, y'know, so we came to an agreement [with WCW management]. They said, 'we want you to be a street thug, and we'll hook you up with Konnan, Rey Mysterio, and anybody else you want'.

"I told 'em, 'I want two more people', so we went to the Power Plant looking for talent to join our group, and Chase Tatum just stuck out. He was big, strong...he had charisma...but he could be an asshole [too]. We needed a good wrestler that would be perfect with us [also], so we picked 'B.A.' - Brad Armstrong."

Collectively, Konnan, Mysterio, Tatum, Armstrong and Thornton - who adopted the on-camera name *Swoll* for his in-ring persona - formed *The No Limit Soldiers*, a babyface stable formed in opposition to Curt Hennig's *West Texas Rednecks*. The storyline, on paper, looked to be quintessential pro wrestling - a 'rap vs. country' feud set to culminate at July's *Bash at the Beach* pay-per-view.

The Soldiers would also be boosted by the presence of 'Da Last Don', Master P himself. His involvement had been used as a bargaining chip by Thornton, who in the process, secured himself a $350,000 deal - with a $50,000 signing bonus - according to the company's talent contract database. "There was a lot of tension because of the money I received," recalls Thornton. "I did get a big contract, and a lot of wrestlers were mad, but I [was] like, 'don't be mad at me because I know how to negotiate!'

"They knew how big 'P' was, because they already knew of him, and then Konnan talking about he was 'bout, 'bout it made it super large. *Monday Nitro* had DJ Ran playing No Limit music [during commercial breaks].

"P and I are [both] from New Orleans, and we knew each other as kids. He and I attended the University of Houston together, so we've known each other for a long, long, long time. We're not relatives [as erroneously reported]. He gave me the opportunity to come work for him, and I took advantage of it - I was his personal trainer and head of security [prior to entering WCW].

"So, we [both] got paid. Master P made $200,000 an appearance. We know how to negotiate - I worked for a guy that turned $10,000 into $500 million.

"I had something that they wanted."

Miller and the Soldiers (who by now added '4x4', a 400-pound monster played by Mike Tyson's former bodyguard, Teddy Reade) made their WCW debut at the *Great American Bash* on June 13th, with a backstage dust-up involving Hennig kick-starting the angle. Meanwhile, on *Nitro* the following night, footage of a press conference announcing the new signing aired in the first hour. "The creative performer of such hits as 'I Miss My Homiez'," deadpanned Gene Okerlund, "is gonna be accompanied at the events by his bodyguard, the massive Swoll...making a very formidable tag team."

"I'm glad to be here," offered Miller, referring to WCW as '*The WCW*' and Eric Bischoff as 'Mr. Eric' in his comments. "I grew up on this - I've always been a big wrestling fan, and to be able to step in the arena with this type of sport...gives me a great honor and pleasure to be here."

"Master P [and] the No Limit Soldiers..." began Bischoff, "their perspective is a very positive one. There's a lot of very positive things that...the music, the philosophy, and their approach to entertainment and life in general, is going to bring to WCW." Later in the show on play-by-play, Bischoff promised the signing was the start of *Nitro*, once again, "changing the world."

Miller's next appearance would be heavily promoted, with the June 21st *Nitro* emanating from *No Limit*'s backyard - the Superdome in New Orleans. In a segment presented live in front of the crowd, the Soldiers hosted a birthday party for Miller's real-life brother and *No Limit* artist, Silkk The Shocker, before the interrupting Hennig

344

received a face full of cake for his efforts. In the eyes of some fans, the ongoing story was becoming increasingly confusing - not only had Hennig apparently developed a Texas accent out of thin air, but he was also being booked as a heel despite being outnumbered by Miller's group.

Aside from confusion, the cake angle created perceptible anger - not necessarily in the stands, but surprisingly, in the locker room. "People got so mad when we threw the cake in Curt Hennig's face," laughs Thornton. "Even the wrestlers got mad. But what they didn't know was that Curt came up with the idea! It was all his idea!"

Although the announced crowd of 17,249 was widely derided as a failure in the wrestling media, Thornton recalls the turnout as being a successful one. "The Mayor and the Governor were at that show. They came to our locker room. I mean, come on...the Mayor *and* the Governor? Everybody came. All my classmates, people I played ball with, family members, neighbors...everybody went there."

Two weeks later, on *Nitro* in Atlanta, the Rednecks were scripted to gain a measure of revenge in a classic 'heat' segment devised by Dusty Rhodes. Consequently, Miller's entire group sold a beatdown at the hands of the Rednecks and fellow villains Steven Regal and Dave Taylor, drawing the wrath of Master P himself.

"Before *Bash at the Beach*, I got jumped by the cowboys in Atlanta," says Thornton. "Dusty told me, 'Randy, you gotta lose. You can't win every match'. So I agreed, and didn't tell 'P' about me being jumped, and he got furious. But it's like I told him, 'do you think I'm gonna listen to a rapper? Or do you think I'm gonna listen to Dusty Rhodes?' [So] basically, Master P threw us under the bus - he stopped making appearances. Management got mad at 'P', so that's when me and B.A. started doing stuff together."

Subsequently, according to numerous sources, a major confrontation occurred backstage at *Bash at the Beach* on July 11th. Based on several accounts, the dispute became so severe that guns were brandished around Bischoff, an allegation that Thornton refuses to confirm. "It's just certain things that shouldn't be told," he says. "I have no comment on that."

The Soldiers triumphed in the eventual pay-per-view clash, but due to Miller's departure, the group quickly disbanded. In the following weeks, Swoll and Armstrong began a short-lived tag-team on *Thunder*, while Tatum slowly faded into obscurity. "If people ever notice, towards the end of our run, Chase would go to the ring by himself," observes Thornton. "We basically turned him loose on Rick Steiner, and Steiner beat the living shit outta him [in a July 26th television title match]. Sid Vicious actually beat the shit outta him [too]. Chase got beside himself...he didn't appreciate what we did for him, so we kinda threw him to the wolves. I kicked him out of the No Limit Soldiers."

Within a matter of weeks, Swoll was out of WCW (receiving, he says, every penny owed on his contract). In some respects, the early exit was a relief for Thornton, who quickly tired of the backstage cliques and, on occasion, a much more serious outrage. "My first match was against [former NJPW and WCW wrestler] Frank Andersson. Frank already told me before I got to WCW, 'you not gonna like it'. I was like, 'huh?' He said, 'your personality is not gonna fit. You're too street'. I still had that street mentality. When we traveled, I traveled first class while a lot of other wrestlers traveled coach. Again, that came back to the negotiation.

"[But] there was a lot of racism. There was a lot of racism, seriously. You have to remember where WCW's headquarters were at - Georgia. [So] when I left there, I was happy to leave.

"I witnessed it and experienced it. I still remember - and I can't say his name - but one of the top bookers didn't know I was in the room, and I heard him say he's tired of this "n----- shit." It was like, 'wow. Did he just say that shit?' The person I'm talking about is a wrestling legend. There became times where we would get to a show, and there would be people with *No Limit* signs and shirts, and they wouldn't even let us wrestle. I was basically getting paid just to go to shows and watch backstage."

346

In a remarkable observation given Thornton's background as a talented athlete, the WCW locker room, he says, was toxic for another significant reason. "I saw so much drugs and stuff going on at WCW that...I did not want to live my life like that. I mean, it's like everybody was a drug addict. Or drugs and alcohol. I would watch these guys just get *wasted - wasted*! It was drugs...steroids...alcohol...guys falling out...getting carried to their room...it was pretty crazy.

"It was worse [than anything experienced playing football]. I mean, shit - you'd be in the locker room, and you'd say, 'oh, my shoulder hurts'. Five guys would give you painkillers!

"It's just part of the business. If you want the work, you have to work. You can't say, 'oh, my shoulder hurts or my back hurts', y'know? It just didn't go like that. When your name was called, you had to work.

"[WCW management] tried to get it under control - they started drug testing them. I flunked a drug test, but everybody smoked weed, y'know?

"I'm not trying to bring those other guys down in any way, but in pro wrestling, we do have a drug problem - big-time. Shit, every week somebody's dyin'. 'Why did they die?' Overdose. Heart attack. Suicide. I just never wanted to be one of those guys. I love livin' on my nice little farm, where I can walk, and play with my animals, and do interviews and talk to people. I'm fortunate.

"I love the fact that I can sit and say that Curt Hennig was a friend. Bobby Duncum was a friend. 'B.A' was a friend - that was my brother. We would talk on the phone every day. I think one of the top 10 people I ever met in my life was Diamond Dallas Page. Randy Savage was one of the nicest guys I ever met in my life, [too].

"I'm a little nappy-haired black kid from New Orleans, Louisiana, and my dream was to grow up to be a pro football player and a pro wrestler. I achieved both of those dreams. [And] I made some great friendships with great people that I'll cherish for the rest of my life.

347

Eric Bischoff, Master P, Dusty Rhodes...they made my dreams come true. I appreciate that."

As for 'P' specifically? "We haven't talked since," reveals Swoll. "I don't have any beef with the man - I thank him for the opportunity. But we haven't talked about it."

Chapter 37:
The Holy Shit File

HE WASN'T USED to this.

He was usually *that guy*, at the front of the room, pontificating eloquently about his business. He wasn't *this guy*, at the back of the room, hoping eagerly for a vote of confidence.

But now, seated on the floor, he could only listen as a concerned spectator. In the distance, Dr. Harvey Schiller was holding court, discussing WCW - and its recent performance - in front of a packed conference room at CNN Center.

The doctor was back in session, and for Eric Bischoff, it couldn't have come at a worse time.

Just weeks earlier, some 1500 miles away in Sturgis, SD, Bischoff was simply a man *in his element*. With Hogan, Nash, and Rodman in tow, he huddled excitedly in the corner of a local tavern, flashing his 'TV' grin as the beers flowed like water. *I feel like I'm in high school*, one staff member observed from afar, unable - evidently - to gain access to the cool table.

That scene was, for all intents and purposes, almost a distant memory now. Suddenly, Schiller was hyper-attentive, but for seemingly good reason, as August had been nothing less than a disaster for WCW. From a programming perspective, *Nitro*'s numbers risked falling into the '2's, and with Hogan and Nash headlining, the nWo fizzling out, and Goldberg again rudderless, fan interest in the product was clearly sinking - and fast.

Grasping at straws, Bischoff went back to his creative well, modifying an idea that had previously been rejected. "He wanted to be on an

349

airplane that got lost," recalls Schiller. "He would fly in to Mexico, his plane would disappear and there would be a search for him.

"I said, 'no, Eric, we can't play around with the FAA. We can't do that'.

"He came up with some concepts that were great, and he came up with some concepts that were a little scary. He was a very, very creative person, and I put a lot of faith in him. [But] that was his idea to get national attention."

In fact, the only attention WCW seemed to attract was negative, particularly in reference to 'Lenny and Lodi' - two flamboyantly dressed 'brothers' known as the *West Hollywood Blondes*. After one *Nitro* appearance from the duo, Brad Siegel received a strongly worded letter from GLAAD - the Gay and Lesbian Alliance Against Defamation - with its media director complaining of the "shocking...promotion of homophobia and [literal] gay-bashing" on TNT. It was the type of scrutiny that even at the best of times, WCW didn't need; in its current state, therefore, the timing was calamitous.

On August 9th, Hogan's babyface turn culminated in Boise, ID, and in a dramatic *Nitro* moment, *Hollywood* became *Hulk* once again. Upon witnessing his reversion to the red-and-yellow getup, the Idaho Center became positively unglued, responding to the Hulkster's return as if it were 1987 all over again. The audience popped with every punch, clapped with every kick, and swooned with every slam, providing a star-studded six-man main event with incredible crowd heat. It was an amazing scene, but questions abounded as to its long-term implications; notably, to what extent WCW could rely on Hogan to counter the fresher stars on *Raw*.

But more significantly, while Hogan's drawing power remained in question, Bischoff certainly had a lot to answer for. Financially, his company was spiraling, suffering an inconceivable loss of $5 million in August alone - the worst monthly performance in its history. The deficiency was so shocking, evidently, that WCW's own accountants reviewed the figures several times, finally preparing an informational

350

report for Schiller. The document came with a label: *The Holy Shit File*.

"In August of '99," begins Greg Prince, "everything in our forecasts - from a revenue standpoint - was in the red. That really goes back to how [Turner's finance division] estimated the pay-per-view revenue."

In other words, the revenue increase for Road Wild '98 - the August pay-per-view featuring Jay Leno - actually turned out to be a double-edged sword. While in its previous incarnations, the event failed to break 250,000 buys, the involvement of Leno sparked an outcome of some 365,000 buys. Consequently, from the perspective of the corporate bean counters, this was now the *new normal*.

"If you go back to 1998," continues Prince, "you can only imagine the good news that was coming in, month-to-month. [TBS] had a 1998 WCW budget forecast, [plotted] versus actual results, which month in and month out - as the company grew by 'gangbusters' - showed things to be on the uptick."

Typically, while there was always fluctuation, the buy rates for WCW's biggest pay-per-views (Starrcade, Halloween Havoc, Bash at the Beach, and so on) could reasonably be anticipated. Therefore, Prince says, Turner accountants would estimate year-to-year performance accordingly, often aiming to grow specific event revenue by a "pretty arbitrary" amount - "5 to 7 per cent, for example."

But in the event that a pay-per-view dramatically *exceeded* prior projections, this in turn raised expectations for successive years. "You might have a number sitting there, and then a pay-per-view goes 'nuts' one year," Prince states. "That would then become their new baseline.

"So there were higher expectations in '99 [from TBS], [like], 'we need to be even better than 1998'.

"On the expense side, it was also in the red. You had an extremely higher fixed expense structure in place. WCW had incurred significant expense in terms of redoing sets…merchandising…everything that was branded with the new logo. We were spending money like crazy on the wrestler payroll.

"So now on paper, we've got increased profitability expectations each month. Revenues are now being projected at an increased level that wasn't happening before, month in and month out - which then would feed even more spending...to try to get back to those revenues. The roller coaster was really starting to accelerate downhill."

Years later, Bischoff disputed the notion of WCW losing $5 million in August, citing internal accounting methodologies as a key factor:

Intercompany allocations and forecasts were used and abused to help various divisions or departments position themselves internally for future budget considerations. The bottom line here is that in August of 1999, WCW was facing the first quarter in eighteen or twenty where we were projecting a loss. This loss was in the neighborhood of $1.5 million. The numbers that were "reported" by the media later were many times higher. When I saw those numbers months later, it appeared to me that management had decided to dump as much of a projected loss on the books as possible for fiscal 1999. This way, management could look as good as possible in fiscal 2000. I'd seen it before, and it didn't surprise me.

In response to Bischoff's comments, Prince is rather candid. "Who's really to say that all these numbers - especially on the expense side - flowing from Turner Entertainment were [accurate]?

"Were they already starting to see the business moving in a negative direction, sending more expense to WCW than maybe was necessary? Did they change their allocation methodology somehow, so that we were getting more expense than we had historically? Who knows. Nobody at our level could speak to that with any degree of certainty."

"Before, the reason it was going so well for Turner," points out Dick Cheatham, "is that cash was coming in 'over the transom'. When the nWo kicked on...man, it just created a viewership that we had never had before. All of a sudden, there was a *ton* of money coming in. If ever there was a time when we made money - if you go back and strip out all the tricked up accounting - that would be it.

"But again, our insane way of keeping books was not meant for decision accounting. For example, the same bunch of MBA's with sharp pencils that [campaigned] against WCW went after the Braves pretty hard: 'the Braves always lose money, let's get rid of it'. Well the problem is, that's not the right way to see it. We *meant* for it to lose money, because Major League Baseball had a surcharge on a team's earnings. So if you *actually made money* - on a standalone basis - Major League Baseball would charge you 7% of your bottom line.

"So our deal was, 'well, find a way to make it look like we're not making any money'. Simple things like, 'we'll sell the broadcast rights to Braves games to TBS for a small amount of money - a dollar, buck-and-a-half, hundred dollars, whatever'. And that way, all the income - the *real income* - is recognized at TBS, not at the Braves."

In his influential book *Creative Accounting*, Ian Griffiths described the general prevalence of such adroitness:

Every set of accounts is based on books which have been gently cooked or completely roasted. The figures which are fed...to the investing public have been changed in order to protect the guilty. It is the biggest con trick since the Trojan horse.

Any accountant worth his salt will confirm this is no wild assertion. There is no argument over the extent and existence of this corporate contortionism - the only dispute might be over the way in which it is described. Such phrases as 'cooking the books', 'fiddling the accounts', and 'corporate con trick' may raise eyebrows where they cause people to infer that there is something illegal about this pastime. In fact, this deception is all in perfectly good taste. It is totally legitimate - it is creative accounting.

"The accounting system at Turner," continues Dick Cheatham, "was kind of a byzantine kind of a deal where...a lot of these guys in other companies couldn't find a way of cutting their expenses. They weren't always doing a very good job, so we had what amounted to intercompany charges.

"Turner Home Entertainment is a good example. They were the ones responsible for selling everyone's product, like Turner Classic Movies - they would sell those movies on VHS, or [DVD] or whatever. The revenue from those sales would be grossed up, sent directly to the company whose product was being sold, and then Turner Home Entertainment would take a block of expenses associated with it...and *charge those to the company.* So in effect, Turner Home Entertainment would be kind of a zero-based company, after you closed your books. It's got no revenue - it's got no expenses - because it's all been closed out to people they were apparently working for.

"I'd say well, 'we've got $3,500 in income from video sales, but we've got $120,000 worth of expenses associated with those sales. Well, I've gotta throw a flag on that - that's bullshit'! Those are the kind of challenges we were constantly fighting with each other about."

Corporate contortionism granted, however, Bischoff was still on the hook for some expensive outlays that showed dubious dividends. Master P's involvement had proven to be a debacle. A partnership with Gene Simmons and KISS, geared towards the development of a wrestler named *The Demon*, reportedly handed over all merchandising rights to the band. And for his part, Dennis Rodman showed little appreciation for being paid $1 million, telling *TV Guide*, "it's money - that's all I have to say. I just don't know why I have to do that damn wrestling shit."

Conversely, even the most ardent of WCW boosters would struggle to find similar profusion in the WWF. If Vince McMahon's company operated, as many wrestlers believed, as if every dollar mattered, it was because - in actual fact - it really did. Functioning without a corporate behemoth to absorb its losses, McMahon was forced to stay carefully within bounds, as opposed to Bischoff, whose reaction to poor decisions - technically speaking - figured to be less visceral. As the economist Milton Friedman observed, "nobody spends somebody else's money as carefully as he spends his own."

A TBS insider, speaking on the condition of anonymity, remembers Bischoff's spending in context with the wider corporate culture. "Eric liked to spend him some dough," he laughs. "He was living the life, using the company private jet...which most Turner execs did [by the way]. But you don't do that if you don't have to - especially when your company is bleeding money a little bit. You don't pay a guy $1 million for one pay-per-view, when you know you're not gonna make it back.

"A million dollars was sort of like Eric's number. It was like, "let's just give away a million dollars - that's nothing'. Everything that was a million dollars [or less] was ok, when the line should have probably been $100,000 dollars - or less.

"There's something about him, though, that makes you believe everything he says. He was handing out these guaranteed contracts that were multiples of previous contracts to guys…and he was telling us that everything was fine.

"But see, the way it was at Turner - for the most part - was that they trusted their guys. If you were showing revenues at 'x'…or projecting revenues at 'x', then your expenses were allowed to rise.

"Eric was a spend first, 'million dollars is my cut off' kind of guy, but I think he did the million dollar thing one too many times."

Indeed, Bischoff would soon instruct Tony Schiavone to plug a contest involving a *million-dollar* giveaway on *Nitro*. It was the latest attempt to turn the ratings around, but Schiavone decided to announce its occurrence with sarcasm, 'overselling' the contest despite Bischoff's pleas otherwise.

But if Schiavone was merely annoyed, reports suggested that Bischoff's production staff were close to a revolt. Morale crashed after news of *New Year's Evil*, a tentatively planned pay-per-view to feature (on December 31, 1999, no less) an oscillating focus between in-ring action, and live music from KISS. The format would bounce back-and-forth - match to song, song to match, and so on - before the main event concluded at exactly midnight on the West Coast. Bischoff envisioned Arizona's 70,000 seat Fiesta Bowl as the perfect venue.

It was a concept that Bischoff had considered for some time - in 1995, for example, he talked of a New Year's Eve show in Times Square -

but with a busy holiday schedule already in the books (and widespread concerns over the Y2K bug), the proposal was universally condemned. "That left a lot of us," remembers Jason Piccolo, a production coordinator for WCW, "like, 'what the fuck?'

"It was on our calendar at one point - so they were planning on doing it. I was in my twenties [at the time], but I looked at it as, 'that's the stupidest idea for a pay-per-view I've ever heard of'. Number one, who the fuck cares about KISS? On top of that…how much money does it take to put a deposit down on a stadium for *New Year's Eve*? And who sits at home on New Year's Eve who is a wrestling fan? That demo is out on New Year's Eve, for the most part."

"WCW already has a Dec. 19 Starrcade PPV and a January PPV scheduled," wrote Wade Keller of *The Pro Wrestling Torch*. "The New Year's PPV is an added event, making it one of three WCW PPVs in the span of about five weeks. For a number of reasons, WCW wrestlers and production staff are more upset by the added PPV than anything in recent memory. A lot of the wrestlers and staffers, who previously believed they would have that day off, had made plans with friends and family to celebrate. Also, there is potential for Y2K computer problems and no one wants to be away from their family and friends during that time.

"There is talk among wrestlers of staging a massive walk-out if WCW management insists they take part in the New Year's Eve PPV."

Meanwhile, morale among the talent was too reaching new lows. In Sturgis, just two hours before their match, Buff Bagwell and Ernest Miller brawled backstage - for real - although thankfully, the tension subsided enough for their contest to go ahead. "Eric called them to his bus and reprimanded who needed to be reprimanded," remembers Sonny Onoo. "They then went out there and cooperated with each other in the ring. That is really amazing to me!"

Some wondered how much of the worsening backstage dissension could have been avoided. "The worst decision was letting wrestling personalities run the program," says Jason Shaya, a former WCW Hotline personality-turned NHL announcer. "Kevin Nash, Scott Hall,

Hulk Hogan...should've had no business playing a role in how the storylines were written, and what would happen on a day to day basis. Imagine you're running a company, but had to wait for the employees to tell you what they felt like doing before they decided to work. It made no sense. There was always a power struggle between various factions...it was unsustainable."

Before *Nitro* on August 23rd, Bischoff decided to give the roster a piece of his mind, organizing another pre-show speech. "We were in Las Vegas," remembers Shaya. "And there was huge turmoil with 'the boys'. Eric called a meeting of every single wrestler in the company, and as they were filing into this small room, Zane [Bresloff] told me to go in and just listen.

"I was standing next to Rey Mysterio [Jr.], and God only knows who else. Eric told everyone he was sick of the bullshit, and [that] if anyone wanted to get out of their contract, that would be fine. He said they could be on *Raw* the next day for all he cared."

To the shock of the room, one wrestler took Bischoff up on his offer. "Raven left the meeting," Shaya says, "and tried desperately to get to the WWF. I think it was all a bluff on his part though, but that was pretty exciting."

After the show, Raven, real name Scott Levy, recalls Bischoff approaching him at the bar, expressing an apparent veneration for his actions and clarifying - despite the earlier rhetoric - that he would not be allowed to sign with McMahon. Raven *would* be permitted, however, to return to *Extreme* Championship Wrestling (ECW), a cult Philadelphia-based promotion with a uniquely rabid fan base. Tantalizingly, Bischoff also informed Raven that his departure thwarted upcoming creative plans - specifically, a proposed storyline involving his portrayal of an 'evil' version of the KISS Demon.

On Wednesday, August 25th, Raven allegedly participated in an unlikely meeting with Brad Siegel. Reputedly, the meeting occurred after a night of Vegas partying with Siegel and Emily Sherman, WCW's VP of international coordination, an on again-off again

357

partner of Scott Hall, and - most importantly - Siegel's niece.

According to Raven, Siegel listened to his ideas in an afterhours club, and then set up a meeting to discuss matters further. In response, Bischoff believed - purportedly - that Raven was looking for vengeance after being denied his WWF option. In any event, the disgruntled star moved on a day later, quickly making a return to ECW in its first nationally-televised show on TNN.

———

Utterly exhausted from the pressure, not to mention the vice-tightening from Turner's financial gurus, Bischoff confided in Bill Busch, WCW's Vice President of Strategic Planning, on Thursday, September 9th. During what he later described as a "heartfelt discussion," Bischoff confessed that he was again considering the option of resigning. Busch responded, according to Bischoff, with an empathetic indication of full support:

Eric, go spend some time with your wife. Rethink this, and come back in the morning.

Chapter 38:
Go Home

As a child in elementary school, Eric Bischoff developed a coping mechanism for classroom monotony. Unless the discussion concerned history or geography, he would consciously tune out the teacher, gaze out of a window, and allow his mind to wander.

More interested in his imagination than the topic at hand, Bischoff loved to see himself steering a humongous ship across the ocean, en route to completing a magnificent voyage around the world. On the off-chance that his instructor delivered even a mildly intriguing utterance, it only stimulated Bischoff's visions further, and thus, perhaps it was here that his creative abilities first flourished.

But he could only see so far. Not in terms of imagination - far from it, in fact - but technically speaking, Bischoff was literally short-sighted. He found it difficult to focus on distant objects, especially when driving, which is where he found himself on the morning of September 10th, 1999.

At about 9:15am, Bischoff's cell phone rang. It was Harvey Schiller, evidently, who in the past had delivered alternately good and bad news through such means. On this occasion, however, his tone was unequivocally ominous: *Meet me in my office*, the Doc requested.

Upon arriving at Schiller's office, Bischoff recalls being told, without ambiguity, to 'go home'. *I have a pay-per-view this Sunday*, Bischoff protested in response. *Not this Sunday, you don't*, Schiller replied. *You need some rest, Eric.*

Having not heard the word 'fired', Bischoff struggled to grasp the implications of Schiller's statement. Moreover, with a contract set to run until early 2002, he doubted TBS would simply pay him to go away.

Schiller continued, Bischoff remembers, attempting to soothe the situation. *You need to go home…you need some rest…take a break, and we'll talk again in a month or two.*

At that moment, Bischoff understood exactly what was happening. *I'm politely being asked to leave*, he thought.

On his way out, Bischoff theorized that veteran financial executive Vicky Miller - acting upon guidance from Bill Busch - influenced Schiller towards pulling the trigger. His belief no doubt strengthened when three days later, Schiller appointed Busch as WCW's new Executive Vice President. "I thought Bill was counseling me," Bischoff wrote years later, "but what he was really doing - *allegedly* - was going to his boss and using that information to position himself."

But according to one of Bischoff's long-time friends, his dismissal occurred for more than one reason. "There was a coup by the [WCW] VP's to oust Eric," states Sonny Onoo, matter-of-factly. "You have to remember that he started as a third-string announcer, and in a short matter of time, he was boss. There was a lot of resentment and jealousy among some of the VP's.

"So there was a coup - that's what happened."

David Crockett, WCW's VP of Production, responded affirmatively when asked if the coup took place. "Yes, yes, yes," he says. "Harvey Schiller…he didn't know anything. He was standing on the podium instead of Bill Shaw. Bill Shaw set everything in motion. It's just like somebody setting up a World Champion football team, and next year, a new coach wins the Super Bowl. He really didn't do squat."

"The line guy Eric [previously] reported to was Bill Shaw," clarifies Dick Cheatham. "He really paid attention to it. He would call me and say, 'what did you think about *WCW Saturday Night*'? I [would say], 'it sucked! It was a series of squash matches!' At that point, Shaw would say, 'I saw exactly the same thing'. He'd pick up the phone and call Eric. He'd chew him out: 'why are we putting stuff like that on television?'

"It ended up with Shaw and Eric having a really good working relationship. At that point, the corporate oversight really helped a lot.

"Later, Terry McGuirk decided that he wanted to hire somebody who really understood sports, and I think underneath everything, he wanted to get someone who would eventually take over the [Turner-owned] sports teams. He hired Harvey Schiller.

"The tragedy is that Schiller had a lot of talent that went to waste. He didn't provide the kind of oversight that Bill Shaw provided, [the kind] that kept Eric Bischoff on track. Bischoff is not a corporate creature, and he needed somebody that was on the 14th floor to provide that kind of support and guidance. I think that was a real problem when Shaw was replaced by Harvey Schiller.

"Harvey really didn't care about wrestling. He didn't care about it, at all. He was there for something else altogether."

When quizzed about Bischoff's departure, Schiller expresses ignorance on the subject. "When I was leaving," he says, "there was some falling out, and to this day, I don't understand what happened or didn't happen. Why he left the company - I don't know."

Crockett laughs loudly upon hearing the Doc's claim. "It had to have his approval! It was a super big deal!

"It took place when I was out of the country," Crockett continues. "I got a call [about it], and I went, 'what?' I could not believe it. It was Gary Juster and Sharon Sidello and Bill Busch. Think about that - the people I named. Who has any [kind of] broadcasting or entertainment background?

"There again, it was just about control. Unfortunately, for Eric, I wasn't there to guard his back."

Within a few hours, Bischoff headed into his private jet and embarked on a fishing trip in Wyoming. Before long, he invited his wife to join him in tranquility, and oddly - perhaps astutely - they both felt relieved.

"That was Harvey showing how little he knew of the business," says Kevin Nash. "They took the one person that had a clue on how to make this thing work, home."

"I thought he was a real 'plus' for us," says Dick Cheatham, speaking of Bischoff. "He took us from an arena-based thought process to a television-based thought process. There's this thing in accounting called cost-volume-profit analysis - it's the study of behavior of cost and revenue, over a relevant range of volume. That's what told us [in 1993], 'god knows, we gotta get out of the arenas, because there's a capacity limit'. I think Eric understood that."

"Eric Bischoff believed that the guys with brand names...still had a lot of value," offers Diamond Dallas Page. "That's the first thing. Then, he did what no-one else ever did - he created the cruiserweight division. It's funny how the WWF took a lot of that [style] later.

"'E' had to deal with a monster amount of egos. Holy fuck! Think about the egos in that era. In a world where it's predetermined, nobody wants to lose! So he was the head babysitter over all of us, at times - me included."

"Eric brought in the best talent in the world," says Kevin Sullivan. "I gotta give him credit where it's due - the nWo was basically his idea."

"Eric was a creative genius," reflects announcer Scott Hudson on the former WCW President. "The nWo angle was an example of what he called the 'umbrella' angle - an overarching storyline underneath which all other storylines operated. It had really never been tried to that extent before.

"Also, the mega push of Bill Goldberg and the re-invention of Sting - from quasi-surfer to 'The Crow' - all Eric. He was never afraid to take chances and to put himself out there for criticism. The old adage says, 'a manager says 'go', and a leader says 'let's go'. Eric was a leader."

"Eric is a man's man," adds Kevin Nash. "You could get in an argument with him, a 'fuck you, fuck you back' thing…then you work the shit out…go downstairs, watch the show back…have a beer, hug him…and go, 'yeah, it worked out!'

"Eric was a different boss than Vince," continues Nash. "When I got to the WWF, some of the agents called Vince, 'Caesar'. You know, 'Caesar wants you to do this…'. Eric wasn't that guy. Eric was kind of like…the head of the Hell's Angels or something. He was a lot more approachable…the perfect person to 'man the ship', at that point."

"I've been around a lot of charismatic leaders in my life," says one former Turner executive. "Eric was one of the best charismatic leaders that I've been around - dude is off the charts."

"I think Eric was brilliant," says Joe Uva. "The characters he created, the way he wove different things into the storylines…his personality on-air. The guy was a genius."

Bischoff himself believes his innovative approach propelled - in no small part - the wrestling industry to unfathomable heights. "My strategic and creative approach," he reflects, "elevated the wrestling industry to a level that it had never seen before, nor has seen since. And that's not hyperbole. That's not my ego [talking]. It's just a fact.

"Nobody could look back at that time…the energy that we created…the numbers and the audience that followed us…I'm largely responsible for that. Going back to sitting in a room by myself with a notepad trying to figure out how I could be different than my competition, because I knew I couldn't be *better* than my competition.

"I think that singular approach and that philosophy, if you will…that strategy…resulted in an era in the industry of professional wrestling that I doubt we'll ever see again. At '33,000 feet', looking down, I feel comfortable saying that, without feeling like I'm full of shit.

"[But] it wasn't just me. There was a lot of input from a lot of people…but [regarding] the nWo, from a creative perspective…to this

363

very day, you can walk into a wrestling arena - or watch it on television - and see people wearing nWo shirts. I can't think of a creative strategy or a creative approach in the history of the wrestling business - other than maybe Hulk Hogan himself - that has the type of endurance that that singular idea had. And to this day, people are trying to copy that formula.

"People are trying to recreate…hell…I did it! I tried to recreate my own success and failed at it. But to this day, that nWo storyline resonates with the audience that weren't even alive when it took place. It still resonates.

"I have to be honest - that makes me feel good. Beyond that, I'm just happy I was able to be a part of it, and was able to feed my family and take care of my kids, based on my participation."

"Now there were things about Eric that - in some ways - were serious flaws," says Dick Cheatham. "Eric wanted to keep everything a secret. Everything had to be really, really secret. What that meant was you [really] didn't have a script - except in your head - and so you didn't have a really tight show.

"When Bret Hart came with us, there was an event we were doing at the Georgia Dome, [for example] and the instruction to Bret is, 'ok, at 9:15, you're gonna go to the ring and talk about Ric Flair for 9 or 10 minutes'. Bret, being the consummate pro - is saying, 'well, what's my motivation? Do I like him? Do I hate him?' The direction he got was, 'ah, just go with it - we'll work around it'. That's too loose…performers don't just invent shit, they gotta have some motivation and guidance about what their character would do. [It's like], Bobby Heenan used to say over and over again, 'I gotta know what's coming so I can set it up'."

Indeed, Bischoff's perceived lack of creative foresight - or perhaps even preparation - has often been cited as a weakness of his approach. As fans would rue endlessly in the years to come, for example, WCW never provided a definitive finale to the nWo narrative (candidly, Bischoff admits that an end point was never determined).

"Whether fair or not," says producer Jason Douglas of the criticism, "that sort of seems like a true statement. I don't recall any fantastic, sustained campaigns...after the nWo and Goldberg's streak."

"I don't think there was an ending [in mind]," confirms Diamond Dallas Page, speaking of the nWo storyline. "Dusty used to call that, 'livin' on the edge of a lightning bolt!'"

"I remember Dusty telling me," adds producer Chris Larson, "'let me tell you one thing about a good storyline, brother. You get on top of it, and ride it like a horse until it falls over dead. Then you get off, and drag it behind you until it starts to stink. Then you go find another one!'"

"A lot of times," contextualizes Professor Sam Ford, "promoters have a great idea for a concept to launch, but don't necessarily think about the end - especially when something is working. Like almost all television or promotion, wrestling has a tendency to find an idea or dynamic that works, and run with it...until they've ran it out of juice.

"That was sort of the case with the nWo. They set up this huge dynamic with the 'takeover', and obviously to see that come to an eventual resolution...would require ending the story in a way that they weren't willing to do - until the nWo shirts stopped selling, and the story got old and bland. Then it's sort of like assisted suicide, rather than an exciting conclusion."

Furthermore, some former TBS and WCW employees question Bischoff's ability as a boss. "I thought Eric was terrific," begins Tom Karsch, TNT's former VP of Sports Marketing, "but I remember starting to hear the visions of grandeur...and things costing way more money. It sounded like things were starting to spiral a little bit - on that level."

"To me," offers producer Joel Edwards, "it seemed like [Eric] was much more of the entertainment figurehead - like the position he played on screen. That's what I saw more than anything else. I'm sure he did a lot more work besides that, but to me, what I saw was Craig

Leathers and the rest of the directors and the writing crew…doing all the rest of it. Bischoff sort of put his stamp on it, and acted like the mercurial 'President' guy as he did."

"Eric was the guy making things grow and explode in popularity," concurs former TBS producer Brendon Hamlin, "but as far as running a company - that side of it was probably…more challenging."

"This was true not only of wrestling, but every Turner company," counters Dick Cheatham. "If you look at who was running these companies, they were either entertainment people…or journalism people…but they weren't really business people.

"For example, Eric went and signed a 10 or 20-year deal with Disney," continues Cheatham. "I said, 'we've gotta unwind this son of a bitch'. It sounds like a good idea, and even people he checked with at corporate said [the same]. The problem was…that is a recordable event - it's called a capital lease. If you sign a 20 year lease, that's gotta get on your balance sheet. I said, 'let's find a way to modify it. We'll make a verbal commitment and we'll just sign one or two year leases'. That way I kept it off the balance sheet."

"I'll be honest," remembers Turner account executive Greg Scordato, "it was hard to separate him as an executive…and the persona he portrayed on TV. However, he seemed intelligent and willing to help our sales efforts - and was even understanding of the sales challenge the programs presented."

"Sometimes I would get Eric Bischoff, 'the on-air talent guy'," remembers TNT's Michael Polydoroff, "and sometimes I would get, 'Eric Bischoff with his hair down'. But by the time I had run my course at the network, Eric was like a friend to me.

"He was a straight shooter behind closed doors, but I was able to sort of break him down, from this kind of hard ridged…very serious…very passionate person…and we ended up having some really great conversations. It was always about the property, but he knew that I cared - and that made Eric care. When Eric knew you cared and put your heart into something, he cared back."

"I do have to give Bischoff a lot of credit," says Greg Prince. "There's probably nobody else that would have had the wherewithal to grow the company, to where he was able to take it.

"One thing I do recall, [though], is that he was always very suspect when an 'office type' would be out on the road at one of the events. I could remember having people accompany me - someone from Turner Risk Management, or someone like that. We would go out, hit a pay-per-view on a Sunday night and be in another city for *Nitro*. I can recall several times where Bischoff would come along, like, 'what are you doing here?' It was indicative of his sense that, 'they're trying to look over my shoulder', or meddle with things.

"I've learned over the years, as I've gotten older, that he probably had a lot of reasons to feel that way."

Indeed, maybe Bischoff was justified in his paranoia, as evidently - even during the good times - the corporate covertness was constant. "There was a point when McMahon wanted to talk about combining the two wrestling groups," reveals Schiller. "I met with him, and they thought about making it into...a mega-type entertainment business.

"We had the meeting...but it would have meant giving up control, and at that point, I don't think either side would have wanted to give up control.

"It was when [WCW] was doing well - later on in my tenure. It was sort of a casual meeting, but it wasn't something that was gonna fit. I think both parties knew that."

And to think, throughout these most epic of wars, Bischoff willingly risked it all: his health, his career...even his safety for World Championship Wrestling.

He could only see so far.

Chapter 39:
A Brave New World

FOR A FIGURE so often seen as a visionary, Ted Turner owed much of his empire to the dustbins of history. Since the 1980s, the Turner strategy of aggregating content that may have otherwise been seen as *old* - the MGM film library and the Warner Bros. cartoon library to cite two examples - had consistently availed itself to be an inexpensive (and effective) means of creating branded television networks. Turner's mastery of broadcast media coincided with an environment whereby viewers consumed programming via a *linear* delivery system; in other words, a direct-flow stream of communication with no tangible means of audience participation.

By the mid '90s, the promise of a future in which viewers could *control* the flow of information (and, potentially, engage with linear media in a responsive manner) threatened to challenge traditional notions of interactivity and narrative. Rather than simply watch an episode of *Seinfeld*, for example, and share reactions with those within the immediate physical space, the scope could exist, it was theorized, for a *complementary* viewing experience involving real-time digital interactions.

Throughout a 16-year career at Turner Broadcasting, Blake Lewin developed many of these ideas. For Lewin, a former Hollywood music licensor whose career trajectory shifted after reading an article about CD-Roms, the concept of *nonlinear* engagement seemed positively disruptive for the time. "It seems obvious now, but back then it was revolutionary," he says. "My whole career at Turner was trying to explore how this interactivity could function in a TV/digital space."

Simultaneously, TBS Inc. was examining how to bring their traditional properties to the next frontier - the World Wide Web. In the summer of 1996, the company formed a small group of web developers - *Turner Online Technologies* - in a rudimentary effort to

368

expose its subsidiaries' content online. The Internet itself was still a decidedly novel innovation; only 20 million Americans had access, and skeptics remained unconvinced of its mass potential. "We are going to see a slowdown in the rate of on-line penetration," predicted one expert quoted in the *Wall Street Journal*. "On-line users are going to become a stable, identifiable group." Aside from the issue of access, statistics regarding Internet usage reinforced perceptions of its limited appeal, with 'light' users - individuals spending less than four hours per month connected - accounting for 80% of all customers.

Meanwhile, a curious Lewin acted to familiarize himself with the new medium. In a casual conversation with Bill Cunningham - one of the web developers hired to exploit the content of Turner's 'old media' divisions - he learned of some unusual activity occurring on a company-run chat server. "[Bill said], 'Man, the chat room just went crazy last night'. I was like, 'what do you mean it went crazy?' He said, 'whenever WCW goes on the air, the chat room gets really, *really* busy!'"

"We started to look at this correlation," continues Lewin, "between what was happening on air, and what was happening in the chat room. Sure enough, it was a one-to-one correlation - people were engaging with each other, talking about [*Nitro*]. The light bulb went off for me. While people are watching television, they want to interact with each other. They want to be part of a bigger audience.

"Today, people refer to this as a 'second screen' [experience], people are 'tweeting' [while watching]...but in my mind, it all goes back to WCW and the chat rooms. It's where we first began to understand that digital communication during linear programming was happening."

———

By the time of his exchange with Blake Lewin, Bill Cunningham moved on to occupy another role - WCW's first-ever Internet manager. After *Turner Online Technologies* dissolved - a casualty of the company's merger with Time Warner - Cunningham considered thoughtfully which Turner division would be particularly suited to online investment. "The Internet was so young," he remembers wistfully. "I was trying to think, 'what do we have that is really a viable product [to develop online]?' I thought, 'classical movies...that's pretty traditional'. 'Children's cartoons...maybe in five or ten years' - the technology just wasn't there to do anything compelling for kids. Wrestling, on the other hand, had *all* the right ingredients.

"Wrestling had obsessive fans who would consume the product, no matter what medium you gave it to them. There was this element of the fan base that was very passionate about their fandom, but also were a bit embarrassed by it. [Therefore], it fit the Internet, because it had these [perceptible] elements of privacy and anonymity."

And so, bolstered with Cunningham's insight, the content skills of Dave Pava, and crucially, support from Tom Hunt, Director of Promotions, and Mike Weber, Director of Marketing, WCW began its initial foray into cyberspace. "The WCW website," remembers Pava, "actually started out as a five page marketing website - almost like an off-shoot of the TNT site. No one really knew a ton about site design, so in the dial-up era, all of these sites were about 2 megabytes big. Eventually, it became a top 20 sports website."

As a result of a partnership with *Compuserve* - the first (major) commercial online service provider - the live chat interface that attracted Lewin offered a transformative experience for web-based fans. *Compuserve* members were provided with special access to a private WCW 'channel', a perk which provided an opportunity to converse in real-time with wrestlers during shows. For a small percentage of viewers, therefore, watching *Nitro* could suddenly become an exercise in *three-dimensional* engagement; for in addition to simply tuning in to TNT, it was now possible to concurrently interact with other fans, and, through a moderator, solicit opinions from the performers themselves. "Some [wrestlers] would do it, and some would not," reflects Cunningham. "It was based on whomever was willing at the time."

Following the successful chat initiative, WCW next looked to establish itself in an infinitely more complicated space - streaming audio. The industry leader in the field, *RealNetworks*, claimed the distinction of having broadcast some of the earliest audio events on the web. Its business model offered the potential to purchase, at a premium rate, unlimited streaming capabilities for live events; conversely, *AudioNet*, a rival company co-founded by future Dallas Mavericks owner Mark Cuban, provided the ability to pay only for the (approximate) bandwidth required. In the dark ages of the web, Cuban, "a huge Hulk Hogan mark," according to Cunningham, built his core business by securing exclusive Internet rights to college radio broadcasts (partner Christopher Jaeb is credited with the initial concept).

As an auxiliary revenue stream, *AudioNet* also functioned as "a reseller," explains Cunningham. "I was their biggest customer at the time. You could say, 'I have an event. It's going to go from this time - to this time. I'll pay you 'x' amount of dollars for the first two hundred simultaneous streams. If we go over two hundred streams, we'll pay [at another rate]."

Despite the resultant audio being relatively pedestrian in nature - backstage interviews and the like - the number of users on WCW.com (originally WCWwrestling.com) consistently pushed the fee into overage territory. "Everyone always underestimated the power of wrestling on the Internet," argues Dave Pava. "It became very obvious from the data that we were getting…that the wrestling site was quietly becoming the biggest site - of all the Turner entertainment sites."

Subsequently, at the suggestion of Tom Hunt, information typically accessed via *analog* means was digitized. "Tom's big idea was, 'we're gonna put the 900-number on the Internet, and sell it'," reports Pava. "It was one of the first ever paid subscription [initiatives] at Turner."

Later, when the Internet team combined an earlier innovation, the chat room inhabited by rabid fans, with an auditory component - wrestlers responding to their questions over a headset - it enabled a real-time dialogue unlike any in the history of the business. "We encouraged the stars to *shoot* - to break character," says Cunningham. "It started to *really* work. We got more and more of an audience, because the aficionados would watch the match, and know enough to ask questions that the wrestlers liked to answer. Their questions were more about the profession, the skill, the talent involved, and less about the storyline."

It would take some time, however, for widespread acceptance of the practice to filter through WCW. The gatekeeper for many top performers appeared to be 'Mean' Gene Okerlund, who much like the wrestlers themselves, initially hesitated to embrace the new format. Eventually, though, Okerlund became an unlikely booster for the 'Internet guys', enabling the participation of mostly the entire roster. "He had relationships with all of the stars," says Cunningham. "If Gene said, 'you should do this', then they would do it. They really listened to him, and so we got more and more of the big talent to cooperate."

Throughout 1997, conversations began regarding the concept of promoting *web-exclusive* WCW events. On June 28th, as a test run for future online offerings, the company broadcast *Saturday Nitro* - an Internet-only transmission of a house show in Los Angeles, CA. "In 1997," recalls Pava, "we had the number three *AudioNet* broadcast, behind only Princess Diana's funeral and the Super Bowl (when asked about the existence of such recordings, Cuban - whose company was later renamed as *Broadcast.com* and sold to *Yahoo!* responds thusly: "I think *Yahoo* got rid of them.")."

In terms of actual stability, the streaming was a moderate success, eventually providing impetus to heavily promote a 'pay-per-listen' card (entitled *Boston Brawl*) on January 31, 1998. At a cost of $7.95, WCW promised candid backstage footage, an hour long Ric Flair documentary, exclusive downloadable games and a salacious main event - Hollywood Hogan vs. Sting in a steel cage match. To pull off the broadcast, two especially difficult problems had to be addressed - first, and at a time of widespread mistrust related to e-commerce, a reliable payment system would need to be established. Secondly, based on *AudioNet*'s modus operandi, it would be critical to accurately estimate the approximate demand in advance.

372

To address the issue of assessing demand, Cunningham's team developed a decidedly unique solution. It was a month after the PC release of *Quake II*, a first-person shooter game permitting players the option to change the appearance of a character - achieved via a customization option known as 'changing skins'. "One of my programmers had the idea to develop WCW Quake 'skins', and give them away - for free - to anybody who subscribed early to the event," remembers Cunningham. "We started doing this, and other giveaways, because we wanted to understand how many people would register. In the first week, we saw something like 20-25,000 people sign up. Keep in mind, this is the late 1990's - that was a *big* number for the Internet!"

In the final 48 hours before the *Brawl* got underway, the Internet team grew fearful of a plethora of users registering at the eleventh hour - similar to the purchase habits observed on conventional pay-per-view. Shortly before showtime, the anxiety compounded backstage when Okerlund - one half of the announce team - left the Fleet Center after suffering a bout of food poisoning (the culprit: a chicken focaccia sandwich at the Marriott). Consequently, on 10 minutes notice, website staffer Chad Damiani was asked to form an unlikely commentary duo with magazine writer Mark Madden.

Customers logging on at 8:30pm EST were confronted with the *layout du jour* - in one frame, a live chat room, in another, a slowly rotating selection of still images, and in a third box, a stream of text updates from WCW.com. Meanwhile, on the audio track, Damiani struggled to perform in his new role. "I was just 'bombing' - I didn't know what do," he laughs. "Mark was just taking over - he was doing all of the talking. [Eventually], I decided, 'you know what...fuck this. I'm just gonna do what I do on the [WCW] hotline, which is make fun of people'. I can remember specifically, Greg 'The Hammer' Valentine had a hammer on the back of his wrestling tights. I was like, 'what a weird thing to do'. Just think about that! He just put a hammer on his ass! Where else but in wrestling would that be considered anything but an invitation?!"

373

Sadly for Damiani, his tongue-in-cheek comments were sailing mostly into the ether. By the start of match two, the audio stream had already cut out, leaving thousands of users to ruminate angrily in the chat room. Nonetheless, his remarks were reaching a particularly entertained audience backstage. "All of a sudden," recalls Damiani, "I hear over my headset, 'hey yo, are we talking about the 'Hammer'? Scott Hall and Kevin Nash had microphones plugged in, and now they are commentating with Mark and I. They're making fun of it too. Most of the show was the four of us - barely calling the matches - just riffing and joking around."

At the recommendation of Hall and Nash, Damiani received a full-time WCW contract offer a week later. In the meantime, however, the company would be forced to issue refunds to every single customer, as despite attempts to purchase greater capacity, the server, streaming system (and incidentally, the payment system) all crashed due to the huge demand. "In spite of all the effort to prepare everyone for it, we still weren't prepared for it," Cunningham laments. "It depends on what numbers you rely on, because you can't say, for example, that every unique IP address would have resulted in a sale...but we had more than 1.5 million unique IP addresses hit the payment site. We had no idea what the real demand could have been - *if* the technology could have handled it.

"It was a complete catastrophe. But my reaction to this was one of elation and joy. I thought, 'well, clearly I've proven that there's a market. Too bad that we didn't make it work the first time, but now we know what we need to do'. You work an angle for a while, produce a house show that's not for broadcast, you put it on the Internet, and you [might] get 2 million people paying 10 bucks each. Nobody heard me...the only thing they heard was the bad publicity. Every meeting I had after that was 'yeah, nice try, but clearly you fucked up'."

"We used *IXL* as the host for that broadcast," remembers Dave Pava. "They did not predict how popular the event would be, and they didn't get the credit card stuff right. The event was a complete disaster."

Ultimately, the pay-per-listen concept would be revived for three more shows during the year, with each experiencing its own technical difficulties (the final event, 'L.A. Melee', sold at the discounted rate of $4.95). In contrast to the production costs associated with television and pay-per-view, the Internet department was running on a severely lean budget - $60,000, according to Cunningham, who earlier had requested a yearly allocation of $1 million. He would soon depart the company, but not before saving a top star some serious dough of his own.

"Randy Savage had put together a site called *MachoManOnline.com*. He was negotiating a contract with some technology company that allowed you to do streaming media. He came up to me because he was curious if the price he was about to pay was reasonable. It was huge - [something] like a quarter of a million dollars for unlimited use, something like that. It was not a small number! He laid the whole thing out for me. I said, 'look, I'm pretty sure we already have a global contract with these guys through Turner. Because you're a property of WCW, we can probably get you in that license contract'.

"Two weeks later, I called the company he was negotiating with, and talked to all the lawyers at Turner. We said, 'look, as long as his site [displays] a Turner logo, and refers to WCW, then they can just link in to WCW-run servers. Even though Randy himself owns the content, we can own the delivery, and therefore, you don't need a new license'.

"So Randy comes up to me in the bar after a show, and I told him the whole thing. I said, 'it's not gonna cost you anything'. He looked at me with that penciled-in beard of his, and goes, 'brother, you just saved me a quarter of a million dollars'. I was like, 'yeah, y'know, don't worry about it'. He grabbed me by the shoulder and said, 'as far as I'm concerned, you're a brother now. Anytime we're in the same town, I'm gonna make sure you have two drinks in front of you - and two girls. If we're in Tampa, it's three drinks and three girls, 'cos that's my town!'"

———

In time, many web staffers became frustrated at management,

specifically regarding their inability to appreciate - and prioritize - WCW's digital growth. "They knew that this thing called the Internet was important, but they didn't understand how," explains Brian Sites, a Multimedia Producer from 1999 to 2001. "They were more than happy to support initiatives like the live broadcasts, because that was close to the world they knew. [But] when I first started, the manager of the website and I bumped heads a lot, partly because she didn't understand the web, but mostly because she didn't understand the product we were selling.

"Part of our role was to be a marketplace for wrestling 'swag', [and so] we would have a featured item every week on the front page. One week, the selected item she wanted us to post was a teddy bear wearing a WCW shirt...because it was cute. When your competitor is hocking personalities like Degeneration X, and The Rock, teddy bears hardly supported our image.

"Keep in mind that the crew running the show all came from a classic pro wrestling background. They understood how to book a 45 minute Ric Flair match, but they didn't get promos - at least not in the way WWF was starting to use them in character development. [Furthermore], they didn't understand how the web, as a vehicle, could further the reach of a wrestler and deepen their [connection] with fans. It was a tough thing to watch at times...we were mostly just kids, fresh out of college, and we didn't know how to navigate those issues."

"In '98," begins Brandon Woodson, formerly the webmaster of WCW.com, "we had mass amounts of traffic (believed to 15,000,000 monthly page views at its peak). More than the Cartoon Network site, more than anyone else within Turner. And we had no advertising on the site. Nobody knew what we had - we had a *goldmine* (case in point: as early as 1996, when nWowrestling.com ran its own 'angle' pretending to hack into WCWwrestling.com, traffic spiked to such an extent that the site overtook CNN.com in page views). I was looking at the overall picture of how this could work, and how this technology could help the company and even affect storylines.

"At one point, management wanted to launch a new website, and they wanted another company to host it. I asked that company probably 10 times, 'do you understand the kind of traffic we get to this site? Can you guarantee that you can host this? 'Yes, yes...', they responded. When we launched the new site, it went down within 10 minutes."

As the digital growing pains continued, a team of videographers and technicians prepared to deal with the next challenge: streaming *video*. "When we first started doing live video webcasts," remembers Sites, "there was no infrastructure to support it. Dial-up was king, so anyone who had the Internet was on either a 28k or 56kbps connection. YouTube, Ustream and all the on-demand providers wouldn't hit the market for another five years. Wifi at the arenas did not exist, nor did access to any wired connectivity.

"In order to do a live [video] broadcast, we needed a satellite uplink truck to blast the signal, and a distribution and service provider like Akamai to link to the broadcast, compress the video in real-time, and feed it out across their network. It was incredibly expensive.

"In the end, what we produced was video the size of a postage stamp. But the content was really interesting, allowing fans to get a glimpse behind the scenes, in a way that had never been done before."

Until the late '90s, most hardcore fans relied on weekly newsletters - *dirt sheets* as referred to in the wrestling business - and expensive paid hotline services to follow the most current behind-the-scenes gossip. While an overwhelming majority of fans, even frequent attendees of WCW and WWF events, knew nothing of the underground periodicals - instead experiencing their patronage as uncritical followers of the week-to-week action - the proliferation of the Internet, coinciding with the boon created by the Monday night ratings competition, soon birthed a limitless number of websites, chat rooms, and rumor boards to support an unremitting coverage of pro wrestling news. More specifically, the crucial introduction of Internet service producers (ISPs) soon democratized the ability to build a website; consequently, thousands of rudimentary wrestling pages abounded on *Geocities, Angelfire* and the like.

"I think the introduction of the Internet," points out Joe Uva, a key Turner executive, "had as much to do with the success and growth of [wrestling] as the product itself.

"Before if you were a wrestling fan, you'd have to go to a news stand and buy a wrestling magazine that was two months old. Now, for a generation of fans who were in their 'tweens', teens and for young adults, it brought them closer to the action and characters."

The need to engage with this growing subset of fans, and, when necessary, confirm or deny the abundance of leaked information, presented an interesting dilemma. While WCW's marketing department found that around 30 percent of viewers regularly visited web-based insider outlets, skeptics retorted with an obvious point: more than two-thirds of fans, therefore, did *not* scour the Internet daily for the latest scoops.

In March of 1999, WCW.com debuted its most inventive project yet - *WCW Live*, a nightly audio broadcast incorporating listener calls and groundbreaking wrestler shoot interviews. Predominately hosted by Jeremy Borash and Bob Ryder, the show quickly established itself as the most streamed audio program in the world, garnering upwards of 50,000 nightly listeners on regular occasions. It complemented a growing range of streaming media available on the site, including 'WCW Hotline' updates and alternate insider commentary – targeted specifically towards the 'smart' audience during pay-per-view events (*so* targeted to such fans, that analysts regularly acknowledged the booker(s) pulling the strings. At the close of Spring Stampede '99, for example, Chad Damiani concluded with the following pronouncement: "Kudos to the booking team and Kevin Nash - it's finally coming together gentlemen!").

"To give you an idea of how far ahead of the curve we were," says Brian Sites, "our sister company, CNN, was only doing on-demand content. I can't be 100% certain, but I don't know of any other entity, or organization, that was doing anything at this level [at that time]."

Indeed, even as late as summer 1999, some Time Warner executives - even heads of divisions - remained resistant to using e-mail. With Wall Street abuzz about the ongoing digital revolution, however, CEO Jerry Levin looked to develop a long-overdue Internet strategy, leading to the formation of *Time Warner Digital Media* in July. "Digital media is [our] most single most important growth area," said Levin upon its announcement.

Recently turned 60, Levin was also thinking about his legacy, particularly as compared to Henry Luce, the magazine magnate and founder of *Time, Inc.* Increasingly, Levin pored over Luce's speeches and letters in the company archives, seeing himself as similar to the man once dubbed "the most influential private citizen in the America of his day."

Inspired by a particular Luce initiative - the pulse-taking *Time* 'News Tours' of the 1960s - Levin decided to organize an 11-day trip to China, designed to position himself and Time Warner as a leader in global corporate responsibility. After all, as Levin himself observed in public comments, "Luce insisted that it wasn't enough for business leaders to pursue efficiency and productivity...[rather, executives should] have a heightened sense of their responsibility to the common good. I share this conviction."

———

On September 22nd, the *Time Warner News Tour* began in Western China. An impressive contingent of 28 board members and executives made the trip, although Ted Turner, upon learning that spouses would not be invited, declined to participate.

I can't last that long without sex, he reportedly complained.

In China, Jerry Levin was greeted like a king, enjoying extraordinary deference from dignitaries far and wide. To coincide with the three-day Fortune Global Forum, his tour made a stop in Shanghai, and amidst an array of corporate titans - including Steve Case of AOL - Levin introduced Jiang Zemin, China's President, as the keynote speaker.

Early in the conference, Levin was approached by Merv Adelson, a Time Warner board member, who brought with him pressing news: *Jerry...Steve Case just whispered something to me about how we should bring our companies together. Has he said anything to you?*

Levin barely knew much of Case, and the part he did wasn't particularly impressive. But one night in Shanghai, after witnessing Case embrace his wife (AOL, evidently, did not adopt a 'no spouse' policy), he considered revisiting the perception. *He couldn't possibly be as cold as I imagined*, Levin thought. *I must have misjudged him.*

Upon returning to America, Levin sat in his Rock Plaza office when the phone rang. *I've been thinking*, said the caller on the other end. *We should put our two companies together.*

Any interest?

Chapter 40:
Vicious Vincent

ON DECEMBER 1ST, 1991, John Arezzi welcomed listeners to *Pro Wrestling Spotlight*, an insider radio show airing on Long Island's WGBB station. "We're going to introduce somebody to you now," began Arezzi, whose weekly broadcast offered fans a rare look behind the scenes of the sport. "One of our sponsors here at *Pro Wrestling Spotlight*...his name is Vinnie Russo."

Unassumingly, thus began the pro wrestling story of Vincent James Russo, a then-30 year old video store owner and Long Island native. Despite being a total non-entity in wrestling - at least, prior to meeting Arezzi - Russo actually possessed a lifelong passion for the spectacle, first becoming exposed as a child to Vince McMahon Sr.'s WWWF. His interest even maintained into adulthood (culminating in enthusiastic road trips to *Wrestlemania IV* and *V*), but interestingly, Russo ranked himself as merely the most casual of wrestling devotees. He professed little interest in the actual matches, or *fake fights* as he would later call them, preferring the elements that built *towards* the predetermined battles instead.

Nonetheless, as a pop culture aficionado and compulsive television viewer, Russo appreciated the entertainment value that wrestling generated. To draw crowds to his store - *Will The Thrill Video* (acquired after convincing Mom and Dad to refinance their home) - Russo organized a series of promotions involving WWF grapplers, including Brutus 'The Barber' Beefcake, Demolition and Jake 'The Snake' Roberts (the latter of which entered the store to find the walls decked out like a snake pit). Eventually, at the recommendation of Andrew Goldberger - the teenage President of a fan club devoted to Jim Cornette, a legendary NWA manager - Arezzi learned about Russo and his interest in wrestling. To stay on the air, Arezzi needed financing, and to help secure the time slot, Russo agreed to cover its

$1,000 weekly cost. Simultaneously, however, Russo's own business was floundering. The arrival of a nearby *Blockbuster* chipped away at his customer base, and ultimately, his daily takings dropped to a paltry $100.

Out of desperation, Russo started to develop, as he would later call it, a "plan to use John Arezzi's resources...to establish [himself] in the wrestling business." With the radio show failing to attract significant sponsorship, or - for that matter - produce any meaningful revenue opportunities, Russo pressed Arrezi to expand the operation. He soon negotiated a deal with WEVD, a station in the heart of Manhattan, after becoming frustrated with WGBB's weak signal and limited listener base. To offset the dramatically higher price tag of $1,500 per week, Russo proposed raising funds via a tried-and-tested method - the publication of a biweekly newsletter.

A decade earlier, Russo's earlier foray into journalism had been controversial. As Editor of the Indiana State University paper, his reporting once provoked the school basketball team to physically retaliate. But ironically, as *Pro Wrestling Spotlight* migrated to its new Manhattan home, controversy was rife in the wrestling world too. The WWF was reeling after a series of drug and sex scandals, and Arezzi, convinced of company wrongdoing, was consistently lambasting Vince McMahon on air. In the March 16th, 1992 edition of their newsletter, a crestfallen Russo expressed his own disgust:

'WWF to face suit alleging child sex abuse'. Is this a sick world we live in or what? I'm deeply disturbed by this story - whether it's true or false, it almost doesn't matter. How could the WWF become involved in something like this? What about all the children that are fans? How will this affect them? How do you explain this to them after they read the article in the New York Post? And how will the WWF handle this? At press time, Steve Planamenta, head of Public Relations for WWF, was unavailable for comment. Unavailable for comment - are you kidding me? As a parent, I want answers! Don't give me your spineless 'unavailable for comment'. What the hell are you guys doing up there in Titan Towers? You think that you can have a secretary say that you are unavailable for comment, and all these allegations are just going to disappear?

...A few weeks ago, I telephoned Steve Planamenta to request an interview with (legendary wrestler) Chief Jay Strongbow for my 'where are they now?' column. Planamenta said he had to think about it, because he wasn't happy with the comments made by [Pro Wrestling Spotlight Weekly] regarding the WWF. He claimed the WWF could take criticism, however our newsletter printed blatant lies about the organization.

...I figured for the sake of our readers and listeners, I was going to make every effort to try and work with the WWF. I took a 'they're right, I'm wrong' attitude. A week has passed since then and I'm certain of one thing: I'm right - they're wrong. There is no working with Planamenta and the WWF - forget it, it's a dead issue.

...I was trying to protect you. I was trying to interview some old-timers to take off the heat and give you some positive publicity. Did you ever think about that? Well hard luck fellas, because you're gonna have a lot a helluva lot of thinking to do now.

In response to the piece, the WWF informed Russo that his presence had been requested - by order of Vince McMahon himself - at an upcoming 'symposium' covering changes to the WWF's steroid policy (a poorly disguised effort, in the eyes of some observers, to quell the mounting controversy surrounding the organization). Realizing that his career prospects in wrestling would be greatly aided by meeting McMahon, Russo accepted, subsequently convincing Arezzi that he had to attend alone. "I realized the whole plan could cave in at any moment," Russo later recalled. "Whether I was ready or not, it was time for me to break away from John and give the wrestling business a go on my own."

Following the symposium, Russo suddenly changed his stance towards the WWF. He notified Arezzi that an affiliation was now possible with the company, causing an argument dissolving their business relationship. *You're missing the chance of a lifetime*, Russo allegedly told Arezzi, shortly before returning to the airwaves with a kid-friendly (and WWF endorsed) show, *Vicious Vincent's World of Wrestling*.

For the next year, Russo was comfortably given access to McMahon's top stars, and soon engaged with listeners through an exaggerated persona modeled on Randy Savage and Ric Flair. In time, Russo and his co-hosts became minor celebrities to their devoted audience, even earning a bizarre booking at a child's bar mitzvah (at the ceremony, Russo devised a rudimentary 'angle' involving Skull Von Crush, his co-host and purportedly, an evil wrestler from Germany).

Eventually, *World of Wrestling* proved to be cost prohibitive, and on a whim, Russo wrote a letter to Linda McMahon - Vince's wife and WWF President - to inquire about writing for WWF Magazine (according to Bruce Prichard, a long-time backstage official, Russo's resume had already been submitted several times). At first, only a freelance position was available, but rapidly, Russo ascended to become Editor of the publication, earning a $60,000 full-time salary.

Unlike his predecessors at the magazine, Russo sought to improve its sense of authenticity by conducting interviews with the performers themselves (rather than - as had been done in the past - writing canned comments in the style of each wrestler). By 1996, two years into the role, he was invited to attend WWF creative meetings - firstly as an observer, based on the pretense that it would create better alignment with the content of the magazine - but ultimately, as a contributing participant. When *Raw* dropped to its lowest ever rating (1.9) in March of 1997, Russo's influence expanded, and by the following year, he was appointed as McMahon's Head Writer.

Concurrent with Russo's ascension was the WWF's unexpected comeback in the ratings war. The Mike Tyson acquisition - combined with the red-hot Austin-McMahon feud, and programming which featured copious amounts of profanity, lewd gestures, and controversy - spurred the company to snap WCW's historic win streak in April 1998. In the heat of competition, Russo became admittedly obsessed with achieving the highest viewership possible, and in the tradition of his idol, Howard Stern, *Raw* increasingly incorporated controversial topics such as racism, miscarried pregnancies, cross-dressing, kidnapping and prostitution.

In June 1998, with the momentum firmly in the WWF's favor, McMahon hired Ed Ferrara, a former script writer for USA Network's *Weird Science*, to contribute to the creative process. In developing their storylines, Russo and Ferrara brainstormed ways to not only progress the WWF's on-screen product, but the entire narrative structure of pro wrestling itself. The duo considered themselves to offer a *thinking man's wrestling*, defying convention and deliberately

384

veering plots in unexpected directions whenever possible.

Scripts for *Raw*, with oversight from McMahon and USA programmer Bonnie Hammer, applied principles borrowed from other television shows; an upcoming commercial break, for example, no longer functioned as simply a break in the action - rather, it represented the chance to tease continuation of a backstage scene. Each episode established a dominant theme in its opening segment, one that would be revisited, reestablished, and ultimately resolved in the final few minutes of the show. Similarly, in opposition to conventional wisdom which stated that star performers should be used sporadically - particularly on television - *Raw* featured the phenomenally popular 'Stone Cold' Steve Austin in up to a dozen pre-taped vignettes. In sum, the changes, along with a dramatic scaling back of time devoted to actual in-ring wrestling, alluded to Russo and Ferrara's ethos to write *as if the viewer held the remote control in hand*. Collectively, the tactics amounted to a strategy known as 'Crash TV'.

In the fall of 1999, and with *Raw* regularly surpassing a 6.0 in the Nielsen ratings, UPN commissioned a second weekly WWF show - *Smackdown*. The prospect of an insurmountable work load loomed for McMahon's writers, who despite adding former WCW staffer Terry Taylor to their committee earlier in the year, were already running on fumes. Working for McMahon meant there was no downtime, *no sick time*, no opportunity to escape the perpetual pressure of the next weekly show. To add insult to injury, the boss refuted any notion of a raise, and in mainstream publications, assumed credit for the WWF regaining its position in mainstream pop culture.

Content concerns notwithstanding (an Indiana University study of 50 *Raw* episodes reported 1,658 instances of crotch-grabbing, 157 obscene finger gestures, 128 moments of simulated sexual activity, and 21 references to urination), it was difficult to argue with Russo and Ferrara's WWF success. While detractors pointed to the convergence of several unique factors - the simultaneous ascension of *two* mega-stars, 'The Rock' and Steve Austin; the talent acquisitions spearheaded by executive Jim Ross, *Raw*'s iconic lead announcer; the Tyson grab followed by WCW's disintegration into organizational chaos - the record showed that WWF revenues tripled ($81.9 million to $251.5 million) since Russo first gained influence. In return, he received an arguably meager compensation package, consisting of a $350,000 annual salary, supplemented by sporadic balloon payments from McMahon.

Therefore, Russo believed his remuneration to be incommensurate with his unending responsibilities, which still included editing WWF Magazine and soon, the writing of *Smackdown* in addition to *Raw*. His wife of 16 years had started to refer to herself as a single parent, and Russo, disconsolate at missing his son's baseball games, requested a meeting with McMahon in September 1999. Upon entering the owner's office, Russo burst into tears - it had all become too much, the proud New Yorker revealed, his family life on the verge of collapse. Realizing that discussion of a lighter schedule - much less an actual vacation - would not be palatable to McMahon, Russo instead considered his escape route.

Inconceivably, and for as long as anyone could remember, Russo had been working at the WWF without a contract. With this in mind, he pleaded to McMahon for a 15-month written deal, and, in light of his previous contributions, a pay increase to $1 million. In response, an unmoved McMahon reportedly made a cold suggestion: *You make enough money Vince - why don't you just hire a nanny to watch your kids?*

Russo would later cite the exchange as the catalyst for his WWF departure. On the morning of Friday, October 1st, 1999, he sent feelers through J.J. Dillon to WCW, which was itself reeling after the displacement of Eric Bischoff some three weeks earlier. After Dillon presented the opportunity to Bill Busch, Russo was informed that there was considerable interest, and at about nine o'clock that evening, he gathered his belongings from the company headquarters in Stamford.

On Saturday, October 2nd, Russo boarded a 10am flight for Atlanta, Georgia, his plans for defection a closely guarded secret. During the afternoon, he traveled to a Marriott hotel to meet with a contingent of

WCW representatives, including Dillon, Busch, and Gary Juster, the company's Vice President of Arenas and Merchandise. Throughout the day, and as reported by Dillon in his autobiography, "Russo did a great job selling himself to [Busch]. [He] told Bill that he had been writing the shows for the WWF, and not Vince McMahon. He also claimed that McMahon would make a cursory glance of the scripts and sign off on them."

Ultimately, the discussion extended into Sunday, allowing the ultimate decision makers to enter the fray: Brad Siegel (bearing a New York Yankees cap) and Dr. Harvey Schiller. "I remember meeting him with Brad," says Schiller of Russo. "I remember he came with a strong resume and background, but that's about it."

Before Russo could fly back to Connecticut, the party tendered its offer - the position of 'Creative Director', a role purportedly promising full control over WCW programming, as part of a three-year deal, effective immediately. In terms of compensation, a generous base salary was proffered, augmented by bonuses for achieving targets related to Nielsen ratings *and* pay-per-view buy rates. In response, a weary Russo, sensing creative fatigue to be imminent, pushed for the pact to expire a year earlier. "I knew at that point that I was already burned out on the wrestling business," he says. "I was looking to give WCW my all for two years, [and] then walk away from the business."

"Bill Busch called me," remembers Dick Cheatham, "and said, 'I just made the greatest decision in the history of WCW'.

"I said, 'oh, Bill, what did you do'?

"He said, 'I just hired the brains behind the WWF'.

"I said, 'who?'

"He said, 'Vince Russo'.

"I didn't know who he was."

387

In his new job, Russo was told he would have to function in line with Turner corporate guidelines concerning televised content. "I knew I was going to have to deal with Standards and Practices," Russo recalls, "but I was cool with that." Moreover, upon his recommendation, WCW agreed to offer his writing partner - also working without a contract for McMahon - a two-year agreement of his own. "I pitched Ed Ferrara in my first meeting with them. He was never originally part of the deal," divulges Russo, whose decision to support his collaborator paid immediate dividends. After reading the fine print, Ferrara insisted on a 'pay-or-play' clause for the twosome, meaning that regardless of circumstances, WCW would be obligated to pay the entire amount promised on each deal. When asked to elaborate on the eventual terms, Russo responds, "[I] don't think discussing my salary is anybody's business but my own. I will say this [however] - I wouldn't have signed a two-year contract with WCW…for less than one million dollars over that time."

Late Sunday, as Russo finally put pen to paper, some rather important business remained undone. In an earlier time, Russo's admiration for Vince McMahon precipitated his employment in wrestling, eventually culminating in their close rapport and even, according to Russo, the growth of a genuine mutual affection. Incredibly, however, their working relationship would now terminate not in person, but rather, in the most *impersonal* of ways - via telephone.

"Effective Sunday, October 3 at 9:45 p.m. ET," began a brief statement on WWF.com, "Vince Russo, one of the creative writers, will no longer be with the World Wrestling Federation. Russo abruptly resigned over the phone and will now be working for WCW."

"Vince felt like Russo stabbed him in the back," says Dennis Brent, Business Manager of WWF Publications between 1998 and 2000. "He thought Russo was like a son, and totally devoted to the company."

Those remaining with McMahon were eventually rewarded handsomely. In mid-October, the WWF launched an initial public offering as a publicly traded company, generating millions in incentives for its loyal braintrust. Clearly a persona non grata, Russo was betting everything on his WCW success, while McMahon - years after railing against Ted Turner - was soon to become a billionaire.

––––––

Similar to how they had rewritten the rule book in writing WWF television, Russo and Ferrara believed a radically novel approach would be needed to 'fix' WCW. In recent months, their creative discussions had touched on a desire to *evolve the business* - a sentiment that conveyed, among other things, frustration with 'traditional' angles and perceived one-dimensional storytelling. But while their previous work had attracted millions of casual viewers, Russo expressed an apparent desire to acknowledge a much narrower audience - the so-called 'smart marks' who frequented online message boards and insider publications. In an interview with the *Pro Wrestling Torch*, Russo insisted the following:

What really changed the wrestling business was the Internet. I was screaming to the WWF five years ago, and nobody wanted to listen to me....they would always come back to me and say 'oh well, there's only one computer in every 20 thousand households'. My argument would be 'oh yeah, there's one computer, but what happens when little Johnny goes onto the Internet and gets kayfabe information? You're going to tell me that the next day, little Johnny doesn't go to school and tell 15 of his friends?

The instant feedback afforded by the web was alluring for those in the creative process. Indeed, for years following episodes of *Raw*, Russo visited chat rooms under a pseudonym, eager to absorb the chatter arising from a just-aired show. He clearly kept a keen eye on the online community, contacting critical columnists with objections to their reports on occasion. After reading an erroneous article on *Wrestleline.com*, Russo began a dialogue with journalist Ben Miller, culminating in his granting of a rare in-depth interview. As part of a wide ranging talk, and after Miller raised a point regarding the presentation of wrestling in Japan, Russo interjected with the following statement:

I'm going to tell you something right now that you will absolutely not agree with, but I've been a wrestling fan my whole life and I will live and die by this. It is hard enough - believe me, I write this shit - it is hard enough to get somebody over. You will never ever, ever, ever, ever see the Japanese wrestler or the Mexican wrestler over in American mainstream wrestling. And the simple reason for that is...even myself, I'm an American, and I don't want to sound like a big bigot or a racist or anything like that, but I'm an American...if I'm watching wrestling here in America, I don't give a shit about a Japanese guy. I don't give a shit about a Mexican guy. I'm from America, and that's what I want to see.

The extent to which Russo's comments would cause controversy remained to be seen. For now, he was focused on familiarizing himself with recent WCW storylines. "I watched the product for a good month out," he recalls. "I felt I had a good grasp of what needed to be done, [in order] to turn around the ratings."

Supremely confident, Russo had also taken to referring to himself by a new moniker: 'The Bill Parcells of Wrestling', according to Miller. "[He said it was] because he could go from promotion to promotion rejuvenating them. I then reminded him that there were 31 NFL teams at the time, but only two wrestling promotions."

———

Before making any attempt to rejuvenate WCW, an honest assessment, Russo believed, would first be required of its on-screen product. With the new creative team set to debut on October 25th - the *Nitro* following *Halloween Havoc* - he observed the October 4th episode with a pained commiseration. In the main event, 50-year old Ric Flair teamed - for the first time - with 46-year old Hulk Hogan, but meanwhile on USA, *Raw* promised a marquee match-up featuring The Rock and Chris Jericho (a match originally booked by Russo prior to his departure). Although there were many difficult decisions still to be made, Russo and Ferrara agreed on one significant measure to be implemented immediately. Flair and Hogan, they reasoned, needed to be removed from television - indefinitely - with a view to facilitate their eventual return in more *appropriate* roles.

Earlier in the night, Bret Hart made his return to in-ring competition, wrestling Chris Benoit in a tribute match for his late brother Owen. Delivering a 28-minute exhibition in technical wizardry, Hart and

Benoit captivated the crowd at the same scene as *Over The Edge* - Kemper Arena in Kansas City, MO. To the purists, the beautifully-paced contest delivered a poignant artistic statement - perhaps Owen had died, because the simplicity of wrestling had died too.

"[It was] a straight-forward, shoot-from-the-hip, wrestling match," Hart wrote in a *Calgary Sun* column. "Pro wrestling in its purest form, just two people telling a story with their bodies. Artistry at its best. It was the kind of match that long-time fans reminisce about and hunger for. And fans who've been around for only a couple of years told me they'd never seen anything like it before."

Hart saluted the sky at the final bell, symbolically saying goodbye to his fallen brother. Meanwhile, WCW - with *Crash TV* imminent - symbolically said goodbye to pro wrestling.

Chapter 41:
The Powers That Be

EN ROUTE TO THE October 11th *Nitro* in Biloxi, MS - ultimately, the last Monday night before taking control - Russo and Ferrara experienced an ominous feeling. They were soon to enter a locker room best described as a lion's den - as outsiders no less - in an effort to discuss creative plans and get 'the boys' on their side. To their surprise upon entering the building, a group of talented young midcarders, including Eddie Guerrero, Chris Benoit and Dean Malenko, greeted them enthusiastically with hopes of moving up the card. Subsequently, the new creative team met with an assortment of top wrestlers - including an hour-long discussion with Bret Hart - in order to sell their vision for WCW's turnaround.

"Part of the plan they [articulated]," recalls Marcus 'Buff' Bagwell, "was that 'the problem with WCW was the person running the show was always *part* of the show'. That's what Russo dogged Eric out about. 'Eric wanted to be in every segment', [and so on]. I love Vince Russo to death - he's a good guy. At the same time, he did promise us something that day. He told me personally that he would never appear on television."

Following an announcement that the writers would be given full control a week earlier than expected - and thus *prior* to *Halloween Havoc* - Russo repeated the pledge on *WCW Live*. Regarding his chances for success, he sounded optimistic about the task ahead, while Ferrara highlighted his "very positive" thoughts on the backstage environment. There was, however, a fairly significant concern lingering in the background, as reportedly, Terry Bollea had rejected their ideas in a closed-door discussion. For now, and especially given the parties involved, no-one was sure of the truth.

The final show of the Kevin Nash booking era - an infamous episode of *WCW Thunder* - occurred on October 14th in Baton Rouge,

Louisiana. Prompting visible confusion on the face of announcer Mike Tenay, Nash greeted fans with an unexpected appearance at the top of the broadcast. "Kevin, I don't understand this," questioned Tenay in the opening segment, "you're retired from professional wrestling. What are you doing here?"

"Well, there's been a lot of people that said I was a horrible booker," replied Nash on the air. "But I've actually booked myself in the best angle of all-time - I'm retired! Since they're paying me big money, they decided that they would be put me on the broadcast team," he smiled, "to try to recoup some of those funds." For the rest of the show, Nash interjected accordingly with a series of uproarious shoot comments (*"That's not Booker T - that's Wesley Snipes!...Sid [Vicious] - six-foot-ten...200, no, 300 hundred, no 591 pounds of menacing steel...Rick Steiner - a man from Detroit, Michigan, who speaks like a southern redneck."*)

"I had a big jug of beer with me," recalls Nash, who was technically 'in retirement' after losing a match at *Road Wild*. "I was drinking the whole show. They always tried to pull these things where they thought they would upset you, and all I did was use their live TV against them. Like, 'you wanna put them in charge? God bless you'. You think someone else can steer the Titanic back to port, after it's taken an iceberg? Knock yourself out.

"They paid me 450 or 500 thousand dollars to book, and I then I pulled myself off the wrestling part...so I made another half-a-million bucks, and I didn't wrestle. I mean, that's how easy it was...I rest my case!"

Finally, October 18th arrived for *Nitro* - the official start of the new era. At their first production meeting, Russo impressed a gathering of backstage staff with his clear explanations and detailed instructions for the broadcast; to some observers, including Tony Schiavone, he came off as almost McMahon-like in his presentation. Characteristically, he and Ferrara had been meticulous in their planning, distributing a lengthy script with more guidance than anyone could remember. In accordance with their philosophy, a much greater emphasis was placed on backstage segments ("my pre-tape workload tripled [for] the first *Nitro* they penned," recalls associate producer Darryl Marshall), and so-called 'cold' matches - bouts occurring without any particular purpose - would be sworn off completely.

Early in *Nitro*'s third hour, Bagwell sauntered to the ring for a match with La Parka, the Mexican luchador with a humorous penchant for swinging a metal chair. After an earlier segment where an upbeat Buff referenced the "two new sheriffs" in charge - reinforcing to viewers that in the new WCW, wrestlers would casually acknowledge the writers' presence on camera - he was now behaving in a manner inconsistent with his usual character. Buff's entrance, which tended to involve a sizable portion of histrionics, curiously came across as jarringly stilted. As the referee signaled for the match to begin, the crowd took notice of Bagwell's reluctance to wrestle, while the announcers - scripted to feign ignorance - speculated as to what was happening.

As the 'contest' reached its conclusion, Bagwell openly encouraged his opponent to cover him for a pinfall, and in a puzzling scene, remained on the mat as the referee counted to three. The live feed quickly cut to a shot backstage, where an assortment of midcard wrestlers applauded the outcome in front of a television screen.

Bagwell exited the ring, gathered a headset, and gazed directly into the camera. "Hey Russo, did I do a good *job* for you?" he asked rhetorically. "Who else can beat me? Why don't you come down and beat me, big man?"

Suddenly, the returning Jeff Jarrett, a second-generation wrestler whose contract with the WWF expired a day earlier, emerged from out of nowhere to nail Bagwell with a guitar. "You wanna talk about stroke, boy?" Jarrett taunted over the house mic. "How's this for stroke?"

Collectively, the sequence of events inferred that the new sheriffs - eager to show WCW's locker room that the playing field was level - instructed Bagwell to lose to a lesser wrestler. During the match,

Bagwell's 'displeasure' with this direction manifested in his going through the motions, and choice to engage only halfheartedly with the crowd. When Buff allowed his opponent to defeat him, his peers reacted positively, hopeful that the occurrence meant good things for their own careers. Finally, after Bagwell sarcastically denounced his scripted loss to the viewers at home, the lead sheriff sent a deputy - one that incidentally, fostered a close relationship with him in a previous company - to do his vengeful bidding.

The self-referential stunt was - like everything else on the show - entirely fictional. But for the scene to make sense to most audience members, prior knowledge, it could reasonably be argued, would be required of at *least* the following:

- Vince Russo's comments in both an insider newsletter, published days earlier, and an online chat session that Buff Bagwell could be the next big WCW star;

- WCW's issues with backstage politics; specifically, the frustration of younger talent who believed previous regimes had favored certain performers;

- Wrestling terminology such as 'job' and 'stroke', neither of which had been uttered (at least flagrantly) on a WCW show previously; *and*

- Jeff Jarrett's prior friendship with Vince Russo during Russo's time as WWF Head Writer.

Assuming that one was aware of the aforementioned backstage happenings, for the segment to fully resonate, they would also have to *believe* that:

- Marcus Bagwell, portraying the Buff Bagwell character, was so upset with being scripted to lose that he visibly acted out his frustration on live television, abandoning the typical depiction of his character;

- Bagwell's fellow wrestlers immediately accepted that the occurrence was real, as evidenced by the reaction captured by a quick-thinking cameraman;

- The director, rather than cutting to commercial, allowed a performer to question the booking decisions of WCW's Head Writer, on air; *and*

- The evil writers were so nefarious that they recklessly endangered one of their top stars (because if, by following the logic of the story, Bagwell went off-script to question Russo's decision, it was unlikely that he could anticipate Jarrett's surprise attack).

To reiterate, fans would not only have to be a) acutely informed as to the inner workings of pro wrestling, but also b) willing to believe that something *real* had taken place within the context of a live *Nitro*. The inherent flaw with this concept, it would seem, is that the most knowledgeable of fans were precisely the group *least* likely to lose themselves in such a manufactured moment. In contrast to *Montreal* two years earlier - when the events appeared real because well, they were - the hardcore obsessives would likely be quick to spot any obvious signs of contrivance.

Alternatively, if the Bagwell-Parka 'match' was *not* designed to trick the so-called *smart marks*, its existence as a standalone 'shock value' type segment (i.e. *that wasn't supposed to happen…*) would logically cause tremendous confusion for viewers, especially those not well-versed in untelevised relationships between writers and talent.

On WCW.com, an incredulous Chad Damiani questioned the internal logic of such a decision. "If our writers want to run an angle involving appearance vs. reality," Damiani wrote, "they have to be very clear about defining the parameters of what's actually real. Example: if Bagwell is working or ignoring an existent script, then unless we are told otherwise, the reality must be that all the contracted wrestlers are a part of the script, told who they are fighting and how their matches will end. Why should I think that only Bagwell must play by these rules? Buff Daddy may be the *stuff du jour*, but he's still a wrestler, just like Norman Smiley, Bam Bam [Bigelow], Kidman and the luchadores. Are these men being instructed as well? And, if they are just playing out pre-written scenes, why should I care who wins and loses?"

In response, Bill Banks, a former WWF staffer brought along by Russo and Ferrara to WCW, defended the move in an online rebuttal. "The Bagwell angle is just one of many currently developing in WCW that cause intrigue, and yes, controversy," Banks argued. "Put Bagwell in there against La Parka in a traditional 'wrestling match', and I say 'eh'. But, add that twist of Bagwell not following the 'script', and I'm interested. Does that break a long held 'kayfabe' tradition in the sport? You bet. Is it controversial? You bet. Will some hate it, while others love it? You bet. Will people continue to talk about and tune in to see what happens next? EXACTLY."

"I was supposed to act like I didn't care that La Parka was beating me," recalls Bagwell. "Should we have ran the angle...or just have Buff win, do his little dance, and pose with his little hat on? It could be that simple. For some reason, Russo always wanted to put the square peg in the round hole. I mean, all you gotta do is, 'Buff hits his Blockbuster [finishing move], Buff puts his top hat on, Buff does his Buff strut, Buff hits a double bicep [pose]', and says 'look at me' in the camera. Everybody's happy.

"My point to Russo was, 'I think there's more people that would rather see me do my little dance and get my hand raised' [in victory]. He thought it was better to have shock value. I said, 'in that case, have La Parka beat Goldberg! If you wanna shock 'em, you can shock the fuck outta them by La Parka beating Goldberg tonight!' Of course, he didn't want to talk about that. I didn't get it - all you had to do was just let me be me."

"In many ways, the nWo started this idea - not of breaking the fourth wall, [per se], but of acknowledging what was happening backstage," says Sam Ford, Professor of an MIT course on professional wrestling. "Eric Bischoff was suddenly on screen, he had betrayed the company...they're talking about contracts...so you could see that evolution.

"I think Russo was also a driving force behind saying, 'people are interested in what's happening backstage'. Especially when the [Montreal Screwjob] happened, [he said], 'we can do one of two things. We could just ignore this, and keep playing the traditional idea of kayfabe, or we could create...', what I would call, a *new kayfabe*. They took the fictional realm that was just on the ringside of the curtain, and broadened it to where the fictional realm now included backstage. But it was still a fictional realm. Vince McMahon goes on screen and acknowledges [the screwjob] in a *coded* way. This is where, I think, the distinction comes up.

"When McMahon said, 'Bret would not do the time-honored tradition on his way out', he's obviously alluding to the fact that Bret refused to drop the title. But he doesn't say, 'Bret wouldn't do the job'. He doesn't break that fourth wall [completely]. He *alludes* to it, and does so in a way that actually creates a new character for himself. They were kind of heading this way anyway, but that was the incident where he said, 'I own the company, and I'm an asshole. I decide who should win, and who should lose'.

"Except, in the on-screen version, McMahon *can't actually make someone win or lose*, so they turn that into him going to ringside and trying to *cause* them to lose through cheating. The story of 'Bret screwed Bret' isn't that the boss decided to change the script, it's that McMahon paid off (referee) Earl Hebner. It's not, 'McMahon tells a [wrestler] he has to lose a match, and the wrestler obliges because he's just a performer'.

"Vince Russo takes that idea, and he starts interfering with people's ability to suspend their disbelief. He did it in ways that seemed fun - for a second - like 'oh wow!' But then you think, well, 'if I'm not suspending my disbelief, and we're openly talking during the performance about the fact that this *is* a performance...how does the narrative continue? Because [that discussion] is happening within the realm of the show itself. And if I'm ironically distanced from

398

everything, how do I play my role as fan?

"Previous versions of [this concept] in WCW had been really successful, because they had drawn on more realism, but kept it fictional. The earlier WCW stuff with the nWo, or even what McMahon did, was *pretending* to give people a glimpse behind the curtain. They were listening to what the fans were finding out, and then fictionalizing a representation of it that made it *feel* more real. But, of course, it was always part of the script."

Despite the bizarre Bagwell angle, the Nielsen numbers seemed to validate Russo and Ferrara's vision - the episode scored a 3.3, the highest rating in five weeks, and critics heaped praise on its fast pace and unpredictable content. At the WCW offices, Bill Busch received a supportive phone call from an unlikely source: Eric Bischoff. "I called Bill Busch," Bischoff later revealed in a March 2000 interview. "I told him, 'great move - it looks like you made a decision that's going to work'. I talked to Harvey Schiller [too]. I said, 'it was pretty good, fast paced...there was a good sense of timing. There were a lot of things that I liked."

Not everyone was convinced. Several weeks earlier, Jim Cornette, a legendary manager, booker, and trainer with a well-documented disdain for Russo, predicted to journalist Mike Mooneyham that the writer would ultimately fail in spectacular fashion. "He has no respect for the wrestling business, or anybody in it," argued Cornette. "He is a great self-promoter who has made all the Internet people believe he is a genius, [and] responsible for the WWF turnaround. He'll be flat out of the business in two years because without the WWF organization behind him, he'll fall flat on his face. [WCW] will pay him until the end of his contract, and then he'll be done. He burned the bridge behind him and he won't be back.

"He knows he doesn't know what he's doing. He knew WCW was desperate, and [he] finally realized it was time to cash in. He doesn't care about being in the wrestling business. He hates wrestling - he likes *entertainment*. He thinks he's a TV writer now, and it's gone to his head."

Amid speculation that the creative team would soon look to 'push the envelope' - a risky proposition given the presence of Turner's Standards and Practices department - the new regime focused on its next major assignment: tweaking the already-booked *Halloween Havoc* pay-per-view in Las Vegas, NV. In the advertised main event, Sting, fresh off a heel turn a month earlier, looked to defend the WCW title in a rematch against Hulk Hogan.

Accordingly, the Sting-Hogan clash had been advertised as the feature bout of the event. However, to play up the online rumors surrounding Bollea's dissatisfaction with his planned new role, he was asked not to appear at the arena before the show began. Halfway through the pay-per-view, Bollea had *still* yet to arrive at the building, causing confusion on the part of backstage staff. At 9:47pm EST - a full hour remaining in the broadcast - Hogan's music then played as announcers Tony Schiavone and Bobby Heenan gazed at their format. Twenty-two minutes had been allotted for the contest - four for the entrances, eighteen for the match - but as Hogan's 'American Made' song echoed throughout the arena, the challenger was nowhere to be found. Improvising, Heenan tried his best to make sense of the delay. "*I bet he's pulling a power play,*" he said. "*I bet he's back there with the Powers [that] Be saying, 'I'm going on last'.*"

"Not many people knew what was happening," recalls Jason Douglas. "I was sitting next to the director, and we were stalling with wide camera pans."

Finally, after Sting solemnly made his way to the ring, Hogan's music restarted. "*He wants to make Sting wait,*" speculated Heenan. With ring announcer David Penzer introducing him again, Hogan finally walked into the ring, laid down, and let Sting cover him for the three count. Following the script, he then immediately got up, walked through the curtain, left out a garage door, stepped into a limousine and exited the building. He had been present at the arena for exactly five minutes.

For Russo and Ferrara, the stunt ostensibly achieved two objectives:

removing Hogan from television (for the foreseeable future, at least), and creating a tsunami of online chatter concerning their 'backstage disagreement'. It was certainly a memorable moment, but not as enduring as another image from the same show. "Burying Ric Flair in the desert," begins Kevin Sullivan, referring to an angle in which 'The Filthy Animals' did exactly that, "if that wasn't a Freudian slip…

"I mean, I took Psychology…and that's Psychology 101 - 'let's get rid of the guy'."

Chapter 42:
Collision Course

IN A SURPRISING DEVELOPMENT to those outside the TBS bubble - although certainly, not to those on the *inside* - Dr. Harvey Schiller resigned on October 29th. Increasingly, his recent tenure as Turner Sports President brought with it accusations of nepotism (resulting first from hiring son Derek as Vice-President of the Atlanta Thrashers), and Machiavellianism (the fallout of two failed bids to take over the Braves and Hawks). *Oh shoot*, joked one WCW staffer upon reading the news, *there goes the most over heel we had.*

But now, Schiller was set to reunite with George Steinbrenner, a longtime associate, former IOC executive and more famously, owner of the New York Yankees. According to a *New York Times* report, Steinbrenner had successfully wooed the Doc to accept a newly created position - President of the 'YankeeNets' - overseeing an amalgamated company handling business interests for two professional franchises.

Around the Turner offices, however, rumors of the move had swirled incessantly since September. In response, Schiller reassured subordinates that there was 'no job to take', and even after the *Times* report, he remained coy to the local Atlanta press. "Am I going to do something else? Yes," he began, using a kind of sermocination that would make Donald Rumsfeld blush. "Is it probably New York? Of course. But I haven't accepted another job yet."

Nonetheless, Schiller was gone, and the consequences were swift. On Tuesday, November 2nd, TBS announced a major strategic reorganization, announcing new responsibilities for several key executives, including Mark Lazarus, the incoming President of Turner Sports. Unlike Schiller in the past, however, Lazarus' duties would *not* include WCW, as according to a company press release, its oversight responsibility now fell to Turner Entertainment chief Brad

Siegel. "These operational alignments," said Terry McGuirk, the Chief Executive Officer of Turner Broadcasting System, "are designed to create a fully integrated sports division. In addition...Brad brings his creativity and programming expertise to bear on our WCW franchise and the networks that air its programming, TBS Superstation and TNT."

So suddenly Siegel - at first a serious skeptic of WCW and later, during the good times, a begrudging booster - added another encumbrance to an increasingly congested plate. As President of TNT (a role he maintained while simultaneously managing TCM, Turner Classic Movies), Siegel's engagement with wrestling grew out of necessity, a 'necessary evil' of sorts that Ted's presence dictated. But a barrage of recent personnel changes, causally consequential in aggregation, helped create the current situation.

At the corporate level, for example, an often overlooked occurrence unfolded on September 14th, 1999, when Bill Burke stepped down as President of *TBS*. "It was simple," Burke explains of his decision. "The 'dot-com' thing was happening, and at the time, the valuations were through the roof. We were [being perceived as] 'old media', and our stocks were falling. People were becoming 'paper millionaires' and all that stuff...it was a weird time.

"Meanwhile, Jerry Levin was trying to figure out how to revolutionize Time Warner...and make *us* a 'dot-com' company. He famously stopped wearing ties to work and all this stupid stuff. But he started these...he called them 'hubs'...[enveloping] all of our digital assets. They were talking about a 'women's hub'...there was 'sports'...and then there was 'news and information' - *CNN.com* and all the 'Time Inc.' websites [like] *Time.com*.

"So Terry McGuirk came to me and said, 'Jerry Levin wants you to leave TBS, and run 'news and information' for Time Warner Digital Media'. I was like, 'wow'. He was like, 'it's kind of an offer you can't refuse, I mean...Jerry wants you to do this'.

"I was like, 'yeah, I can do the 'dot-com' thing and [still] stay in the company', so I was made CEO of 'news and information' - ostensibly in charge of CNN.com and all these Time Inc. websites.

"It was an amazing, *cool* job, y'know, but it was also sad. I really didn't wanna leave TBS and all those people."

With Burke moving on, McGuirk promoted Siegel to President of General Entertainment Networks, reflecting responsibility for both TNT *and* TBS. As part of the deal, Siegel would not only continue oversight over TCM, but also management of *Turner South*, the company's first regional entertainment service launched in October.

Simultaneously, within WCW, the departure of Eric Bischoff had caused a serious domino effect, placing the company on an unlikely collision course with Siegel. First, on September 10th, 1999, Harvey Schiller asked Bischoff to step down. Then, on September 13th, Bill Busch was named WCW's executive Vice-President, accentuating a creative vacuum filled by Vince Russo and Ed Ferrara. On October 3rd, with the approval and blessing of Siegel and Schiller, Russo and Ferrara put pen to paper, but by October 29th, Schiller was done with Turner Sports. In summary, one could only wonder - coup or no coup - just how different things could have been, provided Bischoff escaped scrutiny for several weeks longer.

Technically, Siegel was now the new boss, with Busch handling day-to-day operations and Vince Russo - despite an erroneous perception of 'running the company' - working strictly as Creative Director (combined with possessing influence over 'on-screen' talent acquisitions). In totality, it was the quite the shake-up, perhaps even symbolic given the dissolution of WCW's association with *Turner Sports*. After all, in light of the tropes associated with modern wrestling (heavy violence, foul language, overt sexuality and the like), any guise of legitimacy was becoming passé anyway - a pretentious pretense reflecting a by-gone era.

But WCW still aired on the Turner Networks, meaning its content hinged on review, as ever, from TBS Standards and Practices. Although undoubtedly, the personal tastes of Ted Turner influenced its function, similar departments existed long before cable television. In 1960, for example, NBC censors deleted a relatively risqué joke from *The Tonight Show*, causing host Jack Paar to abruptly resign on-air. "There must be a better way..." mused Paar in an emotional sign-off, "of making a living than this."

Within a month, Paar returned to the show, poking fun at himself in an uproarious monologue. "As I was saying before I was interrupted," he began, "there must be a better way of making a living. Well, I've looked...and there isn't!"

Whereas the Paar spat was handled with humor, WCW-Turner disputes tended to illuminate - at least from one perspective - a palpable, antithetical sense of contempt. Furthermore, the seminal 'Techwood' meeting of July 1998 sparked an unprecedented level of scrutiny, confirms Galen Chandler, former Manager of Live Events for TBS, Inc. "That is when the 'S&P' department started looking more closely at the WCW content," says Chandler, responsible for managing broadcast compliance. "They realized that WCW was not following company guidelines."

In the summer of 1999, the introduction of Lenny and Lodi - an ambiguously gay tag-team eventually revealed to be 'brothers' - only intensified matters further. Seemingly oblivious to the storyline, 'S&P' received a flurry of letters from activist group GLAAD, with one addressed pointedly to SVP Terri Tingle:

Such programming gives license to viewers to ridicule and harass all gay people. How many gay-bashings and gay murders have to be committed in this country for you to remove such hurtful portrayals from your broadcasts?

In response, Lenny and Lodi were ultimately removed from television, and the saga - highlighted memorably by *The Washington Post* ('*TNT Finally Tosses Its Staged Gay-Bashing Spectacle Out of the Ring*', ran the hysterical headline) - led to a significant change. "According to more than one source close to the situation," claimed Lisa de Moraes of the *Post*, "the complaint from GLAAD ...caused Turner bigwigs to remove Bischoff as president of the wrestling organization."

In fact, while the GLAAD complaint was *not* responsible (at least wholly) for Bischoff's firing, it *did* provide the catalyst for TBS to hire a specific, WCW-focused 'S&P' executive. "I was the one hired for this," clarifies Chandler. "Eric was already on his way out and with the new management coming in, the company wanted to get 'S&P' involved at the beginning.

"GLAAD have a lot power in Hollywood. They were threatening to sue, and they were threatening to do a big 'call-out' and boycott - based on the Lenny and Lodi skits that were going on. Then we were starting to get some heat from the PRTVC (Protestant Radio and Television Center) and some other organizations. To avoid lawsuits, I think the idea was to start looking closer at WCW, and try to reign it in a little bit…let the 'heat' simmer down a little bit.

"So I was brought into monitor the [content], working with producers and writers to ensure programming stayed within guidelines. WCW was not alone in this, [incidentally] - with Cartoon Network, [for example], there were lots of infractions…a lot of 'back-and-forth' with scripts and so on.

"The goal was to make sure the programming was correctly identified within the [content] ratings. We were making sure the content conformed to the rating (e.g. TVPG) - that's really what it boils down to."

In regards to the content rating, Siegel approved reclassifying *Nitro* to *TV14*, effectively giving Russo greater room to operate. After all, as Galen Chandler observes, the writer was functioning within a vastly different corporate environment, one inherently more restrictive than his former employer. "Turner Broadcasting liked 'family-style' programming," he says. "Turner were a little bit more conservative [towards content], [whereas] USA - the 'man's channel' were a little more liberal.

"The stuff that was going on [during *Raw*] was pretty incredible. Every show seemed to have [wrestler] 'Mankind' cutting himself…or some horrific thing was happening to him. Barbed wire, baseball bats…just all kinds of craziness.

"Vince was used to working where they didn't have [similar] S&P restrictions. USA Channel was much more hands off, [especially] at the beginning. It sold itself as the 'Man's man' channel, and they enjoyed the ratings that *Raw* was pulling in for them at the time. At Turner, however, you couldn't cross a certain threshold for programming."

In anticipation of the change to TV14, Busch distributed a list of restrictions before the November 1st *Nitro*. "Wrestlers are not allowed to swear without seeking approval," reported *The Pro Wrestling Torch*. "Bloodletting is banned, and male talent is not allowed to physically harm female talent in on-air angles, unless in a match situation."

Moreover, there were more generic - and rather obvious - constraints governing content. "No guns," says Chandler. "No death - no 'on-camera' death. Kind of common sense [stuff]. No urination/defecation. No nudity, of course - things of that nature."

In numerous public statements, Russo has claimed ignorance towards any specific guidelines affecting his writing. "Every week," he complained in one article, "I would ask for an S&P handbook so I knew the rules in advance - but, of course, I was never provided with one, basically because it didn't exist. The rules were made [up] as they went along."

It is a contention that Chandler refutes directly. "He *did* get guidelines," he says. "It may have been delayed, but he did get them. I do know that he didn't have them at first, [however]…the department didn't release them right away."

"There was no rhyme or reason for their stances on certain things," argued Russo in the same piece. "I wanted Roddy [Piper] to call a woman fat, [but] S&P put the kibosh on this…[because] other fat women watching our show would be offended.

"There was a scene that called for Kimberly [Page] to slip a 'mickey' into Ric Flair's drink. While S&P had no issue with the general drugging, they just didn't want the act to be seen on TV.

"Hall and Nash couldn't show up to work drunk, but they were allowed to get high on cough syrup [as part of the show]. These were the things I was constantly dealing with."

In another rejected scene, Russo planned for 'Buzzkill' - a stoner character portrayed by Brad Armstrong, to be found in a room full of smoke (he would later claim it was 'incense'). A segment idea featuring 'Hacksaw' Jim Duggan was also scrapped, whereby the patriotic babyface would be covered in the American flag - following a vicious assault in ring.

But while the aforementioned examples appeared relatively innocuous - at least in comparison to Russo's WWF work - Chandler says there were more serious objections. "There was a thing where they wanted to take Goldberg, tie him to the back of a pick-up truck with a chain, and drag him down the street," he says. "If you recall, there was an incident where that actually happened down South (in a brutal, racially motivated killing in Texas). So we said, 'no!'

"The pressure really came from when things touched on some actual event, or if it was *instructional*. They wanted to take a certain group, [for example], and have them throw Molotov cocktails at a school bus. That's not good. It's like, 'think a little bit beyond that'. Having been in this business for 25 years, [I know that] there are creative ways to do things without crossing the line. That's the easy way in my book.

"If [an idea] has some hint of instruction to it, it puts the company into a liability issue. I don't think that was ever in creative's mind - the liability aspect of things - especially at WCW.

"So there were many challenges working with Vince and Ed [specifically], but mostly it came down to them making script changes at the last minute, which was actually part of their 'MO'. Sometimes there would be warnings - we would say 'don't cut', [for example], but then, of course, somebody would 'cut' (intentionally bleed).

"A lot of times, creative would be like, 'we told 'em not to, but they did it anyway'. Then I would talk to that wrestler afterwards and they would say, 'yeah, I was told to cut'.

"But even with the guidelines, and after things had been written to them about what not to do…there were still situations where they would…try to continue to cross that line."

Regardless, the early returns on Russo and Ferrara - from an objective, ratings-focused standpoint - were promising. "The first two weeks of *Nitro* have drawn ratings of 3.1 and 3.3 in the [head-to-head] time period, [representing] nearly a 20 percent jump from the ten-week average," reported Wade Keller. "The most fascinating aspects of the new booking approach have been the pacing of the program and the use of undercard wrestlers…it hasn't completely hit its stride yet, but the program has the feel of *Raw* with an entirely different cast of characters."

Despite the improvements, the risk of alienating mainstream fans remained a real issue, warned a caustic Keller. "Constant insider references may peak viewers' interest initially," he wrote, "but if it doesn't pay off with a comprehensible storyline eventually, viewers may switch back to the more tangible storylines on *Raw*.

"Russo and Ferrara are working for the first time without the benefit (or hindrance) of Vince McMahon overseeing their work. His vision and experience are missing from their weekly process now."

For his part, McMahon clearly believed the duo were over their heads. "For [WCW] to think that [Russo and Ferrara] were the reason that we are successful is laughable," he told *The New York Post*. "They were part of a much larger creative team."

Mere months earlier, Ferrara was enthralling McMahon with an impression of Jim Ross, the venerable lead announcer for *Raw*. To

409

break up booking meetings, Ferrara occasionally adopted Ross' southern drawl, even mimicking the partial facial paralysis he suffered after two Bell's palsy attacks.

On November 15th, Ferrara took his parody to the TNT airwaves, lampooning Ross as *Oklahoma*, a character briefly introduced in the WWF. It was a cruel cheap shot, especially evident when Ferrara sported a scrunched up face, yelling out Ross' catch phrases at ringside. "[Russo] doesn't understand why anyone liked J.R. and that Southern accent," said Jim Cornette, a WWF official and outspoken critic of the creative team. "And it isn't even Southern, it's Oklahoman."

Ross expressed disappointment at the skit, broadcast as merely the latest - albeit most disdainful - affront in the wrestling war. "I thought that because they were both working here," Ross told journalist Mike Mooneyham, "they knew about when I got sick the last time. I got Bell's palsy just a few hours after my mother passed away. That was a real sudden death, and I was a long way from home (at a WWF pay-per-view in the United Kingdom) when it happened.

"...I thought those guys understood that better, because they were working here when all that occurred. But I guess it just didn't make any difference to them."

Although in later years, Russo profusely expressed remorsefulness over the stunt, he claimed not to understand its implications in a *Wrestleline* interview:

Let me remind everybody. We did the same exact angle when we were at the WWF. Ed Ferrara came out on WWF television, and he did his 'JR' imitations. Everybody at the WWF raved about it, and felt it was the greatest thing they ever saw.

The bottom line is, my god, it just blows me away. When we did the same exact thing when we were in the WWF, everybody was entertained as hell, including JR himself...and nobody thought anything of it. Now all of a sudden, we're the competition, we do the same exact thing...and now it's in bad taste and everything else.

It's not about what the guy looks like, it's about what the guy is saying. That's the

410

angle.

Whereas in subsequent weeks, Oklahoma's routine remained part of *Nitro*, it gradually became toned down, and crucially, any suggestion of Ross' facial paralysis vanished. "There was no defamation at that point," states Galen Chandler. "The character was making fun of him in different ways."

But almost lost in the commotion concerning the initial parody, however, was that it occurred as part of a thoroughly disastrous segment - a 'Pinata on a Pole' match - ostensibly designed to ridicule several Mexican wrestlers. As Oklahoma ranted in Ross' trademark style on commentary, the 'contest' ended with a dangerous post-match run-in, leading to the hospitalization of Juventud Guerrera (separated shoulder), El Dandy (broken collarbone) and Psychosis (injured knee).

For those who blasted Russo's earlier comments about foreign wrestlers ("I don't give a shit about a Japanese guy...I don't give a shit about a Mexican guy"), the 'Pinata' match further ignited accusations of bigotry. "I thought the so-called controversy was ridiculous, and I still feel that way today," says Ben Miller, who published Russo's tendentious remarks. "He was right in most ways. Complaining about not getting pushed when you aren't willing to learn the language is silly.

"[But] Russo was wrong in that there were some Mexican and Japanese wrestlers would could've gotten over - in spite of the language barrier."

Unquestionably, one wrestler with such potential was Juventud Guerrera, a 25-year old luchador from Mexico City. Consistently amazing as an in-ring performer, Guerrera now found himself featured as comedy fodder. Over a dizzying span of several weeks, 'Juvi' was scripted to resuscitate an overweight woman, wrestle to extend his work visa and - perhaps most bizarrely - take a turn as an announcer on *WCW Thunder*.

Meanwhile, at the suggestion of Kevin Sullivan, Russo himself became part of WCW programming. Appearing often as a disembodied voice, situated behind a desk in the style of Larry David's 'Steinbrenner' caricature from *Seinfeld* (ironic, given Harvey Schiller's new job), Russo represented a shadowy force known as *The Powers That Be*.

To Russo's critics, *Nitro* was becoming more a *variety* show than a wrestling event, typified by frequent backstage vignettes, increased narrative complexity, sex appeal, fake retirements and rapid title changes. More than ever, the actual *wrestling* was merely an afterthought, with one episode of *Nitro* offering just 37 minutes of in-ring action (moreover, eight of the nine scheduled matches featured interference, including five straight run-ins to end the show).

While ratings remained steady in November (3.2, 3.4, 3.1, 3.4, 3.1), reports suggested that confusion was permeating the locker room. According to industry gossip, wrestlers were either complaining to Russo about their disposition (in reference to the face-heel delineation, or continuum in modern wrestling), or their ability to use *ring psychology* (in arguing against 'rest holds', Russo suggested that breaking for even 15 seconds could provoke viewers to turn to *Raw*).

Nonetheless, Russo could be credited with reviving interest in the middle of the card, providing a long-needed direction to several characters. "We sat down and made sure," he reveals, "that everyone working the upcoming pay-per-view was covered on the show. From the bottom to the top - every week. We were writing week-to-week, using the ratings as our barometer of what was working."

Interestingly, a hallmark of Russo's writing allowed for wrestlers to engage in multiple feuds - simultaneously. For example, Goldberg was embroiled in a vendetta with Sid Vicious (culminating in their formation of a tag-team together, a take-off on an old Dusty Rhodes angle), in addition to having issues with Kevin Nash, Scott Hall and Jeff Jarrett. "We organically let the show write itself," Russo says. "We just put ourselves in the boots of every performer, and acted like they would, given the situation."

Long frustrated with not receiving credit under McMahon, Russo was apparently becoming, along with Ed Ferrara, "[one] of the more important people in television." While specifically, that particular sentiment belonged to the *New York Times*, other mainstream outlets followed suit, with *Variety* even commissioning a front page story. "The industry has come to regard the two writers," claimed Alex Kucsynski of the *Times*, "as the magic bullet that makes wrestling programs among the fastest-growing shows on television."

The *Times* piece informed its readership of a rapidly changing wrestling world, purporting *Nitro* to be as "carefully scripted as a top-rated soap opera":

Before Mr. Russo and Mr. Ferrara became widely recognized in the industry as the first professional wrestling scriptwriters, wrestling was loosely scripted by a member of the wrestling management known as a "booker" -- usually a wrestler or a former wrestler who booked talent and sketched out rough storylines, while the wrestlers largely ad-libbed their own lines.

But Mr. Russo and Mr. Ferrara work like any scriptwriter on a movie. At the W.W.F., Mr. Russo said, he and Mr. Ferrara would gather in his den, turn on "The Jerry Springer Show" for inspiration and while Mr. Russo's young daughter ran in and out of the room, would write the intricate storylines, dialogue and plots for 16 different segments in a show. The script includes lines for the wrestlers, basic plot outlines and even stage directions, though the wrestlers themselves are allowed to devise the manner in which they dispatch their opponents to the mat. Mr. Russo and Mr. Ferrara's work habits are much the same at the W.C.W., but they are writing from hotel rooms more often.

The storyline, they said, should work seamlessly week to week, 52 weeks a year: there are no seasons in wrestling, no weeks off. They meet almost daily with wrestlers to assure plot lines jibe with the wrestlers' on-stage personalities.

To what extent this complexity benefited WCW remained in question. After all, between *Halloween Havoc* (October 24th) and *Mayhem* (November 21st), Russo and Ferrara booked a convoluted World Title tournament with several bizarre elements, not least of which involved a female wrestler (Madusa) re-entering the contest after elimination. In the end, however, most pundits hailed the eventual outcome - Bret Hart being crowned World Champion in front of a rabid Toronto crowd.

Concurrently, a salacious sexuality began to perfuse *Nitro* and *Thunder*, reflecting a conscious effort to highlight more female stars. In the recent past, the tactic appeared a foolproof method of sparking ratings, but as of late November, WCW's competitor was showing a willingness (albeit reluctantly) to modulate such content. On the December 2nd edition of *WWF Smackdown*, fans also noticed a decrease in beer swilling, innuendo, and profanity, arising from Coca-Cola ending its involvement as a sponsor. "It crossed the line," Coke spokesman Bob Bertini said, "in terms of content - language and character portrayals. We don't have the same content issues with WCW - at this time."

Therefore, it appeared imperative - despite an obvious temptation to 'push the envelope' further - for Russo to stay within bounds. Moreover, with several other sponsors leaving the WWF for similar reasons, some WCW officials were sensing an opportunity. "Given our growth rate in 1998…the fact that wrestling is a cyclical business, and that 1999 is [the WWF's year]," Jay Hassman told *Cable World*, "we anticipate that our business will stabilize and fall more in line with realistic expectations."

In a December 9th memo to all talent, Bill Busch signaled his public support of the new direction:

This has been a year of significant change for World Championship Wrestling. In the last year, we have re-examined all aspects of how we operate our business to improve our product. As we all know, our entire business starts with our television product. In this regard, we have added new members in our creative team resulting in an improvement in our *Nitro* ratings in just a few short weeks. Our commitment to preparation is already evident.

In the same communication, Busch even suggested a previously unthinkable notion, advising of a novel policy to prevent tardiness:

We are now committed to working on our execution, especially where our television shows are involved. In this regard, we need the cooperation and commitment of all of our talent, which includes arriving on-time, prepared and ready for work.

To date, our attempts to get all talent to arrive in a timely fashion have failed.

414

Therefore, stricter enforcement has become necessary. Effective immediately, any contracted talent that fails to check-in by the posted arrival time, will be fined an amount equal to one day's pay, not to exceed $3,000 per offense. In addition to this fine, any no-shows or repeated late check-ins, will be considered a breach of your Agreement and may result in additional penalties up to and including termination.

As a professional, if you are going to be late, you are expected to advise JJ Dillon or the road agent assigned to the event; however, notification to WCW will not automatically excuse the fine. If you experience legitimate travel problems beyond your control with the original flight itinerary booked by WCW, the fine will be waived upon verification of the circumstances. If you change the itinerary booked by WCW and are late due to travel problems, you will be subject to the fine.

We hope that this sends a clear message as to the importance of being professional and arriving on time. If you have any questions regarding the policy, please direct them to JJ Dillon.

Thank you in advance for your cooperation.

In early December, Russo continued to push forward, building towards *Starrcade* with a renewed focus on *Thunder*, the long-derided 'B-show' on TBS. But despite numerous established stars staying on the sideline (Hogan and Flair among them), *Thunder* was beginning to attract interest again, hitting a 2.3 in back-to-back episodes. As for the departed veterans, Russo remained glued to his vision for their reintroduction. "There is a role for these guys in this business," Russo explained to *Entertainment Weekly*, "but it's not the main event."

At the same time, Russo admitted meeting with the Ultimate Warrior, apparently confident of recapturing some early '90s magic (Ferrara envisioned Warrior, dressed in all-white, teaming with Sting in a brand new persona). In another confusing development, rumors of an nWo revival littered the Internet, an apparent refutation of the purported goal to 'elevate' younger talent.

After two months in the job, Russo was starting to feel real pressure, as despite the wave of good press lauding his initial impact, the Nielsen numbers actually showed little change. Upon closer analysis, *Nitro* averaged a 3.2 throughout his first nine weeks in charge (compared to 3.25 over the preceding nine weeks), while *Thunder* averaged a 2.14 during the same period (compared to 2.1 over a commensurate prior period).

415

Observers worried that Russo would invariably panic, especially as *Raw* posted impressive numbers (a 5.8 average, to be exact) in the wake of his WWF departure. Fans soon noticed that some *Nitro* angles resembled recycled WWF plots (on a December 13th show, for example, WCW's officials went AWOL, mimicking a September storyline from *Raw*), while controversy continued to follow his more imaginative content. In one skit, two Italian wrestlers were humiliated with spaghetti, provoking a call from the Italian-American Civil Rights League ("some people thought I made the call," offers Kevin Sullivan. "I didn't.")

As WCW barreled towards *Starrcade*, its programming changes were the talk of wrestling. But news of its shake-up failed to reach Ted Turner, who was evidently preoccupied - and understandably so - with an ongoing dance involving AOL.

Since the China tour in September, Jerry Levin (Time Warner) and Steve Case (AOL) met regularly to discuss a merger, growing closer with each conversation. At first, Case wisely suggested that Levin run the new company, playing to his ego while holding an important trump card. *If* AOL made a formal offer, Case knew, Levin was legally obligated to tell Time Warner's board of directors. *If* such an offer was perceived as AOL *taking over* the company, it would likely be rejected out of hand; however, if presented as a 'merger of equals' - with Levin as CEO moving forward - Time Warner would effectively be trapped.

After all, AOL was worth almost twice as much as Time Warner ($175 billion to $90 billion), meaning that the shareholders of Levin's company stood to gain fancifully if a deal was consummated. In this light, preventing a takeover was potentially *illegal*, a theoretical breach of his fiduciary responsibilities.

Moreover, in comparison to AOL, Time Warner was suddenly being viewed as 'old world', despite its reliable revenue streams (amounting to some $27 billion) and employee base (consisting of 70,000 workers). Meanwhile, AOL, three times more valuable than *Walt Disney Co.*, boasted revenues of only $5 billion, supporting close to 15,000 employees. Crucially, however, analysts noted that on an annual basis, AOL was *doubling* in size, suggesting that despite its lack of assets, it could soon surpass Time Warner in revenue.

Shortly before Thanksgiving, Case met with Ted Turner, still Time Warner's largest (10%) individual shareholder. Turner was both disinterested (arguing in favor of purchasing NBC, part of his long-held ambition to own a broadcast network), and skeptical (especially in regards to 'new media' valuations, which seemed to inflate along promises of *future* growth). Subsequently, Levin began to consider the deal as dead, and Case - privately worried about his company's stock price - returned back to base.

On December 13th, Ted made a surprise appearance on *Larry King Live*, discussing a variety of his business interests - including WCW. Pointedly, Turner blamed Vince McMahon for upping the raunch factor in wrestling, while simultaneously acknowledging that the tactic had worked. "That's how Vince came back against us," Turner said. "He went for more violence…and sex…and language and stuff.

"I think it ought to be rasslin'. That's the business I got into, y'know, slamming each other around…and that's about it."

After listening to a viewer phone call, Turner appeared to learn - apparently for the first time - that WCW was now running the WWF's playbook. "Mr. Turner," began the caller, "as a parent and a grandparent, I would like to see the language cleaned up on the WCW wrestling program - can you help with this?"

"The WCW…" considered Turner in response. "Well…we're supposed to not be using too bad language. I hope you haven't gotten it mixed up with the other wrestling operation that uses worse language than we do. But I appreciate your call.

"I will look into it."

Chapter 43:
Paying Attention

As IT HAPPENED, Ted Turner wasn't the only one paying closer attention. An assortment of industry veterans conveyed their concern over WCW's direction, including Kevin Sullivan and - after admittedly looking the other way at first - J.J. Dillon. "I told JJ," remembers Sullivan, 'the Titanic has hit the iceberg, and we've got two hours to evacuate'."

Dillon reviewed three weeks of *Nitro* episodes, and began to see a troubling pattern. In one such span, 25 of 34 matches ended without a 'clean' finish, with disqualifications (commonly caused by an interfering wrestler) and 'no-contests' (unpopular if used consistently), occurring at a jarring frequency. Moreover, the in-ring action now seemed start *in the middle*, lest the competitors tempt viewers with a chance to change the channel. Provided a match did persist longer than three minutes, *anything* was possible as the culminating spectacle, before a quick cut backstage showcased another 'character-building' segment.

"I'm all for giving Russo a chance to succeed," Dillon recalls telling Bill Busch, "but over a ten-week period of time, he's taken our wrestling product and shrunk it down to nothing. We have no finishes, nobody wins, we're knocking referees down, and we're hot-shotting the shows. If we don't redirect Russo or reel him back in, we're in big trouble."

Meanwhile, in broader media circles, rumors were swirling that something was up between AOL and Time Warner. Quietly, Case and Levin were talking again, and within two days, each side signed a confidentiality agreement, suggestive of an impending union. A contentious stickling point remained, however, as AOL was proposing an exchange ratio of 65:35 - reflective of the relative number of shares given to its shareholders - provided that the merger occurred.

418

Conversely, Levin's advisers argued the deal should be based on revenues and cash flow - rather than prospective growth rates - garnering a very different ratio of 85:15 (in favor of Time Warner).

To split the difference - or more accurately, move towards a *real* 'merger of equals', Levin eventually proposed a 50/50 split. In response, Case moved for a 60/40 breakdown, realizing that further concession would mean - for all intents and purposes - a public admission of AOL's overinflated valuation. Insulted at the terms of Case's offer, Levin simmered out a company memo on December 14th:

Dear Colleague:

Time Warner's robust growth, which should be right in the double-digit range we projected for 1999, reflects our overall strength. But the dynamic consistency of our operating performance shouldn't obscure the fact that the global communications industry is in a period of radical transition. In a breathtaking brief time, a huge digital marketplace has come into being and is expanding exponentially. The technology that defines and drives this new networked community is evolving minute to minute.

We all feel a degree of frustration at the failure of the market to value our company in a way that approximated its superior worth. It's not my purpose to compare Time Warner to a dot-com company. By whatever measure you use - consistent performance growth, free cash flow, range of content, media savvy and creative talent - we're so much more.

Despite a thinly-veiled reference to Time Warner's relative *under*valuation - at least compared with 'dot-com' entities in general - Levin failed to mention the talks with AOL. It was enough evidence that for now at least, the deal was on ice.

If the merger discussions ever hit the press, there was little doubt - under the pen of Vince Russo - that it wouldn't have become part of *Nitro*. Before long, after all, his announcers were referencing Bill Busch, noting the presence of 'the writers' on-air, and calling matches involving the tag-team *Standards and Practices* (portrayed, coincidentally enough, by a repackaged Lenny and Lodi). "We had a brief discussion about that," remembers Galen Chandler, TBS' specific S&P rep for WCW. "It was a phone call. We [determined] that as long as it was within the guidelines, it was fair game."

On a Thursday afternoon before *Starrcade*, Russo was summoned to a large meeting involving Busch, Dillon, Ferrara, Sullivan and Nash, among others. At the outset, Busch implored the room to share their honest feelings about the product, revealing his own concerns in the process. *Don't compromise the in-ring wrestling*, he reportedly declared. *Find a better balance…we have to watch where we're going and the pattern we're developing.*

Russo sat silent as the conversation moved on, utterly dumbfounded as Dillon - a key facilitator in his signing - rattled off his own observed issues. Finally, Russo had seen and heard enough. *I can't believe you guys*, he allegedly thundered, banging his hands on the desk. *You motherfuckers*, he continued, now standing. *You're stabbing me in the back. I can't believe this…after all I've done?*

Things were more unsettled than ever, but the embattled writer hardly had time to digest his political future. *Starrcade* was on the horizon, and with Russo promising "something big…to lead WCW into the next year," fans looked forward to the supposed 'pay-off' of months of storytelling. Instead, Russo simply booked a rehash of the Montreal screwjob, ending the main event with guest referee Roddy Piper ringing the bell early, 'screwing' Goldberg and - inversely - aiding Bret Hart. Scores of enraged fans, seething in disbelief over the abrupt and ambiguous end to the show, flooded *WCW Live* with an unrelenting stream of calls. "This may go down," mused Wade Keller in *The Pro Wrestling Torch*, "as one of the worst PPV finishes of all-time."

On TNT the next night, *Nitro* opened with an elaborate explanation. "The reason that Goldberg was screwed last night," stated Tony Schiavone on commentary, "was because Vince Russo wanted to make up to Bret Hart what happened two years ago in Montreal."

Schiavone's comments set up a dizzying night of insider terminology, culminating in a rematch between Bret Hart and Goldberg. On this occasion, however, Hart revealed himself to be part of the con, joining an assortment of ex-WWF talent (Nash, Hall and Jarrett) in beating down Goldberg. As the foursome celebrated mid-ring, a familiar tune rang through the arena: the nWo entrance music. "Baltimore, Maryland!" exclaimed Kevin Nash. "The band is back together!"

While the announcers valiantly claimed that emotions were running high backstage, in reality, the locker room was almost empty. Morale was certainly dropping, and even the most professional of performers struggled to show enthusiasm. "I don't suck - you suck!" taunted Bret Hart off-mic, the show fading to black. "You're the one that bought a ticket for this shit!"

Two nights later at a *Thunder* taping, disaster struck when Goldberg - scripted to use a pipe to destroy a limousine - called an audible, unleashing his fists to punch out its windows. "Nobody in their right mind," Russo later reflected, "even me...is going to ask a wrestler to bust through a legit limo window with their bare hands.

"An instrument was devised for Bill to conceal in his hand...[but] Bill dropped it prior to breaking the glass, which caused him to finish out the scene [otherwise].

"That night I went to the hospital with Goldberg...and I stayed there with him all night."

The injury was serious - so serious, in fact, that Goldberg was sidelined indefinitely. WCW was suddenly without a key protagonist to thwart the newly-reformed nWo - who much like its previous incarnation(s) - was already in the process of adding members. To close *Nitro* on December 27th, a returning Scott Steiner stole the show, feigning a retirement before joining the nWo instead. "Happy new year from the nWo!" joked a post on DDTDigest.com, a dedicated WCW fansite. "They hope you have a happy and prosperous 1997!"

The new millennium was just days away, but across the world, many were fretting about 'Y2K' - an issue theorized to affect computer systems 'switching over' to the year 2000. Although coverage of the story proliferated throughout 1999, its base premise was known as early as 1985, when Spencer Bolles - a college student posting on the primitive web interface *Usenet* - wondered out loud about its ramifications:

I have a friend that raised an interesting question that I immediately tried to prove wrong. He is a programmer and has this notion that when we reach the year 2000, computers will not accept the new date. Will the computers assume that it is 1900, or will it even cause a problem?

Alongside other reasons (including, notably, the relative scarcity of computer storage), the so-called 'bug' was widely blamed on a lack of prudence, or - perhaps more accurately - a lack of knowledgeable foresight. In that sense, although 'Y2K' was an entirely new concern, it also reflected, rather keenly, a human weakness as old as time itself. As the psychologist Robert Ornstein observed, "human inventiveness has created problems because human judgment - and humanity's ability to deal with the consequences of its creations - lag behind its ability to create."

With respect to the realm of live entertainment - and professional wrestling specifically - this infallibility could be devastating. The absence of a tangible off-season, rather inherently, impaired creators' ability to *reflect*, compounded by an indissoluble production schedule. In other words, unlike other spectacles promoting audience interaction, both the sheer volume of creative output - combined with a built-in synchrony between performance and audience - demanded a tremendous accuracy of predicting fan response. Moreover, from show to show, city to city, fans consumed wrestling *concurrent to its production*, potentially illuminating errors made during the forecasting process.

As MIT professor Sam Ford explains further, "in wrestling, the audience realizes that the performance 'on-stage' is only successful through their performance 'off-stage'.

"They realize that the writers have written a show guessing how they're going to perform, with knowledge that they can reshape the performance...through a decision in terms of how they want to react.

If fans want to begin cheering a villain, [for example], then in theory, they can create a 'face' turn. If fans want to chant 'boring' at the guy who is being pushed, they can help give him a demotion - all through their own 'performance'."

With shows unfolding interactively, dynamically and in *real-time*, wrestling audiences could perhaps be conceptualized as 'focus groups', offering instant feedback relating to creative ideas (with television ratings providing a much broader gauge of success). Conversely, this immediacy could be dangerously intoxicating, insofar as bookers took a *reactive* approach, oscillating wildly in direction from week-to-week. A more fruitful approach, albeit far more difficult, was to adopt a *proactive* strategy, carefully contemplating how narrative developments, 'plot twists' and character turns affected the bigger picture. In short, while leaving room for some necessary deviation, long-term thinking was essential in wrestling, even granting inevitable short-term setbacks along the way.

As Vince Russo often preached, it also required months of engaging, consistent programming to rebuild an audience. In that sense, to borrow from one ancient proverb, each *Nitro* segment represented a single step, part of a thousand-mile journey back to prominence. Meanwhile, a thousand miles removed from Atlanta, Jerry Levin was on a journey of his own.

Perhaps inspired by Henry David Thoreau, whose time around nature formed the basis of *Walden*, Levin spent the holidays in Vermont, deep in contemplation about the ongoing digital metamorphosis. He considered the news that for Time Warner, its 4th quarter numbers were concerning - and declining - reflecting a stock drop of 17% in eight months. In addition, Levin's trumpeted 'new media' division - Time Warner Digital Media - was certifiably going nowhere.

Just weeks earlier, in a reflection on stock prices throughout the '90s, the *Wall Street Journal* highlighted the rise of AOL, citing its 80,000% (!) stock gain since 1989. However, there was no such press extolling the future of Time Warner - it was 'old media', seemed the consensus, a company firmly lost in another age. At some point in the future, Levin thought, he would have no time to act preemptively, and desperate times *did* call for desperate measures. With the clock striking midnight on December 31st, Levin made two dramatic resolutions - one, shave off his beard of 35 years, and two - merge with AOL, even if it meant *less* than a 50/50 split.

The world returned to work on Monday, January 3rd, 2000, and in New York, Levin took the next step forward. *I've thought about it*, he told a select group of Time Warner executives, *and I'm prepared to accept less than half.*

On Thursday, January 6th, 2000, Levin flew to Dulles, VA for an evening dinner with Steve Case, Ken Novack - AOL's Vice-Chairman - and Richard Bressler, Time Warner's Chief Financial Officer. At the opportune time, Levin levied to Case his offer - a 45/55 exchange ratio, in favor of America Online, to merge the two companies. Case smiled, enjoyed some dessert, and then gleefully proffered a handshake: *Deal.*

To consummate the deal, the parties knew that discretion was key. As a company, Time Warner long struggled with issues around press leaks, but more importantly, its pending merger required approval, via each side's board of directors, shareholders and federal regulators.

The very next morning after the dinner, Friday, January 7th, 2000, senior officials at Time Warner received an urgently titled e-mail, demanding their presence at a 'must attend' 10:00am meeting. *Ted must be stepping down*, thought one prominent executive, unaware of the secret talks. Upon learning of the real news, however, Time Warner's brain trust were rhetorically apoplectic: *why exactly are we doing this? What's the point?*

Over the weekend, dozens of lawyers, executives, bankers and accountants worked around the clock, burning through the 'due diligence' phase at a ridiculous clip. On Sunday, the Time Warner board agreed to vote on the proposal at 2:00pm, but shortly before the proceedings, Steve Case threw up a red flag.

Apparently, in documentation concerning projected job roles, Case was being labeled specifically as 'non-executive Chairman' - a mostly ceremonial title with little strategic input. Minutes before the vote, he shared an impassioned phone call with Levin, who reacted dejectedly with a fatigued confusion. *You agreed to take a non-executive role,* Levin reportedly said through gritted teeth.

Insulted at being cast aside - despite previously showing disinterest in operations - Case knew Levin had too much to lose. By the end of their conversation, he secured much more authority than first envisioned, carving out an array of specific duties along the way. "AOL was buying Time Warner: that was the reality," wrote Nina Munk in *Fools Rush In*, a mesmerizing account of the merger and its significance. "It was one hell of a way to begin a marriage of equals."

After all, AOL's shareholders, based on Levin's offer, would receive 55 percent of the new company. According to legend, its own board voted so quickly to approve the deal, several hours were spent waiting for news from their counterparts. In the Time Warner room, meanwhile, despite a peculiar sense of resigned reluctance, its directors voted affirmatively. There had been little time to examine the particulars, and with the exception of Ted Turner, the group tended to back Levin anyway. *Don't you think,* began Ted, observing the faces around him, *we oughtta vote more enthusiastically?*

"And so it was," reported Munk, "that Time Warner's board of directors voted a second time, wholeheartedly approving the sale of their illustrious firm to an Internet company not yet fifteen years old - a company with a single product and with one-fifth the revenue of Time Warner. It was, as the media would soon report, a historic moment."

425

Chapter 44: Mutiny

TOTALLY DISCONNECTED FROM the maneuverings of its parent company, WCW opened 2000 amid fresh optimism (despite posting a loss of $11.5 million in 1999, according to company records). To the delight of Vince Russo, TNT agreed to eliminate the third hour of *Nitro*, instead making possible a two-hour show from 8-10pm. Although the move meant, in a disappointing drawback, that *Raw* could enjoy an hour of *unopposed* television, Siegel and his suits hoped that a "more coherent wrestling show" - as articulated in comments to *MediaWeek* - would become the eventual result.

Furthermore, the cutback figured to increase *Nitro*'s overall rating, as compensatorily, its average would now be derived from only one *opposed* hour. Estimates suggested that a 4.5-4.7 rating could soon be in play, but the initial two-hour shows drew only a 3.3 and 3.5 respectively (exactly equivalent to the first two *three*-hour shows of the Russo-Ferrara era). Wrestlers were diving off balconies, jumping off cages, wielding branding irons and crushing limos, but the gap in viewership remained colossal. Consequently, some wondered if the human cost was even worth it.

"I've been doing everything I can to help WCW compete in the ratings war with the WWF," wrote Bret Hart in the *Calgary Sun*, "and sometimes I find myself going against my personal beliefs in order to be a team player. I ask myself, 'how far do I compromise in order to help WCW beat Vince McMahon,' or do I find a personal victory in not bending at all? I'm having a harder time than people think finding that answer.

"I signed an autograph for a guy who asked me the ever present 'is it fake' question, and I was stunned to realize I'm not even sure I know the answer anymore. Is what fake? The lump on my head is sure real enough.

426

"I could have killed myself screeching out of an arena in a speeding car in [one] scripted scene. I'm flooring it, tearing out of backstage, with no time in the scene to even put on a seatbelt. And it turns out an icy rain had coated the ramp. There I am, careening out of control, towards a trailer truck filled with TV equipment. In the last moment, I somehow veered to safety ("The performers never drove the monster trucks," retorts Jeff Bornstein, WCW's lighting director.)."

"About a week later," continued Hart in the same column, "I was awakened in the middle of the night...by the realization that I had a concussion from when Goldberg kicked me in the head."

Indeed, although seemingly innocuous to the untrained eye, a standing sidekick from Goldberg had initiated - for Hart - a cascade of head trauma that would sideline him indefinitely. "I'd been walking around in a haze ever since," he wrote.

"...so what's the point of all this?

"I'm not sure I know. Maybe the whole wrestling business is pathetic...including me."

With Hart and Goldberg both out, the upcoming *Souled Out* pay-per-view was decimated. To make matters worse, a Nashville doctor then ordered Jeff Jarrett - scheduled to wrestle *three times* at the event - to stay home after suffering his own concussion. Now in desperation mode, Russo presented an alternative plan - vacating the WCW title, only for Tank Abbott (a former UFC fighter-turned WCW midcarder) to win the belt in a surprise battle royal.

The suggestion proved to be ruinous. "Vince Russo," led the *Pro Wrestling Torch* website, "less than four months after signing a two-year contract with WCW, has been removed as head booker and scriptwriter by Brad Siegel and Bill Busch."

"A meeting was held late Friday," wrote Bob Ryder on *1Wrestling.com*, "and a decision was made by WCW management to bring more people into the creative process…and to re-establish a booking committee.

"Russo is said to have been unhappy with the prospect of booking by committee, and expressed his feelings to WCW management."

Elsewhere on the Internet, fans reacted mostly with disbelief, stunned at another behind-the-scenes change. But some were also claiming - in a notion that persisted over the coming years - that Russo's WCW involvement belied a kind of conspiracy, one initiated, supposedly, by Vince McMahon himself.

'RUSSO WAS A PLANT!!!' screamed one user. "He moves Nitro to two hours, leaving the final hour of Raw with no competition. He moves Thunder…he wanted TANK ABBOTT to be WCW champ…he had Goldberg smash in a REAL car windshield with his bare hand…Oklahoma…Juvi at the announce table…you guys, I could go on and on and on and on…"

"There were some rumors," recalls former WCW producer Jason Douglas, "where people said, 'I wouldn't be surprised if this was a deal by Vince McMahon…to have Russo come in and run the company into the ground'. We were doing that 'ok' by ourselves before [Russo] came in, but you would hear people say that."

With up to 20 wrestlers reportedly threatening to quit, chaos reigned backstage before *Souled Out*. "The fallout from the move is enormous," explained Wade Keller, identifying Kevin Sullivan as Russo's replacement. "For one, Sullivan is extremely unpopular with a huge number of midcard wrestlers who believed he had been working against them. Before Russo was removed as booker, a group of more than a dozen wrestlers talked of getting together, and approaching Siegel about having Sullivan removed from the road.

"[Regardless], Sullivan will head a booking committee consisting of Kevin Nash, Terry Taylor, Ed Ferrara, and Bill Banks. Russo has been invited to stay aboard in a more limited capacity helping to write TV. Those who know Russo say they doubt he can accept those

428

circumstances, [however], and he will likely look for a settlement to be released from his contract."

To headline *Souled Out* - and wrestle for the vacant belt - Sullivan and company selected Chris Benoit to face Sid Vicious. Given the history between Sullivan and Benoit, it may have been a surprising decision, but one the matchmaker felt was entirely justified. Nevertheless, having heard whispers that Benoit was unhappy with management, Sullivan asked Vicious to lose cleanly - but only, in a key detail, with his feet placed underneath the ring ropes. In accordance with the rules of professional wrestling, the subtlety provided a means to reverse the outcome - if necessary - depending on the political fallout ahead.

A day later, Sullivan looked positively clairvoyant, as Benoit led a band of disgruntled workers in asking for their release. Subsequently, Mike Graham - the son of Sullivan's mentor, Eddie, and a WCW road agent with deep loyalties to the booker - reportedly pulled a knife on the group before *Nitro*. As a result, and fearing a lawsuit, Bill Busch agreed to offer complete releases to Benoit, Dean Malenko, Eddie Guerrero and Perry Saturn, and just like that, the heart of WCW's midcard was gone.

–––––

On Sunday, January 30th, the Georgia Dome hosted Super Bowl XXXIV, a spectacle made famous for its heavy involvement of 'dot-com' advertisers (not to mention the game's heart-stopping finish). Halfway across the country, Eric Bischoff was watching with family in Wyoming, still processing the events of months past. The next morning, Bischoff took to the skies in a private jet, dropped his brother off in Minneapolis, and decided to stay the night with wife Loree.

That night, the couple ate dinner at Chili's, staying just long enough to see a familiar sight on the television screen. *Monday Night Raw* was playing, and sitting ringside on camera, Benoit, Malenko, Guerrero and Saturn took center stage. *I bet you*, Bischoff remarked confidently to his wife, *WCW will call me in the next week.*

429

Now collectively branded as *The Radicalz,* Benoit and company debuted officially on February 7th. In a damning indictment of their former company's failures, the exiles helped *Raw* destroy *Nitro* 6.5-2.6, and as part of a multi-man main event, their involvement sparked an incredible 8.1 segment rating. Over on TNT, meanwhile, fans were openly being challenged to change the channel, courtesy of a Scott Steiner promo that went completely off the rails:

"When you walked down that aisle last week, I know I wasn't alone...because the people at home, all they did was grab their remote, change the channel to the WWF and watch Stone Cold, a person you and your old friends got fired from here because you're a jealous, old bastard. So Ric Flair, remember this, in this wrestling business, there's never been a bigger ass-kissing, butt-sucking bastard in this business. But also in life, you're the biggest ass kissing, back-stabbing, butt-sucking bastard and you belong where you're at, in WCW, because WCW sucks!"

Completely unscripted, the outburst underscored an increasingly untenable backstage situation. Before a *Thunder* taping in Philadelphia, a dispute involving Scott Hall caused the show to be delayed for 35 minutes. "I wasn't aware of what was going on behind the scenes," remembers ring announcer David Penzer, "but I was saying, 'alright, cameras are rollin' in 5, 4, 3, 2, 1 - make some noise!'

"The pyro went off, and then everything just stopped. It's bad enough to have to kill 30 minutes...but we were in Philadelphia, which is one of the most brutal audiences in all of the world. To get them at that fever pitch...have that pyro go off...and then sit there for over 30 minutes...it was a tough time. Again, I didn't know why - nobody told me why - and I just had to entertain them.

"At one point, I started reading pages out of Diamond Dallas Page's book. It was like an old Andy Kaufman thing. I was taking one on the chin for the company, and getting the crowd to turn on *me* - so they didn't turn on the show."

At the same time - as reflected in Steiner's unsanctioned promo -

WCW's wrestlers seemed to have turned on the company. Suddenly, several top names found themselves sidelined with injuries - some not quite as severe as others - and non-attendance to house shows was reaching epidemic proportions. "For various reasons," remembers Alan Sharp, Head of PR for WCW, "we had arena shows booked and guys weren't able to be on the card. But once you go to a town and you're the headliner...if you don't show up, your 'killing' those towns."

In an unfortunate full circle, WCW was again an embarrassment for TBS - although perhaps this time, to a much greater degree than ever before. "I remember going to a Turner PR conference in early 2000," remembers Sharp, "and someone asked a question about WCW. It was, 'where does WCW fit in?'

"The answer was something like, 'well, at this time, I don't think it would be appropriate to make a comment on WCW'.

"I looked at the person next to me.

"I said, 'do I need to go looking for a job?'"

Chapter 45:
The Next Big Idea

W ITH MORALE PLUMMETING, Siegel summoned the creative team for a late afternoon meeting on Friday, February 25th. Sitting in an office space formerly occupied by Eric Bischoff, the executive implored his staff to set course in a new direction, emphasizing the imminent need to develop two interconnected plans - first, a cohesive set of ideas for Goldberg's return, and secondly, a broader vision of how to revive the on-screen product. *I challenge you*, Siegel reportedly dared as the minutes ticked past 5:00pm, *to find the next big idea*.

On the surface, the mandate appeared to suggest confidence in an overarching storyline, an approach to booking that allowed disparate feuds to unite under a narrative 'umbrella'. Creatively, the nWo years had shown value in such a philosophy, which not so coincidentally, also proved useful in branding WCW to non-adherents of the genre. In those days, Bischoff had been keenly aware of this connection, recalls company stalwart Rob Garner. "I got in a cab one afternoon with Bischoff," Garner remembers, "and we were in New York. I looked over at the cab door, and someone had wrote 'nWo' in the *exact* logo and font. I kinda nudged Eric with my elbow and said, 'look at this - you don't think we're known?' He just laughed at it, like 'oh my god'. Well, later that day, he relayed that story to a group of Turner Ad Sales people."

"I remember driving from Norfolk to Salisbury, Maryland," begins Jeff Bornstein. "I was with David Crockett, and we were on these back roads in Virginia. There was a basketball backboard spray painted with 'nWo' on it...so we knew we'd definitely touched the heart of mid-America."

"Folks were just so attracted to it," marvels Alan Sharp, referencing the nWo - wrestling's original 'cool heels'. "I know their merchandise was incredible. They just had an attitude - this cool, confident, 'we're the baddest folks in the arena' [vibe]."

"When the nWo was created," recalls former TBS producer Brendon Hamlin, "I was like, 'holy cow'. I thought it was an amazing move."

"The nWo storyline was a real hook for quite some time," agrees Aline Weiller, a marketing expert with tenures at TBS, MCA and Coca-Cola. "It really riled up diehard fans...[this] drama involving a group of supposed rogue wrestlers who wanted to take over."

Since the departure of Vince Russo, and more recently - as of early February - the return of Hulk Hogan, critics were increasingly noticing a perceptible aimlessness to WCW programming. While on *Raw*, 'The Rock' was thrilling fans in a weekly battle against the McMahon-Helmsley regime, *Nitro* was stuck recycling a feud between Hogan and Ric Flair, one that had been introduced (and resolved) several times over the previous decade. With Hogan, Flair, and a slew of older talent remaining on the payroll - not to mention the Benoit-led exodus that decimated the midcard - Kevin Sullivan considered his company to be in full rebuilding mode.

But according to Sullivan, while his committee practiced restraint - agreeing collectively to 'do less and do it better' - Siegel's plea indicated a more urgent desire for change. "He wanted an epic, one-week turnaround," the veteran booker recalls. "We told Brad Siegel the truth. We said, 'there's no one-week turnaround, and there's gonna be a rebuilding process for Goldberg.'"

For his part, J.J. Dillon expressed a similar sentiment, noting to Siegel that any request for a grand vision was somewhat unrealistic. "[I said], 'we didn't map out a complicated storyline [for Goldberg]'," Dillon would later write. "We weren't even sure [what to name his character]. He couldn't 'work' and he couldn't 'talk', but we used him because we needed somebody fresh on our roster. We put him on television and had him beat people in less than a minute, because we were afraid he'd be exposed...[but] after pushing [him] for a period of several weeks, he became a huge superstar. It just took on a life of its own,

[and] that's typical of the wrestling business. You introduce a character, allow the fans to watch his story unfold over a period of weeks, and make adjustments depending on how the fans react to each part of the story. So you can't ask for the next big idea. Our business isn't structured that way. It's a form of entertainment unlike any other."

If Goldberg could regain his old mystique - *and* was positioned on a collision course with a credible top heel - Sullivan believed it possible to generate a sizable pay-per-view buy rate before year's end. But Sullivan's penchant for taking the long view clearly placed him at odds with Siegel, and as he traveled home to Miami for the weekend, the booker became convinced that his days were numbered. On Sunday night, February 27th, various insider wrestling sites were reporting that Goldberg had gone incommunicado, an apparent act of protest against the current creative set-up. "He knew I was a dead man," states Sullivan, matter-of-factly.

Monday morning brought news that the most recent edition of *WCW Saturday Night* - historically, a hugely significant program and an institution of Southern wrestling - registered its lowest-ever viewership since records were available. Undeterred, Sullivan continued the rebuild, booking Sid Vicious to submit Tank Abbott in a main event *Nitro* match. While there appeared to be money in an eventual Goldberg clash with Vicious (or, alternatively, a long-awaited singles match with Scott Steiner), the Nielsen numbers suggested that a rapid erosion of the audience was underway. The February 28th *Nitro* scored a 2.1, the lowest in its history, followed by another record low (2.0) for *Thunder* on March 1st.

Despite the concerning slide in ratings, Busch remained supportive, Sullivan claims, even insisting to the matchmaker that Siegel had been convinced of the need for patience. *If you believe that*, Sullivan recalls responding to Busch, *I'll jump off this floor right now. He ain't you, Bill, and that's your problem - you think everybody's honest.*

"Bill was a really nice young man," says Dick Cheatham. "He worked in the accounting operation at WCW before taking over. He was not the controller, because he didn't have the qualifications to be the controller, but he always had the right kind of attitude - 'I'll do whatever I can to help the company'."

"Bill was very down to earth," remembers Scott Sergent, formerly an interactive communication manager with WCW. "He was very 'black and white' - 'this is right, this is wrong' - that kind of thing. No gray areas.

"In this business - and WCW [specifically] - I think the people in charge were 180 degrees from the way Bill would see things. He was maybe swimming with the sharks a little bit, and although he knew his stuff and did everything 'by the book'...he was in a very tough environment."

Determined to right the ship, Busch entertained a J.J. Dillon-led recommendation to pursue Jerry Jarrett as a creative consultant. Although Jarrett had served in a similar role under Bischoff, his dealings with Turner management (including, notably, Ted himself) stretched back much further. "I suppose it all began in the early '70s, when I booked the Atlanta territory for Jim Barnett," surmises Jarrett. "My tenure was very successful in that we developed a following that allowed us to move from the old city auditorium to the Omni. During this time period, I got to know Ted Turner. It would be a stretch to say we became friends, but because he was so intrigued with wrestling, we got on a first name basis. Ted would sit behind me in the booth while I edited the show each week.

"Over the course of time, from the early '70s until the mid '90s, I was asked to manage WCW. I do not know if Ted Turner himself made the suggestions that I come on board. However, my one demand was that the North Tower - Turner management - understand that professional wrestling would not fit into the corporate box. On more than one occasion, I pointed out that Vince McMahon had a corporate structure, but he built the corporation *around* the wrestling business, and did not allow the structure to interfere."

By 2000, however, Jarrett - father of Jeff - divorced himself from the wrestling business, content to run a hugely successful construction company across three states. But with one such project being based in Atlanta, Jarrett saw no downside in traveling to Smyrna to meet with Busch, particularly in light of his son's high-profile position on the WCW roster. After an initial phone call, the two agreed to discuss the proposal further with Dillon on Thursday, March 9th.

At the meeting, Jarrett listened intently as Busch lamented the creative failures of the past year, but armed with the knowledge of WCW's talent costs (forecasted at $40.35 million for 2000, according to a March 1 office memo), the legendary promoter responded by highlighting a larger issue. *You need to go to each of your millionaire wrestlers*, Jarrett recalls stating, *and tell them they have two choices. One is to begin taking orders from the booker...the other choice is to be deemed in breach of contract and fired.*

Above all else, Jarrett advised Busch to stick with his booker. *There is nothing worse than a committee booking a wrestling show*, he told the desperate ex-accountant. *Give your booker a goal, and fire him if he fails to perform.*

As the parties dispersed, Jarrett returned to his business, convinced that his dance with WCW was over.

————

In the meantime, an assortment of WCW talent prepared for a rare tour of England, with weekend house shows scheduled in Birmingham, Manchester and London. Although the market had been, as was the case in most international territories, a WWF stranglehold throughout the '90s, WCW had picked up significant momentum due to the broadcast of *Nitro* and *Thunder* on TNT Europe. In July 1999, the company continued its UK growth through the syndication of a one-hour program, edited specifically for the British audience - *WCW Worldwide*. Although the show consisted mostly of weeks-old matches, bungled together with taped commentary from Scott Hudson and Larry Zybysko, it developed a cult following by virtue of its consistently wacky editing, strikingly bizarre censorship, and infinitely amusing production gaffes (including the particularly infamous occurrence of Zybysko calling his own interference in a match).

With *Worldwide* airing on *Channel 5* - the newest 'terrestrial' or free-for-all station - and a fixed time slot of 7:00pm on Fridays limiting its content, the series became increasingly absurd during the Vince Russo era. After a small number of viewers objected to a weapon being shown on camera, the network responded by utilizing Batman-style visual captions to obscure future violence. When Shane Douglas threatened to 'kick the ass' of an opponent in a pre-match interview, the sound of a cracking whip was inserted in place of the offending word. And as the channel ident signified the end of an episode, it became commonplace for a station narrator to provide a sarcastic comment at sign-off ("Well, that's it for this week…but remember - it's not big - or clever - to hit people with a bat."). Nevertheless, an excitable crowd of 11,812 packed into the Birmingham NEC Arena for the first leg of the 'Nitro UK Tour' on Friday, March 10th.

Inside the arena, fans noted the appearance of various out-of-action stars in the event program, with Kevin Nash, still recovering from an ankle issue, gracing its cover. As matches featuring Norman Smiley, David Flair, Brian Knobbs and Jim Duggan littered the undercard, even a memorable mid-show appearance by Bret Hart could not prevent a growing frustration among the audience. But after Lex Luger defeated Vampiro in the semi-main event, Michael Buffer strolled to the ring to introduce a marquee match-up between two 'old rivals', seemingly alluding to a Hogan-Flair exhibition to close the night.

Within minutes, however, a surge of disappointed patrons headed for the exits when Curt Hennig - introduced to almost zero reaction - emerged from the backstage area to face Flair. As an assembly of angry parents looked on, Buff Bagwell concluded matters with a show-ending promo. *You didn't get Goldberg*, acknowledged Bagwell over the house mic, *and you didn't get Sting, but you got Buff, and he's the stuff!*

437

A similar pattern repeated itself in London the following night, and again in Manchester with the Mamalukes and Harris Brothers headlining on top. And so, despite attracting a cumulative crowd of 38,580 fans over three days - generating a conservative estimate of over $1,000,000 in revenue - the tour would eventually become subject of a *BBC Watchdog* report citing concerns over false advertising.

Less than 24 hours later, the majority of the England crew landed in Providence, RI for the March 13th *Nitro*. Leading up to air time, observers noted the curious sight of Brad Siegel in deep discussions with Hulk Hogan, an ominous sign perhaps of things to come. Back in Atlanta, Bill Busch decided to renew contact with Jerry Jarrett, proposing a sit-down in Siegel's office on Thursday, March 16th. Unbeknownst to Busch, however, Siegel had already determined the way forward, as after several weeks of clandestine discussions, Eric Bischoff was offered the chance to return.

After six months on the sideline, Bischoff possessed no desire to resume his former position, informing Siegel that regardless of any future role, his family were in the midst of a move to Arizona. Assuming he renewed his involvement with WCW, Bischoff wanted to be free to pursue other projects, leading Siegel to propose buying out the two-and-a-half years remaining on his existing deal (believed to be worth exactly $904,250) to tender a *new* contract promising $200,000 for the rest of 2000, and $200,000 for 2001 (with Turner holding an option to renew the pact in 2002 and 2003, at a cost of $350,000 and $400,000 respectively). In short, under Siegel's plan, WCW's former President would receive close to a million dollars - plus subsequent remuneration outlined in the superseding contract - to return as a *creative consultant*, on an *independent contractor* basis, with additional (bonus) compensation available based on pay-per-view and ratings benchmarks. Crucially, TBS would also be obligated to develop three TV movies produced by 'Eric Bischoff Productions', a clause that could be leveraged to create other opportunities in Hollywood.

On Tuesday, March 14th, Bischoff signed the agreement to provide:

Consulting services, as required to TEG (Turner Entertainment Group), with respect to WCW creative matters, including, without limitation, providing creative direction to the creative team, with the goal of improving Weekly Program (i.e. "Nitro" and "Thunder") ratings and Pay Per View buys...

Consultant shall appear in up to (as required by TEG) 70 "Appearances" per year of the Consulting Term (i.e. 70 during the year 2000, 70 during the year 2001 and so on). "Appearances" shall mean televised shows (including Weekly Programs and Pay Per Views) ("Shows") and press events, cable operator and sales meetings and industry events and other promotional appearances (collectively, "Events") as may be designated from time to time by TEG...

If Consultant is required to attend an Event separate and apart from his traveling with the Show, then such appearance shall count as a separate Appearance hereunder. Any Appearance in excess of 70 in any year shall be...compensated at $3,000 per such additional Appearance...

Consultant will travel to Atlanta (at TEG's expense)...as reasonably necessary and required by TEG for overall consultations (but no more than 24 trips per year to Atlanta can be required by TEG)...

Consultant shall [not] have any authority to hire or fire any individual or entity employed or engaged by TEG, WCW and/or any affiliated persons or entities.

On Wednesday, March 15th, Siegel called Bischoff to relay a surprising proposition. With the contract signed, Siegel suggested that his newly-hired consultant consider working with another exiled figure: Vince Russo. The former Creative Director was receiving full pay to sit at home, but with the right amount of oversight, Siegel thought, it seemed plausible that his output could improve. "Brad risked his political capital to bring me back," explains Bischoff. "He brought me back with a deal sweeter than the one I had when I left. That was a big move for Brad, but he wouldn't have done it if he had any confidence in Vince. He was very, very, *very* concerned about it. He said, 'you gotta watch over this guy. Russo is just too dark, and it hasn't worked [with him alone]'."

Although in January, Russo appeared defiant in refusing to work with a committee, he was privately simmering in the basement of his new Atlanta home, surfing the web compulsively for an update on his status. While the checks were still coming - for now - Russo grew increasingly concerned that his stance may have been in breach of contract. A return to the WWF seemed implausible, even preposterous, especially in light of online reports alleging his failures to be the source of much ridicule in Stamford. Now, paradoxically, for a writer whose telling, almost Freudian propensity to create stories around wrestlers fighting for 'their livelihood', he concerned himself only with securing his own. When Siegel finally called - *there's somebody I want you to talk to*, he told Russo, the defeated scriptwriter accepted his only option: working with Eric Bischoff.

Obliviously, Bill Busch moved ahead on the Jarrett plan, presenting the promoter to Siegel on Thursday, March 16th. Busch announced that Jarrett had agreed to become his 'consultant/advisor', accounting for the move by providing a detailed background of the promoter's credentials. At that exact point, remembers Jarrett, Siegel informed Busch that his attempts had been in vain. To the shock of the entire room, Siegel delivered a bombshell pronouncement, divulging that arrangements had been made for Bischoff and Russo to return in creative roles.

Busch responded to the news, says Jarrett, by withdrawing into a fetal position on Siegel's office couch. "I witnessed his delight in reducing Bill to a sniveling person who recoiled to a fetal position on the couch," Jarrett recalls disdainfully. "This is not an exaggeration. I can't recall being in a more embarrassing situation. When one man reveals the content of his character to a stranger - which I was - then perhaps I see the possibility of that character in his future actions. It was one of the saddest occasions I've ever witnessed. Siegel seemed to delight in the humiliation of Bill in front of me."

Betrayed and beaten, Busch returned to his office to compose his resignation letter. His departure would mark the end of a 10-year association with WCW, and more importantly, the dissolution of a recently-signed three year extension. Jarrett left the building soon after, describing Busch as looking 'as down as any human being I've ever seen'. *I must admit*, quipped Jarrett on his way out, *this is the first human castration I've ever witnessed.*

With Busch stepping down, WCW entered an upcoming pay-per-view without an operational leader at the helm - the second such occurrence over the course of six months. On Sunday, March 19th, less than 2,600 paying fans (5,000 total) witnessed *Uncensored* live in Miami, a show headlined by Hogan and Flair in a strap match. Whereas just 12 months earlier, the same exact match-up enticed 250,000 fans to purchase the event on pay-per-view, the 2000 edition drew a measly 60,000 buys - the lowest figure in company history.

The behind-the-scenes shake-up had yet to go public, but late on Wednesday, March 22nd, *PWTorch.com* reported that Bischoff was set to return as WCW 'Vice-President'. Later that evening, Bischoff guested on *WCW Live* to clarify the rumors, noting that some websites were "putting things out that aren't true."

"I *have* been talking to Brad Siegel since January," Bischoff revealed, "off and on about getting my release from WCW. Those conversations, particularly over the last couple of weeks, have evolved into another form of negotiations.

"This has all happened so quickly, so until I know what I am going to be responsible for and how I am going to interact in the office, I don't know. I *am* moving to Arizona...all of those plans are still in place. I made that very clear to Brad several weeks ago, when we first started talking seriously.

"That's why so much of this is premature...[and] it's unfortunate that as much information leaked out as it did...there were too many people involved for it not to leak out, but my intention was not to go public with any information until all of these details were resolved. Right now, we are going public with half a story."

The other half of the story remained Vince Russo. On the morning of Thursday March 23rd, Russo nervously prepared for a clandestine meet-up with Bischoff at *Hops*, a restaurant located almost 20 miles away and therefore, suitably unobtrusive enough to prevent suspicion. Almost immediately, Russo called to memory an attempt to pitch himself, a little over three years earlier, in a phone call to Bischoff -

prior to his involvement with WWF storylines. But while Bischoff could barely place the interaction ("there was just nothing noteworthy about it," he shrugs), Russo held on to a very different memory. He believed Bischoff to have been condescendingly arrogant throughout the call, a perception that soon reinforced itself in-person. Nonetheless, despite those previous differences, the pair agreed on a much-needed course of action - starting completely from scratch. "If [WCW] was a horse, I would just shoot it," Bischoff told the *New York Daily News* of the plan. "That's what we're going to do...we've got to readjust our thinking and give the audience what [it] expects...there's a lot of things that need to be fixed with the show."

At the same time as the covert discussion at *Hops* continued, WCW released a clarifying statement on its website:

Bill Busch has resigned his position as Executive Vice President of WCW. He has made the decision to pursue opportunities outside the company. While we are sorry to see Bill go, we are grateful for his contributions to the organization and wish him the best in his new endeavors. Effective immediately, Brad Siegel will assume oversight of the day-to-day operations of WCW, and will continue in that role until an executive is hired for the position.

In the coming weeks, Eric Bischoff will assume a key role within the WCW creative process. Eric will be working with the writing staff and WCW talent on new story lines and creative direction. We are happy to welcome him back to our corner.

At 12:30pm, Siegel confirmed the reshuffle in an address to WCW's department heads. His next order of business was to inform the current creative committee of the change, literally at the moment of a half-underway booking discussion in Florida. With the news now official, Sullivan knew that the upcoming *Nitro* on March 27th - a 'Spring Break' edition of the show from Texas' South Padre Island - would be his last. He was instructed to avoid furthering any storylines, and more importantly, told to refrain from showing his face backstage.

Within hours, a report on *WrestlingObserver.com* informed fans of the latest developments:

WrestlingObserver.com has just learned that Eric Bischoff and Vince Russo have officially agreed to return and work together in WCW. Russo at one point said he would not have jumped to WCW if Bischoff was in power, but it appears they're working together because they've got common enemies.

On Monday, March 27th, and with Russo providing direction over the telephone, the Spring Break *Nitro* hardly resembled a Sullivan show upon broadcast. In an on-camera statement, Tony Schiavone informed the TNT audience that "Brad Siegel" had made the historic decision to bring Bischoff back as "head of creative," noting that the company also "hoped Vince Russo would return." The proclamation, made as part of a show-long 'hook' to dissuade viewers from skipping the episode, eventually culminated in the announcement that Bischoff and Russo had agreed to work together after all. Critics immediately noted the peculiar internal logic of such a tease, as for the fans 'in the know', word of their secret meeting (and subsequent committal to Siegel) had already been established.

In a WCW.com interview the next day, Russo specifically hinted at potential problems with Bischoff. "We do have philosophical differences," he admitted, "[but] we both want to win...very, very much. Regardless of if we get along...[or] don't get along...we both want to win, and that's why we are here. That's why we are doing this...that's something that we're going to have to constantly remind each other of."

With the WWF preparing for its showcase pay-per-view - *Wrestlemania* - and a mammoth rating expected for the subsequent *Raw*, Siegel approved a one-week hiatus of original WCW programming. The move would provide additional time for Bischoff and Russo to work on their first effort, an April 10th edition of *Nitro* from Denver's brand-new Pepsi Center. "We're gonna come with all guns blazing," promised Russo. "WCW cannot afford to dig themselves in any more of a deeper hole. If this company is going to get serious about competing, that needs to start now."

By Saturday, the 'next big idea' had finally been determined. In a callback to a previously halted storyline in 1999, Russo and Bischoff would lead a hungry herd of young wrestlers - to be christened as the 'New Blood' - against an established old guard of veterans labeled as 'The Millionaires Club'. To capitalize of fans' frustrations with the stale main event scene, the Millionaires would be presented as heels, resentful over 'passing the torch' to unproven lower-card acts. Despite some notable limitations, notably the tens of millions of dollars coming to Hogan, Flair and much of the 40-plus contingent, the concept showed promise - if executed correctly - to enable a gradual turnover of the marquee talent.

In lieu of a regular episode, TNT aired a 'Best of *Nitro*' special on Monday, April 3rd. Watching from Los Angeles, the site of a premiere event for *Ready to Rumble* (a WCW-themed movie that originally cast Bischoff - prior to his removal as WCW President - in an 'evil promoter' role), Bischoff viewed the retrospective not as a blueprint for future success, but rather, a relic of a bygone era. "I watched the *Nitro* anthology last night," he told journalist Dave Scherer, "and there were a lot of things that worked when we launched [the show]. The thing we need to realize now is those same approaches won't work anymore, because the business has changed."

On Wednesday, Bischoff appeared at Mann's Chinese Theatre for the *Rumble* movie premiere, later addressing WCW.com visitors in a special webcast. "I've had the chance now to work with Vince [Russo] for a few weeks, and I'm real excited about it," Bischoff said. "He's a very creative guy, and he's got the discipline as a producer that I think WCW lacked for a long time. I think the combination between his style and mine is gonna be interesting, to say the least.

"Hopefully this movie is successful as everybody anticipates it will [be], and if that happens, success is just gonna breed more opportunities. I talked to Ted the other day - he called me last Friday while I was here - and I know he's just as enthusiastic about WCW as he's ever been. Brad Siegel is a guy that really understands the entertainment business, so there's no doubt about it - we're gonna have a lot of these opportunities."

Concurrent to the webcast, TBS ran the 'Best of Thunder', a puzzling mix of old matches with an equally perplexing theme. Out of the nine bouts chosen for the special, eight ended in disqualifications, a disquieting motif for fans who remembered an infamous run of seven straight *Nitro* main events ending without a decisive winner. "WCW used to get criticized often," recalls Alan Sharp, "for all the 'run-ins'. You would have a match that looked like a 'clean' finish, and in comes the nWo to break it up, [for example]."

To the remaining WCW devotees, it was still questionable how different the 'new' era would be, particularly after a purported 'shoot' interview with Hulk Hogan closed the show.

"The barn is on fire, and somebody needs to throw a bucket of water on it," Hogan observed in a notably muted tone. "When I think about Bischoff and Russo, maybe these are the guys that can help put this fire out...Eric did a lot of good things to make WCW a major player, but as the business got larger and larger - faster and faster - I think we lost focus on the wrestling aspect of this business. A lot of the deals and Hollywood came into play, and Eric was torn in several different directions. With all the good things that he did, I think he got sidetracked, [but] now with him coming back, I think he's learned from his mistakes.

"As far as Russo goes...[he] seems to be a very intelligent human being. I saw what he did in the WWF with the TV-14, the T & A, the violence. I saw him try to implement these things here, and everything went awry. Now, if he's learned his lessons - if he realizes that he has to tone it down a bit...with Eric acting as the filter, they may be one heck of a combination.

"[But] you have to go with what got you to the dance. Whenever Hulk Hogan was on a pay-per-view, whenever Hulk Hogan was on a house show...the numbers went through the roof. The young guys, if they're gonna get established, need to jump on the bandwagon. Young guys like Billy Kidman...[who complain] if they don't get the 'push', they're gonna pack their bags up and go elsewhere. I have the same thing to say to him that I've said before - you couldn't sell out a flea market on your best day. You're not even good enough to be the flea market champion. Until you prove yourself, until you outshine Hulk Hogan, until you out-wrestle Hulk Hogan, until you fight your way...to the top, it doesn't mean anything.

445

"You have to prove you'll go above and beyond to see the Make-A-Wish kids on your days off, you have to prove that you'll sign autographs for an extra couple of hours...you have to work real hard to take my job, because I'm not moving aside for anybody. That's what I have to say to all the fans, and everybody that's been critical of me and my position, and the younger athletes that are so-called 'hungry'. I don't think they're that hungry."

Behind the scenes, and with the blessing of Siegel, Hogan had been slated to feature even more on WCW programming. On Friday, April 7th, he signed an amendment to his 1998 agreement, pledging to build up pay-per-view match-ups by appearing on every *Nitro* and *Thunder* during the preceding month (retaining a minimum guarantee of $25,000 for each show). And so, despite all the rhetoric concerning change, Hogan could rest assured of a continued prominent role, at least until his deal expired in May 2002.

———

Meanwhile, Kevin Sullivan was taking his ousting in stride, enjoying a week in the Florida Keys with Ed Ferrara and his wife. Just prior to Siegel's shake-up, he received a tip-off that his contract was set to 'roll over' for three more years. "It was a guy that was the Head of Acquisitions at Turner," Sullivan reveals. "I befriended him when [WCW] was first bought from Jimmy Crockett [in 1988]. All of the other wrestlers were pretty crude to him, but he was a wonderful guy and was very nice to me. He went out of his way to [contact me], because I was nice to him in '88.

"Now it's over 10 years later, and he came to me and said, 'they're gonna renew your contract for three more years - get it signed'. He told me that AOL didn't want wrestling. I said, 'you gotta be shittin' me!' He said, 'they don't want it, and they don't care about the ratings. It's below them'.

"I said, 'well, I don't think I deserve a big raise'. He said, 'there's a 10 percent raise across the board - just take it'. I looked at him like he

446

was crazy.

"He said, 'just take it, because WCW won't be here in a year'."

Chapter 46:
The Night The World Changed

SEVERAL DAYS IN ADVANCE of the April 10th *Nitro*, TBS and TNT hosted its spring 'upfront' at the Hammerstein Ballroom in New York. The special presentation - designed primarily to introduce new programming to curious ad agency executives - also served to reinforce that Turner's networks appealed to the vaunted 18-to-49 male demographic. While TBS, at least according to the presentation, would remain as 'the network for regular guys', TNT looked to project a more sophisticated image. Its marketing team arranged for appearances from Farrah Fawcett, Alec Baldwin, and Sir Elton John, and although no wrestlers were invited to the party, WCW earned itself a special mention by Brad Siegel. "The world will change Monday night," Siegel promised to the upscale crowd on 34th Street.

The last time WCW changed the world - at least, the *wrestling* world - Hulk Hogan turned heel to form the formidable New World Order faction. But while some remembered his shocking renunciation of *Hulkamania* as an immediate turning point in the ratings war, a closer analysis revealed that *Nitro* viewership actually *declined* in the weeks following his *Bash at the Beach* betrayal. Only over time, with consistently engaging programming, internal TBS support, and perhaps most importantly, *positive momentum*, did WCW leave its competitor in the dust.

There had been a time, long after McMahon had turned the tables, that the occurrence of *Raw* doubling *Nitro*'s viewership garnered attention. But it had now become commonplace, regardless of what Bischoff, Nash, Sullivan or Russo had been able to produce. For that reason, and despite all the criticism of his supposedly short-sighted, 'hot-shotting' booking style, Russo understood that his first show back was only a first step. "If Brad Siegel thinks that in six months...the ratings will be a 6.0, he's out of his mind," argued Russo

448

on *WCW Live*. "Jesus Christ could walk through the door, and he wouldn't get a 6.0 in that time."

Nonetheless, on Monday morning, Siegel boarded a flight to witness the changes for himself. With Russo and Bischoff in tow, he addressed a horde of on-air talent at the Pepsi Center, reportedly emphasizing his long-term commitment to a turnaround. Meanwhile, throughout the hallways of the arena, several staffers were sporting a new promotional shirt, the tag line undeniably inspired by his earlier proclamation:

The Night The World Changed.
April 10, 2000.
Denver, CO.

As the gathering adjourned, an anxious Russo attempted to compose himself. To officially launch the new era, his script called for a scathing soliloquy to open the show, as at the behest of Bischoff, he would now be debuting as an on-screen character. In a revolutionary blend of fiction and reality, Russo prepared to acknowledge the actions of his detractors, referencing backstage politics in the most direct manner possible. The context for his comments would also be a first, as Russo would take center stage in a 'talent meeting' held within the wrestling ring itself. *The announcers should discuss that Vince Russo has called this meeting - invited guests only*, read a note in the episode script.

"*Ladies and gentleman, welcome to WCW Monday Nitro!*" greeted Tony Schiavone in an especially enthusiastic tone. "*Tonight, the mile-high city has the unique distinction to host a landmark event in sports entertainment, for this...is the night the world changed! After a little over four years being on the air, Monday Nitro turns a page on a brand new chapter!*"

After some establishing shots of the crowd and pyrotechnics - '*pyro and ballyhoo*' as referred to in the format - viewers witnessed the peculiar sight of over 40 wrestlers occupying the ring and ringside area. *All talent in street clothes*, instructed a note in the script. *No*

449

gimmicks...talent should be dressed to the nines.

Slowly, and by design, a small contingent of handpicked talent emerged from the backstage area (with journeyman Van Hammer among them, the result of an apparent miscommunication). On commentary, color man Scott Hudson attempted to make sense of the spectacle, referencing the dominant storyline of late 1999: *"Vince Russo - the Powers That Be - has a message for WCW."*

In the center of the ring, Jeff Jarrett took the microphone to introduce Russo, a detail designed to play on his own involvement with the Powers That Be angle. In a plodding monologue, 'The Chosen One' built up the credentials of the returning writer, referring to him as "Vince McMahon's best kept secret." Finally, Russo entered the fray, nervously walking the aisle to an instrumental cover of the Black Sabbath song, 'Ironman'.

But as opposed to the famous reveal in 'The Wizard of Oz', the man behind the curtain seemed remarkably ordinary. For a writer with an unwavering belief in the 'it factor', it remained to be seen how he could justify being on camera. Noticeably, Russo struggled to maintain eye contact with those at ringside, before awkwardly stepping through the ropes and needing only four seconds to reference his former employer. *"After giving six years of my life to the World Wrestling Federation,"* he began, *"I came to WCW with one thing in mind, and that was to beat Vince McMahon at his own game! And you know what? Within a matter of weeks, the new blood in WCW was not only getting back in the game, they were changing the game!*

"And that's when the good ol' boy network kicked in - afraid of change, and more importantly afraid of their jobs - the political BS took place in the back to bring Vince Russo down. And you at home know who you are, 'cause you're watching me now. And then one day, I'm told that there's gonna be a change in direction - a change that I knew sucked! And you know what? I wasn't the only one who knew. Benoit knew...Guerrero knew...Saturn knew...Malenko knew...Douglas knew...and they left! They're gone! Scott Steiner - he knew it, and they suspended his ass! Well you know what? That's all

over now. It's done. Vince Russo is back in charge again. And I wanna turn around now and I wanna say something to everybody in this ring.

"It is over. The 'old boys' management is over. The inflated egos in the back, afraid to lose their spot...it is over. It is the dawning of a new day. It is your opportunity - seize that opportunity!"

In what was presented as a 'swerve', Eric Bischoff suddenly interrupted the diatribe, only to shake hands with Russo after a brief stare down. *"We were both screwed by the same 'good ol' boys' network,"* stated Bischoff in his signature self-assured style. He then subtly stepped back into character, foreshadowing a potential feud with the star he was most associated with.

"Vince is right - those days are over. But it's ok. I don't even mind...because it's giving me a hell of an opportunity to realize the mistakes I've made.

"Mistakes like Scott Hall, Kevin Nash, Sting, Diamond Dallas Page...and oh yeah, let's not forget Sid 'wished he was' Vicious. But...this is the real big one - Hulk Hogan!"

Russo followed with a personal attack on Ric Flair, portending a future angle of his own. *"Ric Flair, you are a piece of shit on the bottom of my shoe!"* he yelled in an insult muted by a TNT censor. *"I'll tell you what I'm gonna do. I'm gonna scrape off that shit, and flush your ass down the toilet personally!"*

According to various sources backstage, Siegel chuckled at the profanity as the shocking open continued. One by one, Russo and Bischoff collected the various championship belts, effectively 'rebooting' the preceding three months of television. To close the segment, Bischoff coaxed Sid Vicious into relinquishing his World Heavyweight title, goading the champion with a reference to a real-life incident. *"What's the matter, Sid?"* Bischoff asked. *"Can't find your scissors?"*

Bischoff repeated the line - an utterance not included in the original script - but the 9,074 fans in attendance failed to react. While to those in the know, the scissors jab alluded to an infamous 1993 altercation whereby Vicious - real name Sid Eudy - stabbed Arn Anderson in an English hotel room, it had never been mentioned on the air previously. And thus, with the segment ending with all titles vacant, *Nitro* was already oscillating between kayfabe and truth at a dizzying rate. "If there is one thing Russo failed to learn from Vince McMahon," observed Wade Keller of the *Pro Wrestling Torch,* "it's that he has the power to create his own universe. By definition, if fans understood all of his shoot references - and that understanding is necessary for his angles to work - then he has to consistently abide by that concrete reality."

Inconsistency - combined with repeated shoot references and a frenetic pace - clearly distinguished the 'new' Nitro:

- Viewers were informed that the 'Millionaires' had been stripped of their entrance music and pyro, but the subtlety was inexplicably dropped by the second match;

- In an apparent meta-reference to Sullivan's booking, Kevin Nash acknowledged the creative changes on-camera (*"what happened to our sweet little rasslin' show?"*), but then immediately sold an attack from the debuting Mike Awesome;

- To finally tie-up an angle from 1999, Bischoff revealed himself as the driver of a mysterious hummer – despite the plot points not adding up;

- Playing off comments in a radio interview, Billy Kidman 'pinned' Hulk Hogan – with Bischoff counting the fall; and

- Shane Douglas - known within the industry for a genuine hatred of Ric Flair - ambushed Flair with an assist from Russo (who in turn, nabbed Flair's watch in an impromptu moment of inspiration). "Whoopie, another Internet angle," mused Dave Meltzer of *The Wrestling Observer.* "Nobody in the building had a clue or cared."

452

In a show-closing angle, Jarrett then walloped Dallas' real-life wife - Kimberly Page - with a guitar, causing a legitimate concussion and complete chaos backstage.

Meanwhile, watching at home, Kevin Sullivan turned off the TV set, never to tune in again.

The 'new' Nitro was officially in the books, and now, only the numbers would show if the world had truly changed.

Chapter 47:
Arquette

"So I WAS supposed to come in," recalls former WCW publicist Jason Glast, "and tell Bischoff what the preliminary ratings were. It was a number that was the best I had seen in a long time, and so I thought he would be excited about it. But when I told him what it was, he didn't speak for about a minute.

"Then…he buried his head in his hands."

Despite the critical acclaim that accompanied the episode ("the best *Nitro* in recent memory…a major success," lauded *The Wrestling Observer*), *Raw* maintained its dominance in the Nielsen numbers, recording a 6.17 rating to *Nitro*'s 3.06. By any objective measure, the figure represented an excellent starting point; however, with the WWF chalking up its 74th consecutive head-to-head win - getting ever closer to WCW's own vaunted streak - Bischoff was feeling less than optimistic.

"Eric said, 'I've failed - this didn't work'," continues Glast. "He was devastated, and I think it was because he was used to - in years past - the numbers being so much higher. For us, it was still an improvement over where it had been, but it was probably a small number [to Bischoff], compared to what he was used to in their heyday."

There would be no time to wallow, however, as Tuesday meant taping the next edition of *Thunder*, this time airing from Colorado Springs. From the outset, it became clear that both Bischoff and Russo would maintain their televised presence, appearing throughout the program and even interfering in the final two matches. But it would be the appearance of the diminutive David Arquette – star of the WCW-themed *Ready to Rumble* movie - that would ultimately become a much greater story.

454

At *Spring Stampede*, the New Blood captured every major title, with Jeff Jarrett finally becoming the World Heavyweight Champion in the main event. In a shocking conclusion to the match, Kimberly Page viciously turned on her husband with the help of Jarrett's guitar, a plot twist with seemingly no prior build-up. Nonetheless, the pay-per-view card and preceding week of programming did enough to entice 115,000 viewers to purchase the pay-per-view, almost doubling the revenue of the previous month. While there was still much work to do - critics pointed to the fact that just 12 months earlier, the same event garnered 255,000 buys - Bischoff and Russo were building some momentum.

The positive trend continued with the April 17th edition of *Nitro*, a show concluding with a 'cliffhanger' ending involving Hogan and Hart. Two days later, with *Thunder* preempted on TBS, Hart praised the recent changes in an interview with *Pro Wrestling Radio*. "I think [Bischoff and Russo] both have very good creative minds," he said. "I think that Eric was always really creative, but he just got burned out. He came back and he seems almost...revamped, reborn.

"I think Vince Russo has a lot of imagination and a lot of great ideas. I never thought that [he] had...a clear opportunity to prove himself which I expressed to him two weeks ago, when I saw him for the first time. A lot of guys were really happy with the job he was doing. There was some questions about some of the content...but I was happy with what they were doing with me. For the first time in WCW, I was very positive. [Russo] got sacked earlier than a lot of us would have wanted, so I'm glad that he's back.

"I think Bischoff and Russo will work really well together. If anything, [the partnership] will lessen the load, [instead of] one person having to put so much thought into [the shows]."

Disappointingly, when the numbers came in, *Nitro* suffered another heavy loss to *Raw* - 6.7 to 2.5. Subsequently, it was decided that the next show feature a title change, traditionally a sure-fire way to drive additional interest. Therefore, in a hastily-put together cage match -

one originally scheduled for the next pay-per-view - DDP defeated Jarrett to end his title reign at just eight days.

In Syracuse the following night, word traveled backstage that *Nitro* had been obliterated by *Raw* again - 7.1 to 3.1. WCW was in town for *Thunder*, and according to the show format, Jarrett was scripted to regain the championship in a tag-team match involving Bischoff, DDP and David Arquette. However, as the pre-show production meeting dispersed, Russo's mind started to wander.

Russo looked to his right at Tony Schiavone. *What are you thinking?* he asked the announcer.

Nothing. What are you thinking? Schiavone replied.

You want David Arquette to win the world title? Russo joked, comedically putting words in Schiavone's mouth.

Well that's a thought, responded Schiavone. *Did anybody think of that?*

Immediately, Russo reformed the meeting, running the idea past "10 to 15" people, he claims, including Bischoff himself. According to Russo, his zany proposal met zero resistance, meaning that in a swerve no-one could see coming, David Arquette would become World Heavyweight champion.

"We were gonna do the predictable thing," Russo told *Wrestleline* a week later. "We were gonna do the tag match, and Jarrett was going to get the title back. [But] I said, 'wait a minute Eric, the whole idea of putting the belt on Page was to be unpredictable. Now we're gonna turn around tonight…and do exactly what everyone thinks we're gonna do - and that's put the belt back on Jarrett!' I said, 'we can't do that - we're predictable again!' So at the building, we came up with the David Arquette scenario.

"I went over to Jeff and said, 'Jeff, sit down. I gotta lay somethin' on ya'. You know, Jeff laughed, because he knows me. He knows how I write television, and he trusts me because he knows I was successful before. So Jeff really didn't have a problem with it."

Russo didn't find Page to be quite as receptive. "When they told me," Page remembers, "I started laughing. I said, 'yeah right, what's the finish?' They go, 'that's what we're gonna do'. I said, 'no, we're not'. I pleaded for at least 10 minutes. I argued, but sometimes...you realize that you're just a character on the fucking show, and you've just gotta move on. That said...I fucking sucked it up and did what I had to do.

"I walked downstairs and pulled David aside. When I told him, he burst out laughing and said, 'yeah right'. I said, 'no dude, they're really gonna do this tonight'. He said, 'no! No! We can't do that!' I said, 'guess what? Yes'. I said, 'If you don't wanna do it, say you don't wanna do it or...guess what dude? You're the world champ'. Then it fucking hit him like, 'are you fucking kidding me? Do I wanna be the WCW world champ? Fucking-a right I do!'"

With *Thunder* being taped, roughly 24 hours would elapse between the title change and its airing. In the interim, WCW released a press release on the company website, effectively spoiling the outcome in a last-ditch effort to recruit viewers. At 11:03pm EST, fans watching TBS witnessed Arquette and Page head to the ring for the tag-team contest. Less than 10 minutes later, Arquette pinned Bischoff to make - as Schiavone breathlessly exclaimed - *"sports entertainment history."*

The viewership figures for the episode would be less than historic, however. Although comparatively, *Thunder*'s 2.72 rating - when stacked up against the sub-2 performances earlier in 2000 - could have been deemed a success, a closer analysis revealed otherwise. In actuality, the segment featuring the title swap scored the *lowest* quarter hour of the night (2.25), suggesting that many viewers tuned in mostly for other segments on the show (or switched to TNT to watch a close Knicks-Raptors playoff game).

From a critical standpoint, the response was unequivocally catastrophic. "The darkest day in WCW history," read the headline at

IGN.com. "In *Ready To Rumble*," mused the subheading, "Arquette's character has a job working with garbage. That's where WCW may as well throw their belt after tonight."

"WCW just called collect on the wrestling business," wrote reporter Chris Sabga, "by perpetrating the single cheapest publicity stunt the business has ever seen. WCW has not only killed any meaning [that] their version of the 'World' title might have had left, [but] they destroyed any credibility the promotion may have had."

"It really [comes] across," observed Dave Meltzer of *The Wrestling Observer*, "as some people using the fact they run the company...[to use] the company and its fans to kiss up to someone for a Hollywood connection.

"It's sort of offensive...to recognize they aren't booking for fans, but booking so if/when this job explodes, maybe they'll have a friend who can get them a television connection."

"I think it's a joke," mused a disgusted Bret Hart, suddenly no longer impressed with the new regime. "I think that anyone who really had a passion for this business...or the profession...[sees it as] a joke. It's an insult to everybody who ever really busted their ass [for wrestling].

"I guess...that's the way wrestling is [now]. Vince McMahon was [WWF] World Champion too, at least for a couple of minutes. I think that if people find that to be entertaining, that's fine, but I wish they would quit calling it professional wrestling.

"I don't have any liking for the concept. It just makes me shake my head at the whole industry in general."

In an interview with *1Wrestling.com*, Jarrett brazenly defended the decision, drawing a parallel to a famous Memphis angle in the '80s. "I think some things repeat themselves," he said. "When we did the Andy Kaufman thing here in Memphis, it worked for my Dad's promotion. So 20 years ago, he was the champion, and everybody cried and moaned and said this was the craziest thing. We're all about creating controversy, good or bad. Old P.T. Barnum used to say, 'bad press is better than no press at all'. So in that aspect, I think it accomplished that."

"Putting the belt on David Arquette - stupidest thing ever," reflects DDP today. "I've never taken more shit from anything than that. Eric had just come back in, and I know he was just trying to work with Russo. I love Vince [now]...me and him are buddies again because we let shit go - there's no use holding on to it. But that was Vince's idea, and it was a bad one. *Really* bad. It is what it is. I had plenty of ideas that weren't great ideas. Not one as bad as that one though!"

"When we were in Florida," offers Kevin Sullivan, "Eddie Graham had two rules. One was that faces and heels couldn't be seen together. The second was if you lost a fight in any public place, you were fired. Guys that wanted to be wrestlers used to [get beaten up by the pros]. Guys used to leave with broken noses and broken faces. One time they beat [a hopeful] so bad, they stripped him of his clothes. I'm not condoning that, but David Arquette winning the world title? Boy, Scott Hall never won the title. Scott Hall never won the World Heavyweight championship, but David Arquette did. Can you tell me what's wrong?"

"This is the *world title*," stresses Robert Kellum, known for portraying 'The Maestro', a heel character on WCW television. "That's the goal of everyone - to be the number one guy in the business. It's like Dusty Rhodes telling Dallas Page, 'if you don't think you can be the world champion, you might as well leave the business'."

Facing unprecedented criticism, Russo reminded his critics of some history. "A lot of people seem to forget," he calmly stated to *Wrestleline*, "that when I started working for the WWF...the last rating they did was a 1.9. That's where they started. When I came in and I started sitting in on writing sessions and talking to Vince, the one thing I started hearing...over and over and over again was... 'you can't do this, you can't do that'. 'A babyface can't do this, a heel can't do that'. That's what I was hearing over and over again, until one day, I finally turned around to Vince and said, 'Vince - we are writing this.

We are creating this. We can do anything we want to do'.

"From that point on…anything that was 'traditional wrestling', anything that you kind of could call the outcome, we went the absolute other way. *Whether it made sense or not* - we went the other way.

"One of the first things that got the WWF over was the unpredictability of it, because things were starting to happen that you never in a million years thought would happen. So basically on a week to week basis, you had to tune in, [in order] to see what was happening. To me, David Arquette was one of those instances.

"A match was made, and within the confines of that match, there was a possibility of David Arquette winning the WCW title. Now the fact of the matter is, there ain't no way that's gonna happen. I mean, how could that ever happen? Well guess what? It did happen. And it didn't happen as a 'hotshot' angle, it happened for a couple of reasons.

"Number one, it is part of the big story. The David Arquette thing is going somewhere, and Eric and I knew that from day one. And also number two, it got people talking about WCW. Negative or positive, they were talking about WCW again, and that's what we need people to do. Nobody has mentioned this, but [before] *Nitro*, somebody hands me a *USA Today* and there it is. Right on the cover of the entertainment section, David Arquette [is shown] winning the WCW title, with a plug for *Nitro* tonight at 8:00pm. Well, that kind of exposure would have never happened [without the angle]."

According to the *USA Today* archives, the 'coverage' of Arquette's win consisted of little more than the following blurb:

Arquette displays neat mat finish (May 1, 2000)
David Arquette, star of the wrestling movie Ready to Rumble, captured the World Championship Wrestling heavyweight championship last week by pinning Eric Bischoff in a tag-team match. He defends the title tonight on TNT's WCW Monday Nitro Live! (8 ET/PT)."

"In my opinion, it was all negative," states Jason Glast of the coverage. "I did not believe that 'any publicity was good publicity'.

460

"David was in *Scream*…he was a mainstream media star…known for being married to Courtney Cox. But it's not the concept of 'wow, that's edgy, that's cool'. It seemed to me like they were just trying to promote this big budget film.

"What I didn't realize - and probably what Russo didn't count on - was it really just mocked the concept of 'ok, this is an *actual* champion. This is an actual professional who does this all the time'. It really was spitting in the face of people who gave the belt any credence whatsoever.

"Usually the champion was somebody who put in incredible time and had perfected their craft…they were physically impressive or they had charisma. It's not the same as an athletic contest…but every champion had *something*. Arquette was a meddling movie star, and I think maybe Russo and all of them got caught up with being impressed with him.

"Maybe they were too enthralled by him and decided, 'hey let's do this to get some publicity', but it made it more of a clown show, in the end."

Interestingly, Glast recalls, the performers themselves responded positively to Arquette. "He put his body on the line, and committed fully," he says. "I remember seeing Page and Arquette [after the match]. I remember they were being driven on the back of a golf cart, and their bodies were just beaten up. They were just beaten to hell. I actually kinda remember a lot of the guys backstage saluting Arquette. I think they gave him credit at the time for being a pretty physically small actor with no previous experience.

"To David's credit, he worked incredibly hard…suffered injuries and gave it his all. He really got into it, committed fully to being this persona, and the way that he did it…they gave him respect for his physical performance. That was my observation, but a lot of times with the wrestlers, what they did in front of your face may not be what they were thinking backstage. But my observation was that they gave the guy credit for really going all out."

After the show, Arquette purchased drinks for the entire road crew, trying hard to conceal his embarrassment. He was later seen recoiling upon learning - in a conversation with WCW staffer Kevin Eck - about the list of wrestlers yet to become champion. "He thought it was as ridiculous as everyone else did," Eck later wrote.

"Whenever I hear those guys who bust David's balls," growls DDP, "I tell them, 'David only made $10,000 off that pay-off, and he gave all of it to [Brian Pillman's widow]. He gave it all to her.

"That changes people's viewpoint on it. I tell people, 'if it was you, you wouldn't have done it, right?' I say, 'fuck you, you would have cut your buddies throat to get that spot'. David was just one of the guys that got that spot.

"It *was* really stupid though!"

Chapter 48:
The BIG Surprise

As a commodity in wrestling, few skills could be as lucrative as *persuasiveness*, an art form unto itself when applied most potently. Certainly, it had always been necessary to influence others, but in the modern era especially, its function took on an entirely new purpose. Due to both technological and industry-specific changes, creative ideas faced scrutiny in a more reactive, interactive and harshly judgmental manner, invoking a necessity to control, essentially, the *narrative of the narrative*.

With his New York accent, measured delivery and rhetorical charm, Vince Russo could be utterly convincing in rationalizing key decisions. "He loved an audience," remembers WCW.com writer Chad Damiani. "If it was the Internet…if he could get five people in the hotel lobby…if he could send out carrier pigeons…[he would do it]."

Throughout his WCW tenure, Russo seemed to particularly value feedback from 'Internet fans', often testing and validating ideas against their comments. "To me," continues Damiani, "if wasn't as much that, 'oh, I'm recognizing this medium' - it was like, 'oh, I still can stay the center of attention. There's a place I can go to make sure fans are receiving my angle *exactly the way I want*."

Interestingly, it's a perception that Russo refutes today. "I was never on the Internet when I worked for [the WWF] or WCW," he says. "Those fans were going to watch no matter what - just like they do today. We were after the casual fans - the mass television audience."

In the case of the David Arquette storyline, the 'mass audience' was responding with a collective yawn. After all, for the 'mainstream publicity' to have any value, an increase in viewership would surely have been expected. Unfortunately, on May 1st - the first televised show since the stunt - *Nitro* dropped to a 2.5 rating, representing a 20% decrease week-to-week. Furthermore, *Raw* posted an unreal 7.4 in opposition, suggesting that while the wrestling audience was growing, new fans were flocking to the WWF - and not WCW.

To reassure concerned fans, Russo continually stressed there was a plan. "If we put the title on a David Arquette," he said, "it's obviously going somewhere. It's obviously part of a story that's going to make sense in the big picture. Again…[there's] a lot of negativity, but that's ok, because they are talking about WCW…and they have no idea of where the story is going.

"I don't know if [the fans] have lost faith in me, because from day one, I've said I'm a story teller."

Therein revealed a key distinction, conceptually speaking, between Russo and those that came before him. Shunning the term 'booker', he instead insisted he was a 'writer', suggesting the former to be an antiquated, antithetical way of producing television. *Bookers start with the matches first*, he would say, *and then work their way backwards. Writers let the story dictate the matches.*

"I'm a writer," Russo clarified, shortly after the Arquette match. "I write stories. I did it at the WWF, and I'm doing it here. I'm not the guy that puts the WCW title up on a pedestal, like Bret Hart does…I've never done that. I'm an entertainment writer - that's what I do.

"Give me the benefit of the doubt and at least…let's see where this thing is going - because obviously it's going somewhere."

"If you listen to interviews with Russo," observes Chad Damiani, "it's always, 'they didn't get it', or it's like, 'if only they let me keep going on this idea…'

"So much of it was like, 'if only they knew exactly what I wanted them to know, we'd make a billion dollars. I think going on *WCW Live* - [while] he had a good relationship with Jeremy and Bob…a lot of

464

that was just like, 'I need to control every element of this angle. I need to talk this through so fans know exactly what to think...and I'm gonna use every medium possible'. In that way, I guess he saw the Internet as valuable, but he didn't consider what might come back at him."

Initially, Russo entered WCW with significant credibility, attained via his consistent, resounding success in the WWF. In many ways, he previously operated in a *supportive* creative environment, benefiting from McMahon's oversight and the incisive genius of Pat Patterson, regarded preeminently as wrestling's greatest 'finish man'. Consequently, when combined with the involvement of other company veterans, Russo's ideas were *filtered*, a notion he despised emphatically.

Now in WCW, however, Russo swam in treacherous waters alone, unable to rely on McMahon, Patterson or - after a falling out in January - Ed Ferrara, his former writing partner still on payroll. Theoretically, while acting in his role as creative consultant, Bischoff figured to monitor matters closely. But according to Russo, his input consisted mostly of 'red-lining' the script, typically done without specifying improvements. "Vince is doing 90 percent of the work," acknowledged Bischoff on *WCW Live*. "My role is broader - a longer term view of where we're going. The best thing I can do for the company right now is let Vince do what he does best."

In hindsight, Bischoff identifies his amenability to Russo as being calamitous. "Despite my legacy...that's been perpetrated by people that make living off perpetrating bullshit," he begins, "I'm pretty open-minded. I wanted it to work. I wanted to compromise. I no longer wanted to be the guy who was ultimately making the final decision. I was perfectly willing and excited to collaborate with somebody who could make the product better and as a result, make my life easier. So there was no unwillingness on my part, but it didn't take me very long to realize there was nothing under the creative hood.

"There was a lot of talk...there was a lot of bluster... there was a lot of, 'I did this in the WWF, I did that...I was responsible for Stone

Cold Steve Austin'. There was a lot of that. But when it came down to sitting down in a room and saying, 'ok what should we do?'…the ideas were very juvenile. They were dark. They had no logic. Most of it was nonsensical, which is why - by the way - they brought me back! Brad Siegel did not want to risk his political capital bringing me back unless he absolutely had to. Even Brad realized, in short order…*everybody* realized that Vince was basically nothing but bullshit. There was nothing under the hood, [and] that's when Brad called me back.

"I came in wanting it to work, for the reasons that I said before. I was making the same amount of money that I had before when I had all the headaches, and actually…I was making more. I had much more freedom - personal and creative. So I came into it with a pretty open mind, and I wanted it to work…but it didn't take long before I realized that, 'this is just smoke and mirrors'. And not even good smoke and good mirrors. It was *bad* smoke and *bad* mirrors."

Still, the fact remained that for Arquette to win the belt, Bischoff had to approve it. As a result, the backlash had become overwhelming, and *Ready to Rumble* - the movie WCW hoped would benefit from the decision - soon bombed disastrously at the box office (losing nearly $12 million overall).

In a mostly disenchanted review, Roger Ebert noted - rather ironically, considering WCW's creative direction - that as *Rumble* deviated away from wrestling, the less interesting it became. "The movie is best," wrote Ebert, "when it deals with professional wrestling, and worst - which is most of the time - when it prefers a wheezy [prefabricated] plot to the possibilities of its subject."

Nevertheless, on *Nitro* and *Thunder*, the weekly plots continued to convolute. On occasion, some of the in-ring occurrences now called for *actors* to be involved, even during scenes seemingly best suited for wrestlers. "I played a police officer in a scene where 'Kronik' became too unruly in the ring," remembers Michael Leslie Miller, an actor of some 15 years' experience. "We were [instructed to] mace, beat, and handcuff these out-of-control wrestlers, and escort them into a waiting police car.

"We were told to 'be careful', though, 'because the mace is real - aim for the chin, not the eyes'." Somebody said, 'excuse me, did you say this is real mace? Why are you using real mace instead of water?'

"[The reply was], 'because we're paying you to go out there and mace them, not spray them with water'.

"As we lined up in the holding area to take our places, we met the two wrestlers that we would be subduing. One of them had some last-minute instructions for us: 'If I get any fucking mace in my eyes, I'm coming back to beat the living shit out of whoever sprayed me'.

"I didn't know what was going on until I watched the video later that night, but a fellow actor tried his best to stay out of the way, successfully huddling into a corner for most of the fight. But one of the KroniK guys hunted him down, picked him up, and tossed him out of the ring like a rag doll. A look of genuine terror came over him, as he grasped desperately for the top rope to break his fall. He caught it with one arm, which caused his legs to flip over his head and crash outside of the ring, while his upper body bounced from the top rope to the second, and finally to the ground.

"Then it was our turn. We got out our clubs and mace, but weren't really prepared for the fight that they gave us. I hit one of the wrestlers two or three times in the back with my club, but I couldn't bring myself to throw a real hit, despite the warnings from the fight coordinator. All of the sudden, I heard one of the KroniK guys saying, 'oh, shit! Who maced me in my fucking face? I can't see a fucking thing! I'm gonna kill you when we get outta here!'

Humorously before the show, Miller also found himself mistaken for WCW's current world champion. "Everywhere I walked, people would stop and look at me...then slowly go back to what they were doing," he says. "It was a little surreal. I had seen David Arquette in Scream, and on some campy AT&T commercials, but the main thing I knew about him was that I apparently looked like his identical twin.

467

Ever since he had married Courtney Cox - who was also from Birmingham - I couldn't go out in public without somebody pointing out how much I looked like him, especially when I was sporting a goatee.

"When I got to Hair and Makeup, the makeup artist suddenly perked up, looked closely at my face, and then returned to her normal, half-comatose state. 'I got excited for a minute', she said. 'I thought you were David Arquette'."

Miller watched the room fill up with wrestlers, and then took his spot against a wall, waiting patiently with the other extras. "A guy came in who looked nothing like a wrestler," he says, "although his outfit made clear he was part of the WCW extravaganza. He was shorter than I was and didn't seem to have much of a wrestler's build, but he was dressed in a bright, garish outfit, a large-brimmed hat, and dark sunglasses.

"I assumed he was the ring announcer, or some kind of promoter. He seemed shy though, and stood along the wall with me and the other extras, rather than in the center of the room with the larger-than-life wrestlers. It seemed [that] we were both a bit intimidated by the testosterone in the room, so the 'announcer' and I stood peacefully next to each other for about five minutes, just watching the action. I wanted to talk to him, and he seemed like he would have welcomed some conversation, but I couldn't think of anything to break the silence.

"Well, I discovered - [upon watching] the replay - that the 'ring announcer' was actually my doppelganger - David Arquette!"

Six days later, Arquette's small stature was on full display, as he defended his title in a 'triple-threat, triple-cage' match at *Slamboree*. Although DDP and Jarrett handled most of the action - a miracle in itself, given Page suffering a serious back injury during rehearsals - Arquette took center stage at the end. In a supposedly shocking swerve, he turned on Page to gift Jarrett the championship, revealing his involvement to be a contemptible ruse.

Ultimately, in step with the movie, *Slamboree* was a financial letdown, attracting only a 0.14 buy rate on pay-per-view (the second lowest mark ever). On *Nitro* the next night, Bischoff boldly attempted to explain the storyline, claiming that contrary to visible evidence, the New Blood had recruited Arquette all along. *"Page,"* Bischoff beamed. *"We wanted you to buy it hook, line and sinker. Just like all these morons in the arena, and all the Internet wrestling experts, who thought it was such as disgrace to put the WCW World Heavyweight title on Mr. David Arquette…*

"I did it for one reason only - to screw you royally!"

Within a week, the title changed hands yet again, with Ric Flair surprising Jeff Jarrett on the May 15th *Nitro*. By now, the Arquette experiment was through, and Bischoff was promising a monumental announcement. In storyline, he missed an episode of *Thunder* - purportedly to conduct some "business in California" - before doubling down on the hype two weeks later. "We had a business meeting," Bischoff told Tony Schiavone on camera. "We had it in Los Angeles, California. There were attorneys present, there were notaries present…there were attorneys for the attorneys and attorneys for the notaries. The fact is, the deal is done. At 11 o'clock this morning, it was signed, it was sealed, it was delivered. One of the largest law firms in Los Angeles have reviewed all the documents to make absolutely certain that there can be no injunctions filed. Nothing can happen that could possibly stop what's going to happen at the Great American Bash on June 11th…*nothing.*

"We are going to change the landscape. We are going to change the face of sports entertainment and wrestling as you and everybody else knows it…and there's not a thing that you…there's not a thing that Vince McMahon…there's not a thing that *anybody* is going to be able to do to stop it."

Almost immediately, the Internet caught fire with speculation, going into overdrive after a *MultiChannel News* report on June 4th:

Hoping to pump some life into its fading World Championship Wrestling unit, Turner Broadcasting System Inc. executives met recently with live-event promoters SFX Entertainment Inc.

Turner Sports spokesman Greg Hughes said executives discussed "promotional opportunities" with SFX.

But one source familiar with the May 25 meeting said SFX appeared to be interested in acquiring a stake in WCW, as executives requested detailed financial information about the company, including a three-year WCW cash-flow statement, a list of WCW employees and titles and information regarding pending WCW litigation.

But almost obscured in the conjecture concerning SFX, the report highlighted the extent of WCW's financial condition:

The talks come as WCW ratings and pay-per-view buy-rates are at an all-time low, despite several management changes. WCW projected that it will post a $61.2 million loss this year, a source said.

WCW has also been a drain on parent company Time Warner Inc.'s earnings. Revenue gains for Turner cable networks were offset by higher programming costs and lower results at WCW, Time Warner said in its first-quarter earnings report.

As ever, Dick Cheatham questions the veracity of such reported losses. "Even when the WCW books showed earnings," he says, "I would question what I was looking at. But at this point, I was no longer associated with [WCW] - I left in '99."

"They wanted to dump as many losses - from as many other divisions - as they possibly could," says Bischoff. "WCW was a very convenient place to do that. WCW wasn't a line item - it was listed under 'other' - so it was easy to reallocate money, without anybody paying too close attention to it.

"I strongly suspect that's probably what happened. That's not to say WCW wasn't losing money - it *was* losing money - but it's doubtful that it was losing [that much]."

Nonetheless, as the impending revelation - now colloquially referred to as 'the Big Surprise' - dawned on WCW and its fans, rumors continued to abound. On Tuesday, June 6th, WCW.com issued the following clarifying statement:

One thing is for certain: Whatever IT is will take place on June 11 at the Great American Bash Pay-Per-View...

...Thus far, no one has the facts on the meetings. Rumors have circulated regarding the possible merger of WCW with another entertainment group, major superstars from another organization jumping to WCW and the debut of a star professional basketball player to the ranks. Thus far, all are just that-rumors! However, if there is ONE clue they have both given us, it's that the meetings have taken place in CALIFORNIA!

...If the hype regarding this announcement is a measure of the truth -- then the WCW, WWF, ECW and every company associated with sports-entertainment will completely change on June 11!

A day later, Bischoff appeared on *WCW Live* to eliminate one scenario, referring to the SFX report as erroneous. "I think it's a smokescreen," he said. "[It's an] opinion from people that don't know what they're talking about. I have friends from SFX [but] a buyout of WCW is not likely.

"WCW is a part of Turner, and isn't going anywhere."

Mike Weber, WCW's Director of Marketing for seven years, moved to take a position with Pace Motorsports - a division of SFX - in the summer of 1999. Therefore, Weber says, he was erroneously credited as having sparked the initial discussions. "I was not involved in it," he recalls. "It would have been an easy assumption though, because of my relationship on both ends. But at that time, SFX was going crazy, buying everything out there...in order to build a conglomerate of sports content, contractual relationships with venues, and sports agents. They were building themselves up to be sold, and ended up selling the whole thing to *Clear Channel* radio. So did SFX have conversations about purchasing WCW? I'd be shocked if they didn't."

In the meantime, Bischoff's creative partner was involving himself like never before. Citing tremendous stress over the ratings, Russo decided to suit up as a wrestler, facing (and defeating) Ric Flair on *Nitro*. Despite prior rehearsals at the Power Plant, however, Russo failed to tuck his chin on a rudimentary maneuver - Flair's Russian leg sweep - and bounced his head violently off the canvas. It would be the first of many concussions for the writer, but he persisted valiantly to complete the match, pinning Flair after enduring his figure-four leg lock for 72 seconds (the result of a production gaffe stifling the release of supposedly incapacitating 'blood' from the rafters).

In terms of a production element, the use of suspended 'blood' was as atypical as possible - notwithstanding an occurrence earlier in the night. "We were getting ready for the show," remembers Production VP David Crockett, "and Eric comes up to me. We were opening up the Philips Arena [that night]. He said, 'David, I've got something for you to do'.

"He has this bag with him - this plastic bag...quart size or maybe a little bit bigger. He said, 'this is [a former WCW referee]. He passed away from cancer, his wife is here, and his dying wish was to be part of *Monday Nitro* [again].

"I said, you *are* kidding me, aren't you?'

"He said, 'no - figure out a way'.

"So I went to my pyro technician. We had these flame projectors and these 'mortar shells'...these things that go off with big explosions. I said, 'what do you think about this?'

"He poured a little bit in each one.

"I just sort of walked towards the back. I wasn't gonna stand out there for the open!

"But...we did it."

Also on the show, Bill Goldberg made a long-awaited return to action, dispatching of Tank Abbott in just two minutes. He was still in the final phases of recovery from injury, but figured to have "some type of role" - based on Russo's verbiage on *WCW Live* - as part of the heavily-hyped *Great American Bash* pay-per-view.

As the *Bash* drew to a close, Goldberg made a dramatic entrance during its main event - Kevin Nash vs. Jeff Jarrett for the WCW title. At first, he looked ready to spear Jarrett, but inexplicably, he then took out Nash instead, gifting 'the Chosen One' a *surprise* victory. *"SURPRISE!"* yelled Mark Madden on commentary, shortly before the camera zoomed in on a crowd sign - *'Goldberg Is New Blood'*.

"And thus," opined *DDTDigest.com* sardonically, "the landscape of sports entertainment is changed for good."

And thus, for the third-straight pay-per-view, WCW provided its fans with a show-closing heel turn. Each twist, inherently devoid of foreshadowing, created a compulsion to retrospectively explain its occurrence, while simultaneously - and logically - diluting the impact each time. "If Russo was managing the local Pizza Hut," writer R.D. Reynolds memorably observed, "you'd order a pizza and they'd deliver a newspaper. Sure, it was a surprise, but it didn't make much sense, nor did you want to order from them again. But it sure fooled you, didn't it?"

Ultimately, the 'Big Surprise' - irrespective of its execution - generated a 0.19 buy rate, just 20,000 buys ahead of *Slamboree*. Therefore, while the *true* state of its books remained questionable, WCW was generating significantly less in a critical area of income.

Internally, staffers were told to expect more aggressive marketing for July's pay-per-view - *Bash at the Beach*. But regardless, something more pressing was going on at TBS. In the wake of the AOL deal (soon to receive shareholder approval), Ted Turner had been pushed aside from his namesake company - despite Jerry Levin's intimations otherwise - preventing his ability (among other things) to influence WCW or its affairs.

Levin once called Turner his best friend, but the 'Mouth of the South' had now been silenced. Apparently ostracized from the new company as well, Ted retreated to his 580,000-acre ranch in New Mexico, receiving a five-page fax shortly thereafter. "Ted Turner," read the fax, "will become Vice Chairman of AOL-Time Warner and will assume the additional title of Senior Advisor."

Ted understood the implication. "Vice Chairman is usually a title," he later told the *New Yorker*, "to give to somebody you can't figure out what else to do with."

Funnily enough, as his wife would later observe, Ted never did like surprises.

Chapter 49:
Oh, What A Night

IT WAS LATE, it was quiet, and Vince Russo lay awake in his basement. *Judge Judy* illuminated the room, but inside, Russo felt nothing but darkness. An insomnia that first gripped him in January was starting to become routine, and even more concerning, the lingering effects of post-concussion syndrome frequently drove him to tears. As the Judge berated another witness, Russo began sobbing, his existence antithetical to that of the brash New *Yawker* on WCW television.

He was getting close to breaking point. With the ratings failing to trend upward, his creative disagreements with Bischoff were becoming more frequent, a development many had predicted as inevitable. As Russo saw it, their disputes tended to arise *after* an angle failed to make an impact, a frustrating recurrence that was destroying their mutual accord. Following the latest flopped segment - this time involving a UFC-inspired cage known as the 'Asylum' - Russo picked up the phone to hear a disappointed Bischoff lodge yet another complaint.

The call ended, and in a fit of rage, Russo launched the phone across the room. His next call, he remembers, would be to Brad Siegel directly. *Let Eric run the ship*, Russo suggested, the 'Dream Team' apparently in tatters.

On Thursday, June 15th, Russo voiced his frustration at the WCW offices, reportedly expressing exasperation with Bischoff, the older talent, and the division he maintained was 'handcuffing' his creativity - Standards and Practices. Less than 24 hours later, and with the consent of Siegel, Russo began a leave of absence, delegating the responsibility of writing television to a group led by Terry Taylor. "The situation has [got] to the point," reported Ian Ross of IGN.com, "where Russo is taking a few days...to consider his future."

With Russo absent for *Nitro* on June 19th, the retired wrestler John Laurinaitis - a huge star in Japan throughout the 1990s - appeared backstage at the behest of Bischoff. His reputation preceded him as one of the premier 'finish men' in the industry, a status that suggested a unique ability to outline the conclusion of a match. 'Johnny Ace' was so talented in this area, Bischoff thought, that his theatrical finishes could almost resemble a three-act structure in their execution. It was a stark contrast to Russo, who according to Bischoff, struggled to comprehend what a three-act structure was.

Meanwhile, in Los Angeles for business but desperate for a reconciliation, Siegel summoned Bischoff and Russo for an urgent meeting. But their June 21st discussion ended in uncertainty, according to Russo, and with no clear plan for exactly how to proceed. With little change to his situation, the former WWF writer returned home, leaving Taylor and the committee in charge for another week of programming.

The second *Nitro* of the makeshift regime produced a stunning angle involving the newly-heel Bill Goldberg. Positioned against the affable fan favorite 'Hacksaw' Jim Duggan, Goldberg appeared to show no remorse in devastating his opponent - a recent cancer survivor - even causing Duggan to cough up copious amounts of post-match blood. In reality, however, Goldberg was fighting an equally tough inner conflict, feeling remorse for his actions after visiting with a sick child backstage.

In the background, the specter of WCW's next pay-per-view loomed - *Bash at the Beach*, traditionally one of the more lucrative events of the year. For the 2000 edition, Hollywood Hogan was once again set to take center stage, facing Jeff Jarrett in a main event clash for the World Heavyweight title. But with all the backstage movement, Hogan was notably absent from television, his match with Jarrett suddenly an afterthought. He maintained frequent contact with Bischoff, but their discussions failed to generate a suitable finish for the bout.

On the weekend leading up to July 4th, Bischoff flew to Wyoming to participate in a family gathering marking the holiday. He was soon informed that Russo was apparently back in the picture, and immediately touched base to review the pay-per-view arrangements. The conversation was cordial, Bischoff recalls, but the one point of contention centered on the marquee match. According to Bischoff, Russo claimed to have no vision for the outcome of Hogan vs. Jarrett, leading to the call wrapping up ambiguously.

Subsequently, Bischoff and Hogan agreed to maintain an open dialogue, with a view to settling the issue on Saturday evening - the night prior to the event itself. In a sad turn of events, however, Independence Day ended with news of a devastating personal loss. Bischoff's father passed away, and for his son, *Bash at the Beach* promptly took a backseat.

Meanwhile, back in the creative saddle, Russo held court over a booking meeting, allegedly asking the room a pointed question: *if we could put the belt on anyone, who would it be?*

The answer was unanimous. According to the committee, most deserving of the honor was Booker T, real name Booker Tio Huffman, a consummate professional and seven-year company veteran. At that precise moment, Russo claims, he decided that regardless of the scheduled card, Booker was to leave *Bash at the Beach* with the title.

In perhaps an audition of sorts, the former Harlem Heat standout immediately squared off with Jarrett on the July 5th *Thunder*, narrowly falling to the champion by pinfall. Particularly observant fans noticed Jarrett wearing a *replica* of the belt for the *Thunder* match, a curious occurrence given what was to come. On Thursday, July 6th, ring announcer David Penzer, a staffer whose responsibilities were gradually increasing over time, received instructions to ensure Booker traveled with a suit for the next *Nitro*.

On Friday, July 7th, standing in the parking lot of a Minneapolis funeral home, Bischoff attempted to finally rectify the main event conflict. He conversed with Russo before the service began, but still, there appeared no resolution in sight. Later in the day, Russo then contacted John Laurinaitis to relay a proposal to Hogan. The proposal detailed the match involving outside interference and a 'DQ' ending to keep Hogan strong, whilst ensuring that Jarrett remained as champion.

Invoking the 'creative control' clause in his contract (with specific language concerning "approval over the outcome of all wrestling matches in which he appears, wrestlers and performs, such approval not to be unreasonably withheld"), Hogan quickly shot down the idea. In response, Russo suggested an expanded scenario - effectively 'doubling the chaos', and conveying Hogan's superiority without booking a title change.

According to Russo, the updated suggestion was received positively. *He loves it*, Laurinaitis allegedly confirmed. But late Friday, in ostensibly a fervent change of heart, Hogan instructed his attorney to fax a letter to WCW's offices, reneging on the outcome after all. The communication failed to reach Russo, however, meaning that the parties traveled to the show with differing assumptions of the booking plans.

After taking care of his unfortunate family business - for the moment at least - Bischoff landed in Daytona at noon on Sunday. He immediately called Russo upon landing, asking clearly, he claims, for the pre-show production meeting to be postponed until he arrived. But when Bischoff entered the Ocean Center, the meeting was practically drawing to a close. "It was clear to me," Bischoff later reflected, "that Russo thought my preoccupation with my father's death [gave] him the chance to...take over everything that was going on."

In response, recalls Bischoff, Russo argued that the decision to start early was a matter of practicality - not malice - representing a genuine effort to get ahead of schedule. At that point, based on his own version of events, Bischoff approached Hogan to suggest an updated outcome: a DQ loss, as agreed to previously, followed by the star taking the belt to set up a subsequent tournament. In accordance with this scenario, a

478

new champion would be crowned at Halloween Havoc, shortly before prompting an impromptu challenge from Hogan – the 'real' champion. "I would feign confusion and try to calm Hulk down," Bischoff later wrote. "There'd be plenty of people and press around. We'd work everyone there, trying to make it look as if Hogan was quitting with the title. That would force WCW to have a tournament to decide the new champion."

According to Bischoff, Russo agreed unequivocally to the strategy, understanding plainly that the events were to lead to a 'champion vs. champion' showdown at *Havoc*.

Conversely, Russo recalls the disagreement persisting, ending in his suggestion - with Hogan and Bischoff present - that the writer "cut a scathing promo" on the star after the match. Subsequently, Russo then proposed booking a bout between Jarrett and Booker T, leading to Booker triumphing as the WCW champion.

It's a notion that Bischoff disputes to this day. "Vince Russo is one of the most delusional human beings I've ever come across," he says with disgust. "There are people that bullshit...and there are people that *believe* their own bullshit - he is the latter. He literally creates things in his mind, and he's very convincing, by the way. He'll talk about them in such a way that you would believe them to be true. He's that delusional. Pathological is probably a better term."

Ultimately, once the match unfolded, it resembled an amalgamation - as described memorably in *The Death of WCW* - of three prior angles. Drawing on the Montreal Screwjob, Fingerpoke of Doom and Halloween Havoc '99, Jarrett simply laid down for Hogan to score the pin (interestingly, as per his own conversation with Russo, Jarrett believed Hogan to be steadfast against doing the match).

Subsequently, in an effort to 'sell' the legitimacy of the angle, Bischoff and Hogan left the building - as planned - even engaging in an argument with production staff. "They got into a limo sitting at a loading dock, next to the television truck," remembers Jeff Bornstein. "Keith Mitchell ran out to Eric and said, 'do you want me to cut his

479

mic?'

"Eric said, 'I don't care if you cut his throat'. The limo took off."

After a short transitional segment, Russo returned to the ring alone. Unloading on Hogan, he took the microphone and ensured his promo was scathing indeed:

"Three weeks ago, I left WCW...and quite frankly, I didn't know if I was gonna come back. And the reason I didn't know if I was gonna come back or not is because from day one that I have been in WCW, I've done nothing - nothing but deal with the bullshit of the politics behind that curtain. The fact of the matter is...I've got a wife, I've got three kids at home, and I really don't need this shit. But let me tell you the reason why I did come back. I came back for every one of the guys in that locker that week in, week out, bust their ass for WCW.

"...And let me tell you who doesn't give a shit about this company, that god damned politician Hulk Hogan.

"Let me tell you people what happened out here in this ring tonight. All day long I'm playing politics with Hulk Hogan, because Hulk Hogan tonight wants to play his creative control card. And to Hulk Hogan, that meant that tonight in the middle of this ring, when he knew it was bullshit, he beats Jeff Jarrett. Well guess what, Hogan got his wish, Hogan got his belt and he went the hell home, and I promise everybody or else I'll go in the god damned grave, you will never see that piece of shit again!

"...Jeff Jarrett is still the official WCW champion, but he will defend that title in this ring tonight. And he will defend that title against the son of a bitch back there who...can't get a god damned break because of the Hulk Hogans!

"I'm talking about Booker T! Booker T and Jeff Jarrett are the two reasons why I'm in this damn stinkin' business to begin with! So tonight in this ring, for the WCW title, two deserving guys, Jarrett and Booker will compete for the WCW title...and tear this god damned

house down!

"And Hogan…you big bald son of a bitch, kiss my ass!"

Shockingly, in a hastily constructed main event, Booker T then pinned Jarrett to capture the WCW title, apparently contradicting plans to hold the aforementioned tournament. After the event, fans checking WCW.com were greeted with a surprising headline - *Oh, What A Night…*, it sheepishly read – while Hogan and Bischoff digested the news later. From their vantage point, it now looked as though Russo – having apparently *gone into business for himself* – had actually managed to double-cross them.

Moreover, in a detail agreed upon by all parties, Russo promised to call Hogan to discuss future plans. However, at the behest of Brad Siegel, he was advised to leave the issue alone, due to the ongoing expense of Hogan's contract. And so, literally overnight, Hogan was gone from WCW, eventually receiving a hefty financial settlement years later.

In the meantime, Russo was promulgating the idea that due to a disagreement with Hogan, Jarrett had been forced to lay down legitimately (conveying the notion even in discussions with coworkers, remembers Tony Schiavone, who was told the same in a private phone call). "I remember watching the video of Jarrett and Hogan's *Bash at the Beach* incident, says one former WCW employee, "when Vince Russo walked by and joined us. I asked Vince, 'was it real?' as we watched his tirade. He looked at me with a flash of anger and asked, "what do you think?"

"He walked out a minute later…and I still don't know if the setup was a work, or if it was truly a shoot."

Finally at his breaking point, Bischoff indicated to Siegel - in no uncertain terms - that he was done with Russo, ending an incredibly turbulent creative partnership. "I'm disappointed that I ever put myself in that position," he laments today. Likewise, Russo regards their differences as too significant to begin with. "Eric Bischoff and I are oil and water," he says. "That has been proven over the years. We are just two very different people who can't work together."

The preparations for another *Bash at the Beach* match seemed to illustrate the creative chaos at play. "They wanted to do a 'graveyard match'," recalls production coordinator Jason Piccolo, "and they came up with the idea late on Wednesday. The thing had to shoot on Saturday - the [week] before the pay-per-view - and they were gonna 'roll' it in, as if it were live.

"They had this huge wish list for the shoot. It had to be in a graveyard…it had to be at night…it had to have multiple cameras across the graveyard…they wanted to have helicopter coverage - all this crazy stuff.

"First of all, from a production standpoint, I have to get everything to a place to shoot - and that has to be a graveyard. I must have talked to at least 20 graveyards at the Metro Atlanta area. I spent all of that Thursday driving around, taking pictures and looking at [different sites]…and to this day, I still don't understand why this particular graveyard let us do it. It's in Decatur, Georgia - a historic graveyard. It's got graves dating back to colonial times, before the civil war. It's on the national register of historic places! So I don't understand why they let us in there - it doesn't make any sense to me.

"Anyway, we find this place, and I rent all the gear. WCW had all these deep pocket deals with their vendors - all of these handshake deals, meaning we had to use this [particular] generator company, we had to use this [particular] audio person for everything. Even though there were people closer - maybe people cheaper - it didn't matter. They had their people and they used their people. So we get all these trucks moving, and I hang up the phone on Friday like, 'this is great'. I just did this thing in two-and-a-half days - personal best, right?

"Then one of the writers - with quotes around it, 'cos I don't know what those guys really were - comes down and is like, 'cancel it! Cancel it all! Cancel it all!' I'm like, 'you can't cancel it. These truck [companies] have already charged our card, because it has to happen first thing tomorrow. They're rolling to the location to unpack. *We're paying them.*

"The writer said, 'no-one called Vampiro to get on a flight from Vancouver, so he can't get here 'til Sunday. We're just gonna do everything next week'.

"I think the whole bill for that shoot was about $75,000, *plus* $20,000 to cancel it."

On Monday, July 10th, the boards of AOL and Time Warner joined in Atlanta for their inaugural meeting. Already, the differences in culture - relative to each organization - were showing themselves to be a concern. Whereas Time Warner - led by Jerry Levin - tended to stick carefully to an agenda, considered thoughtfully upon a three-course lunch, AOL's meetings bordered on anarchy. Speakers drifted in and out of the discussion frequently, stopping intermittently to chomp on Pringles before launching non sequiturs with abandon. "It went on endlessly," Levin later observed of the first joint meeting, evidently losing his enthusiasm. "It was like a fraternity party with people shouting…not what I was used to."

Similarly, Vince Russo wasn't used to being ridiculed. An interoffice memo on July 31st made light of his efforts thus far:

Re: Top Ten Questions Not Asked of Vince Russo

10) Would you like to take this opportunity to claim credit for the return of Cake Day?
9) If the Possum is going to wrestle for us, what reoccurring Saturday Night Live character will he be ripping off?
8) How much did SFX front you for decreasing the value of the organization?
7) Are you going to let Bill hyphenate his name to Banks-Russo?
6) Can you funnel the unwanted talent to the Marketing Department? The New VP of Marketing has numerous openings with lots of opportunity for advancement.
5) When is Hulk coming back?
4) What does the "W" in WCW stand for?
3) How many "young and hungry" employees does it take to screw…up an entire

company?
2) "WCW Creative" -- is it a misnomer or simply a contradiction in terms?
1) Would you know an original idea if it jumped up and bit you on the ass, or would you just think it was the Possum?

A week later, the *Wrestling Observer* reported that after a confrontation with Russo, a prominent WCW employee was quitting:

Matt Williams, who is the Director of Research at WCW, is the latest to leave for another job in the Turner organization. Williams just finished a study of wrestling fans, which apparently went against much of the conventional wisdom within the organization of what people tune in to wrestling for.

The research showed that the reason fans aren't watching the show and the main complaint among those who still are, is the lack of emphasis on the wrestling and too much time devoted to soap opera and non-wrestling related antics on television.

As you can imagine, the results of the study buried [Russo], because it...concludes that the emphasis of those running things may be all wrong and it makes the jobs of the wrestlers' ability to perform more important than the creative end, which is something those in power don't want to hear.

"I reinstated the focus groups at WCW," confirms Williams. "Vince Russo was a nice enough guy, but he had just struck a big contract. He was very confident - very full of himself. Even though he was nice about getting the information, he didn't take it into consideration.

"I guess it's like so many producers in L.A.: 'I know my audience'. It's like, 'yeah, you know 'em so well, that you're gonna be off the air because of your ratings'.

"I don't blame him, because you don't have that job without a big ego. All my findings were taken in a very civil manner, and there was no yelling or [anything]."

According to Richard Steinberg, former Director of Corporate Intelligence for TBS, such rejection of objective data began long before Russo. "We spent a lot of time analyzing the content of various programs," he says of WCW-themed research during his tenure (1989-1995). "We looked at how much of it was 'selling' our pay-per-views, home videos, the 900-lines, [and so on].

484

"Jim Herd wanted Dusty Rhodes to attend a couple of meetings, but Dusty didn't want to attend at all...because nobody knew wrestling better than Dusty Rhodes did!

"He was forced to attend those focus groups, but he spent the whole time laughing about it, cutting jokes, and then walking out during the course of the analytics [section].

"I spent a large amount of time in Dusty's office, where he had these eight-and-a-half by eleven legal pads...stacked from the floor to the ceiling. I asked him what those were, and he said those were the various TV shows [planned out]. He would essentially create stuff on the fly, sometimes with absolutely no meaning or relevance whatsoever. He'd be sitting in a car or on an airplane, throw stuff down on the pad, and that would be the content."

"I know when we did the brand equity study," continues Williams, referencing research completed in 2000, "it was a big nationwide telephone study...500 respondents, or at least in that range. The big brand element that WCW owned was that viewers and fans - of both organizations - viewed WCW as the *pure wrestling organization*.

"WWF was a little more fluff, a little more entertainment. WCW skewed a little bit older, audience wise, because it was the older guys watching it...and having people like Ric Flair and Dusty Rhodes that they had grown up with...getting out there and *wrestling*.

"One thing that I don't think they appreciated was...they had a huge advantage over the WWF in the wrestling element. It's a wrestling show, so you might wanna have wrestling. They were trying to make it more like the WWF, and it's like, 'no. Leverage your strengths!'

"If you're gonna copy them, you're gonna have to be so much better at delivering what appeals to [their] audience. They already *own* that...and for you to mimic it, you're gonna have to do something extraordinary to 'uncement' them from that space, because nobody likes a copycat."

485

One former staffer with knowledge of WCW-related research echoes a similar perception. "My impression was that WCW kept backing itself into a corner of its own making," says the staffer. "They weren't taking into account the feedback that focus groups provided, ideas that weren't represented in the shows, or what it would take to win people back from *Raw*. You end up listening to the people who were going to watch no matter what, rather than the broader audience we should have been shooting for. It was a self-fulfilling death spiral."

"WCW started getting away from what they were known for," continues Williams, "and what they had the most equity in. Sometimes I would see stuff that was brought up in the research - just dumb stuff that they did. It was like a cardinal sin to hit a woman among wrestling viewers - don't put that on the air! I wrote that up in a report, and what happens two weeks later? I think a fairly big star backslaps a woman.

"I'm like, 'holy shit!' Did you not read that this is gonna turn a viewer off - hitting a woman? They would just do stuff like that without thinking."

Contrary to the report of his departure, however, Williams says he did not quit WCW specifically. "It wasn't that I quit," he says. "It was people higher up saying, 'we need him over here (TBS and TNT) now'.

"They were saying, '*WCW is going away*. It's done - so let's get him over here instead'.

———

Before WCW's *New Blood Rising* event on August 13th, Brad Siegel addressed the locker room backstage - a rare occurrence even during the best of times. Effective October 23rd, Siegel advised, *Thunder* (now written mostly by Ed Ferrara), would be taped on the same night as *Nitro* went out live. The decision - merely part of a series of financial cutbacks - meant that WCW could ill afford any unprofessional behavior. As such, Siegel announced that a strict fine system would be implemented, as to provide an incentive for showing up on time.

In the meantime, Siegel continued to focus on a myriad of off-camera incidents affecting WCW - particularly those embarrassing to its parent company. "Right out of the gate," says Buff Bagwell, "who was the first one in trouble? Me.

"The complaints were…I did not do a piss test right when they asked me. The other complaint was that I cussed, and pulled girls' bikinis off at our *Nitro* in South Padre Island, Texas. The third complaint was something kind of simple.

"So here's Buff Bagwell going to meet Brad Siegel. I got my best outfit on, and I'm going to meet the fuckin' boss. So I walk in, go to close the door…but he mashes a button…and *the door closes itself.* I went, 'oh, shit!'

"One of the three things, we got rid of instantly - it was no big deal. The second one was the piss test. I said, 'Brad. Y'all come and piss test us on *Nitro nights*'. I said, 'give me a break - do you know what we're fuckin' doing?'

"I [thought], do they know anything about drugs at all? I said, 'my god, cocaine is three-to-five days'. I said, 'my god, Brad, I'm trying to do a show for TNT…for TBS'. So that got swept under the rug.

"Then the third one, he flops onto his desk a newspaper, and I'm on the cover. I said, 'are you kidding me? That's great! Buff Bagwell's on the cover for something for WCW?'

"The situation was…there was a party going on at a beach, and they were trying to get it going. They sent their talent up there, and it was silence. Crickets. They sent their second round of talent up…crickets, crickets. They're comin' to me every time - 'please Marc, please'. I said, 'can I cuss?' They said, 'no, you can't cuss'. I said, 'no, I'm not doing it'.

487

"Finally, after an hour of getting tortured, they come to me and they go, 'do whatever the fuck you wanna do'. I swear to Jesus Christ - lord, my savior - I get up on the stage, grab the microphone, and I go, *'who wants to see some pussy?'*

"Instantly, the crowd goes nuts. All my bosses are laughing…all the cops on bicycles are clapping and laughing. I point at the first girl, direct her to come out there, and she steps out of her fuckin' bikini. I do that to like three girls, walk off the stage, and the crowd's going fucking nuts. I hand the microphone back like, 'there you go'.

"I said, 'how's that a bad time, Brad'?"

"He said, 'Time Warner doesn't think it's funny'."

"On that one thing, I lost $40,000. $40,000! I sat at home for a month - two pay periods - and didn't get paid. $40,000, brother!"

———

On August 16th, Russo proclaimed that regardless of WCW's fortunes, he was quitting wrestling at the end of his contract - October 2001. "10 months in this company has been [like] 10 years to me - it really has," he told *WCW Live*. "It has literally taken years off my life. But I would never quit…I would never stop chasing that dream…that vision. I've got less than 14 months left on my contract and when those 14 months are finished, I will be as far away from this business as I can possibly get for the rest of my life. And that is a promise."

When asked if there existed any scenario to change his mind - namely, the possibility that *Nitro* would someday topple *Raw* - Russo clarified his thoughts directly. "I am absolutely ruling out that I will stay with WCW, and I am absolutely positively ruling out that I would ever go back to the WWF.

"I am done…as a matter of fact, it's 60 weeks from today. So if you had me on every week, I could be on 60 more times. Look at it that way."

Such definitive rhetoric raised a rather obvious conundrum. "Hypothetical question," wrote PWTorch.com writer Tony Batalla. "In a long-term relationship, would you tell your significant other that [if they] will commit to you, you will put in as much time as it takes....never stop fighting for the dream...take it to the next level...but oh yeah, in 14 months, you're going to disappear and they'll never see you again?

"And in that 14 months...you'd like to play an experiment with one of your top money-makers?"

Batalla was referring to an upcoming angle involving Bill Goldberg, whose heel turn had long been abandoned. "I talked to Brad Siegel," ranted Russo during the same interview, "and whether you believe it's a work or a shoot - I really don't care - but I've had run-ins with Bill Goldberg. I think Goldberg is hurting this company. I think Bill Goldberg is very selfish. If I had my way, Bill Goldberg wouldn't be here.

"Brad Siegel sees things another way...first of all, he thinks the fans like Bill Goldberg, and second of all, Bill Goldberg has a [guaranteed] contract...we [can't] fire him unless he [breaches] his contract.

"So basically, what I'm going to do on Monday - for the first time in the history of this business - we are gonna break more rules, and on live television, I am gonna offer Bill Goldberg a release from WCW. If he signs a release, he'll leave WCW on his own, and then we'll be free and clear.

"[Alternatively], if he chooses to go to the WWF and kiss Vince McMahon's ass like everybody else, than all the better."

Ultimately, Russo offered Goldberg his 'release' to start *Nitro* on August 21st, flanked by Tank Abbott, the former UFC star-turned-comedy wrestler. "All of a sudden, we were breaking kayfabe," remembers WCW producer Jason Douglas, "and Russo's like, 'ok, I'm really gonna do this - this is a *shoot*. I'm really mad - I've got Tank Abbott with me. Well... 'everybody knows' that Tank is a tough guy, but the fans only recognized him as a comedy element with the group '3 Count'."

Later, Douglas remembers, Russo planned to introduce a new role for Abbott: *Tank Sinatra*. "It was communicated to me, I believe, by Craig Leathers," he says. "Craig said, 'we want you to do an infomercial for Tank…singing reworked Frank Sinatra songs.'

"We had Tank singing in front of a maroon backdrop, beautifully lit. Tank was a good sport…he sings along…we do all this work - I think we may [have] cut it together. But I was called into one of our lawyer's offices, and she told me very quickly, '*that* will never see the light of day. Stop what you're doing. I don't know whose idea this was, but the Sinatra group will sue if they even hear about what's going on'."

––––––

To truly make waves in the ratings, Russo argued, WCW needed a significant "publicity stunt," similar to how the WWF utilized Mike Tyson. "We did a huge publicity stunt to put WWF on the map," he asserted. "That was Mike Tyson. [WCW] needs that publicity stunt. I've given good ideas that would have everybody talking about WCW…[but] again, there is only so much I can do. We are going to draw a 2.5 every single week until the public knows that this is a new, different, exciting and cutting edge product."

According to WCW magazine editor Kevin Eck, Russo already had an idea in mind. "He pushed for the company to pay [O.J.] Simpson millions of dollars," wrote Eck years later, "to take a lie detector test, live on a WCW pay-per-view. [It] was based on the fact that Simpson said he would take a polygraph test on pay-per-view for $3 million, which would go toward a reward to catch the 'real' killer. Simpson later said he would keep the money for himself."

In summary, perhaps the most fascinating story in WCW was now the *Vince Russo story*, a fact not lost on the writer himself. "I have written my own [story]," he revealed on *WCW Live*. "Brad Siegel has that as well, and I told him that would be a great 'lead-in' from 8-9. It's the 'Larry Sanders' of sports entertainment. It's a pilot based on my life as a head writer, and what really goes on behind the scenes."

For certain, plenty was always happening behind-the-scenes. After producing a *Thunder* taping in Tucson, AZ, Russo joined a contingent of WCW officials on a red-eye flight back home. As they began to discuss the following episode of *Nitro* - an unopposed show billed as *Russo's Revenge* - one of Russo's colleagues spotted a familiar figure on board.

It was Eric Bischoff, headed for Atlanta.

Chapter 50:
Let Me Buy It

WITHIN A DAY, predictably, news of Bischoff's trip hit the Internet. "Eric Bischoff is meeting in Atlanta with Brad Siegel," reported Dave Meltzer. "This is apparently about something major."

On Thursday, August 31st, Bischoff confirmed the meeting, but denied it was connected - as had widely been speculated - to the prior rumors of a WCW sale. "I met with Brad to discuss projects I'm working on that may or may not involve WCW's participation in the future," he clarified to *1Wrestling.com*. "The meeting had nothing to do with a buyout of WCW."

In response - according to reports - Russo shared a theory of his own in a company office meeting. Since the start of their partnership, Russo claimed, Bischoff had been covertly working to acquire the company. The next major news item concerning Bischoff, however, related to an apparently unrelated business venture:

LOS ANGELES--(BUSINESS WIRE)--Sept. 7, 2000--Hollywood Partners.com Inc. (OTCBB:HLYP - news) announced that Eric Bischoff, a television and film producer and former president of WCW Wrestling, has joined its advisory board.

...Currently, Bischoff is dividing his time between Arizona and California where he is producing and developing projects for television and films. One of these projects involves reality-based "Road Rage," a television show he is currently in negotiations with one of the networks.

"Eric Bischoff is one of the best promoters in the country," said Gene Scher, Hollywood Partners' chief executive officer. "We look forward to working alongside Mr. Bischoff to maximize our promotional and marketing opportunities in the coming months."

"Hollywood Partners was at the tail end of the Internet bubble," remarks Gene Scher today, in reference to the promotions and marketing company. "I was introduced by a mutual friend, Jason

Hervey. WCW was not part of this.

"[It was a] short relationship. Eric was very nice to work with and I found him to be very bright."

Over the coming weeks, Russo then positioned himself as WCW's top heel, significantly increasing his on-screen involvement. First, as part of *Nitro* on September 4th, he featured heavily in a triple-cage match, beating up Sting and Goldberg with a baseball bat. Then, on the September 18th *Nitro*, he earned a World title shot after a fluke pin on Scott Steiner. Finally, seven days later at the Nassau Coliseum - Long Island - Russo entered a cage to challenge Booker T., the WCW champion, in a main event title match.

In his radio days, Russo visited the Coliseum as a fan - even organizing 'meet-and-greets' with the wrestlers - but on this night, he would script himself to take center stage. After a convoluted ending involving Bill Goldberg, Russo - the 'hometown hero' - shockingly defeated Booker to become WCW champion. "In the end," observes Jason Douglas, "it's like, 'who was really the mark?'"

According to WCW wrestler Lance Storm, Booker was under the assumption - based on instructions from Russo - that their match would end in a 'draw'; however, on *Thunder* two days later, the writer revealed a different reality. "*I left the cage before Booker T,*" boasted Russo in a purported shoot interview. "*Therefore - mystery over. I am the WCW champion!*"

At the same time, evidently, Russo plotted for another major storyline to dovetail his direction. In kayfabe, Stacy Keibler (eventually the real-life girlfriend of George Clooney) claimed she was pregnant, setting up a long drama in search of the father. The plot was soon abandoned, but not for a lack of foresight, divulged Russo. "Ric Flair was going to uncover the fact that I...was indeed...the father of Stacy's child," he later wrote on his website, *VinceRusso.org*.

"This bombshell would have turned David Flair against me. After being put in my place by David, he was finally going to forgive Stacy, and David and Stacy were finally going to get married. However, after

493

they were legally married, I was going to return with a second bombshell. That bombshell was that Stacy was the result of a one night Ric Flair fling some 21 years ago. In other words, it was going to be discovered that Stacy was Ric's actual daughter. So the situation was that David and Stacy, who were now married, were indeed step-brother and step-sister."

Viewers would never witness the Keibler story conclude, however, as Russo privately decided it was time to quit - for good. "I knew that October 2nd was my last show," he says, "and I was never coming back."

Russo's reasoning, according to numerous public statements since, revolved around the renewed reports of a WCW sale. "Here you had a company that was in complete turmoil, and nobody from the top was telling anybody anything," he later wrote. "It was at that point that I made the final decision to take my ball and go home, for good. Here I was, giving WCW my all, going out there and performing with a concussion, when all the chatter was about us being sold…that was my 'enough's enough'. It was time to go home and continue on like WCW never even existed in the first place."

And so, backstage before his last program, Russo watched as production personnel, company officials, and talent discussed the latest news:

Mandalay Sports Entertainment, run by former movie mogul Peter Guber, is in serious negotiations to buy Turner's World Championship Wrestling. A deal is expected by mid-October, insiders said.

…In light of the pending AOL acquisition of Time Warner, sources said [Time Warner] has been looking to dump money-losing companies before AOL executives move in. WCW has reportedly lost as much as $80 million in recent years after fickle audiences turned to the WWF.

The sale to Mandalay is being brokered by Eric Bischoff, who ran the WCW in its heyday…

…The scenario being circulated around the offices of Turner Sports is that Mandalay Sports would buy the rights to WCW but would agree to keep it on Turner's cable networks TBS Superstation and Turner Network Television.

Interestingly, a breaking news update on *PWTorch.com* uncovered an intriguing additional detail. 'Mandalay Corporation' was found to have registered the domain *WCWExtreme.com*, perhaps - insiders surmised - in anticipation of a deal being announced (in reality, Mandalay actually registered the domain 15 months earlier, on July 22nd, 1999, as part of its business producing WCW home videos).

Yet evidently, while Russo had been plotting for his title win, Bischoff and Siegel had remained in contact. *Let me buy it*, Bischoff implored to Siegel, confident he could solicit the requisite financing. *No thanks*, Siegel allegedly laughed, *that's not going to work. We will never sell this company, Eric.*

Within a few short weeks, however, Siegel's tune had changed, his talks with Bischoff becoming more substantive. "Everybody kind of looked at it," remembers TBS executive Joe Uva, "and said, 'hmmm. It might be worth more to us if we sell'."

An official announcement seemed only days away, and fittingly, in his favorite city of San Francisco, Russo orated a farewell speech on *Nitro*. *"Last week...I proved to the entire world...that at any given time, I could become the WCW champion. Now the fact of the matter is...I'm not an athlete, nor did I ever claim to be. As a matter of fact, there are many who say Vince Russo has no business being in the ring, and you know what? Maybe they're right. So tonight, being the man that I am...I am going to relinquish my WCW title."*

The next day, Russo announced that instead of joining his co-workers for an upcoming tour of Australia, he was staying in San Francisco instead. "The ratings - I don't give a damn," he said from his hotel room bed on *WCW Live*. "Mandalay - I don't give a damn. Hulk Hogan - I don't give a damn. Vince Russo losing his job next week - I don't give a damn. You think I care about Mandalay? You think I care about Eric Bischoff? I could give a damn. I've got Giant play-offs tomorrow. Nobody is going to rain on my parade tonight."

On Wednesday, October 4th, 2000, Russo visited Pacific Bell Park to watch an MLB play-off game. At one point during the action, he stopped to pose for a photograph, smiling care-free in the sunshine. The photo - since framed - still sits in his home on display.

"Vince quit on us," reflects one ex-WCW producer, speaking under the condition of anonymity. "Australia was the first time I thought, 'we're *really* getting sold now'. I always liked Vince, and I know he really cared about some of the production people. That was refreshing. But we were freaking out, stressing about our jobs, not knowing what was happening…and he just quit."

With Russo under contract for another year, a return to the WWF seemed implausible, particularly given his public assurances of quitting wrestling. But regardless, it suddenly seemed possible that he might have no choice. "Mandalay Sports Entertainment *and* World Wrestling Federation Entertainment are both talking to Turner Broadcasting System Inc.," reported *Multichannel News* on October 9th, "about possibly buying its beleaguered World Championship Wrestling organization…

"A deal could be reached as early as Oct. 17, after WCW executives return from a trip to Australia to produce several WCW cable shows…the source said the deal was contingent on TBS' continued distribution of WCW programming through its cable services."

Ironically, it appeared that the WWF's trademark lawsuit against WCW - quietly settled in July - may have provided the catalyst for such talks (an erroneous notion, says one close source). October 17th came and went, but according to *Multichannel*, the interest persisted:

Just when Mandalay thought it had Turner's World Championship Wrestling down for the three-count, Vince McMahon stepped in to break the hold.

Now Mr. McMahon has his archrivals on the mat as the World Wrestling Federation Entertainment chairman is in final negotiations to buy the once-threatening WCW from Ted Turner--thanks to a clause in a recently settled lawsuit between the two companies stipulating that the WWF gets a first-look and the option to match any offer should WCW be put on the auction block.

With Mandalay virtually locked in as the successor two weeks ago, Mr. McMahon

496

decided to pursue the clause, prompting Mandalay to back out of negotiations.

"When everybody returned to the States [from Australia]," Russo later wrote, "I told Brad Siegel that the…post-concussion syndrome combined with the stress I was suffering on the job was physically, mentally and emotionally killing me. I told him that while the crew was in Australia, I visited my neurologist and he advised me that it was time for me to take time off due to my condition.

"Guess what? I lied. I was bailing out on WCW because WCW had bailed out on me. By this time, it was a known fact to everyone in the company that the nameless and faceless brass were doing everything they could to sell the wrestling division. I was going to be damned to give the same effort I had been giving since the day they hired me, putting my health on the line with every situation, when those in charge couldn't care less about any of us or our families. Pardon my language here, but screw that. I had put everything I had into this company, even my own well-being, and at the end of the day, nobody cared. So I sat myself home in the comforts of my man-cave and waited for the inevitable to happen."

And so, after months of tendentious programming, the Vince Russo era was over. In total, it comprised of 35 *Nitro* episodes, 30 editions of the frequently preempted *Thunder*, and 9 pay-per-views. More specifically, his tenure could be divided into 3 sections:

- The **'Powers That Be' era** with writing partner Ed Ferrara (10/18/99-1/10/00;
- The **'Dream Team' era** with Eric Bischoff (4/10/00-6/14/00, plus Bash at the Beach 2000);
- The **'Blaze of Glory' era**, leading to Russo's eventual sign-off as WCW champion (7/10/00-10/2/00).

The Powers That Be era (10/18/99-1/10/00)
During this time, *Nitro* averaged a 3.21 rating over 13 episodes, a slight **decrease** in viewership - as compared to the preceding 13 shows (3.24).

Thunder averaged a 2.25 rating over 10 episodes, a slight **increase** from the prior 10 regularly scheduled shows (2.24).

3 Russo-produced pay-per-views averaged a buy rate of 0.43, slightly **up** from the

previous 3 events (0.41).

The Dream Team era (4/10/00-6/14/00, plus Bash at the Beach 2000)
Discounting Russo's mid-June-early July sabbatical, *Nitro* averaged a 2.9 rating during this era (10 shows total) - an **increase** from the preceding 10 episodes (2.76).

Thunder averaged a 2.61 rating for 9 episodes, **up** from a 2.21 rating during the prior 9 shows.

Pay-per-view buyrates fell to a 0.2 average, slightly **down** from the preceding 3 events (0.21).

The Blaze of Glory era (7/10/00-10/2/00)
Over 12 shows, *Nitro* averaged a 2.84 rating, the lowest of any Russo-led era. Two episodes (8/28/00 and 9/4/00) aired unopposed, *drawing a 4.2 and 3.6 rating respectively*.

Over 11 shows, *Thunder* averaged a 2.36 rating, down from the previous era (but up from Russo's first run).

The average buy rate for 2 pay-per-views was 0.17, the lowest of any Russo-led era.

Therefore, according to the evidence, Russo - paid an estimated $1,035,000 under his WCW deal (ultimately equivalent to $13,986.49 per show) - made a negligible impact on television ratings, particularly in reference to *Monday Nitro*. Furthermore, pay-per-view buyrates declined dramatically under his tenure, despite the frequent twists and turns accompanying each event. Year-to-year (October 1999-October 2000), monthly house show attendance fell from an average of 4,628 to 1,746, and incredibly, the World Heavyweight title changed 20 times.

For these reasons, among many others, Russo is considered one of the most controversial figures ever in wrestling. "Everybody used to bitch about Dusty Rhodes' booking," says Kevin Sullivan. "He 'made himself World Champion', right? I never heard anybody bitch about Russo becoming World Champion. David Arquette - in his first match - became the World Heavyweight Champion.

"I think [Russo and Ferrara] had a whole different mindset...that they were gonna take this television program, and use it as a pilot for a television show called 'Rope Opera', or something. They made it a

498

comedy, didn't they? Pouring spaghetti on the Italians, [for instance]...it was low-brow humor. Viagra-on-a-pole match. I'm not saying they're wrong, but it was completely against my ideals that I was raised with.

"Wrestling was supposed to be for wrestling fans. I always heard them say, 'people don't wanna see people wrestle for 15 minutes'. Well, I beg to differ. It used to sell out everywhere in the country, and Vince [McMahon] used to have three shows a night. It still said wrestling on the marquee - it didn't say 'Viagra on a pole'."

"I firmly believe [Russo] did the best with what he had," offers Bill Demott, aka Hugh Morrus. "Some it was good...some of it was off-the-wall...we were trying different things...but that was the time of the business we were in.

"I think he was the scapegoat for a lot of things. Vince takes a good beating on the Internet, and from people who feel like they're true wrestling fans. But Vince did his job. If you blame him, then you'd have to blame all the wrestlers who were on top, too.

"I think a lesser man would have fallen apart by now. It's however many years later, and he's still getting beat up by it."

"He had kind of an unenviable task," argues Dean 'Shark Boy' Roll, speaking of Russo. "In baseball, if you bring a guy in to pitch...and bases are loaded with no outs...you're trying to get three outs without anybody scoring. I think Vince walked in to a situation that was similar to that.

"The flip side to that is that he had this reputation, [in terms of] writing stuff for Steve Austin, and The Rock, and Mick Foley...the huge ratings and edgy storylines on *Raw*. He had a reputation for being the *ace relief pitcher*, if you will."

"We had [previously] lost the momentum," acknowledges 'Diamond' Dallas Page, in reference to the time before Russo's arrival. "So could you blame it on Vince? I don't think so. I think that Vince did a lot of things…desperately, trying to grab it back. I would never have wanted to be in his spot. He was in a *really* tough spot.

"[But] again, he wanted to do what they did in New York. He wanted all the young guys to beat all the old guys. Well, if the people don't believe it, it doesn't fucking matter…you can't take what Ric Flair or Hulk Hogan have done in our business - they will be gods forever.

"I was excited [at first]…we were both [basically] Jersey boys…we both used 'bro' every other word! But I wound up hating Russo…fucking *hating* him…but it's like, Sully - at times, I wanted to choke him out and kill him [too]. But I love Kevin Sullivan! He's one of the most charismatic…I love him. He's a sweetheart.

"Were there times I wanted to kill [Sullivan, for example] and he wanted to kill me? Absolutely. But most of 'the boys' let that shit go. Probably the inner voice inside did the most damage to all of us."

"I felt like I tried to give a lot of leeway with [Russo]," says Galen Chandler, the mythical 'Standards and Practices' liaison. "Then at the end, it just kind of got into a thing with Vince. I don't know for sure if he had a 'pay-or-play' contract, but my gut tells me he did.

"For all the calling foul to the Standards and Practices group - 'you're handcuffing me' and stuff like that - there are creative ways to do things. It doesn't always have to be something that crosses the line. That's the easy way, in my book."

"When Russo first got there, he brought a ton of energy," remembers former WCW publicist Jason Glast. "I think a lot of the wrestlers were really fired up and were hoping that he could put us on the right track. But then the storylines that he created were extremely underwhelming, and then when he made himself a centerpiece of it, that seemed like a little bit too 'inside baseball', so to speak.

"I then became a critic of the show - a show that I wanted to be successful. But each week, I would go back and watch it…I would read everything on the Internet…and while Russo was coming up with

500

his storylines…I just thought, 'I understand that you wanna appeal to the smart fans', but it seemed like he went *way* too far.

"His storylines would be either incredibly idiotic and simplistic, or they would be strictly pitched to the fan that would spend hours on the Internet, reading about the inner workings."

"While I dealt with thousands of people associated with the professional wrestling business," states Jerry Jarrett, "none is viewed with more disregard than Vince Russo. He claimed responsibility of the 'Attitude Era' at WWF. Anyone who has ever worked closely with Vince McMahon knows that Vince and Vince alone makes every programming decision."

———

Above all, in hindsight, the impact of Russo's quick demotion in January 2000 - just five weeks after moving his family to Atlanta - could not be overstated. In the years since, fans have often debated as to how different history could have been. "When Russo and Ed [Ferrara] came in," says Kevin Nash, "within three days, J.J. and Dusty and everybody else tried to cut their throats."

"I'm very proud of those [first] three months," says Russo. "We were tearing down the old foundation - which wasn't working at the time - and putting a new one in place. I was very happy with those first three months with Ed."

"The problem with Vince and Ed," offers Alan Sharp, "is that [TBS] never let them do…what they were hired to do. You hire these edgy guys to come up with these outrageous storylines…and then you tie a hand behind their back and say, 'ok - go!'"

For better or worse, Russo was never given the chance to build on that foundation. Subsequently, he fell into a spiral of chaos - both professionally and personally - that drowned him in a state of deep depression. Worryingly, Russo even confessed to understand, for the first time in his life, why some people commit suicide. "It was a horrible period…not only in my career, but in my life," he says earnestly.

Meanwhile, the WWF was on fire, enjoying a magnificent year 2000 - critically and commercially. WCW seemed like a non-entity, and if McMahon had his way, it would soon be stamped out forever.

Chapter 51:
Lenita, Lenita

In SEPTEMBER 2014, CBS Sports announced its intention to revolutionize one of TV's most tried-and-tested formats - the sports talk show - with the introduction of an exclusively female-driven program, *We Need To Talk*. "We've been discussing this and developing it for a long time," divisional president David Berson told the media. "I think the recent news [concerning domestic violence and NFL players]...has probably showcased the need for a show like this." Echoing his colleague's enthusiasm, chairman Sean McManus framed the initiative as being positively historic in a press release. "A sports show featuring all women is long overdue," he said.

Unbeknownst to the plethora of journalists covering the story, the concept - while certainly long overdue - could hardly be considered novel. In 1999, the same year as Brandi Chastain's bare-midriff-and-black-sports-bra celebration at the Women's World Cup Final, Lenita Erickson was looking to capitalize on the growing acceptance - and demand - for female participation in sports media.

"I created the first all-female, ESPN-type show," says Erickson, a former rock musician turned television producer. "I was the anchor, and I had [Olympic swimmer] Dara Torres, [NASCAR reporter] Jamie Little, Lauren Michelle Hill, the playboy model. It was just an exquisite cast.

"At the time, I was dating Gene Simmons. Gene was a very big supporter of my projects, and obviously, he can move mountains. So we pitched the idea across the board, to Fox Sports, ESPN, ABC Sports, NBC Sports, CBS Sports, MTV Sports...[and eventually], we ended up getting picked up by TNN. Within two months, [however], the EVP of Programming was replaced, and the new person wiped out all of his programming. We were shit out of luck."

Despite the evaporation of the TNN deal, Erickson had successfully established herself to the small community of power brokers in sports television. Boosted by her looks, charm, and affiliation with Simmons, she was now a known entity, *on the radar* of executives keen to capitalize on her vision. "George Greenberg, the Head of Fox Sports, said, 'you're on to something so huge, but you're ahead of the game'," Erickson remembers. "He said, 'we can't touch this'."

Meanwhile, in Los Angeles, Brad Siegel was preparing to meet with Leslie Grief, a noted producer in his own right and long-time business partner of Simmons (TNT would eventually premier Grief's series, 'Monday Night Mayhem', in January 2002). "Gene knew that Brad was going to be in L.A. for a meeting with Leslie Grief," remembers Erickson. "I had just come back from New York and a meeting with ABC. Gene said to me, '4:30 - you're walking in to the Havana Cigar lounge, and you're gonna meet Brad Siegel."

To Erickson's delight, Siegel was not only receptive to her presence, but also, expressed support for her brainchild. "He said, 'I love the concept', and I think he liked me, [too]. "He said, 'look, would you be interested in doing a sideshow for the wrestling?' I said, 'hell yeah!' I wanted a deal, y'know."

With Siegel's interest piqued, Erickson decided to propose another of her creations. "I had created this half-cyborg, half-human rock character that was...because I was in music...female à la KISS, but very glamorous and very electronic/heavy metal.

"Brad went crazy over it. He said, 'I can see this as a character in the wrestling arena'. I said, 'I don't wanna be a wrestler'. He said, 'no, you don't have to wrestle. We will make this character be like your alter-ego. Maybe your interviewing these tough wrestlers and you kind of taunt them, and then they get pissed and shove you...then all of a sudden, this alter-ego character comes out'. So that was the [original] plan."

Subsequent to their meeting, Erickson was signed to a WCW contract. According to an October 31, 2000 company memo, her contract called for compensation at a rate of $500 per event - in addition to receiving an annual salary of $125,000. "I negotiated this *hella* guaranteed contract," she confirms. "It was an amazing deal."

In the interim, Siegel and the new recruit had developed a strong working relationship, "throwing ideas back and forth" for other television projects. Concurrently, to get started with WCW, Siegel recommended that Erickson report to its training facility. "At that point, Brad was kinda like, 'I don't know, just go to the Power Plant, and we'll figure it out from there'," she recalls. "I show up and all the people there are like, 'you should apply to be a wrestler'. I said, 'no, I've got a contract - it's done'. I didn't know the relationship between Brad and WCW at the time."

Erickson's meeting with ABC in New York - conducted prior to her initial acquaintance with Siegel - provided an unlikely impetus for her next move. "John Filippelli - the Vice President of ABC Sports - stayed in contact with me over my show and was really trying to be a mentor," she says. "He found out I got the deal down at Turner. [Anyway], it turns out J.J. Dillon and John Filippelli go *way back*. John said, 'when you get down there, ask to meet with J.J., and tell them I sent you'. So while these women [in the Power Plant] are staring at me, like, 'who is this?', I said, 'well, in the meantime, while you're discussing my contract, can I see J.J. please?'"

"J.J. comes out of his office and he's staring at me, like, 'who are you?' I said, 'well, Brad just signed me to a big deal here, and Filippelli told me to ask for you'. He's like, 'come in my office'. He shuts the door, sits down and he goes, 'thank god - they brought you in to take over management, didn't they?'

"I just sat there, I swear to god. My wheels were spinning so fast, because all of a sudden, I realized [that] I just walked in to a hornet's nest without warning. I'm a good businesswoman though, so I looked at him and said, 'possibly. What have we got goin' on here?'

"He goes, 'for all the years Brad Siegel has been the head of Turner, no-one can contact him. So he brought you in. This is awesome!'

"I just went with it. I didn't tell Brad. I didn't say anything."

———

Admittedly, Erickson was a novice in the wrestling business. However, she could already draw some parallels from her day one interactions to the world she had left behind. "I knew nothing about the world of wrestling, except as soon as I got there, it was *exactly* like the world of rock-and-roll. It was such an easy understanding for me."

Erickson's ability to make contact with Siegel - an impossible task for most any WCW employee - made her increasingly attractive to Dillon. "[J.J. said], do you think you can get us a meeting? Let's go in and tell him we want to take over management [together]'. I said, 'yeah, I can get the meeting in a heartbeat, but who's *we*?' He said, 'well, Jerry Jarrett is up in Nashville running his development business, but he would consider coming in on this deal'.

"J.J. was like, 'you don't understand, Lenita. With the millennium [approaching], you could be the first female head of a federation. You could go up against Vince - it would be great TV. This can work'. So I said, 'sure, I'm in'."

Within four days, Erickson says, she was provided with WCW's confidential financial statements, encompassing its entire history under Turner. "I had 12 years of spreadsheets put in front of me," she remembers. "Here I am, in this situation, [thinking], 'I'm taking this company - that's what I'm gonna do'. If this is what they think I'm here for, and Brad didn't level with me...

"I had no idea I was walking into a contract for a company that he was trying to sell. He wanted it gone. I said, 'well, fuck you!'"

Meanwhile, Erickson continued to show up at the Power Plant, her plan still a well-kept secret. "I trained in the Power Plant, worked out, and [otherwise] did nothing. I mean, seriously. I hung out in (the affluent Atlanta district of) Buckhead...(laughs). I trained in the morning with Sarge, under Sarge, and that was it. The whole time I was training side-by-side with these guys, they didn't know what was happening on the other side.

"I traveled to *Nitro* and *Thunder* and was behind the scenes to watch what was going on. Not that I was assessing [things], in truth and honesty. It was because Brad had to sort of explain why I was there. [But] his reasons had nothing to do with my reasons. I know Kevin Nash made a couple comments, [like], 'oh, so is my job in your hands [now]'? I said, 'I don't know...'"

The plot would soon thicken further, as on the November 8th edition of *Thunder*, Erickson's name would be heard on a WCW broadcast. "*I'd like to welcome,*" announced Tony Schiavone, "*the newest member of our broadcast team, Lenita Erickson, who's standing by talking to Bob Sapp, the newest edition to the WCW roster.*"

"That was horrible, so...horrible," Erickson recalls of the segment, so organized as a measure to prevent questions about her contract. "There was absolutely no organization, and I didn't know anything about the wrestler I was interviewing. It was just awful. That was Brad saying, 'help me out here man'. The last thing I wanted was anyone thinking [my contract] was anything but business. At the same time, I couldn't tell anyone what the real business was, what J.J., Jerry and I turned it into. We couldn't breathe a word of that. So now I have some people thinking I'm Brad's bimbo, and I have Brad saying, 'help me out here - just *act* like you're interviewing a wrestler'. I was like, 'you have no idea what I'm really doing'."

With Jerry's son, Jeff, wrestling in a featured position on WCW television, his father made a series of late-night trips to Atlanta, Erickson says, in an effort to brainstorm ideas. "Nobody could know what we were doing, so we would have these covert hotel meetings where we were just drawing up the whole thing. They said, 'honestly, you can call Brad?' It was eleven-thirty at night. I said, 'I can call Brad on his cell right now - we're friends'. So I did. I said, 'Brad, I want a meeting with you - tomorrow'. He was like, 'for *what*?' I said to him, '*you son of a bitch. You did not tell me what you were doing*'. He said, 'what do you care, you're on a guaranteed contract?' I said, 'are you kidding? I'm a workaholic. I don't care that the money's guaranteed. I care that you've wasted my time and didn't level with me.

"So I said, 'here's the deal. We want the company'. He said, '*what the fuck are you talking about?*' He goes, 'what are you doing to me?' I said, 'nothing that you didn't just do to me'. I [reiterated], 'listen, I'm not kidding you - we wanna take over the company'.

"Brad then leveled with me. He said, 'it's for sale. Vince [McMahon] wants it, but Viacom wouldn't allow it'."

In late November, McMahon would himself disclose the role of Viacom - parent company of *TNN* (itself home to *Monday Night Raw*) - in a *Pro Wrestling Torch* interview:

At the last minute, there was a snag with Viacom. Originally Viacom gave us the green light and indicated to us that the price to us in essence would not be severe. So we began negotiations in earnest and good faith with the Turner people and had really good negotiations and I have a good appreciation for that. Then unfortunately, at the last minute - out of the clear blue [sky] - Viacom's price became astronomical, and from there everything broke down because it didn't make any sense for us to pursue that kind of give-back, if you will, to Viacom.

"I said, 'we want a chance'," continues Erickson. "He said, 'who are *we*'? I said, 'we're gonna come in to your office tomorrow, and I'll present the case'. He said, 'I can't believe this. You've got 45 minutes - that's all you're gonna get!'

"J.J. and Jerry are just looking at me going, 'I can't believe this. We actually get to go sit in front of him and present this'. So the three of us go in, and then [Brad] sees J.J. and Jerry. Brad's just like, 'you gotta be shittin' me with this'.

"[But] we had all of the I's dotted, all of the T's crossed. It was an unbelievable presentation. What he said would be 45 minutes went almost two hours in the office.

"[In our vision for WCW], everybody had to be on incentive-based

508

contracts. You cannot just do a blanket contract without incentives. That was a really big thing, because in their finances, obviously, there were troubles with some guaranteed contracts [constructed] with no incentive clauses.

"Jerry and J.J., being what they are in the wrestling industry, wanted to bring back the original [foundational elements of wrestling]. But our pitch was really about putting more control on the wrestlers' performances. We walked out of there feeling really confident.

"Brad called me up about a half hour later and goes, 'I gotta hand it to you - that was a helluva presentation'. He goes, 'I don't know what the hell you think you're doing, but I commend you - you got balls, man!' I said, 'lookit, Eric Bischoff captured lightning in a bottle by doing that $6 million deal with Hulk with no standards, no anything on it'. He sold the farm to capture lightning in a bottle. I go, 'this is your guy?'

"I remember sitting with Bischoff in the office at CAA in Beverly Hills. I just remember him saying, 'well, I already know you're just this amazing woman'. I looked at him and I said, 'how do you know that? You've been sitting across from me for five minutes'. It kinda dumbfounded him. He said, 'well, Gene Simmons said you were amazing'. I said, 'ok, so someone told you I was amazing. That's cool'.

"Brad knew it all. He just said, 'Lenita, you're barking up the wrong tree - I want the company gone. It's going to be sold'. I said, 'then let us buy it! Give us the chance to buy it!' He was just like, 'just quit!' I said, 'no. Let us buy it!'

"At that time, it was going to be the three of us, and [on television], I would run the federation as a female against Vince. That was the whole plan."

As 2000 came to a close, WCW's books showed an inconceivable loss of $62.5 million. Under Turner Broadcasting, it remained a Time Warner entity - for now - but shortly, pending federal approval of the merger, it would become part of AOL-Time Warner Inc.

Behind closed doors, however, Time Warner officials were panicking. AOL's stock, severely damaged after a slowdown in online advertising, had fallen 50 percent in 10 months. There was still time to back out – an apparent 'drop-dead date' of May 31st, 2001 offered a plausible escape route - but Jerry Levin remained resolute. As for the deal, it was too late to change its terms (specifically, that which concerned AOL's shareholders receiving 55 percent of the new company), but similarly, too early to see its consequences.

"When they *announced* the AOL-Time Warner merger," reflects a whimsical former employee - one of thousands ultimately laid off - "AOL was worth more than Time Warner. When the merger *actually happened*, that was no longer the case.

"There was this notion that the AOL merger was going to turn Time Warner into a media company that had never existed before. Their foresight was good, but it was just about 10 years too early.

"There was just no real effort to figure out how to make these companies work together…and how we were going to leverage each other's abilities. Nobody knew how to deal with each other.

"That leads to, 'well…we've got to cut costs'…"

510

Chapter 52:
Fusient

ON THURSDAY, JANUARY 11th, 2001, federal regulators officially approved the AOL-Time Warner merger. In preparation of the merger announcement, Turner Broadcasting had been looking to trim costs, first moving to restructure the operations of Ted Turner's 'baby' - CNN - and incredibly, confirming the sale of its 'red-headed stepchild', WCW. "[AOL-TW] executives have promised Wall Street huge growth in revenue this year," reported the *New York Times*. "[It's] a serious challenge that has grown exponentially with a slowdown in advertising sales in general...CNN and WCW are obvious places to look for savings and efficiencies."

"By then, a lot of people had left TBS," remembers Joe Uva, "in terms of the people who were running it day-to-day. Ted - for all intents and purposes - had been relegated to a Vice Chairman role. Terry McGuirk and Steve Heyer had left. Harvey Schiller had gone on to the YES network. Bill Burke had left...so it was a complete change."

And so, mere hours before the merger was complete, Eric Bischoff - flanked by Brad Siegel and Brian Bedol, a former Time Warner executive – suddenly stepped back into WCW's Smyrna, GA offices. Evidently, staffers soon learned, an investment group named *Fusient Media Ventures* had purchased the operation, with TBS, Inc. maintaining a minority interest and long-term programming rights.

"On the day of the 'big announcement'," remembers Lenita Erickson, "Brad [Siegel] called me up. He goes, "I'm gonna have to pass. Bischoff is gonna get the company'. I started laughing. I said, 'Brad, you mark my words. You mark this day, this time. It's not gonna happen'. He said, 'alright, Lenita - I gotta go'."

In the meantime, TBS appeared to be divesting itself - *operationally* -

from World Championship Wrestling. "Our company - Turner/Time Warner/AOL," said Siegel in an afternoon press conference, "is a very different business than the WWF. That is their business exclusively, [while] wrestling is not our exclusive business. As our company continues to grow and evolve, we realized that wrestling was not a core business for us.

"We felt that it was a critical or important programming asset, but not a core business. We felt that this business can continue to grow and flourish and it was best operated out of the confines of Turner/Time-Warner. I don't think it's throwing in the towel at all. It's an evolution and a next phase, and a smart one. We are still very much in this business, just choosing to evolve it."

Candidly, Siegel admitted that his attempt to manage WCW had been difficult. "I had been running the networks TBS and TNT and Turner South and Turner Classics," he said. "This was a different business than we had been in. Until you come in and sit in the seat, you never know the details and nuances. It was different - that's all I want to say about it. Now I can go back to doing what I do best, and these guys can do what they do best."

In an accompanying press release, *Fusient* identified Bedol as "CEO of WCW Incorporated," with Bischoff returning as WCW President. "Wrestling fans can rest assured," promised Bischoff, "that we will give the WCW the adrenaline shot it needs to once again become the most exciting brand of wrestling in the world."

"We're going to reestablish the WCW as the champion of professional wrestling entertainment," added Bedol. "There is huge untapped potential for the franchise and with Eric Bischoff on board, we will crank everything up to make the WCW franchise even bigger, better, stronger and more entertaining than anything wrestling fans have ever experienced before."

Bedol, co-founder of *The Classic Sports Network* - a remarkably successful initiative that ESPN purchased, in 1997, for $200 million - recalls his WCW interest beginning with a random phone call. "My recollection is that I got a random call - out of the blue - from Eric Bischoff," he says. "He was on a 'fishing expedition', trying to find someone to partner with to buy the business.

"He described it to me as an 'interesting distressed media property'. He expressed that Turner was interested in getting rid of it, and would do so on favorable terms. I didn't know much about the current state of wrestling, but I decided it was probably worth learning more."

Subsequently, Bedol, a wrestling and roller derby fan in his youth, set up a call with Siegel. "I had known Brad for years in the cable business," he says. "We just had an introductory conversation [at first]. They were certainly open to selling it, but may not have been formally marketing it, [at that time]."

To secure its controlling interest of WCW, reports suggested that Fusient eventually agreed to a price tag of $67 million. However, Bedol clarifies that the mechanics involved in the purchase were much more complex. "[The deal] had a pretty complicated structure, that if the sale price was $67 million, we were guaranteed revenue that was close to that," he says. "There were commitments for ad sales, and other revenues...other enhancements. I don't think our true exposure was more than a couple of million dollars. Even though the total sales price was in the 60's, the actual economic risk was very low."

In terms of his proposed role in WCW, Bedol looked forward to working with Bischoff, who as President, figured to handle its day-to-day affairs. "My impressions of Eric were very positive," he says. "He was very professional. One of the things that excited us was moving [WCW] to Vegas.

"One of the reasons that the property was losing so much money at the time was because it was so expensive to tour. [WCW] was losing a lot of money in the touring side of the business, so the idea was to build a state-of-the art wrestling arena in Las Vegas.

"The most serious conversations were with the *Hard Rock Cafe*. We could still do 'mini tours' to big markets - the strong markets - but have a permanent home in Las Vegas, where there were so many tourists that [we] could have a constantly refreshed audience. We were gonna build a very cool physical environment that had built in 'pyro', built in special effects. [So] the notion was to create a new kind of visual experience without the expense of constantly touring."

Creatively, Bischoff planned to methodically remove his top babyfaces from television in 2001, building up Scott Steiner as an unstoppable heel champion. Furthermore, Bischoff suggested taking WCW completely off the air - temporarily, of course - before returning on May 6th for a pay-per-view called *The Big Bang*. At the event, stars such as Goldberg, Kevin Nash and Sting would reemerge, alongside a fresh, novel style of production and a new announce team (including 29-year old Joey Styles, who recalls meeting Bedol to discuss the role). "I was in 'creative' at the end," adds David Penzer. "I think the plan was to take a break, then come back with Goldberg and those guys leading the [charge] against Steiner - [plus] some of the younger heels who were getting hot at the time."

In sum, the changes - "some evolutionary" and "some revolutionary", described Bedol - provided hope of a WCW resurgence. "We won't be satisfied until this is number one again," he said contemporaneously.

"Our goal this time is 100 weeks in a row."

Chapter 53:
It Ain't Over 'Til It's Over

CURIOUSLY, WEEKS CONTINUED to pass, but the sale had yet to finalize. Some outlets were publishing details that *Fusient* - having taken a 'closer look at the books' - were suddenly getting cold feet. "I don't recall that being a factor," retorts Bedol.

On January 29th, *Amusement Business* reported that the Fusient purchase of WCW was subject to a '60-day window', relative to its federal approval. Two weeks later, on February 13th, the FTC granted "WCW Acquisition, Inc." an early termination notice, essentially waving the requirement - instantiated by the *Hart-Scott-Rodino Antitrust Improvement Act of 1976* - that "persons contemplating certain mergers or acquisitions [must] give the Federal Trade Commission and the Assistant Attorney General advance notice, and to wait designated periods before consummation of such plans."

Concurrent to the FTC decision, J.J. Dillon – ostracized from on-camera affairs, but still working as an administrator - received a phone call in the WCW offices. Apparently, an attorney from Fusient had requested his expertise - relative to the nature of WCW's contracts - causing Dillon to respond thusly:

I'm surprised you didn't call Eric Bischoff about this, because he's your wrestling expert...however, you must have been referred to me because you already realize that he doesn't know any details of those contracts.

...As you continue your due diligence process, you may want to inquire why someone with my background and experience in wrestling has been sitting here in an office for the last year - with absolutely nothing to do.

Dillon never heard from the attorney again, but Fusient officials maintained their presence. "They sent people in to shadow everybody in the post-production side," remembers WCW producer Joel Edwards. "They were asking, 'ok, what are you doing? What's your job title?'

"I think they said, 'wow, what a mess', and went away for a little while."

In the meantime, excerpts of an Eric Bischoff interview - posted on WCW.com, no less - confirmed speculation of his long-held intent to buy the company:

I mentioned to Brad last spring when I came back - and I told him quite candidly during our renegotiation process - that it was going to be my intention to purchase the company. Of course he looked at me like I was nuts, because at that time, I doubt there had been any conversation or thought given to it.

...I wanted to be very up front about my intentions so that when the time came, it didn't look Machiavellian in any way - and it was above board.

And thus, considering that he propagated such a notion to coworkers, the still-on-payroll Vince Russo enjoyed a measure of vindication. With WCW in limbo, a petition calling for his return - littered with misspellings - emblazoned *VinceRusso.org*:

To: Fusient Media Ventures/World Championship Wrestling/Eric Bischoff

We the Undersigned, send this as a plea to the new owners of World Championship Wrestling.

...We see hope with Fusient Media Ventures being the new owners of World Championship Wrestling but, we have worries about Eric Bischoff.

Yes Eric Bischoff did change the landscape of wrestling in the mid 90's but over the past few weeks we have noticed that the younger talent has been pushed on the back burner and that the old main eventers who are all close friends of Eric Bischoff are back in the main event. People like Kevin Nash, Diamond Dallas Page, Rick Steiner, and "The Cat" Ernest Miller.

We the fans of World Championship Wrestling, see a familiar trend coming back. This formula has been done in the past and this is what cause [sic] WCW to lose their spot as the top rated wrestling show.

516

…We saw a total of 5 woman talent [sic] released last week. What kind of message is that sending when Eric Bischoff fires 95% of the woman talent? The WWF uses woman talent [sic] with great success. Is the new WCW saying that woman in wrestling [sic] is not to be?

We have heard a rumor that Kevin Sullivan will be coming back. This is a man who worked with a past WCW president to have Vince Russo removed from booking television even as ratings were climbing. After his takeover of booking the ratings dropped intensely and still have not recovered.

We noticed that the guys who were working hard these past months have now little or no airtime on television….What is going on? Was the glass ceiling repaired?

We the Undersigned, ask Fusient Media Ventures to please take a stand and read up on the past history of World Championship Wrestling and understand what did and did not work. Please do not take a back seat and let others run the show.

Talent should be elevated by their work rate and not who they know. Please don't let World Championship Wrestling fall again into the past.

…Eric Bischoff, we have faith in you. You have done it before and you can do it again but please think about what actions you may take. What didn't work in the past will not work today. Vince Russo is a [sic] untapped booker. Please consider this and be the first one to stand up and let him work his best and shine.

Despite not being seen since October, Russo was also in the news for another reason. A series of racial discrimination lawsuits - including the primary case, brought forth by Sonny Onoo (Bischoff's long-time friend and formerly, WCW's international consultant) - cited Russo as having shown a bias against minority talent. Remarkably, the issue stemmed from the writer's published comments (and subsequent actions, argued Onoo) in his September 1999 interview with *Wrestleline*:

I'm going to tell you something right now that you will absolutely not agree with, but I've been a wrestling fan my whole life and I will live and die by this - it is hard enough, believe me I write this shit, it is hard enough to get somebody over. You will never ever, ever, ever, ever see the Japanese wrestler or the Mexican wrestler over in American mainstream wrestling. And the simple reason for that is, even myself, I'm an American, and I don't want to sound like a big bigot or a racist or anything like that, but I'm an American...if I'm watching wrestling here in America, I don't give a shit about a Japanese guy. I don't give a shit about a Mexican guy. I'm from America, and that's what I want to see.

"What he said is pretty cut-and-dry," reflects Onoo, who was let go in the fall of 1999. "You can look at what he said and what happened afterwards, and it's like connecting the dots on a McDonald's happy meal. All of the Japanese and Mexican wrestlers were let go."

Particularly damning to Russo was a suggestion - one he has refuted vehemently ever since - that legal considerations influenced his awarding of Booker T, an African-American, with the WCW title. "I don't know what's in people's minds," responds Onoo on the issue, "but that was certainly interesting. I'll let people make up their own minds about that."

At the time, while fresh off a court hearing regarding his lawsuit, Onoo suggested that post-merger officials were looking into the matter themselves. "It is my understanding," he wrote in mid-February, "that AOL/Time Warner has started its own investigation of many of the alleged incidents of discrimination by the officers of the company...and has begun interviewing current and former workers of [the] company."

Furthermore, rumors of an AOL-imposed 'dead-end' date were making everyone nervous. For months, the gossip went, Siegel had been instructed to 'sell or dump' WCW before March 30th, raising accusations that he deliberately announced the Fusient deal prematurely. "There was a date that was floating out there - for some people within the company," recalls WCW producer Jason Douglas. "I do recall some people that we had worked with at Turner, saying they had heard there was a date that the company was gonna be sold...or something was gonna happen to the company."

———

In January – during the initial Fusient press conference – Siegel outlined that *Nitro* and *Thunder* would continue on Turner-owned television for "many, many years." However, with WCW still in limbo, TBS was undergoing some significant upheaval of its own. On Tuesday, March 6th, AOL-Time Warner (co-COO Bob Pittman specifically) enacted a major change to its leadership:

AOL Time Warner (NYSE: AOL) announced today that it will create a new TV networks group under the Turner Broadcasting System umbrella, which will include both Turner's basic cable networks and The WB broadcast network, and become the world's largest television networks group.

...Jamie Kellner, the CEO and founder of The WB, has been named Chairman and CEO of Turner Broadcasting. In 1993, Mr. Kellner founded The WB Television Network in a joint venture that included Warner Bros., Tribune Company and himself. Previously, Mr. Kellner helped found and build the Fox network as President and Chief Operating Officer of the Fox Broadcasting Company.

As part of a company gathering at the Omni Hotel, Kellner was formally introduced to Turner staff days later. "We're in this big room," recalls one former senior executive. "They played this whole, 'Turner Broadcasting is great!' video to get us all fired up. Then it was, 'now here's your new CEO - Jamie Kellner!'

"He was kind of all crumpled looking, and here he comes shuffling in, kinda hunched over. His first statement was, 'hey, ok, thanks, everybody. I...uh...I'm really tired. I've been flying a lot, and I'm really tired'.

"I'm like, '*this* is my guy?' Come on! Then in a very short period of time, his wife was all involved in the sports teams...buying buses to bring kids from the suburbs to every game, and just all this crazy stuff. It's like, 'why is somebody's wife involved in all of our business'? It's like, 'go away!'

"He was a very weak leader, and I think he was in the wrong job. It was *clear* he was in the wrong spot. It was all being done from above him though, I think."

With Kellner's arrival, long-time Turner executives were now pondering their futures. "It's a great group of people, it's a family," Kellner told a reporter of his new surroundings on March 11th. "It's a good company. I'll try not to mess anything up; I'll tweak it."

Still, agonizingly, even though Fusient personnel were being spotted at WCW shows, the process dragged on. "There was so much speculation going on," recalls Alan Sharp. "I think part of everyone's day was spent in someone else's office - almost as therapy. Everyone was just talking, like, 'what have *you* heard today?'

On March 13th, Siegel - recently returned from a previously scheduled vacation - met with Fusient executives in Atlanta. Notable in absentia was Bischoff, however, who in anticipation of the deal closing - and the increased workload ahead - whisked his family away to Hawaii.

At the same time, fans began to realize that beyond March 26th, exactly zero WCW shows were being advertised. Confusion was widespread, but at 12:59am on Friday, March 16th, wrestling's most preeminent journalist provided an update.

"It appears that at least temporarily," wrote Dave Meltzer on *WrestlingObserver.com*, "the days of World Championship Wrestling may be coming to a close.

"The Fusient deal looks to have fallen through."

Chapter 54:
Two Fridays Apart

IN A REVEALING INSIGHT into political PR, a former White House bureaucrat once commented on the utility of Friday afternoons. "It's where government officials dump stories they want to bury," John Sununu said without equivocation.

Whether intentional or not, Brad Siegel was about to follow the axiom with deadly precision. *"In early January,"* wrote Siegel in a March 16 memo to all employees, *"we told you about an agreement that we had reached to sell WCW and its related assets. At that time, we said that we would apprise you of any changes to the way WCW operates. Effective Tuesday, Mar. 27, WCW programming will begin a period of hiatus. During this hiatus, WCW will review its programming plans and determine the course of future WCW-branded entertainment events.*

"On Wednesday, March 28, please plan to attend an all-staff meeting at 10 a.m. at the Power Plant, at which we will share with you further information regarding WCW plans. In the meantime, I hope that you will maintain the level of professionalism that distinguishes our organization, particularly as we prepare for the upcoming Panama City, Fla. event."

Siegel's memo did little to resolve the ambiguity surrounding WCW's future. While on one hand, the news of an upcoming 'hiatus' aligned with Fusient's plans for a temporary 'shutdown', no indication of causality had been made. A number of possible scenarios remained in play, especially given the rampant speculation, difficulties in closing the sale, and lack of clarification from Fusient since January.

In a persuasive analysis, Wade Keller explored each of the more likely outcomes on his *Pro Wrestling Torch* website:

Scenario A
Fusient takes over WCW as planned. The hiatus is legitimate, and events will resume in May.

Scenario B
WCW is closing down - categorically and definitively - devoid of any transfer of ownership.

Scenario C
WCW is entering a period of evaluation during its hiatus, in order for Jamie Kellner to determine its future viability.

Scenario D
WCW will be - or perhaps already has been - sold to the WWF, with the potential to continue operating as a 'separate' brand or entity.

Scenario E
WCW will be - or perhaps already has been - sold to an investor group unrelated to Fusient.

Concerning alternative suitors, the *Torch* reported that "along with an investor from Boston," a purchase proposal had also been put forward by Jerry Jarrett. Following the Lenita Erickson affair, Jarrett had been working diligently with his financial partner - a former AWA consultant-turned investment banker named John Corcoran - in an effort to secure his own financing, even after Fusient's apparent purchase in January.

Corcoran first met Jarrett when he was still running the Memphis territory in the late '80s. "Jerry had a disproportionate standing relative to other promoters," he points out. "He was very strategic, smarter than most of them, and he recognized the writing on the wall - relative to the expansion efforts of the WWF.

"[In 1988, Jerry] approached the AWA with an eye towards...a merger - ostensibly of equals - but one where he would be buying control over time of the AWA. Among its assets - which included a number of territories [encompassing] a large geographical area - the AWA also possessed a potentially very valuable television contract with ESPN. That made them somewhat unique, and I think Jerry's view was that the combination of the AWA and [CWA - the Memphis territory] would lead to a 'super-regional' player in the Midwest. He thought it could do battle with the WWF.

"His view, and to some extent mine, was that there was probably room for three [national promotions]. That would include the WWF, whatever this Midwest combination would be called, and some version of what became WCW or NWA.

"It got to about as close to a consummated deal as you can get. It broke down at the last minute over unreasonable requirements that Verne Gagne had put in place, relative to maintaining the autonomy of the AWA, and in particular, him trying to make sure that his family members [remained involved].

"Then - in 2001 - the opportunity with WCW came forward."

"Word on the street was that Turner/Time Warner was selling their cash eating elephant," recalls Jarrett. "Corcoran got the financial [statements] from Turner, sent them to me, and the financials confirmed my theory. WCW could not pay its overhead and talent costs, even if they were selling out every arena and continued with top television ratings."

"In regards to Turner [Broadcasting]," continues Corcoran, "they thought it was just another professional sports franchise. There was no real understanding of the uniqueness of professional wrestling.

"The cost structure was similar to what you would see for a professional baseball or basketball team. If we would look at those salaries today, they would still be viewed as large. By the standards of 2000, it was outrageous."

So outrageous, in fact, that according to WCW executive J.J. Dillon, total talent costs exceeded 60% of all revenues in 2000, an unsustainable model given the fixed (guaranteed) nature of that expense. Moreover, to function as a profitable venture in wrestling, it was thought necessary to maintain a percentage closer to *25%*, with an understanding that salaries would increase - in absolute terms - commensurate with an improvement in business.

But according to a source with intimate knowledge of WCW's financial records, there would soon be a chance to address the issue. As of early 2001, only $20 million in salary was earmarked as *guaranteed* for the year, compared to $100 million designated for production costs and 'wrestling operations' combined. Furthermore, many other high-priced deals were set to expire at year's end (although interestingly, Jarrett recalls a suggestion that AOL/Time Warner 'buy out' the outstanding contracts anyway, using a portion of the funds generated from a sale).

"It was to have been a selected asset purchase," Jarrett says of his bid. "I would have not bought the wrestlers' contracts, as WCW would have had sufficient funds from the sale to pay [them off]. My plans were to have a meeting with each talent, and advise them that we would replicate the WWF system - pay based on results."

"He's a rarity," Corcoran says of the legendary promoter, "then - and now - in his ability to understand the underlying economics of the business. WCW needed more the kind of expertise that you would see in the private sector - a 'turnaround' specialist [for example] - but that wouldn't have been appropriate here, because of the uniqueness of the business. You couldn't just bring anybody in that said, 'ok - close this office, sell this and move that'. It's not *that* obvious, and you can actually do more harm doing that kind of thing."

Assuming that salaries were carefully controlled, WCW could have again become, Corcoran argues, "instantly" profitable. "Millions of dollars could be taken out of [the equation]," he says, "without affecting the underlying asset value - this enormous, powerful, global television platform. That was the hidden gem."

After all, despite its well-documented decline, the company still managed to gross $125 million in 2000. "You end up with a company that is hemorrhaging red ink," Corcoran points out, "but has a nice revenue line. You look at that, and you say, 'ok, I like the revenue line, and I'm hoping I can maintain that' - that's the part about keeping the TBS piece going - and in terms of cutting costs, that is an area where Jerry Jarrett would have been involved."

"I would have done more than cut costs," promises Jarrett, "I would have slashed them. John sent me a brief recap of their [financial] condition, and I replied I could turn the company around in one week by slashing payroll and needless expenses."

With its tape library and international distribution, WCW seemed to be well positioned for the ongoing digital revolution ("the library alone could be leveraged forever," laments Corcoran). However, its rumored list of potential suitors (UFC co-founder Bob Meyrowitz, Randy Savage (!), and groups from Germany and Japan) appeared remarkably slim - even for the time.

"I tried to get Bill Shaw and some investors to buy it," reveals David Crockett. "Bill was retired. He said, 'David, if I do this…it will shorten my life'. I said, 'Bill, just give me a year'.

"I would have liked to have run it. It would've worked - I know it. But they wouldn't sell…to us, [anyway]."

"If they were trying to sell it today," clarifies Corcoran, "the list of suitors would be much larger, because there's a whole lot more you can with the distribution of content.

"There were also very unrealistic expectations about the underlying value of the asset…that bore no relation to reality. Off the top of my head, my recollection is that they wanted $100 million for it. So even to put forth a letter of intent, you had to be at a level that just didn't make any sense."

Nonetheless, as word of Siegel's memo leaked online, the group's offer - "$70 million", according to Jarrett - remained on the table.

But then: Saturday, March 17th brought with it a shocking revelation. Despite the unresolved ownership situation, TBS suddenly announced that there would no hiatus; on the contrary, it was unreservedly canceling all future WCW programming. "We've come to the decision," said TBS spokesman Jim Weiss, "that professional wrestling, in its current style, is not consistent with the upscale brands we've created with TNT and the SuperStation TBS…therefore, we've made the decision that we're no longer going to carry professional wrestling in its current style."

Weiss declined to confirm if the Fusient deal was off - noting instead there were "several options" for a WCW sale - but later Saturday, reports indicated that TBS was already moving on. Its officials designated March 21st as the final *Thunder* show, meaning that *Nitro* on March 26th - ironically, the annual 'Spring Break' special from Panama City - would function as the concluding WCW program on TNT.

In response, theories of an elaborated ruse abounded online, fueling hopes of TBS cooperation in a WCW 'relaunch' storyline. "At this point," wrote Dave Scherer on *1Wrestling.com*, "I don't know if people thinking that way are just holding out hope for WCW to live on, or if it could actually be true. If it is a work, the only possible thing they could be looking for is publicity."

On Sunday, a weary band of performers, producers and office staff came together for *Greed*, WCW's latest pay-per-view at the Jacksonville Memorial Coliseum. Given all the distractions, a perceptibly ominous feeling permeated the broadcast, and consequently, the end product suffered. "That event was terrible," remembers Joe Uva. "Really bad."

Monday morning named the apparent culprit of the cancellation - new TBS head Jamie Kellner. The *New York Times* even suggested it was his call alone - *Turner Drops Wrestling in First Decision by Its New Chief*, read the headline - while the paper described the Fusient deal as "off":

The cancellation of wrestling [marks] the end of an era at Turner Broadcasting, the cable franchise built by Ted Turner, in part, on the strength of professional wrestling.

Mr. Turner, now the vice chairman of AOL Time Warner, began showing matches of the World Championship Wrestling league on his first television station, WTCG-TV in Atlanta, in the early 1970's. He later used wrestling to attract viewers to TBS and TNT.

But the league has fallen on hard times. Though it was, at one point, the dominant wrestling franchise on television, in the last couple of years, it has consistently lost in the ratings to the World Wrestling Federation, which was first on USA network and later on TNN and MTV.

With high production costs and expensive contracts for wrestlers, World Championship Wrestling is estimated to have lost tens of millions of dollars.

Turner Broadcasting said in January that it would sell its controlling interest in the league to Fusient Media Ventures, a fledgling media concern, but that it would continue to show wrestling on TNT and TBS for years to come.

Everything changed two weeks ago when Jamie Kellner, the chief executive of WB network, became the head of TBS, executives at AOL Time Warner said.

In the years since 2001, wrestling lore has positioned Kellner's call in terms of a personal vendetta, with one account alleging of his "hatred" for the genre. However, in a statement that is sure to surprise fans, Kellner outright disputes that perception. "I grew up a fan of wrestling, and once tried to make a deal with Vince McMahon at a different network," he says.

According to Brian Bedol, Kellner's hand was forced by a condition embedded in the Fusient deal. As part of its purchase agreement, Fusient retained the right to 'program' a Turner time slot (believed to be on the TBS network) – irrespective of WCW's future existence.

"We structured a deal that was great for us," Bedol reveals, "but Jamie might have decided it wasn't so good for Turner. We had negotiated into the deal certain rights to the time slot, in case WCW was canceled.

"We retained the right - for a period of time - to continue to 'program' the time slot.

"We looked at [the time slot] as a valuable asset, because if we were going to pay all this money for the property, we didn't want to take on the risk of it being canceled.

"Of course, Turner couldn't be in the position where they had a valuable time slot with a guarantee [essentially] never to cancel the show in it. So my recollection is that when Jamie came in, he looked at that as being something that they weren't willing to give."

Furthermore, the *Times* piece alluded to two additional factors at play: firstly, the specific influence of Brad Siegel ("*[AOL executives said Mr. Kellner, in consultation with the president of Turner Entertainment, Brad Siegel...decided that wrestling should be canceled sooner rather than later.*"), and secondly, the desire of Kellner to signal a change in audience demographics ("*It was the first programing move made under Mr. Kellner's leadership, and is an indication that he wants to attract more affluent viewers to TNT and TBS.*")

Both elements were, in fact, closely interrelated. On February 10th, 2000, at a time when WCW was attempting to stabilize after its latest creative shake-up, Siegel hired Steve Koonin to oversee the day-to-day operations of TNT. Koonin, known for a striking resemblance to the diminutive 'Newman' character on *Seinfeld*, arrived at the network after 14 years of marketing genius at Coca-Cola, where he was widely hailed for developing the successful 'Always Coca-Cola' ad campaign. Upon arriving at TNT, however, Koonin realized that his input would take on a much greater scope.

Since its launch in 1988, TNT was regarded as one of cable television's success stories, but by 2000, its executives believed change to be imminent. The proliferation in cable TV options meant that it risked being viewed as a general 'variety' network, broadcasting everything from WCW to historical dramas and Westerns. Of course, there had always been concerns over TNT's vague brand identity (as evidenced by the near-ubiquitous condemnation of *Monday Nitro* in the first place), but in the new media landscape, these concerns risked becoming an *identity crisis*. As such, its marketers and programmers touted a pointedly instructive buzzword: *focus.*

In short, TNT lacked a clear identity, becoming a general entertainment network in the process. In response, Koonin, now tasked with developing a *brand initiative* for the network, spearheaded a research project to get started. His team interviewed 1,500 respondents about their viewing habits, with the resultant data informing a process called *audience segmentation*. One segment of the audience (identified as 'The Drama Club') reported an attraction to programming described as 'emotionally engaging', while an opposite group ('Sitcom Lovers') reported more a willingness to 'feel good' when watching television. "It was such a clear road map to differentiate the networks," reflected Jon Marks, the lead researcher on the project. "We needed a drama network, which is what TNT became. We [also] needed a comedy network, which is what TBS became."

Over the course of several months, TNT used the findings to develop a so-called 'Meat and Potatoes' growth strategy. The 'Meat' of the equation would be the 'Drama Club', whose affluent members could be targeted to grow ratings across similar programming. In turn, this internal consistency could leverage the 'Potatoes' portion, comprised of two additional segments ('Cable Potatoes' and 'Broadcast Potatoes') both of whom reported heavy viewership habits (in the case of the 'Cable Potatoes', over 45 hours per week).

As an ancillary tactic, TNT proposed appealing to a segment identified as 'Sports Junkies' with limited sports and 'action' inventory, but otherwise conceding this group to another network. As Marks observed, "[Branding] imposes a sense of internal discipline, which is very important. It acts as a filter to help you narrow down the best choices. If you don't have a cogent brand for your network, any idea can be a good idea."

A remaining audience segment - 'High Brows' (light TV viewers with discriminating tastes) - would be conceded entirely. Therefore, TNT, with a targeted focus towards its 'Drama Club', aimed to position itself as '*100 percent dramatic entertainment that makes you think and feel*'. To illustrate the new direction, its staff eventually determined an instructive slogan: *We Know Drama.*

On September 27th 2000, at the same time Vince Russo was WCW champion, some 200 executives and associates traveled to Florida for a corporate retreat. As part of the proceedings, Koonin hired conductor Boris Brott to deliver a powerful, direction-affirming experience. As if to underscore the importance of harmony, Brott taught the entire TNT staff to play Beethoven's 'Ode to Joy', leaving Koonin to explain its motif. *We all need*, Koonin indicated, observing agreeing eyes around him, *to play off the same song sheet.*

Following the retreat, TNT identified its integral characteristics - what it hoped to represent as a network, and what it didn't. While Booker T. and Jeff Jarrett fought in a 'San Francisco 49ers' match - utilizing blow-up dolls and other props in a *Nitro* main event - the network looked to follow-through on its *personality statement*: '*TNT is not juvenile, mindless, predictable, frivolous [or] superficial*', read the document. '*TNT is contemporary, meaningful, suspenseful, exciting, [and] powerful*'.

Therefore, once Kellner called off the Fusient deal - unwilling to give up a time slot for "multiple years," according to Brian Bedol - therein lied the chance to (publicly) signify change. Suppositionally, positioning the fallout as the *cancellation of wrestling* provided a convenient way to start the re-branding process. "The story we told was that it didn't fit the TNT rebrand," says Scot Safon, TNT's SVP of Marketing. "That was somewhat true...but it was also because the show couldn't make money - given how tough it was to sell and how expensive it was getting to run."

"TNT's management wanted to position TNT as a high-quality network," summarizes Jon Marks, SVP of Research at Turner, "targeted to affluent city/suburban residents.

"That's not the WCW viewer. Its audience was downscale and rural-skewing, plus the content was perceived as being lowbrow and juvenile (in September 2000, an analysis of WCW's audience composition revealed that 32% of its fanbase were unemployed, with 42% of its viewers working in 'blue-collar' fields. Of the entire *Nitro* audience, only 11% completed four years of college).

"In fairness, wrestling was becoming a sport that drew entire families to arenas…and most of the viewers were young, and therefore many years from reaching their peak earning potential. But it was very disruptive to audience flow, and most TNT programming had a much older and more female-skewing audience. WCW viewers wouldn't watch TNT original movies or much else on the network, and vice versa. Even the NBA, which also had a young male audience, had minimal audience duplication with WCW. The one was urban and African-American, while the other was largely rural and White.

"A lot of advertisers wouldn't get near WCW or WWF, despite the fact that they did a great job reaching young males - one of the hardest demos to find on television. Content issues [were] the main reason. The 1990's were a decade when many advertisers were reluctant to sponsor shows with sex, violence, salty language, or other controversial content. Terry Rakolta and the Parent's Television Council organized boycotts. Even though they never really caught on with consumers, they did spook advertisers and their agencies - [and] wrestling got caught in that net. Over time, [WCW] grew its base of advertisers significantly, but back then, there were a lot of mainstream advertisers that wouldn't go near it.

"In 2000, we conducted a ton of research to identify a new brand position for TNT, [and decided] that we would turn it into a drama-oriented network. We put a lot of thought into whether sports still had a role in the portfolio. We decided that sports is very dramatic, and *did* fit the new brand promise…but wrestling isn't a traditional sport. It's not a true competition, and it didn't 'touch the heart and mind', which was our new mantra."

531

"[WCW] was our top-rated show by more than double anything else, and we dumped it," Safon said in 2002. "Can you name another network that canceled its top-rated show? I don't know if consumers noticed that we dropped wrestling from our schedule, but it said *everything* to the staff. The notion that we [could] be a drama brand while still keeping WCW on the schedule...who are we kidding?"

———

Meanwhile, with the Fusient pact dead - at least, for the time being - an opportunity emerged to take advantage of an accounting rule, one that would reflect positively on the AOL-Time Warner balance sheet. In the post-merger environment, the new conglomerate was able to 'write down' money losing operations, essentially eliminating those losses because of their irrelevancy moving forward.

"My recollection," says Jamie Kellner, "is that [WCW] was losing money, and following the AOL-Time Warner merger, we were allowed to purchase account the losses if we moved within 12 months.

"These were difficult times with a turbulent economy and an ad recession. There were many non-core businesses where similar decisions were made."

"Think about it in the context of what was going on at that time," begins Greg Prince, WCW's controller. "You've got a new corporate owner coming in to play. Purchase accounting would allow them to identify discontinuing operations - or operations they didn't view as being vital - [relative] to what the new, larger, combined company was gonna look like.

"They had the ability within accounting rules to say, 'we're gonna take this little collection of assets and businesses' - let's say it was WCW and some other non-performing movie studios, or whatever - and 'we're gonna divest ourselves of these'.

"So purchase accounting gave them the opportunity to do a couple of things.

"Rather than consolidating the operating results, in a consolidated income statement every month - for quarterly reporting purposes and in their annual 10-K [statement] - they wouldn't have to. All those entities deemed to be 'non-essential', or designated to be discontinued operations...would only be reflected in their income statements in a *single line item*. It wouldn't be combined with all their ongoing entities.

"It's almost like quarantining the bad news, if you think about it. 'Alright, we've got a loss for discontinued operations' - some big fat number with a lot of zeros on it - and there's a little footnote or disclaimer in the financial statements. [It could say], 'these were the discontinued operations...this is the plan to wind them down, or dispose of 'em', blah, blah, blah.

"[Through this method], they would be able to estimate what their planned future losses were gonna be, and collapse those in to that number they reported in a single line item."

And so, in the final analysis, says Kellner, "it was all numbers."

"It really *was* financial," offers Scot Safon today, "but here's why. WCW grew fast and it had a lot of ratings success...but ratings success only matters if you can monetize it.

"Turner's ad sales teams had a tough time monetizing those ratings. They weren't aligned with anything else they were selling - from a content standpoint or a demographic standpoint. Turner's premium sports sponsors didn't want to be associated with it, and Turner's entertainment advertisers didn't want to buy it either, as the demographics weren't in line with theirs."

"Ad Sales couldn't package it with [anything else] at the time. Maybe today, you could put it with *truTV* and *Adult Swim* and E-Sports, and go after certain advertisers in a big way. But WCW as a standalone wasn't enough."

"If you asked people at WCW," says Michael Polydoroff, formerly TNT's Marketing Project Manager, "they would say, 'the network doesn't care about us. We're making them money hand over fist, and bringing in millions of people'. Their perception was, 'the ratings are good - so we're the golden child of the programming schedule'.

"Of course, what they didn't realize is that we weren't making money hand over fist, because no-one wanted to advertise."

"Those WCW ratings," adds Safon, "were [also] turning some of the talent into big stars, who then started negotiating for higher salaries. The moment it became a star-driven, production-value driven spectacle, the bigger the costs and the smaller the margins.

"By the end, it was just not going to be a big business for Turner - so they just shut it down. It was the margins that killed it more than anything else, I think."

And so, the removal of Fusient's time slot effectively opened the door for two desirable outcomes: a dramatic 'kick-off' to TNT's re-branding efforts, *and* the ability to make AOL's corporate bean counters happy.

However, Corcoran believes that Turner management made a fatal error in their decision making. "By signaling [publicly] that they didn't want to continue the programming," he says, "they essentially rendered [WCW] unsellable. I remember speaking with Brian Bedol about this. It's confirming of just the gross stupidity of the Turner organization, relative to this kind of an asset, and their ability to continually shoot themselves in the foot."

As memorialized indelibly in a 2004 documentary, Bischoff joked that without a television contract, WCW was worth "20 bucks." Corcoran goes even further, noting that "from a strict economic standpoint, I could argue that if the entity was losing millions of dollars on a monthly basis, it wasn't worth anything."

Still, as of midday on Monday, March 19th, Jim Weiss portrayed TBS as being in the driving seat. "There are two points I want to make," the Turner spokesman told Alex Marvez, as a cavalcade of cancellation coverage sent shockwaves around the wrestling world. "WCW is going to be sold. We have options.

"The other point is that we've decided professional wrestling in its current incarnation just isn't appropriate for the high-scale, up-scale brand that we have built on TNT and TBS Superstation. We're no longer interested in carrying the product."

"Up-scale" was clearly the buzzword *du jour*, but fans hoped for some plainer messaging on *Nitro*. Late in the afternoon, an update on WCW.com informed viewers to expect an announcement from Eric Bischoff on the telecast - apparently via telephone - in what was now being called a 'season finale'.

At close to 9:00pm EST, Bischoff called into the O'Connell Center in Gainesville, Florida. He sounded positively dismayed:

"For those of you in the arena and all of you watching around the country this evening, I very much would have [rather] chosen to be there, tonight in person if I could be...but given everything that's going on tonight, that's just not possible.

"Many of you may know that for the past six months, I've been working with a group of people whose goal it was - and is - to acquire World Championship Wrestling, and to grow it once again to becoming a competitive, dominant wrestling organization worldwide.

"But recently, we've hit a couple...roadblocks, that may be in fact, brick walls. And while it is still in my power, I want to do something befitting what could very well be the last night of wrestling on the Turner networks.

"Given the fact that wrestling has been such an important part of Turner's history over the past 29 years, I've been thinking over the

535

weekend on what I could do…to provide as exciting a program as this historic event should be.

"To that end, I want to make an announcement now that next Monday night in Panama City is indeed going to be a 'Night of Champions'. By that, I mean every championship will be up for grabs…

"…And given the historic nature of this occasion and my relationship with this company for nearly ten years, I wanna personally extend an open invitation to any former - and I mean any former - World Heavyweight champion in WCW to join us in Panama City, and don't be afraid to bring your boots with you."

For Bischoff and Fusient, there would be one final chance. For months, Bischoff had been in negotiations to provide either *Nitro* or *Thunder* - preferably *Thunder* - to one of the Fox networks, with the remaining prime-time show staying with TBS. It was a fact that had not been disclosed during January's press conference. "I know personally," says Diamond Dallas Page, "that Bischoff did not want to stay on TBS - or TNT. He wanted to take it somewhere else."

If - and for all intents and purposes, it was an impossible if - WCW could still find a home on Fox, the Fusient deal, in some incarnation, was salvageable. "WCW will be sold very swiftly," Jim Weiss told the press on Tuesday. "I am sure of that. Fusient is still in the picture, but I can't say for sure who will end up with WCW. It's too early to tell."

Evidently, however, Fox Sports Net would not be an option. "I got a call from George Greenberg, who was the VP of Fox Sports Net," reveals Lenita Erickson. "I hadn't talked to George in [several months], but he calls me up and goes, 'hey Lenita, you were down there working at Turner, weren't you? With WCW?' I go, 'yeah, why?' He goes, 'well, I got a meeting coming up in 20 minutes. This guy - Eric Bischoff - says he owns the company and wants to give us the programming'."

("[I] don't remember much of the conversation," offers Greenberg, when asked about his dealings with Erickson, "but she was smart, articulate and very marketing savvy.")

"I said, 'no George, he does not own the company - not at all'," continues Erickson. "I said, 'he's gonna try to secure programming so he can secure financing to buy the company'. George went, 'oh, hell no!' He shut it down - boom. Turned him down.

"Brad called me that night, like, '*what the fuck did you do?*'

"I said, 'I told you…mark this day, mark this time and mark my words - It's not happening'."

"He was like, 'Lenita!'"

For Bischoff, the FX network - based on consistent indications of interest, emanating mostly from executive Peter Liguori - remained a Hail Mary option. "I know that 'Bisch' was panicking, trying to get them to [reconsider]," recalls DDP. "He said to Brad, 'don't let them cancel it - give me at least a couple of weeks'."

Perhaps in the fictional realm of wrestling, it may have been possible to script a feel-good ending. But in the realm of reality, television deals - such as the one discussed with FX - tended to consummate under vastly different conditions. Quite simply, both the time-sensitive nature of negotiations, plus the inability of FX to effectuate terms rivaling TBS' original commitment - proved insurmountable as obstacles.

Put differently, Fusient was out.

"When a program (wrestling on the Turner networks) is 29 years old," laments Page, "and you've got that many people attached to it…maybe you don't just cancel it. Maybe you give Eric Bischoff a [real] chance to take it to another network."

By Tuesday afternoon, all mentions of WCW were scrubbed from the Fusient website. Several hours later, the group issued a one-sentence statement on their home page:

Fusient Media Ventures has terminated its efforts to purchase the WCW as a result of the decision by Turner Broadcasting Systems to no longer carry wrestling programming on its networks.

Subsequently, online speculation intensified that the WWF would end up with the company. "We are holding discussions with AOL Time Warner," said company spokesman Gary Davis, "about the possibility of acquiring WCW."

Meanwhile, Jerry Jarrett still couldn't get a reply - nor would he ever receive one. On Wednesday, *Thunder* completed its run on TBS with a whimper, ending with a group shot of WCW's production team on the entrance ramp. *Fans,* signed-off Tony Schiavone, somehow maintaining his enthusiasm, *it's been a great run on Thunder*!

On Thursday, the sale to WWF seemed all but complete. WCW's 'Board of Directors' (believed to be a ceremonial assortment of TBS executives, identified as such for legal reasons) voted to amend its business name to "Universal Wrestling Corporation" - the corporate name used to purchase Jim Crockett Promotions in 1988.

Come Friday morning, as per a press release on the WWF website, it was official:

World Wrestling Federation Entertainment, Inc. (NYSE: WWF) today announced its purchase of the World Championship Wrestling (WCW) brand from Turner Broadcasting System, Inc. (TBS Inc.), a division of AOL Time Warner.

The purchase of WCW creates a tag team partnership with the World Wrestling Federation brand that is expected to propel the sports entertainment genre to new heights.

In keeping with the company's strategic alliance with Viacom, new WCW programming is anticipated to air on TNN in the near future. The possibility of cross-brand storylines and intrigue, however, may start as early as Monday night during WWF Raw Is War on TNN and the final performance of WCW Monday Nitro Live on Turner Network Television (TNT).

The binding agreement provides World Wrestling Federation Entertainment with the global rights to the WCW brand, tape library, and other intellectual property rights.

"This acquisition is the perfect creative and business catalyst for our company," said Linda McMahon, Chief Executive Officer of World Wrestling Federation Entertainment. "This is a dream combination for fans of sports entertainment. The incendiary mix of World Wrestling Federation and WCW personalities potentially creates intriguing storylines that will attract a larger fan base to the benefit of our advertisers and business partners, and propel sports entertainment to new heights."

"The acquisition of the WCW brand is a strategic move for us," said Stuart Snyder, President and Chief Operating Officer for World Wrestling Federation Entertainment. "We are assuming a brand with global distribution and recognition. We are adding thousands of hours to our tape library that can be repurposed for home videos, television, Internet streaming, and broadband applications. The WCW opens new opportunities for growth in our Pay Per View, live events, and consumer products divisions, as well as the opportunity to develop new television programming using new stars. We also will create additional advertising and sponsorship opportunities. In short, it is a perfect fit."

Appearing on the *Between the Ropes* radio show, Kevin Nash provided his immediate reaction. In the final analysis, argued Nash, WCW suffered a "slow, agonizing death," showing a fatal inability to follow up on the nWo idea. Astutely, he observed that while the WWF maintained its pay-per-view numbers during *Nitro*'s ascendancy, WCW's own buyrates collapsed once *Raw* took control. Concerning the likelihood of a farewell appearance in Panama City, Nash left no doubt as to his plans: "*not a chance.*"

Meanwhile, at precisely 3:34pm, Siegel penned another memo:

-----Original Message-----
From: Snyder, Tracey
Sent: Friday, March 23, 2001 3:34 PM
To: *WCW (TBS)
Subject: Announcement

March 23, 2001

To: WCW Staff
From: Brad Siegel
RE: WWF announcement

Today, World Wrestling Federation Entertainment, Inc. is announcing that we have reached an agreement for the sale of WCW. This agreement with WWF holds tremendous potential for the WCW brand and assets. The press release announcing the news is attached.

As we told you last week, WCW programming will not appear on TNT and TBS Superstation after March 27. We will share more information with you about the WWF's immediate plans for WCW in the all-staff meeting scheduled for Wednesday, March 28, at 10 a.m. at the Power Plant.

Thank you.

Chapter 55:
Conspiracy

GIVEN THAT THE financial terms of the WCW purchase were not immediately made public, it would be four months until the final cost was known. But when WWFE eventually outlined the component parts of the deal - within a 10-K filing for the SEC - the response was one of widespread disbelief. Apparently, Vince McMahon had managed to eliminate his competition for a mere $4.3 million:

In March 2001, the Company acquired substantially all of the intellectual properties and certain other assets of World Championship Wrestling (R) (the "WCW (R)"), including the trade name, tape library, and other intangible assets from a subsidiary of AOL Time Warner for [$2.5 million]. In addition, the Company incurred certain related costs to acquire these assets of approximately [$1.8 million]. Intellectual properties and certain other assets acquired, in addition to the related costs to acquire these assets, will be amortized over 10 years.

Within several days, ex-WCW employee Bob Ryder issued a widely disseminated response online, alleging of deliberate sabotage, collusion and cooperation between Siegel and the WWF:

Brad Siegel took steps to make sure the company was of no value to anyone except the WWF...

..While Fusient was still at the negotiating table [and negotiating in good faith], Siegel was contacting his friend Stu Snyder at the WWF to figure out what needed to be done to make sure the WWF got the deal.

Siegel and Stu Snyder (the top WWF exec who brokered the deal) were friends and co-workers when Snyder worked with Time Warner. It is widely believed that Siegel offered the job of WCW President to Snyder near the end of the Busch era, but that Snyder turned it down and went to work with the WWF.

When it became obvious that the only way the WWF could get back in the hunt to buy WCW would be if the shows were cancelled...that's exactly what Siegel made sure happened.

Siegel sabotaged his own company by convincing Kellner to cancel the shows. He did that *after* he made a call to Stu Snyder, and found out the only way he could make a deal with the WWF was to cancel the shows...

...Once the shows were cancelled, that narrowed the potential buyers to one.

The Fusient offer was still on the table until the shows were cancelled.

There were at least four offers from people who were willing to pay much more than the WWF paid...and they were ignored repeatedly."

Ryder called for a criminal investigation into the matter, centered around the claim that Stuart Snyder, an associate of Siegel, provided knowledge of the WWF's requirements for a deal. The notion persisted over the next decade, culminating in a vague passage in *The Death of WCW*:

Hey, remember when we mentioned Stuart Snyder earlier? Around this time, the WWF flew him in to Atlanta. Why? Why do you think? "The most surreal moment was flying into Atlanta on the WWF jet," Snyder [said]. "I said, 'there's no way we're going to keep this quiet, flying on a WWF jet into the home of Turner Broadcasting." Sure enough, their limo driver asked if he was there to buy out WCW.

He simply smirked.

Interesting.

A variety of other accounts - both formal and informal - have also made similar allusions to a conspiracy. In J.J. Dillon's autobiography, *Wrestlers Are Like Seagulls*, Snyder (identified as "Stu Schneider") is mentioned in a discussion of the WCW sale:

We couldn't help but look at the fact that Brad Siegel's fraternity brother, Stu Schneider, was the President of the [WWF].

For his own part, Kevin Sullivan has consistently made reference to an 'inside man' that enabled a swift WWF purchase. Today, Sullivan maintains a similar perspective. "They sold it to Brad's fraternity roommate," he says. "Pretty strange, don't you think?

"If this was a lawsuit, wouldn't the judge have to rescind himself from the case? Hello…nobody at TBS thought about saying, 'hey Brad, you might have [a conflict of] interest in this, to go and sell it to Vince, while there may be somebody else wanting to buy this'."

With all the conjecture, Snyder's involvement has become the stuff of legend. But despite being known to most fans in name only, his career in film and live entertainment superseded the WCW sale by nearly two decades. After graduating from Binghamton University in 1981, he rose the ranks at MGM UA to become Head of Sales for its home video unit, later joining LIVE Home Video/Carolco Pictures as a Vice President. At the time of Snyder's departure in 1993, the company was a major player in the home entertainment business, grossing $450 million in annual revenue.

His success attracted interest from Turner Broadcasting, and over the next four years, Snyder developed its home video division to a $500 million juggernaut, representing a 25-fold increase in business. In 1997, following the Turner-Time Warner merger, he advanced to become CEO of Feld Entertainment, a global live show production company.

In regards to his hiring at the WWF, Snyder describes a fairly typical process. "They were in search for a President and COO [in 2000], and [so] I was contacted through an industry headhunter," he says. "I interviewed for the position." When asked if he was offered a similar role at WCW first, Snyder responds with an unequivocal "no."

During his mid-90s tenure at Turner, and later in his role at Feld, Snyder enjoyed watching the developing wrestling wars. "Ted Turner wanted to compete in wrestling, and was willing to put the resources of his company behind that effort," he says. "[Ted] went out and signed major superstars, committed the company to programming content, and anyone who knows Ted Turner knows he likes to compete. So it was his desire and vision for the company, and the marketplace."

When asked to describe Ted personally, Snyder first uses the word practically synonymous with his character. "Entrepreneurial," he says. "Risk taker. No fear. Smart. Intelligent. Passionate. He always had great instincts, and knew what the future trends and future opportunities were all about. He surrounded himself with executives that were able to do two things: [firstly], challenge him to make wiser decisions, and also to execute on his vision and strategy."

He stops short of comparing Vince McMahon to Ted, however. "Not going there!" Snyder laughs. "But I will share this: they share a lot similar traits, in regards to [being] visionaries and individuals who know their businesses very well. They are both willing to take risks, learn from mistakes, and really enjoy competing."

Snyder regards the advent of cable television as key to explaining McMahon's success. "I perceive wrestling as always being popular," he begins, "but because it was a local phenomenon, it was always popular within ones locale.

"In New York, or the North East, Vince and his Dad really controlled wrestling - what is affectionately known as 'sports entertainment' now - and then you had the South East being controlled by another group, and so forth.

"But I think what happened from a [media] landscape point of view was really cable. Cable enabled Vince to see the future and say, 'this is something that could be done on a national level, and consolidated'. [In other words], this phenomenon...enjoyed by millions on a local basis, now could be shared on a national level. Stars could [then] be made from a national perspective - not just locally.

"Ted obviously had that same vision with cable, [in terms of] what he was looking to do, and what he did do with CNN, with TNT, and buying libraries to find content for his cable channels.

"So from a phenomenon standpoint, cable television and more opportunities for content clearly help to drive this very popular format."

In regards to WCW and the WWF, Snyder struggles to think of a similar example of head-to-head competition. "Nothing comes to mind, immediately," he says. "The uniqueness of this back and forth between the two organizations…was the fact that you had two strong entrepreneurs also leading them. At the core, they weren't just necessarily corporate identities competing - these were personality driven [entities].

"A lot of people like to position it as 'Ted vs. Vince', or 'Vince vs. Ted', so you had that little drama to the storyline. You had a business that was driven by storylines - in terms of what was happening [on screen] - but fans also loved the storylines from the two organizations behind the scenes. From a consumer facing standpoint, nothing comes to mind that had that kind of appeal. Certainly from an industry standpoint, there were rivalries and challenges. I mean, Ted always had those exciting war of words with Rupert Murdoch at the time, but that was more *industry* than consumer. This was really about viewers, fans and consumers."

In discussing the WCW purchase, Snyder first contextualizes the issue. "I experienced the growth of WCW from a Turner perspective," he says, "and [then] being with WWF at the time, I had watched and observed what had been happening with WCW. I don't think it's any surprise that towards the time that I arrived at WWF, WCW had dropped in ratings and popularity. I think that is a pretty well known fact.

"So from my perspective, observing what was happening, I wasn't surprised when Turner [Broadcasting] made the decision to explore other opportunities for WCW. I had always expressed an interest that in the event that anything ever happened with WCW [under] Turner Broadcasting, I would be - on the behalf of WWF - interested in having conversations. It's as simple as that."

On the subject of collusion with Siegel, Snyder dismisses the perception wholly. "From my standpoint - not true," he says. "It had already come to us that the show was being canceled, so we had nothing to do with that…I had nothing to do with that decision - them canceling the show.

"Clearly, it's a known fact that Brad and I worked together at Turner. That part is true, but the other element is not true."

545

Once the cancellation was made official, Snyder recalls, the WWF were actively "re-approached" - a reference to the abandoned talks in October 2000 - in an effort for Turner management to gauge their interest.

"I can't speak to why the sale price [was so low]," says Snyder. "We were re-approached to see if we were interested. An offer was floated to us...we ended up negotiating a little bit, and we settled on an agreed upon price."

Snyder's contention that TBS solicited the WWF - *after* canceling *Nitro* and *Thunder* - appears to align with John Corcoran's memory of the timeline: "by publicly signaling that they didn't want to continue the programming, they essentially rendered [WCW] unsellable."

Furthermore, as Brian Bedol highlighted, the "$67 million" offer made by Fusient was much more intricate than first reported. For that reason, he does not view the final sale price as surprising. "We had a pretty complicated structure," said Bedol, "that if the sales price was $67 million...we were guaranteed revenue that was close to that. There were commitments for ad sales, and other revenues and enhancements...I don't think our true exposure was more than a couple of million dollars. So even though the total sales price was in the 60's, the actual economic risk was very low."

———

Today, Snyder maintains a philosophical outlook on the outcome of the wrestling war. "I think it was a great time for the industry," he says. "I think that it was exciting for the fans, it was exciting for the companies, and the employees of both organizations. And it was exciting to watch these two organizations compete against each other - better programming came out of it.

"WCW had some great shows, and for a period of time, it was winning the competition. But I think its success, and what they were doing [themselves], I speculate, led to its decline. As with anything in this genre, the more extreme or risky you get...[especially] if you're under

546

a corporate umbrella, it gets a little complicated.

"That enabled WWF to reinvent itself with the Attitude Era, so what came out of this was great success for both companies, and for the fans, just an enormous win. By the time that we bought WCW, I looked at it as an opportunity...*we* looked at is as an opportunity from the standpoint of the library of matches, the library of content that was there.

"It was exciting times."

———

Various contemporaries of Siegel dispute the notion that he 'sabotaged' WCW, in order to ensure a quick sale via Snyder. "I think Brad really wanted to save the property when he was put in charge," says long-time TBS producer Brian Welch. "I spoke to him personally about it several times and he was very disappointed - and frustrated - that he couldn't keep it afloat. Ultimately, he said the numbers didn't add up...and it was a simply a smart business decision to unload it, and take the loss."

"I always liked Brad," offers Eric Bischoff. "I still respect him a great deal. He was just in a horrible spot...a horrible, horrible position. He was under the same kind of [corporate] duress that everybody was under at that time. He's got some of the stigma on him [for WCW's collapse], which he doesn't deserve."

"Brad was a cool dude," says Kevin Nash. "I always got along with him, because Brad *got it.* To the end, I always felt he was an ally."

"I would certainly say," says Michael Polydoroff of TNT, "that Brad had a vision for WCW to do well. He was the President of the network, so he was very supportive of that partnership. While I don't know he saw it as the future of the network - it was probably not in the 10-year vision - he did see the revenue potential, and where it could sit in its own niche."

"I love Brad and he's a dear, long-time friend," begins Lenita Erickson. "I respect him madly, so let me be careful what I say. I know that he vehemently despised having wrestling on programming - it's not his cup of tea. That being said, he's also a very numbers-oriented person, and he knew they had good ratings for a time.

"A lot of people inside WCW never really had the chance to know Brad. He's a brilliant, brilliant businessman...but it just happened to be something that was not up his tree, so to speak. There were a couple of times - when I traveled on *Thunder* - that he traveled to meet the wrestlers and try to be [the boss]. I used to tell him, 'come on, man', from the sidelines. I know there were times he would mention certain wrestlers, and be in awe of them, actually. So it was just a weird dynamic. Business is one thing, personal is another.

"What I believe is this: business is harsh and cruel. There's always going to be a discrepancy between those 'under' and 'over' - I've been both. But I tend to see it fairly, in that big business is hard to do. When you're running a superstation, and you're in charge of hundreds of millions of dollars...you're sometimes not there to take care of people's personalities, [their] worries and that kind of thing. That sounds horrible, and I don't mean it that way....but I believe that Brad does what Brad does best. That's why he has continued to run networks, and stay at the top of his game for as long as he has. So I have mad - *mad* respect for his business skills.

"Personal skills? Eh.

"He could use a coach."

Chapter 56:
One Monday in Florida

W HEN HURTLING TOWARDS the inevitable, time distorts. It speeds up, slows down, stretches and compresses until assuredly, it expires. Once nothing, it becomes everything. A simple smile takes on new meaning. Words of wisdom linger longer. The loudest look could last forever.

And then, it hits you. Conscious effort notwithstanding, you grapple with an unconscious refrain:

This is it.

Time flies, but memories stay grounded. It's why looking back on a painful 'goodbye' - even with the passage of months, years, or even longer - greets us so vividly upon recall.

For a handful of souls, such send-offs are communal. On the surface, the heartache is shared, but in the moment, it only compounds. Some can never talk about it. Others close their eyes, weary to revive a painful post-mortem. A minority can emote the flagrant finality. "It was…a death," recalls David Crockett. "A death."

Standing amidst an ethereal backdrop, at once hopeful but *heavy*, Crockett prepared to extemporize a eulogy. Conjecture aside, he knew - *they* knew - that this gathering was final. While surely, there would be some meet-again-soons, call-you-on-Sundays, and let's-stay-togethers, it would never quite be like this again.

In short, *this was it.*

"I just wanted to thank everyone," Crockett says of his speech, delivered backstage before the final *Monday Nitro.* "We all had such a wonderful life. We were family, and the family wasn't gonna be together again.

"[I said], 'we can definitely be proud of what we accomplished. We did so many things that no-one thought we could do'. [Because] everybody stepped up - *everybody*. Just to be able to adapt…I don't think a sane person could have handled it."

Standing adjacent to Crockett was Shane McMahon, sent by his Dad - alongside a small contingent of WWF officials - to oversee the end of *Nitro*. "It's like they were expecting us…," Crockett begins, "…I don't know what. We weren't gonna sabotage anything."

With McMahon looking on, Crockett summoned a stirring soliloquy, making reference to his father, the Crockett territory, and WCW's creation itself. Ironically, while his protests against the original Turner purchase were unsuccessful ("[JCP] was part of my heritage," he says), it was a stance that now seemed prophetic. "[In '88], I didn't wanna go in to a corporation," Crockett recalls. "You get lost."

Deftly, and with an aplomb reminiscent of his own father, Shane spoke next. Somewhat convincingly, he described the situation as the 'blending of two great companies', offering an olive branch so often promised in Stamford, Connecticut: *opportunity*. Some wanted to believe him. Others couldn't believe their eyes.

Meanwhile, at nearby *Club La Vela* - a familiar locale hosting an unfamiliar ambiance - spring break revelers raved all around. Similar debauchery, according to legend, first took root in Ancient Greece, and later, rather famously, in Ancient Rome. Like all great empires, however, both eventually declined - a consequence of infighting, overexpansion and instability - perhaps the universal symptoms, some wondered, of unchecked success.

Backstage, the gladiators waxed philosophically. Some of it was caught on camera - Dustin talking about Dusty, Flair about Sting, Booker T, in a departure from the mood, talking of the future. Coworkers rushed to take photos with each other, faces old and new combining for one last embrace. A terse order soon broke up the procession: *set up some space for the WWF people*, they were told.

An hour before air time, fans participated in a special pre-show on WCW.com, calling in to the broadcast with sadness in their voices. Hosts Jeremy Borash and Bob Ryder offered their own thoughts on the passing scene, remaining hopeful that somehow - in some incarnation - WCW would survive. At about 7:20pm EST, the voice of one particular caller pierced through the airwaves. He sounded especially familiar, but also dejected, opting to deliver a statement rather than ask a question. "Listen…" began the caller, identified by Borash as 'Vince from Atlanta'. "I just wanted to wish you two guys a lot of luck. "Whatever happens with…your careers, I really enjoyed listening to *WCW Live*.

"And, if you don't mind, I'd like to give a shout out to my friends on *VinceRusso.org*…"

For the first time ever, TNT agreed to 'simulcast' its feed with *USA*, enabling the *Raw* transmission to be duplicated - at specific moments - with the live *Nitro* broadcast. Effectively, this arrangement removed autonomy from WCW over its final program, and allowed McMahon to end the *Nitro* era on his own terms. Moreover, according to online reports, he would be given the final 17 minutes - uninterrupted - to do as he pleased.

But with the sale now official, McMahon and the WWF controlled *Nitro*'s content regardless. His henchmen requested the show script on Sunday night, but showed up on Monday with a radically different format, rewriting planned matches, segments and videos in the process. One element that would survive, among only a handful, was the scheduled main event bout between Ric Flair and Sting (attributed, in later years, to a mandate from McMahon himself).

Back in Cleveland, the site of *Raw*, the mood was unmistakably "tense," recalls former WWF writer Pete Doyle. "It was kind of like knowing you're gonna win a big game or award. You know it's coming - it's in the bag - but until it happens, it's just anxiety.

"[It was] a very secretive day, and some things [were planned] that 'creative' wasn't even in on. Not many of the WWF roster knew Shane was in [Florida], until some of the WCW talent called their buddies at WWF that day, [asking], 'Shane McMahon is here - are we fucked?'"

In a circular tribute to historical events (namely, his shocking appearance on TBS in 1984), both shows started with a surreal sight: Vince McMahon, ostensibly in 'character', gloating over his purchase of WCW. *"Imagine that,"* he boasted, standing in front of a display showcasing the WWF's logo. *"Me - Vince McMahon. Imagine that. Here I am on WCW television. How can that happen?*

"Well, there's only one way. You see, it was just a matter of time before I, Vince McMahon, bought my competition. That's right. I own WCW...

"...[so] what is the fate of WCW? Well tonight, in a special simulcast, you will all find out. Because the fate - the very fate of WCW - is in my hands."

McMahon's opening remarks set the stage perfectly for a rebuttal. It would come from none other than Ric Flair, who for all his trials and tribulations, remained WCW's favorite son. *"Did I - did I - woooo! Did I...happen...to hear...Vince...McMahon...say...*

"He...was going...to hold...WCW, in the palms of his hands? Is that what he said?

"Does that mean that you are gonna hold Jack Brisco, Dory Funk, Harley Race, the Road Warriors, Sting, Luger, the Steiners, Bagwell, Ric Flair, Steamboat...does that mean you're gonna hold us all in the palm of your hands? To coin a phrase, I don't think so!

"You know, at 12 o'clock today, someone very special to me said, 'do not go onto that show tonight, knowin' it's the last time you'll ever be on TNT or TBS'...she said to me, 'don't go out there and cry - don't go out there and say you're sorry'...

"...I'm not! I've been fourteen times the world champion, in one of the greatest - you got it! The greatest wrestling organization in the world, WCW!

"...As a matter of fact, we have run neck and neck with you, Vince McMahon, for years! For years! And just for trivia, Vince McMahon, do you know that in 1981 - when you were trying to become an announcer - your dad was on the [NWA] board of directors, and [he] voted for me to be the world champion! Woooo! How 'bout that?

"And ever since that day, I have been a limousine ridin', jet flyin', kiss stealin', wheelin' dealin', son of a gun, that along with the whole WCW dammit all...kissed the girls worldwide! And made 'em cry.

"...It's always been WWF vs. WCW in the 'office'. The 'boys' have gone out there, night in and night out, doing everything they could to be the very best at what they chose to do in their life!

"...[so] we're not going anywhere! You can't hold us in your hand and predict our life! We're WCW! We've bled and we've sweat... when was the last time you wrestled for an hour, cut yourself five times...bled for forty-five minutes...when were you there? You weren't! You weren't! You were never in the dressing room, on the road forty days and forty nights...bleedin', sweatin', goin' to the next town...

"...in closing, let me say this. In all my years in this sport, my greatest opponent with this company has been Sting. So tonight, if we're going out, we're going out on a high note. Stinger - the Nature Boy wants you right here, because...to be the man, you've gotta beat the man, and Sting - I'm. The. Man. Woooo!"

Flair's promo came across as *especially* real, but in a business founded on blurring lines, it was merely another great performance. Desperate for WCW to close, Flair later scoffed at the notion that he was sincere, emphasizing that after all, he was simply playing his part. "Nothing could be further from the truth," he wrote, several years later, in reference to his televised comments.

On a night of unavoidable heartbreak, however, the first match provided viewers with a reprieve. Despite rumors indicating otherwise, Scott Steiner dropped the WCW title to Booker T., who after eight long years of dedication, closed the company with both Heavyweight belts. *"Give him all the hardware!"* yelled announcer Tony Schiavone, his voice breaking. *"He's the man!"*

Booker's win may have been a feel good moment, but its emotion paled against what was to come. With less than 30 minutes of air time remaining, Flair walked to the ring, conceivably for the last time. *"Very few men,"* lionized Schiavone on commentary, *"in any walk of life...can say they've had the career of Ric Flair. He's done it all.*

"We have no idea if we will ever be bringing you World Championship Wrestling again. [It's] the last night on TNT. And here comes a man who has meant everything to many fans around the world, Sting..."

"When it was in vogue to jump from World Championship Wrestling to the World Wrestling Federation," added color commentator Scott Hudson. *"...this man...was loyal! He bled WCW! He slept WCW!"*

For the next eight minutes, Sting and Flair showcased the chemistry that WCW so often relied on, taking fans on a nostalgic trip down memory lane. Backstage, as the competitors worked through their tried-and-true routine, an emotional group of witnesses huddled around the monitor, struggling mightily to fight back tears. At one stage, even Schiavone appeared to be overrun with sentimentality, perhaps being transported - however briefly - to his time as a young fan. *"We've seen it so many times..."* he observed as Sting mounted his offense, *"but god we love it - each and every moment!"*

Post-match, in a touching moment that couldn't be fabricated, the competitors embraced. In later retellings, many witnesses described the scene as being more than poignant, or even touching; rather, given the circumstances, history and uncertainty ahead, it was *moving* - perhaps the most legitimate few seconds ever in pro wrestling.

"It's been an emotional roller-coaster for all of us, fans," Schiavone said in a heartfelt final address.

"The uncertainty of our jobs...our future...of what we love...of what we breathe...of what we live. We don't just work for WCW - we live WCW - and I know Flair, Sting and the fans would agree."

And then, abruptly and without warning, the picture faded to Cleveland. "Watching Vince appear on the jumbo screens," remembers former WCW producer Chris Larson, "...it was a tough pill to swallow. But this was Vince's victory lap, and he was going to make the most of it."

At the height of the wrestling wars, McMahon once told a reporter that above all, his job was to influence perceptions. In concert with this philosophy, he gleefully used his time on TNT - under the guise, naturally, of his on-screen persona - to deride WCW, its performers and even Ted Turner himself:

"Time Warner can't sell this property to anybody else, because nobody really knows what to do with it...Time Warner is practically begging me - they're practically begging me to buy WCW, and I have agreed.

"There's only one small caveat...they've signed the contract...but I'll sign it this Sunday on pay-per-view at WrestleMania. I'll sign it when Ted Turner himself walks down the aisle at WrestleMania and delivers the contract in front of me."

Masterfully, McMahon managed to leverage his own issues with Turner, ridicule his rivals, and - after a show-closing swerve featuring son Shane - further a storyline leading up to *WrestleMania*. *"The deal is finalized, and the name on the contract does say McMahon..."* taunted Shane. *"However, the contract reads 'Shane McMahon'. I now own WCW!"*

In reality, just as Ted Turner couldn't save WCW, neither could Shane. It may have taken thirteen years, half a dozen bosses, and a handful of executives overseeing the worst merger in history, but finally, Ted's *rasslin'* was no more.

Unable to lead, and never one to follow, he could only get out of the way.

Epilogue

On WEDNESDAY, March 28th, 2001, WCW officially began the process of closing down. As per Brad Siegel's memo, its employees were summoned to the Power Plant in Smyrna to receive "further information" about the WWF purchase, although Siegel himself - not that it was lost on those in attendance - failed to attend.

In anticipation of being fired, some particularly savvy staff members took preemptive measures ahead of time, securing valuable mementos from the 'Log Cabin' facility. Even still, much of the company paraphernalia remained on display as the workers filed in, destined to end up in a WWF warehouse. "They gathered everyone in the back area, where we had the wrestling school," notes Rob Garner. "All the banners from the pay-per-views were hanging back there. I'm standing there, looking at all that history around me, and here's someone from WWF standing in one of our rings. It was so weird just being there, knowing it was over."

Alongside an unidentified WWF representative, Loretta Walker - Turner's Vice President of Human Resources - addressed the group upon arrival. According to several witnesses, Walker advised that all positions would be terminated, effective March 30th, with severance packages forthcoming. Employees recall the WWF rep saying little, aside from a vague promise of 'opportunity' and an acknowledgment of WCW 'as great competition for all these years'.

While before the meeting, there remained some hopeful optimism - perhaps owing, at least somewhat, to Shane McMahon's allusion of a 'merger' - the hope soon vanished once staff were given boxes to collect their belongings. They were organized into groups of 10, told to remove everything from their desks, and instructed to see a Turner rep to discuss severance paperwork.

However, as the group were about to find out, their work computers and e-mail accounts were already shut down (causing writer Bill Banks, after a year of effort, to lose an almost-finished novel in the process). Pagers and cell phones were confiscated, meaning there would be no chance to retrieve important work contacts. A Turner rep, apparently affected by the unfolding scene, turned to a colleague in concern. Audible to all in the vicinity, he couldn't help but to ask a pressing question: *do you think people are upset?*

"They had police there checking us," David Crockett says. "All the phones were cut off, and the computers [were too], supposedly to stop us downloading anything, or taking anything.

"They locked the whole place down, and you were searched by a policeman. A WWF guy was there...and I didn't even know who he was. I had several boxes [with me], and he said, 'you can't take that stuff'. I said, 'yes, I can - it's *mine*!' It really was an insult."

"We stood in line while security checked through everything in our boxes," remembers Chris Larson. "It was a rather rude way for [things] to wrap up."

Concurrent to the office clearing, an important transaction was in progress, one that was integral to the WCW sale itself. "A WWF employee demanded to know where the tape library was, and instructed everyone not to take anything," reports an anonymous former employee. The tapes, reportedly disorganized upon retrieval, ultimately became a cornerstone of the *WWE Network*, launched in February 2014.

Interestingly, according to another source, a section of the exit paperwork attributed not the WWF purchase as causing WCW's shutdown, but rather, the AOL-Time Warner merger. In any event, the deal was done, and there was no going back - a fact underscored when everyone left the building. "Our ID cards were immediately deactivated," says the source.

"It was a real sad experience," remembers Greg Prince. "I was having a tremendous time working at WCW. It was a real challenging, fun and exciting work environment. But I can recall sitting in the building in Smyrna, and having the Turner HR people over from downtown. They gave everyone the news, and people were crying, because a lot of those people had been in WCW forever. They were looking at it like, 'there probably isn't a different option for me within Turner Broadcasting'."

In fact, there had been rumblings - even assurances, some say - that some WCW staff would be reassigned, a promise that helped cushion the blow of being terminated. Inevitably, however, in perhaps the final parting shot of TBS' association with wrestling, nothing ever materialized.

Postscript

WCW was eventually integrated, albeit rather clumsily, into WWF story lines that summer. In a missed opportunity lamented in countless books, articles and commentaries, only a handful of top stars made the transition over, and the 'invasion' failed to resonate with most fans.

As part of AOL-Time Warner, WCW - under the reclassified name of *Universal Wrestling Corporation (UWC)* - technically continued to exist post 2001, a measure necessary to deal with its countless unresolved lawsuits. Incredibly, UWC survived as an entity until December 5th, 2017, when it was finally absorbed back into Turner Broadcasting. Humorously, a TBS web page purporting *WCW Thunder* as being 'on hiatus' also survived the 16 years.

While still relatively popular, and perhaps even thriving on an independent level, pro wrestling has failed to regain its mainstream following of the mid to late '90s. "There aren't necessarily 'hard and fast' reasons," reflects Professor Sam Ford, "to explain why it happened - when it happened - other than the right combination of factors.

"You had the right personalities…the right writing team, who were capturing a cultural zeitgeist…and the rise of Internet culture, which I think did play a role. Both promotions responded to that [phenomena], and wrestling did something it never did before – it 'played with the curtain'.

"But the competition played a major role, too. The fact that you had two major networks and two major companies pouring resources - not just in to putting on a good show - but trying to beat one another. It meant that in some ways, they lost their logic, but [ultimately] to the benefit of the fan."

"Having competitive elements on television is really important," agrees Dr. Harvey Schiller. "It was always 'us against them', and

560

'them against us'. Everybody knows what happened when WCW disappeared - the ratings for the other group went down."

"They still can't get away from that era of guys," argues Kevin Nash, "because the business has never been hotter. It's why the Rolling Stones still show up at the Super Bowl every eight years. It's hard [though] - because the [WWE] Network still plays that era. When I do a signing, I've got 10, 11, and 12 year old kids that throw up the Wolfpac sign...or have an nWo shirt on. The Network doesn't tell you that this was 85 years ago...it just says, 'this is the Monday Night Wars'."

According to Jack Encarnacao, co-host of the popular *Lapsed Fan Wrestling Podcast*, the industry has failed to surpass its 'Monday Night Wars' peak - both in terms of artistic merit and cultural significance.

"It used to be better in this time period for a few reasons," he says. "One - the hyper competition for talent imbued wrestlers with a higher value in the minds of fans, and forced bookers to go all-in on creating new stars when people left. Bookers couldn't afford to fight the crowd in this era, [in order] to force something they didn't want down their throats. And that made for more excitement and constant 'freshness' when guys would jump ship.

"Wrestlers were also allowed to go further in their promos - in terms of saucy language, violent rhetoric, and adult themes - at a time the cultural zeitgeist was characterized by Jerry Springer and South Park.

"Also, the talent that defined this era was perhaps the last to come up at a time when you learned how to get yourself over. This embedded in them the right instincts to make their matches and promos engrossing for the fan. They weren't left flat-footed when crowds didn't respond as anticipated, a huge problem today for guys who essentially train to remember scripts and hit certain spots, and are more focused on the hard camera than the jeering fans in the arena."

When asked to articulate its ubiquity during the Monday Night Wars,

Encarnacao says wrestling was "on the pop culture map in the late 90s. It had young males by the balls. You'd see WWF merchandise as often as you'd see South Park merchandise.

"Mainstream media couldn't stop doing stories about how edgy it was. The Stone Cold character captured the angst of a waning Generation X, and the nWo and DX updated what it looked like to be rebel cool. In [2018], what makes wrestlers cool registers only with wrestling fans - there are way less characters that an outsider can recognize as special.

"And there's too much wink-wink, we're-all-in-on-the-joke' stuff in how wrestling is presented today. I think there's so much instant social media reaction to these guys that they think they're killing it - even if no one outside of that bubble gives a shit about them - which should be the overriding goal. The modern feedback loop is a bad thing for something like wrestling. It takes the eye off the prize, or obfuscates what the prize really ought to be."

When asked about the impact of WCW's death on pro wrestling, Jerry Jarrett responds solemnly. "If you sense some lingering resentment on my part because of the total failure of WCW," says Jarrett, "you are correct.

"The death of that company changed the landscape of professional wrestling - at least for my lifetime. I hold professional wrestling in a special place in my heart, because it is - as I've often said - 'Shakespeare for the masses'. It is the only form of theater that many will ever see. It taught that good prevails and evil is well...evil to so many young people. Vince McMahon does not claim to be professional wrestling, and in fact, his promotion is not professional wrestling. Pro wrestling died with the death of WCW."

"As a wrestling fan," adds Diamond Dallas Page, "and as one of 'the boys', I wanted both companies to be around forever. The last thing anybody wanted was one monster monopoly."

Bill Behrens, wrestling's 'power agent' to many top stars, believes

562

there were numerous industry changes post-WCW. "Because WCW ended," Behrens observes, "TNA started and is still in business [under the name Impact Wrestling] 16 years later. But the 3-5 million people that watched WCW TV did not move to WWE - nor TNA. In WCW's absence, WWE stayed number one and changed its business substantially, going public, creating a new distribution platform with the [WWE] Network, and launching new brands like NXT, to fill some of the gap."

"Pro Wrestling, as a programming genre, is considered to be at the lower end - broadcast or cable," says Garth Ancier, former EVP of Programming at TBS. "[But] WWE is a non-commercial success on SVOD (Subscription Video on demand). Subscribers like it, so the WWE SVOD channel - where consumers pay for access without commercials - is a big success. I applaud their success."

While reflecting on the last wrestling boom, ex-WWF President Stu Snyder cites *fragmentation* as a crucial change since the *Nitro* era. "Today's landscape, first of all, is so fragmented," he says. "I'm not so sure you could necessarily see the same popularity [for wrestling] again, although I never say 'never'.

"But today's viewers are different, between short form video, to long form cable, over-the-top platforms...it's so fragmented in terms of how folks are getting their content.

"In addition, since that time, *new* events have taken place. MMA has exploded, from the standpoint of competition for viewers, and also for purchasing dollars. So I think everything now is a little more complicated...but at the end of the day, it's still all about exciting content.

"If someone comes along with exciting content, and wants to compete, I'll never say 'never' about the opportunity for that. [However], what makes it a little tougher is the cable landscape. Could you ever see cable companies competing again like they did? You had WCW on the Turner networks and WWF on the networks of Viacom, at that time. Could you ever see that again?

"Possibly, but it was also personality driven at that time. Boy, that was lightning in a bottle. I'd like to believe it could be done again. I know people are always gonna keep trying with new formats, new shows, and new ideas - always."

One of the personalities Snyder alludes to is, of course, Ted Turner. Fittingly, as someone often described as a 'dying breed' - considering his self-determination, bombastic nature, and unapologetic leadership - he is now concerned mostly with conservation. According to the *Ted Turner Expeditions* website, "his focuses have shifted from cable ratings and baseball standings to species conservation and nuclear weapons eradication, among many other passions. Turner hopes for a simple, yet momentous legacy – 'to leave this world a better place for future generations to come'."

Upon receiving requests related to this project, Ted Turner's office issued the following statement to the author:

Although Mr. Turner has very fond memories of his time as owner of WCW, he now devotes his time almost exclusively to the work of his foundations and existing business partnerships...we appreciate your understanding, and wish you success with your book project.

Of Mr. Turner's prior employees, relatively few declined an interview request for this project. One of those few was Bradley Siegel, former President of Turner Entertainment Networks and from 2000-2001, the figurehead of WCW. In a brief telephone conversation, Mr. Siegel first agreed to speak on-the-record, subject to attorney approval, but subsequently indicated - through a third-party - that he "no longer wished to participate."

Eric Bischoff shocked the wrestling world by eventually signing with Vince McMahon, working purely as an on-screen talent from 2002 to 2007. In 2010, he took part in an attempt to reignite the Monday Night Wars, joining TNA Wrestling in an Executive Producer role. However, after less than three months of the ratings contest, despite Bischoff's prior suggestion that "history was repeating itself," TNA bowed out of competing directly with the WWE.

564

As of the publication date, Bischoff maintains a cordial relationship with the WWE, and was profiled in a popular 2016 documentary, *Sports Entertainment's Most Controversial Figure*. When asked if he would change anything about his WCW tenure, he said the following:

"Some of this is the luxury one has of retrospect, and '20-20 hindsight'," Bischoff begins.

"I really wish I could've been smarter and more sophisticated in my dealings with the corporate side of my company. I wished I would've had the foresight to really understand the dynamic that happens when one company buys another company. Because I had never been in that position before - I had no idea. I took everything at face value. When Gerald Levin said...at the beginning of the Time Warner-Turner merger, 'this is why I'm so excited about these two companies coming together - because Time Warner needs the entrepreneurial instincts that the Turner organization brings to the table', I believed it. But nothing could be further from the truth. It was exactly the fucking opposite.

"But I believed it. So I wish I would've been smart enough to see the handwriting on the wall, and to see that that's not how it works. How it really works is that all those entrepreneurs in Turner were now going to start wearing wing tip shoes, and dark blue suits, and white shirts, and red ties - to be just like their Time Warner counterparts. It wasn't the merging of the entrepreneurial spirit of Turner into Time Warner, it was the corporate environment of Time Warner overwhelming and killing the entrepreneurial spirit that Ted Turner built his company on.

"That's what it really was. I know that now, but I didn't know it then, and I wish I would've been smart enough to have a better perspective on what was likely to happen. Because I would've handled things differently. I wouldn't pick the same battles that I [ended up picking]. I wouldn't have taken certain positions as aggressively as I did, had I known what was really going on. And oh - by the way - Ted Turner didn't know it either.

"He didn't know he was getting the carpet pulled out from underneath him, once AOL [came in to the picture]. He didn't know that there were people that he thought were his partners - and his peers - working secretly to undermine him, to take away the control and power he had of his own company. So I feel badly that I wasn't smarter or didn't have a better vision or more experience, but at the same time, Ted Turner himself didn't either. So I try not to beat myself up over it.

"I've learned that if I were ever in the same situation again - believe me - I would look at things much differently than I did back then. And I wouldn't take things at face value. That's probably it, really. There's millions of other things, but that's the most prominent one."

Acknowledgements

Firstly, to my wife, Aysha, for your undying love and support. I simply could not have done this without your encouragement, sacrifice and help. You are truly one of a kind, both as my soul mate and mother to our baby boy.

He is beautiful, and so are you.

This project has benefited from the kind and gracious assistance of many people, and hopefully, all will be mentioned here (!). A special acknowledgment is due to Neal Pruitt, whose insight and knowledge are to be admired. Neal was frequently cited as "one of the good guys" in these interviews, and it's easy to see why.

So to Neal: thanks so much for believing in the concept, and putting up with all of my questions. I truly appreciate it.

In one of our earliest conversations, Neal spoke glowingly about the WCW production team - "one of the greatest crews of all-time," in his estimation. After speaking with many of these people, I don't doubt his judgment for a minute. I learned a little something (or, in many cases, a lot of something!) from each interaction, but I'd especially like to thank Jason Douglas, who first answered my queries in 2015.

During our initial conversation, I asked Jason a series of questions about a department completely unrelated to his position, showing a (relative) lack of understanding at the time (at least, compared to now - I hope!). Nevertheless, Jason never made a big deal about it, and it was only having listened back to our talk that I realized the error. So Jason - thanks for your patience and all of the insight. It was tremendously helpful.

Rob Garner was the first interviewee for this project, way back in January 2015. He was instrumental in improving my baseline knowledge of the WCW-TBS relationship, and provided an excellent springboard for discussions with others. Thank you.

Of this whole endeavor, one of the most enjoyable experiences was visiting Bill Burke (formerly TBS Network President) in Portland, Maine. I am still struck with how enthusiastic, engaging and positive Mr. Burke was, and appreciate his valuable understanding of the TV business. What a great guy!

I am also grateful to Eric Bischoff, who spent time - over two separate days - responding to my questions thoughtfully and articulately. His willingness to be interviewed was extremely helpful, especially in understanding the contextual factors at play. Thank you very much for the time.

To Dick Cheatham: I appreciate the great conversation, humor, and crash course in accounting (!). If you have any ideas for another book, please let me know, because I'd love to continue talking!

To Greg Prince: Thanks for being so detailed in your explanation of the TBS financial structure.

To Brian Sites: Thank you for helping with my understanding of the Internet division, and the mechanisms involved in web broadcasting. The hot chocolate wasn't bad, either!

To Jason Glast: You were kind enough to interrupt your vacation to talk, and then were available to meet in San Antonio. I learned a lot from speaking with you - thanks!

To Diamond Dallas Page: Congratulations on your post-wrestling success, and thank you for the time. Many interviewees cited you as a positive influence in their career, which says a lot. Thanks again.

To Kevin Nash: I appreciated your willingness, while recovering from surgery, to speak with me on the phone. Thanks for being so gracious with your time.

To Buff Bagwell: One of the best storytellers I had the pleasure to interview. Thanks for taking my call and listening to the pitch to begin with. I appreciate it.

To Kevin Sullivan: Learning about the mechanics of booking was fascinating. Thanks for a very insightful talk.

To David Crockett: Thank you for the insight on the WCW production process, JCP history and environment at Turner. It was a great pleasure speaking with you.

To Jerry Jarrett: Your thoughtful answers provided much clarity, in regards to both the history of wrestling and its performers. Many thanks indeed.

I also would like to specifically acknowledge: David Penzer (the only man at every *Nitro*!), Michelle Baines, Chad Damiani, Lenita Erickson, Luther Biggs, Pat McNeely, Phillip Kidwell, Bill Cunningham, Galen Chandler, Dave Pava, Joe Uva, Mike Ciraldo, Neill Cameron, Sonny Onoo, Richard Turner, Randy Thornton, Sean Bresloff, Scot Safon, Bill Behrens, Andy Gillentine, Ben Miller, Stephen O'Laughlin, Ray Lloyd, Howard Helm, Brian Fritz, Sam Ford (fascinating insight), Germaine Gioia, Jack Encarnacao (brilliant), Bill Demott, Chung deh Tien, Alan Sharp, Mike Weber (available for conversations three years apart), Bobby Blaze (great stuff on the life of a wrestler), Jason Shaya, Brad Lanoue, Jeff Lawrence, Vince Russo, Jason Weiner, Matt Williams, Andre Freitas, Jeff Bornstein, Brendon Hamlin, Michael Polydoroff, Sanders Keel (good call getting Raven on the cover), Bryan Barrera (go to WCWWorldwide.com), 'nWo Wolfpac TV', Kyle Shiely, Jon Marks, all the interviewees (over 120 in total) - and those who gave their time on an off-the-record basis. *Apologies if I forgot you!!*

In large part, NITRO is the culmination of many hundreds of hours talking to key TBS and WCW employees. I was also fortunate enough to have access to various company records and materials to supplement my research. Therefore, the outcome is a highly original book that hopefully - at the risk of sounding hyperbolic - has added greatly to fans' understanding of this time period.

So finally, a big thank you to YOU - the reader. I hope that you have

569

enjoyed reading NITRO as much as I did writing it. Please feel free to drop me a line via e-mail (guyevanswcwbook@gmail.com) or social media (@WCWNitroBook). Who knows…maybe there will be more to come.

Guy Evans

June 2018

New York, NY

"Either lead, follow, or get out of the way."

Sources and References

Books

Baker, A. (2003). *Contesting Identities: Sports in American Film.*

Bibb, P. (1997). *Ted Turner: It Ain't As Easy As It Looks.*

Bischoff, E. (2006). *Controversy Creates Cash.*

Burke, B. and Turner, T. (2008). *Call Me Ted.*

Clarke, B. And Crossland, R. (2002). *The Leader's Voice: How Your Communication Can Inspire Action and Get Results!*

Culp, C.L. and Niskanen, W. A. (2003). *Corporate Aftershock: The Public Policy Lessons from the Collapse of Enron and Other Major Corporations.*

Deford, F. (2014). *Five Strides on the Banked Track.*

Dillon, J. (2005). *Wrestlers Are Like Seagulls-From McMahon to McMahon.*

Dixon, J., Henry, J. and Reynolds, R.D. (2016). *Titan Screwed.*

Dixon, J. (2014). *Titan Sinking.*

Dylan, B. (2004). *Chronicles, Volume One.*

Goldberg, B. (2000). *I'm Next! The Strange Journey of America's Most Unlikely Superhero.*

Griffiths, I. (1986). *Creative Accounting: How to Make Your Profits What You Want Them to Be.*

Hart, B. (2007). *Hitman: My Real Life in the Cartoon World of Wrestling.*

Jarrett, J. (2011). *The Best of Times.*

Jericho, C. (2007). *A Lion's Tale: Around The World In Spandex.*

Lipschultz, J. (2018). *Free Expression in the Age of the Internet: Social and*

Legal Boundaries.

McQueeney, W.T. (2012). *Sunsets Over Charleston: More Conversations with Visionaries, Luminaries, and Emissaries of the Holy City.*

Mooneyham, M. and Assael, S. (2004). *Sex, Lies, and Headlocks: The Real Story of Vince McMahon and World Wrestling Entertainment.*

Mould, B. (2013). See a Little Light: The Trail of Rage and Melody.

Munk, N. (2004). *Fools Rush In: Steve Case, Jerry Levin and the Unmaking of AOL Time Warner.*

Ornstein, R. E. and Ehrlich, P. R. (2000). *New World New Mind: Moving Towards Conscious Evolution.*

Pfohl, L. (2013). *Wrestling with the Devil: The True Story of a World Champion Professional Wrestler - his Reign, Ruin and Redemption.*

Reynolds, R.D. and Alvarez (2014). *The Death of WCW: 10th Anniversary of the Bestselling Classic.*

Reynolds, R.D. and Alvarez (2004). *The Death of WCW.*

Ries, A. And Trout, J. (1993). *The 22 Immutable Laws of Marketing.*

Riley, P. (1988). *Showtime.*

Ruder, D.S. (2008). *Strategies for Investing in Intellectual Property.* Beard Books: Hopkins, MN.

Russo, V. (2010). *Rope Opera: How WCW Killed Vince Russo.*

Russo, V. (2005). *Forgiven: One Man's Journey from Self-Glorification to Sanctification.*

Sowell, T. (2005). *Black Rednecks and White Liberals.*

Thoreau, H. D. (1854). *Walden.*

Wertsch, M. E. (2006). *Military Brats: Legacies of Childhood Inside the Fortress.*

Ziglar, Z. (1984). *Secrets of Closing the Sale.*

Newspaper and Magazine Articles
Adalian, J. and Dempsey, J. (1998). NBC, Turner Wrestle with NBA options. *Variety.* December 23, 1998.

Auletta, K. (2001). Ted Turner: The Lost Tycoon. *The New Yorker.* April 23, 2001.

Baldwin, K. (1999). Ring Leader: Vince Russo. *Entertainment Weekly.* November 12, 1999.

Bates, J. (1995). Bill Gates Again at No.1 on Forbes Wealthiest List. *The Los Angeles Times.* October 2, 1995.

Bedell, S. (1982). Ted Turner Challenges TV Networks. *The New York Times.* October 17, 1982.

Browning, E.S. (1999). Goodbye to the Golden Decade. Now What Will the '00s Bring? *The Wall Street Journal.* December 13, 1999.

Cady, S. (1977). A Brash Captain Outrageous: Robert Edward Turner 3rd. *The New York Times.* September 19, 1995.

Carter, B. (1998). Cable and Broadcast Networks Clinch Over Wrestling Ad Revenue. *The New York Times.* August 17, 1998.

Carter, K.L. (1995). Grunting for Dollars. *Philadelphia Inquirer.* June 27, 1995.

Dawson, G. (1993). Nielsen Meters Gauge a Penchant for Fibbing. *Orlando Sentinel.* April 8, 1993.

De Moraes, L. (1999). TNT Finally Tosses Its Staged Gay-Bashing Spectacle Out of the Ring. *The Washington Post.* October 12, 1999.

Dean, D. (1967). The Nielsen Rating for a Box of Spaghetti: Competitors Claim Nielsen's Methods are Outdated. *The New York Times.* July 30, 1967.

Denberg, J. (1997). Sunday Special: Another arena for Rodman. *The Atlanta Journal Constitution.* March 16, 1997.

Diamos, J. (1997). Rodman's Kick is Costly: 11 Games and $1 Million. *The New York Times*. January 18, 1997.

Doolittle, L. (1997). Rodman Coming to Daytona to Kick Butt. *Orlando Sentinel*. June 27, 1997.

Drucker, J. (1999). King of the Ring. *Cigar Aficionado*. Nov/Dec 1999.

Emerson, B. (1999). 35 Million Viewers Can't Be Wrong. *The Atlanta Journal-Constitution*. April 13, 1999.

Flint, J. and Beatty, S. (2001). WB Network Chief Kellner Takes Over Turner Operations at AOL Time Warner. *The Wall Street Journal*. March 7, 2001.

Forman, R. (1997). Bad as He Wants to Be: Anti-Hero Hulk Hogan is Bent on Destroying World Championship Wrestling. *Chicago Tribune*. August 13, 1997.

Gabler, N. (1995). The Culture Wars: The Democratic Spirit's Romance with Trash. *The Los Angeles Times*. June 4, 1995.

Goldwyn, R. (1993). Ted, Jane and The Braves Coming to Town. *Philadelphia Daily News*. October 5, 1993.

Gross, D. (1998). WCW blames injuries for Sunday pay-per-view snafu. *Savannah Morning News*. October 29, 1998.

Haddad, C. (1993). Ted Turner is Launching a Classic Movie Channel. *The Baltimore Sun*. October 31, 1993.

Harris, L. (1998). Hold On to Your Remotes: The New Taboo TV Coming This Fall Uses Explicit Violence, Daring Subject Matter and Raunchy Language to Hook Viewers, Build Ratings. *The Atlanta Journal-Constitution*. August 2, 1998.

Helmore, E. (1999). No Limits for Master P. *The Guardian*. October 16, 1999.

Hobson, W. (2016). UFC, which took mixed martial arts from fringe to mainstream, sells for $4 billion. *The Washington Post*. July 11, 2016.

Kerr, P. (1989). Now It Can Be Told: Those Pro Wrestlers Are Just Having Fun. *The New York Times*. February 10, 1989.

Kleinfeld, N.R. (1989). This Is Not Real. *The New York Times*. November 26, 1989.

Kloer, P. (1998). Channel Surfer TV Tour Talk: Truth Out There Somewhere. *The Atlanta Constitution*. July 28, 1998.

Kuczynski, A. (1999). Wrestling, Once Ad-Libbed, Is Now As Carefully Scripted As A Top-Rated Soap Opera. *The New York Times*. November 22, 1999.

Landler, M. (1995). Time Warner to Sell Stake in Rap Label. *The New York Times*. September 28, 1995.

Landler, M. (1995). Turner to Merge into Time Warner; a $7.5 Billion Deal. *The New York Times*. September 23, 1995.

Leydon, J. (1996). Santa with Muscles. *Variety*. November 17, 1996.

Lieberman, P. (1998). The Ultimate Grudge Match. *The Los Angeles Times*. November 15, 1998.

Katz, R. (1998). Steve Heyer Boosted at TBS. *Variety*. January 28, 1998.

Marvez, A. (2003). Bresloff Was A Good Man to Have in Wrestling's Corner. *South Florida Sun-Sentinel*. June 27, 2003.

Marvez, A. (1998). 'Monday Night Raw' Huge for WWF, USA. *Atlanta Journal-Constitution*. August 17, 1998.

Marvez, A. (1996). Monday Nitro Will Expand to 2 Hours. *Dayton Daily News*. May 12, 1996.

Mooneyham, M. (2001). Bischoff Faces Tougher Task This Time. *Charleston Post and Courier*. January 14, 2001.

Mooneyham, M. (1999). JR Parody Bottom of Barrel. *Charleston Post and Courier*. November 9, 1999.

Mooneyham, M. (1999). Vince Russo Joins WCW. *Charleston Post and Courier*. September 16, 1999.

Mulligan, T. (1996). Turner-Time Warner Merger Approved by Shareholders. *The Los Angeles Times*. October 11, 1996.

Patton, J. (1999). The General Awards the Best, Worst of '98. *The Miami Herald*. January 7, 1999.

Pearlman, J. (1999). Goldberg is the WCW's Hottest Star, But He's Still Bitter About his NFL Career. *Sports Illustrated*. April 19, 1999.

Povich, S. (1931). Why Wrestling Has Stolen the Show from Boxing and Who is Responsible. *The Washington Post*. August 16, 1931.

Robichaux, M. (1996). In This Corner, Ted 'Hulk' Turner, in the Other, 'Titan' McMahon. *The Wall Street Journal*. February 12, 1996.

Rosenthal, P. (1995). Turner Explodes on Media Violence. *The Los Angeles Daily News*. July 11, 1995.

Russo, R. (2001). TBS, TNT Smack Down Wrestling. *Orlando Sentinel*. March 20, 2001.

Rutenberg, J. (2001). Turner Drops Wrestling in First Decision by Its New Chief. *The New York Times*. March 19, 2001.

Rutenberg, J. (2001). TBS to Sell Major Stake in Its Wrestling Franchise. *The New York Times*. January 12, 2001.

Sack, K. (1996). ATLANTA: DAY 6; Atlanta Bristles at all the Criticism. *The New York Times*. July 25, 1996.

Salem-Fitzgerald, D.J. and Philips, C. (1996). Crusaders Launch Round 2 In War On Nasty Lyrics. *Orlando Sun-Sentinel*. May 31, 1996.

Sandomir, R. (1998). Long Before Murdoch, There Was Ted Turner. *The New York Times*. March 8, 1998.

Scherer, D. (2000). Trimming the Fat is WCW's Top Job. *The New York Daily News*. August 19, 2000.

Schultz, J. (1999). Yankees Woo Chief of Turner Sports. *The Atlanta Journal and The Atlanta Constitution.* October 30, 1999.

Scott, J. (1999). 'Smackdown': Coke Ad Cut Hits Home at WWF. *The Atlanta Journal and The Atlanta Constitution.* November 30, 1999.

Severo, R. (2004). Jack Paar, Unpredictable TV Host Who Kept Americans Up Late, Is Dead at 85. *The New York Times.* January 28, 2004.

Smith, R. (1948). Gorgeous George Gets Hair Curled. *The Washington Post.* November 7, 1948.

Strauss, N. (1998). How a Gangsta Rapper Turns Entrepreneur; At 28, Master P Has Created One of the Biggest Independent Labels. *The New York Times.* May 13, 1998.

Strydom, M. (2014). Ted Turner Loathes Rupert Murdoch, so What Will He Do About CNN? *The Daily Telegraph.* May 16, 2014.

Truell, P. (1995). For Advisers, Turner Plan is Already a Big Deal. *The New York Times.* September 7, 1995.

Weber, T. E. (1996). Who Uses The Internet? *Wall Street Journal.* December 9 1996.

Wood, D. B. (1996). Drumbeat of Criticism Continues as Rap Music Moves in New Direction. *The Christian Science Monitor.* June 26, 1996.

Trade Journal Articles
Donohue, S. (2000). Turner Meets with SFX on WCW. *Multichannel News.* June 4, 2000.

Higgins, J. (2001). A Gentler Jamie Kellner? *Broadcasting and Cable.* March 11, 2001.

Kimelman, J. (1995). Viva Hulk! *Financial World.* February 14, 1995.

Linnett, R. (2000). Siren Song. *Advertising Age.* May 15, 2000.

Mandese, J. (1994). The 10 Most Expensive Prime-Time Ad Buys. *Advertising Age.* September 19, 1994.

McAdams, D. (2000). WCW Getting Bischoff Facelift. *Broadcasting and Cable*. April 9, 2000.

McConville, C. (2000). Guber Wrestles for WCW; Mandalay Sports Out To Buy Franchise From Turner. *Electronic Media*. October 2, 2000.

Mickle, T. (2013). An American Original. *SportsBusiness Journal*. March 11, 2013.

Muret, D. (2001). WCW Road Shows May Cease After Purchase by Fusient Media Ventures. *Amusement Business*. January 29, 2001.

Osterman, J. (1998). WCW Grapples for Dollars. *MediaWeek*. January 19, 1998.

Reynolds, M. (1999). A Banner Year for Events. *Cable World*. December 6, 1999.

Schlosser, J. (1998). Wrestling with Success. *Broadcasting and Cable*. August 17, 1998.

Shermach, K. (1997). Wrestling on a Peak; Keeps One Eye on Valley. *Marketing News*. May 12, 1997.

Technology Law Alert (1999). Spammer Trespasses and Infringes. January 1999.

Umstead, T. (2001). Three-Count Looks Near for WCW. *Multichannel News*. March 16, 2001.

Umstead, T. (2000). WCW May Work With Rival. *Multichannel News*. October 9, 2000.

Umstead, T. (1999). NBA Deal Nixes WCW, NBC February Date. *Multichannel News*. January 17, 1999.

Umstead, T. (1998). Starrcade Sets WCW Wrestling Record. *Multichannel News*. January 11, 1998.

Academic Journal Articles
Gillentine, A. (2000). Professional Wrestling Fans: Your Next-Door Neighbors? *Sport Marketing Quarterly*. Volume 9 (3).

Online Articles

Cable News Network (1999). Martha, WWF, Satyam Gain. *CNN.com*. October 19, 1999.

Carpenter, J. (2014). "Long Overdue" All-Female Sports Talk Show Set to Debut Tonight. *SportsBusinessDaily.com*. September 30, 2014.

CBS News (1998). Dennis Rodman Sues The WCW. *CBSNews.com*. November 27, 1998.

Chartier, J. (2000). Dot.coms ready Bowl game. *Money.CNN.com*. January 28, 2000.

Cornette, J. (2009). The "Write Stuff". *JimCornette.com*. April 24, 2009.

Daly, W. (2014). Sonny Onoo Discusses His Time in WCW, Working with Ernest "The Cat" Miller, nWo and More. *Wrestling-News.net*. March 3, 2014.

DDT Digest (2000). Great American Bash – Sunday, June 11th 2000. http://www.ddtdigest.com/updates/2000062p.htm. June 11th, 2000.

DDT Digest (1999). WCW Monday Nitro - December 27th, 1999. http://www.ddtdigest.com/updates/1999124m.htm. December 27th, 1999.

Devenish, C. (1998). Militia Claim Victory Thanks to Debut Single. *MTV.com*. April 20, 1998.

Eck, K. (2017). WWE, WCW Both Wanted to Work With O.J. Simpson After His Murder Trial. *SportingNews.com*. July 21, 2017.

Fensom, M. (2013). Take 5 with Jersey Shore Native Diamond Dallas Page. *NJ.com*.

Frances, E. (1999). Wrestling Hero Owen Hart Will Be Remembered as a Class Act. *Slam! Sports*. May 26, 1999.

Geuder, M. (1999). Team Seeks to Pin Down Professional Wrestling Fans. *MSStade.Edu*. February 2, 1999.

Giri, R. (2017). DDP Talks Goldberg Getting Knocked Out During Their Match, Almost Beating Goldberg for WCW Title. *WrestlingInc.com*. March 28, 2017.

Golianopoulos, T. (2015). The Missed Shot That Was Master P's NBA Career. *Complex.com*. August 6, 2015.

Handy, A. (2005). Interview: Blake Lewin on Launching GameTap. *Gamasutra.com*. June 22, 2005.

Hart, B. (1999). I Was Seeing Ghosts. *Slam.Canoe.com*. October 9, 1999.

Hausman, N. (2017). Eric Bischoff Reveals Contract Details and How Much He Paid for Jimi Hendrix's 'Voodoo Child' to Use in NWO Theme. *Wrestlezone.com*. May 26, 2017.

IGN Wrestling (2001). Press Release: WCW Sold to Fusient. *IGN.com*. January 11, 2001.

IGN (1998). THQ's Revenge Explodes in the Charts. *IGN.com*. November 13, 1998.

Ivanovic, R. (2013). Underrated and Underappreciated Wrestler Series: Gorgeous George. *CagesideSeats.com*. May 1, 2013.

Keller, W. (2015). Random Thoughts: Memories of Attending First Nitro, Circus Aspects of WWE, Austin with Edge & Christian. *WadeKeller.com*. September 4, 2015.

Manjoo, F. (2009). Jurassic Web. *Slate.com*. February 24, 2009.

Mickle, T. (2013). An American Original. *SportsBusinessDaily.com*. March 11, 2013.

Nash, K. (1999). Kevin's Forum. *KevinBigSexyNash.com*. February 16, 1999.

Nash, K. (1999). Kevin's Forum. *KevinBigSexyNash.com*. January 9, 1999.

Nash, K. (1999). Kevin's Forum. *KevinBigSexyNash.com*. January 6, 1999.

Nash, K. (1999). Kevin's Forum. *KevinBigSexyNash.com*. January 1, 1999.

National Park Service (2018). The Fascinating History of Alcatraz Island. *NPS.gov.*

Onoo, S. (2001). Commentary for 02.10.01. *WCWUniverse.com.* February 10, 2001.

Page, D. (2017). Letter to My Younger Self. *ThePlayersTribune.com.* November 28, 2017.

Reinhard, H. (2018). 5 Questions with: Diamond Dallas Page, Yoga King and Former Wrestling Champion. *Weightwatchers.com.*

Ross, I. (2000). WCW Thunder Ratings Breakdown. *IGN.com.* April 27, 2000.

Russo, V. (2015). Exclusive: You Have No Idea How Close McMahon vs. Bischoff Was to Happening. *Wrestlezone.com.* February 5, 2015.

Russo, V. (2014). 10 Reasons Why WCW Was Its Own Worst Enemy. *WhatCulture.com.*

Ryder, B. (2001). Siegel Sabotaged His Own Company. *1Wrestling.com.* July 30, 2001.

Shoemaker, D. (2013). Wrestling's Greatest Shoots, Volume 5: Brian Pillman vs. Kevin Sullivan. *Grantland.com.* August 6, 2013.

Turner Broadcasting System, Inc. (1999). Turner Broadcasting System, Inc Announces Strategic Reorganization of its Turner Sports Division. November 2, 1999.

Ward, M. (2014). Terry Taylor's Lifetime in Wrestling Celebrated with Industry's Top Award. *Slam.Canoe.com.* May 20th, 2014.

World Wrestling Entertainment (2016). Big Bang: The Untold Story of the WCW Pay-Per-View That Almost Happened. February 19, 2016.

Other Interviews
Alvarez, B. (2006). Interview with Bob Mould. April 7, 2006.

Apter, B. (2011). Interview with Bill Goldberg. June 18, 2011.

Arezzi, J. (1993). Interview with Eric Bischoff. February 6, 1993.

Austin, S. (2014). Interview with Eric Bischoff. May 7, 2014.

Garcia, L. (2017). Interview with Eric Bischoff. April 24, 2017.

Landsberg, M. (1998). Interview with Eric Bischoff. *Off The Record*. March 18, 1998.

Keller, W. (2009). Torch Talk with Eric Bischoff.

King, L. (1999). Interview with Ted Turner. December 13, 1999.

Miller, B. (1999). Interview with Vince Russo. *Wrestleline.com*. September 30, 1999.

Public Broadcasting Service (2000). Interview with Milton Friedman. October 1, 2000.

Russo, V. (2016). Interview with Kevin Nash. May 11, 2016.

Russo, V. (2014). Interview with Debra Miceli. August 13, 2014.

Russo, V. (2001). Live Chat with Fans. *VinceRusso.org*. April 16, 2001.

Ryder, B. (1998). Interview with Eric Bischoff. April 1, 1998.

Ryder, B. (1998). Interview with Kevin Nash. March 15, 1998.

Ryder, B. (1997). Interview with Eric Bischoff. October 7, 1997.

Ryder, B. (1997). Interview with Eric Bischoff. February 19, 1997.

Ryder, B. (1996). Interview with Eric Bischoff. October 12, 1996.

Skakel, E. (2016). Interview with Eric Bischoff. March 31, 2016.

Winfrey, O. (2012). Interview with Ted Turner. January 30, 2012.

Weisler, C. (2013). How To Brand a TV Network: Q&A with Turner's Jon Marks. *Mediapost.com*. September 12, 2013.

Wrestling Media

1Wrestling.com
Pro Wrestling Torch
WCW Magazine
WCW Hotline
WCW.com
WCW Live!
WCW Reload
Wrestling Observer Newsletter
Wrestleline.com
WWF.com

Podcasts and Radio Shows

83 Weeks with Eric Bischoff
Between the Ropes
Between the Sheets
Bischoff on Wrestling
JJ Dillon Show
Keep It 2000
MLW Radio
Neal Pruitt's Secrets of WCW Nitro
Pro Wrestling Radio
Pro Wrestling Spotlight
Ringside with David Penzer
The Lapsed Fan Wrestling Podcast
Vince Russo's The Brand
What Happened When with Tony Schiavone

Court cases

Bollea v. World Championship Wrestling (2000).

Easterling v. World Championship Wrestling (2000).

Onoo v. World Championship Wrestling (2000).

Titan Sports, Inc. v. Turner Broadcasting, et al. (1996).

Video releases

ESPN (2011). Scott Hall: The Wrestler.

Hitman Hart: Wrestling with Shadows (1998)

Kayfabe Commentaries (2007). Guest Booker with Kevin Sullivan.

RF Video (2014). Interview with Eric Bischoff.

RF Video (2007). Interview with Kevin Nash and Scott Hall.

Ultimate Insiders (2004). Interview with Vince Russo and Ed Ferrara.

World Wrestling Entertainment (2016). *Eric Bischoff - Sports Entertainment's Most Controversial Figure.*

World Wrestling Entertainment (2015). *Monday Night War: Shots Fired.*

World Wrestling Entertainment (2004). *The Monday Night War: WWE Raw vs. WCW Nitro.*

SEC filings
Turner Broadcasting System Inc. *Form 10-K/A.* SEC file number 001-08911. February 28, 1995.

World Wrestling Federation Entertainment. *Form 10-K.* SEC file number 0-27639. July 27, 2001.

Printed in Great Britain
by Amazon

41272728R00336